Praise for *Soldier Spies*

"A thorough study of Israeli military intelligence corps'
reconnaissance and espionage activities in the Middle East from
the earliest Zionist settler organizations in Palestine to the present.
It is well researched with a very readable narrative, a must read for
any one interested in the modern trends in espionage as well as
interest in Israeli military strategy."

—*The Reader's Review*

"*Soldier Spies* is a rich and well-documented history of Aman,
Israel's military intelligence, easily as critical to the country's
survival as the better-known Mossad (overseas intelligence) and
Shin Bet (internal security)."

—*The Jerusalem Report*

"[A] notable addition to the English-language literature on the Israeli
armed forces . . . Katz, himself a veteran of the intelligence corps
and an experienced military writer, has researched thoroughly and
written clearly from a strong but not uncritical pro-Israel stance. His
numerous pen portraits of key figures in the long and tortuous
development of the corps are most memorable, and the whole book is
invaluable for larger Middle East and current-affairs collections."

—American Library Association *Booklist*

"Katz has drawn on official histories, war records, recently declassified documents, and interviews with former and present intelligence officers, to compile this definitive book on Israel's Military Intelligence—a story heretofore untold."

—The Jewish Star

"A critical history, warts and all. The style is journalistic, with excellent documentation and a useful bibliography, including Hebrew sources. Written for general readers, this volume does not focus narrowly on intelligence in a technical sense. However, the intelligence perspective and the minute detail add a dramatic flair that will interest those who seek to learn more of contemporary Israeli history."

—Choice Magazine

"Well worth reading, if only for the glimpses it affords of the mysterious world of Israeli intelligence gathering and its impact upon the IDF and the society it protects. The insights into some of the astounding Israeli intelligence coups of past decades, as well as the type of men and women who pulled them off, seem almost the stuff of myth."

—The Friday Review of Defense Literature

Soldier Spies

Israeli Military Intelligence

Samuel M. Katz

PRESIDIO

Paperback edition published in 1994

Published by Presidio Press
505 B San Marin Dr. Suite 300
Novato, CA 94945-1340

Library of Congress Cataloging-in-Publication Data

Katz, Samuel M., 1963-
 Soldier spies : Israeli military intelligence / Samuel M. Katz.
   p.   cm.
 Includes bibliographical references and index.
 ISBN 0-89141-526-2
 1. Military intelligence—Israel—History—20th century.
 2. Israel. Tseeva haganah le-Yisra'el. Agaf modi' in—History.
 3. Israel—History, Military. I. Title.
 UB271.I8K37   1992
 355.3'432'095694—dc20   92-4880
                                                   CIP

Typography by ProImage
Printed in the United States of America

To Sigi and Yoav, my two lights of inspiration.

CONTENTS

PREFACE

T his book examines the history of Israel's largest, most important, and most enigmatic intelligence service. A'MAN, the Intelligence Branch of the Israel Defense Forces, lacks the glamour and public image of the MOSSAD and the SHIN BET, yet A'MAN is the State of Israel's true shield. By executing its mandate of gathering, analyzing, and disseminating accurate intelligence, A'MAN protects the Jewish state from conventional—and unconventional—attack. The history of Israeli Military Intelligence is the history of the Jewish state and, in many regards, the Jewish people—Israel is a country always on guard, always vigilant. In victory, however, A'MAN cannot join in the exhilaration of national success. The soldier spies of Israeli Military Intelligence operate under a permanent veil of anonymity. Yet in the case of failure, they usually are made the national scapegoat. Since they are the most exposed, and the most egalitarian, of all Israel's intelligence-gathering and espionage services, they are also the most scrutinized. A'MAN carries an enormous burden upon its shoulders. It is as unenvious an organization as can be found in any nation's military order of battle.

It must be noted that this book, in its manuscript form, has undergone a security examination by the IDF Military Censor's Office. In certain cases, words and even entire passages have been deleted by the censor's pen. It must be stressed, however, that *only* information deemed damaging to Israeli military security has been removed from this book. It is not the mandate of the censor's office to suppress an author's thoughts, criticisms, or political opinions. Freedom of expression is never controlled in Israel, only information that can damage the security of the Jewish state. Citizens of North America and most of Western Europe are usually apprehensive about censorship. They view censorship as an activity of "big brother" government, infringing on a citizen's right to hear differing ideas, and exerting bureaucratic control over the expression of views not in accordance with the government line. But the citizens of North America and Western Europe do not find their physical survival constantly threatened. They have not endured six major wars and over forty years of terrorism. They have not been forced to don gas masks at the siren's sound and lock their families in sealed rooms to await a missile, with a possible chemical or biological payload, aimed at their homes. For Israel, *military* censorship is a requirement for existence. Information can damage a nation's security. It can endanger lives. And that is not the intention or objective of this book. It is also interesting to note that the IDF Military Censor's Office is an integral part of Israeli Military Intelligence.

A book of this nature could not have been completed without the assistance of a great many friends, some of whom must remain anonymous. I wish to thank Yosef Argaman, Joseph S. Bermudez Jr., "Mike," Dan David, and Brigadier-General Ephraim Lapid for all their help, advice, and time. I wish to thank Lieutenant-Colonel Shai Dolev and the staff of the IDF Military Censor's Office in Tel Aviv for their quick review of my manuscript, and I thank the staff of the IDF Spokesman Photographic Unit for the assistance with illustrations. Thanks also to my editor at Presidio Press, Joan Griffin, for her extreme patience, faith in this project, and ability to turn a sometimes mysterious text into a cohesive book. I would like to offer a very special thanks to my father-in-law, Mr. Nissim Elyakim, for his efforts as messenger and liaison on my behalf. His efforts were crucial to the production of this book, as were, in true family fashion, the assistance I received from my two sisters in-law, Ms. Sharon Elyakim and Mrs. Smadar Castoriano. Lastly, I wish to offer a very warm thanks to my wife, Sigalit, for her remarkable patience, moral support, and invaluable assistance—at all hours—in the materialization of this project.

INTRODUCTION

E ver since Joshua dispatched his two spies on a reconnaissance mission to Jericho, espionage has been a way of life in the Middle East. Yet no nation in that torrid region has been able to coordinate its human and technological national resources into as effective an intelligence shield as has the State of Israel; the prevailing image of efficiency and sometimes ruthless dedication is rooted in reality. The State of Israel was born in the aftermath of war and tragedy. Surrounded by a ring of well-armed hostile Arab nations the young nation quickly formed a triumvirate of intelligence bodies: a foreign espionage agency, the MOSSAD; an internal counterintelligence force, the SHIN BET; and, lastly and most importantly, Israel's Military Intelligence arm.

The most flamboyant and romanticized member of the Israeli intelligence community is, of course, HA'MOSSAD LE'MODE'IN U'LE'TAFKIDIM MEYUCHADIM ("the Institute for Intelligence and Special Tasks"). Born out of the controversial remnants of the mysterious Foreign Ministry's Political Department, the MOSSAD, as it is most commonly known, was formed on April 1, 1951. Its first director, the shadowy Reuven Shiloah, was considered a one-man intelligence dynamo.

From its humble genesis the MOSSAD soon blossomed into a professional organization, staffed by dedicated servants and capable of the most impressive coups and operations. The MOSSAD in its early years helped smuggle thousands of Jews out of Iraq. Perhaps most importantly, it forged a firm and binding relationship with the Central Intelligence Agency (CIA), especially with the legendary James Jesus Angeleton. Eventually commanded by Israel's most revered spy master, Isser Harel, the MOSSAD earned an international James Bond type of image, pulling off such capers as the kidnapping of Nazi war criminal

1

Adolph Eichmann from Buenos Aires, Argentina, and "convincing" a religiously persecuted Iraqi MiG-21 pilot to defect to Israel with his then top-secret warplane.[1] The MOSSAD was also in the vanguard of Israel's highly successful war against Black September—a conflict waged from the streets of Europe to the Beirut shoreline—culminating in the assassination of Ali Hassan Salameh, the mastermind of the 1972 Munich Olympics Massacre.[2] Most recently, the MOSSAD snared Israeli nuclear traitor Mordechai Vanunu by setting up a classic sexual sting operation and having him smuggled from Europe to face a behind-closed-door trial in Israel. According to foreign reports, the MOSSAD was also behind the brilliantly executed assassination of Palestine Liberation Organization (PLO) deputy chieftain Abu Jihad in his Tunis villa in April 1988.

The MOSSAD, however, has also been embroiled in some bitter failures. In its quest to hunt down the perpetrators of the Munich Massacre, a MOSSAD hit team operating in the sleepy Norwegian resort town of Lillehammer mistakenly gunned down a Moroccan waiter. In the uncontrollable chain of events that followed, several MOSSAD agents were arrested, tried, and sentenced to prison terms.

The Lillehammer debacle was embarrassing, but not as damaging as the MOSSAD's supporting of the Christian Phalangists in Lebanon—a mistake, it can be argued, which eventually dragged the Israel Defense Forces (IDF) into a most brutal and costly Lebanese quagmire. One of the MOSSAD's most prominent agents and leader of the notorious hit teams, Mike Harari, went from the MOSSAD station chief in Mexico City to become the indispensable right-hand man to Gen. Manuel Noriega in Panama.[3] The MOSSAD was deeply entrenched in the Iran-Contra affair, and it even went to court in 1989 to block an Israeli newspaper from publishing unfavorable articles about its more inept operations in the 1980s. In the fall of 1990, the MOSSAD suffered one of its most embarrassing failures when a revenge-bent disgruntled recruit, Victor Ostrovsky, wrote a telltale exposé, which—although it intertwined obvious fiction with historical fact—opened a Pandora's box of sensitive secrets that had the Israeli government reeling. The State of Israel went to court, unsuccessfully, to have the book banned in Canada and in the United States; the failed legal move made a below-average book on Israel's mysterious espionage agency into an international best-seller.

The SHERUT HA'BITACHON HA'KLALI ("General Security Services"), commonly known as SHIN BET and SHA'BA'K, is Israel's counterespionage force. It is no less important than the MOSSAD but has been romanticized far less. The SHIN BET developed a reputation as a fierce and unrelenting counterintelligence force—and, in the later years, counterterrorist force—mainly as a result of the legendary dedication, success, and zeal of its first chief, Isser Harel. In the tumultuous political environment of Israel's early years, Isser Harel and the SHIN BET hunted down Soviet-bloc and Arab intelligence agents with great success, including the arrest of Lt. Col. Israel Be'eri, the official historian of the 1948 War, and a seasoned KGB agent who not only provided his Soviet handlers with important information on the State of Israel's security apparatus but on the North Atlantic Treaty Organization (NATO) as well. SHIN BET also arrested Professor Kurt Sita, a Czech physicist who was spying on Israel on behalf of the STB, the Czech espionage service. SHIN BET officers even planted bugging devices inside the ambassador's office in the United States Embassy in Tel Aviv in 1954. Several foreign assignments were also executed, including a dominant SHIN BET role in the capture of Adolph Eichmann.

When Israel captured the Gaza Strip and the West Bank of the Jordan River from Egypt and Jordan, respectively, the SHIN BET's three departments—Protective Security (responsible for guarding Israeli embassies and safeguarding the lives of the prime minister, other officials, and the Israeli defense industry), Arab Affairs (tasked with monitoring subversion among Arabs in Israel and the Occupied Territories), and Non-Arab Affairs (clearly the most important SHIN BET division and the one responsible for counterespionage, surveillance of foreign diplomats, and combating political subversion)—were pressed into a new type of war that they were ill-prepared to face and hopelessly outnumbered to wage: Palestinian terrorism.

On the foreign front, SHIN BET security efforts made El Al, Israel's national airline, virtually hijack-proof following the seizure of an Israeli craft to Algeria in 1968 by Palestinian terrorists. SHIN BET masterfully exploited a network of informants to crush an extremely dangerous and heavily armed Palestinian terrorist offensive in the West Bank and Gaza Strip. But the SHIN BET's reputation for efficiency also brought it one of ruthlessness and, in the case of a young Circassian Moslem officer serving in the IDF who was wrongly accused of passing information to the PLO, paranoid-inspired brutality. When SHIN BET agents, under the direction of its commander, Avraham Shalom, beat two Palestinian terrorists to death following a bus hijacking in April 1984, the organization's veil of public anonymity faded into an embarrassing scandal. When the SHIN BET failed to predict and, later, control the Palestinian Intifadah in 1987, it was subjected to further public scrutiny and criticism.

Although both the MOSSAD and SHIN BET have been instrumental players in the incessant campaign to safeguard Israel's national integrity, no Israeli intelligence force has been as important to the survival of the State of Israel as the arm of TZAHAL (Hebrew acronym for TZAVA HAGANAH LE'YISRAEL, or "Israel Defense Forces"), responsible for gathering, analyzing, and disseminating military intelligence. Certainly, no member of the Israeli intelligence community has been as brilliant, controversial, and maligned. The ability of the IDF General Staff's AGAF MODE'IN—better known by its Hebrew acronym A'MAN ("Intelligence Branch")—to react to intelligence obtained on Arab conventional military threats has been the cutting edge in spectacular military victories, such as the 1967 Six-Day War. Failures in the intelligence-gathering and analysis process have led to close calls with defeat, such as the 1973 War. Clearly the largest Israeli intelligence agency, A'MAN is part of the IDF General Staff and is under direct control of the IDF chief of staff and the defense minister. Like the relationship between the U.S. National Security Agency (NSA) and the CIA, A'MAN lives in the MOSSAD's shadows while laying the groundwork for Israel's intelligence success.[4]

A'MAN's resources include everything from remotely piloted vehicles and sophisticated eavesdropping devices to the masseur employed by Egyptian President Nasser.[5] A'MAN has employed political connivers, criminals, and conscript Israeli soldiers. Some of the most promising espionage agents recruited by A'MAN—legends such as Eli Cohen and the "Champagne Spy," Wolfgang Lotz—later advanced into the ranks of the MOSSAD to become important agents in Israeli history. Other A'MAN agents, who even in death remain anonymous, have had even greater impact on Israeli victories, both past and present.

What makes Israeli Military Intelligence so unique is its direct connection to the Israel Defense Forces. Unquestionably, the IDF has been the most important force behind the building of the State of Israel and its subsequent struggle for survival. As a citizen army, the IDF has absolute—and religiously followed—egalitarian ideals purposely designed for its citizen army's dependency on universal conscription and annual reserve duty. For such ideals to govern the behavior and guidelines of an espionage service is quite unique. Because A'MAN is part of the Israel Defense Forces, its activities, methods, and doctrines follow the tenets of the IDF; this is also expressed in its reliance on innovative responses to unfavorable military circumstances, including the use of elite force units for delicate "special operations." Israel's vast manpower resource from the Jewish diaspora of Arabic, English, Russian, and other language native speakers has made it possible to employ conscripts, including women soldiers, for most sensitive tasks. As part of the IDF, A'MAN also controls the subordinate air force and naval intelligence divisions—two branches of the IDF that utilize intelligence-gathering techniques specific to their own needs.

According to a CIA document captured in the Teheran Embassy titled "Foreign Intelligence and Security Services: Israel," "Israel's Military Intelligence is charged with the collection, production and dissemination of military, geographic and economic intelligence, especially on the Arab nations, and security in the IDF [abbreviation for Israel Defense Forces] and the Administered Territories." A'MAN commands four sections: Production, the Intelligence Corps, Foreign Relations, and Field Security/Military Censorship. There are an estimated seven thousand personnel (conscript soldiers, career officers and NCOs, and civilian analysts) employed by A'MAN.[6]

The MACHLEKAT HA'HAFAKA ("Productions Department") is the largest and one of the most vital elements of the Intelligence Branch. It has three divisions: Regional, Functional, and Records. The Regional Division's three desks (Western: Egypt, Sudan, and Libya; Eastern: Iraq, Syria, and Lebanon; and Southern: Jordan and the Arabian peninsula) produce target studies on the surrounding Arab nations.The Functional Division deals with Near Eastern economic matters, Inter-Arab relations, the Palestinians, Near Eastern international activities, and enemy doctrines. The Records Division catalogs and disseminates intelligence reports to their respective offices.

The primary function of the Productions Department, however, is the effectuation of the daily intelligence reports and bulletins and, most importantly, the preparation of the National Intelligence Estimate—a very thick document, submitted every year to the prime minister, which contains all of A'MAN's predictions and evaluations for the coming year. A'MAN, in fact, is the sole channel through which an integrative intelligence evaluation is brought to Israel's policymakers.[7]

Many have argued that intelligence evaluation is a crapshoot, a gamble in which the odds are no better than fifty-fifty. In the past few years, A'MAN's annual predictions, in fact, have been consistently incorrect. Both the 1967 and 1973 wars were not predicted; A'MAN failed to provide an indication that Egyptian President Anwar as-Sadat would visit Jerusalem and, remarkably, whether his trip was genuine or a trick. Nor did A'MAN warn of the onset of several strategically threatening arms deals between the People's Republic of China, Syria, and Saudi Arabia, or, of course, the eruption of the Intifadah.

HA'MAN ("Intelligence Corps") is entrusted with the overt and covert labors of intelligence-gathering. This is a far-reaching responsibility that touches virtually all aspects of the trade, from running agents into enemy territory to gathering valuable bits of political and military intelligence from open sources, such as the Arab radio, television, and print media. HA'MAN's divisions are Collection, General Headquarters, Training, Organization, Logistics, Personnel, and Research and Development.[8]

Collections is certainly the most fascinating department. From its inception, Israeli Military Intelligence has run agents into the treacherous abyss of the neighboring Arab countries; some have met with great, though anonymous, success, whereas the operations of others have led to politically destructive scandals. The Arabic-speaking conscripts of the "Open Sources Unit," known by the Hebrew name HATZAV ("Quarry"), have also been involved in some dramatic breakthroughs: They uncovered that war would erupt between Egypt and Israel in 1973 via an unlikely source—an interview with PLO Deputy Commander Abu Iyad in a Lebanese fashion magazine!

The Intelligence Corps is also responsible for all SIGINT, COMINT, ELINT, and VISINT gathered via atmospheric and landline interception. Their publicized successes have included recording a politically damaging telephone conversation between Jordan's King Hussein and Egyptian President Nasser during the Six-Day War to eavesdropping on the radio traffic of the *Achille Lauro* hijackers and the Palestine Liberation Front (PLF) commander, Abu Abbas.

A'MAN is responsible for IDF military attachés sent throughout the world and for counterintelligence activities back at home. The BITACHON SADEH ("Field Security") and HA'TZENZURA HA'TZVA'IT ("Military Censorship") divisions are two of the most important and respected Israeli military intelligence forces. They decide whether to allow the name of a senior officer, an Israeli Air Force (IAF) squadron emblem, or a unit's numeric designation to be published; they also, for military and security reasons, can prevent the publication of such facts as where Soviet Jews assemble for their flights to Israel. For the most part, their word is law.

Finally, the success or failure of A'MAN is not determined by the countless man-hours of labor of its agents, soldiers, and analysts—either behind enemy lines or in the bustling offices of the IDF headquarters (HQ) in Tel Aviv—but by its commander: the director of Military Intelligence. Historically, the A'MAN director is one of the most capable IDF generals, chosen because of his exploits as an elite unit commander, or for his brilliant analytical mind. The head of A'MAN is usually being groomed for the post of IDF chief of staff, though very few are eventually chosen for the top posting.* The past two A'MAN directors, Lt. Gen. Ehud Barak and Maj. Gen. Amnon Shahak, are two of the IDF's most decorated, respected, and flamboyant soldiers. Barak, A'MAN commander from 1983 to 1985, was, according to published reports, the commander of SAYERET MAT'KAL, the IDF's ultrasecret General Staff reconnaissance force. He not only participated in some of Israel's most spectacular military operations, but is the most decorated Israeli soldier in history; the stories behind those medals, however, remain a highly guarded state secret. Major General Shahak, a veteran paratroop and reconnaissance commando officer, commanded some of the IDF's most brilliant operations.

But the position of director of Military Intelligence is a precarious one. He is obligated—either at the behest of the policymakers or by his own initiative—to supply the most reliable intelligence and evaluations to the political leaders. Yet, when the defense minister or prime minister chooses to ignore, or go against, the professional intelligence recommendations, the A'MAN chief is usually scapegoated and has but one recourse: resignation. Because A'MAN, as part of the IDF, is an absolutely apolitical body, several directors

---

*On April 1, 1991, Lt. Gen. Ehud Barak was named the IDF chief of staff and Maj. Gen. Amnon Shahak was named his deputy.

of Military Intelligence have been placed in impossible positions: Being accurate and convincing the political hierarchy are sometimes totally separate realities.

The personality of the A'MAN director can make all the difference in the success or failure of Israel's intelligence-gathering efforts. The very professional demeanor of Maj. Gen. Aharon Yariv, for example, personifies the skill and affirmative nature of Israeli intelligence even to this day; the political leadership during his tenure tended to rely on every word he said. On the other hand, Defense Minister Arik Sharon overrode A'MAN objections and continued Israel's adventure with the unreliable Lebanese Christian Phalangists. Major General Yehoshua Saguy, who served as the director of Military Intelligence during the Lebanon debacle, chose to express his dissatisfaction by being silent. Others have been more outspoken. Major General Amnon Shahak, for example, was a firm believer that the Intifadah was being run by the PLO, and when his political bosses refused to agree, he went so far as to meet with a senior supporter of the PLO in the Gaza Strip.[9] Yet the most indicative clue as to the lone-wolf status of A'MAN'S chief is the fact that his identity is public knowledge, unlike the heads of the MOSSAD and the SHIN BET, who remain anonymous figures.

Like all elements of the Israel Defense Forces, A'MAN was not created overnight, but developed from the embryonic military organizations of preindependence Palestine. A'MAN evolved in an army that in the beginning could not supply its men in the field with standard uniforms, but became a fighting force so powerful, professional, and dedicated that many consider it to be the most able in the world. The threats that face the State of Israel today have also evolved, from a small-scale regional conflict to an international conflagration in which both conventional and terrorist means are employed. As was seen in Operation Desert Storm—the type of conflict the Middle East might see in the coming decade—a future war against the Jewish state may involve chemical, biological, or possibly nuclear weapons.

Like all of Israel's combat arms, A'MAN has paid a heavy price in the endless years of war. Near the gates of the Intelligence School, just north of Tel Aviv, stands a monument to the 360 members of the Israeli intelligence community who have fallen in the line of duty.[10] Unlike other monuments of its kind, there are no names carved into this solid granite wall: A transparent veil of anonymity personifies the life, and death, of an intelligence soldier.

Notes: Introduction

1. Amnon Kaveh, "ha'mossad tichnen et a'rikat ha'mig 21 ha'iraqi," el ha'matara, 10 (1989): 4.

2. Michael Bar-Zohar and Eitan Haber, *The Quest for the Red Prince* (New York: William Morrow Company, Inc., 1983), 215–222.

3. Yossi Melman and Dan Raviv, *The Imperfect Spies: The History of Israeli Intelligence* (London: Sidgwick & Jackson, 1989), 374.

4. *Ibid.* 216.

5. Various ed., "President Nasser's and Sadat's Masseuse Who Spied For Israel Passed Away," yisrael shelanu (April 20, 1990): 9.

6. Yossi Melman, ed., *CIA Report on the Israeli Intelligence Services* (Tel Aviv: Zmora Bitan Publishers, 1982), 69.

7. Gideon Doron and Reuven Pedatzur, "Israeli Intelligence: Utility and Cost-Effectiveness in Policy Formation," *Intelligence and Counterintelligence*, Vol. 3, No. 3 (1989): 352.

8. Jeffrey T. Richelson, *Foreign Intelligence Organizations* (London: Cambridge Univ. Press, 1988), 212.

9. Various ed., "One of the PLO Heads in the Gaza Strip Met With The Director of Military Intelligence," yisrael shelanu (New York, July 13, 1990): 6.

10. Various ed., "Memorial To Israel's Intelligence Community," *IDF Journal*, Vol. III, No. 1 (Fall 1985): 4.

CHAPTER 1

LAYING THE FOUNDATIONS:
THE COVERT TRAILBLAZERS

The onset of the First World War raised the hopes of many Jews worldwide, especially those inspired by dreams of a Jewish state in Palestine. With the world's major powers participating in a mad dash to dominate old empires and rule new territories, Theodore Herzl's concept of a Jewish homeland seemed tangible; clearly, with the borders about to be dramatically redrawn in the wake of the conflict, there could easily be room for a Jewish state in Palestine. There had been a steady flow of Jewish immigrants to Palestine since the late 1880s, with the greatest number reaching the holy land in 1903–04. The OLIM—Hebrew for "those who ascend" and the term for those who immigrate to the Jewish homeland—were idealistic socialists, mainly from Czarist Russia, who were determined to build their own paradise among the swamps, deserts, and economic misery of Ottoman-controlled Palestine. Hopelessly outnumbered by the local Palestinians and mistrusted by the ruling Turks, the newcomers to Zion kept to themselves and their land. They drained the swamps, irrigated the arid landscape, and constructed the framework for their Jewish paradise. But they quickly learned the realities of their new home.

Armed attacks by marauding gangs of Palestinians and Bedouins were commonplace. Several security forces were established to guard their homes and fields; at first the Jewish settlers hired Circassian Moslem and Bedouin gunmen but later took up arms themselves. Both of the early Jewish defense groups, BAR GIORA (named after a famous Jewish fighter who battled the Romans in 70 A.D.) and HASHOMER ("the guard"), were passive organizations with very little grand vision for the future. Many of HASHOMER's guards, accepting the presence of the Turks in Palestine, even served as officers in the Ottoman army.

By 1916, Palestine was in total chaos. The war with the British throughout the Ottoman's crumbling empire had taken its toll on the colony; hunger, poverty, and violence by Turks against the Jewish residents spread throughout the land.

In Zichron Ya'akov, an affluent and educated Jewish family, the Aaronsons, had taken the initiative for promotion of a Jewish homeland by volunteering to spy for the British. The ring's leader and the family's oldest son, Aaron, was a well-respected botanist whose name and experimental greenhouse in the seaside village of Atlit was world renowned. The Turkish military commander in Palestine had named young Aaronson the province's chief inspector in the struggle against locust swarms.

The spy ring named itself NILI (the acronym of the Hebrew words for "the eternal one of Israel does not lie") and consisted of Aaron, his brother Alexander, his sister Sarah, and several loyal friends. Aaronson set out for Egypt to establish his necessary contacts with British Military Intelligence; within a matter of weeks, reliable and invaluable intelligence information began to flow from Zichron Ya'akov and Atlit to British HQ in Cairo.

The British mistrusted the NILI ring and showed great skepticism concerning their loyalties; a spy ring that refused to accept money as payment was, after all, suspect.[1] Aaron Aaronson, however, was gambling that the British would prevail in the Middle Eastern campaign and was anxious to see a Turkish departure from Palestine. Aaronson also possessed the political insight to realize that in any peace conference to follow the war, the Jews would fare better if they took an active role in the conflict.

The NILI ring utilized ingenious and elaborate codes in Hebrew, English, French, and ancient Aramaic phrases to pass intelligence data concerning Turkish troop strengths and movements on to the British. Atlit, the eventual home to both the British and Israeli naval commandos, served as a convenient cover while also providing the Jewish community in Palestine (the YISHUV) with its sole contact to the outside world.

But the bustling activities of the Aaronsons eventually compromised the security of the NILI spies. The ring was successful until whispers of their existence began to circulate among the Jewish community in Palestine. Absolute secrecy, the crucial element for the survival of any spy organization, was lost. Even the impassioned Zionists of HASHOMER opposed the efforts of the Jewish spies working for his majesty, because they feared that the Turkish reaction would be brutality against the Jews of the YISHUV. Although political infighting would become a trademark of the Jewish forces of preindependence Israel, it was not the downfall of the NILI ring. A homing pigeon, who reached the Turks instead of the British, would eventually destroy the Aaronson intelligence-gathering efforts. Instead of heading toward Egypt, the bird, with a coded message tied to its foot, landed on the beach at Caesarea and was retrieved by a Turkish officer. Palestine's military commander demanded that the Jewish spies be found either dead or alive at all costs, and within days a Turkish dragnet searched the countryside.

Inevitably, the Turks' search operation yielded its human dividends. The NILI spies were captured, tortured with unprecedented brutality (including being subjected to the bastinado, a Turkish form of flogging), and executed. Sarah Aaronson immortalized herself by committing suicide rather than reveal NILI's secrets to the Turks. But the doomed NILI ring had served an invaluable purpose to the Allied cause; from the south, the roar of the British army's guns could be heard, and the unstoppable force of Gen. Edmund Allenby's legions reached the gates of Palestine. In November 1917, news of the British Balfour Declaration, confirming Great Britain's support for the establishment of a Jewish state in Palestine, reached the YISHUV. Clearly the NILI spies had not died in vain. But their espionage legacy was even more important. Their ingenuity, courage, and determination became the precedent for the intelligence-gathering forces of the Jewish state.

The lack of security that eventually compromised the functional and physical existence of the NILI spy ring was due to many factors, the most important of which was perhaps the group's lack of espionage experience. Fueled by Zionist zeal, as opposed to skill and training, the NILI ring had shortcomings that were not lost to the founding fathers of the HAGANAH (Hebrew for "defense"), the Jewish army of preindependence Israel. The HAGANAH was formed in 1921 as an answer to increased attacks against the small, though growing, Jewish population of Palestine. Although the HAGANAH was the true embryo of what would eventually develop into the Israel Defense Forces, it was much more than a military force. It was a nation-building entity tied to every aspect of Jewish aspirations for statehood; the HAGANAH was an inseparable element of David Ben-Gurion's Jewish Agency and its all-powerful "Political Department." The Jewish Agency was the political body responsible not only for the day-to-day running of Jewish life in Palestine, but also its political makeup—providing support for its emissaries sent abroad on all sorts of covert missions—and, perhaps most importantly, the overseeing of Jewish immigration —both legal and illegal—to Palestine.

Militarily the HAGANAH faced enormous challenges. As poorly armed and outnumbered as a force could be, the HAGANAH was an illegal entity under the British Mandate and had to conduct its very difficult tasks of forming and maintaining a force under arms in absolute secrecy and with extremely limited finances. Accordingly, the HAGANAH relied on a series of covert organizations to keep its operations running and its sphere of influence growing. "Palestine, in fact, seemed a state inundated with covert organizations—each more secretive than the other."[2]

There was RECHESH ("the acquisition"), a secretive office that obtained weaponry and munitions from anyone and anywhere. One of their first documented operations was the successful smuggling of three hundred pistols and seventeen thousand rounds of ammunition from Vienna in 1921.[3] Although this type of operation might pale when compared to the high-tech, daring feats of Israeli intelligence in recent years, it set the tone for how Israel's intelligence operations—and covert military operations—would be run in the future. Dummy companies were established in major cities in Europe and beyond; networks of reliable and false-flag informants were found worldwide, as were elaborate escape plans, consisting of false identities, forged passports, and connections at border crossings and ports of entry throughout the world, from London to Limassol.

The twin organization to RECHESH was the even more secretive MOSSAD LE'ALIYAH BET* ("Institute for Immigration"), tasked with organizing illegal Jewish immigration to Palestine—through any means possible and at all costs—usually by means of nighttime boat landings on the Palestinian coast.

The commander of both the RECHESH and the MOSSAD LE'ALIYAH BET, in the years prior to the Second World War, was the remarkable Shaul Avigur, one of the founding fathers of the State of Israel and the Israeli intelligence community even though he operated primarily from Geneva and Paris. Known for his eighteen-hour days and fanatic regard for detail, Avigur would become the role model for the Israeli intelligence agent of the future. At the same time, the other Jewish groups within Palestine seeking Israel's independence all maintained their own semiprofessional, highly mysterious intelligence-gathering cells, including Menachem Begin's right-wing extremist IRGUN underground.

The HAGANAH's other two secret organizations were the mysterious HA'MACHLAKA HA'TECHNIT ("Technical Department," also known by its Hebrew acronym HA'MA'CHAT, or needle) and a small unit known as the SHERUT YEDIOT ("Information Service"), or SHA'I, as it was commonly called. Although the SHA'I was the weakest, and some say most neglected, element within the HAGANAH in the early years, it faced crucial challenges vital to the YISHUV's survival. The HAGANAH desperately needed intelligence data on the capabilities, intentions, and shortcomings of the various armed Arab groups roaming Palestine in order to prevent, and defend against, attacks—either individual acts or mob type of pogroms—on Jewish settlements and institutions. The SHA'I also had

---

*Not to be confused with the MOSSAD LE'MODE'IN U'LETAFKIDIM MEYUCHADIM of later date.

to contend with the "British question"—the capable British Mandatory police, Criminal Investigation Department (CID), and counterintelligence operations mounted against the HAGANAH. Against both the Arabs and British, the SHA'I utilized informants—smugglers, prostitutes, roaming Bedouins, and blackmailed police officials—to gather any tidbit of information it could obtain, from the military Order of Battle of a British force operating in a particular area, to plans for the next British raid against a HAGANAH arms cache. Massive dossiers were complied and meticulously cataloged in the secret HAGANAH regional headquarters throughout Palestine, while copies were transferred for safekeeping to the offices of the *legal* Jewish Agency. The amount of information gathered was enormous; Palestine was a nation surviving on rumors, fear, and suspicion.

The SHA'I also had to contend with divisive internal threats. The numerous Jewish Communist organizations operated according to directive from Moscow, often against the best interests of the Jewish state. There were also Jews, and many members of the HAGANAH, who served as informers for the British authorities and even the various Arab interests. Such varied and far-reaching threats required a capable and dedicated intelligence and security service, but the HAGANAH, in its SHA'I, possessed neither. Intelligence on the community's military predicament and internal security situation was gathered in a local, incidental, and haphazard manner.[4]

This weak link in the HAGANAH's ability to provide accurate intelligence to its units (and political hierarchy) was best illustrated by one of the most serious incidents of violence between the Jews and Arabs: the 1936–39 riots. While monitoring Arab telephone communications—a practice begun in the middle of the 1929 disturbances—Jewish telephone operators and HAGANAH spies (members of a special SHA'I Listening Unit) heard military attacks being carelessly talked about on the lines, and also discovered a connection between German and Italian intelligence and the Palestinian Arab nationalists. But the HAGANAH's intelligence apparatus was unable to analyze this data and thus prevent or prepare to meet determined Arab mob attacks against Jewish settlements and targets.[5] The HAGANAH's intelligence forces not only failed to maintain a productive surveillance on the forces and leaders of the armed Arab groups but, more importantly, failed to infiltrate these organizations and hinder them through either assassination or interdiction.

Although the HAGANAH's intelligence failure during the riots had severe implications—hundreds of Jews were murdered in the riots and thousands injured—it made Eliahu Golomb, the HAGANAH's legendary commander, realize the need to solidify an active, innovative, and efficient intelligence service for the struggle of independence that would surely follow. Most of the HAGANAH's Arabic-speaking agents during the riots at the time were stringers, either courageous members of the Jewish Agency's "Arab Department" or agents in other bureaucratic posts desperately needed in the field.

There was also an effort, in June 1939, to form a reactive intelligence and operations force when several HAGANAH commanders formed HA'YECHIDOT LE'PEULOT MEYUCHADOT ("Special Activity Units").[6] These very secretive units operated primarily as an antiterrorist retaliatory force, but one of their other functions was counterintelligence. They dealt harshly with spies, informants, and traitors. Although the challenges faced by the Special Activity Units were very real and dangerous, the Jews' *next* fight, however, would be even more difficult—Hitler and the Second World War.

When Nazi Germany invaded Poland on September 1, 1939, and Britain and France declared war on Germany two days later, the Jewish leadership in Palestine faced a moral and military dilemma. On May 17, 1939, the British had issued the infamous "White Paper," which restricted Jewish immigration to Palestine in light of European Jewry's perilous existence; this was considered, in many circles, an act of war demanding a harsh HAGANAH response. Ben-Gurion realized, however, that the fight against Hitler was of epic proportions and, in his now legendary summation of the Jews' plight, he promised to fight Hitler as if there were no White Paper, and fight the White Paper as if there were no Hitler. That view led to a marriage of convenience between the British and the HAGANAH; they had found a common enemy even though both camps maintained differing objectives.

To mount this effort, the Jewish Agency (which by 1940, with all its covert departments and operations, resembled a defense ministry more than a prestatehood political order) together with the full support of the HAGANAH High Command formed the SHERUT HA'YEDIOT HA'ARTZIT ("National Information Service"). The new national intelligence service adopted the popular SHA'I acronym. Many noted Israeli scholars view its creation as the true genesis of Israeli military intelligence, even though it has been argued that a Jewish military intelligence entity had existed in Palestine since 1909, when the HASHOMER society monitored neighboring Arab villagers. In June 1940, a special SHA'I Arab Department was founded. Commanded by Ezra Danin, it conducted systematic intelligence-gathering and evaluation for the HAGANAH on Arab military capabilities and intentions.[7]

The new SHA'I maintained close links with British intelligence and, in fact, tried to model its style and organization along the lines of MI-4, British Military Intelligence; MI-5, the Counterintelligence Branch; and, MI-6, the foreign espionage service. For several years prior to the outbreak of the Second World War, British intelligence assisted in the formation of the HAGANAH's military intelligence group. The relationship began during the 1936 riots when both the HAGANAH and British intelligence fought the Arab bands that were terrorizing much of Palestine. In 1936, British intelligence dispatched a young, religiously zealous captain to Palestine to combat this escalating tide of Arab guerrilla warfare. His name was Orde Charles Wingate and his influence on the Israel Defense Forces, and the covert brand of special operations for which they are now infamous, was profound.

Wingate was sent to Palestine to utilize the irregular warfare skills he had learned in the Sudan to halt repeated Arab guerrilla attacks against the Iraqi Petroleum Company pipeline, which ran through northern Israel into Haifa—an ultrastrategic economic target for British interests. A devout Christian reared on the Bible, Wingate was a passionate supporter of the Zionist cause, and he went to great personal effort to convince both the British High Command and the Jewish Agency of the need to arm the Jews; he wished to become commander of the Jews' first army in two thousand years. Through this eccentric British officer's tenacity and persistent, though frustrated, attempts to speak Hebrew, the HAGANAH slowly grew to trust him. He would endear himself to the HAGANAH and eventually become known as HA'YEDID ("the friend").

Wingate formed a mixed British-Jewish counterguerrilla force, known as the Special Night Squads (SNS). He taught the SNS troopers to operate in small, highly mobile units and to think of being outnumbered as a military advantage. Most importantly, he taught his eager Jewish troopers to always enter a battle with the upper hand, which could be achieved through accurate intelligence and surprise. He taught his men to bring the fight into the enemy's territory. Among Wingate's pupils were such legendary Israeli soldiers as Moshe Dayan and Yigal Allon—two future IDF chiefs of staff. Wingate's combat doctrine of "turn the night into your own" soon became the dominant theory of Israeli military thought and the standard practice of the IDF's elite and intelligence units.

Wingate's unflinching support for the HAGANAH's plight angered the Arabist-minded British, and eventually led to the disbandment of the Special Night Squads; it also resulted in Wingate's eventual removal from Palestine, although by then a military relationship had developed between the HAGANAH and the British. When war broke out in Europe, that relationship was expanded by the British Special Operations Executive (SOE) of the British army, which did not find itself bound by the anti-Zionist policies of the Mandatory government. According to Nicholas G. Hammond, SOE, "A decision was reached by Winston Churchill not long after Dunkirk to make use of the Jewish resistance power in Palestine for the war effort. The prevailing thought among the senior British military commanders at the time was that everything must be done in the Middle East to hamper the Germans' advance. Even though this military relationship with the Jews might have severe implications for British forces at a later date, winning the war against Hitler was the primary objective." [8]

The men chosen to commandeer this relationship were A. W. Lawrence, a professor of archaeology and the brother of T. E. Lawrence*; Nicholas

---

*Lawrence would eventually leave the SOE group because of his unabashed sympathies for the Arabs.

Hammond, a professor of Greek history at Cambridge University; and Henry Barnes, an adventuring and eccentric soul. From the Pension Wolstein, a small hotel on Mount Carmel in Haifa, the three, together with a small contingent of Gaullists who established a radio transmitter to beam propaganda into Vichy Syria, launched an effort that would eventually serve as the backbone for the Israeli army and her military intelligence.[9]

Although the Jewish Agency was initially reluctant to cooperate with the British in such an overt and, some feared, compromising fashion, the arrangement went into an operational phase. Through their base in Haifa, the SOE brought HAGANAH ships to raid the Lebanese and Syrian coasts, and also explosives, weaponry, funding, and, certainly most crucial, training in military tactics, espionage tradecraft, and the proper organization of an intelligence force. A special camp, code-named Me-102, was soon established for German-speaking HAGANAH agents, who would be smuggled into Europe for intelligence-gathering and sabotage operations against the Nazis.

This marriage of mutual convenience was as much a game of political wills as military necessity. British intelligence commanders cared little about the HAGANAH's fight for Zion or about Whitehall's policies concerning the possibilities of a Jewish homeland. They realized that the HAGANAH was utilizing its new found legal status and British funds to build up arms reserves, establish a sophisticated communications network, and train thousands of HAGANAH personnel. The defeat of Hitler was of paramount importance, however, even beyond the future of Palestine.

What the SOE received in return from HAGANAH personnel was intelligence unattainable anywhere else in the world. The Jews of Palestine were a conglomerate representing almost every nation in Europe, and their linguistic expertise was invaluable to the SOE, which desperately lacked such language-skilled personnel. From its headquarters in an unobtrusive building on a side street in the port city of Haifa, SHA'I case officers interrogated new arrivals to Palestine from Czechoslovakia, Poland, Germany, Belgium, France, and the Netherlands. Under SOE guidance, the SHA'I officers collected maps, documents, picture postcards, and a mass of verbal testimony that was of crucial importance to the ability of the British Military Intelligence to mount campaigns behind enemy lines.

For the Jewish Agency, the Allied effort was also providing valuable benefits. During the early stage of the war, Palestine became a depot for the Allied forces. Recruits from all over the British Empire came for military training to the Jezreel Valley and Galilee plains, and for rest and relaxation at the beachfront promenade of Tel Aviv and the exotic nightclubs of Yafo. Military units from the Nazi-occupied nations of Europe also assembled in Palestine, turning the holy land into the staging ground for the liberation of their vanquished homelands.[10] Soldiers from Poland, Greece, Czechoslovakia, France, and Yugoslavia all trained in Palestine, and agents from the HAGANAH, SHA'I, RECHESH, and MOSSAD LE'ALIYAH BET took advantage of this international conglomeration of recruits to ferret out reliable allies for possible use after the war—markers that would most certainly be called in at a later date.

Yet there were problems with this influx of foreign servicemen in Palestine. The most serious difficulties the HAGANAH encountered involved the four divisions of "Free Poles" who made their way to Palestine via the Soviet Union, Persia, and Iraq. Many of the Poles, including the legendary General Sikorski, were devout anti-Semites who overtly assisted the British in their efforts to halt illegal Jewish immigration and expose HAGANAH arms caches. In fact, several directives from the office of Gen. Wladyslaw Anders, commander of the 2d Corps, instructed his troops to help the authorities deal with the "Jewish problem." In addition, the Polish army's secret police, the Dwojka, assisted the British CID by infiltrating the Jewish community of Polish exiles and by offering arms to the Arabs.[11] SHA'I countered with infiltration operations of its own, sending Polish-speaking natives undercover to compromise Polish military officers, as well as conducting "false-flag" operations with agents posing as British and Arab nationalist agents.

Throughout the early relationship between the HAGANAH and the SOE, it was clear that the British did not intend to arm an entire Jewish army, or even a full battalion; they set limits, both in arms and finances, from which the HAGANAH was supposed to draw and support its manpower. The HAGANAH, however, would arm and train three times the number of soldiers mandated under the SOE arrangement. This was best illustrated in early May 1941 when, with the German army already occupying Greece and Yugoslavia and operating in the North African desert, it appeared that the Nazis would move on Palestine. As a desperate stopgap measure, an elite Jewish guerrilla—fifth-column type—force was created jointly by the HAGANAH and the SOE. Called the PAL'MACH, the Hebrew acronym for PLUGOT MACHATZ ("Strike Companies"), it would become the most important step in the building of the Israeli army years later, as well as defining that army's reliance on small-unit reconnaissance formations to conduct commando and intelligence-gathering operations deep behind enemy lines. The PAL'MACH's commander was the rambunctious Yitzhak Sadeh. The burly native of the Crimea was one of the HAGANAH's most innovative and unconventional commanders. In 1936 he had created the Field Companies, a functional elite patrol force, at a time when the HAGANAH could not even field conventional combat units. Sadeh understood the strategies of warfare in Palestine, and supplied his Field Companies with a small, though highly effective, intelligence service of Arabic-speaking officers.

Sadeh was determined that the PAL'MACH would go into action immediately and, once again, prove that small units and accurate intelligence could defeat much larger armies. The PAL'MACH's first SOE-inspired campaign was against the Vichy French in Lebanon and Syria—a harbinger of the future for the State of Israel. With the Germans occupying the isle of Crete, a mere five hundred miles from the Lebanese shore, British Intelligence had good reason to believe that the Germans would move into Lebanon, with the blessing of the Vichy French, which would position a force poised to advance through Iraq and Iran toward India—a catastrophe of unimaginable proportions for the British.[12] Accordingly, the Allies planned to invade Syria, with the PAL'MACH in the forefront. Their first action was also one of the more mysterious and tragic chapters in PAL'MACH's history.

Since 1940, the SOE had been training a group of Jewish frogmen in great secrecy in Tel Aviv's Exhibition Park. The group was intended to serve as an elite intelligence warfare strike force, primarily, it is believed, for action in Europe, where they would be infiltrated by amphibious means. The unfolding events in Lebanon and Syria, however, reshaped the military priorities. On the night of May 18, 1941, twenty-three of these HAGANAH frogmen set sail, along with British Maj. Anthony Palmer, from northern Palestine on the HMS *Sea Lion*, a motorized Coast Guard craft; the objective was the destruction of oil refineries in Tripoli, Lebanon. The team disappeared without a trace, and to this day no one knows what became of them. Some reports indicated that they were seized by an Italian submarine, brought to internment in Italy, and later executed.[13] The failed operation was so covert that the families of the fallen were not even informed of their loss until much later.

The British were also training different elements of the YISHUV in intelligence and sabotage tradecraft, including the right-wing extremist IRGUN underground, commanded by the wily Menachem Begin. When the Second World War broke out, the anti-British IRGUN declared a cease-fire and many of its officers were released from detention, including two commanders, Ya'akov Meridor and David Raziel. The SOE called on the IRGUN for assistance when the pro-Nazi Rashid Ali al-Gailani, together with the support of the Grand Mufti of Jerusalem, Haj Amin Husseini, took power in Iraq through a coup d'état on April 1, 1941. The IRGUN had conducted operations worldwide and had maintained an excellent network in Iraq, especially in Baghdad. Their time for action came in May, when Rashid Ali's men began to bombard the Royal Air Force (RAF) base at Habbaniya, and a pogrom in Baghdad resulted in the deaths of more than 150 Jews.

The SOE wanted the IRGUN to destroy Ali's supply dumps. Raziel and Meridor agreed to lead the team personally, to gather intelligence and sabotage key Iraqi positions. The IRGUN team also had as one of its objectives the assassination of the Mufti, the spiritual leader of Palestinian Arab nationalism, the brainchild of the brutal 1936–39 Arab riots, and, based on his conduct while in the company of Adolf Hitler, a Nazi war criminal.[14] Tragically, however, Raziel was killed on May 20, 1941, when a Luftwaffe fighter-bomber scored a direct hit on his automobile. The IRGUN mission was abruptly terminated.

The British later moved against Rashid Ali, utilizing Transjordan's highly professional Arab Legions, but the IRGUN missed its golden opportunity to rid itself of the Mufti; he found sanctuary in the Japanese Embassy in Teheran from where he would later embrace Hitler.

The SOE's intelligence training, however, was not lost. Many IRGUN officers would eventually translate their newly learned skills in the fight against the British and, following Israeli independence and the IRGUN's acceptance into the Israel Defense Forces, as intelligence agents serving in A'MAN.

With British attention removed from Iraq, newly formed segments of the PAL'MACH were sent into action. Elements of Sadeh's Arabic-speaking intelligence force, which by 1941 had returned to HAGANAH and Jewish Agency control, were reinstated into the PAL'MACH into what became known, under their SOE classification, as HA'MACHLAKA HA'SURIT ("Syrian Platoon"), an intelligence-gathering force composed entirely of Arabic-speaking Jews who could pass themselves off as Arabs.[15] Dressed in clothing unique to Bedouins, the Lebanese, and Syrians, the disguised Palestinian Jews infiltrated into Vichy territory and monitored French military movements, unit strength, and their order of battle. The information was duly relayed to the SOE through David Hacohen, the HAGANAH's (as well as the PAL'MACH's) liaison with British Intelligence. Should full-scale conflict erupt, the men and women of the Syrian Platoon, commanded by Yigal Allon, were also to serve as fifth-column guerrillas, disrupting Vichy lines of supply and communications as well as initiating a psychological warfare campaign.

When the Allies invaded the Vichy-controlled Levant, the Jews of the SOE's Syrian Platoon were instrumental players. As a result of their frequent cross-border intelligence-gathering forays behind enemy lines, the intelligence soldiers of the Syrian Platoon were able to map and range targets for Allied air power and artillery strikes, and secure key routes of advance, including the seizing of bridges.* Their reconnaissance missions uncovered roads that the British did not know existed and located French military roadblocks and ambushes. On the basis of the intelligence obtained by the PAL'MACH, the French were taken by surprise when the Allies mounted the invasion.[16] Most importantly, the Jews proved their worth as scouts to the advancing vanguard of an Allied task force composed of British, Australian, and a token Free French contingent, which made its way through the mountain passes to invade Lebanon and Syria on June 8, 1941. Among those serving as scouts during the offensive were Yigal Allon and Moshe Dayan, who, during the battle for a Vichy

*For such cross-border intelligence-gathering forays, the PAL'MACH enlisted the support of Druze and Circassian Moslem guides. This practice was continued following Israeli independence when the IDF utilized these minorities in the State of Israel as soldiers in the indigenous "Unit 300" and as guides for military intelligence operatives crossing the borders into enemy territory.

police fort, lost his eye—one of the most famous war wounds in history! Many Allied commanders were quick to compliment the Jewish fighters on their skill, courage, and determination, but the PAL'MACH officers were not interested in faint praise. Instead of compliments they opted for rewards, and many Allied commanders, unaware of the struggle for Israeli statehood, gave the Jews captured French weaponry. These guns, pistols, and explosives were smuggled back to Israel for later use against both the British and Arabs.[17]

Originally, when the PAL'MACH was created on May 15, 1941, the British sanctioned the creation of nine PAL'MACH battalions with a total of 1,080 men and women under arms. Later that summer, two PAL'MACH training camps were established at Kibbutz Ginosar and Beit Oren. Yitzhak Sadeh knew that once Lebanon and Syria were secure, the prosperous relationship between the SOE and his Strike Companies would cease under political pressure, and they would be forced to go underground. So he pushed his men and women harshly; they lived in the most spartan conditions, training incessantly, and surviving in the field without the luxuries of quartermasters, cooks, and orderlies.

But the war worsened for the Allies. As Rommel's Afrika Korps made its steady advance through the North African desert toward Egypt, worst-case-scenario contingency planning for a probable Nazi invasion of Palestine was entertained. The British prepared for an evacuation from Palestine while the Jews prepared for what could be the death of their nation. A desperate plan was even formulated to turn the area between Mt. Carmel and the mountains of western Galilee into a modern-day Metzada (this was the fortress overlooking the Dead Sea where, in A.D. 73, 960 Jewish zealots besieged by the Roman Legions committed suicide rather than submit to slavery). The "fortress," part of the contingency known as the Carmel Plan, was to be supplied by British submarines and airdrops. In the British scheme of things, the enclave would serve as a base from which PAL'MACH units would harass the might of the German war machine. The twenty-four SOE-trained HAGANAH men and women, as part of a special intelligence unit commanded by Moshe Dayan, would operate secretive radio equipment and relay back to London intelligence data on German troop movements.

Within weeks of the setbacks in the North African desert, the SOE supported more than three hundred PAL'MACH fighters for elaborate commando and intelligence warfare training; the HAGANAH deviously managed to train three times as many commandos. They trained at an impromptu base located at Kibbutz Mishmar Ha'emek, in the Jezreel Valley. The PAL'MACH fighters were taught to fight with what was available rather than what was tactically advisable. Under British guidance, they honed their skills in demolition, cold killing, and marksmanship; after all, ammunition was a scarce commodity. They were trained in every weapon to be found in the area, from the German MP-38 Schmeisser submachine gun to their issued British Stens. The PAL'MACH fighters developed their own unique form of martial arts, known as KRAV MAGA ("close-quarter battle"), and were even trained to withstand capture, interrogation, and torture at the hands of the Gestapo.

Throughout the course of the SOE training, the PAL'MACH developed its own brand of innovativeness and ingenuity for guerrilla warfare and intelligence operations; the PAL'MACH was, in fact, the proving ground of the HAGANAH. Since the Jews of Palestine came from more than sixty nations, their ability to masquerade as members of any nationality became a trademark of Israeli intelligence operations. Three unique language-based PAL'MACH units had profound impact on the later development of IDF Military Intelligence.

The most fascinating was HA'MACHLAKA HA'GERMANIT ("German Platoon"), commanded by two of Sadeh's longtime comrades, Shimon Avidan and Yehuda Ben Hurin. Both commanders searched the ranks of the HAGANAH for recruits, and more than sixty people volunteered. In all, the platoon was composed of only forty-five fighters, because most volunteers failed to pass the grueling physical and emotional entrance examinations. Both Avidan and Ben Hurin chose their *soldaten* and intelligence warriors well. One of their most promising fighters was a German Jew named Avraham Seidenwerg, a man who years later, as an agent of A'MAN, would be the infamous Third Man in the disastrous "Lavon Affair." Another German Platoon member, Dan Laner, became a parachutist for the SOE (serving as liaison with Yugoslav partisans) and eventually a major general in the Israel Defense Forces.[18]

Originally, the German Platoon was designed as a harassing force to attack German rear columns should they succeed in invading Palestine. When Rommel's advance halted, the German Platoon became a first-rate intelligence force, which was the cutting edge of British special operations in North Africa and the Mediterranean. The German Platoon was composed *entirely* of Jewish refugees, escapees from Germany and Austria who, with fair hair, Aryan features, and language skills, could masquerade as German soldiers in deep-penetration intelligence operations behind German lines. Their training base at Mishmar Ha'emek resembled a German army installation, and the soldiers of the German Platoon spoke only German (Hebrew was strictly forbidden). In PAL'MACH tradition, they conducted frequent brutally paced forced marches through the Jezreel Valley countryside, the most harsh being a five-day march throughout the entire country.

The sight of armed men sounding off in German alarmed many of the local residents, but such was Palestine during the Second World War. The German barracks, a series of damp caves in the Jezreel Valley, were decorated with Nazi posters and flags and the songs of the Afrika Korps, the Luftwaffe, and the Kriegsmarine. In their spare time, platoon members wore German army uniforms and read Nazi publications. For these fighters to speak the language and wear the uniform of their hated homelands required supreme emotional discipline.

After being properly, and intensively, indoctrinated into the art of irregular warfare, the platoon was sent to SOE headquarters, in Cairo, Egypt, for additional training. Wehrmacht defectors, SOE experts, and Afrika Korps POWs taught their Jewish pupils everything there was to know about being a Deutscher *soldaten*. In the classroom, the role of the German soldier was studied, from basic training in Bavaria to service in the Western Desert. They became proficient with every weapon in the Nazi arsenal, from the MP-40 submachine gun to the K-98 Mauser rifle. They were taught the intricacies of German military life and day-to-day procedures: rank insignias, pay scales, even the most popular brothels and watering holes. It was a fantastic irony that Jews, most of whom had escaped the Nazi terror only a few years earlier, were now emulating their former persecutors.

The most capable members of the German Platoon were dispatched, as German soldiers, into British prisoner of war (POW) camps, where they were able to mingle with other Germans interned by the British and gather impressive amounts of intelligence data that SOE interrogations and aerial photographs were unable to uncover.

Another unit of the German Platoon was trained and intended to execute a most audacious plan—to infiltrate the desert wasteland and blow up Rommel's headquarters.[19] Other German Platoon commandos served with Capt. David Sterling's Long-Range Desert Group (LRDG) in the Western Desert. There were even plans for a large force of German Platoon parachutists to jump into Germany and Austria and conduct intelligence-gathering reconnaissance forays.[20] When the British ordered the PAL'MACH disbanded in 1943–44, the German Platoon became the intelligence element within the Jewish Brigade, which fought in Italy. Following the war, HAGANAH, SHA'I, RECHESH, and MOSSAD LE'ALIYAH BET operatives were sent into Europe to facilitate the smuggling of Jewish refugees into Palestine.

A much smaller "Balkan Platoon," made up of HAGANAH fighters who hailed from the Balkan States, also served alongside the SOE and commandos from the British Special Air Service (SAS) in the Greek isles and Yugoslavia.* And, it has been rumored, there was a "Romanian Platoon," which had as its principal objective the destruction of the oil fields at Ploesti.

Yet the first, largest, and most important (for the struggle ahead) PAL'MACH platoon to be conceived was HA'MACHLAKA HA'ARAVIT ("Arab Platoon"). The Arab Platoon already had its own cadre of officers and agents at the ready; they dated back to Yitzhak Sadeh's Field Companies intelligence unit, the SHA'I's Arab Department, and the SOE's Syrian Platoon. The Arab Platoon

---

*Many members of the Balkan Platoon later served as parachutists for the SOE and were dropped into Central Europe to relay intelligence and forge contacts with the trapped Jewish communities in Hungary and Czechoslovakia.

was composed of Jews from the Middle East diaspora who were taught to act, speak, and think like Arabs. They were instructed in the teachings of Islam, and the Arab histories and traditions. Their commander was Yerucham Cohen, who, in spite of the disadvantage of his fair complexion and red beard, proved to be a natural in intelligence operations. The force donned Arab dress and was dispatched to Syria, Lebanon, and Transjordan to be in place should the Nazis succeed in conquering Egypt and the remainder of the Middle East.

Yerucham Cohen's Arab Platoon was a purely volunteer force; the fighters did not receive pay and were supported by family and friends. The platoon was trained quite extensively for irregular warfare, but they proved to be superb intelligence agents as well. From Beirut to Damascus, from the Galilee hills to the bustling marketplace of Hebron, the agents of the Arab Platoon established their covers, infiltrated pro-Nazi groups, and faithfully reported their activities back to their SOE handlers (their SOE liaison was Major Hammond) by utilizing top-secret radio transmitters.

Three of the Arab Platoon's best operatives—Akiva Feinstein, Shaul Elgavish, and Moshe Adaki—were planted in Beirut, the platoon's principal base of operations, in 1942. Yerucham Cohen supervised his agents throughout the Levant with extensive travel. Although the Arab Platoon was highly successful in its covert intelligence-gathering operations, there were incidental problems in establishing identity, which could have led to tragic results. According to Yerucham Cohen, "When we arrived in Beirut, I responded to a waiter's question in a restaurant with the word *aiwa*, meaning yes. But in Beirut one should say, *ah*. When he heard the word *aiwa*, he said, 'You are a Palestinian. . . .' In Tripoli, a twelve-year-old boy asked me if I wanted my shoes shined. He was apparently an expert in his trade. He kneaded the leather of my shoe, feeling it well, and then told me: 'This shoe was bought in Haifa!' " [21]

Sometimes their luck ran out. Once, in Damascus, sympathizers of the platoon were arrested and, when tortured by a particularly sadistic Syrian detective, gave up Cohen and his men. They were freed only after the intervention of their SOE liaison, Major Hammond. [22]

Although such heart-stopping events were frequent, the Arab Platoon was viewed as a highly effective force. The British also held the platoon's commander, Cohen, in high regard, even training him in great secrecy in Egypt to undertake an underwater sabotage mission against a German warship. The operation was never executed and, when it was clear to the British that their Middle Eastern empire was no longer threatened by the Germans, the Arab Platoon was officially disbanded. In actuality, it went underground, only to resurface a few months later as one of the most important elements in the history and operational formation of an active Israeli military intelligence force.

NOTES: CHAPTER ONE

1. Yigal Allon, *Shield of David: The Story of Israel's Armed Forces* (London: Weidenfeld and Nicolson, 1970), 39.

2. Stewart Steven, *The Spymasters of Israel: The Definitive Inside Look at the World's Best Intelligence Service* (New York: Ballantine Books, 1980), 4.

3. Yehuda Slotsky, KITZUR TOLDOT HA'HAGANAH (Tel Aviv: Israel Defense Ministry Publications, 1978), 105.

4. Isser Harel, BITACHON VE'DEMOKRATIA (Tel Aviv: Edanim Publishers Ltd., 1989), 74.

5. *Ibid.* 75.

6. See Yehuda Slotsky, KITZUR TOLDOT HA'HAGANAH (Tel Aviv: Israel Ministry of Defense Publications, 1978), 292.

7. Hagai Eshed, MOSSAD SHEL ISH ECHAD: REUVEN SHILOAH—AVI HA'MODE'IN HA'YISRAELI (Jerusalem: Edanim Publishers, 1988), 58.

8. Yigal Lossin, *Pillar of Fire: The Rebirth of Israel—A Visual History* (Jerusalem: Shikmona Publishing Company, Ltd., 1983), 299.

9. Nicholas Bethell, *The Palestine Triangle: The Struggle between the British, the Jews and the Arabs 1935–1948* (London: Andre Deutsch Limited, 1979), 102.

10. See Yigal Lossin, *Pillar of Fire*, 297.

11. Ephraim Dekel, ALILOT SHA'I (Tel Aviv: Israel Defense Force "Ma'arachot" Publications, 1953), 252.

12. See Nicholas Bethell, *The Palestine Triangle*, 104.

13. Alex Doron, "TA'ALUMAT YORDEI HASIRA: HA'TIK NISGAR," MA'ARIV SOF SHAVUAH (December 9, 1988): 29.

14. Colonel (Res.) Tzvi Elpeleg, HA'MUFTI HA'GADOL (Tel Aviv: Israel Ministry of Defense Publications, 1989), 65.

15. Tzika Dror, HA'MISTA'ARAVIM SHEL HA'PAL'MACH (Tel Aviv: Hakibbutz Hameuchad Publishing House, Ltd., 1986), 12.

16. Mordechai Noar, ed., HA'HAGANAH (Tel Aviv: Israel Ministry of Defense Publications, 1985), 140.

17. Yaakov Markovitzki, HA'YECHIDOT HA'YABASHTIYOT HA'MEYUCHADOT SHEL HA'PAL'MACH (Tel Aviv: Israel Ministry of Defense Publications, 1989), 61.

18. See Nicholas Bethell, *The Palestine Triangle*, 104.

19. See Yaakov Markovitzki, HA'YECHIDOT HA'YABASHTIYOT, 67.

20. See Yigal Lossin, *Pillar of Fire*, 331.

21. *Ibid.* 331.

22. Yeruham Cohen, *By Light and in Darkness* (Tel Aviv: Amikam Publishers, 1969), 36.

CHAPTER 2

THE TRANSFORMATION OF SHA'I

T he 1943 British High Command directive, ordering the PAL'MACH to return their British-supplied arms, appeared to signal the end to the Second World War "marriage of convenience," which the HAGANAH hoped would provide the foundations of a capable Jewish military force—not only for the conflict against the British, but the later struggle against the Arabs. The British decision came at the worst possible time: The Strike Companies were on the verge of training nearly three thousand fighters—a formidable contingent. The PAL'MACH's intelligence forces, mainly the Arab Platoon, had flourished with British funding and support; the leadership of Yerucham Cohen and the abilities of its agents were laying the groundwork for a capable military intelligence infrastructure. The Arab Platoon continued to work for the HAGANAH and SHA'I, operating in compartmentalized cells and preparing routes throughout the Middle East through which the MOSSAD LE'ALIYAH BET could smuggle Jewish refugees into Palestine via Turkey, Syria, and Lebanon. HAGANAH Chief of Staff Eliahu Golomb also expressed his displeasure with the termination of the British relationship, since it cut short the development of a viable military intelligence entity. While the SHA'I was a capable intelligence-gathering force and counterintelligence agency staffed by dedicated agents, it lacked the military framework—complete with military-trained units—needed to conduct long-range reconnaissance operations.

Oddly enough, just as British Intelligence appeared to no longer need the eager Jewish fighters, a new use for them was discovered from a most obscure source for service in a treacherous arena of operations.

MI-9 (or Military Intelligence 9) was the British military intelligence body responsible for coordinating the escape, and hiding, of British POWs; its civilian name was Evasion and Escape. Initially a small force, MI-9 expanded as the Allies moved to the offensive and the aerial campaign against Nazi-occupied Europe increased in size and scale. The principal recipients of MI-9 assistance were, of course, downed airmen—men whose lengthy training demanded that they return to active service as soon as possible.

The commander of MI-9 was a career intelligence officer, Lt. Col. Anthony "Tony" Simmonds, who had served in Palestine during the riots of 1936–39. Simmonds was a strong supporter of the Zionist cause, and during this tour in Palestine, he had forged a close friendship and working relationship with Reuven Zaslani, one of the first officers of SHA'I. It was Zaslani who had urged cooperation, at least on the intelligence front, between the British and the Jews of Palestine. In 1943, Zaslani fervently and persistently supported sending Jewish agents into Nazi-occupied Europe to assist Allied Intelligence.[1]

Reuven Zaslani remains to this day one of the most admired and mysterious members of the Israeli intelligence community. Some have said that he was born a secret agent; he reveled in secrecy, mystery, and the Israeli trait of self-imposed censorship.[2] Known as the founding father of Israeli intelligence, Zaslani was unique among the early Israeli statesmen because he was born in Jerusalem, not Eastern Europe. Born Reuven Zaslanski, he was a serious and gifted student—talents not lost to David Ben-Gurion and the commanders of the HAGANAH. He first Hebracized his name to Zaslani; later he would change his name to Shiloah (SHALIAH is the Hebrew word for emissary, which fitted with his secretive and well-traveled life-style with the HAGANAH).

Reuven Zaslani's first foreign assignment came in 1931, when he was dispatched to Baghdad and planted as a deep-cover operative; his job was as a schoolteacher, a position that allowed him to forge an extensive network of informants and agents. It was during his posting to Iraq that Zaslani came into contact with the Kurds, a non-Arab and often persecuted minority in the Middle East. In the oppressed Kurds, Zaslani envisioned a future ally for the Jews: He dreamed of eventually forging espionage alliances with all the non-Arab minorities of the Middle East.[3] This would become known as the "peripheral philosophy" of Israeli intelligence and, as discussed in Chapter Thirteen, materialized with Israeli military assistance to the Kurds, intelligence cooperation with the shah of Iran, and the ill-fated relationship with the Lebanese Christians in the years prior to the 1982 invasion.

When Zaslani returned to Palestine in 1934, he helped create the SHA'I and served as liaison between Ben-Gurion's Jewish Agency and the British. It was here that his contacts were established and strengthened; the relationship expanded when the Second World War erupted and he was among the first HAGANAH officers to openly call for active Jewish involvement. Reuven

Zaslani was deeply influenced by the practices of British Intelligence, especially by Brig. Gen. Dudley Clark, the commander of the A Force, the shadowy organization that oversaw the operations of MI-9, and another intelligence unit known as "Deception." Clark, a career intelligence officer who served in Palestine during the 1936 riots, was a firm believer in "strategic deception," a tactic of never conceding one's strengths, weaknesses, or intentions by maintaining a strict blanket of security over military installations and combatants alike, and, of course, by releasing false signals to the enemy whenever possible. This strategy would be religiously deployed by A'MAN in the years to come.

Strategic deception was also one of the objectives when, in 1943, Reuven Zaslani, as head of the SHA'I, and Zeev "Dani" Shind, one of the commanders of the MOSSAD LE'ALIYAH BET, signed an agreement with Lieutenant Colonel Simmonds to form a unit called "Land of Israel Parachutists," a literal translation of its Hebrew name. Primarily, the force was meant to set up way stations in Central Europe for Allied airmen who were shot down during the bombings of industrial and strategic targets, especially the Ploesti oil field in Romania.[4]

Their true HAGANAH objective, however, as set forth by Reuven Zaslani and the SHA'I command, was to help smuggle Jews out of Romania, in particular, to safe haven in Turkey. The Jewish Agency had for years been adamant about using the capable fighters of the HAGANAH to help save the Jews of Europe. Such large-scale and *overt* involvement, however, was seen as politically undesirable by the British; concern over Arab reaction, even though the Palestinians tended to side with Hitler, was of paramount importance in the corridors of Whitehall. Nevertheless, on January 20, 1943, Reuven Zaslani met with General McCary, chief of staff of the British Middle Eastern Command in Cairo, and offered five hundred "Land of Israel Parachutists," all natives of Central Europe, for intelligence missions behind German lines. Zaslani was frustrated by British rebuffs of his contingencies to save the Jews of Europe militarily; therefore, he tried to form a PAL'MACH type of commando force to be created and dropped into Poland, where they would supply arms to the Jewish resistance organizations in the ghettos and create serious military problems in the German rear.

The British remained apprehensive about accepting full HAGANAH and SHA'I assistance. Zaslani had to look elsewhere for a sympathetic ear and tangible results. He turned to the Office of Strategic Services, better known as the OSS.* Zaslani hoped that Washington would help form the Jewish intelli-

---

*This was not the first, nor last, contact between the OSS and the SHA'I. In 1941, Zaslani met with Gen. William Donovon and other figures in the American intelligence community concerning sanctioning a force of "Israeli" intelligence agents to

gence and commando force, but the British intervened, claiming that the Jews
were their responsibility and the Americans had no business with them.[5]
The relationship between the SOE and the HAGANAH was, in fact, deterio-
rating at a rapid pace. The turning point came in March 1943, when a force
of PAL'MACH fighters attacked the SOE training facility atop Mt. Carmel in
Haifa and stole a vast quantity of arms that the British had previously con-
fiscated from them. This operation led the British to look elsewhere for help,
and, in Syria and Lebanon, the SOE turned to Armenians, Circassians, and
Maronite Christians.

In the end, only two hundred fifty "Land of Israel Parachutists" volunteered and very few were ever dropped behind Nazi lines in Greece, Italy,
Hungary, Romania, Bulgaria, Slovakia, and Yugoslavia. The Jewish parachutists,
along with Tito's guerrillas, faced Bosnian Moslems drafted by the Grand
Mufti of Jerusalem on behalf of the Nazi SS (the Tito regime would later
declare Haj Amin Husseini a war criminal). Of the thirty-four Israeli parachutists who were dropped into Europe, twelve were captured and seven executed,
including Hanah Szenesh, who became a stoic symbol of martyrdom, and Enzo
Sereni, one of the commanders of the MOSSAD LE'ALIYAH BET and a parachutist instructor who was captured in northern Italy and sent to his death in the
Dachau concentration camp.

The effectiveness of the Israeli paratroopers, and their dedication—which
allowed them to fill a dual role with dual loyalty—was absolute and ad-
mirable. In Yugoslavia alone, the Israeli parachutists were able to save one
hundred twenty-four British and American airmen who had bailed out after
their aircraft were hit by German air and ground fire. The success of their
activities in Central Europe was proof of the strict and, some say, zealous
training and briefing. The parachutists knew their land of destination as though
they had left it only a week before: They wore typical clothing; they knew
the train schedules and fares; and they knew who, and who not, to trust. The
detailed preoperation groundwork became a trademark of Israeli intelligence in the years to follow. In addition, most of the parachutists remained
in Europe at the war's end and helped facilitate the illegal immigration of
countless refugees to Palestine. Many would continue their intelligence work
years later for the MOSSAD, the SHIN BET, and, of course, A'MAN.

---

be parachuted into Europe, but the British demanded that such contacts cease. According to Reuven Shiloah's biographer, Hagai Eshed, Zaslani had forged close contacts with American intelligence agents while sipping cocktails in Cairo officers' clubs
and nightclubs. The OSS had also contacted SHA'I regarding German-speaking Jewish agents to be used in Soviet-occupied Austria. A special relationship would soon
develop between Zaslani/Shiloah and the CIA, especially with James Angeleton, and
was the beginning of a unique and close military relationship with the United States
intelligence and military community.

The end of the war in Europe also led to the final chapter in the military relationship between the intelligence agencies of the HAGANAH and Great Britain. For the Jews, the British connection had been highly prosperous: SOE training, funds, and equipment—as well as combat experience—had allowed the SHA'I to develop from an intelligence force primarily concerned with political threats, to a force—with the formation of the PAL'MACH—capable of long-range military operations and intelligence-gathering forays. Most importantly, the years with British intelligence served as a laboratory for the tactics, strategies, and means by which the espionage services—especially the intelligence arm of the Israel Defense Forces—of the future State of Israel would operate.

Aspects of these "laboratory years," as some have called it, were evident in some of the smaller SHA'I intelligence units, such as the MISRAD HA'CHAKIROT ("Investigations Office") commanded by Gideon Rafael. Together with the Military Intelligence 4 ("MI-4") contingent in the Middle East—known as SIME, or "Security Intelligence Middle East"—the primary task of the Investigations Office was the interrogation of new immigrants to Palestine, especially those arriving through Turkey via Syria. The British and SHA'I feared that German Military Intelligence would infiltrate agents to Palestine disguised as Jewish refugees. Another, and more important, task of the SHA'I's Investigations Office was assembling evidence on Nazi war crimes and criminals for use at later legal proceedings, such as the Nuremberg trials following the war. They compiled a ledger of the property stolen by the Nazis from individual Jews and Jewish communities throughout Europe. This information was utilized following the war to prove Jewish compensation claims, and these funds helped subsidize the Jewish state in its early years, especially in defense purchases.

Another important aspect of the cooperation between the Jews of Palestine and the British during the Second World War, which had a profound impact on the creation of the Israel Defense Forces and its intelligence arm, was the Jewish Brigade Group, formed on September 20, 1944. Although they wore British uniforms and carried British weapons, the soldiers of the brigade were, in fact, Israel's first conventional fighting force, equipped with its own staff, services, supporting arms, and cadre of NCOs and officers. Many distinguished members of the Israel Defense Forces came out of the brigade. In all, five thousand were trained and sent to northern Italy, where they saw limited fighting in a neglected front of the Western European campaign.

The soldiers of the Jewish Brigade found themselves in a most difficult moral dilemma. Having heard about or visited the Nazi death camps, these Jewish soldiers thirsted for vengeance. In a Europe where six million of their brethren had been slaughtered, many of the soldiers awaited their chance to murder a Nazi and rape a German woman.[6] Fearing such acts of revenge, the British rescinded their original plans to have elements of the brigade police Germany during the Allied occupation. As a result, the brigade remained in Italy, Belgium, and Holland for garrison duty—far from any contact with the

Germans. Even so, the HAGANAH High Command was resolute not to let any Nazi criminals slip through Allied lines!

Even though many of the soldiers in the Jewish Brigade were not serving fighters in the HAGANAH, a small group of Jewish Brigade officers formed a small clandestine force known as HA'NOKMIM ("the Avengers"). The group centered around Israel Carmi, a Long-Range Desert Group veteran, who was assigned to a brigade intelligence unit sanctioned with rounding up Nazi officers hiding around the brigade's headquarters in Treviso, Italy, so that they could be turned over to the British.[7] Carmi was a veteran of Yitzhak Sadeh's Field Companies and Orde Wingate's Special Night Squads. During the war, he volunteered to serve in the British army, where he was recruited by the SOE for a special unit, the Special Interrogation Group, for operations behind German lines in the Western Desert; it was here that he learned the skills of commando operations, as well as the inescapable labyrinth of treachery involved in counterintelligence work from several Abwher agents in their ranks. Joining this covert campaign of retribution were Haim Laskov, an eventual IDF chief of staff, and Meir "Zaro" Zore'a, an eventual IDF major general, as well as dozens of veterans of the German Platoon who were attached to the brigade as scouts, saboteurs, and intelligence agents. They were all well-trained intelligence officers.

The Avengers' operations began with a captured SS captain who, when promised that his life would be spared, compromised the whereabouts of his fellow officers in hiding. With a well-detailed list of all the Nazi officers in hiding in northern Italy, the Avenger squads, protected by their British uniforms and identification papers, went to work. There is no official body count, but moderate estimates place the number of executed Nazis in the hundreds. Although political directives from Jerusalem called for trials to be held, the soldiers in the field did not see the need for the formalities of a tribunal. They checked and cross-checked every Nazi they executed, never killing a man unless there was irrefutable proof of his guilt (the notion of eliminating the very guilty would become a standard of many Israeli intelligence antiterrorist operations in the following years).

The Avengers had kept their activities secret not only from their fellow brigade members (the HAGANAH already boasted a well-taught tradition of keeping those privy to classified information to the absolute minimum), but also from the British, who surely would have ceased this maverick operation.

The Avengers continued their operations until the winter of 1946, when the brigade was disbanded and repatriated to Palestine. Most of the members returned home, where they were conscripted into the ranks of the HAGANAH for the struggle ahead; others remained behind in Italy, where they proved instrumental in Operation Bricha ("the flight"), the complex and highly covert human smuggling ring that brought Jewish refugees to Palestine.

*   *   *

As the war in Europe ended, the *true* struggle for Israel's independence began. In the intelligence campaign of spies, terrorists, and informers, Palestine reverted to its prewar days of chaos. The destruction of Nazi Germany also destroyed the gentleman's agreement that treated the British White Paper with indifference. As the various Jewish liberation movements in Palestine moved toward armed struggle against the British, a vicious and highly controversial cycle of fraternal infighting, treason, and murder rocked the YISHUV's intelligence community. It all started with an obscure group whose actions shocked even bloodstained Palestine at a time when a political solution to the Arab-Israeli question was being discussed by the British.

On November 6, 1944, Lord Walter Edwarde Guiness Moyne, the British minister of state of Middle Eastern Affairs and an ardent anti-Zionist, was assassinated in Cairo by two gunmen of the LOHAMEI HERUT YISRAEL ("Fighters for the Freedom of Israel"), more commonly known as the LEHI, or Stern Gang. A volatile and extreme group, the Stern Gang had actually approached the German Embassy in Ankara, Turkey, in January 1941, and offered to "assist in the conquest of Palestine and its delivery from the British to the Germans, in exchange for a Jewish state and the transfer of the Jews of Europe to that state." [8] The murder of Lord Moyne infuriated the British, and a vigilant roundup of Stern Gang, IRGUN, and HAGANAH agents began; those caught, including a future MOSSAD station chief and Israeli Prime Minister Yitzhak Shamir, were exiled to Eritrea and Kenya. Many of those seized by the British, however, had been captured, compromised, and handed over by the SHA'I. It was known as the Saison ("open season").

The Saison was carried out by SHA'I liaison officers, including Teddy Kollek (an intelligence officer and future Jerusalem mayor), who met daily with officers from the CID. The HAGANAH would detain the "Jewish dissidents," interrogate them, then either release them or hand them over to the authorities. Using SHA'I records, squads of PAL'MACH fighters traced Stern Gang and IRGUN suspects and, after the go-ahead from SHA'I HQ, arrested them. SHA'I agents would often identify suspects for the British, primarily to prevent accidental arrest of their own undercover agents; the SHA'I, however, gave up only "unimportant fish." IRGUN commander Menachem Begin, who was forced into hiding, viewed the Saison as a shameful betrayal of the Jewish war of liberation, and many HAGANAH officers despised the fact that their cause was working against itself. But HAGANAH cooperation with the British—at this stage of the struggle—was crucial. The assassination of Lord Moyne polarized British opinion and warranted a "Union Jack iron fist," which might very well have crippled the HAGANAH's capabilities against the most important adversary in the region—the Arabs.

On March 9, 1945, the SHA'I resumed transmissions of its illegal radio network, KOL YISRAEL ("Voice of Israel"), to relay instructions and warnings to its agents throughout the Middle East. By V-E Day, the SHA'I's principal intelligence-gathering efforts, as well as selective acts of sabotage, had been directed against the British—both in the espionage and counterintelligence arenas. Through coded messages and seemingly innocent personal greetings, deep-cover SHA'I operatives maintained constant communications with headquarters while at the same time providing the Jewish population with propaganda; Voice of Israel often publicized anti-British messages, including the mentioning of remote acts of British barbarity and violence against Jews as rallying cries for anti-British resistance.[9] SHA'I also used its radio facilities to monitor British military radio transmissions; in many cases, SHA'I's monitoring of the British lines informed the HAGANAH High Command of either the success or failure of its offensive military operations before messengers returned to Tel Aviv. This real-time intelligence allowed HAGANAH forces to coordinate their escape-and-evasion tactics by knowing where British forces were heading, where roadblocks were positioned, and what moves the British commanders were discussing. They also jammed British military transmissions to Royal Navy vessels hunting down illegal immigration ships. KOL YISRAEL enraged the British. Most baffling was their inability to ever locate the SHA'I transmitter. The CID brought in elaborate equipment from England, as well as Scotland Yard signal-tracking experts, but found nothing; the transmitter was located on a very mobile and well-traveled truck!

SHA'I's British Department was responsible for the "strategic deception" aspect of the campaign. It not only gathered and disseminated intelligence data on British military and police intentions, but leaked a wide variety of farfetched and false rumors; one such tidbit was vastly overestimating the HAGANAH's Order of Battle. SHA'I was also tasked with the security of the HAGANAH's primitive weapons-manufacturing industry, known as TA'AS, as well as its well-hidden arms caches, or *slicks*, where the invaluable commodity was stored. SHA'I's internal security apparatus forbade even senior commanders of the HAGANAH from knowing where arms workshops were located. SHA'I ensured that negotiated arms deals were not British traps; its agents were planted as postal workers and customs inspectors to help facilitate the smuggling of weapons and ammunition.[10] Determined not to have any of its few installations compromised, agents were *carefully* screened and informants dealt with harshly.

There were also SHA'I sabotage operations, including attacks on British naval vessels, and SHA'I assistance to the MOSSAD LE'ALIYAH BET, mainly in operations against the Royal Navy. False rumors of immigrant ship landings were filtered to Royal Navy HQ, leaving unhindered the beaches where real landings were transpiring. The SHA'I's most successful operation was the capture in May 1946 of the CID's dreaded "Black List," a painstakingly compiled top-secret collection of the names and addresses of thousands of HAGANAH, SHA'I, PAL'MACH, and other underground operatives throughout Palestine. SHA'I photographed the files, put the endangered agents in hiding, and returned the files before the British were the wiser. By the time the CID, the red berets of the British 6th Airborne Division, and police units went into action to round up those on the list, it was rendered absolutely useless. According to General Barker, commanding officer of the British army in Palestine, the SHA'I was a "perfect intelligence system."[11]

The one force entrusted and prepared to serve as a military intelligence–gathering force for the struggle of independence was, of course, the PAL'MACH. Militarily, the PAL'MACH was the HAGANAH's cutting edge, a force of the elite young men and women of the Jewish community. With its British-taught discipline and Zionist dedication and indoctrination, the PAL'MACH's spectacular operations belied its small numbers, precious few arms, and outnumbered status. It can be argued that the PAL'MACH was a commando, as well as an intelligence, force. Their most potent intelligence weapon for a campaign against the Palestinian Arabs was the SHACHAR ("dawn")—the Arab Platoon.

The British decision to end its relationship with the PAL'MACH in 1943, along with Yigal Allon's decision to resign his command of the Syrian Platoon, signaled the deployment of SHACHAR against Arab objectives. During its years of service with the British, the Syrian Platoon agents were the Jewish state's first cross-border covert operation warriors. Their operations in Syria and Lebanon were important not only in the data brought back to the British, or to their HAGANAH handlers in Jerusalem, but also because Syria and Lebanon were a testing ground where the techniques for going deep-cover inside enemy territory were established, examined, and perfected. The thriving cities of Beirut, Tripoli, and Damascus were, of course, easier to infiltrate than the mountains of Galilee and the Judean hills, where the local villagers would identify and deal with strangers more effectively. Yet for a Yemenite Jew to blend into the day-to-day life of Beirut was in itself an achievement; success in Beirut was a stepping-stone for being dispatched to the Palestinian cities of Hebron, Nablus, and Jenin. Infiltrating themselves into this closed society, the men and women of the force conducted long-range reconnaissance forays throughout hostile territory, mapped out strategic targets, and prepared for a guerrilla struggle, setting the stage for the war of liberation against the Palestinians and the other Arab nations.*

---

*Another task of the SHACHAR was to establish contact with the large and prosperous Jewish communities of Lebanon and Syria on behalf of the MOSSAD LE'ALIYAH BET.

In the spring of 1943, the SHACHAR department was officially established; its commander was the wily Yerucham Cohen. SHACHAR, also known as the MISTA'ARAVIM ("Arabists"), was made up of veterans of the joint SOE/PAL'MACH Syrian Platoon and SHA'I's Arab Department; they were taught to become Palestinian Arabs and operate freely throughout the Middle East. At their training base in Kibbutz Alonim, in the western Jezreel Valley, they conducted "conventional" military exercises and honed their skills in sharpshooting, martial arts, field survival, and reconnaissance techniques. They were also instructed in seamanship and evasive high-speed driving techniques. The soldier/spies of SHACHAR learned Arabic—Palestinian Arabic with the Filastin accent —at a hurried pace. Colloquial Arabic was taught with a distinctive Palestinian accent, and classical Arabic was taught with the use of unique Palestinian idioms and grammar. The magnanimous rabbi, or instructor, of the force was Shimon Somech, a Baghdad native, who had studied religious practices from a famous sheikh at Jerusalem's ancient Al-Aqsa mosque in 1943. Somech wanted his force to be exceptional actors twenty-four hours a day, seven days a week—living their roles in a volatile and fatalistic theater.[12] One important aspect of their training, urged by Yerucham Cohen, was to view the local Arabs not as hated enemies but as respected opponents, peoples whose culture and habits greatly and ominously resembled those of the Jews.[13]

The standards set by SHACHAR for its agents were incredibly rigid and demanding; of the thirty volunteers who made up the first course, very few were proficient enough in their espionage and military tradecraft to be dispatched on operational assignments. Oddly enough, however, their first true operation involved revenge and psychological warfare. In the early part of 1944, two Jewish girls from a kibbutz near Beit Shean were brutally raped by Muhamed Sarghusi, an Arab from a nearby village. Dressed in local garb, agents from SHACHAR escorted a force of PAL'MACH fighters for retaliation. They infiltrated into Beit Shean and apprehended Sarghusi. According to the legend—which first appeared in 1950 in MA'ARACHOT, an esteemed journal of Israeli military thought—the force exacted retribution by castrating the young Arab. Among those participating in the raid were two NCOs who eventually reached the crank of general in the IDF.[14] Such actions, as well as several spectacular operations in which SHACHAR agents, disguised as local Arabs, stole weapons from local Arab villages and British police stations, served as psychological warfare. The local Arabs could no longer trust their own; even their sacred territory was vulnerable to infiltration.

The principal objective of SHACHAR was to plant its deep-cover agents for espionage tasks during peacetime, and sabotage operations during wartime. The agents were dispatched to strategic targets and locations, and popular workplaces where they would find it easy to blend in, such as the port and oil refineries of Haifa, the potash mining facilities along the Dead Sea, British army camps around the Gaza Strip, and private businesses in Ramla, Yafo, and Haifa. Oddly enough, the total secrecy required for the success of deep-cover agents and their operations often posed dangerous and difficult quandaries. The "Sea Section"—the budding naval commando force of the PAL'YAM, or "Sea Companies," the PAL'MACH's emerging naval force—had planted its own intelligence agents in the Haifa facilities; the possibility of two PAL'MACH agents recognizing each other, or even acting against each other, was very real.

SHACHAR agents opened their own small business establishments, mainly bookstores and newspaper stands, in Arab towns and villages. Once entrenched in a location, the agents formed a psychological, political, and economic portrait of their surroundings and duly sent the findings to PAL'MACH headquarters, where the material was analyzed and passed on to SHA'I HQ. SHACHAR agents also infiltrated the various Palestinian military organizations, such as the heavily armed nationalist group known as the N'jada, and gathered invaluable insight into their objectives and capabilities. The agents faced enormous operating challenge: Their financial allowances were miniscule—only fifteen Palestinian pounds a month—which had to cover the cost of open intelligence sources (books and periodicals), indigenous clothing, and the dues to various enemy political and military organizations. The most important task of the SHACHAR agents was to provide accurate and *untainted* intelligence and not the selective brand of material that the SHA'I's Arab agents and informants so often obtained.

The other mobilized PAL'MACH force entrusted with gathering intelligence—such as determining enemy strengths and troop deployments, topographical surveys, and map drawing—was the unheralded 7th Reconnaissance Platoon. The Hebrew word SAYERET ("Reconnaissance Force") has become one of the most important of all Israeli military terminologies; reconnaissance units are the elite within an elite brigade or division and are entrusted with the most sensitive and dangerous behind-enemy-lines operations. The various paratroop, infantry, and intelligence reconnaissance units of the Israel Defense Forces would conduct many of the most spectacular military operations of the postwar era. In the PAL'MACH, however, the reconnaissance unit, and soldier, played a more significant role. According to Benny Marshak, one of the founding members of the PAL'MACH: "The task of the reconnaissance soldier in every army is to seek out and discover the enemy—in the PAL'MACH, the recon soldier's task also included discovering his homeland." [15] Because Palestine was under the control of the British, and because the Jews, let alone armed units of the PAL'MACH, were unable to roam freely through many sections of the country, there were severe intelligence gaps.

Originally, the reconnaissance capabilities of the PAL'MACH, and, of course, the HAGANAH, lay primarily with the 7th Reconnaissance Platoon. It was a small force of physically fit soldiers who trekked the countryside alone, or in small bands of two or three; they were usually accompanied by a Bedouin or Circassian guide. They ventured deep into the heart of enemy territory around Nablus, Jenin, Ramallah, the Jordan Valley, and the Hebron hills, and learned to become self-sustaining combat entities—able to survive and perform in the wild while conducting surveillance. Eventually, the PAL'MACH commander, Yigal Allon, called for each PAL'MACH company to possess a reconnaissance platoon whose task would be to scout and become familiar with the area in which the company would be operating.

In 1941, the PAL'MACH had several reconnaissance squads, operating primarily in Syria and Lebanon, but they were small and sanctioned for specific missions with an Allied expeditionary force for backup. At the time when the words *El-Alamein* and the *Carmel Plan* were in the thoughts of British commanders in Palestine, the PAL'MACH established several rear bases in the wild from where their small units would wage the SOE-financed guerrilla war of survival. In 1945–46, however, they were to set the stage for Israel's inevitable war of liberation. Accurate *field* intelligence on opposing military strength, as well as on the terrain and structure of the battlefield, was urgently required by the HAGANAH; that responsibility fell on the reconnaissance soldiers, who had learned virtually all aspects of the topographical and geographic landscape with their accurate surveillance apparatus—their eyes and feet!

The primary tasks of the PAL'MACH's reconnaissance units were to train a whole force of scouts, trackers, and guides who could lead PAL'MACH fighting units to any location in Palestine; to know the different regions of the land and to accurately map out the terrain; and to organize and lead forced marches of new PAL'MACH units in territory where they would be likely to face Arab forces in the inevitable conflict for independence.

One of the most ambitious intelligence-gathering projects that the HAGANAH High Command set for the SHACHAR and the 7th Platoon was what became known as the "Village Files." The Village Files operations were meant to gather voluminous and accurate intelligence on *only* those Arab villages that possessed strategic significance. The intelligence gathered included all pertinent topographical and geographic information; identification of major buildings, important offices, and homes of local officials, religious sheikhs, and political organizers; water sources; bridges; physical and geographic obstacles; and points of access and departure. SHACHAR agents, meantime, would gather the important information concerning a village's political makeup—its position vis-à-vis the Jews, and whether it was a home base to a guerrilla or an army of liberation unit. To protect their identities, the SHACHAR agents were equipped with numerous forged identification documents, including passports stolen from the British.

The SHACHAR and reconnaissance units that conducted the intelligence-gathering forays usually consisted of a four-man team: a commander, a note taker, a navigator, and a map sketcher. Each team was equipped with three maps of the targeted village: one general map of a 1:5,000 scale and two targeting maps in 1:20,000 scale. Complementing their efforts were the men of the "Pilots' Platoon" of the PAL'AVIR ("Air Companies"—the PAL'MACH's air arm and the predecessor to the Israeli Air Force)—based in Kibbutz Na'an, near Ramle. Utilizing mechanically dubious Pipers, the pilots would conduct early-morning and late-afternoon flybys of Arab villages, roads, and other strategically important areas. Aerial photographs were taken and given to the PAL'MACH scouts, who, in turn, made corrective notations to the photographs, adding their own comments.[16] Naval commandos from the PAL'YAM's Sea Section provided maritime intelligence of port installations and defenses of many of the Arab villages along the Mediterranean coastline.

These were, indeed, dangerous missions, requiring courage and skill. The Arab villages were lawless entities, and there was nothing the PAL'MACH or British forces could do to save an operation gone bad. Most villagers were heavily armed and active in some sort of armed group, and they knew the surrounding hills and roads with the shepherds' instincts. The reconnaissance soldiers, on the other hand, operated in small and isolated groups. They carried very little by way of firepower, usually a British or HAGANAH-produced Sten 9mm submachine gun, which, even on a day without wind, was highly inaccurate. Most of the agents and soldiers realized that capture meant torture and death. Their most powerful weapons were their cunning wits and the endurance of their legs.

The contribution of SHACHAR agents and PAL'MACH reconnaissance fighters in the PAL'MACH's ability to mount military operations was immeasurable. The mapping out of targets, determining enemy strengths, and conducting close-up reconnaissance were the deciding factors in many of the PAL'MACH's most spectacular and successful attacks against British army installations throughout Palestine—and beyond. The first such attack was a raid on the police fort at Givat Olga, on the Mediterranean coast almost halfway between Tel Aviv and Haifa, on January 20, 1946. A force of sappers from the PAL'MACH's 2d Battalion disguised themselves as painters and proceeded to destroy the facilities.

The most ambitious operation, however, was what became known as Operation Merchandise or "Night of the Bridges," a determined response to British interdiction of illegal Jewish immigration from Europe. On the night of July 17, 1946, PAL'MACH units destroyed ten of the eleven bridges connecting Palestine to the outside Arab states across the Lebanese border, the Golan Heights, and the Yarmuk and Jordan rivers. The raid's preparatory groundwork was conducted by SHACHAR agents and recon troopers who, through nighttime forays and daytime surveillance, gathered the data that the sappers needed to destroy the bridges—including architectural information, sentry routines, and routes of escape.[17] Similar operations, including the sinking of several British naval vessels by the PAL'YAM, were preceded by similar and extensive intelligence-gathering efforts.

In 1946 as well, the HAGANAH expanded its aggressive though still limited military intelligence capabilities by coordinating and unifying its reconnaissance and intelligence forces—primarily the SHACHAR and the 7th Platoon. The SHACHAR commander, Yerucham Cohen, was appointed the PAL'MACH's intelligence staff officer. Haim Ron, a veteran scout who—legend has it—knew every inch of the Negev Desert, was named PAL'MACH reconnaissance staff officer and commander of the 7th Platoon, which was soon expanded into a company. Their primary task was to supply PAL'MACH HQ with accurate tactical intelligence.[18] The creation of these new units, as well as a new "Intelligence Department" within the HAGANAH High Command, was to play an instrumental role in the struggle against the Arabs, in both retaliatory and conventional military operations. The creation of such units, attached to battalions and brigades, would also become an integral element of IDF combat intelligence units in the years to follow. As an obvious extension of the newfound importance placed in tactical battlefield intelligence, the SHA'I, in concert with the HAGANAH and PAL'MACH field commander, organized a course for thirty intelligence officers.[19]

By 1946, Palestine was in the throes of the violent spasms so typical of the postwar wars of liberation. Arab attacks against both the Jews and the British, British retaliation operations against the Jews, and, of course, HAGANAH and IRGUN attacks on the British and Arabs (such as the infamous July 22, 1946, bombing of the King David Hotel in Jerusalem) signaled that British control of the land had vanished and a political settlement—which would lead to inevitable bloodshed—was forthcoming.

To prepare for full-scale war, SHACHAR began dispatching its agents, who by 1947 numbered only thirty-three (eighteen conscripts and fifteen reservists), to the neighboring Arab countries. Agents were infiltrated across the border into Lebanon, Syria, Jordan, and Egypt to prepare targets for PAL'MACH hit-and-run attacks. They prepared profiles of opposing military strengths, troop deployments, and the psychological resolve of the locals for war. Two of the most favored targets for SHACHAR operations were the Golan Heights and the Jordan Valley—on both sides of the river. SHACHAR spies traveled through the inhospitable terrain of the Jordan Valley to monitor the formidable Arab Legion, preparing vast studies of their bases so that retaliation and hit-and-run raids could be planned in PAL'MACH HQ. SHACHAR agents examined the logistics of the Arab Legion and visited key towns and cities, such as Salt and Petra. Three SHACHAR agents, in fact, traveled to the capital of Amman to witness the coronation ceremonies of Emir Abd'allah as king of Transjordan.[20]

Quneitra, the capital of the Golan Heights, was also a popular espionage target. The best day for reconnaissance was market day, when the important strategic location swelled with merchants and shoppers. SHACHAR agents who infiltrated into Syrian territory provided their handlers with routine geographical and topographical information, as well as portraits of the local citizenry and their support or resistance to Arab war calls. When, in November 1947, the United Nations declared its historic resolution for the partition of Palestine into a Jewish and an Arab state, the PAL'MACH High Command ordered its agents to photograph Syrian army bases and installations, monitor the battalion markings on tank transports, and report on all moves made by the Syrian military. SHACHAR agents also made it to the Syrian capital, Damascus, and followed the movements of the "Army of Liberation," an Arab League–sanctioned force commanded by the charismatic hero of the 1936 riots, Fawzi Qawuqji. The accurate and highly detailed information they funneled back to Tel Aviv proved invaluable; SHA'I estimates were highly inaccurate, severely overestimating enemy strengths and deployments.

With the departure of British forces from Palestine scheduled for May 1948, along with the declaration of Israeli independence, SHACHAR and 7th Company troopers were pulled in out of the cold. It would be a historic time for the Israeli intelligence community, and one of the most critical times in the embattled history of the State of Israel.

Notes: Chapter Two

1. Hagai Eshed, MOSSAD SHEL ISH ECHAD: REUVEN SHILOAH—AVI HA'MODE'IN HA'YISRAELI (Tel Aviv: Edanim Publishers, ltd., Yediot Aharonot Edition, 1988), 78.

2. Yossi Melman and Dan Raviv, *The Imperfect Spies: The History of Israeli Intelligence* (London: Sidgwick and Jackson, 1989), 45.

3. *Ibid.* 47.

4. See Hagai Eshed, 80.

5. *Ibid.* 82.

6. Michael Bar-Zohar, *The Avengers* (New York: Hawthorn Books, Inc., 1967), 21.

7. Benny Morris, "Revenge," *Jerusalem Post International Edition* (Weekend Supplement, July 22, 1989): B4.

8. Connor Cruise O'Brien, *The Siege: The Saga of Israel and Zionism* (New York: Simon and Schuster, 1986), 246.

9. Ephraim Dekel, A'ALILOT SHA'I (Tel Aviv: Ma'arachot Publications, Israel Defense Forces, 1953), 84.

10. Yigal Allon, *Shield of David: The Story of Israel's Armed Forces* (London: Weidenfeld and Nicolson, 1970), 166.

11. *Ibid.* 167.

12. Yaakov Markovitzki, HA'YECHIDOT HA'YABASHTIOT HA'MEYUCHADOT SHEL HA'PAL'MACH (Tel Aviv: Israel Ministry of Defense Publications, 1989), 33.

13. Ezra Danin, "HAKAMAT HA'SHAI HA'ARAVI," MA'ARACHOT, No. 294–295 (July 1984): 33.

14. Yerucham Cohen, *By Light and in Darkness* (Tel Aviv: Amikam Publishers, 1969), 57.

15. See Yaakov Markovitzki, HA'YECHIDOT, 107.

16. Yerucham Cohen, "HA'MISTA'ARAVIM—HA'MACHLAKA HA'ARAVIT SHEL HA'PAL'MACH," MA'ARACHOT, No. 297 (January 1985): 44.

17. Yehuda Slotsky, KITZUR TOLDOT HA'HAGANAH (Tel Aviv: Israel Ministry of Defense Publications, 1978), 395.

18. See Yaakov Markovitzki, HA'YECHIDOT, 39.

19. See Ezra Danin, "HAKAMAT HA'SHA'I HA'ARAVI," MA'ARACHOT, No. 294–295 (July 1984): 35.

20. See Yaakov Markovitzki, HA'YECHIDOT, 45.

CHAPTER 3

OUT OF THE SHADOWS: THE UNHOLY GENESIS

T hroughout the early-morning hours of June 30, 1948, several battered staff cars and converted taxicabs pulled up alongside 85 Ben-Yehuda Street, a nondescript apartment building along one of Tel Aviv's more fashionable, sea-hugging boulevards. The men who headed for the building that day all bore signs of extreme exhaustion, emphasized by their drawn expressions and nervous chain-smoking. Entering a five-room flat identifiable only by an engraved sign proclaiming "Counseling Services," they passed the scrutiny of a tommy gun–toting sentry. The apartment was, in fact, the regional SHA'I headquarters; the men assembled on that humid summer day were the new state's top spies, the finest minds of all the shadowy figures who had helped guide the Jewish state toward independence. They were the "field marshals" of the covert war of nerves and shadows that had helped realize independence, and they were now slated to command the new state's intelligence services.

The men gathered at 85 Ben-Yehuda Street included Binyamin Gibli, the SHA'I commander in Jerusalem; Avraham Kidron, the Galilee and northern region SHA'I commander; Isser Harel, SHA'I's Tel Aviv commander; David Karon; and Boris Guriel. Chairing the meeting was a giant of a man, Israel Beeri, the forty-seven-year-old commander of the SHA'I, who because of his height was known by the nickname Isser HA'GADOL ("Isser the Big"). After briefing the assembled—who were sitting around a large oak table reading newspaper accounts of Israel's worsening military situation—Beeri began to discuss the historic day's agenda: the total overhaul of the State of Israel's intelligence community.[1]

Israel's intelligence community was no longer underground. It had come out of the shadows to guide the nation through its darkest and, perhaps, final hour. The genesis would not be an easy one, and the transition would be marked by controversy and bloodshed.

Ben-Gurion and Shiloah had realized, as far back as October 1947 with the first rumblings of conventional military action between Jewish and Arab forces, that the future state's intelligence apparatus would have to be seriously overhauled. In November 1947, Ben-Gurion had convened a meeting to examine and restructure Jewish Palestine's somewhat ambiguously deployed intelligence community. On November 29, following the announcement of the UN-sponsored partition plan, the SHA'I began extensive field operations to gather data on Arab leaders and the forces they commanded.

While the PAL'MACH's SHACHAR agents proved invaluable, their numbers were limited (although the ground, territory, and subjects they *could* cover were extraordinary). Exacerbating the situation was the fact that the SHA'I was suited for *gathering* intelligence, but not for immediate (or long term, for that matter) assessment and dissemination of intelligence to the ground troops. And, although the SHA'I's Arabists were expert in following the movements of Arab leaders, such as the Grand Mufti, King Abd'allah, and Fawzi Qawuqji, they were inexperienced in evaluating military matters, such as troop movements and arms supplies. After several meetings with Ben-Gurion and David Shaltiel, the ex–French Foreign Legionnaire who commanded SHA'I in late 1947, and Eliahu Sasson, the head of the Arab Branch in the Jewish Agency's Political Department, Reuven Shiloah came to the conclusion that the HAGANAH's intelligence arm would have to become more familiar with military requirements. He suggested that a special photoreconnaissance unit be formed and a failsafe communications link be established between SHA'I headquarters in Tel Aviv and the "Arab Desk" of the Jewish Agency's Political Department in Jerusalem.[2]

At the insistence of Yigal Yadin, the HAGANAH's Operations chief (and second IDF chief of staff), intelligence responsibilities were shared between SHA'I and a new department within the HAGANAH's Operations Branch, which was known by its Hebrew designation "AGA'M/3." Yadin's primary concern was to prepare the groundwork for an intelligence force within the General Staff that could meet the needs of all its forces. In the first half of 1948, the HAGANAH fielded six conventional infantry brigades: the 1st GOLANI Brigade; the 2d CARMELI Brigade; the 3d ALEXANDRONI Brigade; the 4th KIRYATI Brigade; the 5th GIVA'ATI Brigade; the 6th ETZIONI Brigade, along with the 7th Armored/Mechanized Brigade and the 8th Mechanized Brigade. There were also three regional PAL'MACH brigades: the NEGEV Brigade, operating in the southern desert; the HAREL Brigade, deployed in the ultrastrategic Jerusalem and Etzion-bloc area; and the YIFTACH Brigade, operating in the mountainous eastern and upper Galilee region. Although these forces lacked even the basic fundamentals for sustaining combat operations, such as sufficient training and arms supplies, their most serious weakness was a desperate lack of field intelligence; it was a weakness that Yadin hoped to correct with an influx of newly commissioned intelligence officers trained by the Operations Branch.

The brigade intelligence officer was a new entity in the HAGANAH, and his duties had to be defined—he would still be subordinate to the regional SHA'I commander. In January 1948, in a hastily convened course taught by Zerubavel Arbel, ex-PAL'MACH officer and one of the founders of Israeli reconnaissance strategy, the HAGANAH's first intelligence officers studied topography; the principles of battlefield tactics; identification of enemy weaponry and unit heraldry; the tasks of an intelligence officer; and cooperation between the intelligence officer and the air and naval units, the signal corps, and special forces. Many of the instructors in the course were veterans of the British army, and all the manuals and training guides had been stolen from the British and quickly translated into Hebrew.

The most important aspect of intelligence work taught in that first course was prisoner interrogation. The new intelligence officers attached to the HAGANAH's brigades and battalions were ordered to dispatch small reconnaissance forces at night to kidnap enemy soldiers. This was the most accessible form of information, as well as the most accurate and reliable. According to HAGANAH HQ directives, *only* the battalion or brigade intelligence officer, along with his regional SHA'I counterpart, was allowed to talk to prisoners.[3] The information obtained from the prisoners—sometimes easily, and sometimes following forceful inducement—proved invaluable.

In late 1947, the first "volunteers" from Syria and Iraq had begun infiltrating into West Bank towns and villages as part of the "Salvation Army" being formed by the Mufti and Qawuqji; similar bands began to establish strongholds in Jerusalem, Haifa, and Yafo—a poor Tel Aviv suburb mainly populated by Arabs. Interrogated Arabs confirmed SHA'I suspicions that larger, highly organized military units of the Salvation Army were preparing to cross the frontiers of Palestine in order to attack Jewish towns and settlements. These units, numbering thousands of men, included hundreds of well-trained professional soldiers: Arabs who served in units of the Palestinian police force; deserters from Arab armies who also brought along their weapons; military officers from Syria, Iraq, and even Turkey who were "imported" for their knowledge, to train elements of the Salvation Army; and ZARIM ("foreigners")— European guns for hire who, like many Czech and Polish officers, had remained in Palestine following their service to the Allies. There were also many British deserters whose military service was motivated by pure profit, and, ominously for the HAGANAH, former officers of the SS and Wehrmacht.[4] The Israelis, of course, had ZARIM of their own. There was Col. David "Mickey"

Marcus, an American volunteer who was tragically killed by one of his men, and Col. Fred (Harris) Grunich, an American officer who, posing as a journalist in Arab countries, provided the SHERUT MODE'IN ("Intelligence Service") with invaluable firsthand intelligence reports.[5]

The beginning of the end of Brittania's rule of Palestine afforded HAGANAH HQ greater freedom in conducting intelligence-gathering operations. With British forces withdrawing in significant numbers, the few aircraft that the HAGANAH possessed were able to operate without interference from the RAF. Aerial reconnaissance, in fact, became one of the most important tools in the HAGANAH's quest to locate and track the Arab bands roaming the Palestinian countryside. AGA'M/3 slowly developed a system—albeit highly primitive— where intelligence gathered was distributed to field commanders. AGA'M/3's position as part of the Operations Branch was particularly useful in this regard. As the senior commanders sat in HAGANAH headquarters in Ramat Gan, a Tel Aviv suburb, plotting troop movements and offensive operations, the small intelligence arm was amply represented in the planning. Several operations, however, were mounted against the advice of the intelligence experts. Such was the case of Operation 35, a two-night, multiregional preemptive strike by PAL'MACH units against Arab guerrilla positions in Yafo; the destruction of two bridges along the northwestern frontier; and an attack against the Arab village of Sasa'a, located on the Lebanese border, a base of operations for guerrilla bands that had infiltrated from Syria. The Intelligence Department had warned against such initiative operations, arguing that they would provoke open conflict. The opposite transpired, however; the offensive set back the Arab military momentum in marked fashion.

As the situation in Palestine worsened, and the British withdrawal proceeded apace, the countdown toward May 14—the day designated as the birth of Israel—lessened to weeks and days. It became obvious that the UN-sanctioned partition of Palestine would not be honored; full-scale war for control of all of Palestine was an absolute certainty. Yet, in this dangerous period, the HAGANAH's intelligence reports were still ambiguous. The SHA'I and AGA'M/3 continued to operate separately, assessing each Arab nation and guerrilla force with very little coordination between the two agencies. The SHA'I, and its Arab Division in particular, faced enormous difficulties in preparing for the inevitable conflict. Since the UN partition decree, the Arab informers, the SHA'I's most prized source of intelligence, were becoming fewer and fewer. The "meet" between handler and agent, which usually took place in the middle of the night in a cave or wadi, or on an isolated stretch of desert, had for years been the SHA'I's workshop for gathering information. The breakdown of British rule, however, led to the assassination of several prominent Arabs who, either for profit or political gains, had sided with the Jews. Also, the infiltration of heavily armed individuals from Iraq and Syria preaching Arab nationalism served to promote a catalytic wave of patriotism. These factors kept the Arabs from assisting the Jews. The absence of these Arab agents, with ties to relatives and political officials throughout the Middle East, led to severe gaps in the intelligence dossiers being compiled for analysis. These gaps haunted HAGANAH commanders: They had no way of knowing what the *actual* military plans of the neighboring Arab states would be once Israeli independence was declared.

One Arab agent, however, did remain loyal to the SHA'I—and to Isser Harel, his former handler, in particular. His name was Hassan El-Batir, a seasoned operative who had worked for SHA'I for several years. He was engaged to a Jewish woman, which could account for his loyalty to the Jewish cause. As a last-minute gambit, he was dispatched to Amman amid the chaotic scenario of withdrawing British forces, fleeing Palestinian refugees, and pitched battles between PAL'MACH units and marauding Arab bands. He returned two days later to report that the signs were clear and foreboding: King Abd'allah was preparing for a full-scale invasion.[6]

It was on May 14, as hundreds of thousands of newly declared Israelis were dancing the hora in the streets, that the definitive intelligence was received that the Arab Legion, joined by more than four thousand Iraqi soldiers, planned to cross the UN-sanctioned borders to invade the infant state. News of the invasion force's attack routes, through Jericho and Ramallah toward the central lowlands, came too late for any serious preemptive strike—not that the HAGANAH possessed the means for such an attack, in any event.

When war did, in fact, erupt, the beleaguered HAGANAH command-and-control infrastructure could not concern itself with long-term intelligence-gathering operations, and the responsibility was delegated—through desperation rather than choice—to smaller units. In the south, where a massive Egyptian army had made its move across the Negev and along the southern Mediterranean coastline toward Tel Aviv, aerial reconnaissance was performed by the PAL'MACH's "Negev Squadron." They provided real-time intelligence to HAGANAH HQ by courageously hovering above battlefields in small and extremely slow Pipers; they radioed in the "play-by-play," and also analyzed the events below and warned isolated Jewish settlements—mainly kibbutzim and moshavim—about impending Egyptian advances.[7] Aerial reconnaissance capabilities increased dramatically when the first combat aircraft reached Israel, primarily Avia S-199s (Czech-produced copies of the World War II–vintage German Me-109G). With greater speed and range, reconnaissance sorties of the SHERUT AVIR ("Air Service"—in late May 1948 it became known as the HEYL HA'AVIR, or "IDF/air force") could be flown along the frontiers bordering Lebanon and Syria; along the Jordan River above the Allenby and Damiah bridges; and north, toward the Sheikh Hussein Bridge in the Beit Shean Valley. When the first MA'HA'L ("foreign volunteers") pilots—from Canada, the United

States, Great Britain, and South Africa—arrived in Israel, their wartime experience led to bolder intelligence-gathering flights.

Less than twenty-four hours after David Ben-Gurion formally declared Israeli independence, the fighting forces of five Arab nations—Egypt, Transjordan, Syria, Iraq, and Lebanon—invaded the infant Jewish state in conjunction with various Palestinian guerrilla forces that had been crossing the borders since late 1947. Tel Aviv was bombed by Egyptian Dakotas, Jerusalem lay victim to an unrelenting siege, and the agricultural settlements in the desert were cut off and isolated. Two weeks later, with the forces of the HAGANAH outgunned, outnumbered, but standing fast, the formation of the TZAVA HAGANAH LE'YISRAEL, better known as TZAHAL (the Hebrew acronym for "Israel Defense Forces"), was announced as a replacement to the HAGANAH. The governing hierarchy of the new Jewish state, which for years had operated in covert arenas, through guile, guts, and sheer cunning, now had their most difficult task before them—the salvation of that nation.

As the war was fought, severe problems continued not only in gathering long-term intelligence but in relaying the information to the brigade commanders. On the eve of the battle for Latrun, the strategic crucible overlooking the main Tel Aviv–Jerusalem road, the 7th Armored Brigade was fed intelligence from the General Staff indicating that they would be encountering only scattered elements of the Arab guerrilla bands. They, in fact, encountered the crux of the Arab Legion, more than five thousand well-trained soldiers commanded by British officers and equipped with armored cars and heavy artillery. The ensuing carnage was horrifying. Tens of thousands of Israeli soldiers became casualties. The situation was so severe that new immigrants—just off refugee ships from Europe—were issued uniforms and guns and rushed into the fray. The debacle at Latrun convinced many top Israeli military leaders, including Yitzhak Sadeh, that military intelligence (AGA'M/3) was actually *sabotaging* Israel's war effort. An overhaul of the feuding and ineffective intelligence-gathering apparatus was desperately needed.

At the historic meeting at 85 Ben-Yehuda Street, Israel Beeri informed his colleagues that HA'ZAKEN, the Hebrew term for "Old Man" and the affectionate name for Prime Minister David Ben-Gurion, had ordered that the SHA'I disband; its infrastructure and personnel would be split into a triad, to form a new intelligence community.[8] A foreign intelligence service would be responsible for gathering political, economic, and military intelligence *outside* the boundaries of Israel. This espionage service would be under the command of Boris Guriel, a Latvian native who, as a Palestinian-Jewish soldier in the British army during the Second World War, had been captured by the Nazis. The espionage service under his control would be known as the "Political Department" of the Israeli foreign ministry, a dubious term for a mysterious and highly independent spy office.

An internal intelligence and security agency was also mandated by the "Old Man," and it would become known by the initials of its full title, SHIN BET, short for SHERUT HA'BITACHON HA'KLALI ("General Security Services"). The SHIN BET's commander would be the legendary Isser Harel, known by the nickname Isser HA'KATAN ("Isser the Little"), for his short and stocky physique. The Russian-born Harel had been a distinguished SHA'I security officer and was known for his uncanny intuition and dedication to patriotic service. As SHA'I's Tel Aviv station chief, he commanded surveillance operations of the right-wing liberation movements, such as the IRGUN, which refused to abide by the authority of Ben-Gurion and the HAGANAH (similar and, it is believed, more aggressive operations also were mounted against the hard-core Jewish Communist organizations). Harel was a wise choice for the posting, since he was one of the very few to vocalize his beliefs that threats to Israel were particularly dire when originating from within. He had made a lasting name for himself in the handling of the June 1948 *Altalena* affair, an attempt by the IRGUN to smuggle a ship (actually an ex–U.S. Marine Corps LST, purchased in New York for $75,000) loaded with arms past a UN cease-fire blockade. The failed attempt nearly led to civil war—HAGANAH and IRGUN fighters battled each other along the Tel Aviv seashore promenade while the Arabs were tightening their noose around the Jewish state. Ben-Gurion ordered the SS *Altalena*, moored off the shore of Tel Aviv, sunk, and the IRGUN to be incorporated into the IDF. The man responsible for that delicate undertaking was Isser Harel.

Shaul Avigur's, MOSSAD LE'ALIYAH BET, mysteriously, remained intact; this was odd since immigration to the State of Israel was now legal and under open auspices. The agency would not last very long, however, and would soon combine its activities with another MOSSAD.

The largest and most important Israeli intelligence entity would belong to the Israel Defense Forces. Initially it was called SHERUT MODE'IN and was commanded by Isser Beeri, who by 1948 had assumed the rank of lieutenant colonel in the new IDF. The SHERUT MODE'IN, which eventually would become known by its initials—SHIN MEM—was responsible for four primary areas: combat intelligence, field security of operations and counterintelligence, communications intelligence, and censorship. In the newly formed IDF General Staff, the SHIN MEM would be represented by the Operations Branch of the General Staff and would oversee the dissemination of intelligence data to frontline units.[9]

The creation of the SHIN MEM came at a most crucial junction in the 1948 War. Israeli forces were about to seize the initiative on both the northern front—in Galilee against Iraqi, Syrian, and Lebanese forces—and on the southern front, where the PAL'MACH's reconnaissance and commando units harassed the Egyptian advances. The all-important Jerusalem front, however, where the IDF fought the elite Arab Legion, was desperate.

The SHIN MEM's new commander, Lieutenant Colonel Beeri, was an anomaly, and perhaps the wrong man for the task. Born in Poland, Beeri was a ten-year

HAGANAH veteran, but he had joined SHA'I only in 1947, and had come out of absolutely nowhere to become its commanding officer. Known for his tall frame and haunting eyes, Beeri believed that Israel had to be a "perfect society," and he loathed corruption—either monetary or political. This moralistic facet of Beeri's personality bordered on fanaticism, and contributed to one of the more tragic aspects of Israeli military intelligence, one that would have severe ramifications for future intelligence chiefs and the operations they sanctioned.

The SHIN MEM was also having difficulty adapting to its new position as a branch of the month-old IDF. Spies once addressed by oral titles were now officers and NCOs; they had to wear the standard IDF khaki drill and conduct their day-to-day intelligence operations within the framework of the IDF's strict codes—even in the midst of full-scale war. This set the stage for the shameful episode that ensued.

In the early part of the 1948 War, the heavy guns of the Arab Legion were scoring accurate hits on strategic Israeli targets around besieged Jerusalem—in particular, a munitions plant—and SHA'I's Jerusalem commander, Binyamin Gibli, could come to only one viable conclusion: There *had* to be a traitor in the Israeli section of the city who was relaying targeting information to the Jordanians and, more importantly, to their British commanding officers. A witch-hunt ensued. Anyone with military knowledge and close British connections was suspect, and that logic led to the arrest of Capt. Meir Tubianski. An employee with the Jerusalem Electric Company, Tubianski had been a commissioned officer in the British army Royal Corps of Engineers during the Second World War, as well as a HAGANAH commander. He was, nevertheless, an Anglophile, known for close relationships with his British bosses, and such circumstantial evidence was sufficient in these desperate times.

On June 30, only hours after Isser Beeri had convened the now-historic meeting at 85 Ben-Yehuda Street, he joined Gibli, David Karon, and Avraham Kidron, and they traveled to the village of Beit Jiz, a HAGANAH stronghold along the Tel Aviv–Jerusalem road. In an abandoned, shell-cratered house in the village, Tubianski was being held under armed guard, his feet tied together, hands cuffed, and a gag placed over his mouth. In an impromptu military tribunal, Beeri and his three SHA'I subordinates served as investigators, prosecutors, and judges. After a cruelly paced tirade of accusations and verbal abuse, the top brass of Israel's new military intelligence force declared Tubianski guilty of treason and sentenced him to death by firing squad. He was executed hours later, without being given a blindfold or the opportunity to scribble a last message to his wife and family. Even by the standards of a military force less than a month old, this was far from the norms of military protocol.

The killing of Capt. Meir Tubianski was a frightening example of how several men could corrupt the absolute powers of a covert intelligence agency. In fact, no mention of the killing was ever supplied to David Ben-Gurion, who, as acting prime minister and defense minister, should have been informed of the incident. Although the murder of a Jew was a highly charged and potentially decisive action, this was *not*, however, the first time such an incident had occurred. On June 25, 1940, for example, Baruch Carmi, a Haifa traffic policeman, was murdered by three men from the HAGANAH's elite Special Company, a pre-PAL'MACH covert unit. He was killed because it was feared he was an informer, relaying information of illegal Jewish immigration to the British Criminal Investigation Department (CID).[10] In the winter of 1946, Binyamin Korfirst, an active member of the radical LEHI, was executed by a PAL'MACH assassination squad acting on the orders of a HAGANAH field court, which convicted him of supplying the British with intelligence. The death sentence was kept secret for many years, and his family was told that he died a hero in a military operation.[11] In the Tubianski case, the prime minister learned of the execution only when his grieving widow, Lena, sent an impassioned and logically reasoned letter telling of her suspicions and pleading for justice. Outraged, Ben-Gurion duly ordered an official inquiry, which eventually cleared Tubianski's name. Yet the killing of the Jewish engineer was not the only act of unbridled zealousness that eventually destroyed Isser Beeri and his Military Intelligence service.

On the same day that witnessed the birth of the Israeli intelligence community and the tragic kangaroo court of Meir Tubianski, another sad chapter in the day-old SHERUT MODE'IN was unfolding in the northern port city of Haifa. In a secluded room near the docks, intelligence agents were involved in the torture of a taxi owner and black marketeer named Yehuda Amster. He was seized on May 15, 1948, in order to gather evidence that the mayor of Haifa, Abba Khoushy, was a traitor to the Zionist cause. After two and a half months of incessant physical abuse, Amster relinquished nothing and, much to the chagrin of Beeri, was released. The obsessive nature of Beeri's Military Intelligence department frightened many officers in the IDF, who felt that fear, suspicion, and informants were hardly the successful recipe for creating a national defense force capable of defeating a numerically superior enemy. Ben-Gurion, who had been kept in the dark about much of Beeri's activities, eventually learned of the abuses of power, and steps were taken to revamp the Military Intelligence service only a few months after it was formally sanctioned.

Beeri's reign of terror ended after the killing of a wealthy Arab, Ali Qassem, in the summer of 1948. Qassem had been an agent of the SHERUT MODE'IN for several months and was ordered to infiltrate the various Palestinian Arab militias and provide information on their strengths, weaknesses, and intentions. Since the SHA'I's creation in the 1930s, the use of Arab agents—especially those volunteering their services for financial rewards—was frowned upon. The Jews had traditionally mistrusted Arabs as two-faced and treacherous—a view that dated back to the days of the first settlers to Palestine and land deals gone wrong. The apprehension in employing Arab agents proved correct in Qassem's case, however; he was found to be not only a double agent, but a *triple* agent, offering his services to the British as well. Beeri ordered SHIN MEM officers to capture Qassem and execute him; he was shot in the head point-blank with a 9mm pistol.

Qassem's bullet-ridden body was discovered in a shallow grave in early December 1948 at the foot of Mt. Carmel in Haifa. The police opened an investigation and later learned of SHIN MEM complicity. After discovering that it was Beeri's orders that resulted in the Arab's death, Ben-Gurion summoned the IDF chief of staff, Lt. Gen. Ya'akov Dori, to his Tel Aviv war room and ordered the sacking of Beeri. "Isser the Big" would claim to his dying day that Ben-Gurion had, in fact, sanctioned all the killings and detainings, but Beeri's days as Military Intelligence chief were over.[12] He was indicted for manslaughter in the death of Ali Qassem and removed from his post. One month later, after it was discovered that he had forged documents in the Yehuda Amster incident, Beeri was removed from the IDF, his rank of lieutenant colonel reduced to that of a lowly private. Eventually, Beeri was charged with the murder of Meir Tubianski and, following a closed-door trial in October 1949, convicted of the crime; punishment was a token *one-day imprisonment!* In 1958, he died of a heart attack—a broken and bitter man.

The case of Isser Beeri sent shock waves throughout the Israel Defense Forces. His fanaticism, mistrust, and role as judge, jury, and executioner went against every rule by which the IDF, and the State of Israel, tried to operate. Although Isser Beeri was an accomplished intelligence officer—and, many of his colleagues have said, instrumental during the dark days of the spring of 1948—his usurping of power had set a dangerous precedent. This kind of behavior had to be eliminated from the vocabulary of the Israeli intelligence community if the State of Israel was to follow its course of moral integrity. The real truth learned from the incident was that nobody, not even Ben-Gurion, understood that controls needed to be placed on the intelligence community.[13]

In writing the history of the SHERUT MODE'IN, the Isser Beeri scandal tends to overshadow some positive and highly dramatic chapters in the early days of Israel's Military Intelligence. There was the excellent work of SHA'I, and later the SHIN MEM, in the besieged city of Jerusalem. Under incessant Jordanian artillery and sniper fire, the Jewish quarter of the old city of Jerusalem was in a precarious struggle for survival. One of the PAL'MACH's premier formations, the HAREL Brigade, commanded by eventual IDF Chief of Staff and Israeli Prime Minister Yitzhak Rabin, had been fighting heroicly against the British-led Arab Legion. The ability to supply these forces with accurate field intelligence fell, in most cases, to the SHA'I station commanded by Yitzhak Navon (later president of the State of Israel). Among other noted exploits, they tapped Arab communication lines, including telephone conversations (in Turkish, no less) between the Grand Mufti from his lair in Cairo and military commands in Jerusalem, and forged documents that allowed SHA'I agents access to Arab sections of the city. In the street-to-street and house-to-house fighting of the battle for Jerusalem, many agents were killed. Many were captured, their identities remaining anonymous even following brutal interrogations.

Another of the SHIN MEM's considerable accomplishments was its successful "Listening Unit." In May 1948, a listening post was established in General Headquarters in Ramat Gan, to support several smaller posts that the SHA'I had established throughout the country, as well as those that the PAL'MACH agents had hastily set up in the field. Although, like anything Israeli, the creation of the listening post in Ramat Gan met with its share of skepticism and budgetary infighting, it reaped invaluable rewards. In July 1948, the Listening Unit finally succeeded in breaking the Egyptian military codes that forces in the field used to communicate with headquarters in Cairo. The unit's commander, Mordechai Almog, turned over the information to the SHERUT MODE'IN chief; this knowledge greatly altered the manner in which the Israeli offensive in the Negev was conducted. As a result of this success, the IDF's perception of the Listening Unit immediately changed, and funds were cleared for Almog's force to travel abroad and obtain sophisticated equipment.[14]

The Listening Unit scored another major victory in October when, following Operation Yoav, an attempt to liberate the Negev Desert and southern Israel from Egyptian forces, Egyptian forces were trapped in what became known as the Faluja Pocket. The Listening Unit monitored all Egyptian communications between the trapped forces and the regional headquarters in Rafah, near the Gaza Strip, then relayed the data to field commanders and the IDF General Staff. The information was used to terminate attempts to smuggle weapons and ammunition across the Israeli siege lines. The ability of the Listening Unit, as well as other SHIN MEM forces, to gather real-time intelligence was a significant factor in the pocket's eventual collapse in November 1948. In fitting fashion, the Egyptian commander surrendering the forces, Col. Es-Sayid Thaha Bei, was escorted to Israeli headquarters by Yerucham Cohen, one of the forefathers of Israeli Military Intelligence.[15]

During the first battles in Operation Yoav, SHERUT MODE'IN officers interrogated hundreds of Egyptian prisoners and sifted through thousands of documents and records abandoned in the field. The most important document seized was a roster of all officers in the Egyptian military—their names, addresses, political affiliations, academic scores, and other personal notations. When a captured officer was brought in for questioning, the interrogator would first ask the soldier's name, rank, and serial number, and then would begin asking the flabbergasted prisoner extremely personal questions.[16]

Also assisting in Israel's intelligence war effort in 1948 were the SHACHAR agents of the PAL'MACH, who continued to infiltrate deep behind enemy lines and follow the Arab bands, relaying their findings back to headquarters.

In its historical perspective, the Beeri incident underscored the difficulties encountered when an underground intelligence service was forced to restructure itself along conventional military lines, while at the same time combating an overwhelming military invasion and politically devisive (and threatening) internal elements. Beeri's relentless pursuit of moles and traitors left him with little time to conduct the day-to-day business of creating a military intelligence entity—such responsibilities as recruitment and training of personnel, acquisition of financial resources, and incorporation of the force into a military command infrastructure. Also neglected was the invaluable aspect of a military intelligence force's ability to supply its units in the field with data.

The man tasked with reforging the Order of Battle of Israeli Military Intelligence was Chaim (Vivian) Herzog. Born in Belfast, Ireland, in 1918, Herzog was the son of the nation's chief rabbi. A graduate of London University and Cambridge, Herzog immigrated to Palestine at the age of seventeen and promptly volunteered to serve in the HAGANAH. When the Second World War erupted, Herzog enlisted in his majesty's armed forces; he served in a mechanized unit and, later, as an intelligence officer in an armored brigade. He served in Maj. Gen. Brian Horrocks's legendary 30th Corps and participated in the D-day invasion and the liberation of Western Europe. Horrocks, in fact, labeled Herzog as the finest intelligence officer in his command. He ended his military service in the British army with the rank of lieutenant colonel.[17] In the years 1947–48, Herzog served as the chief of the Security Department in the Jewish Agency, and during the first months of the 1948 War, as the operations officer for the elite 7th Armored Brigade. One of the few tank formations with operational armor in the IDF Order of Battle, the brigade received its baptism of fire in the battle for Latrun, where ad hoc brigades and battalions were mowed down by Arab Legion firepower. In this battle, Herzog witnessed—firsthand—the need for accurate and reliable intelligence: Data on enemy strengths, ammunition supplies, and deployments could have helped save thousands of Israeli lives.

Although Isser Beeri had a personal disdain for "Anglophiles," he named the ex–British army officer as the deputy chief of the SHERUT MODE'IN. Herzog immediately put to use his organizational talents. By August 1948, he, along with Beeri, presented their plan to the IDF chief of staff.

Initially, the IDF's "Intelligence Service," through Beeri's grand vision, was to perform four primary tasks: (1) form and maintain a system by which intelligence data on enemy troop strengths, intentions, capabilities, and industrial support complex is gathered, as well as information on the enemy's home front, its political leadership, and the will of its people to sustain armed conflict; (2) process this information and extract reliable fact from tantalizing summation, and work together with the other intelligence services (that is, the SHIN BET and the Foreign Ministry's Political Department); (3) pass on the obtained intelligence to the military commanders in the field as fast as possible—through secure channels; and (4) implement *strict* field security defenses to prevent the enemy from gathering information on IDF forces, installations, and strengths through education, field security, and counterintelligence units, and through an all-powerful Military Censor's Office, which would examine all media, literary, and photographic works pertaining to the security of the State of Israel.

This four-point plan to incorporate a military intelligence entity into the new state's defense forces and political infrastructure was the blueprint for a true IDF intelligence entity. The subsequent sacking of Beeri, and Herzog's assumption of command, altered these contingencies. On March 24, 1949, Herzog ordered that the SHERUT MODE'IN be split into two separate and distinctive departments. First, there was HEYL MODE' IN ("Intelligence Corps"), a branch of the Israel Defense Forces like any other service, that is, the air force, the navy, the armored corps, and the artillery corps. The Intelligence Corps would be staffed by conscript soldiers and commanded by a small cadre of professional officers and NCOs; the Intelligence Corps CO would, of course, chair the General Staff. The second department, known simply as the MACHLEKET MODE'IN ("Intelligence Department"), would also be represented in the General Staff forum and would be answerable to the Operations Branch of the IDF, from which the "Intelligence Service" was run.[18]

The Order of Battle of Herzog's twin military intelligence forces consisted of units known at first by the initials of the SHERUT MODE'IN, or SHIN MEM, followed by a numerical designation. The system was later changed, with each unit designated by the word MOD (or "Intel"), or Section. The military intelligence force of the Israel Defense Forces consisted of the following.

MOD 1, commanded by Lt. Col. Binyamin Gibli, was known in generic terms as combat—or field—intelligence. It oversaw intelligence officers attached to the different combat units in the field, and commanded the Intelligence Corps' "Research Department," which was responsible for processing and assessing incoming intelligence. Section 1 consisted of what became known as the "Desks," a separate desk or office for every hostile nation (Egypt, Jordan, Syria, Iraq, et cetera).

MOD 2 was the small, though highly important, Listening Unit. Based on the SHA'I's similar force, it was entrusted with signals intelligence (SIGINT). In 1948 SIGINT was a primitive undertaking. Its responsibilities included electronic monitoring of Arab military communications; IDF field communications, including Morse and coded transmissions; recording enemy communications signals; and code-breaking and translations. The unit was commanded by the SHA'I's Listening Unit commander, Maj. Mordechai Almog.

MOD 3, commanded by Avraham Kidron, was the ubiquitous BITACHON SADEH ("Field Security") command responsible for keeping the secrets of the IDF personnel and installations safely in Israel. Although a bureaucratic force when compared to combat units within the Intelligence Corps, Field Security would have a profound impact on the future of the Arab-Israeli wars and Israel's ability to win the intelligence puzzle.

MOD 4 was better known as HA'TZENZURA ("the censor"), the IDF's Military Censor's Office. It was entrusted with keeping what was deemed *classified* military, political, and economic news from being printed and reported in Israel, or transmitted abroad by foreign journalists and authors.

MOD 5, which would later be known as HATZAV ("Quarry"), was the unit assigned to gather positive intelligence from open and literary sources, such as newspapers, periodicals, journals, books, films, and radio programs. Even in 1948, MOD 5 boasted an extensive library. The true lifeblood of the unit, from its inception to the present, was Arabic-speaking Israelis, mainly those with roots in the Arab diaspora.

MOD 6 and MOD 7 concentrated on "physical," or topographical and geographical field intelligence, and obtaining maps and aerial reconnaissance photographs. The unit, originally part of the fledgling IDF Engineer's Corps, was staffed by veterans of the PAL'MACH's 7th Reconnaissance Company who, by 1948, were seasoned veterans in such work.

MOD 8 was the "Technical Department," commanded by Haim Ya'ari. More a "desk" than a military unit, the Technical Department was responsible for technological development, the production and development of "tradecraft" gadgetry, the refinement of existing off-the-shelf equipment, and the preparation of documentation. It was known as Israel's "intelligence laboratory."

MOD 9 was the overt foreign body within the Intelligence Corps, tasked with maintaining communications between the chief of staff and the military attachés dispatched to foreign lands. MOD 9's members participated in counterintelligence work, as well, since this section was entrusted with the care of foreign attachés stationed in Tel Aviv and Jerusalem.

MOD 10, also known by its Hebrew acronym KA'TA'M ("special operations officer"), was one of the most secretive of the Intelligence Corps units. It was responsible for handling agents, operatives, and "maintained" sources across Israel's boundaries.[19]

MOD 18 was the special operations group of the Intelligence Corps for operations in Arab lands. It consisted primarily of PAL'MACH's Arabists, now under full IDF command and control.*

---

*On October 15, 1948, at the orders of Ben-Gurion, the PAL'MACH disbanded. They were, on the whole, extremely political and supported a left-wing party opposed to Ben-Gurion. Many esteemed Israeli military commanders appreciated the "built-in" special forces element the PAL'MACH offered the IDF, but after the *Altalena* affair, Ben-Gurion was determined to rid Israel of *all* politically volatile armed groups. The units of the PAL'MACH were duly incorporated into the IDF.

Following the war, the officers of the Intelligence Department played a significant role in the cease-fire and disengagement talks with Jordan, Egypt, and Syria. There were, of course, power plays, which plagued the development of IDF Military Intelligence; an example is an attempt by the IDF/navy to assume the army's intelligence responsibility. There were conflicts of control, command, and responsibility, and ambiguity as to what the role of the intelligence triad would, in fact, be. But a true *Israeli* intelligence community at last had been formed; it would experience extreme growing pains in the years to follow.

NOTES: CHAPTER THREE

1. Hagai Eshed, *One-Man "MOSSAD": Reuven Shiloah, Father of Israeli Intelligence* (Tel Aviv: Edanim Publishers, Yediot Aharonot Edition, 1988), 120.

2. Lt. Col. (Res.) Dr. Yoav Glover, "HAKAMAT HA'MODE'IN HA'TZVAI," MA'ARACHOT, No. 294–295 (July 1984): 20.

3. *Ibid.* 22.

4. *Ibid.* 23.

5. *Ibid.* 29.

6. Michael Bar-Zohar, *Spies in the Promised Land: Isser Harel and the Israeli Secret Service* (Boston: Houghton Mifflin Company, 1972), 38.

7. Yerucham Cohen, *By Light and in Darkness* (Tel Aviv: Amikam Publishers, 1969), 105.

8. Yossi Melman and Dan Raviv, *The Imperfect Spies: The History of Israeli Intelligence* (London: Sidgwick and Jackson, 1989), 45.

9. Oded Granot, HEYL HA'MODE'IN: TZAHAL BE'HEILO ENTZYKLOPEDIA LE'TZAVA U'LE'BITACHON (Tel Aviv: Revivim Publishers, Ma'ariv Library, 1981), 13.

10. Moshe Geva, "ULAY BICHLAL LO HAYA ASHEM" ("Perhaps He Wasn't Even Guilty"), YEDIOT AHARONOT ("7 Days" Weekend Supplement, June 26, 1990): 30.

11. Shlomoh Nakdiman, "HUTZA LE'HAROG BE'YADEI HA'PAL'MACH," YEDIOT AHARONOT (SHABBATH July 3, 1987): 3.

12. Amos Nebo, "ISSER HA'GADOL" ("Isser the Big"), YEDIOT AHARONOT ("7 Days" Weekend Supplement, April 7, 1988): 8.

13. Stewart Steven, *The Spymasters of Israel* (New York: Ballantine Publishers, 1980), 18.

14. See Oded Granot, HEYL HA'MODE'IN, 21.

15. See Yerucham Cohen, *By Light and in Darkness*, 195.

16. See Oded Granot, HEYL HA'MODE'IN, 26

17. *Ibid.* 17.

18. *Ibid.* 18.

19. There has been some confusion as to the exact designation of many units of the Intelligence Service and, later, Intelligence Department. The esteemed historian Lt. Col. (Res.) Dr. Yoav Glover has listed the following as the SHERUT MODE'IN's Order of Battle: SHIN MEM 1, Combat Intelligence; SHIN MEM 2, Listening Unit and Code-Breaking; SHIN MEM 3, Field Security; SHIN MEM 4, Military Censor; SHIN MEM 5, Intelligence Research Center; SHIN MEM 6, Topographical Intelligence; SHIN MEM 7, Intelligence Library and Research Department for foreign (non-Arab) armies; SHIN MEM 8, Technical Department; SHIN MEM 9, Military Attachés; SHIN MEM 10, Open Sources Department; SHIN MEM 18, Special Operations Branch.

CHAPTER 4

THE FIRST YEARS:
FROM DEPARTMENT TO BRANCH

T
he IDF's intelligence units performed admirably during the 1948 War of Independence. Interservice coordination, which is the true factor behind the success of a military intelligence service, was beginning to appear. The fledgling IAF—which had gone from aging Piper Cubs to ex-RAF Spitfires—was not only providing the ground forces with invaluable support, but with aerial reconnaissance as well. The PAL'MACH had graduated from the small piston-engine aircraft, such as the Auster Mark 5,[1] which it used to prepare its prewar "Village Files," to high-flying, well-armed aircraft such as ex–U.S. Army Air Corps B-17G Flying Fortress bombers. These planes, as part of the infamous "69 Squadron" based at Ramat David, flew intelligence sorties throughout the Middle East in their respites from bombing such targets as Gaza, Cairo, and Amman. Such long-range aircraft, later to include the Bristol Beaughfighter Mark TF10, played an essential role in gathering real-time field intelligence. The PAL'MACH's efforts were made possible by the uncanny ability of RECHESH agents abroad to "liberate" special high-altitude photographic equipment and Leica cameras from post–Second World War arsenals. Although the IAF had very few—six, to be exact—proficiently trained fighter pilots, the obvious need for intelligence-gathering sorties was given top priority by officers in the Operations Branch.

Yet it was in the naval arena that the coordination with IDF intelligence achieved the most valuable rewards. The collaboration between the SHA'I, later the SHIN MEM, and the IDF/navy, known in Hebrew as the "HEYL HA'YAM," proved that the IDF's intelligence arm was not only successful in the collection of data, but in the operational use of the material obtained.[2] During the course of the 1948 War, the SHA'I* obtained a secret document from British Intelligence concerning a signed, and paid for, arms deal between Syria and Czechoslovakia for ten thousand rifles and ten million rounds of ammunition; at the time, this equaled the total arsenal of the IDF and the PAL'MACH, and was perceived to be enough material to equip three infantry battalions.[3]

The information incensed Israeli military leaders. Not only was Czechoslovakia *Israel*'s principal arms supplier—as well as a transit point for arms shipments directed toward Israel—but the Czechs were seen as a staunch ally, one whose military expertise and Zionist-leaning policies would help see the Jewish state through its darkest hour. Most importantly, however, the Czech-Syrian arms deal would drastically, and perhaps fatally, alter the balance of power in the chaos of the war-torn Middle East. When, in March 1948, the information was received that the arms shipment was to be transferred to the Syrians via Beirut using a civilian Italian tramp steamer, the SS *Lino*, the green light for military action was issued by HAGANAH HQ in Israel. The operation, ominously, was code-named "Operation Bandit."

From the outset, the operation's masterminds were MOSSAD LE'ALIYAH BET commander Shaul Avigur (who remained in his Geneva headquarters) and the commander of HAGANAH forces in Europe, Nachum Shadmi. The HAGANAH had years of experience operating in Europe, especially in Czechoslovakia, where it had bought Avia fighter aircraft, Mauser rifles, and many of the explosives the IDF was utilizing at the time. The Czechs were also in the process of training a few dozen PAL'MACH commandos to become parachutists. Operations in Italy were also quite routine, especially since many Jewish Brigade veterans had remained behind to establish MOSSAD LE'ALIYAH BET and HAGANAH bases of operations. The headquarters chosen for this delicate operation was the San Giorgio Hotel in central Rome: There, several nondescript men carrying forged travel documents hustled about.

At first, the HAGANAH, SHA'I, and MOSSAD agents thought of bombing the *Lino* from the air while the ship was on the open seas; bombers and transports that RECHESH personnel purchased overseas frequently refueled in Italy before their last leg to Israel. All the men in the San Giorgio had to do was locate the *Lino* and produce a bomb that could destroy the ship. HAGANAH aircraft

*There has been some controversy as to the true originator of the gathered intelligence. Some sources claim that agents serving the MOSSAD LE'ALIYAH BET, in fact, obtained the information; others have claimed that RECHESH was the true source. Sources deemed reliable, however, indicate that it was an agent of the HAGANAH's (later the IDF's) intelligence arm that gathered and disseminated the information.

available in Italy at the time included Ansons and C-46 Commandos; these planes were not bombers and did not even have bomb doors! The only feasible operational plan was to fly at a low altitude over the ship and roll a homemade explosive device out the door. Such a military operation, highly dependent on luck, was deemed unacceptable, and another means of destroying the *Lino*'s cargo was sought.

One small factor delaying direct action, particularly an aerial bombing, was determining the exact location of the *Lino*. It was believed to be somewhere in the Adriatic Sea—between Italy and Yugoslavia—but for all intents and purposes, the ship and its ten thousand rifles seemed to have vanished. Avigur ordered the HAGANAH aircraft undergoing maintenance in Italy to become airborne—the pilots were to tell the Italian air-traffic controllers that they had to perform some in-flight system checks on the aircraft before proceeding toward Israel—and try to locate the elusive cargo ship. Also, several volunteer pilots with naval experience, from America, Britain, and Holland, were brought to Italy specifically to conduct private reconnaissance flights over the Adriatic. Finally, when Avigur's men in their Rome hotel rooms were close to panic, the *Lino* was finally found. By then, however, severe storms had grounded the HAGANAH aircraft, and the intricate plan was scrubbed. In the end, this seemingly bad bit of luck played directly into the HAGANAH's innovative hands.

The severe weather that gripped the Adriatic on April 1 caused the *Lino* dangerous mechanical difficulties; the ship had to dock in the small Italian port of Molfetta for urgent repairs. With the target now stationary, the HAGANAH task force opted to immobilize it legally while its destruction was planned and executed. One member of Avigur's team, Ada Sereni (widow of Enzo Sereni, one of Reuven Shiloah's "Land of Israel Parachutists"), telephoned the *Corera de-la Sera*, a newspaper loyal to Italy's Christian Democrats, and reported that the arms aboard the *Lino* were meant for a Communist coup against the government.[4] Within twenty-four hours, news of the ten thousand rifles was on every front page throughout Italy, and the *Lino*'s skipper, Captain Pietro, was arrested and taken to Bari for interrogation. Avigur realized that time was of the absolute essence; it would be only a matter of days before the authorities established the true ownership of the *Lino*'s cargo and the ship was allowed to proceed unhindered to Beirut.

Initially, Ada Sereni wanted to enlist the assistance of ex–Italian navy frogmen to destroy the *Lino*. Mussolini's naval commandos had been one of the few bright spots on the failed Italian war effort, and many of these veterans had expressed pro-Zionist sympathies and had assisted illegal Jewish immigration to Palestine following the end of the Second World War. Several of these former Fascist underwater commandos, including a firebrand-wielding officer named Fiorenco Capriotti, had gone to Israel to help train the IDF/navy's fledgling commando forces.[5]

Munya Mardor, one of the HAGANAH's chief sabotage officers, and Yosef Dror,* a founding father of the IDF/navy's elite naval commando forces, objected to "outside" intervention—citing security protocols—and demanded to take care of the *Lino* personally. The two planned to utilize the primitive explosive device that had originally been packaged to drop by air on the *Lino*. There were severe operational difficulties, however. The Royal Navy, in its postwar duties, was involved in the defense of the Italian coastline, and one of their primary objectives was to monitor ships that might be holding illegal Jewish refugees en route to Palestine; coincidentally, a Royal Navy destroyer had moored next to the *Lino*. The two PAL'YAM frogmen would also have to be sure that the explosive device did not damage Bari harbor or other ships; this might change the Italian's laissez-faire attitude toward Zionist activities in its territory. Also, time was a dwindling commodity. The *Lino*'s captain was ironing out his difficulties with the authorities. Dror and Mardor reconnoitered the harbor extensively, marking down all shipping and truck movements, isolating deserted spots along the harbor wall, and determining where guards patrolled. Most importantly, they observed the schedules of the local fishermen and what attention was paid to their comings and goings.

The first attempt to sink the *Lino* met with failure. On April 8, the sapper squad loaded its gear, including the crudely modified limpet mine and sulfuric-acid detonator, into a dinghy and set out for the *Lino*'s mooring, but they were picked up by the searchlights of a Coast Guard craft, and the mission was aborted. The following night, the exhausted and anxious saboteurs returned, only to find that Coast Guard activity around the *Lino* had intensified. Luckily, they found out that the reason for the hustle and bustle was that the Royal Navy destroyer was preparing to set sail. The sappers crouched in their barely seaworthy dinghy until the British warship was out of sight. The *Lino* was now alone and vulnerable. The mine was attached to the ship's hull and the detonator set. At 0400 on April 10, a drop of sulfuric acid detonated the explosive agent and the *Lino* was sunk in a thunderous blast. Most

---

*Yosef Dror was, in fact, a member of the PAL'YAM ("Sea Companies") elite "Sea Section," the designation for its elite underwater sabotage unit. Space limits a full history of the PAL'YAM, but it was one of the most influential of the PAL'MACH units in forming IDF Military Intelligence, and the IDF's special forces capabilities, as well. The Sea Section not only conducted numerous sabotage operations against the Royal Navy's sea blockade of Palestine, but also executed several impressive intelligence-gathering forays against Arab shipping lanes and port installations. As part of the PAL'MACH's 4th Battalion, the unit entrusted with special operations, the Sea Section was on the cutting edge of many of the innovative military tasks performed by the PAL'MACH before, during, and after the 1948 War, as well as being the recipient of the most talented minds and bodies the PAL'MACH could recruit.

of the HAGANAH and MOSSAD LE'ALIYAH BET personnel had escaped to within four hundred kilometers of Bari and awaited the news of the *Lino*'s destruction by coded signal.

On April 10, Avigur sent two brief telegrams to Tel Aviv from his Geneva lair. The first one simply said, "The Benjamin Isma'ilite has set. Details to follow. Regards to our friends." The second telegram was more ominous. It said, "Please prevent disclosure of the perpetrator's identities."[6]

The sinking of the *Lino*, a brilliantly executed intelligence operation, was not the end of Operation Bandit. The Syrians eventually assumed legal ownership of the vessel and recovered much of its cargo. The rifles and ammunition, which had been heavily packed in protective grease, were still fully functional. Colonel Fou'ad Mardom, from the Syrian army's Quartermaster's Unit, was dispatched to Italy to oversee the recovery operation and the final receipt of the cargo in Syria. The dredging operation and cargo retrieval, carried out under the watchful eyes of Colonel Mardom, took weeks. Unbeknownst to him, a contingent of SHA'I intelligence officers from the newly declared Jewish state was monitoring the whole operation. They had bribed the proper officials, and made sure that they knew everything there was to know about the *Lino* and its cargo. When Colonel Mardom leased a 250-ton, ex–Italian navy corvette, the SS *Argiro*, to ferry the guns and ammunition to Syria, the second phase of Operation Bandit went into effect. Why not divert the arms to Israel; after all, who needed the guns more than the IDF!

Luckily for the Israeli operation, Colonel Mardom had not adhered to strict security guidelines while conducting his day-to-day activities. He was not an espionage agent and his inexperience at such work was fatally obvious. He spoke frequently to strangers, telling them enticing details concerning his mission; in addition, to charter the *Argiro*, he even used a shipping line with close ties to the Jewish Agency.

At dawn on August 19, 1948, the *Argiro* set sail for Alexandria, its first port of call. The IDF/navy, however, had had several months to prepare for this phase of the operation and were ready and waiting in ambush. The importance of seizing these weapons was evidenced by the fact that the IDF General Staff had dispatched the *only two* warships in the IDF/navy, the INS *Wedgewood* and the INS *Haganah*, for the interdiction mission.

In the open seas, the *Argiro*, sailing with two "last-minute replacements," mysteriously suffered engine difficulties. Hours later, a small fishing vessel pulled up alongside the *Argiro*; two men boarded the Italian merchant vessel, saying that they had been dispatched from Cairo to oversee the operation. With four HAGANAH agents now on board—with weapons and ammunition smuggled onto the ship before it left port—the hijacking of the *Argiro* was completed in a matter of moments, without any violence. The two "Egyptian government representatives" ordered the ship's captain to change course for

Tel Aviv. The IDF/navy ships arrived hours later and the transfer of the *Argiro*'s cargo commenced, a laborious process that took nearly two weeks.

On the night of August 29, the two IDF/navy vessels reached their home base of Haifa under a great veil of secrecy and heavy security. The eight thousand weapons and eight million rounds of ammunition (a portion of the cargo was lost following the *Lino*'s destruction) were quickly removed from their crates and rushed to IDF forces fighting in Galilee, Jerusalem, and the Negev Desert—forces who, until then, had been defending their positions with crudely assembled Molotov cocktails and were under strict orders not to fire their weapons in automatic bursts in order to conserve ammunition.

Operation Bandit was a brilliant intelligence operation with crucial military significance. It not only demonstrated the ability of Israeli intelligence to operate far from the boundaries of the State of Israel, but also the new state's capability to mount intelligence operations with clear and viable military objectives in mind.

The PAL'YAM sappers returned from their successful operation abroad to fight the bitter battles of the 1948 War. The crew of the *Argiro* was treated as royalty and, following a wartime tour of the country, was returned to Italy; nationals from a nation that had turned a blind eye to intelligence operations on her soil were treated well by the State of Israel. Colonel Mardom suffered the ultimate punishment for his failure: He was executed even though the Israelis offered the Syrians full details of the operation in order to spare his life.[7]

Operation Bandit was one of the new state's most successful undertakings. But this close-knit force of spies, handlers, and controllers also endured bitter losses. In the fight for Israeli independence, the HAGANAH, the IRGUN, and the IDF lost more than six thousand killed and tens of thousands wounded. Only five members of the intelligence services lost their lives,[8] a seemingly miniscule number by comparison. It was significant, however, considering the *value* that each fighter possessed in his (or her) long-term training, elaborate cover, and skill in covert operations.

On May 22, 1948, two of the SHACHAR's most experienced agents, Lt. David Mizrahi and Lt. Ezra Hurin, were arrested by the Egyptian military after they had infiltrated behind enemy lines following the initial Egyptian invasion on May 15. The two were brutally tortured and, following a show trial that lasted less than two hours, executed by a firing squad of twelve Egyptian soldiers.[9] The importance of their contribution in relaying data on enemy troop movements cannot be overestimated; the work of these two men remains awe-inspiring to this day. (In its zenith, the SHACHAR operated at only 3 percent of the SHA'I's total budget, yet contributed much more than was invested in them; such disparity, it is believed, stemmed from the prejudice on the part of the Ashkenazi [European Jews] toward their Sephardim [Oriental Jews] brethren from the Arabic diaspora.)[10]

Not all of Israel's fallen agents received the dignity of a martyr's death by firing squad. Some were buried as Arabs, assuming the identity of their cover even in death. Such is the case of Nagib Ibrahim Hamudah, or, as he was known in his IDF files, 1st Lt. Ya'akov Boke'i. One of MOD 18's most capable officers, Boke'i, like most of his colleagues in the unit, began his intelligence career in SHACHAR; he was recruited (upon his return to Israel) from his native Syria in 1945. His handler in SHACHAR was Ya'akov Nimrodi, a legend in the Israeli intelligence community. He later became a private arms merchant who would feature prominently in the Iran-Contra scandal. Nimrodi considered his Syrian-born agent, "a natural for the delicate operations in Arab lands—even though Boke'i had blonde hair and striking blue eyes, hardly the criteria for a deep-cover agent in the Middle East." [11] Following the creation of the IDF Intelligence Service, Boke'i was dispatched into Syria and Jordan for deep-cover operations. Infiltrating across the wartime frontiers was not a difficult undertaking and he remained in the cold, usually for three months at a time. During the 1948 War, he operated unhindered.

The chaotic refugee situation between Jordan and Israel afforded MOD 18 the opportunity to send two of its best agents, Boke'i and a young man who is identified only by the name "Ephraim," *back* into the cold; their targeted country was Syria. Although the northern border between Israel and the Republic of Syria was far from hermetic, it was still a risky undertaking to send an agent across a fortified no-man's-land. The Syrians were vigilant along their border with Israel; to have an agent captured so close to Israel risked political and military embarrassment. Infiltrating into Syria from Jordan, however, was much simpler, a routine border crossing relying on the quality of forged papers.

When a prisoner and refugee exchange between Israel and Jordan was announced in January 1949, the opportunity to send in the two agents appeared brilliantly convenient; between five thousand and six thousand Jordanian soldiers and Palestinian refugees would be leaving Israel. (The planting of bogus POWs was a practice the British first sponsored with the PAL'MACH's German Platoon and is continued, it is believed, until this day by the IDF Intelligence Corps.) Following intensive training, which established their covers, at MOD 18 headquarters in the SHA'I's "Green House," * the men were supplied with impeccably prepared documentation, including birth certificates,

*The Green House in Yafo, coincidentally, had also once served as headquarters for the Arab guerrilla forces commanded by legendary leader Hassan Salameh, who was killed by IRGUN forces on May 30, 1948, during the battle for Ras el-Ein, an Arab village of strategic importance. There had been several unsuccessful attempts by both the SHA'I and the PAL'MACH to assassinate Salameh, but they both met with dismal failure.[12] Salameh's son, Ali, rose through the ranks of the PLO, eventually serving as head of its much feared counterintelligence force, the Razd. As head of Black September, Ali Salameh commanded the 1972 Munich Olympics Massacre.

high-school report cards, work permits, and military service IDs and dog tags. According to several reports, these forgeries were all produced at the SHA'I HQ. After a hearty send-off from MOD 18 HQ, these men were thrown into a detention camp along with other refugees who were under suspicion of being Arab Legion deserters. No one was informed of their true identities, not even the military police guards who regularly beat the prisoners; Boke'i and "Ephraim" were not spared and would both carry severe scars of their treatment.

Following their stint inside the detention center, the agents were sent to the main POW camp inside the huge IDF military compound at TZRIFIN, where they were introduced to "fellow" Jordanians about to be repatriated. MOD 18 handlers kept constant surveillance on the two men and briefed and debriefed them in interrogation sessions in which, once again, the two SHIN MEM agents had to suffer physical abuse in order to not raise suspicion as to their true identities. Their stay in the TZRIFIN POW camp was not only crucial preparatory work, but turned out to be an intelligence bonanza for the IDF. Sitting in their squalid holding pens along with other Arab soldiers, Boke'i and Ephraim listened attentively to countless stories and battle accounts and other enticing tidbits; this firsthand data—forged into the agents' memories—proved invaluable.

On May 4, 1949, Boke'i, now fully immersed in his identity of Nagib Ibrahim Hamudah, joined six hundred Jordanian soldiers in Jerusalem, preparing to cross the barbed-wire concertina barriers and heavily mined no-man's-land in front of the old city's Mendelbaum Gate. As he stood in line, holding his few personal possessions, a team of MOD 18 watchers faithfully followed his progress until he was out of sight. Unbeknownst to IDF intelligence, however, the Jordanians (with, it is believed, British intelligence assistance) had assembled a comprehensive list of all its personnel held by the IDF. Heavily armed Arab Legion soldiers ringed the narrow Ottoman-built gate while intelligence officers checked the names of all those returning home. The individuals whose names were not on the list were taken aside and led away for interrogation. It is likely that such a fate befell Boke'i, although it was also reported that another Arab in the assembled lot identified him as an Israeli agent to the Jordanian soldiers on duty. Nevertheless, Boke'i was captured and, after refusing to disclose any information about himself, he was suspected of being an "Iraqi Jew" and an Israeli spy. He was brutally tortured in Jerusalem's Hakisha Prison and transferred to Amman for further "attention," which included the bastinado, starvation, and sensory deprivation. Refusing to betray his nation, Boke'i was sentenced to death and hung on August 9. He was buried in a nondescript grave under the name Nagib Ibrahim Hamudah.

The death of Boke'i was a devastating loss to IDF intelligence and a personal tragedy for his handlers, who assumed responsibility for his capture and eventual execution. The loss of one of their own remained an open wound for years;

following the 1967 War, captured Jordanian soldiers, policemen, and intelligence agents were questioned about the location of Nagib Ibrahim Hamudah's grave by Intelligence Corps interrogators and A'MAN agents, some of whom had served with Boke'i in the PAL'MACH, but no new information was gathered. To this day, Boke'i's body remains in a grave somewhere in the West Bank, or in Jordan proper, awaiting a deserving Jewish burial with full military honors.

The unique esprit de corps of the IDF's young intelligence community helped see it through the difficult 1948 War, but its tasks in the years following independence were just as trying, if not more so.

When Colonel Herzog was appointed the IDF attaché for the United States and Canada in April 1950, Col. Binyamin Gibli was named head of the Intelligence Department. A strikingly handsome individual with Nordic features, Gibli was known for his charisma, glamor, and popularity among the lower ranks; he was an odd contrast to the dowdy Eastern European Jews who dominated the Israeli defense community. He was also an odd choice for the position of Military Intelligence chief. A HAGANAH veteran and a member of the British-sanctioned Settlement Police, Gibli rose through the ranks of the underground hierarchy, eventually commanding SHA'I's Jerusalem section during the 1948 War. As Jerusalem station chief, Gibli had chaired the kangaroo court of Meir Tubianski. Many saw him as an officer of questionable virtues and judgment, and many thought he should have been court-martialed along with Beeri! Instead, Gibli, a skilled politician even in the alleged apolitical environment of the IDF, testified at Beeri's trial. His appearance sealed Beeri's fate and led many Beeri loyalists in the SHIN MEM and, later, the Intelligence Department to forever hold him in disdain. Ben-Gurion, however, liked Gibli, and at the time, that was enough to guarantee anyone's posting.

Gibli sought sweeping, penetrating changes in the makeup of IDF intelligence. Herzog had established the Intelligence Department along British lines: In the British army, the chief of Military Intelligence is on the Operations staff, subordinate to the chief of Operations. Gibli wanted this system modified to resemble the American or French systems, in which Military Intelligence is a separate branch and answerable to the chief of staff. Such a move, beyond its immediate impact on the structure of the IDF, would further empower Gibli and, most importantly, make him a general—possibly, one day, even chief of staff.[13]

Gibli also sought control of *all* foreign espionage operations, an arena that was in the hands of Boris Guriel's Foreign Ministry Political Department and its flamboyant Operations chief, Arthur Ben-Natan. In his power play against the Political Department, Gibli found a sympathetic ear in the IDF's second chief of staff, Lt. Gen. Yigal Yadin, one of the nation's most esteemed soldiers. Yadin was considered a soldier's soldier in the true Israeli sense, one who adhered religiously to the IDF's egalitarian beliefs. Along with Gibli and much of the socialist element within the Israeli hierarchy, Yadin disdained the Political Department's expensive life-style abroad—the tailored suits, endless restaurant bills, and presidential suites in the finest European hotels—while in Israel, food was rationed, and tens of thousands of immigrants lived in filthy transit camps overrun by disease and despair. Their detractors felt that Guriel and Ben-Natan's high-class tastes made them non-Israeli; but it could be argued that the Political Department's agents had to frequent locations of power, capital, and prestige in order to obtain *political* intelligence. Military Intelligence, on the other hand, was restricted in its use of overseas operations (through a 1949 Defense Ministry memorandum). Gibli chose to ignore these limitations, however. A civil war in the shadows soon ensued.

In 1949, Reuven Shiloah, sensing these rifts in the new nation's security and intelligence services, tried to prevent future problems by forming a "coordinating body." It was called the VA'ADAT ROSHEI HA'SHERUTIM ("the Committee of Service Chiefs"); of course, he was its chair. Initially, the VA'ADAT was made up of Shiloah; MA'MAN ("Intelligence Department") chief Herzog; Political Department boss Guriel; SHIN BET commander Isser Harel; and chief superintendent Yehezkel Shahar, commander of the National Police Special Branch. (Although the police were not privy to state secrets, at the time they did constitute the nation's largest *security* force.[14]) Although the first VA'ADAT sessions were useful in charting the progress of ongoing operations, coordinating activities, and airing opinions, it eventually became clear that there was severe discord within the Israeli intelligence community. Intelligence chiefs openly lambasted one another; levied charges of moral indiscretion, treason, and other more colorful accusations of impropriety; and vowed to end the others' power. It became known as the "Revolt of the Spies."

The Political Department felt that several of their spectacular intelligence coups, such as obtaining the Syrian army's war plans and Order of Battle, offered proof of their ability, and their rights of exclusivity, in foreign operations. Military Intelligence, however, claimed that *their* obtaining of a top-secret Iraqi document—a study of the 1948 War—was evidence of their abilities and responsibilities for conducting foreign espionage operations.[15] When Shiloah tried to seek a compromise between the Political Department and Military Intelligence, his first attempt met with embarrassing failure. The case in point involved an opportunity by the Political Department to have an agent operate in Cairo as "Consul General for the Republic of San Salvador"; the agent would then be protected by the protocols of diplomatic immunity.[16] Gibli's Military Intelligence was allowed to choose the operative, but the agent botched his cover immediately, and a golden opportunity for risk-free intelligence-gathering was blown. This escalated the verbal war between the Political

Department and the IDF. The situation was exacerbated when Gibli found a willful ally in SHIN BET boss Isser Harel, who also held the Political Department in contempt for their lavish extravagance and lack of continuous productivity.

Because the Israeli intelligence organizations operated in spite of the other, instead of in the national interest, total chaos ensued. Each organization dispatched its agents abroad with the hope of outdoing and undercutting its rivals. Europe was inundated with Israeli agents. The security services of such countries as Italy and France, which were extremely friendly with the newly formed Jewish state, were bombarded by requests for liaison, support, and information—all from different agencies and for similar targets. The services also encroached on the "sacred" territory of the other; according to several reports, Military Intelligence conducted surveillance of Political Department operatives, and, in a move against the SHIN BET, the Political Department became involved in counterintelligence by breaking into Eastern-bloc embassies in Tel Aviv. The situation was intolerable and embarrassing to David Ben-Gurion, who ordered Reuven Shiloah to end the crisis once and for all.

Shiloah had been sent to Washington with Colonel Herzog in 1950, and he was deeply influenced by the organizational attributes of the newly formed CIA. His solution for Israel's revolt of the spies was to disband the Political Department and give Military Intelligence *all* foreign special assignments. Realizing that the new arrangement meant death to their careers, as well as those of their loyal operatives, Guriel and Ben-Natan simply folded the Political Department's operations: Agents resigned and files for ongoing operations were destroyed; years of work vanished in politically motivated spite.

In Israel, however, this was the cost of doing business. Out of this obvious mess arose an agency called "The Central Institute for Coordination," and later, "The Central Institute for Intelligence and Security"; it later became known as HA'MOSSAD LE'MODE'IN U'LE'TAFKIDIM MEYUCHADIM ("The Institute for Intelligence and Special Tasks"), or the MOSSAD. It would be Israel's CIA, but at its inception it was tasked only with the *collection* of intelligence; it did not possess an operations department. The MOSSAD was directly under the control of the prime minister, and Ben-Gurion chose Shiloah as its first head when the organization was formally sanctioned on April 1, 1951. By chairing both the VA'ADAT as well as the MOSSAD, Shiloah was preoccupied with internal infighting and not with the day-to-day running of an espionage service.

In February 1953, Shiloah's career ended in disgrace following a disastrous operation in Iraq where, it appeared, Gibli's Military Intelligence, Shiloah's MOSSAD, and Avigur's MOSSAD LE'ALIYAH BET were all working separately to arrange the same operation—involving the covert immigration of Iraqi Jews to Israel. According to Ya'akov Frank, one of the operatives recruited for the mission, "The right hand knew nothing of what the left hand was doing. . . . We were fortunate that the Iraqis were worse than we were!" [17] Although more than 150,000 Iraqi Jews were flown to Israel in an impressive covert operation, the infighting for control of the mission illustrated a fundamental lack of concern for the agents in the field. The Iraqi Muchabarat ("Secret Service") seized more than a hundred Jews suspected of assisting in the operation and eventually executed two of them. After this debacle, Isser Harel, whose integrity was held in awe by Ben-Gurion, was named the MOSSAD chief while also remaining in control of the SHIN BET. This made him the most powerful man in Israel.

With its new exclusivity in foreign—or active—operations, the Intelligence Department faced numerous tactical difficulties. In the 1948 War's aftermath, many Arabic-language journals stopped reaching Israel; this deprived Military Intelligence of invaluable open sources of intelligence. Open intelligence was a crucial element in the department's ability to determine Arab military intentions as well as Arab political scenarios: A photograph in a magazine showing one leader refusing the traditional embrace of another leader could provide greater insight into a political situation than a thousand man-hours of spy work. The Military Intelligence spy desks, MODS 10 and 18, were also considerably weakened following the War of Independence. With borders now sealed, albeit not hermetically, dispatching agents and recovering them from enemy territory became a precarious undertaking indeed. The end of the war also meant that the most valuable source of intelligence in the Arab world, the local Jewish populations, were now persona non grata in Middle Eastern capitals. In Egypt, the premier target country for Israeli intelligence, thousands of Jews had been placed in detention during the 1948 War, and most had immigrated to Israel following the 1949 cease-fire accords. In the early 1950s, the intelligence coming out of Egypt had dwindled into piecemeal increments that were, on the whole, unreliable: Attention and resources had to be diverted to more profitable locations.

The IDF's Intelligence Department faced operational hardships in the 1950s, which continue to this very day and typify Israeli intelligence work. IDF Military Intelligence is the only intelligence service in the world that *cannot* maintain overt physical contact with a targeted (or Arab) nation. Every country utilizes spies and agents to gather intelligence on neighboring nations, or to subvert political institutions in their own national security interest. To accomplish this feat, "sleeper" agents are dispatched into strategic locations and controlled by legally sanctioned diplomats and military attachés in that nation's embassy; information is transferred by dead drop or other coded means and then returned to the operating nation by protected and coded radio transmissions, or by the sanctity of the diplomatic pouch. Israel possessed no such luxury. The neighboring Arab nations never recognized the State of Israel, never made a nominal peace with her, and never established even the lowest order of diplomatic relations. There was no Israeli embassy in Amman or

Damascus, where the representing IDF attaché could view military exercises or recruit local officers with impunity. (After all, with diplomatic immunity, the penalty to a blown embassy spy was merely expulsion.) Since Israelis were not allowed to visit these Arab nations as tourists, students, or businessmen, the acquisition of open sources of intelligence from university libraries and industrial facilities could not be done routinely. There were not even telephone or postal links between Israel and her Arab neighbors. Israel was truly an island.

In the field, MOD 2's ability to monitor signals intelligence was prohibited by geographic ranges and the lack of sophistication of the equipment deployed by both sides. The Israeli Air Force's Intelligence Department was extremely limited in its range and abilities. With the PAL'MACH disbanded, the IDF no longer possessed an elite force to conduct cross-border intelligence-gathering forays; its role as nation builder had transformed the IDF of 1950–1952 into a mediocre, even incapable and unreliable, fighting force. As a result, Military Intelligence had to rely almost exclusively on human intelligence ("HUMINT") for the steady flow of accurate intelligence the IDF required to keep its strategic edge in the tense peace that followed the war.

The exodus of Jews from the Arab diaspora both helped and hampered military intelligence capabilities. Although the expulsion of much of Egyptian Jewry and the successful Operation Magic Carpet arrangements, which saved the Jews of Yemen and Iraq, depleted these Arab nations of potential military intelligence agents, these new immigrants, many of whom were wealthy merchants and educated professionals, provided a wealth of intelligence on their native Arab lands. Nevertheless, new agents had to be found, cultivated, and dispatched.

MODS 10 and 18 turned to their Arabic-speaking personnel, mainly SHA'I Arab Desk veterans and the former warrior/spies of the PAL'MACH's Arab Platoon and SHACHAR. These men were veterans at intelligence work. Through their past operations on behalf of the HAGANAH and Jewish Palestine's other underground network, they had already established links with informers and agents who, as a result of the new geographical boundaries forged following the 1949 Armistice Arrangement, now lived in Jordan, Lebanon, Syria, and Egypt. The ex-SHA'I and ex-SHACHAR agents were now professional officers in the IDF, and it was their responsibility to seek out the talent in their ranks and train the next generation of Israeli intelligence agents. The new blood came predominantly from new Arab immigrants, principally from Syria, who had been conscripted into the IDF.[18] They were monitored upon their entrance into IDF service; those with extraordinary talents were recruited almost immediately. Others volunteered and underwent difficult acceptance examinations. For all those who were recruited from Arab lands, MOD 3, or Field Security, conducted elaborate background checks.

In their book *Men of Secrets, Men of Mystery*, Rafi Sitton and Yitzhak Shoshan, both former IDF Military Intelligence officers and natives of Syria, offer unique insight into the making and existence of an Israeli intelligence agent. Intelligence Corps basic training was a fascinating combination of military and espionage indoctrination. Along with the drills, weapons training, and preparatory work for combat, which was standard for all soldiers, Intelligence Corps conscripts spent time in more specialized fields suited to their future tasks. Some spent time in the "Journalist Section," where Arab journals and newspapers were read and scrutinized for any tidbit of intelligence. This afforded the Arabic-speaking natives the opportunity to immerse themselves in the language and it taught the young conscripts how to sift through available material and gather from it valuable sources of intelligence.

Recruiting natives from target nations for intelligence work was a difficult procedure. Many times, Military Intelligence had to rely on "false-flag" operations, in which the recruited agent believed he was offering his services to, or was being paid by, a more politically agreeable power; but this could not always be carried out. The State of Israel did not represent any beliefs or ideals other than a permanent home for the Jews. Zionism was not a universal philosophy like communism, so, unlike the Soviet Union, Israel could not rely on political ideals to recruit espionage agents. Unlike the West, which could promise freedom to oppressed peoples, Israel did not represent a cherished ideal or irrefutable right to Arabs. The only exception, the only true nonprofit motive for an Arab citizen to spy on behalf of Israel, was religious freedom. There were dozens of small religious sects scattered throughout the Middle East—the Copts in Egypt, the Druze in Lebanon and Syria, and the Kurds in Iraq—who were treated with disdain and suspicion in their native lands; they were monitored by the secret police, barred from travel, and, for the most part, forbidden to hold significant military rank.

Sex was another tool for purposes of recruitment or blackmail, but in the traditional Arab cultures, its use had its obvious limitations. Women in the Arab world were not permitted to hold important government postings, and men did not bother to hide their mistresses. Money could also be used as a lure, but it tended to attract unreliable elements; and, in any case, IDF Military Intelligence had very limited funds. This operational difficulty was best phrased in a popular saying in Military Intelligence headquarters: "The Arab has yet to be born who will join Israeli intelligence for the sake of Herzl's beard!" (a reference to the symbol of the founding father of modern Zionism).[19]

Recruiting Arabs as agents was attended to in meticulous fashion. SHA'I veterans had learned an invaluable lesson in the dark days of the preindependence underground: The charisma of the handler was many times more important than the cause, or espionage service, he represented. If a handler could cultivate a warm friendship with an agent and develop loyalties, the agent would feel as though he was operating with complete backup and support, even when risking his life alone in hostile territory. Potential recruits were thoroughly screened before being approached. Their family histories were checked, school grades examined, and intelligence quotient and political affiliations scrutinized. The job of GAYAS HA'SOCHNIM ("agent-recruiter") was one of the most important within the Military Intelligence framework.

Besides the idealistic and political barriers that separated Israel from the Arab world, the geographical barriers made intelligence work extremely difficult. In the early 1950s, cross-border espionage operations meant Jordan. Although Israel did not have access to the Jordan River bridges, and the West Bank was secured by fortified defenses, there were gaps in the borders that afforded one-time crossings; the most popular spot was Jerusalem. Following the 1948 War, Jerusalem, the City of David, was divided in much the same way as Berlin, except that there were no Checkpoint Charlies in Jerusalem, only a no-man's-land guarded by thick, impassable rows of barbed-wire concertina, antipersonnel mines, and Jordanian snipers. The snipers' eagle eyes and M-1 carbines would pick off anyone, from a military official to a schoolgirl, who came too close to their side of the fence. The State of Israel's capital, Jerusalem was a heavily armed camp where the day-to-day life of nearly a hundred thousand citizens was conducted amid patrolling half-tracks, occasional mortar shells, and fear that a full-scale conflagration would erupt. There were gaps in this impervious border, however—holes known only to smugglers and intelligence agents.

When a "meet" was scheduled in Israeli territory, Military Intelligence rarely informed the authorities. It was on a need-to-know basis, and for security precautions very few people—even senior officers in the army, the police, and the border guards—needed to know. The agent and the handler met one-on-one, and only one of the handler's assistants came along for added security. The handlers wore civilian garb and carried only sidearms and a knife secured in their trouser leggings. They would choose a spot along the fortifications that divided Jerusalem and wait at the prearranged time in a safe house for the agent to arrive. Sometimes, agents were delayed for several hours, even several days, and each safe house had to have an ample supply of food and amenities. It also had to be nondescript to avoid unwanted attention from curious neighbors. The most popular neighborhood was Jerusalem's poor "Samuel the Prophet" district, which overlooked much of the Jordanian section of the city. There was always the danger that the meet would be a trap: The agent could, in fact, be working for both sides, and might bring along some company to escort the Israeli handler back to Jordan.

When an agent finally arrived, the interrogation would begin at a relaxed pace. SHA'I and SHACHAR veterans had learned in their years in the field to be quiet, attentive, and never press the agent for details; if a good rapport had been established, the agent would in good time tell everything he knew. This practice was adhered to religiously, although each handler knew and respected the individual habits and personalities of his particular agent. Interrogations were usually administered by two Military Intelligence officers, one playing the serious professional and the other, usually the lower-ranking assistant, offering understanding and friendship (an espionage version of the "good cop–bad cop" routine). Some interrogations were recorded; at the time, however, the Intelligence Department's operating budget limited the number of recording devices that were available. At the end of the interrogation, the question of financial reward would come up. Since the Intelligence Department had limited funds, and since the IDF had always frowned upon utilizing agents whose sole motive was profit, agents were paid nominal fees. Intelligence Department headquarters believed that beginning with a small payment and slowly increasing the scale always brought in better "merchandise." Some agents were rewarded for their efforts with sexual favors—a prostitute was sometimes offered as a going-away present before the trip back into the cold.[20]

Operations against Jordan achieved impressive results, especially since the professional Jordanian military was seen as one of Israel's most dire threats. Intelligence efforts were primarily restricted to *Jordanian* military and political developments, since the Palestinians living in the West Bank had yet to factor into the equation. There were, nevertheless, sideshows typical of Jerusalem of that era.

One of the oddest Intelligence Department operations was the 1951 hunt for one of the most notorious gangsters in Jerusalem's history: Mustapha Samueli. A resident of the village of Nebi Samuel, a Jordanian border strongpoint on the Tel Aviv–Jerusalem road, Samueli was described as a psychopath even by his friends. During the Second World War he had served as an intelligence agent for the German Abwher.[21] During the years of peace that followed the 1948 War, Samueli regularly crossed the "no-man's-land" to commit acts of robbery, extortion, rape, and murder in Jewish Jerusalem: His calling card was a German MP-38 Schmeisser 9 mm machine gun, which he carried at all times.

In addition to his "professional" activities as a criminal, Samueli was also a well-paid agent for the Jordanian Intelligence Service and was regularly assisted in his cross-border crime sprees by the Jordanian military. Since Jerusalem was a mixed city of Arabs and Jews, Samueli was able to blend into the local population. He monitored IDF troop movements in the city, as well as defenses and other security installations. As a result, a criminal matter became one of national security, and his case was transferred to the IDF and the Military Intelligence for special attention.

The two Intelligence Department officers entrusted with hunting down the "Big Thief," as Samueli was known in Jerusalem folklore, were men still known only by their code names of "Abu-Assaf " and "Abu-Aharon." They were ex-SHA'I officers with extensive experience in the Jerusalem area. They first crossed the frontier and tried to root out Samueli utilizing the enticing financial reward of fifty Jordanian dinars (approximately a six-month salary for a mid-level Jordanian civil servant). Many would-be agents rose to the occasion, assuring the two Israeli intelligence officers that Samueli was indeed dead, and demanding the rewards, or at least an advance. Samueli, feeling the uncomfortable pressure, decided to print his own obituary in the popular Jerusalem newspaper *Palastin*. Abu-Aharon and Abu-Assaf were not convinced. They duly ordered one of their own agents to print a highly emotional sympathy letter in the paper, proving that by paying a nominal fee, any bit of news could be published.

Eventually, Samueli's megalomaniac personality sealed his fate. He boasted about where his next act of robbery would occur in Jerusalem, and an agent in the crowd immediately reported the news back to his handlers. IDF infantry units in the area were summoned, and a heavily armed ambush was prepared; in the ensuing firefight, Samueli was killed. He died, however, with guns ablaze. The following day, thousands mourned Samueli's death in a huge funeral in East Jerusalem; the Intelligence Department followed suit by paying for the publication of a *real* obituary on the pages of *Palastin*.

While conducting its activities with virtual impunity across the poorly defended Jordanian frontier, the Intelligence Department was sometimes assisted in its operations by the most benign of acts—such as a royal decree by the young King Hussein offering a Jordanian passport to all Palestinians in the West Bank. This revelation afforded Military Intelligence the opportunity to obtain a plentiful supply of authentic documents that it could later use in Jordan, and in other Arab nations as well.

Israel was not the only country in the region to conduct cross-border intelligence missions. The smugglers and criminals who frequently crossed the Syrian and Jordanian borders to rob agricultural settlements in Israel were often recruited by the Arab intelligence services. They photographed military installations and sifted through their trash, gathering invaluable information on troop strengths, personnel, and future operations. Perhaps the most serious threat to Israel came in the south, where Egyptian intelligence agents crossed the desert frontier at will and monitored IDF activities.

In response to Egyptian military intelligence operations, the IDF created small, highly mobile reconnaissance formations to combat these covert infiltrators. At first, the small and short-lived IDF Cavalry Corps patrolled the desert, but they were soon replaced by members of the Minorities Unit, known as Unit 300, a force of Druze, Circassian, and Bedouin soldiers who volunteered, and were later conscripted, to serve in the IDF. In August 1951, OC (officer commander) Southern Command Maj. Gen. Moshe Dayan created a force of scouts, trackers, and commandos known as Unit 30, to prevent Egyptian intelligence agents from infiltrating into Israel, and also to conduct cross-border retaliation raids.[22] Eventually, the infamous Unit 101 commanded by Maj. "Arik" Sharon would inherit this responsibility (and this unit would forever alter the concept of Israeli combat intelligence). Later, these units were augmented by a Southern Command reconnaissance force of Bedouins and Jews called SAYERET SHAKED ("Almond Recon"), which patrolled the penetrable frontier with extreme skill and determination.

The Arab intelligence effort against Israel also prompted MOD 3, responsible for field security, into immediate and decisive action. Military installations were soon decorated with posters extolling the virtue of the security-conscious soldiers; the password soon became KOL HA'KAVOD LE'HAYAL HA'SHOMER SOD ("All the honor to the soldier who keeps a secret"). Undercover snare operations were conducted to punish soldiers who were careless with military secrets; harsh examples were made of those guilty of the smallest infractions. In the years to come, these efforts would expand markedly in their scope, sophistication, and importance.

During his tenure as commander of the Intelligence Department, Gibli pushed to improve the IDF's intelligence-gathering and -analyzing capabilities. His principal objective in the structural overhaul was to obtain *new* sources of intelligence—sources so vital that they would make up for the IDF's outnumbered status. One of Gibli's major targets for improvement was the department's Listening Unit, MOD 2. The "ears" of the IDF had more than proven their worth, and now, in a period void of full-scale war, the unit received an influx of funds, personnel, and technical assistance. The most important addition was the production by the Technical Department (MOD 8) of small listening devices to be attached to telephone lines; these devices were planted in enemy territory during cross-border forays by reconnaissance units and reaped a wealth of real-time intelligence data, as MOD 2 Arabists listened in on operations conversations between field commander and headquarters.

The other cog to receive special attention by Gibli was the IAF's small intelligence component. In 1951, the IAF was still not adequately equipped to defend the Israeli skies or conduct effective reconnaissance and aerial-photography flights. There were only six combat-trained pilots in the IAF, the foreign volunteers having left Israel after the war, and there were only sixty operational Spitfires in the IAF's inventory. (A shipment of an additional twenty P-51 Mustangs from the Swedish Air Force and some ex-RAF Mosquitos would later bolster this force.) The only aerial-reconnaissance aircraft with photographic equipment was a short-range Spitfire, which usually pushed beyond its safe operational ceiling; many sorties flown against the Egyptians encountered constant antiaircraft fire and, on many occasions, the depletion of fuel supplies.[23] Gibli pushed the IAF to add reconnaissance aircraft to their shopping list of fighter aircraft that the Defense Ministry had dispatched throughout the world.

On December 28, 1953, Gibli's grand organizational vision paid off when MA'MAN, the Intelligence Department, received increased responsibility and command influence by officially becoming A'MAN, or the Intelligence Branch. The announcement was made in a special memo to Intelligence Department officers by Lt. Col. Yehoshofat "Fatti" Harkabi, the acting intelligence commander for Gibli, who was then completing his studies abroad.

> On this day, the Intelligence Department ceases to be a part of the Operations Branch and has become a branch, to be called A'MAN, within the General Staff. This change has come, primarily, to reinforce the importance of the Intelligence Corps to the IDF Order of Battle. The change of status, with everything it entails, is an essential step in *our* development which is as important as was establishing the foundations of an IDF military intelligence entity in the very beginning. The importance of this event is not limited to the Intelligence Branch, but extends to the entire Intelligence Corps. Yesterday, what used to be the Intelligence Corps and Department, which today is the Branch, were, and are, linked and combined; the senior A'MAN officers are simultaneously senior staff officers in the Intelligence Corps. The change of status will also be observed, within time, in the extended units of the corps. This change is not a cause for celebration; the meaning of it is an increase of responsibility and demand from all the intelligence soldiers to increase their efforts. For our state, which has been under siege since it was established by enemies who seek its destruction, intelligence is the first line of defense. We, who live in the center of the tumultuous Middle East, must know and so recognize everything which transpires around us. This objective of ours is the prophecy of intelligence; this is the cornerstone of the state security and its existence. This vision we shall always keep in front of us and we shall walk towards its light and see its way. Our ears are going to be attentive to every whisper and our eyes and mind shall be open to enlighten ourselves and understand everything to its full extent. We shall develop within ourselves love and fanaticism to intelligence work and we shall continue to fulfill its objectives.[24]

Harkabi's emotional declaration was typical of the reaction within the IDF. The formation of A'MAN, the IDF's intelligence Order of Battle, which remains intact to this day, had a profound impact on the IDF's view of military intelligence.

There were now five principal components of Israeli intelligence. The two military intelligence forces, A'MAN and HA'MAN (Intelligence Corps), remained responsible for gathering and disseminating intelligence data on enemy forces and their commanders and combat units; surveillance of enemy forces and their positions, movements, and intentions; and research and analysis in military, strategic, and national security matters. The remaining tasks, such as military censorship, field security, and foreign liaisons, remained intact. The MOSSAD would have the responsibility for foreign espionage operations; the SHIN BET continued its tasks of counterintelligence and internal security; the Police Special Branch assisted the SHIN BET in delicate cases that endangered national security; and a newly sanctioned institution called the Foreign Ministry's Research Department would be tasked with gathering "legitimate intelligence," or intelligence gathered overtly abroad by diplomats and military attachés. Another force would be created later, a mysterious office in the Defense Ministry known as LA'KA'M (acronym for "Science Liaison Bureau"), which would be responsible for overseeing development in the nuclear sphere.

The formation of A'MAN meant increased responsibility in research and analysis. Under Herzog, the Intelligence Department had allotted these functions to the various desks that covered each target nation. The researchers tended to be academics, mainly Western Europeans, or YEKKIM (a derogatory Yiddish word reserved for the stubborn, snobbish, and sanitary German Jews). Few of them spoke Arabic, and fewer understood the Arab mentality. With their academic backgrounds, they tended to be too analytical, often calculating probable strengths on mathematical formulas rather than common sense; as a result, intelligence reports were often inaccurate, sometimes overstated by 30 to 40 percent. If A'MAN was to function successfully, its research and analysis capabilities would have to be consolidated into a force of well-trained, intellectually disciplined Arabists and military experts.

The creation of A'MAN signaled the end of an era, one dominated by HAGANAH recollections and the ways of the past. In retrospect, one Intelligence Corps senior officer had this comment about the early days: "Perhaps what made the first years of the Intelligence Department so crucial and so successful was the fact that the conscript soldiers and professional officers had to perform above and beyond the call of duty because they had so little to work with." [25] For the IDF, the creation of A'MAN would be a tumultuous thrust into the future.

NOTES: CHAPTER FOUR

1. Dani Shalom, KOL METOSEI HEYL HA'AVIR (Tel Aviv: Bavir Aviation Publications, 1990), 111.

2. Ian Black, "The Origins of Israeli Intelligence," *Intelligence and National Security*, London, Vol. 3, No. 4 (October 1987): 153.

3. Yosef Argaman, "Robbing the Bandit," BAMACHANE (December 28, 1988): 23.

4. *Ibid.* 24.

5. Uri Milstein, HA'HISTORIA SHEL HA'TZANHANIM KERECH DALED (Tel Aviv: Schalgi Ltd., Publishing House, 1987), 1412.

6. See Yosef Argaman, "Robbing the Bandit," 23.

7. Shmuel Segev, "HEM NIKBARU BE'SHEMOT A'ARAVIM" ("They Were Buried With Arab Names"), MA'ARIV Daily (May 31, 1985): 20.

8. Yerucham Cohen, B*y Light and in Darkness* (Tel Aviv: Amikam Publishers, 1969), 67.

9. See Ian Black, 153.

10. Eitan Haber, "KTZIN MODE'IN YISRAELI NITLA BE'YARDEN KE'A'ARAVI," YEDIOT AHARONOT SHABBAT (April 27, 1982): 4.

11. Michael Bar-Zohar and Eitan Haber, *The Quest for the Red Prince* (New York: William Morrow and Company, Inc., 1983), 88.

12. See Eitan Haber, "KTZIN MODE'IN YISRAELI NITLA BE'YARDEN KE'A'ARAVI," 5.

13. Stewart Steven, *The Spymasters of Israel* (New York: Ballantine Books, 1980), 31.

14. Yossi Melman and Dan Raviv, *The Imperfect Spies: The History of Israeli Intelligence* (London: Sidgwick and Jackson Ltd., 1989), 52.

15. See Stewart Steven, 36.

16. Oded Granot, HEYL HA'MODE'IN: TZAHAL BE'HEILO ENTZYKLOPEDIA LE'TZAVA U'LE'BITACHON (Tel Aviv: Revivim Publishers, 1981), 18.

17. See Yossi Melman and Dan Raviv, 63.

18. In the limited number of accounts that have been published by ex-IDF Military Intelligence officers, an overwhelming number of the agents have been Syrian Jews. The majority of Syrian Jews, mainly from Aleppo and Damascus, immigrated to Israel prior to 1948, and they quickly established themselves as true "blue and white" Israelis. Yet their penchant for intelligence work perhaps can best be analyzed by a Syrian Jew's ability—because of the unique linguistic characteristics of the accent resembling those of Syrian Moslem, Lebanese, and Palestinian dialects—to pass themselves off as Syrians, Lebanese, or Palestinians. Iraqi or Yemenite Jews, for example, would face greater difficulties in achieving this deception. In his fascinating book *The Aurora's Butterfly*, ex-Military Intelligence Maj. (Res.) Eliahu Rika, a

Syrian Jew, elaborates extensively on his ability to pass as a Lebanese Arab while planted deep-cover in various Middle Eastern capitals.

19. Rafi Sitton and Yitzhak Shoshan, ANSHEI HA'SOD VE'HA'STAR ("Men of Secrets, Men of Mystery"), Tel Aviv: Edanim Publishers, Ltd., (1990), 117.

20. See Yossi Melman and Dan Raviv, 115.

21. See Oded Granot, 31.

22. Yosef Argaman, "HA'MALKODET" ("The Trap"), BAMACHANE (June 10, 1987): 24.

23. See Uri Milstein, Vol. 4, 1503.

24. Alex Doron, "TAYAS RIGUL," MA'ARIV SOF SHAVU'A (March 30, 1990): 44.

25. See Oded Granot, 30.

CHAPTER 5

THE AFFAIR IN EGYPT

A mysterious unit in the IDF's intelligence forces was responsible for the most sensitive, dangerous, and important espionage missions to be sanctioned in Arab lands. The enigmatic force, known simply as "Unit 131," had been in existence since the inception of the Political Department, though few outside the Israeli hierarchy knew of its existence. At an unknown juncture following the 1948 War, and, it must be added, after brutal infighting between the IDF and the Foreign Ministry, Unit 131 was transferred into the Intelligence Department's Order of Battle. Within a matter of months following the formation of A'MAN, it would become embroiled in one of the most sensitive and embarrassing political scandals ever to grip the Jewish state.

Since MODS 10 and 18 of Military Intelligence operated primarily across the Jordanian frontier, the only military intelligence force scrutinizing the developments in Egypt was the few photoreconnaissance aircraft of the IAF's 115th Squadron,[1] which flew sorties over Sinai and the Nile Delta. They photographed Egyptian Air Force bases, antiaircraft installations, and other strategic targets that would "interest" the air force in a future conflict. Although these Mosquito pilots tended to "hotdog" a little too often—risking being shot down for a souvenir photograph of the pyramids was common—they were the only viable source of active intelligence-gathering conducted by the IDF against Egypt at the time. They provided accurate reports on Egyptian military developments and the Egyptian Air Force—specifically, the number and type of aircraft were counted and chronicled; flight schedules were monitored; and details on the logistical operations of a major enemy air base were compiled. Two sorties, in particular, are worthy of mention for their audacity and results. The first, on September 3, 1953, was carried out over Alexandria. Military and economic targets were discovered and identified, including numerous top-secret bases and installations, which discredited previous Military Intelligence estimates. The second mission, conducted a day later, was flown over Cairo at an altitude of twenty thousand feet; the aircraft remained over the capital for nearly two and a half hours, observing and collecting data. The success of the reconnaissance flights impressed senior Defense Ministry officials, and additional sorties over Egypt, as well as Jordan, northern Syria, and even as far away as the H-3 desert airstrip in Iraq, were sanctioned.[2]

Human intelligence (HUMINT) operations against Israel's most powerful enemy, however, had been a Political Department responsibility. The primary objective of Unit 131 was to conduct covert long-term operations in Arab lands. Although these special operations were never formally outlined, they are believed to have included sabotage, fifth-column activities, even assassinations. Since these activities involved both military and political objectives, Unit 131's activation was to be sanctioned only following an agreement between MOSSAD chief Reuven Shiloah and Maj. Gen. Mordechai Maklef, the IDF's deputy chief of staff, in an arrangement known as the "Two Committee."[3] The Two Committee would not only decide when Unit 131 would be called upon, but what its mission would be, what limitations would apply, and what the likely political implications would be. The latter was a crucial point of agreement, because scapegoats and fall guys had to be found for a mission gone bad.

Unit 131's operatives were to be sleeper agents according to the classic definition; they were to act as a base, a friendly bastion in enemy territory to assist other agents who were dispatched into the target nation. The intelligence they gathered was to be of a passive nature, and they were not—under any circumstances—to risk their cover in order to obtain information: the intelligence gathered was not as important as their presence in an enemy nation. Most importantly, perhaps, they *were not* to perform violent operations—any criminal or terrorist act that would result in police or security forces' attention. Primarily, Unit 131 control agents were to recruit locals (indigenous Jews), who were reliable, psychologically and ideologically resolute, and whose careers and family histories were nondescript—their routine day-to-day existence should not arouse any suspicion.

Egypt was one of the more difficult Arab countries for Unit 131 to penetrate. Unlike Jews from Morocco, Syria, Iraq, and Yemen, Egyptian Jewry had not had the luxury of centuries in which to establish their roots, adopt elements of the culture, or even attempt to assimilate. Jews began to arrive in Egypt in the late nineteenth century; Egypt served as a convenient transit point for Yemenite Jews traveling to Palestine and Ottoman Jews looking for new opportunities in the confines of the empire. During the First World War, many Palestinian Jews migrated south toward the relative prosperity of Egypt in order to escape starvation and economic desperation; many Russian Jews unable to gain entrance into America also settled in Egypt. Jews were not allowed Egyptian citizenship and were called the *hawagat* ("gentlemen"), a respectful term for foreigners not allowed to integrate into Egyptian society. The eighty thousand Jews confined themselves to ghettos in Cairo, Alexandria, and three Suez Canal cities. Their children attended Jewish schools and were treated by Jewish doctors and hospitals; business was conducted with other Jews—or foreigners; and the language spoken was French or Ladino, *not* the Egyptian dialects of Arabic.[4]

Jewish segregation from mainstream Egyptian society increased when the Israeli question enveloped the area in full-scale bloodshed. It was, after all, a matter of distinction for an Egyptian Jew to donate time, money, or activities on behalf of the Zionist cause; when Egypt invaded Israel on May 15, 1948, that distinction became the target for rage. Members of the Moslem Brotherhood attempted to instigate pogroms against Egyptian Jews, often to the blind eye of police officials. The police harassed the Jewish community, arresting hundreds of innocent individuals suspected of Zionist activities. In fact, there was much Zionist activity transpiring on Egyptian soil, even at the height of the 1948 fighting. Agents from the MOSSAD LE'ALIYAH BET conducted their business of organizing Jewish emigration to Palestine virtually unhindered; they trained many young and zealous Egyptian Jews to organize classes in Jewish history and Hebrew. This practice began during the Second World War when soldiers of the Jewish Brigade trained in the Egyptian sands, and their emissaries began to preach to the local Jewish leaders the realism of returning to Zion. By 1950, more than half the Jews of Egypt had left their homes for sanctuary in the Jewish state. Thousands, however, remained behind.

The predicament of the Jewish population in Egypt was one of the incentives for Unit 131 to expand its original objectives of sleeper cells, and create a "last resort response force" of fifth-columnists. The man behind the mysterious Unit 131 was Lt. Col. Motke Ben-Tsur, an old hand at covert operations. He had served as an undercover HAGANAH representative in Iraq, and during the 1948 War served as a company commander in the PAL'MACH'S HAREL Brigade, which distinguished itself in the battle for Jerusalem. (Because so many senior officers emerged from that brigade, it has been called the "Chiefs of Staff Brigade.") Unit 131 was answerable to the chief of Military Intelligence, but Ben-Tsur generally was subordinate only to the chief of staff, Lt. Gen. Yigal Yadin, and his deputy, Maj. Gen. Mordechai Maklef.

In 1951, Shlomoh Hillel, a Military Intelligence agent who had served the MOSSAD LE'ALIYAH BET with great distinction in Iraq, was sent to Egypt with a forged Persian passport to seek out potential intelligence agents among the more "talented" young Jews of Egypt. With MOSSAD LE'ALIYAH BET files at his disposal, Hillel observed the young Jews in action as they conducted Zionist activities. Hillel made note of those who showed initiative, intelligence, and intuition—three important traits for any espionage agent—and compiled massive dossiers. The elite of the elite were singled out, and those names were transferred to Military Intelligence HQ in Tel Aviv.

Hillel was soon joined by Avraham Dar, a Unit 131 agent and Hillel's eventual replacement; he had been sent to Egypt to form an espionage ring of sleeper agents. Avraham Dar was born in the British port of Aden, in Yemen. His father had been recruited by British Intelligence during World War I, so Avraham learned the secrets of tradecraft at an early age. Although his dark Arabian features were pronounced, Avraham's "Queen's English" was impeccable and he was able to pass himself off as a British subject with little difficulty. Dar was a sailor and ex-PAL'MACH officer who fought with distinction in the PAL'YAM elite Sea unit during the 1948 War. He was a capable espionage professional who, in 1949, was selected to become the deputy commander of the IDF/navy's small Intelligence section. Nevertheless, many in the Israeli intelligence community felt that Dar lacked decisive leadership qualities and did not possess the analytical mind required for a delicate intelligence operation.[5]

For this mission, which would eventually adopt the code name Operation Susannah, Dar's cover persona was John Darling, a Gibraltar-born sales representative of a British electronics firm. With the young Jews of Egypt organized into youth movements, it was not difficult for "Darling" to locate, observe, and recruit them. Amazingly, the MOSSAD LE'ALIYAH BET *still* operated in Egypt, and their representatives maintained extensive files on those young individuals whose display of leadership, Zionist zeal, and intelligence "might" serve useful in the future.[6]

With the intimate knowledge of Egypt at his disposal, Darling utilized the MOSSAD LE'ALIYAH BET's office* to approach two prominent Jews and recruit them to lead the spy rings. The first was Dr. Moshe Marzouk, a physician at the Cairo Hospital; he was placed in charge of the Cairo group. A twenty-four-year-old Alexandrian schoolteacher and mathematics prodigy, Shmuel "Jacques" Azar, led the ring in that city. These two highly dedicated Zionists quickly enlisted the help of compatriots who they knew could be relied upon for dangerous undertakings. When given the opportunity to offer their services for

---

*In his book *The Spymasters of Israel*, Stewart Steven mentions that Darling was assisted in Cairo by a secretive Jewish organization known as "Together." Although there is little evidence to substantiate the existence of a group called Together, it is probably the code name of the local MOSSAD LE'ALIYAH BET office.

the Jewish homeland, these young Egyptian Jews disregarded the danger to themselves and their families and volunteered for what was considered *the* honored and noble cause.

Before his departure from Egypt in August 1951, Darling had formed the basis of two distinct cells of sleeper agents. He was a passionate man who convinced these eager disciples that their value to Israeli security was supreme. He instilled in them the belief that one well-placed agent could do the work of an entire division—and Israel had very few divisions to spare! He returned to Israel after successfully completing his mission, although he still hadn't a clue as to how his people would be utilized.

The ingenious cover of a travel agency was produced for the two cells. This type of business bustled with activity, with countless strangers coming and going. A travel agency could also obtain legitimate travel tickets and documentation without attracting unwarranted suspicion.

Marcelle Ninio, one of the first to be recruited by Dr. Marzouk, was responsible for maintaining the travel agency in Cairo. Called the Grunberg Reisboro, it occupied one floor of the impressive Immobilia Building in Cairo with a branch office in Alexandria as well. Before officers in Unit 131 had ever conceived of the Egyptian operation, the Grunberg Travel Agency had served as a MOSSAD LE'ALIYAH BET transit station for Egyptian Jews en route to Israel. Ninio was, in fact, one of the most important members of the ring because she served as the link between the Alexandria and Cairo cells. A vivacious beauty known for her charm, vitality, and athletic figure, Ninio was extremely popular and maintained a long list of loyal friends. Another member of the Cairo cell was Robert Dassa, a visionary Zionist and a man who, many say, was more Egyptian than the natives because of his passionate interest in Arab history and culture. Leading the Alexandria cell was the rambunctious Victor Levy (the "tough guy" among the recruited), soft-spoken Philip Nathanson, Meir Zafran, and Eli Na'im. They didn't view themselves as spies, but as conscripted soldiers.[7]

In early 1952, the Egyptian cells had the opportunity to prove their worth as soldiers when they were brought to Israel, via France, for military and espionage training. Their departure from Egypt was a difficult emotional experience for them. Indeed, being part of the cell had meant wrenching changes. For years they had been active in Zionist activities, yet Avraham Dar had ordered them to cease their pro-Israeli involvement immediately: They had to become nondescript, faceless, and causeless members of Egypt's Jewish population. They had to desert their social lives, which were centered on Zionist functions, and cultivate a different set of companions. Friends and families viewed them as traitors, and they had to endure the isolation and ridicule. But they were to become warriors for the State of Israel, and that was more important than anything.

The first one to arrive in Israel was Victor Levy, who many believed was the strongest—both physically and psychologically—of the agents. He stayed in a small Tel Aviv pension for nearly two months awaiting the start of his instruction, which would be conducted at a secret army base near Ramle. He was the sole pupil in the special course, taught in English. Levy soon became proficient in sabotage, explosives, planting mines, reconnaissance, target identification, codes, and intelligence tradecraft. He was trained to shake surveillance, to observe proper security procedures, and, most importantly, to withstand a brutal interrogation. A few weeks later, Moshe Marzouk joined the course, as did the others.

The course was commanded by Gideon Mahanaimi, a Unit 131 veteran; the deputy commander and chief sabotage instructor was Natan Rahav. Both men were extremely impressed with the dedication displayed by the agents, especially their Zionist ideals; very few Israelis, even old-time pioneers, could compete with the nationalistic spirit shown by these new recruits. Their logistics officer, Martin Hauser, accompanied the spies throughout their frequent travels in Israel. He escorted them to various kibbutzim, the Sea of Galilee, the Negev Desert, and, of course, divided Jerusalem. Hauser was also the officer responsible for seeing his agents off on their return to Egypt.

Although the Unit 131 instructors worked with utmost determination to prepare this group of agents for operational readiness, it was clear to everyone involved that the Cairo and Alexandria agents were rank amateurs. An ex-PAL'MACH officer, who, at the time, was working for Isser Harel's MOSSAD, looked at the ring with impending doom, characterizing the operatives as "gentle, idealistic and sensitive city dwellers who were more impressed with the concept of *what* they were doing than the work itself."[8] According to Natan Rahav, the group's sabotage instructor, the spies kept to themselves and refused to share any emotion or personal insight with their Israeli mentors. Their zeal, however, remained resolute. Toward the end of their training, which was meant to be on a level equal to an IDF officers' course, the group unanimously demanded not only to be *conscripted* into the IDF, but as commissioned officers. The request was sincere and deserving, and the Susannah spies were made second lieutenants. Pride in this accomplishment would bring them through many dark hours.

It should have been evident in the intelligence training facility that there would be problems. The key to the true success of any espionage ring is its compartmentalization. Cell members must be secluded from one another, and kept from knowing the identities, physical descriptions, or any other bit of incriminating evidence that might link a captured agent to the others in his group. It is the golden rule of tradecraft, but, in the case of the Cairo and Alexandrian cells, it was completely ignored. The agents in the A'MAN training facility were introduced to one another: Everyone knew everyone else—

where they lived, what they looked like, who their acquaintances were. Some of the agents were already good friends from high school, college, or from a Zionist youth movement; all had connections to either Dr. Marzouk or Shmuel Azar. Exacerbating this invitation to disaster was the use of rented flats as a substitute for dead-letter boxes and cutouts. Amazingly, the agents were not even provided with cover stories. Nor were they given intense countersurveillance instruction or viable escape routes in the event their ring was uncovered. Why these mistakes were made is not known, but perhaps the Israelis had little regard for the Egyptians, or, possibly, Unit 131 commander Ben-Tsur never really felt that the cells would be activated.

It was, in retrospect, an amateurish undertaking underscored by the fact that A'MAN possessed little experience in this facet of intelligence warfare. It was to be an entirely Military Intelligence undertaking, and, with the exception of the odd MOSSAD or SHIN BET agent brought in for observation, none of the more experienced outside sources were to be tapped. Following the course, sabotage instructor Natan Rahav submitted a top-secret report to his superiors stating strongly that the agents should not be considered fully operational, and recommending that they *not* be involved in violent operations and certainly not in the deployment of explosives.[9]

There was, however, one impressive surprise, and his name was Eli Cohen.[10] Born to a Syrian-Jewish family in Alexandria in December 1924, Cohen had distinguished himself as a student, not only concentrating on Jewish culture but on the vast and grand history of the Arabs and their languages. In 1944, he joined the Zionist Youth of Alexandria; working for Israel became his life's vocation after the execution in Cairo of two Stern Gang terrorists for assassinating Lord Moyne.[11] Later, he was recruited for HAGANAH operations and then for the Susannah ring by Shmuel Azar, where he became one of the key logistical support personnel; he evaded torture and imprisonment, although he was questioned by the authorities. Several years later he would return to the forefront of Israel's war in the shadows against the Arabs and become A'MAN'S, and certainly the State of Israel's, most famous, successful, and ill-fated spy.

In late 1952, the Susannah spies returned—in well-spaced intervals—to Egypt, via Italy and France, all utilizing Grunberg Travel Agency tickets. This signaled the beginning of the difficult portion of their assignment: the "hurry up and wait." They had been told to lie low for a year, but after two months the sleepers received their "wake-up call." Events in Israel and Egypt had accelerated their activation and dictated their objectives.

Impending signs of revolution in Egypt had been evident for some time. Following its disastrous performance in the 1948 War, the Egyptian military, long known as a hotbed of political dissent, polarized into factions of nationalists, religious fundamentalists, and Communists. Revenge against Israel was a popular war cry, but so, too, was the anticolonial fervor that had gripped much of the postwar Third World; they were outraged with British and French ownership of the ultrastrategic Suez Canal—the most valuable piece of real estate in all of Egypt and, many say, in all of Africa. Taking advantage of this momentum, a group of army officers seized power on July 23, 1952, forcing King Farouk to abdicate his throne in favor of his infant son, Ahmed Fuad II. The coup's leader was a charismatic officer, Lt. Col. Gamal Abdel Nasser, one of the few war heroes to emerge from the 1948 fighting. His deputy was Lt. Col. Anwar as-Sadat, who, during the Second World War, was imprisoned by the British as a Nazi agent. By 1953, Nasser had consolidated his power in Egypt, ousting the highly respected Gen. Mohammed Naguib, who the coup organizers had initially chosen as the country's president, and clamping down on the activities of the Moslem Brotherhood, fanatically inspired fundamentalists who wished to turn Egypt back into the throes of a strict Moslem nation.

The rise of Nasser to the pinnacle of power in Egypt was received optimistically at first in Jerusalem. A new ruler in Egypt might pave the way toward a peace treaty and coexistence; a secret dialogue was even established between the Israelis and the new Egyptian strongman.[12] Nasser, however, was a pragmatic man, one who relied on a rallying cry; he recognized the yearning for revenge, and the destruction of Israel topped his political and national agenda. A bold and powerful orator, Nasser took on the title of "leader of the Arab world," and incited nationalism and revolution to all those he reached, promoting an armed Palestinian struggle to destroy Israel. His views found sympathetic ears throughout all classes and religious circles in the Arab world, from clerics to the fellahin peasants, to philosophical intellects and devout Marxists. Not since the days of the Grand Mufti of Jerusalem, Haj Amin Husseini, had the Arabs had such a firebrand as a leader and the Jewish state such a formidable foe. War with Egypt seemed inevitable, hence the activation of the Unit 131 saboteurs.

The Unit 131 sleeper cells in Egypt were considered by many in the IDF to be a last resort: a guerrilla force to be put into action only in the case of a dire threat to the State of Israel. Their principal operational objective, during a full-scale conflagration, would be psychological warfare, to unravel the fabric of security and stability in Egypt. They were, however, never meant to instigate a war or promote a volatile political situation in Egypt. The sleeper cells found themselves in the midst of another volatile situation, however—an upheaval at the highest level of Israeli politics.

On December 7, 1953, the patriarch of the Jewish state, Prime Minister and Defense Minister David Ben-Gurion, did what he had promised to do for nearly three months: He resigned and retired to the seclusion of a self-imposed political exile at his home in Kibbutz Sde-Boker in the Negev Desert.

Although clearly not *loved* by everyone in Israeli politics, he was revered as the founding father of the Jewish state—the man who, politically, had brought it from the underground to independence. His departure from government sent shock waves through the KNESSET, the Israeli parliament, but its greatest impact was felt in the Defense Ministry and the IDF, in particular. Ben-Gurion, along with a close-knit circle of visionary confidants, had helped forge the Defense Ministry and the IDF into a powerful institution more than capable of meeting the nation's defense requirements—from national defense to talk of even dispatching an IDF contingent to join the United Nations effort in Korea.[13] Ben-Gurion was the IDF's guardian angel. The sight of the Old Man, dressed in loose-fitting fatigues, visiting troops in the field, empowered the simple soldier with an overwhelming sense of pride and worth. Now, without Ben-Gurion's guidance and sense of national direction, both the Defense Ministry and the IDF found themselves rudderless, when, with the Arab world uniting behind Nasser, they could ill afford such a distraction.

Ben-Gurion's replacement was Moshe Sharett, a career diplomat and Labor party loyalist with impressive credentials. He was not, however, of Ben-Gurion's stature. Sharett did not evoke confidence or even decisiveness. It was clear that, unlike Ben-Gurion, Sharett's word would not be considered law.

The new man at the Defense Ministry, much to the objection of just about everyone in Ben-Gurion's ruling circle, was Pinhas Lavon. Such party stalwarts as Golda Meir strongly urged Ben-Gurion to reconsider his decision. In spite of an intellect bordering on genius, Lavon delivered sharp-tongued verbal barrages and had an abrasive style that made his foes shudder in fear, and greatly limited the number of power players who viewed him as a friend. His lack of ministerial experience was also an important factor in his unpopularity, as was his disdain for Prime Minister Sharett. The two men despised each other. It was hardly the ideal environment for advancing Israel's national security policies.

Lavon was at odds with the IDF, too. He regarded them as bureaucratic buffoons in parade uniforms and often criticized the army and its senior commander with blazing ferocity; the army viewed him as a dangerous man psychologically unfit to head the nation's defense policies. Chief of Staff Lt. Gen. Mordechai Maklef resigned over Lavon's appointment, and was replaced by one of Ben-Gurion's favorite sons: Lt. Gen. Moshe Dayan—one of Israel's most controversial national icons. The director general of the Defense Ministry was a young Labor party loyalist named Shimon Peres. Another lackluster individual, Peres was, however, highly intelligent and capable and, above all, ambitious. Completing this picture was, of course, A'MAN chief Gibli, who, along with Dayan and Peres, was extremely fond of Defense Minister Lavon. They admired the new confrontational—even bullying—style of the post–Ben-Gurion defense community. Gibli also believed that Lavon would be receptive to the A'MAN viewpoint of special operations.[14]

The Two Committee, which had been established in 1950 to coordinate Unit 131 operations between the IDF and the MOSSAD, was supposed to reduce the level of competition and animosity between the two intelligence agencies. But there were still bitter debates over who maintained the exclusive right for launching special operations, who would choose the targets, and who would issue final authorization. Before A'MAN could initiate any special action, it had to receive the approval from Isser Harel's MOSSAD. Since the MEMUNEH ("trustee") of the MOSSAD was answerable to the prime minister, and the director of A'MAN was subordinate to the defense minister, obvious challenges to Sharett's authority would be mounted.

The battle for control over special operations and Unit 131 lasted throughout 1953. The IDF officer in the forefront of the struggle was acting A'MAN chief Yehoshofat Harkabi, temporarily replacing Gibli, who was completing his studies abroad. Harkabi, described as the intellectual vision of A'MAN, met with the General Staff to discuss IDF exclusivity in the special activities of Unit 131. With Pinhas Lavon's full backing, he fired off a memo to MOSSAD chief Harel on February 18, 1954, advising him that: "The military hierarchy is determining that Unit 131 is subordinate to the command and control of the Director of A'MAN and through him, the Chief-of-Staff."[15]

Isser Harel did not give up the struggle. In a heated meeting with Lavon on February 26, 1954, he urged that the guidelines of the Two Committee be adhered to honorably. His efforts failed, and when Gibli returned from his studies in March, cooperation between the MOSSAD and A'MAN had reached an all-time and dangerous low.

The bitter war between A'MAN and the MOSSAD was not restricted to interservice sensitivities: There was also an extremely bitter fight over the operations of Unit 131 within the IDF. The "old warriors"—veterans of the PAL'MACH—applauded the innovative, unconventional style of Unit 131; operations in the enemy's rear, after all, were the *Israeli* way of defeating a numerically superior enemy. Others in the IDF command structure argued that the IDF was too small, ill-equipped, and vulnerable to commit to misguided foreign adventures. They contended that in wartime such operations contributed only marginal results and, if conducted without political insight, could do more damage than good. It was this conflict of control that would undermine Operation Susannah from the start and betray the idealistic sleeper agents in Egypt.

Another strike against the "Egyptian Base," as many in A'MAN have termed it, came from the case officer who replaced Avraham Dar/Darling. His name was Avraham Seidenwerg, an Austrian Jew who, upon arrival in Palestine, Hebracized his name to Avri El-Ad. A paratrooper in the British army during the Second World War, El-Ad joined the HAGANAH and, later, the PAL'MACH, where he excelled as an officer in the HAREL Brigade during the brutal hand-to-hand fighting for Jerusalem; remarkably, he reached the rank of major by age twenty-two.

Although he had the potential to become a senior commander in the IDF, El-Ad was arrested by the military police for stealing a refrigerator in a captured Arab village and having it installed in his home. It was behavior that the IDF despised and he was immediately court-martialed; he was stripped of his rank and reduced to a lowly private first class in the reserves. He was disgraced, and his marriage soon fell apart. The dishonorable discharge from the IDF also guaranteed that his chances of finding lucrative employment were nil. Hopeless and miserable, El-Ad was approached by Avraham Dar and Ben-Tsur, who saw this desperate man as *perfect* material for a dangerous mission in enemy territory. Working for Unit 131 was the opportunity for El-Ad to rectify the mistakes of his past; successful completion of the assignment would guarantee his future in Israel. After all, he had nothing to lose.

Unit 131 went to great lengths to ensure that El-Ad had a foolproof cover story before entering Egypt. He adopted the name Paul Frank and would masquerade as a wealthy West German businessman and former SS officer. To bolster his cover story, he traveled to West Germany to procure an authentic West German passport and even underwent an excruciatingly painful medical procedure to reverse his circumcision so that, if captured and interrogated, he could not be immediately identified as a Jew.[16]

In December 1953, Frank sailed to Cairo from Hamburg. Armed with his West German passport,* handsome Aryan features, and excellent acting abilities, "Paul Frank" was able to pass himself off as an ex-SS man; he had authentic Nazi documentation and even a photograph of himself in black uniform. His impressive charade was short-lived, however, for as a case officer, he proved to be a dreadful failure. Either by treacherous design, negligence, or inability, he failed to follow even the most basic and logical of security guidelines.

Frank's first mistake was insisting on knowing every agent in both the Cairo and Alexandria rings—a tragic error for any controller—and wanting to participate in their operational planning and activities. Many in the group were troubled by Frank's relaxed attitude toward security concerns. Shmuel Azar, for example, frequently argued with Frank, pleading with him to establish escape routes for the spies should something go wrong. Frank always promised them that everything would be all right, saying that there was no need to worry. Under the code name "Robert," he even visited the agents in their homes while their families were present. In fact, many of the Susannah-ring families were eager for the visits from "Robert the Spy."

*In their book *The Imperfect Spies: A History of Israeli Intelligence*, authors Dan Raviv and Yossi Melman claim that the Israeli intelligence community was, in fact, utilizing genuine passports supplied to them by the West German Intelligence Service, the Bundesnachrichtendienst, or BND. The West German government developed a close relationship with the Jewish state, mainly as a result of guilt over the Holocaust.

Another A'MAN agent, Meir Bennett, was roaming through Egypt at the time, although he was not connected with the Susannah ring. The thirty-seven-year-old Hungarian-born Jew of German descent had arrived in Palestine in 1935 and was recruited for Avigur's MOSSAD LE'ALIYAH BET. His reputation as a brilliant operative became legendary in the Israeli intelligence community as he served throughout Europe and in a number of perilous missions to Iraq.[17] Bennett was wounded during the 1948 War and went on to join the IAF as a junior officer. He was eventually recruited into the ranks of IDF Military Intelligence, where he continued his excellent work, reaching the rank of major quite quickly.

In 1951, Meir Bennett, now utilizing the first name Max, was dispatched to Egypt on business unrelated to the Susannah spy ring. He was masquerading as a German expatriate, a man with close Nazi connections who sought asylum in the sympathetic political atmosphere of Egypt. Max Bennett, the former Nazi official, now represented a West German firm that manufactured prosthetic devices for crippled soldiers. The cover story was so fantastic, it was absolutely believable. His "profession" brought him into close contact with the Egyptian military; Bennett even established a close friendship with Gen. Mohammed Naguib, the Egyptian president. Later, Bennett became the chief engineer in Egypt for Ford Motors, the major supplier of materials to the Egyptian military at the time. His access to military officers and installations was unprecedented, and proved to be an intelligence bonanza: The full details of the data he filtered back to Israel remain classified to this day.

The true story behind Bennett's eventual connection to the doomed group remains unclear; every book written on the Israeli intelligence community reports a different version. It appears that what connected Max Bennett to the Susannah espionage and sabotage ring was bad luck and bad intelligence work.

A break had developed in Bennett's communication network to report back to Israel and, impatiently, A'MAN ordered him to make contact with elements of the El-Ad ring, in particular, Marcelle Ninio, the ring's communication officer. They first met in March 1953, at the exclusive Bijelle Café. She identified Bennett as the unobtrusive man reading a book and sipping Turkish coffee.[18] Following the initial contact, in which Bennett informed Ninio that she would serve as his liaison in Egypt, she visited his fashionable flat in the Zamalek Quarter once a week. According to Marcelle Ninio, he even supplied her with a Leica camera, which Dr. Marzouk was to forward to members of the Alexandria cell. The "human contact" was a fatal breach of espionage tradecraft, one that a seasoned agent, such as Bennett, should have avoided at all costs.

Communications between Unit 131 and their Egyptian cells were conducted in Paris sidewalk cafes. France was a favorite operational ground for the Israeli intelligence community. The MOSSAD station chief in Paris at the time was Yitzhak Shamir, the ex-LEHI (Stern Gang) commander who became Israeli prime minister. Shamir conducted extensive intelligence operations on French soil, and the SHIN BET regularly utilized Paris as an arena for security and sting operations to bring traitors back to Israel, such as the 1954 case of ex-SS officer Ulrich Schneft. He assumed the identity of a Jewish Holocaust survivor, immigrated to Palestine as a refugee, and served in the IDF, eventually achieving the rank of lieutenant. He later offered his services to Egyptian Military Intelligence and was seized in Paris by SHIN BET agents who brought him back to Israel, where he was imprisoned and later expelled from the country.[19]

A'MAN also used the fashionable boulevards of Paris. Unit 131 commander Ben-Tsur met his control and deep-cover agents in Paris; in his sidewalk-cafe meetings he provided his men—and women—with instructions, equipment, and funds. Ben-Tsur frequently met Avraham Dar/Darling in Paris, as well as Paul Frank and Max Bennett. In June 1954, Ben-Tsur met Frank on the Boulevard St. Germain and the final outline of Operation Susannah was fully detailed. Although the sleeper cell supposedly possessed up-to-date radio transmitters, it was decided that dates and targets would be identified through coded messages on KOL YISRAEL, Israel's national broadcast network. On June 29, Frank returned to Alexandria with the official activation of his network.

The purpose of a fifth column during a military conflict is clear: to sabotage key political, economic, and military installations, and to psychologically weaken enemy defenses and resolve. Yet it was clear that the Susannah ring was intended to be much more than a fifth column, since it would be activated without the imminent outbreak of war. Its members would become politically inspired saboteurs, an underground force meant to weaken the Egyptian regime. It would be the first time that the IDF force (Unit 131 was, after all, part of A'MAN) would operate in order to achieve political objectives.

The Egyptian nationalist fervor catalyzed by Nasser led to demands that Great Britain and France relinquish their ownership and control of the Suez Canal. The Israelis feared that, should Nasser solidify his standing as a world leader, the British and French would be forced to acquiesce and provide Nasser with a victory that would threaten Israeli national security. In 1954, it appeared that British Prime Minister Winston Churchill was preparing to sign away the canal. The only possible hope of stopping this was to discredit the Egyptian nation, making it seem to be united only by its violent hatred for the West. The actions of the Susannah ring would fuel the fire.

On July 2, 1954, the eager spies finally received orders from Tel Aviv. Their first target was to be a series of mailboxes in the main Alexandria post office in the El-Ramel District; its destruction would hopefully be blamed on the Moslem Brotherhood. Victor Levy and Philip Nathanson walked into the facility and, without any difficulty, slid their homemade explosive device down a narrow mail chute. They calmly walked outside into the bustle of the city's thoroughfare. Minutes later, a muted thud emanated from the Victorian building; damage, however, was minimal. Worse, the Egyptian censors forbade any mention of the incident in press reports. The spectacular eruption of anti-Western violence that was to ruin Nasser's image worldwide never made it to the print, electronic, or celluloid media.

Tel Aviv was undaunted by this lack of publicity, and the group received further coded instructions via KOL YISRAEL on July 10. The cryptic radio messages, reminiscent of the Free French broadcasts on the BBC during the Second World War, instructed them to attack an American and a British installation. Hitting dual targets was a bold move. New bombs had to be made, involving the risky purchase of sulfuric acid and other chemicals. Also, attacking Western targets was sure to attract greater police and security service attention. On July 14, incendiary devices were planted in the American libraries in both Cairo and Alexandria; Robert Dassa and Shmuel Azar struck in the capital, while Victor Levy and Philip Nathanson attended to the target in Alexandria. This time the Middle Eastern News Agency did carry details of a new wave of terrorism that had gripped Egypt. Although the news items were eagerly picked up by the Israeli press, the attacks sparked little concern anywhere else.[20]

The July 14 attacks indicated to Paul Frank that his agents were, indeed, capable of simultaneous attacks. This feeling of bravado prompted him to recommend further bombings. His reports found a receptive ear at A'MAN headquarters in Tel Aviv, which was impatient for immediate results. The agents were, naturally, quite nervous about accelerating their attacks since it increased the chances of their capture. According to Victor Levy, when interviewed during a staged reunion of the Susannah survivors for Israeli television: "There was serious debate among all concerned regarding the new flurry of activity, and the lack of escape routes should anything go wrong, but Paul Frank assured us not to worry."

The most audacious day of operations was scheduled for July 23: Revolution Day. The plan called for the Cairo team, Dassa and Azar, to plant hastily constructed explosive devices in the Rivoli Theater and in the check-in room at the main railway station. Their homemade bombs proved to be duds; the detonators failed to properly activate the incendiary agents and little, if any, damage was done. Frustrated by their failure, they returned to their homes to await news from Alexandria.

The Alexandria team of Levy and Nathanson was to plant two bombs, hidden in eyeglass cases, in the city's Rio Cinema. But tragedy undermined the operation—and the ring. While waiting in line to purchase tickets for the feature film, the device in Nathanson's coat pocket suddenly ignited in a blinding burst of smoke and flame. In excruciating pain, caused by the burning device, Nathanson frantically attempted to extinguish the blaze without attracting attention. Unfortunately, his agony was witnessed by dozens of horrified moviegoers. Captain Hassan el-Manadi of the Alexandria Special Police rushed to Nathanson's aid, and helped put out the flames. Although burned over a good portion of his left side, Nathanson tried, in vain, to explain his predicament— he claimed that a box of matches he was carrying had mysteriously exploded. The policeman quickly discovered the smoldering remains of the explosive device and summoned reinforcements. Philip Nathanson was immediately taken into custody. Levy had escaped; racing toward the sea, he threw his bomb into the Mediterranean. It was now only a matter of time before the entire group would be exposed.

Initially, Nathanson, a quiet nineteen year old, withstood the intense questioning of the Egyptian authorities. He had been given morphine to dull the pain of the burns, and this helped him withstand the first few hours of incessant beatings, hair pulling, and other acts of barbarity. At one point, more than thirty Egyptian police, military, and Muchabarat officials supervised and participated in the torture of Philip Nathanson. Then the soothing powers of the morphine evaporated. He tried to buy as much time for his comrades as possible, but eventually the agony was too much. Victor Levy was arrested seven hours later. He, too, was severely tortured—without the benefit of morphine. For forty-eight hours, the most capable hands in the Egyptian secret police attended to Levy, but the rambunctious agent gave them nothing. Then, unable to withstand the pain any longer, he gave up his comrades.

Within days, the Egyptians had exposed the unprofessional ring and arrested most of the spies: Dr. Marzouk, Shmuel Azar, Robert Dassa, Meir Zafran, Meir Meyuchas, Eli Ya'akov and Caesar Cohen. Marcelle Ninio was placed under immediate surveillance following the interrogation of Nathanson and Levy; she was arrested at the popular Nile Delta vacation spot of Ras el-Bar and taken to Cairo's notorious Am-Hasa Prison. The ringleader, Paul Frank, managed to remain in Egypt for another fortnight; for some reason he was not placed under surveillance. He sold his car and escaped to Europe.

The circumstances surrounding Frank's miraculous escape from Egypt remains to this day one of the most controversial aspects of Operation Susannah. Although he claimed to have evaded the Egyptian authorities through guile, many have argued that he was, in fact, a double agent and that *he* gave up the ring, either to save his skin or by design. (This theory was gingerly broached by Victor Levy in an interview on Israeli television on the twenty-fifth anniversary of their trial; he professed his belief that there was a double agent among them. For reasons unknown, however, he would not elaborate any further as to the identity of this traitor.)

The Egyptians followed their counterespionage coup with mass arrests of Egyptian Jews—especially relatives, friends, and business associates of the Susannah agents. The homes of the arrested were ransacked and their families terrorized. The police uncovered a bonanza of incriminating evidence, including chemicals used to produce bombs, funds, and coded documents. More than forty employees of Cairo's Zilcha Bank, where Caesar Cohen worked as manager, were also arrested and tortured. The Egyptians proved to be especially capable in this field, gathering confessions and incriminating statements through crude psychological torture. Accused spies were dragged in front of a firing squad and blindfolded as the sergeant at arms ordered his men to aim and fire. The mental anguish of such an experience had immediate and permanent effects.

Tragically, the man least involved with Operation Susannah would suffer the most. Under harsh Egyptian interrogation Ninio gave up Max Bennett. The Egyptian police raced to his home and stripped him naked; upon seeing that he had been circumcised, they cruelly beat him and dragged him off to prison. He was tortured with zealous barbarity but confessed to nothing—not even being an agent for A'MAN. The Egyptians believed that he was, in fact, a West German national who had been recruited by Israel; they never even suspected that he was an Israeli national. Bennett was, however, the highest ranking spy among the group, or in Egypt, for that matter; if he were forced to talk, he might permanently endanger the security of Israel.

On December 21, 1954, only ten days after the trial of the Susannah spies commenced in a crowded Cairo courtroom, Max Bennett produced a shaving razor out of his personal belongings and slashed open his wrists—he died an hour later. His body was flown to Rome, and then secretly transferred to Israel following intensive A'MAN efforts. His family was given only the sketchiest information concerning his death. According to Yossi Melman and Dan Raviv, Israel only acknowledged Bennett's association with A'MAN in 1988: At a secret and private ceremony in the defense minister's office in Tel Aviv, one of Israel's most neglected spies was posthumously awarded the rank of lieutenant colonel. The other Susannah operatives received the same rank in a more public forum, which was televised nationally and included praise and acclamation from the Israeli president, Chaim Herzog, a man intimate with the dangers and anonymity of intelligence work.[21]

On January 27, 1955, the military tribunal in Cairo published its verdict. The two cell leaders, thirty-six-year-old Dr. Marzouk and twenty-six-year-old Shmuel Azar, were sentenced to death by hanging: Their sentence was carried out on January 31, 1955. Victor Levy, Robert Dassa, and Philip Nathanson were sentenced to life imprisonment. Marcelle Ninio, after a failed suicide attempt of her own, received fifteen years in prison; Meir Meyuchas and Meir Zafran each received seven years of incarceration. The inevitable end to a doomed espionage ring had finally come.

News of the debacle had been carefully censored in Israel. While foreign press accounts chronicled the Jewish spy ring—their capture, trial, and execution of their sentences—the Israeli public, through the efforts of the Military Censor's Office, received no mention of the disastrous chain of events in Egypt. Inside the Israeli hierarchy, however, the debris of Operation Susannah was creating infighting and scandal the likes of which had never before been seen in Israel. The nagging question was who gave the order? Who was responsible for this disaster? Who *really* sanctioned the awakening of the sleeper cell, and whose career would be ruined in order to save political face. Prime Minister Moshe Sharett professed having no knowledge of the sleeper cell. (This lack of knowledge of such a secret mission was what Reuven Shiloah's Two Committee was meant to avoid.) Defense Minister Lavon took most of the blame, admitting that there was, indeed, an A'MAN sleeper cell operating in Egypt, but he denied ordering its activation. He stated that the attacks had transpired prior to his issuing the necessary authorization[22] and he suggested that perhaps the IDF chief of staff, Lt. Gen. Moshe Dayan, might be responsible. Dayan, eager to preserve his Teflon image, quickly distanced himself from the activities of the Intelligence Branch, saying that such special operations were the sphere of influence of A'MAN; Gibli, however, claimed that he had received his orders from superior commanders in the General Staff and the Defense Ministry. Even Isser Harel entered the fray by stating that the MOSSAD had no idea of the operation in Egypt, or what was transpiring in A'MAN HQ and at the Defense Ministry.[23] The political denial, scandal, and deceit continued to not only divide opinion and hinder cohesion within the Israeli intelligence community, but within the Israeli political system, as well. The incident eventually brought down the government of Prime Minister David Ben-Gurion in 1962, when it was finally uncovered, in spectacular fashion, by the Israeli media. The first casualty of the crisis, however, was Pinhas Lavon, who resigned two days after the hangings of Azar and Marzouk in Cairo; his departure from the Defense Ministry was inked in a scathing letter to Prime Minister Sharett. It was clear that a cover-up with enormous political and military implications was underway, and the prime minister ordered an investigation headed by the former president of the Israeli Supreme Court, Yitzhak Olshan, and the IDF's first chief of staff, Lt. Gen. (Res.) Ya'akov Dori, to seek the truth. Unlike most of the participants involved in the Operation Susannah scandal, both men were revered for their impeccable integrity.

The Olshan/Dori committee had two versions to work with: facts uncovered through the Susannah ring trial in Cairo, and those gathered from interviewing the key players in the Defense Ministry, A'MAN, and Unit 131. In the ensuing labyrinth of closed-door hearings, anonymous tips, and suspicions, it became clear that documents had been forged and destroyed. It appeared that conclusive evidence on *who* actually gave the order might never be found. Accusations were heard that the Defense Ministry's director general, Shimon Peres, and Moshe Dayan were party to a dangerous conspiracy, as were charges that Lavon had lied to the committee, and to his subordinates in the IDF and A'MAN, in particular. Everyone summoned to testify had an alibi, an excuse, and, in typical Israeli fashion, a pronounced opinion. The most explosive testimony came from the case officer of the doomed ring, Paul Frank, who, now back in Israel, returned to the identity of Avri El-Ad. In his accounts, Gibli was termed the "Senior Officer," Ben-Tsur the "Reserve Officer," and El-Ad, in a reference to the Graham Greene thriller, was the "Third Man." [24] Finally, the Olshan/Dori committee summarized that they could not conclude beyond a reasonable doubt that the senior officers in A'MAN did not receive their orders from the Defense Ministry.

The Olshan/Dori committee's ambiguous findings had immediate implications; as a result of Lavon's resignation, the subsequent affair was termed the "Lavon Affair." The ex–defense minister returned to political life as head of the trade union movement and was replaced by the Old Man, a resurrected David Ben-Gurion, who returned to his cherished Defense Ministry. A'MAN director Binyamin Gibli was forced to resign, but not in disgrace; he returned to "regular" service and served in Northern Command headquarters, later distinguishing himself as the commander of the GOLANI Infantry Brigade during the 1956 invasion of Sinai. He would never make general, as he had once envisioned when A'MAN was created, because of his role in the Susannah scandal. Unit 131 commander Ben-Tsur was also forced out of his posting and resigned from active service; he was replaced by Lt. Col. Yosef Harel.

The whole affair eventually became known as the ESEK BISH ("dirty business"). The disgraceful term aptly described the tragic effects of the infighting within Israel's intelligence community: Had relations and cooperation between A'MAN and the MOSSAD been better, the "dirty business" might never have happened. The ascension of Yehoshofat "Fatti" Harkabi as A'MAN director helped diminish the feud between Isser Harel and the IDF, and forge a close-knit relationship of mutual assistance between the two services.

The case of Avri El-Ad, however, remains a controversial and painful mystery. Following the events in Egypt, he remained an A'MAN agent, even though questions as to his loyalty perpetuated a bitter controversy. Major General Harkabi continued to believe in El-Ad, but others in the intelligence establishment led a crusade, orchestrated by MOSSAD and SHIN BET chief Isser Harel, to "break him." The fact that El-Ad had been recruited as a desperate man made him a natural suspect as a double agent. The fact that a petty theft charge had ruined his brilliant military career made revenge seem a viable motive.

Even though he was under suspicion, El-Ad was dispatched to West Germany for further special duty. Harel, who never believed in El-Ad, had SHIN BET agents in Europe follow him without notifying anyone in A'MAN. The surveillance team's findings were explosive: They saw El-Ad meet with officers from Egyptian Military Intelligence in Vienna; in Bonn, they saw El-Ad pass sensitive intelligence documents to an officer from the Egyptian Military Attaché's Office. With the irrefutable and painful truth before him, Harkabi called El-Ad back to Israel, where he was immediately detained by the SHIN BET. For nearly a year, SHIN BET interrogators tried to get El-Ad to confess to being a double agent and betraying his agents in Cairo and Alexandria. The experienced intelligence officer, however, could not be forced into admitting his guilt. In 1959, following one of the most secretive trials in Israeli history, Avri El-Ad was convicted on security violations. He was sentenced to the notorious Ramle Prison, shared later by Adolph Eichmann. Released in late 1967, he left Israel, moved to California, and wrote a book entitled *Decline of Honor*, in which he claimed that Isser Harel had framed him.

While the political infighting went on in Israel, the forgotten victims of this sordid affair were left to rot in Egyptian prisons. Not protected by legal appeals, the Red Cross, Geneva Convention, or any other international human rights organizations, the imprisoned spies were routinely tortured and beaten by the prison guards, including Hamza Basion, the prison warden whose nickname was the "Butcher of Cairo"; the title gave a clear indication of his sadistic nature, especially when dealing with enemies of the state. The men were also subjected to physical abuse at the hands of the Moslem Brotherhood, which was to receive blame for the Operation Susannah deeds. Although Marcelle Ninio remained closemouthed regarding her confinement, it was clear that she fared worse than her male comrades. Young, beautiful, and an infidel in an Arab/Moslem prison, she attempted suicide several times, which provides some insight into her terrible plight. Since the Israeli government denied connection to her fallen spies in Egypt, efforts to gain their release were negligently minimal, especially when compared to the internationally sponsored attempts to gain the freedom of Eli Cohen from Syria in 1965. The Israelis even rebuffed an Egyptian offer to exchange the spies for Egyptian officers captured during the 1956 War, as Moshe Dayan feared that such a move would be politically damaging to Israel.[25]

The one man who refused to forget about the Susannah spies was Avraham Dar. He had learned of their capture from his commander, Ben-Tsur, on July 25, 1954. Unit 131 had only learned of the ring's destruction from an article in the Cairo daily newspaper, *El-Ahram*. Courageously, Dar returned to Egypt to try to contact his ill-fated ring, but security around the spies was almost hermetic. He quickly left Egypt and traveled to Europe, where he recruited legal assistance, in both England and France, for the agents; these A'MAN-sanctioned lawyers would also be able to send back information on the morale of the captured agents.

Whereas many in the Israeli hierarchy preferred to forget about the incident in Egypt, Dar never lost hope. He planned operations—both covert and military—through which they could be released, but his elaborately conceived contingencies, when presented to the IDF commanders, fell on deaf ears. Only in 1956, when Great Britain, France, and Israel were conceiving the groundwork for their invasion of Egypt, did a truly viable option for the Susannah ring's release materialize. Dar formulated an exchange program with the French military: He would supply them with secret intelligence data that A'MAN possessed on Egypt and they would provide him, and two comrades, with an armed escort to the prison where the spies were held.[26] Dar and his comrades went to Cyprus, which was a staging point for the British and French invasion forces, and received uniforms of French Foreign Legionnaire sergeants. The three A'MAN agents fought with the French forces in Port Said, where they were to await the arrival of the lead IDF units advancing from Sinai, then head into Cairo. The fighting bogged down, however, and Dar's force was stranded. They made the best of their predicament: Racing through the Suez Canal region, Dar's team gathered the Jews of the area and brought them to a rendezvous point where they were transported by IDF/navy vessels to Israel.[27]

Chances for release of the Susannah spies remained optimum following the 1956 Suez War. The IDF captured more than six thousand Egyptian soldiers during the blitz into Sinai, including the commander general of Gaza. Chief of Staff Dayan, however, traded them for one Israeli POW, a pilot named Yonatan Atax, without even pushing for the release of the nine spies rotting in Tura Prison. Remarkably, the incarcerated spies were able to remain dedicated and focused. They survived the ordeal by participating in sports (their "Spies Basketball Team" won several championship medals), psychological discipline, and the hope that they would one day be free; Meir Zafran endured his torment by creating lithographs depicting his torture sessions.

For Dassa, Levy, Nathanson, and Ninio, freedom came in February 1968. During the lightning-fast 1967 Six-Day War, the IDF had captured more than five thousand Egyptian soldiers, including hundreds of senior officers and several generals; the release of these ranking officers, many of whom were personal friends of President Nasser, ensured eventual freedom for the Susannah spies. This time, the IDF, led by MOSSAD chief Maj. Gen. Meir Amit, refused any prisoner deal unless the Susannah spies were included; in fact, he threatened to resign if Prime Minister Levi Eshkol did not do everything possible to secure their release.[28] The four were returned to Israel by way of Zurich, on a Red Cross flight, and then to an awaiting IAF flight to Lod Airport. They received a subdued welcome from Israeli officials, then had more emotional reunions with both Meir Meyuchas and Meir Zafran, who, after finishing their prison terms, had made ALIYAH ("ascension to the holy land") to Israel. Just as important as their freedom was recognition from the army they served. In a ceremony charged with pride (and relief), the released spies were awarded the 1956 and 1967 War campaign ribbons and promoted to the rank of major. Wearing their

Class A khaki dress uniforms, Intelligence Corps unit tags, medals, and new rank, the spies were driven to Jerusalem to view Israel's victory parade. The climax of their return into the society for which they so loyally sacrificed their freedom was a meeting with David Ben-Gurion.[29]

The survivors of the "dirty business" remain a proud symbol of courage—not only in Israel. A supreme compliment was paid to them by their former enemy when a movie of their ordeal was produced by Egyptian television. Following the 1978 Camp David accords, several of the spies even returned to Egypt. Today, all have gone their separate ways, enjoying the anonymity of civilian life. Once a year, however, on the anniversary of their release from Egypt, the spies gather for a feast. They are joined by the other Israeli prisoners of war, several pilots, and naval commandos who were freed with them that day. The Susannah spies had passed letters to these captured Israeli soldiers during their incarceration, urging them to remain strong and positive. The indomitable human spirit of these people allowed them to put this trying experience behind them, but the Susannah incident would haunt A'MAN for years to come. Perhaps American President Dwight D. Eisenhower best expressed the realities of intelligence warfare when, at the inauguration of CIA headquarters in Langley, Virginia, he stated: "Victories are not suitable for publication and defeats not suitable for proper explanation."[30]

NOTES: CHAPTER FIVE

1. Major Yitzhak Steigman, TOLDOT HEYL HA'AVIR—ME'A'ATZAMAUT LE'KADESH (Tel Aviv: Ministry of Defense Publications/Air Force History Branch, 1990), 318.

2. *Ibid.* 111.

3. Oded Granot, HEYL HA'MODE' IN: TZAHAL BE'HEILO ENTZYKLOPEDIA LE'TZAVA ULE'BITACHON (Tel Aviv: Revivim Publishers, 1981), 35.

4. Aviezer Golan, *Operation Susannah* (New York: Harper and Row, 1978), 4–5.

5. Yossi Melman and Dan Raviv, *The Imperfect Spies: The History of Israeli Intelligence* (London: Sidgwick and Jackson, Ltd., 1989), 52.

6. See Oded Granot, HEYL HA'MODE'IN, 35.

7. The television show HAYIM SHE'KA'ELEH, hosted by Amos Etinger, from the Israel Broadcast Service as seen on Israeli television on December 27, 1989, and on the New York cable station "Shalom America" in May 1990.

8. Stewart Steven, *The Spymasters of Israel* (New York: Ballantine Books, 1980), 79.

9. In the book *The Imperfect Spies*, authors Dan Raviv and Yossi Melman imply that Eli Cohen was one of the Egyptians brought to Israel in 1952 for espionage training. Although he was, indeed, recruited to assist the ring as a radio operator, noted author Shmuel Segev, in his book *Alone in Damascus: The Life and Death of Eli Cohen*, points out that he was first brought to Israel for intelligence training *only* in 1955.

10. Ben Dan, *The Spy From Israel* (London: Vallentine, Mitchell and Co., 1969), 13.

11. Colonel Trevor N. Dupuy, *Elusive Victory: The Arab-Israeli Wars 1947–74* (New York: Harper and Row Publishers, 1978), 131.

12. Moshe Zak, "TZAHAL: SHTEI ETZBA'AOT ME'MELCHEMET KOREA," (April 20, 1988): 6.

13. See Stewart Steven, *The Spymasters of Israel*, 73.

14. See Oded Granot, HEYL HA'MODE'IN, 37.

15. See Yossi Melman and Dan Raviv, *The Imperfect Spies*, 66.

16. See Aviezer Golan, *Operation Susannah*, 37.

17. *Ibid.* 37.

18. Yosef Argaman, ZE HAYA SODI BE'YOTER (Tel Aviv: Ministry of Defense Publications, 1990), 43–54.

19. See Yossi Melman and Dan Raviv, *The Imperfect Spies*, 69.

20. See Oded Granot, HEYL HA'MODE'IN, 38.

21. Various ed., "Lavon Affair Remembered," *IDF Journal* (spring 1988): 4.

22. See Yossi Melman and Dan Raviv, *The Imperfect Spies*, 70.

23. Yair Amikam, "HA'ESEK BISH HAYA LE'LO YEDIOT HA'MOSSAD," YEDIOT AHARONOT (April 23, 1980): 4.

24. *Ibid.* 4.

25. See Yossi Melman and Dan Raviv, *The Imperfect Spies,* 70.

26. Yitzhak Ben-Hurin, "MERAGEL VE'GENTLEMAN," MA'ARIV SOF SHAVUA (December 22, 1989): 8.

27. *Ibid.* 10.

28. Various ed., "IYEM LEHITPATER M'ROSHUT HA'MOSSAD K'DEI SH'ESHKOL YIFA'AL LE'SHICHRUR A'ATZUREI HA'PARASHAH," HADASHOT (March 9, 1989): 6.

29. See Aviezer Golan, *Operation Susannah,* 375.

30. Eitan Haber, "HEM NIKBARU BE'SHEMOT A'ARAVIM," MA'ARIV (May 31, 1985): 20.

CHAPTER 6

DOUBLE JEOPARDY 1954:
"I HAVE NOT BETRAYED MY COUNTRY"

T he demise of the Susannah spy ring in the summer of 1954 was a tragedy for IDF Military Intelligence. The fiasco in Egypt underscored the inherent dangers of covert espionage activities on enemy soil, and the results of poor political supervision and a lack of bureaucratic responsibility. Yet there were other facets of A'MAN intelligence-collection efforts that did keep the State of Israel forewarned of enemy capabilities, intentions, and positions.

One of the most important tools employed by A'MAN was the use of elite, commando-type units to conduct deep-penetration reconnaissance forays inside enemy territory. These forces were also called upon to execute other covert tasks that required speed, stealth, and terminating firepower. The importance of these reconnaissance units to A'MAN's overall agenda was profound and irrefutable. This more conventional military espionage differed markedly from the activities of the deep-cover spies, but it could prove equally as dangerous.

Being a vastly outnumbered entity in the Middle East, the IDF was forced to consolidate the best of its conscripted forces into small, specially tasked units capable of inflicting more damage than their numbers would reasonably indicate. The practice of deploying elite forces for hit-and-run retaliatory and intelligence-gathering operations first began with the joint British and HAGANAH Special Night Squads commanded by Capt. Orde Wingate; it continued later with Yitzhak Sadeh's Field Companies and, most significantly, with the PAL'MACH in the Allied campaign for Syria and Lebanon in 1941 and the struggle against the British between 1945 and 1947. During the 1948 War, the PAL'MACH achieved legendlike status and became the role model for all future Israeli special forces units. In 1948, for example, Moshe Dayan formed an ad hoc mechanized force of commandos, known as the 89th Commando Battalion, which, among other achievements, captured the ultrastrategic airfield at Lydda (now "Lod"), as well as the city of Ramle. The IDF/navy possessed two special forces components—the Underwater Sabotage Unit and the Special Craft Force—which performed brilliantly during the conflict, including sinking the Egyptian navy flagship, the destroyer RENS *Emir Farouk*, on October 21, 1948. In the Negev Desert, the GIVA'ATI Brigade created the 54th Battalion, a elite force of jeep-borne raiders that modeled itself on the British Long-Range Desert Group, adopting the name SHU'ALEI SHIMSHON ("Samson's Foxes").

When Prime Minister Ben-Gurion dismantled the PAL'MACH in 1949, fearing that they would one day subvert the Israeli democracy through force, the IDF entity was meant to carry on the PAL'MACH's legacy with its small group of fledgling paratroopers.[1] In 1948, several PAL'MACH officers had been sent secretly to Czechoslovakia for parachutist training; the instruction was, oddly enough, carried out in a former SS base in the Carpathian Mountains. When these "airborne officers" returned to Israel in September 1948 to create the TZANHANIM ("paratroopers"), its twenty-eight officers and two hundred thirty-eight volunteers were too insignificant in number to contribute to the fighting in the War of Independence; in any case, they were considered too valuable an entity to even risk in combat.

Early on, however, it was clear that the paratroopers were *not* living up to expectations. Officers were being killed in alarming numbers in training accidents, and the foreign volunteers who had initially flocked to the unit (mainly adventure-seeking Second World War veterans from America, Britain, and South Africa) proved to be divisive elements. Also, many of the Israeli paratroopers had forgotten that their mandate was to become the IDF's true cutting edge; instead, they spent their days "moonlighting" at the Haifa shipyards and carousing at a nearby Women's Corps training facility. When, in 1949, Capt. Yehuda Harari, the paratroopers' second commander, arrived at the Mt. Carmel training base, he found the facility unguarded, the grounds littered with garbage, and the elite of the Israeli armed forces sitting around half-naked and drunk, playing pinochle. It would take some time before the paratroops were truly ready to conduct special operations.

The initial failure of Israel's airborne option prompted the IDF General Staff to look elsewhere. There were attempts to expand the scope of the Minorities Unit 300; indeed, the Druze, Bedouin, and Circassian soldiers were effective and highly motivated, but, in the xenophobic minds of the Israeli hierarchy, they were not suitable material for intelligence operations because they were "Arabs."[2] Attempts also were made to transform an element from the 1st GOLANI Infantry, a brigade turned into a national melting pot for North

African immigrants in the early 1950s, but this, too, met with disappointing failure. As the IDF developed from its born-in-battle genesis, other elite units were soon formed, such as Unit 30 and Almond Recon, but they were small in size and too specialized in security operations throughout the Israeli frontier to be considered candidates for intelligence work. Eventually, the one force that would come forth to meet the IDF's unique needs was a short-lived, extremely effective group of recluse adventurers, scouts, and commandos. Known as Unit 101, it was commanded by the most controversial man ever to wear the IDF uniform: Maj. Ariel "Arik" Sharon.

Unit 101, which adopted its name in honor of the American 101st Airborne Division, was created on August 5, 1953. It was sanctioned as a retaliatory strike force capable of inflicting "biblical justice" on those who perpetrated terrorism against the Jewish state; in 1953, this meant Palestinian infiltrators who crossed the loosely defended frontiers and committed acts of nationally inspired murder and mayhem. Sharon was a perfect choice to lead Unit 101. As rambunctious a soldier as could be found, the burly Sharon was a maverick—a man who did things his way and only his way, and he always got them done. A fearless man, he was also charismatic: His courage inspired undivided loyalty and performance from the men under his command. Incidentally, the first operation in which Sharon led what would become the nucleus of Unit 101 was the "incited" ambush that led to the death of Mustapha Samueli.[3]

Ben-Gurion was so impressed with the capabilities of Major Sharon's ad hoc commandos—as well as their ability to conduct intelligence-inspired operations—that he authorized Chief of Staff Lt. Gen. Mordechai Maklef to form a retaliatory strike force to conduct top-secret operations for the General Staff.[4] Word of this exciting new force spread quickly in the IDF, and soon Major Sharon's headquarters was inundated with volunteers seeking adventure in their monotonous military service.

Unit 101's first volunteer, Meir Har-Zion, would also become its most famous. A legendary scout with the NA'HA'L ("Fighting Pioneer Youth," a force of soldier/ farmers that settled volatile frontier posts in heavily fortified kibbutzim) Infantry Brigade, Har-Zion had already earned a reputation as a skilled and fearless warrior. Before being conscripted into the IDF, he frequently had cut through Jordanian territory on camping trips from Jerusalem to the Dead Sea desert oasis of Ein Gedi. He could read the terrain like the back of his hand and trek through seemingly impassable mountains and wadis with silence and speed. Most importantly, he was, like Sharon, a fearless man. Har-Zion also brought many of his more zealous comrades from the NA'HA'L to Unit 101, and they, in turn, brought more friends. Within weeks, Unit 101 consisted of fifty proven fighters who would soon convince the Arabs that they were mightier than a brigade.

For the soldiers of Unit 101, the term *field intelligence* was not a military formality but the currency of day-to-day life. Their home base at Camp Staph, located in the Jerusalem hills, was configured to resemble an Arab village, which allowed the fighters to familiarize themselves with the physical appearance of a common target. To gather intelligence they did not rely on A'MAN bureaucrats, IAF photoreconnaissance flights, or topographical studies: Fighters simply "visited" the target in audacious cross-border forays. When a village was targeted, Unit 101's intelligence squad geared up for a forced march and set up encompassing surveillance around the area. They identified buildings, roads, and possible ambush positions, compiling a wealth of data before returning to base.

Arik Sharon would greet each return with boisterous praise and a feast of roasted lamb. These trips into enemy territory soon became legendary in the IDF as well as in the Arab capitals, where news of this new *Ja'ish al-yahud* ("Jewish army") received apprehensive attention. Jordanian, Egyptian, and Lebanese soldiers were routinely kidnapped and interrogated; police files in border villages were lifted; Unit 101 fighters brazenly stopped vehicles on main thoroughfares to search passengers and steal documents. To add insult to injury, the commandos often returned with souvenirs of their efforts—Jordanian police uniforms, weapons, and, on one occasion, the local commander's camouflaged Land-Rover. The value of reconnoitering enemy territory was not lost to A'MAN headquarters, who envisioned grand objectives for Unit 101.

When a retaliatory or preemptive strike against a village harboring or supporting Palestinian infiltrators was ordered, Unit 101 proved ruthless and dynamic. Objectives—be they Egyptian garrisons or Jordanian villages—were attended to in a meticulous and prejudicial fashion. The commandos always attacked at night. Before infrared equipment and low-light goggles became the mainstay of night warfare, the arrogant fighters of Unit 101 turned night into day. The psychological impact of their blazing tommy guns illuminating the darkened Levantine sky was immense; Arab soldiers and fedayeen guerrillas feared them greatly. Arik's commandos were achieving supermen status.

One mission, however, went too far. Operation Shoshana was the code name for the retaliatory strike against the Jordanian West Bank village of Kibya, located just two kilometers from the Israeli frontier, south of Jerusalem. The strike was sanctioned after three Israeli civilians were murdered by Palestinian terrorists who used the village—with Jordanian army assistance—as a base of operations. On the night of October 14, 1953, a combined force of Unit 101 commandos and paratroopers from the 890th Battalion attacked the town. The fighting was fierce, though the Israeli attackers quickly seized the initiative and quelled all resistance. The noise of exploding grenades and automatic-weapon fire led most of Kibya's villagers to flee into the surrounding hills. Believing that all of the villagers had fled, the Unit 101 commanders did not conduct a time-consuming house-to-house search before the village homes were destroyed as a retributory measure. The commanders were wrong: many villagers had, in fact, remained behind. The next morning, the news of sixty-nine civilians killed reached a stunned Israel, and a wave of outrage and condemnation engulfed the Israeli political and military establishment. Even though Ben-Gurion was *publicly* outraged by the massacre at Kibya, he was *privately* pleased with its results; he was quoted as saying, "It's not important what the rest of the world will say, it's important what the Arabs will think."[5] Still, to placate public demands, the rogue force would have to be merged with the more conventional 890th Paratroop Battalion. Arik Sharon, of course, would remain at the helm.

With the influx of Unit 101 commandos, the paratroopers improved their abilities to mount special operations. Former scout Har-Zion—the only soldier in IDF history to be commissioned an officer *without* undergoing the mandatory stint in BA'HAD 1, the IDF Officer School—became the force's reconnaissance and intelligence officer. Operations on behalf of IDF Military Intelligence flourished because the TZANHANIM was the only force in the IDF that could reliably mount regular cross-border intelligence-gathering missions. With the paratroopers at their disposal, A'MAN operations increased in scope and boldness.

Nowhere was this cooperation more evident than in the activities of MOD 2, or A'MAN's eavesdropping unit. In the early 1950s, A'MAN's Technical Department had produced a listening device that tapped into enemy telephone lines and relayed the conversations back to reception posts inside Israel. Israel's use of such technology was considerably enhanced in 1948 when a series of four secure "red lines" were established between Israel and Jordan to conduct covert negotiations between Jordan's King Abd'allah and Israeli leaders.[6]* During the 1948 War of Independence, the SHA'I and the Intelligence Department had made extensive use of tactical listening devices. As was previously discussed, MOD 2 monitored the telephone conversations of the Palestinian Grand Mufti and his supporters, and also communications between ranking Arab Legion officers in Amman, Jericho, Hebron, and Jerusalem and their commanders in the field; and in the campaign against the Egyptians, the field communications of forces trapped in the Faluja Pocket were monitored continually.

---

*These links, according to authors Yossi Melman and Dan Raviv in their book *A Hostile Partnership: The Secret Relations Between Israel and Jordan*, were reestablished in the mid-1950s between Jordan's King Hussein and Israeli Prime Minister Ben-Gurion as a Middle Eastern version of the "red phone." The "red lines" were used to reduce the threat of full-scale war between the two antagonistic nations.

Following the war, MOD 2 faced many challenges that its small units were ill-prepared to meet. The armistice agreement and separation of forces agreement signed in 1949 distanced frontline Arab units from Israel's borders. This geographical separation was, of course, a respite to IDF frontline forces but created an unacceptable operating environment for the MOD 2 radiomen. The ranges separating Arab and Israeli forces were, in most cases, too great to successfully and continuously monitor wireless radio communications. Unable to hear the radio traffic between Arab headquarters and forces in the field on a constant basis, MOD 2 was hindered in its ability to determine regular radio frequencies, unravel codes, and thus predict troop and artillery coordinates. As a result, new sources of communications intelligence (COMINT) and signal intelligence (SIGINT) had to be found; this, of course, meant tapping into *conventional* telephone lines.

Accessing telephone and cable communications lines was a well-known art. The Germans had managed to tap the underwater telephone cables that connected Great Britain and the United States during the Second World War, and in the postwar era, the NATO powers had tapped the Soviet lines underneath divided Berlin.[7] For the IDF, however, tapping into Arab telephone lines presented extreme difficulties. Eavesdropping on enemy telephone lines could not be accomplished from the safety and security of Israeli territory, as it had been during the 1948 War. Accurate intelligence was necessary: The lines had to be traced and charted. To execute this task, cross-border forays would have to be sanctioned. Such operations, if successful, would prove invaluable, yet one failure could spark an international incident that might lead to full-scale war. And to maintain the telephone and telegraph tap, frequent cross-border operations would be required to check on the equipment. It was a risky undertaking, but A'MAN HQ felt that the potential results were worth any possible political and military repercussions. In retrospect, another factor may have played a role in this bold decision: Since A'MAN did not possess an elite combat entity of its own, other IDF units would have to execute the operations.

When a top-secret undertaking was deemed necessary, the General Staff and A'MAN called for the services of the paratroops' elite reconnaissance entity, SAYERET TZANHANIM ("Paratroop Recon"). Created in the aftermath of Unit 101, and commanded by Lt. Meir Har-Zion, the SAYERET was much more than the battalion's indigenous commando element: They were the best of the best—every red beret strived for the opportunity to be part of the SAYERET. Har-Zion's SAYERET TZANHANIM also functioned as the paratroopers' intelligence force, a component that could infiltrate into enemy territory without attracting unwanted attention from enemy forces—or from "regular" IDF troops manning frontier positions, for that matter. They never attacked a target in the conventional sense: They became intimate with it through personal reconnaissance, then exploited the objective's weakness, attacking with lightning speed and accurate use of firepower. The SAYERET commandos regarded the entire Middle East, or at least Israel's neighboring countries, as their own backyard, and would even conduct "routine" training operations, such as forced marches and target practice, in enemy territory. This not only helped the reconnaissance commandos gain experience, but it proved to the General Staff that as a force, they knew no boundaries. (When these reconnaissance commandos were released from active duty, their impressive attributes were not lost to A'MAN, MOSSAD, and SHIN BET recruiters, who actively sought their talents for future work in the more covert echelons of the Israeli intelligence community.[8])

After intense debate in the A'MAN hierarchy regarding sanctioning telephone-tapping operations, with A'MAN commander Gibli demanding the deployment of phone taps and Dayan remaining conveniently neutral, the final decision fell on Defense Minister Lavon's shoulders. After analyzing the data and studying personnel files on the reconnaissance paratroopers being considered for the mission, Lavon gave A'MAN the green light. The target would be the nation that was most difficult to penetrate: Syria.

Five paratroopers from SAYERET TZANHANIM, led by Sgt. Meir Ya'akobi, were "volunteered" for the operation. At the time, the SAYERET was involved in joint-security patrols along Israel's volatile frontiers. The chosen five, who were among the finest soldiers within the reconnaissance force, learned of their proposed participation in this new aspect of intelligence work during an informal meeting with Har-Zion in his spartan office. Har-Zion, a commanding officer renowned for his courage under fire, was a difficult man to refuse, especially when a soldier was offered such an "honorable assignment"—crossing into Syria on behalf of A'MAN. The five men did not need much persuasion. They were rushed to Tel Aviv for another interview with MOD 2 officers, then hastily trained in the technical aspect of the tapping device. Their instruction culminated near the seedy sand dunes north of the city, where, amid beachgoers and ladies of the evening, the five paratroopers were taught to install the device. The most difficult aspect of the training was learning to climb the telephone poles carrying full battle kit.

The tapping device was made of two principal elements. The first was a long black wire, which was to be attached to the top of the telephone pole's communication cables; it would transpond signals back to a receiver in Israel. The second part of the device was its mechanical brain—a small transmitter that was to be buried a few meters underground and adjacent to the telephone pole. Because the device was considered top secret, a small, though highly powerful, explosive charge was built into its mechanism. It could be set off if the team of installers was captured, and as a booby trap, it would kill any enemy soldiers who had the misfortune of examining it too closely.

The devices would be attached to the telephone lines that connected Syrian fortifications along the Golan Heights. Overlooking the Sea of Galilee, and much of central Israel, for that matter, the volcanic plateau of the Golan Heights was one of the most strategic vantage points in the Middle East; whoever controlled the Heights controlled vast stretches of contested territory. Syrian artillery batteries had continuously and indiscriminately shelled the town of Tiberias and the many kibbutzim that surrounded the Sea of Galilee; these attacks had killed dozens and proved a security dilemma to which the IDF had little response. Air strikes were inconsequential, since the Syrian gun positions were carved deep into rock—they even proved impervious to napalm. Knowing Syrian intentions ahead of time would prove to be a remarkable advantage. Any venture into the treacherous zone, with its great concentration of Syrian troops, was considered a suicide mission, however, and, the A'MAN officers in charge of the operations followed the developments of the squad with great anxiety and trepidation.

The SAYERET force, confident of its abilities, attended to the task calmly, as if crossing the heavily fortified frontier into Syria was routine. After a hearty meal in Kibbutz Dan—which was so close to the border that Israeli farmers and Syrian soldiers often eyeballed one another across the pastures—the group trekked through a safe patch of woods, cleared of antipersonnel mines, to the other side of the frontier. Used to carrying well over eighty pounds of equipment each, the five-man squad was laden down with additional supplies of ammunition, explosives, and survival gear. Climbing up the narrow volcanic roads that led to the Syrian fortifications, the squad operated in total silence; with stealthlike movements they slipped past Syrian military squads that vigilantly patrolled the area in search of "Israeli spies." With little difficulty, Meir Ya'akobi's men succeeded in planting the eavesdropping device on a telephone pole between Ein Fit and Za'aura—on the road connecting the fortifications. Once the device was installed, they radioed back to HQ to see if it was functioning correctly. With an affirmative reply from their MOD 2 handlers, they returned to Israel and, after swearing to absolute secrecy, resumed operational duty with their unit.

The eavesdropping device proved extremely successful. In Kibbutz Dan, MOD 2's Arabic-speaking soldiers sat around tape recorders and radio switchboards—the cumbersome headsets became part of their uniform. While recording the Syrian telephone activity around the Golan Heights fortifications for later analysis, MOD 2 personnel made lengthy notations; they identified the local use of slang and voice inflections, and made other comments they felt were important. The device, however, was not a modern, self-sufficient piece of equipment. It required maintenance, repairs, and battery replacements. This task fell to Meir Ya'akobi's squad of full-time paratroopers/part-time intelligence agents. Sergeant Ya'akobi was considered by all his superiors to be one of the finest soldiers they had ever commanded; Arik Sharon said of him, "A sergeant like him could easily command Lieutenant Colonels."[9] Most importantly, his leadership reassured the nervous intelligence officers in Northern Command.

Throughout the fall of 1954, Ya'akobi's five-man force, now including two members of the GOLANI Infantry Brigade—Lt. Meir Moses and rifleman Uri Eilan—crossed into Syria to maintain the device. Their forays became routine—too routine, many would say in retrospect. The infiltrations into Syria were always executed at night, but, for reasons unknown, the squad crossed into Syria at regularly scheduled intervals; it was a breach of security guidelines that not only enhanced the ability of the Syrian military to intercept them, but proved to be an invitation to disaster.

Their cocky, confrontational style resulted in additional risk. The manner in which they checked on their work was audacious. The only way that headquarters could ensure that the eavesdropping mechanism was working properly was to monitor telephone traffic; even on the fortified Golan Heights, the Syrians tended to sleep at night, willing to gamble that an Israeli attack would not preempt their good night's slumber. Ya'akobi's squad, therefore, had to wake up the Syrian fortifications. They preferred to do this in an explosive fashion. The squad would hurl a few grenades around the officers' barracks, which ensured a flurry of angry telephone activity to all positions atop the Heights. Or, when they felt the need for a "little" excitement, Ya'akobi's squad would fire their weapons in mad and desperate bursts at the Syrian fortifications; after their Schmeisser submachine guns' barrels would almost melt, they would jubilantly dash back to the safety of Israeli lines. The sounds of unrelenting automatic-weapon fire would so frighten the Syrians that emergency war contingency plans were sometimes discussed on the telephone lines, all to the delight of MOD 2 Arabists who listened in. Such exploits earned the team the endearing nickname the "Wake-up Squad."

The success of the team was awe-inspiring to many senior IDF officials, but Ya'akobi and his men were never allowed a glimpse into the gold mine of intelligence that "their device" brought to Israel. This was done for obvious security considerations—the possibility of the squad ending up in Syrian captivity remained a real possibility.

On the night of December 8, 1954, the mixed force of recon paratroopers and GOLANI infantrymen once again crossed the border into Syria. The squad was commanded by Lt. Meir Moses, and included Ya'akobi as the chief scout, with Gad Kastelanitz, Jackie Lind, and Uri Eilan for fire support and communications. As on all nights in which they ventured into Syria, the full moon illuminated their path; as on the other nights, they followed a predetermined path and crossed the frontier at a fairly regular time. But this night was to be different.

The five-man squad labored in the cold winter air up the volcanic peaks and around endless boulders. They passed a local police fort bustling with activity; its powerful searchlight raked the surrounding area but failed to pick up the five hulking figures walking at a feverish pace along the tree line. The squad was within fifty meters of the fortification at Tel Azzaziat when the sound of rifles being cocked broke the night's silence. It took only seconds for Moses and Ya'akobi to realize that they had fallen victim to a Syrian ambush. "The Syrians must have expected us for some time," Gad Kastelanitz would later recall. "They even moved boulders to advantageous firing positions in order to facilitate the ambush." [10] The Syrian commanding officer shouted, *"Min hada?"* ("Who's there?"), to which a surprised Ya'akobi replied, *"Nahna min el A'arab!"* ("We are Arabs!"). The Syrian patrol did not believe the foolish masquerade. The squad quickly hit the dirt to prepare for a firefight, but the Syrian patrol, which greatly outnumbered the Israelis, swooped down on them in seconds. The Israeli men were placed face down on the cold, muddy path; the Syrians placed the barrels of their French MAS-36 rifles to the heads of the shocked Israeli soldiers, while the commander contacted headquarters in the Golan Heights capital of Quneitra and notified his superiors of the evening's important news. The telephone lines atop the heights were bustling that fateful night—communications activity that was monitored by MOD 2 back in Israel. For the second time in six months, a disaster had befallen A'MAN.

The routine nature of the cross-border incursions had, perhaps, blunted the soldiers' alertness; it was lax regard for the enemy that betrayed their efforts. Yet the five men were also betrayed by their A'MAN handlers. The IDF's inherent inability to view the Arabs as competent soldiers and counterintelligence agents resulted in a feeling of invincibility; as a result, the five men were not even supplied with cover stories to protect their identities. In fact, even after the five Israeli soldiers were taken by jeep and force-marched to the Syrian police station in Quneitra, they failed to take their predicament seriously. Uri Eilan was mumbling in Arabic to annoy the Syrian guards, and several soldiers joked about the thumbnails and Chinese water tortures they were about to endure. [11] The laughter ended, of course, when the first interrogation began. Initially, all they disclosed were their names, ranks, and serial numbers. These were the toughest soldiers in the IDF: ex-NA'HA'L, Unit 101, and GOLANI fighters who prided themselves on eighty-kilometer forced marches and dangerous exploits. They may have compromised themselves, but they were not about to surrender the secrets of the operation.

The capture of the intelligence squad sent shock waves through the upper echelons of A'MAN and the IDF General Staff. The failure of Military Intelligence to execute delicate operations in 1954 had been epidemic and extremely costly. Many in the halls of the KIRYA—the huge complex in the heart of Tel Aviv that houses the IDF General Staff and the Defense Ministry—felt that there might even be a security leak in their midst, or worse, a double agent. Was it a case of treason, or had the intelligence squad's luck simply run out? Questions regarding the capture of the five recon troopers caused sincere concern in A'MAN circles and sparked utter outrage in the General Staff. Chief of Staff Dayan was particularly infuriated by the squad's seeming cowardice. At a closed-door session with the General Staff, Dayan said to his deputy, Maj. Gen. Haim Laskov: "Israeli soldiers do not give up without putting up a fight— no matter what the circumstances!" The feeling seemed to be that it was better to die for Israel than become a politically embarrassing prisoner.[12] Once again, Dayan's self-righteous morality, and what some paratroop veterans have termed a pompous sense of loyalty, would interfere with the freeing of Israeli intelligence soldiers held in Arab prisons.

The true reason why the squad surrendered remains a mystery to this day. While some have theorized that they simply refused to fight their way out of the situation, there were rumors that because all the brutal close-quarter killing that Ya'akobi had encountered as part of Meir Har-Zion's SAYERET, he wanted to avoid face-to-face bloodshed at all costs.[13] Others believe that Meir Ya'akobi and Lieutenant Moses did not want to risk the lives of their men in what surely would have been a suicidal act of resistance. Outnumbered and hopelessly outgunned, they could not have survived a firefight. The stigma of cowardice, however, would haunt the five men for many years.

From Quneitra, the captured intelligence team was transferred to Al-Mazeh Prison, notorious throughout the Middle East as one of the most brutal prisons, located in the heart of ancient Damascus. The five Israelis' first encounter with incarceration was actually quite benign: a kindhearted, sixty-year-old Circassian sergeant offered them mint tea and Bedouin cigarettes. The men were placed in solitary confinement, in narrow cells three meters high. Although the media has embellished accounts of their imprisonment with tales of exhaustive questioning sessions complete with electric-shock torture and the bastinado, the treatment these prisoners received was humane when compared to the mutilations many Israeli POWs endured at the hands of the Syrians in 1967 and 1973. According to Gad Kastelanitz, "The only torture was sensory deprivation. We were separated from each other and not allowed to sleep, sometimes, for several days. There were, however, no brutal beatings." The Syrians, in fact, treated them with kid gloves; it was believed that a prisoner exchange under United Nations auspices was imminent.[14]

However, other accounts indicate and, in all probability, prove that several of the Israeli prisoners were, indeed, tortured in blood-chilling fashion. Still, after several months of intensive questioning, the Syrians had yet to learn the truth behind the force's mission on the Golan Heights. They tried a psychological ploy, telling one Israeli that a comrade had already broken under interrogation and had supplied them with the required information. The

Syrians hoped to convince at least one of the unbreakable Israelis to talk. Fearing that he would not be able to withstand torture and might eventually give up classified information, Uri Eilan, the young idealistic kibbutznik, hung himself in his prison cell on January 13, 1955. Hoping to avoid certain Israeli retaliation should news of a murdered POW reach Tel Aviv, the Syrians returned his body to Israel a day later, where he was buried at his home in Kibbutz Gan Shmuel. Remarkably, Eilan had managed to scribble a small note and hide it in the lining of his uniform; it was discovered when the military rabbis were preparing his corpse for proper Jewish burial. His note, which would become a fundamental element of Israeli folklore, simply said: "LO BAGAD'TI!"— "I have not betrayed!"

Eventually, the Syrians did learn about the telephone-tapping device. An Arab native of Haifa who was living in Syria was brought to Al-Mazeh Prison and identified Lieutenant Moses, also a native of the city, as an officer in SAYERET GOLANI, the GOLANI Brigade's reconnaissance force. Soon, the secrets of the squad's mission began to be revealed. Moses and Ya'akobi both realized that it was only a matter of time before the Syrians discovered the device, so they hatched a daring and suicidal plan. Ya'akobi volunteered to take the Syrians to the telephone pole and show them how the device worked. A UN observer would be brought along to ensure the safety of the Israeli soldiers. Ya'akobi planned to detonate the explosive booby trap and destroy the device, killing himself and several Syrian guards. The severe weather conditions—bitter cold, incessant rains, and mud slides—that had gripped northern Israel, Lebanon, and the Golan Heights in January and February of 1955 had made the detonating mechanism inoperative, however. The Syrians seized the device intact and a disheartened Ya'akobi was returned to the confines of his prison cell. It would be his home and hell for the next thirteen months.

Although Dayan was not pressing for the release of the four remaining prisoners in Syria, Eilan's suicide set off a political time bomb in Israel. In the halls of the KNESSET, Israeli politicians demanded a military operation to free the captives. Senior A'MAN officers also pressed the General Staff to act on behalf of "their" men in Damascus, and Paratroop Brigade commander Arik Sharon pushed for the authorization to conduct a military move—if not to free *his* men, then at least to capture Syrian soldiers for an eventual prisoner exchange. The Defense Ministry was preoccupied with the fallout of Operation Susannah, and the green light for action was received only following the resignation of Pinhas Lavon and Ben-Gurion's return to the Defense Ministry. Although, once again, the saving of Israeli intelligence personnel became secondary to political concerns, the paratroopers refused to forget about one of their own.

On the night of December 11, 1955, the IDF struck on the Golan Heights. Ostensibly, the raid was a retaliatory strike against Syrian artillery fire that had been directed against Israeli police vessels on the Sea of Galilee, yet it was clear to all involved that the operation, code-named ALEI ZA'IT ("olive branch"), was designed to obtain the release of the Damascus prisoners. While a combined force of infantrymen from the GIVA'ATI and NA'HA'L brigades joined the paratroop battalion in an attack against a series of Syrian fortifications along the eastern bank of the Sea of Galilee, Meir Har-Zion's reconnaissance force engaged the Syrian barracks in order to kidnap as many enemy soldiers as possible for a later "use." [15] The battle was fierce, and Har-Zion's SAYERET gave little quarter: In the four hours of close-quarter battle, the Syrians lost fifty dead and nearly a hundred wounded.* Although the Israelis suffered six combat fatalities of their own, they captured twenty-nine Syrian officers and NCOs and brought them back to Israel.

On March 29, 1956, a prisoner exchange took place on the B'NOT YA'AKOV Bridge, which separated Israel and Syria over the Yarmuk River; the bridge served as a Levantine version of the Glienicker Bridge separating East and West Berlin—the sight of numerous prisoner exchanges in both reality and fiction. The four Israeli prisoners were swapped for *forty* Syrians under the supervision of UN peacekeeping officers, International Red Cross representatives, and intelligence agents on both sides of the border. Unfortunately for all those involved, the soldiers' return to Israel was not the end of the chapter.

The five repatriated soldiers were met with joyous celebrations and reunions with families and friends. Days later, SAYERET GOLANI Lt. Meir Moses and SAYERET TZANHANIM 1st Sgt. Meir Ya'akobi were court-martialed. Chief of Staff Dayan apparently had hoped to convince the rest of the IDF that it was better to die in battle than become a prisoner of war. The paratroop commander, Sharon, was outraged by the diabolical plot to discredit his men, who, he felt, had already proven their courage above and beyond the call of duty; he battled on behalf of his men even though it could have seriously endangered his blossoming military career.** A long list of decorated Unit 101 and SAYERET TZANHANIM veterans testified on Ya'akobi's behalf: They labeled him a true Israeli hero.

The trial was a kangaroo court. Lieutenant Moses lost his commissioned rank for twelve years, until December 1968, when captured Syrian files revealed that he had, indeed, attempted to destroy the device. Meir Ya'akobi

---

*In the battle, First Lieutenant Har-Zion was awarded the I'TUR HA'OZ ("Courage Decoration") for leading the force through impassable terrain and under heavy enemy fire.
**Although never publicly mentioned, it is believed that Dayan held Sharon's testimony against him for many years; it might be one of the reasons why Dayan, while serving as defense minister, passed over Sharon as a potential chief of staff candidate in 1972.

received a dishonorable mention to his record, and was demoted to the rank of corporal. The proud recon paratrooper was humiliated and resolved to right the wrong perpetrated against him, no matter what the price. Although as a one-time POW he was released from compulsory service, Ya'akobi demanded to return to the SAYERET as a conscript; proving his courage became an obsession. Tragically, as a heavy machine gunner, he was killed in the battle for Mitla Pass on November 1, 1956, after parachuting into this ultrastrategic gauntlet with the SAYERET.[16]

The saga of this five-man squad working for A'MAN has become an integral part of Israeli legend. Books, films, and documentaries retold the tragic story of Eilan and Ya'akobi, giving the ill-fated soldiers martyr status. The internal political and military fallout following the incident, similar to the lingering effects of Operation Susannah, remained an open wound for many years. In A'MAN headquarters, many painful questions remained: Was the device's intelligence value greater than the lives of five men? What was the "true" contribution of the device to the intelligence-gathering efforts of the day? Were all the necessary steps taken to ensure the security and safety of the squad while in enemy territory? Why weren't the men provided with false identities and cover stories?

Although a sensitive issue to this very day, the installation of a listening device on the telephone pole outside the Tel Azzaziat fortification on the Golan Heights did, in fact, represent an innovative and aggressive effort by A'MAN to increase the scope and quality of the military intelligence data gathered from neighboring Arab states. It also represented a respectable degree of improvement in A'MAN's technical abilities to conceive and produce items that would enhance intelligence-gathering capabilities. Most importantly, the doomed eavesdropping device marked the beginning of close cooperation between A'MAN and the IDF's elite units. In fact, the efforts of one have become an integral part of the other; the various commando and reconnaissance forces within the IDF have developed into mobile, on-call intelligence squads, trained to scout enemy territory and bring back HUMINT, SIGINT, COMINT, and VISINT (visual intelligence) rewards unattainable through other means. In the years to follow, the IDF's YECHIDOT HA'NIVCHAROT ("Chosen Units," the term used to cover all of Israel's special forces) became the Intelligence Branch's rapid deployment force, performing their joint military and intelligence tasks throughout the Middle East.

1. Uri Milstein, HA'HISTORIA SHEL HA'TZANHANIM KERECH ALEPH (Tel Aviv: Schalgi Ltd., Publishing House, 1985), 87.

2. Although the minorities, that is, non-Jews and non-Palestinian Arabs, of Israel have made great advances in the IDF, several sensitive tasks are still closed to them; these include the air force, several branches of the IDF/navy, and the Intelligence Corps. Many in the IDF and the Israeli political community are attempting to correct this situation, arguing, quite justifiably, that if a Druze, Bedouin, or Circassian is a worthy enough citizen to serve in the paratroops or GIVA'ATI Brigade, or as a scout along one of the volatile frontiers, he should have the opportunity to serve in *any* branch of service where his talents and intelligence can be best utilized.

3. Samuel M. Katz, *Follow Me! A History of Israel's Military Elite* (London: Arms and Armour Press, 1989), 35.

4. *Ibid.* 35.

5. See Uri Milstein, HA'HISTORIA SHEL HA'TZANHANIM, 232.

6. Natan Ro'y, HEYL HA'KESHER VE'HA'ELEKTRONIKA: TZAHAL BE'HEILO ENTZYKLOPEDIA LE'TZAVA U'LE'BITACHON (Tel Aviv: Revivim Publishers, 1982), 26.

7. Oded Granot, HEYL HA'MODE'IN: TZAHAL BE'HEILO ENTZYKLOPEDIA LE'TZAVA U'LE'BITACHON (Tel Aviv: Revivim Publishers, 1981), 40.

8. In the back pages of BAMACHANE, as well as in all the major Israeli daily newspapers, "mysterious" advertisements for employment frequently appear; they seek out those about to be released from active duty who are in search of "challenging and sensitive positions for government agencies both at home and abroad." While some of the ads, like those for the National Police Border Guard antiterrorist unit, the YA'MA'M, indicated which service the ad is for, others just indicate a post office box, somewhere in Tel Aviv or Jerusalem, and require the response come from an elite unit veteran—preferably an officer.

9. In their book *Inside the PLO* (William Morrow, 1990), authors Neil C. Livingstone and David Halevy erroneously indicate that the five men chosen by A'MAN to infiltrate into Syria were, in fact, members of the top-secret SAYERET MAT'KAL, a unit formed, according to foreign sources, in 1957—three full years after the incident in Syria. This trend in crediting SAYERET MAT'KAL for *each and every* IDF commando raid is as much fiction as an opportunity to attract publicity when "routine" commando operations are discussed.

10. Sarit Fuchs, "MEIR YA'AKOBI: PETZA PATUACH," MA'ARIV SOF SHAVU'A (November 28, 1986): 8.

11. Talma Admon, "GAD ZOCHER" ("Gad Remembers"), MA'ARIV SOF SHAVU'A (July 6, 1990): 9.

12. See Sarit Fuchs, "MEIR YA'AKOBI: PETZA PATUACH," 10.

13. See Talma Admon, "Gad Remembers," 10.

14. *Ibid.* 10.

15. *Ibid.* 11.

16. See Uri Milstein, HA'HISTORIA SHEL HA'TZANHANIM, 363.

CHAPTER 7

THE SHORT AND BLOODY ROAD TO WAR: 1955-56

N asser's rise to power in the revolution of 1952 catalyzed the possibilities of war between Egypt and Israel. Pan-Arabism, Nasser's glorified
dream for the Arab and Moslem people, could not exist as long as
a Jewish state prevailed in the Middle East, nor could Pan-Arabism gain momentum as a political entity—from the Kurdistan hills in Iraq to the Atlantic coastline in North Africa—as long as Arab pride, at a low ebb following
the 1948 War, was not reinstated. Yet Nasser knew that a full-scale "conventional" conflagration against Israel would result in yet another Arab loss;
the Egyptian army, in particular, had lost a large segment of its officers' cadre
following political purges of the Communists and Moslem Brotherhood from
its ranks after the revolution. As a result, Nasser initiated a bold strategy that
linked his thirst for vengeance with the plight of the Palestinian peoples—
the real losers in 1948. Forgotten, betrayed, and desperate, the Palestinians
would become, with Egyptian and Jordanian military assistance, a vengeful
and violent entity that would make life in Israel unbearable. Guerrilla warfare, after all, was the trademark of military affairs in the postwar world. It
was a strategy designed to seriously weaken Israel and lead to a Pan-Arab
war of Palestinian liberation that would destroy the Jewish entity once and
for all. The war between Israel and the fedayeen ("Men of Sacrifice") had
begun. It is a war that continues to this day.

In spartan facilities in the Sinai Desert and the Gaza Strip, Egyptian Military
Intelligence agents attended to the training of poor and illiterate Palestinian
and Egyptian (mainly Bedouins whose services were rented) males, recruited

out of the squalor and misery of the refugee camps. They were taught the art of sabotage, murder, and subversion. Unlike Israel's Susannah spies in Egypt, the fedayeen were never meant to passively assist deep-cover intelligence agents, nor were they to become fifth-columnists, or even a first-strike offensive element in the event of war. Their sole objective was murder and destruction, which, it was hoped, would lead to the political and moral destabilization of the Israeli political system. In 1952 alone, there were 3,742 illegal border crossings into Israel; these infiltrations resulted in nearly a hundred Israeli deaths.[1] The attacks, however, were not orchestrated by Egyptian authorities, although they assisted the perpetrators. The motive in many of these acts of violence was theft, rape, or looting, and although the Jews of Israel were targeted because they were the hated Zionist enemy, there was no nationalist-inspired organization or backdrop to this activity. Things would change dramatically in 1955.

For IDF Southern Command, which was responsible for protecting the Gaza frontier and Sinai border, as well as the southern stretch of territory shared by Jordan and Israel, this threat presented an impossible predicament. Settling southern Israel with new immigrants was a high Israeli national priority, but it was a most difficult objective to accomplish when daily acts of murder and mayhem created an aura of insecurity and fear. The kibbutzim of the Negev Desert—agricultural masterpieces where the desert was made to bloom—were forced, as a result of the infiltrators, to become armed camps; work in the field was attended to with both a plowshare and a Czech Mauser rifle. This situation was exacerbated by increased infiltrations from the Jordanian frontier, which, because of its mountainous terrain, was harder to defend and secure. It was not a military threat that could be terminated through air strikes, or by a singularly destructive retaliatory raid; Gaza and the West Bank had been targeted on countless occasions by Arik Sharon's Unit 101 and, later, by the 202d Paratroop Brigade. A more selective target had to be found. It would have to be a target whose destruction would limit, if not destroy, the fedayeen's ability to mount operations. That target was Lt. Col. Mustafa Hafaz.

The Egyptian military in the 1950s was a force constructed on political nepotism, and it was a breeding ground for Young Turk movements.[2] The intelligentsia of Egypt tended to shy away from military service; officers were chosen primarily for their political loyalty at first to the reign of King Farouk, and then to President Nasser. One man whose integrity and skill were not compromised by these privileges was Lt. Col. Mustafa Hafaz, a Military Intelligence officer who, when assigned the "Palestinian Desk" in 1949, was the first Egyptian military officer authorized to run large-scale espionage rings against Israel's southern frontier. It was a task that achieved substantial success, in spite of denials by the Israeli officers of the time! Mustafa Hafaz was a rarity in the Idarat Muchabarat al-Askariya ("Egyptian Army Intelligence") in that he was a firm believer in egalitarian ideals. He cared little for the trappings of rank and privilege, and cared for his men's welfare and happiness in much the same manner as his Israeli counterparts had learned to do in the IDF Officers' Course. He disdained his comrades who obtained postings through class or political payoff; his disinterest in Egyptian politics made him an enemy of the zealous junior officers who blindly followed Nasser, and a favorite of senior commanders in Cairo who knew he posed no threat to the regime. Hafaz's loyalty was to the Arab cause—nothing else. Most dangerous for Israel, he had one of the most brilliant analytical minds found in the Egyptian military—and it would be used solely against the Jewish state.

Mustafa Hafaz's personality was especially unique for an officer serving in an Arab intelligence entity. Even though—in Egypt and many other Arab nations—Military Intelligence was responsible for collecting military information beyond the nation's borders, the internal security services, responsible for safeguarding the *regime*, would usurp its power and meddle in all facets of intelligence work, including those directly under Military Intelligence jurisdiction. This was tolerated by regimes that viewed the internal security service's ambition as proof of loyalty; they used this premise of regime preservation to eventually gain control over many areas of Military Intelligence and become the most dominant element in the nation's intelligence community.[3] When Nasser ascended to power in 1952–53, he had targeted Military Intelligence for a purge.

From the small, heavily guarded "Gaza Bureau" office, Lieutenant Colonel Hafaz directed fedayeen activity with cunning guile and cold-blooded skill. He understood that the Palestinian's weakness was his government's gain, and it was not difficult to find recruits amid the utter desperation of the refugee camps, which his service carefully kept in a deplorable state. Mustafa Hafaz also understood the Israelis; his admiration for the Israeli military refuted the claims of Egyptian propaganda. Unlike many of his counterparts in military HQ in Cairo who were plotting the destruction of the Jewish state in an ennobled jihad ("holy war"), Lieutenant Colonel Hafaz respected the Jews—their strengths as well as weaknesses. Hafaz viewed Israel's poorly fortified frontiers as their soft underbelly, an invitation for armed incursions. His elaborate network of agents inside Israel, and the nomadic Bedouin tribes who could reconnoiter targets with great ease, provided Hafaz with an accurate picture of the strategic workings of the Israeli frontier; as a result, his fedayeen attacks were quite successful and grew bolder.

A most important point for his political bosses in Cairo was the fact that the Palestinian infiltrators were "outraged civilians," *not* Egyptians. This provided Egypt with legal cause of denial to the United Nations observers who inspected the aftermath of fedayeen attacks and—on the other side of the border—the sites of IDF retaliation.* Any activation of paramilitary or irregular forces was a violation of Paragraph 2 of the armistice agreement of February 24, 1949, between Israel and Egypt.[4]

Lieutenant Colonel Hafaz also understood the military tactics of sabotage and attempted a successful two-front assault against Israel. Egyptian fedayeen who crossed into Israel from Gaza would perpetrate their crimes and then cross the frontier into Jordan. At a safe house along the disputed frontier, the fedayeen were met by Lt. Col. Saleh ed-Din Mustafa, the Egyptian military attaché in Amman. For Israel, the uninterrupted travels of heavily armed infiltrators on both the Egyptian and Jordanian frontiers proved to be the casus belli for eventual full-scale military involvement. Hafaz also dispatched increasing numbers of Bedouins—eager to commit acts of murder and robbery—into Israel. Unlike the Palestinians, the illiterate Bedouins proved worthless as intelligence agents but invaluable as perpetrators of heinous acts of barbarism. They murdered civilians in brutal fashion, kidnapped and mutilated Israeli soldiers hitchhiking home on leave, and opened machine-gun fire on a bus traveling near Tel Aviv. On February 25, 1955, following a particularly vicious attack in Rechovot, a town south of Tel Aviv, Israel had clearly reached the point of no return.

The IDF General Staff had tried once before to terminate Mustafa Hafaz's flourishing enterprise. In 1953, a sapper squad from Arik Sharon's Unit 101 had crossed the border into Gaza and demolished the home of Lieutenant Colonel Hafaz. The operation—which proved Egypt's inability to secure its *own* frontier—failed, however, since Hafaz was not at his residence but supervising a mission in the field. Following the murderous attack in Rechovot, the IDF retaliated again, this time using Arik Sharon's paratroopers. The operation, code-named Black Arrow, was the largest retaliatory strike of the period. Bypassing routine targets, such as homes of suspects, the Israelis audaciously

---

*Many Israeli intelligence and security officers believed that UN observers were openly collecting intelligence in Israel and relaying it back to Egyptian Military Intelligence officers. Although emphatically denied by UN officials, this Israeli charge is substantiated in top-secret memos of the time, which implicate UN officers, from such countries as Yugoslavia and India, as agents for the Egyptian Muchabarat. Nevertheless, beyond denials, UN peacekeeping forces continued to support the enemies of Israel, the most blatant examples of which were found in UNIFIL ("United Nations Interim Forces in Lebanon"), a force created in the aftermath of Israel's March 1978 mini-invasion of southern Lebanon, known as Operation Litani. United Nations officers regularly turned a blind eye to Palestinian terrorists utilizing their territory to cross into Israel, and one Nigerian major even smuggled weapons for the PLO into Israel—all under the protection of UN diplomatic cover.

attacked Egyptian military headquarters, as well as a rail station and a heavily guarded water tank. The Israelis killed thirty-six Egyptian soldiers; they lost eight of their own, including a company commander, Maj. Sa'adiah Elkayam. Operation Black Arrow was meant to send a message to Egyptian Military Intelligence that acts of sabotage and murder would no longer be tolerated. It was also the first true step toward war. The Israeli attack, ordered just a few days after Shmuel Azar and Moshe Marzouk were hung in Cairo, was a clear indication of the worsening relations with Egypt, and it was one of the factors behind Nasser's alliance with the Warsaw Pact, and the subsequent signing of the Czech-Egyptian arms agreement.[5] 1955.

An interesting footnote to the Gaza raid was the unique marriage between Arik Sharon's paratroopers and A'MAN officers throughout the IDF chain of command, from battalion level to the General Staff. This relationship was especially successful with the intelligence sections attached to both Central Command and Southern Command, the two bodies whose responsibilities included Egypt and Jordan. Utilizing a strategy that began with the PAL'MACH's "Village Files," Sharon's lieutenants assembled a vast wealth of data on the Jordanian and Egyptian frontiers, including detailed—sometimes even intimate—information on every town, installation, and potential target. A'MAN was particularly helpful in organizing these archives for Sharon, but when their material was lacking, the rambunctious paratrooper commander dispatched his own battalion and, later, brigade, intelligence officer, Gideon Mahanaimi, into unfriendly territory for personal and reliable reconnaissance. Scouts were infiltrated into targeted areas for surveillance, and radiomen set up mobile camouflaged eavesdropping stations in the hills and ravines to monitor the lines of communication. Mechanically questionable Piper Cubs were also employed, with Mahanaimi and the 890th Battalion commander, Maj. Rafael "Raful" Eitan, often flying the photoreconnaissance sorties themselves.[6]

Although the raid in Gaza created much publicity on the prowess of the paratroopers, Operation Black Arrow failed to provide even a short-term solution to the fedayeen problem, and led the IDF General Staff to search elsewhere for a permanent solution. Lieutenant Colonel Hafaz's death warrant had been signed!

Israeli Prime Minister David Ben-Gurion was vehemently against "officially sponsored" intelligence-style assassinations as a matter of course for Israeli national policy. He argued that Israel had to perform at a moral level above that known to the Arabs, and that survival of the Jewish state depended on the morality of its policies. Many in Ben-Gurion's inner circle of political and military advisors, however, had survived Hitler's Europe and wanted to fight the Arabs on equal terms. They believed that survival meant the ends justified the means—especially in a Middle East where "Talmudic" reason would not prevent murder and destruction: It was realpolitik with explosives.

Lieutenant Colonel Hafaz's counterparts in the "shadowy war of the minds," the officers working for A'MAN in the Southern Command, labored at a feverish pace to plan Hafaz's termination.

The man in charge of ending Lieutenant Colonel Hafaz's illustrious career was Colonel R., one of the most brilliant and experienced minds that A'MAN possessed. Although security considerations have kept his identity secret to this day, it is known that Colonel R. began his intelligence career in the HAGANAH's elite PAL'MACH ("Strike Companies"), where he served as an intelligence scout for the legendary 3d Company.[7] Working with Colonel R. was Major S., a graduate of the Scottish University in Jerusalem, whose identity also remains a state secret. In official accounts of this undertaking, however, it is mentioned that he is a Yemenite Jew and was a control officer of the failed Operation Susannah; he, therefore, is *assumed* to be Avraham Dar. Their intelligence office in the IDF Southern Command consisted of twenty officers, all known to one another by code names beginning with the Arabic *Abu* ("father of"). For a number of years they had been under intense pressure from their superiors to follow and monitor the movements of Lieutenant Colonel Hafaz. It was the beginning of A'MAN's war against state-sponsored terrorism.

The director of A'MAN at the time of the fedayeen offensive, Maj. Gen. Yehoshofat "Fatti" Harkabi, faced enormous difficulties in fulfilling his role; he had achieved the posting, after all, following Binyamin Gibli's forced resignation in the wake of Operation Susannah. He had to instill a new pride in the beleaguered entity, as well as make it an effective organization. When news of the signing of the Czech-Egyptian Arms Pact of 1955 reached Israel, it caught everyone in the Israeli intelligence community completely by surprise, especially A'MAN. (Unlike Unit 131's fiasco in Egypt, however, this new revelation was a MOSSAD embarrassment.) This development prompted Harkabi, who was also the commander of the Intelligence Corps, to create two new units.[8] The first unit, called HA'MADOR HA'TECHNI ("Technical Section"), had as its sole task the study of Soviet weaponry—a direct by-product of the Warsaw Pact's embrace of the Arab cause. The second new unit, HA'MADOR HA'BEINLE'UMI ("International Department"), quickly established ties and a working relationship with the military intelligence services of foreign powers—mainly the French and British, and, in following years, a close-knit working relationship with the various intelligence and military agencies in the United States.

A'MAN director Harkabi also enhanced his branch's image and aura of reliability by providing daily intelligence reports to the prime minister and the chief of staff. It became an honored routine, and Ben-Gurion took unabashed advantage of it: He would summon Harkabi to his office during all hours of the day and night—especially at night—to question his intelligence chief's observations.

While he was fastidious in his day-to-day tasks, Harkabi was not a charismatic or particularly decisive individual; he differed greatly from his predecessor, Gibli, whose resolute style would lead him to easily sanction a "hit" operation. An educated and soft-spoken man, Harkabi was considered by many to be one of the most intellectual officers ever to serve A'MAN. Born in Haifa in 1921, Harkabi joined the British army during the Second World War, where he fought with the Jewish Brigade's 2d Battalion. After service in the IDF during the 1948 War, Harkabi joined the Foreign Ministry, where he supervised the department responsible for Asian affairs. He was, in fact, the liaison between the Foreign Ministry and the IDF and in 1949 served as an officer during the armistice talks between Israel, Jordan, and Egypt, in Rhodes. According to one intelligence officer, "Harkabi was a diplomat in khaki drill." [9] The most infamous proof of this was his covert meetings with King Abd'allah across the Jordan River, where a peace accord between the two nations was aggressively sought; hopes were crushed in 1951, however, when the king was assassinated in Jerusalem. [10] Harkabi firmly believed in coexistence with the Arabs, and his agreement with Ben-Gurion concerning the moral implications of deadly force initially endangered the proposed assassination of Hafaz. Almost daily funerals in Israel, however, proved to be the mightiest argument for decisive action.

The force tasked with the implementation of the planned assassination, the intelligence unit assigned to the Southern Command, was as poorly supplied and logistically neglected as any rear unit in the IDF. From its spartan command center in Beersheba, the unit had the enormous responsibility of collecting material on Egypt—Israel's most powerful and largest enemy; yet reliable telephone lines and vehicles were considered prized luxuries. Nevertheless, the men were under intense pressure from Chief of Staff Lt. Gen. Moshe Dayan and A'MAN director Harkabi to emulate the innovative commandos of Unit 101 and bring the war onto the enemy's territory.

In the Southern Command, the principal source of intelligence activity centered on agents—mainly Arabs who would provide tidbits of data for a price. The roaming Bedouins had never allowed the barbed-wire concertina that separated Israel from Egypt to hamper their movements: They crossed the border with virtual ease. It was a situation that proved profitable to both Israeli and Egyptian Military Intelligence services. There was, of course, the danger of double agents, and Lt. Col. Mustafa Hafaz proved extremely capable in running these treacherous souls. A'MAN utilized a system of checks and balances—with other agents inside Egyptian territory—to help them determine the veracity of the spies in their employment. Once a traitor was found, he was not executed or imprisoned; he was used in devious plots to drive the Egyptians frantic. A famous example of one of Hafaz's double agents was Sheikh Mohammed, a Bedouin from the Negev who was discovered to be working for both A'MAN and the Idarat Muchabarat al-Askariya. The commander of the A'MAN Southern Command office, Maj. Ya'akov Nimrodi, played this treasonous spy like a violin. Although most details of this operation remain classified, it is known that the false information channeled through Sheikh Mohammed kept the Egyptian security services busy looking for "invisible" Israeli spies in Cairo while true agents were left untouched.[11]

After mounting an intensive intelligence-gathering effort against the fedayeen in Gaza, utilizing Arab agents trained in Israel to operate communications and photographic equipment, Colonel R.'s intelligence unit came to the conclusion that killing Lieutenant Colonel Hafaz could not be done by a commando type of operation, like the failed Unit 101 attempt three years earlier. Hafaz was heavily guarded, and very cautious. At first, the intelligence officers planned to mail a booby-trapped package to Lieutenant Colonel Hafaz from a post office in Gaza, but the plan was rejected after it was concluded that a Gaza postmark might arouse suspicion. The next plan called for Lieutenant Colonel Hafaz to receive a basket of poisoned fruit from an appreciative officer at Egyptian military HQ, but the risk of mistake, of someone else eating the fruit, was too great; it contradicted the IDF's strict policy of TOHAR HA'NESHEK ("purity of arms"), which forbade killing innocents. In any case, Lieutenant Colonel Hafaz would probably suspect such a gift of having a Tel Aviv return address! Colonel R. knew that they needed a "special" package to deliver the deadly payload. It had to be very important, very tempting, something that could easily get through Hafaz's tight ring of bodyguards, and something that Lieutenant Colonel Hafaz would be sure to handle personally. When news of a double agent inside A'MAN's Southern Command network reached Colonel R., the loose ends came together.

His name was Suleiman Et-Tlalka, and he was a volunteer to the ranks of Israeli Military Intelligence. The twenty-five-year-old Bedouin from Rafah was a ruthless spy known for his cunning personality. He had been recruited and controlled by Lieutenant Colonel Hafaz for quite some time. The Israelis had suspected that Et-Tlalka was both "batting and bowling," but his true identity was confirmed when his Israeli controllers asked him to provide them information regarding a certain Egyptian base in the Gaza Strip that they were interested in attacking. A photoreconnaissance flight ordered the following day revealed that the base garrison had been tripled—a fact that exposed Suleiman Et-Tlalka's true color. Colonel R. understood that manipulating a double agent was tricky, but he saw a way to use him in the termination of Lieutenant Colonel Hafaz. He summoned Et-Tlalka and ordered him to deliver a package of "new code books" to Israel's "master spy" in Gaza, Lutfi El-Achawi, the Gaza's police chief—a man who had never worked for the Israelis. Colonel R. was confident that Et-Tlalka would take the package straight to Lieutenant Colonel Hafaz.

The biggest problem for Colonel R.'s intelligence unit was authorization.

They were careful not to embark on any "independent" operations, especially after Operation Susannah. Initially, Major General Harkabi was skeptical about the double-agent plan; the ramifications of its unsuccessful execution could be yet another damaging scandal for a'MAN. Yet with Colonel R. providing him with the target, the method, and the means, Harkabi was finally convinced. After obtaining a carefully prepared booby-trapped package from the Intelligence Corps Research and Development Department, Colonel R. rushed the device to Southern Command HQ—in such haste that he ordered his *commandeered* driver to run over the motorbike of a military policeman who had foolishly tried to issue the intelligence team's jeep a speeding ticket on the Tel Aviv–Beersheba Highway!

At a safe house near the Egyptian frontier, Colonel R. and his staff cultivated Et-Tlalka's feelings of self-worth by passionately explaining the importance of the delicate assignment he was about to undertake. To make sure that Et-Tlalka's prying nature would not result in the detonation of the intricately constructed bomb, they showed him a notebook with codes in English, then told him they were wrapping it, in a copy of *The Commander and the Man*, by German Field Marshal Gerd Von Rundstedt, in an adjacent room. As the sun set over the Mediterranean on July 11, 1956, Colonel R. and two case officers escorted Et-Tlalka to the border in a nondescript car, passing several armed checkpoints whose sentries had strict instructions not to be overly curious. After a handshake and an *insh* Allah ("God willing"), the double agent headed into the twilight. When Colonel R. looked through high-powered field glasses to follow the movements of his treacherous messenger, he noticed Et-Tlalka heading in the direction of Gaza, not south toward the home of Police Chief El-Achawi.[12]

Suleiman Et-Tlalka reached Lieutenant Colonel Hafaz's headquarters just before midnight and found the Egyptian spy master in friendly conversation with a group of subordinate officers over cups of dirt-colored Bedouin coffee. It had been six years since Hafaz had been assigned to the Palestinian Desk in Egyptian Army Intelligence, and he had just returned from a visit to Cairo, where his commanders had praised his loyalty and impressive operations record.

Initially, the heavily armed sentries outside Hafaz's HQ refused to allow the raggedy-looking Bedouin to see their commander, but after hearing that the man at the gate "claimed" to be holding invaluable intelligence material, Hafaz ordered Et-Tlalka in at once.

At first, Lieutenant Colonel Hafaz refused to believe that chief inspector El-Achawi was an Israeli agent. He had worked side by side with the fedayeen and Egyptian Army Intelligence, and was considered above suspicion—which, of course, would make him an intriguing suspect! As Lieutenant Colonel Hafaz clutched the package, he suddenly recalled that there had indeed been speculation that El-Achawi was dealing with the Israelis in order to protect his hashish-smuggling enterprise. As he opened the parcel with great anticipation, a small note with Arabic scribbles fell to the floor. Then a thunderous blast killed the thirty-four-year-old lieutenant colonel; also dead were Et-Tlalka and Maj. Sha'aban Haridi, Hafaz's deputy and a most capable intelligence officer in his own right. Hafaz was buried with full military honors in his native Alexandria.

On July 13, 1956, in a small and unobtrusive article in the prominent Cairo newspaper *El-Ahram*, the death of Lt. Col. Mustafa Hafaz was announced. Cause of death was attributed to a "Zionist" land mine, which was detonated by his Russian-made jeep in the Gaza Strip. Of course, the article portrayed Lieutenant Colonel Hafaz as "one of the heroes of the Palestine War, who fought hard to liberate her from illegal Zionist occupation." The Israeli press had a different version of the story. The respected daily DAVAR reported that Lieutenant Colonel Hafaz, the head of Egyptian-sponsored Palestinian terror attacks, was murdered by Palestinian refugees who sought revenge for the hundreds of refugees he had sent to their deaths in pointless guerrilla raids against Israel.[13] The article also mentioned that Lieutenant Colonel Hafaz was primarily responsible for the vast amount of Jewish blood spilled by the murderous gangs of Palestinian terrorists dispatched by the Egyptians. As a result of *strict* orders issued by both the Israelis and Egyptians, neither obituary revealed the true account—that Lieutenant Colonel Hafaz was, in fact, assassinated by A'MAN.

On the same day that the booby-trapped copy of Von Rundstedt's *The Commander and the Man* fatally detonated in the hands of Lieutenant Colonel Hafaz, the Egyptian attaché in Jordan, Col. Saleh ed-Din Mustafa, received a small parcel in his "secured" Amman office. Wrapped in coarse brown paper of a type commonly sold in Amman, and adorned with authentic Jordanian postmarks, was another copy of Von Rundstedt's book along with papers that read: "TOP SECRET: Jordanian-Israeli Armistice Committee." Anxious to uncover the secrets now in his possession, Colonel Mustafa quickly removed the remaining wrapping. A furious explosion knocked him to the ground. He was rushed to an Amman hospital with both arms blown off, and he died a week later.[14] Had the Egyptian military communications network been more sophisticated, news of Hafaz's death would have reached Amman, warning Colonel Mustafa of Israeli intentions. But it didn't. In one day Egypt lost two of its most capable soldiers in the war against Israel.

For A'MAN and the State of Israel, the double assassinations proved a remarkable success. The fatal blasts in Gaza and Amman sent a message to the Arab world: Israel would utilize all resources available to her to combat the dire threat that organized terrorism posed to her existence. Fedayeen raids stopped for ten years.

Even though the A'MAN offensive against terrorism—one of its few successful operations in the 1950s—diminished the ability of the fedayeen to perpetrate acts of terrorism inside Israel, Israel was still on a road to war against Egypt. Nasser's growing military power and the increased superpower involvement in the Middle East proved to be the fuel for conflict. British and French aspirations, the last gasp of dying empires, were the spark.

The IDF had realized for some time that military operations in the Sinai Desert, the formidable barrier separating the Egyptian heartland from Israel, would become a necessity in the next inevitable conflict. During the 1948 War, in fact, IDF forces had pushed toward El Arish and points inside the desert, but retreated following the 1949 Armistice Agreement. From the first days of the Intelligence Department to the creation of A'MAN, IDF Military Intelligence had conducted intelligence-collection operations concerning Sinai, but these consisted mainly of photoreconnaissance and occasional shallow-penetration forays. Now, with the threat of war looming, the IDF General Staff needed precise topographical data on Sinai in order to formulate any offensive strategies.

One of the first objectives of any Israeli incursion into the Sinai Desert would be the neutralization of the Egyptian guns at Sharm es-Sheikh—a strategic spot commanding the Straits of Tiran, which joined the Red Sea to the Gulf of Aqaba; the waters were crucial to Israeli shipping heading into the port of Eilat. In April 1950, however, the 12th Arab League Council decreed an embargo against Israel and, more importantly, a passive state of siege against Israeli sea and air traffic. The huge guns eventually positioned at Sharm es-Sheikh provided muscle to the Arab decree; Israeli vessels sailing in international waters to Eilat were constantly attacked by cannon volleys. Indeed, some Israeli vessels—for example, the INS *Bat Galim*—were also seized by Arab naval forces.

Sharm es-Sheikh was, as a result, an important economic as well as a military target. Located at the southern tip of the Sinai Peninsula, hemmed in by a labyrinth of mountains, sand barriers, and wadis, it proved to be a difficult military objective. Since war could break out literally at any moment, the IDF General Staff desperately needed exact and immediate intelligence on routes and geographical landmarks from the Israeli frontier south to Sharm es-Sheikh.

A plan was developed, known as Operation YARKON, the brainchild of Chief of Staff Dayan. It was the IDF's first true integrated operation, incorporating land, sea, and air elements. A squad of reconnaissance infantrymen would be ferried by an IDF/navy vessel to the oasis at Dahab, located midway between the Israeli frontier and Sharm es-Sheikh on the Gulf of Aqaba coast. The force would reconnoiter the passes to determine whether or not an armored and mechanized advance could be performed. The IAF's Intelligence Section had dispatched numerous photoreconnaissance flybys of the roadways, and they had concluded that a path suitable for armored vehicles did, indeed, exist. These were the days before satellite imaging, however, and although aerial photographs could determine the physical aspects of an area, they could not determine with certainty if armored vehicles could traverse the terrain. If a direct armored path to "Sharm" was impossible, then alternatives had to be quickly formulated by the military planners in Tel Aviv.

A'MAN had yet to establish its own rogue force of intelligence gatherers and commandos, so once again, soldiers from other elite units were recruited for this delicate assignment behind enemy lines. Chief of Staff Dayan decided that the team should come from the GIVA'ATI Infantry Brigade. The brigade's commander, Col. Haim Bar-Lev, who eventually became IDF chief of staff, was tasked with selecting six of the brigade's finest soldiers; he sought volunteers throughout the battalions and received five officers and an NCO. The man who would lead the reconnaissance foray was Lt. Col. Asher Levy, the commander of the brigade's 51st Battalion. The force's deputy commander would be Maj. Emanuel "Manno" Shaked, the 51st Battalion's deputy commander and a future chief officer of the IDF's Infantry and Paratroop Forces. Other members of the team were 1st Lt. Aharon Luvliner, a company commander in the 52d Battalion; 1st Lt. Yigal Halmi, the communications officer; 2d Lt. Yoram Lipsky, a platoon commander in the 52d Battalion; and Sgt. Dov Simchoni, a scout in the brigade who was known throughout the IDF.[15]

To survive the unforgiving environs of the Sinai Desert, the six men underwent rigorous physical training, during which their endurance to heat, dehydration, and the elements was monitored by curious military physicians and nervous intelligence officers. The instruction and physical conditioning lasted for nearly four months. Decisions were made as to what each infantryman would carry. Water, the staple of survival in the desert, would take precedence over ammunition. Each man would carry two canteens on his utility belt and an additional five in his rucksack. The reconnaissance unit would need every drop of this precious commodity. They had to cross a formidable amount of territory in a relatively brief period—in an area with a great concentration of Egyptian military units. They would sail for the Sinai coast from the IDF/navy's base at Eilat, on the northern point of the Gulf of Aqaba, to the shoreline oasis at Dahab, where they would land at night. From there, the force would proceed north for approximately seventy kilometers, through mountains with peaks up to twelve hundred meters high, toward another desert oasis at Ein Fortega, where they would be picked up and evacuated in dramatic fashion by six IAF Piper Cubs. The whole operation, with or without contact with enemy forces, was to last no longer than forty-eight hours. No deliberate contact was to be made! The discovery of an IDF intelligence force so far inside Egypt would most certainly lead to a full-scale conflagration.[16]

On the night of June 9, 1955, an IDF/navy vessel, the INS *Eilat*, landed the force of reconnaissance infantrymen on the Dahab coast, after a nearly disastrous encounter with an Egyptian naval vessel. The six men raced ashore in a manner reminiscent of the Allied D-day landings on the Normandy beaches. They had released the safeties on their Czech-produced Mauser rifles, expecting to encounter at least an Egyptian sentry or a Bedouin. None appeared. The force commenced its grueling itinerary, ascending the hard rock cliffs and marching through the deep sand in 125-degree Fahrenheit heat. They quickly finished off their water supplies and were resupplied by aerial drops from the low-flying C-47 Dakotas, which also served as a primitive, though effective, airborne command, control, and communications platform. (It was impossible to keep the water pleasant tasting, since it was stored in tin canisters to survive the impact of the parachute drop, and the metal absorbed the unrelenting desert heat.) Navigating the planned route through the twisting desert hills, they realized they had to complete their mission in the allotted time; otherwise, they might not survive the elements. After learning that a company of Sudanese infantrymen was in pursuit, the team called in their rendezvous with the six Pipers on a mountaintop landing strip. Operation YARKON had been a success: the data was rushed to A'MAN headquarters.

The Egyptian sponsorship of fedayeen activity moved Israel toward war. Intelligence-gathering forays such as Operation YARKON made a conflict feasible, and the signing of the 1955 Czech-Egyptian arms agreement made it inevitable. The strategic alliance between Israel and France, however, was what made the conflict politically viable.

That Israel had succeeded in establishing a close-knit working military relationship with the French (in the 1950s a major superpower) was in itself an anomaly. Israel's small size, her policies of national security at all costs, and her lack of natural resources meant that she was not one of the emerging nations courted by the superpowers. West Germany *had* to maintain an intangible bond with the Jewish state; after all, friendship with the Arab states would be perceived as an extension of the Holocaust. The special relationship between Israel and the United States had yet to be formulated; at this time only the groundwork for a strategic arrangement existed between James Jesus Angleton's Central Intelligence Agency and representatives of the MOSSAD and A'MAN in Israel's Washington Embassy.[17]

The French, however, were more pragmatic about their dealings in the region. Adhering strongly to the Arab phrase "The enemy of my enemy is my friend!" France set as her primary objective the swift defeat of Nasserism. The Suez Canal question and the president of Egypt's support for the Front de Liberation Nationale (FLN), the Algerian National Liberation Front, had been very costly to the French treasury and, in Algeria, to French lives. France found Israel a useful ally in the struggle against the Arabs. Israel was pro-Western, its military was strong, and it was ideally situated as a possible springboard for French interests. The French ambassador to Israel, Pierre Gilbert, viewed the alliance with such seriousness that he was the only diplomat in Tel Aviv who bothered to learn Hebrew. Since Israeli independence, in fact, France had served as a sort of frontier outpost for Israeli intelligence operations; MOSSAD station chief Yitzhak Shamir established particularly close bonds with the French services. France had also seen to it that Israel had the tools of war with which to wage the next conflict; these contacts were nurtured through A'MAN auspices by Col. A. Neshri, the IDF military attaché in Paris, and finalized by A'MAN's deputy director, Col. Yuval Ne'eman.[18] Covert shipments of military supplies reached Israeli harbors and airfields. They included deliveries of AMX-13 main battle tanks, artillery pieces, and, most importantly, combat aircraft (*jets!*), such as the Ouragon and Mystere IVA.

On October 21, 1956, a French Air Force DC-4 Skymaster secretly lifted off from an IAF base in southern Israel with a flight plan to Paris. The aircraft carried a precious cargo of dignitaries, including Israeli Prime Minister Ben-Gurion, IDF Chief of Staff Dayan, Arthur Ben Natan (the ex–Political Department staff officer and a MOSSAD representative in Djibouti), and the managing director of the Defense Ministry, Shimon Peres.[19] They had been invited to France to coordinate the invasion of Egypt and the violent political- and military-sponsored demise of President Nasser, who was a thorn in the backsides of both nations. The meeting was held in a quaint villa in the Parisian suburb of Sèvres, around a shiny oak table, and was chaired by French Prime Minister Guy Mollet. Defense Minister Maurice Bourges-Maunoury, Foreign Minister Christian Pineau, and several other high-ranking military and intelligence officials decorated the room with their combination of military and civilian dress. Also attending the meeting was British Foreign Secretary Selwyn Lloyd and an army of his advisors and confidants.

British and Israeli collusion in formulating invasion plans of an Arab nation was indeed amazing. Israel's relations with the most powerful European superpower, Great Britain, were in a state of, according to one retired Israeli intelligence official, "vengeful tension." The British, happy to be rid of the Palestine question and the resulting high body count, had reverted to its more profitable ties with the Arabs, especially with Jordan and Iraq, assisting them militarily and with intelligence data and support; they did, however, supply the IDF with arms and aircraft, as well. The Israelis, on the other hand, had long regarded the British as conspirators with the Nazis in perpetrating genocide, since they had not allowed more Jews to immigrate. When IDF retaliatory raids against Jordanian towns on the West Bank resulted in heavy Arab casualties, the British had, in fact, threatened Israel with war. The Jewish state actually was targeted through aerial reconnaissance flights, and a full listing of all the IAF's airfields and installations was issued to Royal Air Force squadron leaders for possible attack. The preparations were meticulous. In a document labeled "TOP SECRET—U.K. EYES ONLY" and dated August 2, 1955, the British Ministry of Defense listed fourteen target groupings (airfields, rail lines, rail facilities, roads, headquarters and camps, assembly areas, ammunition and supply stores, fuel facilities, military defenses, electronic installations, electric power installations, waterways, port areas, and amphibious landing sites) for massive aerial bombings.[20] Nevertheless, British hatred for Nasser and a desire to retain ownership of the Suez Canal superceded their hostilities toward the Jews.

The unlikely allies began to plan the assault against Egypt. The first contingency, a seemingly legal one, called for the Israelis to dispatch a merchant vessel into the Suez Canal, knowing only too well that the Egyptians would seize it. This would be the casus belli for massive Israeli military action. France and Britain, arguing that Egypt was violating Israel's maritime rights and the legitimacy of the Suez Canal, would intervene with force.[21] The plan, however, was never agreed to.

In the end, the following arrangements were finalized in the Sèvres Conference. (1) On October 28, 1956, the eve of the proposed assault, the French Air Force would position three antiaircraft batteries around Tel Aviv and Haifa; two fighter squadrons of F-84 Thunderstreaks and Mystere IVAs would be stationed at IAF bases and take an active role in Israel's air defense. (2) Israel would commence the hostilities on October 29, and race toward the canal. France and Britain would then issue a twelve-hour ultimatum, demanding that both Israel and Egypt withdraw 120 kilometers from the canal zone. (3) If Egypt refused to remove its forces from the canal, it would find itself in a state of war with both Britain and France; the first objective would be the destruction of the Egyptian Air Force. (4) No matter what the final conclusion of the military undertaking, Israel would receive a guarantee that the Straits of Tiran would no longer be blocked to Israeli shipping, and the Gaza Strip would cease to be a base for fedayeen operations against Israel.[22]

French military cooperation with Israel was so strong, in fact, that Major General Harkabi was even allowed to open an Intelligence Branch representative office in the French capital; this, of course, crossed the veiled boundary of Isser Harel's MOSSAD and SHIN BET and angered the wily spy master. His complaints to Ben-Gurion went unanswered. Israel would be at war in less than a week.

The 1956 Sinai Campaign, or Operation KADESH, as it became known in the IDF's vernacular, was Israel's second war in eight years. It was one of the oddest military campaigns the Jewish state has ever fought, and the first and only war that Israel has waged in accordance with an Allied military effort. Unlike the other conflicts that have engulfed Israel, the 1956 campaign is considered a primitive effort fought *without* the sweeping intelligence warfare that characterized later conflicts. It was, nevertheless, a war whose success was dependent on surprise and security—and it was an impressive campaign by the soldier spies of A'MAN.

In a matter of hours following the final and seemingly faultless planning at the Sèvres Conference, A'MAN officers coordinated a swift and convincing effort to make it appear that war with Jordan, not Egypt, was imminent. The rumor mill, always a bustling commodity (or liability) in a military environment, was squeezed for all it was worth. Senior officials, always anonymous, quoted tidbits of tantalizing information on Arab military intentions and definitive Israeli responses; "well-placed" rumors that Iraqi units were about to enter Jordan for a "final assault" on the Jewish state were also filtered to the headline-hungry press. The fact that a joint Arab military front against Israel had been formed, consisting of Egypt, Syria, and Saudi Arabia, and commanded by Egyptian Defense Minister Abdel Hakim A'mer, heightened the possibility of war—full-scale regional conflict. Politicians in Washington and Moscow were extremely nervous.

Israel Defense Forces units were moved to the Jordanian frontier, very close to the watchful eyes of Jordanian military officials and United Nations observers. Units from the National Police Border Guards, the MISHMAR HA'GVUL, were dispatched to border villages to maintain curfews and security operations in the "likely" event of war.[23] Israel Defense Forces soldiers positioned along the frontier were equipped for full-scale combat; even reservist units, middle-aged men toting rifles and heavy rucksacks, were brought to the front lines. When the MILU'IM ("Reservists") were called up, it was a clear sign of impending war. On October 28, the reservists were, in fact, mobilized in Israel, only strengthening the belief that Israel was preparing an assault on Jordan. Leaves were canceled, a security cover was placed on most IDF installations, and emergency stores of supplies and ammunition were readied. The Israeli deception was so successful that United States President Dwight David Eisenhower cabled Prime Minister Ben-Gurion expressing his concern regarding the mobilization of Israel's reserves. According to authors Yossi Melman and Dan Raviv, these false signals were enhanced by the CIA and James Angeleton, who many considered Israel's representatives in the United States. Israel's false-information campaign was so believable that on October 29, 1956, less than twenty-four hours before war erupted, the Iraqis placed a division on full alert at Habbaniya (also known by its British designation H-3) for possible movement into Jordan should Israel attack.[24]

The Egyptian army firmly believed that war would not involve them directly. Surprise would be total and devastating.

The fact that A'MAN was able to play such a skillful and devious game with Jordan reflected on a philosophy of operations that, in the years to follow, would become a focal point of international awe. Unlike other military forces that rotate their personnel to different positions throughout their careers as serving officers, the IDF and A'MAN, in particular, preferred the use of MUMCHIM ("experts") in sensitive positions; these were officers who sacrificed their potential futures as senior commanders to dedicate their talents and skills to one particular role. For example, the commander of the Jordanian Desk at the time was the fascinating Lt. Col. Ze'ev "Biber" Bar-Lavi a man renowned for knowing more about the Jordanian military than King Hussein. For years he accumulated a wealth of information from radio intercepts, intense research, and human intelligence sources and interviews, and developed an intimate knowledge of the kingdom and the day-to-day operations of its military and security services.* Similar MUMCHIM existed throughout the IDF territorial commands and in A'MAN HQ, men who knew the neighboring Arab nations as well as someone who had lived in either Syria, Lebanon, or Jordan for his entire life.

During A'MAN's massive effort to convince Jordan that she was about to be attacked, the IAF mounted an intensive photoreconnaissance campaign over the sands of Sinai. Mosquito PR-16s flew countless reconnaissance sorties over strategic points in the desert, mapping out and pinpointing strategic targets and monitoring last-minute Egyptian troop movements. This intelligence-gathering effort was an integral facet of Israel's opening salvo of the war: the parachute assault on the ultrastrategic Mitla Pass.

The IDF plan for the conquest of the Sinai Desert, and providing a reason for British and French military involvement, centered around the capture of a strategic gauntlet in the middle of the desert mountains: the Mitla Pass. Whoever controlled the pass controlled the route to the canal, so its capture was essential. A vanguard of armor and mechanized infantry forces would burst across the frontier from southern Israel, and the planned timetable made it imperative that they proceed toward the canal unhindered. The para-drop into the pass, the first and last full-scale parachute assault attempted

---

*According to a story in Oded Granot's volume to the TZAHAL BE'HEILO IDF Encyclopedia series, Lt. Col. "Biber" Bar-Lavi, in the days just prior to Operation KADESH, convened a staff meeting in A'MAN's Research Department. When a colleague asked "Biber" why he seemed so troubled, the lieutenant colonel responded, "The Jordanians have been searching for a missing case of ammunition for several months and *I don't have the heart to tell them where it is!*"

by the Israel Defense Forces, was the prize of Maj. Rafael "Raful" Eitan's 890th Paratroop Battalion, part of the 202d Brigade commanded by Col. "Arik" Sharon. Being tasked with Mitla's capture was a reward for the battalion's brilliant execution of retaliatory strikes against the fedayeen. The jump was going to be either their finest or most disastrous hour. Accurate intelligence would be the deciding factor.

The original plan for the capture of the Mitla Pass, as conceived by the OC Operations Branch, Maj. Gen. Meir Amit (a future commander of both A'MAN and the MOSSAD), called for the 890th Battalion to be dropped into the western approach of the pass—the easiest location from which to defend against a determined counterattack. On October 6, however, a photoreconnaissance sortie revealed the existence of sixteen shacks similar to the type used by the Egyptian garrison; on another reconnaissance flight flown on October 28, the photographs showed an additional twenty-three tents around the Mitla Pass. The discoveries resulted in intense debate among the minds in A'MAN's Egyptian Desk. Several officers argued that the installations indicated a major Egyptian military presence, and the prevailing conclusion—which was passed on to the Operations Branch—was that a new landing zone (LZ) for the 890th Battalion had to be found. That LZ was the Parker Memorial, a local and nondescript landmark near the approach to the Mitla Pass.

The military predicament that Raful's paratroopers might encounter was important for another reason. The landing of parachutists into the Mitla Pass, coined Operation Press, would be the opening move in the invasion of Egypt and a point of no return. Should anything go wrong at the last minute, the red-beret jumpers of the TZANHANIM would be isolated deep behind enemy lines with little firepower. Per the terms of the Sèvres Conference, the paratroopers at Mitla would be vulnerable to Egyptian air attack for thirty-six hours—until British and French warplanes pounded Nasser's air force into oblivion; to avoid being labeled the aggressor, Israel could not destroy Egypt's air power in a preemptive move.[25] A'MAN's analysis and the operations of the brigade intelligence officers were crucial to the survival of the battalion.

In the early-morning hours of October 29, 1956, the IDF's D day, the IAF Intelligence Section commander, Maj. Moshe Meller, ordered Mosquito PR-16s to fly by airfields in Sinai and along the Suez Canal to see if the Egyptian Air Force was on alert; the fear was that one of the European partners had leaked some face-saving information to the Egyptians. The flights also buzzed the Mitla Pass and determined that the tents and huts did not belong to the Egyptian military, but were the hastily set up living quarters of civilian engineers working on roadway construction. The photographs indicating this new development were clear and irrefutable. They were rushed from the Mosquito's home base at Hatzor Air Base to the Ekron Air Base, home to the C-47 Dakota squadron that would ferry the 890th Battalion to battle.

At 1330, as the paratroopers stood at attention in their combat fatigues and parachute harnesses for the departure inspection, Raful was asked if he wanted a last-minute change in the battalion's LZ due to the new intelligence data acquired regarding the Mitla Pass; the new revelation indicated a severe operational-stage intelligence failure. The answer was an immediate and resounding NO! Raful, a careful and courageous officer, argued that his commanders had prepared for a landing on the eastern approach to the pass and a new LZ would provide an inoperable working environment. New intelligence or not, Operation Press would go on as planned.

At 1400, a flight of P-51 Mustangs took off from the Ekron Air Base for the preemptive portion of the Mitla landings. Flying at low altitudes, sometimes just fifty feet above the desert sands, the Mustangs' propellers sliced through telephone cable lines and, in effect, cut off Egyptian forces in Sinai from their commanders in the mainland. It was a bold move, but one that the planners in the Operations Branch and A'MAN knew was crucial to the success of the operation.[26] One hour later, sixteen C-47s,* each carrying twenty-five paratroopers and their gear, lifted off from Ekron; they were protected by flights of subsonic Mysteres. Two hours later, Raful peered through his field glasses toward the Mitla Pass while his men prepared defensive positions and aimed the sights of their Uzi submachine guns for any possible target. Operation KADESH was underway.

For Israel, the war lasted eight days. The paratroopers in the Mitla Pass fought a brutal battle with a determined force of Egyptian infantrymen, which resulted in extremely heavy casualties. Its inevitable aftermath was bitter controversy inside the psyche of the IDF.

The eight days of combat was the IDF's first true performance as a *modern* fighting machine, one relying on "nearly" state-of-the-art equipment, such as the AMX-13 and "Super-Sherman" tanks, and Mystere and Ouragon jet fighters. The fighting illustrated the IDF's ability to operate with a fair degree of sophistication—the parachute drop in Mitla was proof of that—and coordination between different branches of the service. The Armored Corps' elite 7th Brigade sliced through the Sinai Desert all the way to the Suez Canal at Ras A-Sudr with lightning speed; the 37th Brigade succeeded in capturing Abu Agheila in a brilliant pincer move; and the 27th Brigade took El Arish, the capital of Sinai, and raced along the desert's Mediterranean coast to Kantara. The 1st GOLANI Brigade seized Rafiah while the 9th Mechanized Brigade, utilizing the data compiled during Operation YARKON, raced down the Red Sea coast of the desert peninsula to seize Sharm es-Sheikh and end Nasser's naval

---

*Interestingly enough, the lead Dakota was copiloted by Lt. Yael Finkelstein, a female officer.

blockade. The IAF, utilizing a combination of jet and piston engine aircraft (including the hulking B-17G Flying Fortress) bombed targets throughout the Sinai Desert, while the small IDF/navy fought and won a major sea battle off the coast of Haifa, when the Egyptian Navy flagship, the ENS *Ibrahim El-Awal*, was seized intact. The war cost the IDF 190 dead—a very dear price for such a small army.[27]

The British and French began Operation Musketeer, their participation in the invasion, with an aerial assault on Egyptian Air Force bases. They targeted the Il-28 bombers, in particular, which Israeli Prime Minister Ben-Gurion feared would be used to decimate Tel Aviv, Jerusalem, and Haifa. The Royal Air Force utilized air bases in Cyprus, while the French, when not preoccupied with assisting in Israel's air defense, used IAF bases for the preemptive aerial strikes against Egyptian targets. On November 5, British paratroopers were dropped on Suez and, once the city was neutralized, ground forces landed by sea. The French parachuted forces into Port Fouad and Port Said; they quickly gained control of their portion of territory, encountering minimum resistance. Militarily, the campaign to regain control of the Suez Canal was not much of a contest.

Politically, however, the British, French, and Israeli invasion was a disaster. The Soviets threatened London, Paris, and Jerusalem with missile attacks, while in Washington, President Eisenhower deplored the unprovoked use of force against Egypt. President Nasser remained in power and became the champion of the Arab world; his image was transformed from that of a local leader to an Arab hero, along the lines of Saladin, who had stood fast against overwhelming military pressure. The British and French had suffered their final defeat in a series of postwar challenges to their roles as world powers; their dominating presence in the Middle East would not be felt again. For Israel, its image as an embattled nation was severely damaged by its being labeled an aggressor. Israel did achieve all of its objectives, however. When IDF forces finally pulled out of Sinai in the winter of 1957, they left with Israel's shipping integrity guaranteed through a United Nations Emergency Force (UNEF) charged with keeping the peace in what became, through a Security Council agreement, the demilitarized Sinai Desert. Nasser had, indeed, been *temporarily* contained.

With Egypt no longer an immediate threat to the State of Israel, a situation that would last for only a year or two, A'MAN could focus its energies on more aggressive and enticing projects.

NOTES: CHAPTER SEVEN

1. Edgar O'Ballance, *Arab Guerrilla Power: 1967–72* (London: Faber and Faber, 1974), 18.
2. Eliezer Be'eri, *Army Officers in Arab Politics and Society* (Jerusalem: Israel Universities Press, 1969), 217.
3. Ya'akov Caroz, *The Arab Secret Services* (London: Corgi Books, Transworld Publishers Ltd., 1978), 62.
4. *Ibid.* 67.
5. Danni Sadeh, "HA'PLISHA LE'A'ZA," YEDIOT AHARONOT (February 27, 1989): 7.
6. Oded Granot, HEYL HA'MODE'IN: TZAHAL BE'HEILO ENTZYKLOPEDIA LE'TZAVA ULE'BITACHON (Tel Aviv: Revivim Publishers, 1981), 49.
7. Yosef Argaman, "KACH CHUSAL MUSTAFAH HAFAZ," BAMACHANE (November 4, 1987): 40.
8. See Oded Granot, HEYL HA'MODE'IN, 46.
9. Interview with former Israeli intelligence officer, Haifa, May 22, 1990.
10. Avi Shlaim, *The Politics of Partition: King Abdullah, the Zionists and Palestine 1921–51* (New York: Columbia University Press, 1989), 293.
11. See Oded Granot, HEYL HA'MODE'IN, 46.
12. See Yosef Argaman, KACH CHUSAL MUSTAFAH HAFAZ, 41.
13. *Ibid.* 37.
14. See Ya'akov Caroz, *The Arab Secret Services*, 64.
15. Col. (Res.) Avraham Eilon, HEYL HA'RAGLIM (GOLANI VE'GIVA'ATI): TZAHAL BE'HEILO ENTZYKLOPEDIA LE'TZAVA ULE'BITACHON (Tel Aviv: Revivim Publishers, 1982), 176.
16. Uri Milstein, HA'HISTORIA SHEL HA'TZANHANIM (Tel Aviv: Schalgi Ltd., Publishing House, 1985), 463.
17. Yossi Melman and Dan Raviv, *The Imperfect Spies: The History of Israeli Intelligence* (London: Sidgwick and Jackson, 1989), 77.
18. Maj. Yitzhak Steigman, TOLDOT HEYL HA'AVIR ME'ATZMAUT LE'KADESH 1949–1956 (Tel Aviv: The Air Force History Branch, Ministry of Defense Publications, 1990), 168.
19. *Ibid.* 358.
20. Col. (Res.) Professor Yuval Ne'eman, "KESHER I'M HA'TZARFATIM VE'HA'BRITIM BE'MA'ARECHET SINAI," MA'ARACHOT, No. 306–307 (December 1986–January 1987): 29.
21. *Ibid.* 32.
22. *Ibid.* 33.
23. On October 29, 1956, the day the war began, Border Guards securing the border village of Kfar Kassem, located in the "Triangle," killed forty-nine

civilians and wounded thirteen more. The tragic massacre illustrated how dangerous and costly such a campaign of misinformation could be.

24. See Oded Granot, HEYL HA'MODE'IN, 55.

25. See Maj. Yitzhak Steigman, TOLDOT HEYL HA'AVIR, 196.

26. *Ibid.* 198.

27. Yechi'am Fadan, ed. "BITACHON YISRAEL: 40 SHANA LU'ACH IRU'IM," SKIRAT HODSHIT, Vol. 35, No. 3–4 (April 25, 1988): 52.

CHAPTER 8

A Special Unit: Modernizing A'man

As A'man looked past its performance in the 1956 Sinai War and prepared
for a third decade of operations, several acute deficiencies needed
to be addressed. First and foremost, A'man's ability to provide *accurate* information to the prime minister, defense minister, and chief of staff
concerning the military developments of neighboring Arab states had to be
enhanced and refined. Soviet influence in the Egyptian and Syrian militaries
had become pronounced, and placed the IDF in an inferior strategic position;
also, the creation of the much feared, though short-lived, United Arab Republic in February 1958, uniting Syria and Egypt, weakened Israel's quantitative pursuit of military parity, although Israel always believed that it maintained
a qualitative edge over the Arab military forces. There were additional developments in the Middle Eastern balance of power, like the appearance of
ex-Nazi scientists working for Nasser on a ballistic missile program, which
troubled A'man analysts greatly.

On the international scene, A'man was making impressive strides in establishing ties with the few friendly powers who would *overtly* associate
themselves militarily with Israel; covert ties were, of course, forged with just
about everyone else. A'man, under the direction of Prime Minister/Defense
Minister David Ben-Gurion, had engaged in extensive intelligence-gathering
operations in North Africa and parts of Asia since the early 1950s. The contrived "outflank" strategy tried to contain Israel's principal enemies by arranging alliances and operating understandings with such nations as Ethiopia (which bordered Egypt and Sudan), Turkey (which touched both Syria

141

and Lebanon), and Iran (which overshadowed both Jordan and Iraq). Since the North African nations (Morocco, Algeria, and Libya) were either colonies or monarchies, they provided A'MAN and the MOSSAD with convenient ties in what otherwise was a hostile region.[1]

Closer to home, there was still the problem of monitoring enemy frontiers and planning those "special operations" that helped make Israel's numeric inferiority less of a liability. The cases of the ill-fated eavesdropping device planted on the Golan Heights by the joint paratrooper/GOLANI task force in 1954 and of Operation YARKON in 1955 illustrated how conventional military intelligence–gathering operations *behind* enemy lines had to be executed by non-A'MAN and Intelligence Corps personnel. Although these units were certainly combat ready and highly capable, their training did not facilitate constant intelligence work, nor did the security-conscious officers in the Field Security Section of IDF Military Intelligence trust the average infantryman, paratrooper, or tank soldier enough to dispatch him on top-secret operations. Indeed, with the worst-case scenario of Meir Ya'akobi's ill-fated squad fresh in everyone's memory, the requirement of a special type of fighter capable of special tasks in a most dangerous and dire environment seemed immediate, though unaddressed. The IDF/navy did possess what it considered to be an elite force in its HA'KOMMANDO HA'YAMI ("Naval Commandos"), which specialized in seaborne operations and underwater sabotage, but the commandos had little experience in ground operations—not enough to serve as the *sole* commando/intelligence element of A'MAN. There had been serious talk in IDF/navy command about handing the HA'KOMMANDO HA'YAMI over to the Ministry of Defense as a rogue force of underwater warriors and intelligence agents, separate from the IDF command structure and subordinate only to A'MAN and the MOSSAD.[2] These plans were discussed in the General Staff and in the hallways of the KIRYA in 1954—until the "dirty business" turned the innovative minds of the Israeli defense community to a more conservative bent.

The idea of a special commando force capable of meeting many of Israel's unique intelligence needs had been, after all, the calling card of the PAL'MACH and its Arab Platoon. In 1953, Unit 101 inherited this short-lived exclusivity. Between the dismantling of Arik Sharon's maverick squad of retaliatory warriors and the 1956 Sinai Campaign, a revolution took place in the security thinking of Israel's leaders that led to the eventual resurrection of such a force. The rise of the fedayeen had convinced even the most faithful optimists that a period of peace would not follow conflict, and that the Arabs would initiate bloody and incessant wars of attrition against the Jewish state. There would be no peace treaties, no cross-border commerce and travel; a status quo of hostilities, casualties, and turmoil would, it appeared, forever haunt the State of Israel. Retaliatory strikes, such as the weekly attacks against Egypt and Jordan that had preceded Operation KADESH, were not the answer;

the Arabs had learned defensive measures against these rather primitive, though courageously mounted, operations. Israel Defense Forces casualties, in fact, had gone from costly to unbearable. New tactics had to be formulated, with new weapons and with a new, intelligence-gathering focus.[3]

Prior to the 1956 War, Chief of Staff Dayan gave permission to Paratroop Brigade commander Sharon and his reconnaissance genius Meir Har-Zion to form an elite unit from the brigade's *best* battalion for special tasks inside and beyond the Israeli frontiers. The force was to be called on to execute delicate operations that no other IDF entity could be trusted to perform. The prospect of such a force excited many in A'MAN headquarters who believed it would be a great benefit in their day-to-day labors. The plans were temporarily halted in 1956, however, when Meir Har-Zion was critically wounded while commanding a raid against the Jordanian police fort at A-Rahawa on September 11, 1956, in what was known as Operation Jonathan. In the raid, twenty-nine Jordanian soldiers were killed and Har-Zion was the lone Israeli casualty. He was saved during a dramatic battlefield surgery, but the bullet that ripped through Meir Har-Zion's neck greatly reduced his physical abilities, and ended the brilliant military career of a man who Moshe Dayan had said was "the greatest Jewish warrior since Bar-Kochba fought the Romans."[4]

The desire to create a top-secret intelligence-gathering entity was rekindled following Operation KADESH when a large-scale paratroop assault was successfully executed in the Mitla Pass. If such a feat could be achieved in large numbers in combat, then certainly, it was argued in A'MAN HQ, it could be refined and perfected on a small scale during the gray periods of peace that followed Israel's wars. The reiteration of this notion came with the Israeli Air Force's acquisition of a small helicopter fleet, consisting of French Hellers and, most importantly, the Sikorsky S-55 in 1956 and the Sikorsky S-58 in early 1958.

In 1957, Har-Zion's unit was finally sanctioned. Its combat doctrine would rely on the belief that "It is worthwhile to fight and die for accurate data and intelligence. Forewarned intelligence was not a bonus or a candied dessert, but a dire prerequisite for Israeli survival that had a dear price."[5]

The true founding father of this ultrasecretive force—which, according to foreign reports and simple deduction, was called SAYERET MAT'KAL ("General Staff Reconnaissance Unit")*—was Maj. Avraham (Harling) Arnan. After his death from a prolonged illness in 1980, he was called "an anonymous force behind the security and preservation of the State of Israel." Born in 1931, in Jerusalem, Arnan volunteered for the PAL'MACH at the age of seventeen and

---

*Several press accounts have even gone so far as to give SAYERET MAT'KAL the numeric designation of Unit 269.

fought with the HAREL Brigade in the bitter close-quarter battles for Jerusalem in the 1948 War. His secretive nature made him a natural for intelligence work, and he was recruited by A'MAN, where he commanded a clandestine unit that employed SHTINKERIM (loose Hebrew slang for "informants") to obtain and verify intelligence information. Working with informants—Arabs who sold state secrets for a hefty profit—convinced Arnan that *waiting* for intelligence to arrive and relying on dishonest individuals were not acceptable ways for the State of Israel to formulate its defensive posture. Involvement in this dirtiest end of the intelligence business led the innovative A'MAN officer to conceive new methods of *active* intelligence-gathering, by which the nation's best and most capable soldiers would be sent into enemy territory to bring back the desired data under any circumstances—without excuse of danger or damaging political implications. His vision would eventually become a force of "on-call spies" who relied on lightning speed, firepower, and cold-blooded courage.

Initially, Arnan's quest to form his own elite unit was seen as a nuisance by some members of the IDF General Staff who were unimpressed with promises of spectacular feats and decisive operations. They nevertheless decided to humor Major Arnan, allowing him the funding and rubber stamps needed to create his force. Their main objective in giving in to Arnan was to keep him in the desolate training environs of the Negev Desert and *far* away from IDF HQ in Tel Aviv.

The original personnel who helped bring the unit from the pages of top-secret A'MAN memos to fruition came primarily from Unit 101's boisterous veterans. They were adventurous souls who, although assimilated back into the IDF, had never found their niche in the large and suffocating confines of battalion- and brigade-sized formations. They were, indeed, mavericks—men who thrived on being a cut above everyone else, and who performed above and beyond the call of duty as long as the duty was on their terms. With proper leadership, they were capable of just about anything; the man to bring out the best in them was, of course, Meir Har-Zion.

Recalled from the hospital with a severe disability, Har-Zion joined Arnan and helped create one of the most important and remarkable military entities ever to serve the State of Israel. Even with his limp and subdued physical presence, Har-Zion was still a supreme soldier; he marched faster and farther than the most physically fit soldier in the unit, and pushed himself and, as a result, his men beyond the scope of human endurance. Whereas a fifty-kilometer forced march in the desert sun without the "luxury" of water might seem to be harsh training, a hundred kilometers inside enemy territory could be a realistic scenario and one to which the fighters had to become accustomed. They were, in fact, taught to routinely do what had never been done before. Arnan saw to it that his fighters received the most modern, even nonissue, weapons available on the market, and Har-Zion saw to it that they knew how to use them with deadly accuracy. It was, nevertheless, a small unit; it was said that the entire force could fit into the cargo area of a Land-Rover.[6]

As a result of the miniscule size and untested status of this new unit, very few senior officers in the IDF General Staff took the unit seriously. The IDF chief of staff, Lt. Gen. Haim Laskov, had to be bullied into giving his final authorization for the unit's creation, and at many junctures Arnan's reconnaissance force was threatened with bureaucratic termination.

At first, Arnan tried an obvious Byzantine tactic to guarantee the survival of his unit: *bribery!* Employing "spies" to discover what the chief of staff fancied, Arnan sent Laskov a *shabariyah*, a gigantic curved Arabian scimitar emblazoned with gold and jewels, as a Chanukah present. When this childish gesture failed, Arnan tried once and for all to convince the chief of staff that they were, indeed, a special force.

To achieve this ambitious objective, Arnan conceived a most devious and sadistic plan. One of the unit's original soldiers, Eli Gil, who was also known by his nom de guerre "Da'ud" ("David" in Arabic), was dressed as an Arab by Arnan and dispatched on foot to the northern frontier with a bag full of IDF documents stamped SODI BE'YOTER ("top secret"). Only Arnan, Laskov, Da'ud, and the commander of the Israeli National Police knew of the undertaking. For days Da'ud roamed the border with Syria until he was finally arrested by a heavily armed Israeli Border Guard squad; they subsequently beat him mercilessly in impromptu interrogation sessions. Da'ud's ordeal continued for two weeks. He did not break. The battered fighter was released. Arnan received his unit with a contemptuous "I told you so" to the chief of staff.[7]

Even before Arnan's elite unit began to flourish and expand, A'MAN was learning the value of special forces intelligence-gathering operations. On July 9, 1958, a small force of IDF/navy naval commandos conducted a top-secret intelligence-gathering mission into Beirut harbor.[8] A'MAN and the small IDF/navy Intelligence Section had for years neglected—through lack of reliable sources and limited funding—active intelligence-gathering operations against enemy shore installations and shipping targets. The seizure of the *Ibrahim El-Awal* off the coast of Haifa during the 1956 War reinstated interest in naval theater operations. The intelligence data required for possible offensive naval action against a Mediterranean facility, however, was not the type that a deep-cover espionage agent could readily provide. Although an agent could inform his controllers of enemy shore defenses, shipping patterns, and the number and identification of vessels in a harbor, the underwater topography could be discovered only through personal contact; the depth of the water, stability of the harboring facilities, and possible escape landmarks had to be determined personally by the attack force.

Skepticism followed the "Navy's Batmen" (their nickname was a result of their bat-winged unit insignia) much as it surrounded Avraham Arnan's

General Staff reconnaissance unit. Although they had performed with great skill and dedication during the 1948 War, the naval commandos were a small and neglected entity; at their home base on the Mediterranean coast, they conducted their day-to-day operations anonymously in the shadow of the IDF/navy. Many ex-PAL'MACH officers filled the HA'KOMMANDO HA'YAMI's ranks, and the force garnered a reputation for daring lone-wolf operations.

The 1958 mission into Beirut harbor was meant to lay the groundwork for a possible naval attack against Lebanese shipping should another full-scale conflagration erupt. The foray came at a time when Lebanon was in its first spasms of internal violence and bloodshed; factional fighting between the ruling Christians, under President Camille Chamoun, and Druze leader Kamal Jumblatt had engulfed the nation in violent turmoil. As a result, the raiding party, ferried to Beirut by an IDF/navy torpedo boat staffed by a select crew, consisted of the naval commandos' top people, including Ze'ev Almog, a future commander of the IDF/navy, and several expert sabotage and demolitions officers.

Navigation to Beirut, the Paris of the Middle East, was an effortless exercise, since the neon lights of the casinos and the well-lit avenues illuminated the sky. The underwater reconnaissance mission was attended to with routine ease. The divers, utilizing special and secret equipment, charted the harbor facility and made notations for future reference. The operation went unhindered until an alert Lebanese gendarme, manning a sentry post on shore, spotted a suspicious object floating nearby. Suspecting an Israeli attack, he opened fire. Lebanese patrol boats quickly entered the open seas in pursuit of the Israelis, described in the panic-inspired Lebanese reports as an "entire flotilla"! (One week later a flotilla would, indeed, appear off the Lebanese coast, although it belonged to the United States Navy's Sixth Fleet, which landed five thousand marines onto the Beirut shores to save the Lebanese administration in that nation's first civil war.)

With the obvious exception of the last-minute excitement, the mission in Beirut harbor had been a total success. Chief of Staff Laskov was impressed with the exploits of this unheralded force, and interest in elite units increased significantly. Major Arnan's force, meanwhile, intensified its training regimen.

To expand his small unit, Arnan sought the best minds and bodies serving the IDF. Soldiers did not volunteer into the unit; Arnan personally picked each potential candidate and then volunteered *him* into the force. He went to great lengths to question each candidate—his "interrogation" sessions soon became infamous throughout the IDF—even though the unit did not really exist! According to published accounts, Arnan would arrange a "meet" between himself and a potential recruit in a true spy-movie setting. He would tell the candidate to wear a specific article of clothing and stand in a public place and hold a folded newspaper tucked smartly underneath his arm. Any aberration from Arnan's original instructions resulted in a failing score and a terminated meeting, leaving the candidate standing on a street corner for hours wondering what had, indeed, transpired.

Arnan did not seek robots, nor did he pursue gung-ho men eager to kill; men who wore their hatred for Arabs on their sleeves were also rejected. His recruitment process resembled that belonging to an espionage service rather than a military unit; his people weren't supposed to do it all, but instead fit nicely into the machinery of a cohesive and balanced unit. The first soldiers included the "advisor" Har-Zion, the infamous Micha Kaphusta, and "Jibli the Little"—all Unit 101 veterans. They, in turn, brought friends and comrades who were combat veterans seeking adventure and, most importantly, a challenge. A recommendation from a soldier "already inside" was sufficient to guarantee a preliminary interview with Arnan for possible service with the unit.

Arnan was one of the first senior IDF officers to appreciate the value and integrity of new immigrants from the Arab diaspora. These newcomers to the State of Israel, mainly from Morocco, Yemen, and Iraq, were sent into tent-city ghettos or desolate frontier towns by the political establishment; their young men, upon reaching the age of conscription, were thrown into infantry formations, especially the 1st GOLANI Infantry Brigade, where they were to fight and learn citizenship in a khaki-colored national melting pot. Often disadvantaged and bitter, these men would, through design and self-pity, become an underclass. Arnan, however, realized that these Arabic-speaking soldiers were crucial to Israel's intelligence war. He also understood that these men were proud and tough, and when placed in a family environment would excel beyond all expectations. Later, Arnan was convinced to recruit the "Blondes"— a derogatory term for the European, or Ashkenazi, Jews, especially for the elite socialists from the kibbutzim—although he would send them to Bedouin tribes in the Negev Desert for Arab orientation. It was clear to all involved that once Arnan had approved a soldier for service in the reconnaissance formation, he was released from the IDF proper and had enlisted into a very private army.[9]

Arnan was a true believer in the sacrosanct relationship a nation shared with its military and security forces. This bond depended on a capable, aggressive, and incessant intelligence-gathering campaign. No sacrifice was too great to achieve the upper hand. Arnan's spiritual mentor was the infamous Capt. David Sterling, founder of the British Special Air Service (SAS). Arnan's bible was Sterling's book, *Who Dares Wins*. According to Emanuel Rosen, a respected Israeli military journalist, a "Who Dares Wins" sign decorates the unit's mess to this very day.

Slowly, the secretive reconnaissance force achieved some respect and even assistance. Supporters included the new director of A'MAN, Maj. Gen. Chaim

Herzog,* OC Central Command Maj. Gen. Meir Amit, and Col. David "Dado" Elazar, commander of the IDF's Armored Corps. Arnan and Elazar, a future chief of staff, had been comrades in the PAL'MACH and were close friends; "Dado" supplied him with covert shipments of petrol, rations, vehicles, and, most importantly, one Ehud Barak, who became one of the unit's most important soldiers.

One of Arnan's "Blondes," even though he had dark brown hair, Ehud Brog (the family name prior to it being Hebraized to BARAK, or "lightning") was a product of the hardworking, physically strong idealists who literally transformed the wastelands of Palestine into an agriculturally productive society. Born in Kibbutz Mishmar Hasharon in the Hefer Valley in 1942, Barak grew up amid fighting for independence against the British and struggling for survival against the Arabs. Upon his conscription into the IDF in 1959, Barak, like many *kibbutznikim*, volunteered for the pilots' course, the IAF being the most prestigious branch within the IDF. The IAF's acceptance rate for flight training, however, was stringent, and Barak didn't pass the initial examinations. He was placed in a mechanized infantry formation, the 52d Battalion.[10]

In the battalion, he quickly proved himself to be a superb soldier, an inspiring leader, and a fierce individualist. His disregard for the rules and trappings of rank did not go unnoticed in the close-knit command echelons of the IDF. The young corporal was soon monitored as a potential "volunteer" for Major Arnan's top-secret reconnaissance unit. Arnan had heard about the infantryman from the 52d, and went to Kibbutz Mishmar Hasharon to find out more about this mysterious young man. The kibbutz elders labeled Ehud "a small, lock-picking bastard!"[11] The lock-picking bastard would become not only the unit's most influential soldier, but its heart and soul; the reconnaissance force would develop around the talents and abilities of Ehud Barak.

With a close-knit esprit de corps established around Arnan's cultlike personality, the unit began to mold itself into a capable fighting formation. Most importantly, it became the Intelligence Corps' "operational and professional branch." Major Arnan, in fact, became the "godfather" of the Intelligence Corps— a man who could "take care" of the most unpleasant situations. Any new gadget to enter the IDF's combat vocabulary—such as a folding stock for the Uzi submachine gun or a nylon watch cover to reduce glare during nighttime operations—all originated with Arnan's force of intelligence warfare com-

---

*Harkabi was forced to resign over a bungled mobilization exercise on April 1, 1959. The public was to receive advance warning of the "practice" call-up in order to prevent panic and chaos, but miscommunication between Harkabi, his Field Security command, and the OC Operations Branch led to an announcement of impending doom with no advance warning. Panic and controversy followed, and Ben-Gurion demanded Harkabi's resignation.

mandos. Through their work with Uri Yaron, commander of the IAF's first helicopter squadron, the force refined its own unique methods of infiltration and exfiltration, long-range intelligence-gathering forays, and hard-hitting commando strikes. The helicopter proved to be a tool with limitless application for the reconnaissance unit, enabling them to reach almost any target in the immediate vicinity. Once they reached their target, however, the commandos would be on their own until the whirlybirds picked them up for the quick hop home. Coordination between the intelligence gatherers and their fleet of aerial taxis became critical—one could not survive without the other.

Oddly enough, the importance of an active intelligence-gathering unit was made evident in 1960 during a severe breakdown in A'MAN's ability to prevent an enemy surprise attack with its early-warning capabilities.[12]

On the night of January 31, 1960, the IDF conducted its first large-scale retaliatory raid following the 1956 War. This time, however, the target was not the Gaza Strip or the Hebron hills, but the Golan Heights and the Syrian position at Tewfiq, a deserted town towering above the Sea of Galilee and Kibbutz Tel Katzir. Earlier, in January, Syrian soldiers and artillerymen, disguised as peasants, had infiltrated into the demilitarized zone and initiated a daylong bombardment of the surrounding Israeli agricultural settlements. An Israeli military response was expected, and the raid, code-named Operation Locust, was carried out by a GOLANI Brigade task force. Dozens of Syrians were killed and tension in the area was elevated to a war frenzy.

In a show of Arab solidarity, and to prevent Israel from attacking Syria or diverting the Jordan River's waters, the Egyptians secretly sent a huge military force into the demilitarized Sinai Desert. The moves began on February 18, 1960. Under cover of darkness and in total radio silence, the Egyptians moved their 2d, 5th, and 7th Infantry Brigades and elements of the 4th Armored Division toward the Israeli frontier. Nasser's gambit was a complete success. Not only were the United Nations' observers unaware of the Egyptian moves, but neither were the Israelis! Only on February 23, after a series of intelligence reports reached A'MAN HQ, did Maj. Gen. Chaim Herzog order a newly acquired Sud.Aviasion S0.4050 Vautour IIB aircraft to conduct a photoreconnaissance sortie over the desert peninsula. It was almost too late.

The findings shocked and outraged the Israeli defense community. Not only had the IDF lost track of the Egyptian 4th Armored Division for several hours, but in the end, more than five hundred Egyptian T-54/55 main battle tanks (MBTs) were counted spread out along the Israeli frontier; two additional infantry divisions were also discovered along the Um Katef–El Arish–Rafiah line. The IDF Southern Command had only twenty frontline tanks in position to meet any Egyptian attack.

Immediately, the General Staff ordered the IAF placed on full alert. Combat units, including the GOLANI Infantry Brigade and the elite 7th Armored Brigade, were rushed from the northern frontier to assume defensive positions in the south; a partial mobilization of the reserves was also ordered. War seemed imminent. Two huge armies had gathered in the desert sands to do battle, but common sense prevailed—a war of nerves replaced a war of destruction. The Egyptians withdrew. President Nasser once again reaffirmed his position as leader of the Arab world, while a sigh of relief was sounded in IDF HQ in Tel Aviv.

For A'MAN, Operation Broom, the code name of the mobilization, was a traumatic experience. Intelligence material gathered on Egypt from various reliable sources was ignored, and "expensive" intelligence-gathering activities, such as photoreconnaissance flights, were compromised for budgetary reasons. Bureaucratic differences between the Intelligence and Operations branches complicated a coordinated effort. It has been argued that the situation revealed a lack of A'MAN experience in dealing with a surprise attack.[13] Thirteen years later, A'MAN's inability to deal with the threat of surprise attack would haunt IDF Military Intelligence in an irreversible manner that would make Operation Broom seem inconsequential.

To ensure that enemy movements were never concealed for long from A'MAN eyes, SAYERET MAT'KAL was finally brought into the IDF's operational Order of Battle. On August 1, 1963, the unit was dispatched on its first operational assignment deep into Syrian territory. The mission, commanded by 2d Lt. Ehud Barak—who was fresh out of the officers' course—was assisted by Uri Yarom's helicopter fleet; it was the first time an IAF whirlybird was used in an intelligence operation.[14] Although full details of the mission remain classified to this day, it was a complete success and proved that Major Arnan's unit was A'MAN's cutting edge. Second Lieutenant Barak* received the first of his four TZA'LA'SHIM SHEL HA'RA'MAT'KAL ("Chief of Staff Citations"): a medal issued for a unique act of courage.[15] The unit's intelligence-gathering raid, declassified only in 1990, was the last the public would hear from the secretive force for nearly a decade.

A'MAN-sanctioned intelligence operations against Syria and Egypt, however, intensified in dramatic fashion.

*Lieutenant General Ehud Barak is the IDF's most decorated soldier and, at the time of this book's writing, is the IDF chief of staff.

NOTES: CHAPTER EIGHT

1. Neil C. Livingstone and David Halevy, "Israeli Commandos Terminate PLO Terror Chief," *Soldier of Fortune* (December 1988): 76.

2. Uri Milstein, HA'HISTORIA SHEL HA'TZANHANIM—KERECH DALED (Tel Aviv: Schalgi Ltd., Publishing House, 1987), 1,426.

3. *Ibid.* 1,545.

4. Eilan Kfir, TZANHANIM CHI'R MUTZNACH: TZAHAL BE'HEILO ENTZYKLOPEDIA LE'TZAVA ULE'BITACHON (Tel Aviv: Revivim Publishers, 1981), 31.

5. Emanuel Rosen, "HA'ISH SHE'HIMTZI ET HA'YECHIDA HA'MUVCHERET," MA'ARIV SOF SHAVU'A (September 19, 1990): 42.

6. *Ibid.* 44.

7. *Ibid.* 44.

8. Shlomo Mann and Sheni Payis, "SHLOSHA TZA'LASH'IM MEE'BEIRUT," BEIN GALIM, No. 181 (August 1990): 17.

9. See Emanuel Rosen, "HA'ISH SHE'HIMTZI," 44.

10. There have been differences in several accounts as to whether Ehud Barak was a veteran of the 82d Battalion or the 52d Battalion. The IDF is traditionally closemouthed concerning its forces' numeric designations.

11. Yosef Walter, "MU'AMAD LE'RA'MAT'KAL: YESH BARAK," MA'ARIV SOF SHAVU'A (January 24, 1986): 6.

12. Oded Granot, HEYL HA'MODE'IN: TZAHAL BE'HEILO ENTZYKLOPEDIA LE'TZAVA ULE'BITACHON (Tel Aviv: Revivim Publishers, 1981), 65.

13. *Ibid.* 67.

14. See Uri Milstein, HA'HISTORIA SHEL HA'TZANHANIM, 1,550.

15. See Emanuel Rosen, "HA'ISH SHE'HIMTZI," 44.

CHAPTER 9

THE SUPER SPIES

The 1960s was the most remarkable decade for Israel's intelligence community, especially for A'MAN. It was a period of rapid expansion, both in the threats faced by Israel and in the military might that Israel acquired to meet the new dangers poised along its frontiers. The decade would prove to be a turning point not only for the region, but for the entire world; the reverberating effects of what would transpire in 1967 are *still* felt throughout the globe.

The decade began in both celebrated and tumultuous fashion for Israel's intelligence community. On May 11, 1960, in one of the most remarkable operations ever conducted by a nation's intelligence services, a joint MOSSAD/SHIN BET force kidnapped "Ricardo Klement" as he was walking to his home in a Buenos Aires, Argentina, suburb. Ricardo Klement was, in fact, the notorious Col. Adolph Eichmann, one of the highest officials in the Nazi regime to have escaped Allied justice in the Nuremberg war crimes trials; as logistical architect of the Holocaust, Eichmann was one of the most wanted Nazi war criminals. The Jewish state felt a moral obligation to hunt down these men and bring them to justice. The ability of its intelligence agents to locate the elusive Eichmann, secretly bring him to Israel from underneath the protective noses of his Argentine hosts, and put him on trial was viewed in the world community as an incredible feat. In a riveting trial Eichmann was found guilty and hung, and his ashes were spread across the waters of the Mediterranean.

The SHIN BET also scored several notable achievements at the start of the decade, the most important of which was the arrest of Dr. Kurt Sita, an agent for the Czechoslovakian foreign intelligence service, the S+B. Sita, born to a Gentile family in the Sudetenland, had been a prisoner of the notorious Buchenwald concentration camp simply because his wife was Jewish. He was recruited into Czech intelligence because of his genius in mathematics and physics. Sita had studied in London and then in the United States, where he became a professor of physics at Syracuse University, in New York State. The FBI expelled him on the grounds of being a Communist spy and he sought refuge in Brazil. Oddly enough, he was eventually invited to become a lecturer at Israel's prestigious Technion Institute, situated high atop Mt. Carmel, in Haifa. At the Technion, Sita was in contact with the most advanced scientific minds and data in Israel's possession, including highly sensitive military and nuclear science statistics. His arrest, on June 16, 1960, came two days before Israel's experimental nuclear reactor at Nahal Sorek, near Rechovot, became operational.[1]

In the A'MAN camp, the 1960s was a decade of transitions. The nearly disastrous effects of Operation ROTEM, in early 1961, sent shock waves through the IDF General Staff. Israel, caught by absolute surprise by intensive Egyptian military buildup in Sinai, faced a most dangerous situation where her Military Intelligence service had failed in providing an early warning to the Israel Defense Forces of impending attack. Chaim Herzog, one of the most respected figures in A'MAN history, was quietly coerced to resign. He would, however, be replaced by an equally remarkable figure in the future of Israeli intelligence: Maj. Gen. Meir Amit.

Meir Amit was born in 1921 in Tiberias on the shores of the Sea of Galilee. In 1936 he joined the HAGANAH and served as a NOTER ("mobile settlement policeman"). A talented soldier who was a natural-born commander, he served as a company commander in the HI'SH ("Field Corps") and, during the 1948 War of Israeli Independence, fought against Syrian and Iraqi units in the battles for the Mishmar Ha'emek, the Jezreel Valley, Tzemach, Ein Gev, and Kibbutz Degania. During the fierce close-quarter battle for Jenin, in Jordanian territory, Amit was seriously wounded while leading a charge against a heavily fortified enemy position.[2]

Meir Amit's military past, in fact, was more suited to combat commands than leading an intelligence service. After graduating from New York's Ivy League Columbia University in 1950, he was awarded the command of the 1st GOLANI Infantry Brigade upon his return to Israel; it was a posting where he excelled in his ability to coordinate and lead the men and material in his command into combat. Amit was one of the practitioners of the "follow me!" method of IDF command tactics. His courage and logistics talents were not lost to the IDF General Staff and, in 1951, Amit was appointed head of the Operations Department in the General Staff. In 1954, he became the commander of AGA'M ("Operations Branch") and was instrumental in the planning—both covert and overt—that preceded the 1956 Sinai Campaign. He was, in fact, the IDF's second in command and was Chief of Staff Dayan's aide-de-camp during the Sinai Campaign. The IDF's success was, in many ways, his own, and, in 1958, he was rewarded with the important posting of OC Southern Command, where his abilities, it was hoped, would help rally IDF forces to defeat a new wave of Egyptian espionage and infiltration operations mounted against the southern Israeli frontier. Once again, Meir Amit displayed a courageous and tenacious brand of command and achieved the respect of his troops, and the admiration of his political and military bosses, as well. He seemed destined for the top rung of the Israeli command ladder.

During routine airborne training maneuvers, however, Meir Amit was critically wounded in a parachuting accident and remained in a hospital bed for more than a year. It was a wound, many say, that kept him out of the chief of staff's chair, although it would secure his role in another most important posting: the director of A'MAN.

Major General Meir Amit's ascension to the top position in A'MAN on January 1, 1962, commenced a period of great controversy and conflict within the closed-door ranks of the Israeli defense community. Amit, a soldier's soldier who disdained all pursuits of individual power or political glory, was appalled by the relationship between A'MAN and the remainder of the IDF, which was mainly a result of the "dirty business" in 1954 and Operation ROTEM in 1961. Many in the IDF, from the conscript private to senior staff officers, openly mocked A'MAN's abilities (or inabilities). They were likened to desk-jockey bureaucrats incapable of predicting a war even after it had been fought![3] This disturbed Amit greatly. A man who had spent his entire military career in *combat* service, Amit understood the inseparable bond between combat forces and their intelligence entity: In his mind, successful military operations depended on highly accurate intelligence.

Another flash point in the halls of the KIRYA was friction between the new A'MAN director and the MOSSAD boss, Isser Harel. It was reported that Meir Amit was outraged by Isser Harel's political purges of "undesirable elements" within the Israeli defense community. These included national security–inspired witch hunts against such diverse institutions as left-wing newspapers, black marketeers, and smugglers.[4]

Meir Amit was particularly annoyed by Harel's massive manpower deployment of MOSSAD agents in search of a small boy, Yosef "Yossele" Schumacher. Yossele had been kidnapped by his grandfather—an ultraorthodox fanatic who disdained Zionism—in order to provide the boy with a proper orthodox education. The hapless child was smuggled to New York City, and the case became a top Israeli news story. Harel became obsessed by his quest for the child and, many have argued, dedicated too much effort to this routine abduction case. Although Yossele was eventually found in a religious enclave in Brooklyn, New York, many in A'MAN mocked the MOSSAD for spending time on a campaign against the ultraorthodox Jews while Arab states prepared for full-scale war against Israel. As A'MAN director, Major General Amit firmly believed that *all* of Israel's intelligence-gathering efforts should concentrate on the immediate threat facing the nation: the bordering Arab states of Egypt, Jordan, Syria, and Lebanon. Israel was not in a position to conduct "frivolous" intelligence endeavors that centered around the personal crusades of the MOSSAD chief.[5]

Although the capture of Adolph Eichmann was seen as a national coup, and the "rescue" of little Yossele appeased a nation's curiosity, these preoccupations did, indeed, reduce the amount of foreign intelligence being gathered, disseminated, and analyzed. This gravely reduced A'MAN's capabilities to provide an all-inclusive picture to the prime minister and chief of staff as to ongoing developments. An example of this dangerous scenario was seen on July 21, 1962: Revolution Day in Egypt.

The military celebrations for Egypt's national holiday were mighty and awe-inspiring. On Cairo's Revolution Boulevard, freshly painted rows of Soviet-made T-54/55 main battle tanks, 130mm artillery pieces, and armored car troop carriers were paraded with much pomp and ceremony. Egyptian Air Force MiG-17s flew above the sun-baked plaza, as did flights of Ilyushin Il-28 bombers—the principal long-range weapon in Nasser's arsenal.

Another flight on Revolution Day worried the Israelis greatly. On a desert firing range, the Egyptians test-launched four ballistic missiles: two copies of the el-Zafir ("the Victory") and two copies of the el-Kahir ("the Conquerer"). The firing, which was surrounded with great fanfare, was followed by an impassioned speech by Nasser in which he promised that the missiles would *obliterate* Israel's principal cities. Of course, Egypt was not the sole nation in the region to possess such rockets. On July 6, 1961, Israel had launched an indigenous rocket, the SHAVIT ("Comet"). The el-Zafir's range of 175 miles and the el-Kahir's range of 350 miles were, however, impressive. Nasser's claim that they could hit targets south of Beirut was taken seriously.

The launchings caught both A'MAN and the MOSSAD completely by surprise. The existence of the missiles was discovered through routine news coverage. An infuriated Amit was quoted as saying: "What are we spending our intelligence budget on if we are getting our information from a public speech of Gamal Nasser? If that's the case, all we need is a portable radio!"[6]

Israel had known of Egyptian attempts to produce its own series of surface-to-surface ballistic missiles as far back as 1961. The Egyptians had actively pursued a missile option to the IDF's qualitative superiority by importing materials from Switzerland; several prototypes of missile propulsion systems had, in fact, been tested in a wind tunnel in the Swiss Alps. Yet A'MAN had not predicted that the missiles would become operational—or even in the advanced experimental stages—by 1962. They posed a threat to which Israel had no viable response, and this prompted Prime Minister Ben-Gurion to seek American-produced HAWK surface-to-air missile batteries from President John F. Kennedy.

Another troubling aspect of Egypt's budding missile program, known as the "Bureau of Special Military Programs" and under the control of Army Intelligence, was the fact that the minds behind the Egyptian warheads were ex-Nazi scientists recruited by Nasser. The Israeli intelligence and security services had kept tabs on the large number of German scientists, especially since many of those newcomers to the land of the pyramids were ex-SS officers guilty of war crimes; these included Leopold Glim, Gestapo commander in Warsaw, and SS Gen. Oscar Dirlewanger, one of the founders of the notorious Mauthausen concentration camp.[7] The Germans had established a thriving colony in Egypt and would develop a prosperous technological and industrial colony for the production of President Nasser's weapons of mass destruction, as well as indigenous Egyptian fighter and bomber aircraft. Nazi scientists working toward the destruction of the Jewish state evoked harsh and bitter memories of the Holocaust. Isser Harel was determined to thwart the Egyptian effort at all costs; it would become another one of Harel's personal crusades. The Egyptians, with German assistance, had also stockpiled a substantial arsenal of chemical weapons, which they threatened to use against Israel; they would, in fact, deploy these weapons against Yemeni royalists during the bitter campaign in 1963. The possibility of German-designed missiles delivering chemical warheads to the streets of Israel was an Armageddon scenario for the Jewish people. (It was a scenario that, tragically enough, the State of Israel would be forced to endure once again when Saddam Hussein launched thirty-nine SCUD missiles against Tel Aviv and Haifa in January and February 1991.) Ben-Gurion was naturally outraged by the failure of his intelligence agencies to detect Egyptian developments, thereby delaying implementation of the required and decisive preventive contingencies by the IDF and other security forces.

Under orders from Isser Harel, the currency deployed for terminating Nasser's missile program would be a deliberate and deadly plan of package bombs, similar to the ones A'MAN employed against Egyptian Military Intelligence Colonels Hafaz and Mustafa in 1955. It was known as Operation Damocles, the sword of Damocles hanging over the head of the German scientists. It would be Harel's last great coup.

Through an elaborate network of agents, the MOSSAD tracked the German scientists in Egypt and provided up-to-date information on their activities, movements, and locations. Several bombs did, indeed, deliver their fatal payloads. On March 15, 1963, however, two MOSSAD agents were arrested outside a Basel, Switzerland, hotel after they had threatened the daughter of one of the German scientists. The unwanted publicity embarrassed Ben-Gurion, and the wily prime minister was forced to reconsider his intelligence chief's tactics. The sword of Damocles was proving to be a dull penknife.

Harel responded to this challenge by utilizing the services of Israeli journalists, generally an independent-minded group, to publicize German complicity in Egypt's attempt to destroy the Jewish state. This, too, proved to be a disastrous undertaking. News led not only to fear and panic on the Israeli home front, but hampered Ben-Gurion's attempt to forge close-knit relations with West Germany, a relationship that might have led to economic and military assistance. Ben-Gurion ordered Harel to cease his crusade against the German scientists. The feisty spy chief refused, however, and opted to enter into a battle he could not win.

Anger and friction had come to characterize the once-infrangible relationship between the Old Man and his rambunctious spy master. Harel was angry over Ben-Gurion's choice of Shimon Peres to head Israel's super-top-secret nuclear program.[8] These two most powerful and stubborn men appeared on a collision course—one that could produce only one victor. Their paths crossed on March 25, 1963. Hoping to reaffirm his position as guardian of the Israeli intelligence community, Isser Harel submitted his letter of resignation to Ben-Gurion, confident it would not be accepted. It was!

One day later, the director of A'MAN, Major General Amit, was summoned to Ben-Gurion's office to learn, to his utter surprise, that he would become Israel's new spy chief and MOSSAD MEMUNEH. Israel, the MOSSAD, and, most importantly, A'MAN were entering into a new age—the true golden age of the Israeli intelligence community where its character would forever be established.

Ben-Gurion's choice of Meir Amit to lead Israel's foreign intelligence service was not a request; he ordered the A'MAN director to accept the posting. And it was not a move meant to appease the career intelligence agents who had served the MOSSAD so faithfully since the State of Israel's inception. Ben-Gurion did not want a spy chief with a monopoly on power and fear. Instead, Israel needed a calm, apolitical commander with unimpeachable credentials. The IDF and A'MAN, in particular, were the perfect recruiting depot.

There was a profound difference between A'MAN (as an integral element of the IDF) and the MOSSAD. The MOSSAD took pride in being an independent entity, a proud "civilian" body where intelligence, innovativeness, and utter genius had helped keep Israel's head above threatening waters for more than a decade. The IDF was, of course, a universal entity, an egalitarian body composed of conscripts and citizen-soldier reservists who sacrificed their civilian existence for yearly stints of khaki drill, border patrols, and potential combat. When, on March 26, 1963, Maj. Gen. Meir Amit walked into MOSSAD's headquarters in his full Class A IDF uniform—campaign ribbons, silver metal parachutist wings, and epaulet insignia—he created a furor. Harel's secretaries and his legion of loyalists openly wept inside the headquarters, while many senior agents threatened a collective strike. A revolution was nearly transpiring in the MOSSAD; yet, according to authors Yossi Melman and Dan Raviv, Meir Amit was placed in his new posting in order to "clean the stable" in the wake of Harel's legacy.

Amit understood that for Israel to maintain the upper hand against the Arabs, the nation could not tolerate infighting and petty bickering between the MOSSAD and A'MAN. As the new MOSSAD director began valiant attempts to mend all gaps between the two services, he met with intensive opposition from both sides. MOSSAD agents objected to the sacking of Harel and began a letter-writing campaign to express their displeasure and disgust with the fate of their former commander; they were equally outraged with the ascension of Major General Amit, a *military* man, to the MOSSAD reign of command. Amit, accustomed to the IDF's shared responsibility of command, ensured that this letter campaign was crushed; the signatory parties were eventually replaced. A'MAN personnel who rejected Meir Amit's new "outside" job were lambasted in Defense Ministry memos and *ordered* to join forces with the guardians of the state.

Amit's first days as MOSSAD director were hectic and filled with duplicity. Shuttling between A'MAN and MOSSAD headquarters, one of Amit's first acts was to restructure the MOSSAD along more effective and productive lines, emulating efficiency and frugality that were unwritten laws in the IDF. When he finally left the IDF and A'MAN a few months later, his most important move was to transfer Unit 131 into the MOSSAD's Order of Battle. This change would have impressive implications not only for A'MAN, but for the State of Israel. The move, in many ways, helped to consolidate Israel's "unique" HUMINT capabilities prior to the 1967 Six-Day War.

Human espionage remained the cornerstone of Israel's intelligence-gathering efforts. While the "dirty business" in Egypt had proved that running agents inside an enemy nation was a precarious undertaking, the dispatching of both MOSSAD and A'MAN spies continued. A'MAN was still determined to have deep-cover agents planted in Arab capitals. In 1956, their hopes were pinned to a most controversial and, some have said, abhorrent figure: Mordechai "Motke" Kedar.

Kedar was born Mordechai Kravetski in Poland in 1930. Abandoned at birth by his mother, he immigrated to Palestine along with his maternal grandfather and grew up in Hadera, a small rough-and-tumble town located halfway between Haifa and Tel Aviv. Without parental supervision, he grew up on the streets; his education was in the small cafes frequented by black marketeers, smugglers, and pimps. That he became a small-time and ruthless hood came as no surprise; he was, after all, a product of his environment. In 1948 he was conscripted into the IDF/navy, but deserted after a short time due to dangerous behavior. He returned to Hadera and his criminal ties even though he was also enrolled as a student of the law in Jerusalem's prestigious Hebrew University. Israeli police say he was involved in numerous robberies, cases of extortion, and even murder.[9]

Kedar's psychopathic behavior brought him to a famed Tel Aviv psychiatrist who, many have said, was in urgent need of psychiatric care himself. The good doctor, Dr. David Rudi, was also a talent hunter for A'MAN. Noticing certain redeeming qualities in the Hadera hood, he made arrangements for him to meet Maj. Gen. "Fatti" Harkabi. The A'MAN director's assessment of Kedar was a positive one, and the young man was introduced to the world of military espionage. He was formally recruited by A'MAN's elite Unit 131, and trained at a top-secret facility in central Israel.

For several years it appeared as if Kedar had simply vanished. His wife received only sporadic postcards from exotic locations throughout the world, informing her of his well-being. He was, in fact, traveling the world in order to establish an irrefutable cover story for his eventual and ambitious mission: to be planted as an expatriated European/South American businessman operating in Egypt.

Kedar's background work involved establishing front companies, opening bank accounts, and making contacts—all accomplished with generous supplies of A'MAN funding. Argentina was the favored location for this work, since it boasted a large European colony as well as many Arab emigres. As an open business community, it was well suited for international commerce and the quiet comings and goings of businessmen and their finances. Argentina was a perfect staging point for establishing the identity of an intelligence agent about to go into the cold. With a large and flourishing Jewish community, and free of the suspicion that would have been encountered in an Arab state, Argentina was also well suited for the operations of Israeli intelligence. Since the country was not an *overt* supporter of Nazi criminals in hiding, Jews posing as Germans ran less risk of encountering stringent identity checks.

In early 1957, shortly after being sent to South America with $15,000 American dollars and a forged European passport, Kedar was suddenly ordered back to Israel. After an elegant first-class flight via Paris to Tel Aviv (unlike most Israeli intelligence operatives abroad, Kedar prided himself on the luxuries associated with expense accounts), Kedar suddenly found himself being arrested by three heavily armed National Police Special Branch officers supported by SHIN BET officials. One of the most embarrassing chapters in Israeli Military Intelligence was underway.

According to the Israeli charges, Kedar had brutally murdered one of his intelligence contacts, a wealthy Argentinian Jew, stabbing him more than eighty times and then robbing him of a substantial sum of money. His trial was held in a desolate building in a citrus grove, under *extreme* IDF protection; it was a frightening reminder of the events that had preceded the execution of Meir Tubianski in 1948. Kedar was taken to Ramle Prison and held in absolute secrecy. The jailers did not know his identity, and his meager cell was marked simply with the letter *X*. The Israeli government covered up, in what they considered to be a humane manner, the heinous crime committed by one of its intelligence agents. In his book *Security and Democracy*, former MOSSAD/ SHIN BET chief Isser Harel, the man who actively ensured that Kedar would not be heard from until the end of his twenty-year prison sentence, said, "*We do not kill our own agents*—for this there are judges and courtrooms. The British services may eliminate people. We do not. This is, however, one of the dangers of employing men with criminal histories for sensitive intelligence assignments." [10]

(In 1974, after seventeen years in Ramle Prison and seven years in solitary confinement, Mordechai Kedar was released. He was interviewed by numerous Israeli journals and papers, but mention of his name, his crime, and his connections to IDF Military Intelligence was prohibited by A'MAN's IDF Military Censor's Office. In a 1990 interview from his lavish Los Angeles, California, exile, he spoke of his ordeal for the first time: "What I would like to do is get on a plane, go to the house of Isser Harel, and pump a bullet into his head." [11])

The mistakes, and lessons, of the Kedar case were forgotten in the early 1960s as two brilliant A'MAN junior spies were being trained; they would develop into the most celebrated espionage agents ever to serve the Jewish state. Their contribution to Israeli security was so profound that it is still felt today. They would both, however, suffer defeat, and one of them would pay the ultimate price for failure. The two agents were victims of their own overzealousness; they knew that the Jewish state relied on the work of a "master spy" to compensate for the harsh security challenges it faced. Israel's master spies were Eli Cohen and Wolfgang Lotz.

One of the most important lessons the painful "dirty business" in Egypt had taught A'MAN was that the use of local Jews for espionage assignments in their home country could have tragic repercussions. It was an operational taboo, a scenario to be avoided at all costs. The uncovering of a local Jew as a serving Israeli spy endangered the indigenous Jewish population, who could be persecuted by the government and attacked by irate citizens. An espionage assignment was not meant to precipitate a pogrom! Using Arabs as spies in other Arab countries also presented problems and was frowned upon by the intelligence planners of A'MAN, as well as the MOSSAD and the SHIN BET. Arabs are a diverse people separated into many unique and thriving chauvinistic cultures, with different languages and dialects. Indeed, the PAL'MACH's Arab Platoon had learned of such difficulties during the struggle for independence when attempting to infiltrate Iraqi and Yemeni Jews into Beirut, Damascus, and Amman as natives. It took a most capable and courageous agent to succeed at such a masquerade. In the 1960s, that agent was found. His name was Eli Cohen. His legendary James Bond type of exploits transgressed the boundaries of the Middle East, and he became known internationally as a master spy.

Eli Cohen was born in Alexandria, Egypt, on December 26, 1928. His parents, Syrian Jews from the thriving town of Aleppo, had always instilled in their educationally minded son the traditions of the Jewish people, of Zionism, and of the culture of Syria's Jewish community, in particular. His yearning for Zion was expressed in self-sacrifice: In 1949, his three brothers and parents moved to Israel, while Eli remained behind to coordinate Jewish activities.* He was one of the few "Marzouk-Azar" recruited youths connected with the Susannah spies who was left unscathed by its tragic finale, even though he was questioned in brutal fashion by the Egyptian Muchabarat. Officers in Unit 131 sensed something very special and promising about this young intellectual, and grand plans were envisioned for him.

In the summer of 1955, Cohen was brought to Israel from Egypt for secretive intelligence training. His journey was through the back-door route of Greece, and his arrival in Israel was attended to with absolute secrecy. He did not see his family in Israel, but was rushed to a seaside hotel and, supplied with a pseudonym, kept in hiding for several weeks. He was taken to the same Unit 131 training facility that had served as home to his doomed Susannah compatriots in 1953, and was inducted into the world of espionage with intensive personalized training. Unlike the Susannah spies, Eli Cohen was not to serve the Israel Defense Forces as a fifth-columnist and certainly not as a saboteur. He would become Israel's chief intelligence operative in Egypt.

Unfortunately for A'MAN's planners, Cohen proved to be a "blown" individual from the outset. Upon his return to Egypt in 1956, he was placed under Muchabarat surveillance and, during the opening hours of the 1956 Operation KADESH, was detained by Egyptian authorities. In the ensuing chaos that followed the conflict, he reached Israel on February 8, 1957, after being expelled from Egypt along with the remainder of the Jews from Alexandria.[12]

A new immigrant to Israel, Eli Cohen believed that his services as an intelligence operative would be urgently required. He offered himself to Is-

---

*According to an article in the IDF's weekly magazine BAMACHANE ("In the Camp"), there is a question whether or not Eli Cohen was recruited into Israeli Military Intelligence back then, since many have reasoned that this could have been the only true reason for him to remain in Egypt.

raeli Intelligence twice, and was rebuked both times. He felt that he wasn't even needed in the defense of the Jewish state, since he wasn't conscripted for military service but placed in a reserve Israeli Air Force formation as a logistics clerk.[13] Like most new immigrants, he attempted to settle into the day-to-day life of a civilian, seeking employment and acclimation into Israeli society. On August 31, 1959, he married Nadia Majald, a Baghdad-born beauty, and took an accounting job in the Tel Aviv branch of a department store chain. Life appeared to be quiet, routine, and uneventful. For a man who had witnessed the destruction of his childhood friends and his social infrastructure as a result of a failed intelligence operation, anonymity and a quiet life were a welcome respite.

In 1960, however, a man whom Nadia called the "Angel" (because of his handsome and benevolent appearance) knocked on the door of the Cohens's Tel Aviv home and forever changed their lives, as well as the fate of the State of Israel.

The "Angel" was, in fact, an A'MAN headhunter, a talent scout looking to rerecruit Eli Cohen back into the ranks of its special force—Unit 131. The need for the services of someone like Eli Cohen—an elegant and intelligent man who spoke Arabic, English, and French—was a reflection of the troubling events transpiring on Israel's eastern and northern frontiers. The February 1, 1960, IDF raid against Syrian gun positions at Tewfiq underscored the fragility of Israel's Syrian front. The continuing political competition between Ba'athist Syria and King Hussein's Jordan exacerbated this sense of tension and impending danger with Israel's most radical and unpredictable neighbor. Syria had been looking to dominate her southern neighbor by undermining Jordan's political will; these goals were addressed primarily with terrorism. On August 29, 1960, the Jordanian prime minister, Haza'ah Al-Majali, was assassinated when Syrian Muchabarat agents succeeded in planting a powerful explosive device in his Amman office.*

Syria had, indeed, become the radical Arab nation. Its active and violent anti-Israel policies were meant to coalesce a splintered and a racially diverse (often fratricidal) populace into a cohesive and well-controlled political entity. With large shipments of Soviet-supplied weaponry, which included modern MiG-21 "Fishbeds," T-54/55 main battle tanks, and scores of heavy guns,

---

*According to noted Israeli author Shmuel Segev in his book *Alone in Damascus: The Life and Death of Eli Cohen*, Jordan's King Hussein was so angered by the Syrian move that he planned for war against his fellow Arab state. The king had approached Israel's prime minister, David Ben-Gurion, to seek guarantees that Israel would not invade Jordan while King Hussein's legions were invading Syria. Israel, realizing that the Jordanian military was incapable of inflicting any harm on the Syrians, sought both British and American involvement to stall any such moves.

Syria posed a momentous threat to the State of Israel. A closed society with limited access to the Western *and* the Arab worlds, Syria was an enigma to the Israeli intelligence community.

Eli Cohen's abilities as an intelligence warfare operative had been noted by A'MAN officers, who perhaps had a desk job envisioned for this reliable recruit. Yet his Aleppo background made him a suitable choice for infiltration into Syria. Initially, however, Eli Cohen vehemently refused Angel's offer for intelligence work. Citing his new marriage and his satisfaction with the anonymity of civilian life, Cohen, age thirty-four, turned down the alluring promise of "international travel and adventure." When promised that intelligence work did not necessarily mean leaving the boundaries of Israel or being exposed to physical danger, Cohen still refused, saying that he did have steady employment and he was not at all interested in working for A'MAN. A few days later, under circumstances not fully explained to this day, Cohen was fired from his accountant's job. Unemployed, out of money, and with a family, Cohen graciously accepted the 350 Israeli pounds a month he was offered by Angel. Eli Cohen was back in A'MAN's sphere of special operations.[14]

Initially, the "gold star" next to Eli Cohen's name at A'MAN HQ, even before he formally accepted the extortionlike offer, sanctioned him for possible espionage activity in his native Egypt. His controllers attempted to create a new identity for him, that of a rich businessman whose wealth and prestige would facilitate the flow of intelligence, much like Max Bennett before his fatal connection to the Susannah spies. Upon realizing that the Egyptians maintained meticulous registers of their citizens, and that Cohen had, indeed, been under Egyptian police surveillance, A'MAN sought new plans for Cohen's espionage future. What made the Alexandrian so attractive to A'MAN controllers were his high IQ, photographic memory, unbreachable integrity, and, most importantly, the social qualities that afforded him acceptance and maneuverability in foreign surroundings. Relentless psychological examinations also revealed some negative—and possibly foretelling—information about him, including an exaggerated sense of self-importance and a high level of internal tension.[15]

When, in 1960, the need for a spy in Syria became a military necessity, the connection between Cohen's abilities and A'MAN's requirements converged into an operational scenario. His training was extensive and exhaustive. He was taught high-speed evasive driving techniques, weapons proficiency (especially with a wide variety of small arms), topography, map reading, sabotage, and, most importantly, radio transmissions and cryptography. These skills were instrumental in ensuring the safety and survival of one Kamal Amin Ta'abet: Eli Cohen's new identity. One of the most difficult tasks for Eli Cohen was to learn the intricate and unmistakable phonetic tune of Syrian Arabic; prior to his intelligence training, his Egyptian accent was undeniable. According to several reports, his mentor at the Unit 131 training facility was a legendary figure named Sam'an, an Iraqi-born Jew who, during the 1948 War, was the SHACHAR's chief expert on Arabic language and traditions, and Moslem customs.[16]

The well-researched files in Unit 131 HQ were used to formulate Eli Cohen's Syrian identity: Kamal Amin Ta'abet was born in Beirut to Syrian parents; his father's name was Amin Ta'abet; his mother's name was Sa'adiah Ibrahim.[17] In 1948 the family moved to Argentina, where they opened a successful textile business. Kamal Amin Ta'abet's return to Syria would be the fulfillment of a lifelong patriotic dream of returning to his roots.

After careful deliberations in A'MAN HQ, the decision to send Eli Cohen into the cold was made. The document was signed by the A'MAN director, Major General Herzog.

On February 3, 1961, Eli Cohen took off from Lod Airport, near Tel Aviv, on an El Al flight to Zurich, where he switched his Israeli travel documents and became Kamal Amin Ta'abet. He was driven to the airport in a Ministry of Defense staff car. His wife was allowed to see him off. She was told that Eli would be working on a top-secret arms-procurement program for the Ministry of Defense and would be placed in absolutely no danger. It was a masquerade that Nadia Cohen would believe until her husband was captured in Damascus.

In Zurich, Eli Cohen boarded a flight for Santiago, Chile, which had a transit stop in Buenos Aires. This point was imperative because it provided an undocumented entry into Argentina. As a transit passenger his passport would not be stamped in the airport, and he would not be required to register with the police; the Argentinians, of course, were not expecting one of the passengers to leave his ticketed flight and pass through the customs barrier. This evasive move was important for another reason. In the politically volatile period following the MOSSAD/SHIN BET kidnapping of Adolph Eichmann, Argentina was not a hospitable environment for Israeli intelligence operatives.

Days later, Cohen met with his control officer, a man known only as "Avraham." They conducted their briefings in crowded Buenos Aires cafes. Slowly Kamal Amin Ta'abet developed into a distinctive character. With scrupulous attention to detail, a generous budget, great care, and a theatrical ability that a Shakespearean actor would have envied, Cohen became a prominent and respected "Arab" businessman in the Argentine capital. He attended local Arab social and cultural meetings. He frequented the numerous Arab nightclubs in the city, where he was known as a man who tipped well and who never missed an opportunity to profess his patriotism toward Syria. He was also a prominent supporter of the city's local Arab newspaper, *La Bandera Arabe* ("The Arab Flag"); he befriended its editor, Al-Latif El-H'ashan, and paid for a year's subscription with cash.[18]

His friendship with El-H'ashan brought profound dividends, especially with Syrian diplomats and military attachés working out of the embassy. Through these contacts Eli Cohen met Syria's new military attaché to Argentina, Col. Amin El-Hafaz. A bright officer who had commanded the training section in the Syrian army General Staff, El-Hafaz had been ousted from Damascus because his zealous Ba'athist party leanings made many of Syria's military and political leaders extremely nervous. Since 1949, Syria had been host to seven military coups d'etat; power was exchanged on numerous occasions to Pan-Arabists, socialists, and fanatic fringes of Nasserism and Ba'athist party politics. Cohen's contacts were nurtured in lavish dinner parties at the Syrian Embassy, located in the luxurious lower city section. The zealous nationalism of Kamal Amin Ta'abet was expressed to any receptive ear. He professed his desire to visit his native Syria and invest large sums of his Argentine money in the Syrian economy; this potential foreign capital made him a popular commodity with the crooked Syrian government officials. When he announced to his new friends that he was planning, for the first time, to visit his native land, he was equipped with letters of introduction, addresses, and promises of Byzantine support for any endeavors he might wish to accomplish in Syria.

"Avraham," his A'MAN controller in Buenos Aires, was impressed with the abilities of this amazing spy. Details of his activities were conveyed to Tel Aviv, and arrangements for Kamal Amin Ta'abet's visit to Syria were accelerated. Eli Cohen's success went beyond even the wildest expectations of his A'MAN handlers. The commander of Unit 131, who had sent men into enemy territory many times, acknowledged that "Not every agent was willing to travel to Damascus." [19]

Nine months after his secret arrival in the Argentine capital, Eli Cohen came back to Israel. He was allowed to spend some time with his wife, Nadia, but the majority of his time was spent in Tel Aviv perfecting his cover story and being briefed on A'MAN's requirements of him in Syria, as well as last-minute intelligence data needed for his mission. This was the TACHLIS ("real thing") of his mission. The danger would now truly begin. In late 1961, Eli Cohen left Israel for Italy, his staging point for entry into Syria. This time, as he left Nadia, he realized that he might not be coming home ever again.

On January 1, 1962, Eli Cohen boarded the liner *Astoria* in Genoa for the short journey to Beirut and then Damascus. [20] His first-class quarters and ability to part with money made him a favorite among the wealthy Arab passengers on board. One of those influential Syrians, in fact, was so taken by Kamal Amin Ta'abet's financial resources and patriotic zeal that he offered to drive him from Beirut to Damascus; this allowed Eli Cohen to enter Syria without any scrutiny. Within days, Kamal Amin Ta'abet renounced his Argentine home, vowing never to leave Syria. He rented an apartment in the exclusive Abu-Ramana quarter of Damascus—in a building that overlooked the Syrian army General Staff and was adjacent to accommodations where the Syrian military housed many of its elite guests. [21] His dangerous masquerade had begun.

On the morning of February 25, 1962, the Unit 131 communications officer on duty at A'MAN HQ in Tel Aviv received the first broadcast from Eli Cohen. It was met with hugs and cheers in a military office usually devoid of emotion. A bottle of Israeli champagne was even opened in celebration.[22]

Eli Cohen reported to his handlers in meticulous fashion. He had set up an antenna along a pipe outside his study window; coded signals were tapped in deliberate bursts to develop a pattern that would become his signature. Any deviation from the norm would signal danger. Regular transmission schedules were established and Cohen was ordered not to broadcast long messages; the Syrian Muchabarat might be able to trace a prolonged electronic signal.

A millionaire playboy who was happy to provide lucrative loans to government officials, Kamal Amin Ta'abet was one of the most requested party guests on the Damascus nightlife circuit. Politicians flocked to his side for advice and expensive French cognac. The "husband hunters" among the Damascus rich and influential flocked to the handsome Ta'abet, hoping that their almond eyes, Byzantine beauty, and olive skin would secure a future of wealth and power: He became the most sought-after bachelor in the Syrian capital. He did not object, in fact, to the idea of a ladies' man reputation. He had seventeen lovers in Syria, all dazzling beauties with a fair degree of family power. Eli Cohen and his handlers believed that these women would help him escape in a time of crisis.[23]

Yet it was his prowess in the halls of power, not in the bedroom, that made him a most valued asset for Israeli Military Intelligence. His friends in the Syrian Air Force often "ordered" him to visit them at their offices or at the air bases. Indeed, Eli Cohen was able to get "up close and personal" with the men and machines of the much-vaunted Syrian Air Force. He talked to pilots, asked them how they planned to defeat the IAF in air combat, and was even given technical briefings on their MiG and Sukhoi aircraft, as well as the weapons systems they carried. Hoping to one day secure business dealings with Kamal Amin Ta'abet, the Syrian Air Force pilots explained, in impressive detail, their tactics and, in some cases, secret tricks they had learned from the Russians. All this information was, of course, supplied to Tel Aviv with meticulous accuracy; Cohen possessed a truly photographic memory. Remarkably, he also supplied his Unit 131 officers with a list of all the pilots in the Syrian Air Force. In June 1967, it would become a scorecard of death.[24]

Other military officers who befriended Cohen took him to numerous weapons facilities, arsenals, and training camps. During a party or business meeting (which usually entailed Ta'abet handing over an envelope filled with cash to a corrupt official or army officer), all Cohen had to do was vocalize his concern regarding potential Israeli attacks against Syria and he was ushered around top-secret facilities with the pomp and ceremony of a visiting head of state.

The most important installations to which Eli Cohen was taken were on the Golan Heights—the impregnable volcanic plateau that hovered majestically above northeastern Israel, from which the Sea of Galilee and much of central Israel could be easily seen in artillery gunsights. In any future conflict, it was considered Israel's number-one priority target—and for good reason. The Syrians had established a series of heavily fortified gun emplacements and forts, which would create a gauntlet of cannon and machine-gun fire against attacking Israeli forces; the artillery trap was so overwhelming, the Syrians believed it was deterrence enough to any Israeli military move. More importantly, its 130mm guns and mortars subjected the kibbutzim and moshavim to incessant and murderous artillery barrages.

The Golan Heights was Syria's version of the Maginot line—a top-secret first and only line of national defense. Nevertheless, Kamal Amin Ta'abet succeeded in visiting each and every position. With senior staff officers acting as guides, Eli Cohen was provided an in-depth intelligence briefing of monumental proportions. He was even photographed with his Syrian military friends at a top-secret defensive position on the Heights, looking into Israel. He also photographed, in his mind, the positioning of every Syrian gun, trench, and machine-gun nest in each Golan Heights fortification; tank traps, designed to impede any Israeli attack, were also identified and memorized for future targeting. During his business trips to Europe, on the premise of visiting a dummy front company, Cohen would take a quick flight to Israel and report personally to his superiors, as well as see his wife and family. The information he gathered was used to construct three-dimensional models of the Syrian positions. They would be used on June 9, 1967, to seize the Golan in an awe-inspiring blitz.

One of the most important aspects of Eli Cohen's reports back to Israel was his scrupulous objectivity. Many spies in the field tended to provide their handlers with information they *wanted* to hear rather than what was actually transpiring. Eli Cohen refrained from this practice of espionage editorializing. He sent only fact; when speculation or guesswork was involved, he went to great lengths to insist that such information be accepted as such.

Beyond the military intelligence he sent back to Israel via his secret transmitter, Eli Cohen was also able to obtain, analyze, and disseminate incredible quantities of data on Syrian political developments, especially the bitter and divisive infighting between the Nasserites and Ba'athists. This was actually the sphere of responsibility of the MOSSAD, yet the ability of Kamal Amin Ta'abet to infiltrate the higher echelons of Syrian power transgressed anyone's operational domain. The political intelligence that Eli Cohen was able to transmit was exceptionally useful when, on March 8, 1963, a coup d'etat by Ba'athist military officers helped pave the way for Gen. Amin El-Hafaz to grasp the reigns of political power in Syria. El-Hafaz was an old acquaintance of Kamal

Amin Ta'abet from his days in Argentina, and the relationship between the ruler of Syria and Israel's master spy reaped unanticipated rewards. According to accounts published in several Lebanese newspapers, Kamal Amin Ta'abet was being considered for the post of Syria's deputy defense minister.

The change in leadership in Syria had great impact on Eli Cohen—the man and the spy. He had been horrified by the brutal Ba'athist purges of Nasserites from the Syrian government and military; the indiscriminate murder and big brother type of informing that ensued shook the foundations of Syrian society.[25] Signs that Eli Cohen was faltering in his steadfast approach to espionage tradecraft were apparent in several radio transmissions when he asked his A'MAN communications contact to call his wife and tell her that he would be returning to Israel shortly. His was a most demanding charade—one that clearly could not last for an extended period of time. He began to feel threatened in Syria, especially in the company of Col. Ahmed Su'edeni, the commander of Syrian Military Intelligence. The ruthless colonel, known for trusting absolutely nobody and able to extract confessions through inhumane acts of torture, disliked Ta'abet greatly; he was, in fact, *extremely* jealous of the newcomer from Argentina.

Unfortunately for Eli Cohen, his apprehension about life in the cold and desire to terminate his mission came at a time when a new military threat to the State of Israel, the Palestine Liberation Organization, was emerging with the support of the Syrian military. This was also the time that Unit 131 was transferred to the MOSSAD Order of Battle. (The battle for control of the waters of the Jordan River was developing between the Syrians and Israelis at the Dan River tributaries, and Tel Aviv needed as much data on the Syrians as could possibly be gathered.)

Upon his return to Israel in November 1964, Eli Cohen expressed his fears to his new handlers in the MOSSAD, but they pressured him to return to Damascus one final time. Israel now needed its man in Damascus more than ever. An exchange of control in the midst of an espionage assignment, however, is considered fatal in tradecraft rule books.

In hindsight, Eli's return to Syria was an accident waiting to happen. According to several accounts, his transmissions soon became routine and lengthy— even cocky. Some say this came as a result of the ease through which he was able to infiltrate into the top echelons of the Syrian leadership; others blame it on an almost suicidal tendency—sometimes seen in a person who has been in the cold for too long. Whatever the true reason, Eli Cohen's disregard for security compromised his activities and, eventually, his life. His broadcasts were so long and frequent that embassies nearby complained to the Syrians that their own radio transmissions were encountering interference. The MOSSAD should have ordered him back to Israel, but the information he was supplying was unbelievably valuable.

Colonel Su'edeni, meanwhile, was zeroing in on the spy in the Syrian capital with the help of Glavno Razvedyvatelnoe Upravlenie (GRU, the Russian acronym for Soviet Military Intelligence) personnel who were sent to Syria to operate highly sophisticated radio-tracking devices. Apparently, the Soviets were extremely nervous about classified material, especially concerning their modern weapons systems, reaching Israel and, inevitably, NATO intelligence files. After much field work, the source of the radio transmissions originating from Damascus was finally traced. On a dark winter's day in January 1965, Colonel Su'edeni led a squad of Syrian intelligence officers and commandos to the man he had long suspected. They burst into Kamal Amin Ta'abet's apartment in the middle of a transmission to Tel Aviv.

For the next few days, the Syrian colonel attempted to force Eli Cohen to send false information back to Tel Aviv. He refused, even though this increased the frequency and ferocity of the beatings he received. Finally, on January 24, Colonel Su'edeni ordered the badly beaten Israeli spy to transmit a message to his handlers in Tel Aviv. It read:

FOR PRIME MINISTER LEVI ESHKOL AND SECRET SERVICE CHIEF TEL AVIV FROM SYRIAN COUNTERINTELLIGENCE SERVICE
Kamal Amin Ta'abet and his friends are our guests in Damascus. Assume you will send all his colleagues. Will give you news of his fate shortly.
SYRIAN ESPIONAGE SERVICE [26]

Now there was no doubt. One of Israel's most successful espionage agents was in enemy hands.

Several accounts of Eli Cohen's torture state that his interrogators had been taught by the Gestapo. After all, the Syrian Muchabarat had been trained and guided by Alois Brunner, a former SS officer and convicted Nazi war criminal who was held responsible for sending more than 120,000 Austrian, German, French, Slovak, and Greek Jews to their deaths during the Holocaust. Brunner had arrived in Syria in 1955, after escaping from Europe to Egypt.[27] The Israelis had known of the Syrians' penchant for torture since the "listening device" incident in 1954. No rational officer in either A'MAN or MOSSAD headquarters expected Eli Cohen to be able to withstand the brutal physical and emotional torture. Eli Cohen, however, proved them wrong. A man reared on the Zionist dream was not about to betray his nation, even though he had lived in Israel for only a brief four years. He refused to break and give his interrogators any information of value.

Eli Cohen's trial was a farce and a mockery; its decision and verdict were, of course, predetermined. The judge, Colonel Dili, personally assaulted the accused in both physical and verbal barrages. More than five hundred names, all contacts and friends of Kamal Amin Ta'abet, were mentioned at his trial; these hapless individuals, all innocent of knowingly assisting an Israeli intelligence agent, were also put on the docket. The Syrians were concerned that Cohen had worked as part of an elaborate network of agents, and the spy hunt in the Syrian capital was extensive and unforgiving. Eli Cohen refused defense counsel; a French lawyer did lobby for the opportunity to defend the Israeli spy but the Syrian government would not give him an entry visa. The trial ended on March 19, 1965; Cohen's death sentence was announced on May 1. The signatory to his execution orders was President El-Hafaz, the man who had befriended Eli Cohen and had even accepted gifts from the generous "Argentine expatriate."

Meir Amit labored with passion and frustration to help save his prized intelligence agent. The norms of international espionage dictated that captured spies were imprisoned until eventually swapped. Amit had been shaken by the IDF's lack of concern for the fate of the Susannah spies, and he was determined to save this man, *his* man, at all costs! Israel recruited influential world leaders to petition on behalf of the doomed spy, including French President de Gaulle, British Prime Minister Wilson, American President Johnson, and even the Pope. The Syrians stood fast in their determination to execute Cohen. The Israelis even offered the Syrians valuable intelligence data, including news of a developing coup against President El-Hafaz, but the Syrians were so outraged by the success of the Israeli agent that they were determined to make an example of him.[28]

At 0330 on May 18, 1965, Abu-Saliman, the chief executioner of Damascus, placed the noose around the neck of Eli Cohen in Martyr's Square; in a humanitarian gesture, Cohen was executed only after he was allowed a brief prayer with the city's chief rabbi, Anadivu Cohen. The execution was witnessed by more than two thousand Syrian army officers and televised to a national audience. Cohen's body was left hanging for several hours as jubilant crowds passed by screaming anti-Israeli slogans.

In Israel, following the cruel play-by-play broadcast of Eli Cohen's execution, there was a period of national mourning. Posthumously, Cohen was promoted to the rank of lieutenant colonel. Although he could not witness the rewards of his ultimate sacrifice, he had, according to Maj. Gen. (Res.) Meir Amit, "succeeded far beyond the capabilities of most other men." [29]

Eli Cohen was not the only trained and sanctioned A'MAN agent who returned a wealth of data to Tel Aviv. One of Cohen's anonymous contemporaries would also achieve the status of master spy.

Wolfgang Lotz was born in Germany in 1921 to a Jewish mother and a Christian father. After his parents' divorce and the tumultuous rise to power of Adolf Hitler and the Nazis, both mother and son moved to Israel. Wolfgang's name was changed to Ze'ev Gur-Aryeh and he studied at an agricultural school for new immigrants. When he was sixteen, he volunteered for service in the HAGANAH and developed a fierce reputation guarding the Ben-Shemen forest near Jerusalem on horseback—horses were his true passion. During the Second World War, he volunteered to serve in the British army, where his knowledge of Hebrew, English, Arabic, and, most importantly, German was particularly useful. In the 1948 War, he was commissioned with the rank of lieutenant, and placed in command of an infantry platoon made up of new immigrants, mainly former refugees detained on Cyprus, who spoke little Hebrew and had received very little military training. They fought on the bloodied hills known as the Burma Road, which eventually connected the besieged capital of Jerusalem with Tel Aviv.

Following the war, Ze'ev Gur-Aryeh was approached by the MA'MAN for potential intelligence work. Unlike many German Jews who were labeled by the unflattering term YEKKE, meaning snobby and fanatically neat, Gur-Aryeh was outgoing, rambunctious, and extremely confident. With reddish blond hair, blue eyes, and strikingly Aryan features, he didn't even look Jewish. Some said he didn't even act Jewish. In fact, at the young age of twenty he had already been divorced twice—an unheard-of occurrence in the Jewish community.[30]

After intensive training at Unit 131 facilities, Ze'ev Gur-Aryeh was transformed back into Wolfgang Lotz. He was sent to West Germany to shore his cover story: A wealthy businessman, he had served in Hitler's Wehrmacht as a loyal and dedicated soldier and had later emigrated to Egypt. This was almost identical to Max Bennett's modus operandi in the early 1950s; although Bennett was fatally implicated in the Susannah spy ring, his cover as a West German businessman held up through the investigations and interrogations, and even survived his death by hanging. According to authors Yossi Melman and Dan Raviv in the comprehensive study of Israel's intelligence community, *The Imperfect Spies*, Wolfgang Lotz's cover was assembled, coordinated, and maintained by the West German BND intelligence service; an agent, code-named Waltraud, worked with Lotz in Egypt. Waltraud was an attractive blond woman whom Lotz had married in Germany while his cover story was being assembled.[31] Although never acknowledged, the scenario seems credible, since Gur-Aryeh was married when he departed Israel for West Germany and bigamy was not considered a policy in A'MAN tradecraft.

In Egypt, Lotz easily infiltrated the country's thriving German colony and, most importantly, the Egyptian military. Since his father had been a German of Christian faith, Lotz was entitled to obtain a German passport, which he used to enter Egypt. A playboy with a taste for alcohol and extravagant parties, and the habit of flashing around large sums of cash, Lotz became a favorite among the high-ranking Egyptian officers who flocked to his home. His friends, to whom he often loaned substantial funds, included members of the Egyptian police, counterintelligence sections, and the Muchabarat. He also rubbed elbows with prominent members of Egypt's fledgling armament-producing programs. Like Eli Cohen, the information Lotz transmitted back to Tel Aviv was unbelievably intimate and detailed. Egyptian troop, armor, and air force deployments, designations, and dispositions were observed, recorded, and dispatched to Israel. A comprehensive and highly accurate Order of Battle concerning the Egyptian military was obtained.

Lotz enticed and snared his contacts through his lavish life-style. His financial reports to his A'MAN, and later MOSSAD, handlers were the subject of much shock and ridicule. Thousands of dollars were spent on furs, champagne, caviar, and jewels; his appetite for luxury earned Lotz the endearing name of "the Champagne Spy."

For nearly five years, Wolfgang Lotz sent his handlers vital information. He was incredibly successful and remarkably reckless. In the end, his recklessness compromised his mission. On February 22, 1965, as Wolfgang and Waltraud Lotz returned to their Cairo home, they were set upon by six heavily armed men of the Egyptian secret police. Less than one month after the Soviet GRU specialists in Syria had helped nab Eli Cohen, a similar contingent had tracked and located the transmissions emanating from the Lotz's residence. Through a brutal interrogation and sensory deprivation, Lotz managed to keep his cover secure: He was a German who had been duped into working for the Israelis. Since he was not circumcised at birth, he wasn't suspected of being a Jew, which most likely spared him the fate that befell Eli Cohen. Hundreds of Lotz's associates and friends were rounded up as well, but they knew nothing of his activities or true identity. In a show trial, which lasted from July 21 until August 21, 1965, the Egyptian Supreme Court presented *ten* charges, all of which carried the death penalty. His life, however, was spared. He was sentenced to life imprisonment and incarcerated along with numerous Egyptian military men and intellectuals who had been convicted on espionage charges —including several who had worked for British Intelligence and the CIA.

On February 3, 1968, Wolfgang Lotz was freed from his lifetime sentence. He was exchanged, along with the Susannah spies and other captured IDF personnel, for five hundred Egyptian POWs, including several generals.[32]

It is clear that the activities of both Eli Cohen and Wolfgang Lotz—two A'MAN agents eventually placed under the control of the MOSSAD—helped pave the way for Israel's lightning victory in June 1967. These two men provided information that enabled the operational planners in the IDF to classify enemy strengths, locate and prioritize targets, and, most importantly, provide the General Staff and the prime minister with an accurate assessment of what the enemy's moves, capabilities, and tactics in a future war would likely be. Although there were other Israeli agents operating in Arab countries prior to the Six-Day War, the volume and quality of the information that these two men smuggled out remain awe-inspiring even to this day. Their results far surpassed the capabilities of space satellites and high-tech electronic spook devices.

It must also be understood that A'MAN's intelligence-gathering efforts prior to the Six-Day War did not rely solely on these two super spies. Conventional intelligence-gathering means were employed, and with great skill. Intelligence Corps radiomen continued to intercept, monitor, and analyze enemy communications; elite-unit reconnaissance forays were mounted; and photoreconnaissance missions were flown by the Israeli Air Force. These operations were escalated following the Arab League Summit of January 1964, where three threatening propositions were advanced: (1) to create a united Arab command to deal with liberation of territory; (2) to execute diversion operations to deprive the State of Israel of water sources; and (3) to create an armed, as well as political, Palestinian response to Israeli aggression— hence the creation of the Palestine Liberation Army (PLA) and the Palestine Liberation Organization (PLO).

A'MAN's vigilance and responses to these threats were a never-ending task. Small teams of combat intelligence soldiers conducted ambushes to seize the Palestinian guerrillas or Syrian artillerymen who protected water-diversion projects; the ensuing interrogations usually reaped valuable rewards. Israeli Air Force Piper Cubs, carrying Intelligence Corps personnel with 8x30 and 7x5 field glasses, buzzed enemy positions, braving dense and, in some cases, deadly antiaircraft artillery (AAA) fire. The threat of the new Palestinian guerrillas, the new fedayeen, forced A'MAN officers, and especially its Operations Section, to deal with a growing threat of saboteurs, murderers, and intelligence operatives entering Israel. Organizations had to be infiltrated, their tactics and doctrines studied, and capabilities assessed. From January 1965 to the start of the Six-Day War on June 4, 1967, the PLO mounted 122 attacks and operations; these resulted in fourteen Israeli dead and sixty-two wounded.[33]

There was also one MOSSAD operation that proved of enormous military intelligence value to the Israel Defense Forces. In 1966, the MOSSAD was able to establish contact with Capt. Munir Redfa, a Maronite-Christian and an Iraqi Air Force MiG-21 Fishbed pilot. The MOSSAD approached him through a sexual snare, although the religious discrimination he and his family had been subjected to by Iraq's Moslem majority had helped pave the way for cooperation with the Israelis; his disdain for the Iraqi government's indiscriminate aerial bombings of the rebellious Kurdish minorities* sealed his decision to help the Israelis. What *they* wanted most was his plane: the top-secret Fishbed.

To convince Redfa that they meant business, the MOSSAD arranged a meeting between him and the IAF OC, Maj. Gen. Mordechai "Motti" Hod, in Paris. During the chin-wag, Hod showed Redfa a fully detailed roster, to prove that the IAF knew the names of *all* Iraqi combat pilots, the names of their Soviet instructors, and details of the air bases and air defenses. In this top-secret meeting, the operational details of the defection were mapped out and coordinated. Redfa was understandably apprehensive and nervous. Hod and the MOSSAD agents realized that failure would mean a brutal end to the life of Redfa, his family, and, in all probability, his entire village.[34]

On August 15, 1966, after his family had been smuggled out of the country with the assistance of Kurdish guerrillas, Redfa boarded his MiG-21 fighter and proceeded to fly across the predetermined route—over Jordan—toward an IAF base in southern Israel. The operation was a brilliant success. The West got, for the first time, an intimate look at the Soviet's top-of-the-line fighter interceptor, and the IAF was able to form a tactical response to the most prolific aircraft in the Egyptian and Syrian air forces. The MiG, eventually adorned with a Star of David, the IAF's emblem, and the "007" (James Bond) designation, became a symbol of Israel's remarkable HUMINT abilities. Today, this MiG-21 is an exhibit at the IAF's new museum at the sprawling Hatzerim Air Force Base in the Negev Desert.

On April 7, 1967, when military clashes between Syria, Israel, and Jordan had indicated that a full-scale conflagration was imminent, a flight of IAF French-built Mirage IIIC interceptors ambushed a flight of Syrian MiG-21s flying over the Sea of Galilee. In a spectacular dogfight, the Mirages blew *six* of the much-vaunted MiGs out of the sky without suffering a single loss. Some experts would later comment that the Israeli pilots had become more intimate with the Fishbed than even their Arab counterparts.

Israel's "intelligence" sword and shield had proven to be an invaluable asset. In two months, it would also prove to be Israel's most potent weapon.

*A'MAN had extensive contacts with the Kurdish rebels in Iraq; after all, the saying "The enemy of my enemy is my friend" was traditional law in the Middle East. A'MAN's role with the Kurds concentrated mainly on weapons supplies and training in exchange for intelligence. The relationship was strong and cordial.

NOTES: CHAPTER NINE

1. Yossi Melman and Dan Raviv, *The Imperfect Spies: The History of Israeli Intelligence* (London: Sidgwick and Jackson, 1989), 129.

2. Avi Battleheim, GOLANI: TZAHAL BE'HEILO ENTZYKLOPEDIA LE'TZAVA ULE'BITACHON (Tel Aviv: Revivim Publishers, 1982), 42.

3. Interview with IDF intelligence officer, Tel Aviv, May 1990.

4. See Yossi Melman and Dan Raviv, *The Imperfect Spies*, 115–143.

5. Oded Granot, HEYL HA'MODE'IN: TZAHAL BE'HEILO ENTZYKLOPEDIA LE'TZAVA ULE'BITACHON (Tel Aviv: Revivim Publishers, 1981), 68.

6. Stewart Steven, *The Spymasters of Israel* (New York: Ballantine Books, 1980), 159.

7. *Ibid.* 160.

8. See Yossi Melman and Dan Raviv, *The Imperfect Spies*, 143.

9. *Ibid.* 136.

10. *Ibid.* 136; also see Isser Harel, BITACHON VE'DEMOKRATIA (Tel Aviv: Edanim Publishers, 1989), 284.

11. Leah Etger, "MORDECHAI KEDAR: ROTZE'ACH O'CHAF ME'PESHA," YEDIOT SHEVA YAMIM, (January 13, 1990): 9.

12. Shmuel Segev, BODED BE'DAMESEK: CHAYAV VE'MOTAV SHEL ELI COHEN (Jerusalem: Keter Publishing House, 1986), 50.

13. *Ibid.* 51.

14. Ben Dan, *The Spy From Israel* (London: Vallentine, Mitchell and Company, Ltd., 1969), 72.

15. See Yossi Melman and Dan Raviv, *The Imperfect Spies*, 166.

16. Ian Black, "The Origins of Israeli Intelligence," *Intelligence and National Security*, London Vol. 2, No. 4 (October 1987): 153.

17. See Shmuel Segev, BODED BE'DAMESEK, 66.

18. *Ibid.* 73.

19. Yosef Argaman, "ELI COHEN: PEREK HA'SHE'ELOT," BAMACHANE (June 13, 1990): 18.

20. See Stewart Steven, *The Spymasters of Israel*, 203.

21. Eli Ben-Hanan, *Our Man in Damascus: Eli Cohen* (Tel Aviv, Steimatzky Ltd., 1972), 57.

22. See Shmuel Segev, BODED BE'DAMESEK, 106.

23. *Ibid.* See photograph supplement showing Cohen on a beach with one of his lovelies.

24. See Yossi Melman and Dan Raviv, *The Imperfect Spies*, 167.

25. Anne Sinai and Allen Pollack, *The Syrian Arab Republic* (New York:

American Academic Association for Peace in the Middle East Publications, 1976), 26.

26. See Stewart Steven, *The Spymasters of Israel*, 205.

27. *The New York Times*, October 29, 1985, A3.

28. See Yosef Argaman, ELI COHEN: PEREK HA'SHE'ELOT, 19.

29. Various Ed. "MODE'IN: ALMONIM BE'BDIDUT AYUMA," MA'ARIV YOM HA'A'ATZMA'UT (May 9, 1989): 2.

30. Wolfgang Lotz, *The Champagne Spy* (New York: St. Martin's Press, 1972), 15.

31. E. H. Cookgridge, *Gehlen: Spy of the Century* (New York: Random House, 1971), as quoted in Stewart Steven, *The Spymasters of Israel*, 71.

32. See Wolfgang Lotz, *The Champagne Spy*, 229.

33. See Oded Granot, HEYL HA'MODE'IN, 75.

34. See Yossi Melman and Dan Raviv, *The Imperfect Spies*, 162.

CHAPTER 10

A'MAN'S COMING OF AGE: THE 1967 SIX-DAY WAR

"Know thy enemy"
A catchword of Maj. Gen. Aharon Yariv, A'MAN's director during the 1967 War

T he illustration in the magazine, one of the many weeklies put out by the Egyptian government, expressed the view of millions of Arabs since 1948. In eye-catching color, the full-page spread showed an Egyptian soldier, in full fatigues and carrying a machine gun, liberating the holy el-Aqsa mosque in Jerusalem while stomping on a blood-soaked Israeli flag. "Liberation *is* at hand," the caption read. "The *Zionist Infidel* will be pushed into the sea."

In A'MAN HQ, the soldier sleuths in HATZAV translated the article, and promptly sent it out for review and analysis.

Wars have different ways of beginning—they can erupt in a spasm of uncontrolled madness, or they can fester through minor acts of violence into one final expression of conflict. Since 1956, the Middle East had been following the latter course in truly bloody fashion. From the sporadic fedayeen incursion into Israel, to the execution of the A'MAN/MOSSAD master spy Eli Cohen, and the attempts to divert the waters of the Jordan River away from Israel, chances for a full-scale Middle Eastern war escalated with each passing hour. On November 13, 1966, a major trip wire was pulled.

Tension between King Hussein's Jordan and Israel had been mounting since 1964, when the newly formed Palestine Liberation Organization began to express itself militarily with attacks into Israel. Between 1965 and the end of 1966, an increasing number of terrorist infiltrations had prompted the IDF to mount retaliatory operations meant to destroy Palestinian bases, as well as the protective ring of Jordanian troops that surrounded each guerrilla encampment. When, in November 1966, an Israeli jeep detonated a land mine planted in the Arava desert, near the Jordanian frontier, killing three paratroopers, Israeli retaliation was swift and harsh. In what became known as Operation Step, a force of paratroopers, reconnaissance commandos, tanks, and half-tracks crossed the frontier into Jordan and raided the village of es-Samua; they killed dozens of terrorists and Jordanian soldiers in the day-long battle. Although the raid amounted to a mini-invasion of Jordan, King Hussein did nothing—even after a Hawker Hunter fighter, the pride of the Royal Jordanian Air Force, was shot down by the IAF.[1] Through its raid, the IDF announced to the Arab world that it would do what was militarily necessary—even if not politically acceptable—to keep her integrity secure: *even* if it meant war. Operation Step also demonstrated to the Arabs their military impotence, which, following Eli Cohen's infiltration into the intimate circles of Syrian power and the 1966 defection of the Iraqi MiG-21, was escalating at an alarming rate in the eyes of the enraged Arab masses.

On April 7, 1967, the Arab military inability was once again displayed; this time, however, it was Syria's turn. Since the early 1950s, Syrian artillery encampments dug into the volcanic rock of the Golan Heights had pummeled Israeli agricultural settlements. Sometimes the artillery attack consisted of a lone 130mm shell lobbed at a kibbutz farmhouse or lunchroom; sometimes it was a barrage lasting a full day. On April 7, the barrage, directed at Tel Katzir, was particularly fierce. Israeli Air Force commander Maj. Gen. Mordechai "Motti" Hod dispatched a flight of Super Mysteres to take out the Syrian guns. In a swift chain of events, the Mysteres were intercepted by a flight of Syrian MiG-21s, which, in turn, were placed inside the gunsights of a flight of IAF Mirage IIICs. Over the Golan Heights the IAF would prove itself second to none. Six MiG-21s were blasted out of the sky to no Israeli losses. In an ominous statement meant to deter any escalation of hostilities, IDF Chief of Staff Lt. Gen. Yitzhak Rabin warned Syria that Israel would *not* remain passive in the face of provocations.[2] Red flags were raised in Damascus—and in each and every Arab capital—as the Ba'ath regime felt Israel would exploit Syrian military weakness to mount an invasion through the Golan Heights. With Egyptian President Nasser being the indisputable leader of the Arab world, all eyes turned to Cairo. On May 15, 1967, Nasser placed the Egyptian army on full alert. The 1967 Arab-Israeli war was about to begin.

Since the end of the last Arab-Israeli war, the 1956 Sinai Campaign, the IDF and the Israeli defense establishment had been gearing themselves for a larger confrontation between Arab and Israeli. Superpower involvement in the arming of the Arabs and, in 1962, President Kennedy's decision to sell batteries of HAWK surface-to-air missiles to the IDF fanned the flames in an area heading toward war. Every nation in the region knew that the next conflagration would be the bloodiest yet fought. Predicting when war would come became one of the most important tasks assigned to A'MAN.

In 1967, the A'MAN director was one of the most able men ever to serve the Israel Defense Forces. Aharon Yariv was born in 1920, in Moscow, and emigrated to Palestine in 1935. A born leader, Yariv became a serving officer in the HAGANAH, where he was affectionately known as "Ahrele." He later volunteered into the British army for the fight against Hitler; in his majesty's service he attained the rank of captain. A charismatic officer whose abilities were noticed above his personality, Yariv was dispatched to Europe following the Second World War to help facilitate the smuggling of Jewish refugees from Europe; he also worked for RECHESH as a covert arms procurer and was eventually accepted for the Jewish Agency's "Institute for Advanced Studies," the training ground for the State of Israel's future diplomatic corps. When the battle for Israeli independence began in 1947, he served as the adjutant to HAGANAH Chief of Staff Ya'akov Dori, as well as its Operations director; he was also the personal translator and guide to Col. David "Mickey" Marcus, an American officer who volunteered to help organize the infant IDF into something resembling a conventional fighting force. During the 1948 War, Yariv served as a deputy battalion commander in the ALEXANDRONI Infantry Brigade, as well as the battalion commander in the CARMELI Brigade, which liberated Nazareth. His tactical brilliance and inspiring intelligence were not lost to senior IDF commanders, who elevated Yariv to the head of the Operations Branch of the General Staff in 1951. He was also the first Israeli graduate of France's Military College.[3] In 1957, Colonel Yariv was named the IDF's attaché to Washington, D.C.—a posting that enabled the analytically minded officer to observe firsthand the importance of strong military alliances, as well as interservice intelligence cooperation between the Western world's espionage and intelligence-gathering services. After a brief stint as commander of the crack GOLANI Infantry Brigade, Yariv joined Maj. Gen. Meir Amit's A'MAN in 1961. Yariv was as well-rounded an officer as could exist at the time in Israel, and his battle experience, foreign exposure, and uncanny understanding of Middle Eastern dynamics made him a natural choice to succeed Meir Amit when Amit assumed control of the MOSSAD in 1963. Yariv would be A'MAN's director for a record-setting nine years.[4]

Although the winds of war were, indeed, blowing in the Middle East in the spring of 1967, nobody expected conflict to erupt so soon. Especially A'MAN.

According to A'MAN predictions, the earliest date that the Egyptian army could launch a major military campaign against Israel was 1969–70, and this depended on a politically stable Syria and a major contribution by the Jordanians. Oddly enough, due to "mysterious" technical reasons, A'MAN failed to provide its regular annual assessment for the year 1966–67.[5] The Israeli prime minister, Levi Eshkol, had a different understanding of what *could* happen. He felt that war could break out at any moment and that the IDF needed to be cognizant of the imminent danger, whether or not it materialized.

When, in April 1967, tension between Israel and Syria was escalating on an hourly basis, A'MAN still believed that should Israel be forced to mount a large-scale operation against Damascus, Egypt, the principal military power in the Arab world, would *not* intervene.[6] Expert predictions, like the desert sands, would shift with time.

The one man within the Israeli defense establishment who felt that the tensions with Syria were a harbinger of worse to come was IDF Chief of Staff Yitzhak Rabin. As Operations chief in 1960, Rabin had been caught in the confused grip of Operation ROTEM—when Egypt had moved covertly into the Sinai and, even when the armored column's movements toward the Israeli frontier were uncovered, the IDF had been unable to determine Nasser's ultimate intentions. In 1967, however, the similarities with ROTEM were very few indeed.

In the early-morning hours of May 15, 1967, the Egyptian army began to cross the Suez Canal and ferry frontline infantry and tank forces into Sinai. Unlike 1960, when the Egyptians had entered secretly so that their eventual withdrawal could be low-key and honorable, there was no radio silence in this operation, no secrecy; in fact, the sight of Egyptian tanks in a bright sand camouflage en route to push the Jews into the sea was covered with great glee by the Arab media. When, a few hours later that day, the IDF learned that the Egyptians had begun to move men and equipment into the demilitarized Sinai peninsula, Rabin was determined to avoid a repeat of the chain of events that nearly led to a full-scale war.

Rabin summoned A'MAN director Yariv to his office in the KIRYA and, convinced that some kind of military clash was imminent, telephoned Maj. Gen. Yisrael "Talik" Tal,* commander of the 84th Armored Division. The two generals conducted the following—now infamous—conversation:

Rabin: "Do you remember ROTEM?"
Tal: "I remember."
Rabin: "Well, we have a repeat of ROTEM now. Talik, *roll* immediately!"[7]

Hours after this half-minute talk between the chief of staff and the division commander, columns of IDF Centurion and Patton main battle tanks were

---

*One of the founding fathers of Israel's armored forces, Yisrael Tal would later go on to conceive, design, and help see the materialization of the MERKAVA ("Chariot") series of main battle tanks. These armored fighting machines take into consideration crew survivability over speed, and are considered one of the best tanks in the world today.

loaded on their transporters and rushed from their bases in the Negev Desert to the Egyptian frontier to bolster the nation's thinly spread defenses.

Initially, however, A'MAN did not view Nasser's move into the UN-controlled Sinai with great foreboding. As in 1960, it was thought that Nasser would order his army and tanks to withdraw after a show of force had helped put Israel in its place. The officers in A'MAN HQ were still sticking to their opinion that Egypt could not possibly mount a full-scale war until 1969–70, even though the Soviet Union, the principal arms supplier and ally of both Syria and Egypt, was stirring up major problems in the region. Perhaps wishing to instigate a conflict in order to humiliate Israel, or to instill a sense of invincibility in the Arab camp, the Soviets gave the Egyptians and Syrians false information about nonexistent IDF troop movements and about American intentions. Apparently, the Soviets did not believe Israel could win a war with Egypt. A conversation, relayed back to A'MAN director Yariv, between Moshe Sneh, the leader of the Israeli Communist party, and the Soviet ambassador in Tel Aviv went something like this:

Sneh: "Of course Israel will win the war!"
Soviet ambassador: "Who the hell is going to fight? The espresso boys and the pimps of Dizengoff Street?" [8]

On May 16, 1967, a calm confidence still permeated the hallways of A'MAN HQ. The reason: Egypt's 4th Armored Division, the elite fighting formation of Nasser's army, had yet to cross the Suez Canal. A'MAN's research and assessment officers believed that without that fighting force, Nasser had no chance of mounting any type of offensive military action. These same officers, however, still hadn't a clue as to the Egyptian president's intentions.Was he putting on his poker face? Was he trying to instigate a brief war in order to reinforce his position in the Arab world? To confuse the harried soldier spies in Tel Aviv, Nasser ordered a squadron of Ilyushin-28 bombers, a Soviet-made combat aircraft capable of carrying a two-thousand-kilogram payload, into the Sinai air base of Bir-Thamade. Tel Aviv was only a three-minute flight from Bir-Thamade, so A'MAN's intelligence would have to be good. If Egypt was planning something, the IDF needed to know. Also on May 16, the IDF conducted a secret mobilization of some of its reserve forces and key intelligence personnel. The call-up would make it politically difficult for Nasser to cut his losses and run back to the border, but, more importantly, it would limit Israel's losses should a surprise attack occur. Indeed, losses could be heavy. According to reports, Egyptian forces in Sinai were equipped with poison gas.[9] Chemical weapons were particularly feared by the IDF, since Nasser already had used them in the Yemen Civil War.

During the beginning of the crisis, the soldier/archivists at HATZAV disseminated incredible amounts of data on Arab intentions as relayed through government-controlled newspapers, magazines, and radio broadcasts. According to the public line it appeared as if the Arab world was preparing for the final solution to the State of Israel. Still, the popular belief in A'MAN HQ was that the Egyptians were bolstering their defenses in Sinai in case a full-scale war between Israel and Syria erupted; the deployment of Egypt's 2d Division along the El Arish–Kusseima line was viewed as 100 percent defensive in nature.[10]

The guessing game continued and intensified. On May 18 a new twist was thrown into the chaotic equation when United Nations Secretary General U Thant capitulated to Nasser's demand that the UN peacekeeping force evacuate Sinai. This could mean only that war was imminent, but at an IDF General Staff meeting, Egypt's moves still were viewed as defensive (in the most optimistic light) and ambiguous (in the most realistic sense). According to A'MAN director Yariv, after consultation with his most respected "Egypt Desk experts," Nasser's moves left him with only four viable options: (1) provoke Israel into a full-scale conflict in which the Jewish state would be labeled as the aggressor and suffer damaging political consequences; (2) continue the political brinksmanship ("a potentially deadly game of 'chicken' played with tanks and cannons" was how one A'MAN officer viewed this posture); (3) launch a massive invasion of Israel, from the Gulf of Aqaba to Gaza, in which the destruction of the Jewish state was envisioned; and (4) economically ruin Israel by initiating a static war of attrition (or of nerves!) in which the IDF would have to remain mobilized for a lengthy period of time.

Whatever the scenario, developments did not bode favorably for Israel.[11] Yariv ordered the further mobilization of reservist KA'MANIM ("Intelligence officers") and additional photoreconnaissance flights. Special orders were issued to the IDF Military Censor's Office to pay special attention to any mention in the press of IDF troop deployments or the call-up of reservist units. War, it appeared, was unavoidable. But when? Who would fire the first shot?*

In the next few days, bad news continued to flow into A'MAN HQ. Intelligence reports—supported by extensive coverage in the Arab media—indicated that three infantry and engineering brigades originally stationed in Egypt had boarded transport aircraft and were headed toward Sinai; already, six full

---

*Since June 1967 there has been great speculation as to whether or not Nasser *actually* intended to attack Israel. In the book *Dangerous Liaison* by husband-and-wife team Andrew and Leslie Cockburn, who painted a sensationalized picture of the covert relationship between Israel and the United States, the assertion is made that both the CIA and the MOSSAD knew that Nasser was not in a situation where he could or would attack Israel; he was sitting on the fence waiting for the winds of Arab radicalism to pass with time. According to this new twist on an already controversial aspect of the war, the CIA gave Maj. Gen. Meir Amit the impression that they were not only behind any Israeli preemptive strike, but would help support Israel with any political fallout that would follow the anticipated IDF victory.

Egyptian divisions were poised for action throughout the sandy abyss of Sinai. Israel knew it still possessed the qualitative edge, but its tenure was precarious and dwindling moment by moment. On May 20, Egyptian units took over heavy gun emplacements in the Straits of Tiran at Sharm es-Sheikh, Israel's commercial gateway to Asia and Africa. Every Israeli cargo ship, vessels that ferried the precious fuel and raw materials from Iran and Africa, were now at the mercy of Egyptian gunners. But would Nasser close the Straits? A'MAN staffers viewed this as unlikely since it provided Israel with a legal casus belli.[12]

Two days later, Nasser made an announcement to the world's media that shocked nearly every Israeli citizen—the Straits would be blockaded! At a General Staff meeting later that evening, Yariv addressed the who's who of the Israeli military and Prime Minister/Defense Minister Eshkol. He stated that if Israel did not act, there would be no credibility to the nation's deterrent power; the Arabs would interpret this as weakness *and* take advantage of every opportunity to assail Israel.[13]

The A'MAN director understood that the tide of war—or the mere illusion of it—had overcome the usually pragmatic Egyptian president. He had been swept to the threshold of war by a militarily weak and politically fragile Syria, by the bankroll and armaments of a mighty superpower, and by the thirst for revenge among his masses. Only a preemptive Israeli strike could turn possible annihilation into victory. Yariv proposed that Israel act militarily and at once; his motion was seconded by Operations Branch OC Maj. Gen. Ezer Weizman (an ex-RAF and former OC IAF who had brought the HEYL HA'AVIR into a period of supersonic excellence) and by a hesitant Lieutenant General Rabin. The prime minister attempted to press the United States, England, and France in a last-ditch diplomatic effort, but high-level cables from Washington to Cairo would have little effect as long as 40 million Egyptians were stirred into a war frenzy by their own government. War was now definite. On May 24, the Egyptian army's 4th Division began to roll into Sinai.[14]

War with Egypt was now expected. It would be a hard-fought conflict, according to A'MAN predictions, but there was little doubt that Israel would avail. On May 30, however, King Hussein of Jordan paid a surprise visit to Cairo, accompanied by Prime Minister Saad Jamaa, Gen. Amer Khammash, the Royal Jordanian army's chief of staff, and Gen. Saleh Kurdi, the OC Royal Jordanian Air Force. The purpose of this reconciliation—severe problems existed between the Pan-Arab socialism of Nasser and the monarchist pro-Western Hussein—was to conclude a mutual defensive pact bringing Jordan into a joint military command with Egypt. An Egyptian, Gen. Abdul Moneim Riadh, was named commander of Arab forces on the Jordanian front.[15]

It was now evident that Israel would not be fighting for mere political face, nor would this war be a minor skirmish in a long history of bloodshed. It would be a three-border war—four if Lebanon became involved. Israelis, made nervous and anxious by the events now controlling their lives, attached themselves to radios and listened for rumors. Hospitals and schools taped their windows shut in preparation for air raids; trenches were dug along the main streets of Israel's principal urban centers; and bomb shelters were examined by civil defense officers to make sure that emergency supplies of water, food, and medicines were well stocked. The city's bus stations looked like military bivouacs as tens of thousands of men, carrying kit bags and weapons, headed off to their military units to prepare for battle. A sense of national urgency brought out the best in the Israelis—much like Britain during the early days of the blitz. Everyone knew that with the exception of 1948, this was the greatest threat to Israeli existence that had ever been mounted. Nearly 100,000 Egyptian soldiers equipped with the latest Soviet materiel were less than a two-hour drive from Tel Aviv; Jordanian heavy artillery batteries—the dreaded American 155mm "Long Tom"—could hit virtually any area around Tel Aviv; and Syrian commandos—seen on filmed newsreels skinning live snakes with their teeth, then cooking the poor beasts—were within striking distance of Galilee and northern Israel.[16]

For years, Israel had prepared for the contingency of a full-scale Arab-Israeli war, one that would involve nearly every Arab nation—from Morocco in the west to Saudi Arabia and Iraq in the east—pitted against the IDF. To combat this eventuality, Israel developed the "Peripheral Defense," finding allies and forming alliances with the various non-Moslem and non-Arab elements within the Middle East. Fearing a joint Jordanian-Iraqi front, extreme effort was made to court the Kurds militarily. A proud mountain people whose ethnic roots date back thousands of years to the dawn of Mesopotamia, the Kurds have longed for an independent homeland for nearly a thousand years; when in the seventh century they converted to Islam, they were forced to become a minority—second-class Moslem citizens—in an Arab Middle East and Moslem Turkey. In 1961, Kurdish leader Mustafa Barzani founded a force of Peshmerga (the Kurdish word for "those who face death") guerrillas to mount an organized resistance to harsh Iraqi rule in Kurdistan. The civil war in Iraq was brutal: The Peshmerga fought fiercely and the Iraqi Air Force countered with heavy artillery strikes and napalm attacks by Soviet-made bombers. Israel openly supported Mustafa Barzani's rebels, realizing that supporting the Kurds was an excellent opportunity to weaken Iraq, one of the Arab world's largest military machines, and hamper its abilities to wage war against the Jewish state. The MOSSAD had supported their military campaign, as did A'MAN.

The relationship with the Kurds afforded Israel invaluable firsthand intelligence on the Iraqi army. Covert visits were arranged between the Kurds and IDF officers; those sent included Capt. Arik Regev, an up-and-coming reconnaissance paratroop officer, and Maj. Gen. Rechavem "Ghandi" Ze'evi, deputy commander of the Operations Branch.[17] Through its work in Kurdistan and through the MOSSAD's networks, A'MAN was able to assemble an intimate portrait of the Iraqi military—an extensive Order of Battle to the platoon, and how many planes were flown by its air force as well as the names of most of its pilots. What it did not know were the intentions of the Iraqi leadership. Would they join in the fighting if Egypt attacked Israel? How much of their army would they dispatch to Jordan?

Whether Jordan would fight was another critical question. The man responsible for evaluating the moves of Jordan's King Hussein and assessing the capabilities of its military was the commander of A'MAN's Jordanian Desk, Col. Ze'ev "Biber" Bar-Lavi—a man considered by many in the Israeli intelligence community to know more of what was going on in the Hashemite kingdom than the king himself![18] "Biber," a PAL'MACH veteran, had joined the IDF Intelligence in 1948 in the Jordanian Section and remained there for over twenty years. (Many A'MAN desk officers remained at their posts for lengthy tours of duty, each becoming as good an expert as could be found on a particular nation, army, or unit.) Yet Biber, too, had a difficult time predicting King Hussein's moves in this ever-escalating crisis. In fact, he predicted that King Hussein would keep out of the war, and duly sent a memo to Yariv indicating that the central front should remain quiet. Yariv, however, had a gut sense about what would transpire and, according to reports, told his trusted officer to "wake up and realize that this is a new ballgame now."[19] Israel Defense Forces armor and infantry units were moved all along the elongated and circular frontier with Jordan, preparing to fight against what was considered to be the toughest of Israel's foes on the Middle Eastern battlefield—the British-trained Jordanian Legion.

Increased intelligence assets also were devoted to the Jordanian front. Yet as thousands of IDF forces were rushed to the border, it became harder for the Intelligence Branch to run its agents across the no-man's-land in divided Jerusalem. Spies were the principal means of gathering intelligence on Jordan, but with so many prying eyes everywhere along the frontier, it was virtually impossible to keep the "meet" between agent and handler a secret. According to Rafi Sitton, a K'TZIN LE'TAFKIDIM MEYUCHADIM ("Special Tasks officer"), "agent running did continue up until 48 hours before the eruption of hostilities."[20] In fact, an Israeli courier dispatched through Jerusalem's Mendelbaum Gate was sent to King Hussein to instruct him that Israel would not enter into hostile actions against Jordan if the king refrained from attacking Israel. Sitton was responsible for the flow of information relayed to A'MAN HQ through the agents who slinked their way between Jordan and Israel. These agents, according to reports, represented a wide range of talent and personalities—from low-ranking Jordanian army officers to the usual profiteers, smugglers, and pimps. Even with the reports filtering in to the Jordanian Desk, Col. "Biber"

Bar-Lavi was unable to formulate an accurate assessment as to what Jordan's moves would be. Its deployments throughout Jerusalem, the West Bank, and the Jordan Valley were both defensive and offensive in nature.

There were also misgivings and uncertainties regarding Syria's role in any impending conflict. Although a series of skirmishes with Syria had catalyzed the process and brought the Middle East to the brink of full-scale war, there were many in A'MAN HQ who believed that Syria would sit this one out, as it did in the 1956 War. If Israel won the war quickly, Syria could claim to the Arab world that it had tied down large numbers of Israeli forces in the north; if the Arabs won quickly, Syria could enter the war at an opportune instance when the rewards clearly justified the price. The commanding officer of the Syrian Desk, Lieutenant Colonel "Micha," an expert on the Damascus regime who would eventually spend more than thirty-five years at his post, was also at a loss in determining decisions from Damascus.[21]

The indecision, uncertainty, and anxiety continued into June—it was not a matter of if there would be war, but a question of when. Prime Minister Eshkol still hesitated to issue the green light and authorize a preemptive strike, being naturally concerned with Israel's precarious political position should it strike first. Eshkol was, however, reassured as to the IDF abilities by the A'MAN director. During a historic cabinet and military meeting on June 2, Yariv addressed Israel's decision makers. Although not allowing his colleagues to know any details of the means employed and the sources tapped, Major General Yariv shared A'MAN's extensive knowledge of the enemy's deployment, and morale, and their conclusion that the Arabs could not win a war. Yariv described how the Egyptians were rushing so many men and machines across the Suez Canal that some units were roaming the Sinai desert without water, food, and uniforms. Israeli Air Force OC Major General Hod added that his fighter squadrons knew exactly where each and every Egyptian combat aircraft was located.[22] Many details of Yariv's speech, including intimate details of the enemy's command-and-control apparatus, remain classified to this day. It was clear, however, that the IDF was tired of waiting for the diplomatic community to produce a miracle.

The final push that propelled Eshkol to war was the transfer of Egyptian commando units to Jordan on June 3. This signaled the onset of covert cross-border sabotage attacks, which would precipitate an Egyptian first strike. The fact that several commando units, the elite of the elite within the Egyptian military, had been deployed around the town of Eilat, which borders Aqaba and is Israel's sole shipping lane to the east, indicated that a strike against this strategic location was imminent. Israel's government was now united. The cabinet—which consisted of twenty-one ministers from seven different political parties—voted on June 4 to go to war. The Middle East would never be the same.

Israel's blitz on June 5, 1967, against Egyptian forces in the Sinai and against Egyptian Air Force bases throughout the country, has become legend. In one strike, the Israeli Air Force annihilated one of the most powerful aerial armadas outside of Europe and did so brilliantly. Next in line would be the air forces of Syria, Jordan, and Iraq; in less than twelve hours, Arab air power was history. With the skies over the battlefields no longer contested, IDF ground units were able to move with lightning speed. Within three days, Israeli soldiers were bathing in the Suez Canal and the city of Jerusalem was liberated. On the sixth day of the war, the Syrians no longer controlled the Jordan River tributaries or the strategic Golan Heights, and their ability to harass the Galilee settlements existed no longer. The Six-Day War was an epic Israeli victory.

The capture of the Gaza Strip and the Sinai desert, the West Bank of the Jordan River including the city of Jerusalem, and the Golan Heights came as a result of the accurate and reliable intelligence data made available to Israeli combat troops. It is safe to assume that in no time in the history of modern warfare has a nation been equipped with such an intimate portrait of the enemy's disposition, deployment, abilities, and inabilities as was the IDF at 0740 on the morning of June 5, 1967—the time when the code words "SADIN ADOM" ("Red Sheet") were heard in thousands of Israeli communications headsets and the order to roll was given.

A'MAN's ability to monitor, track, and gain a real-time portrait of Arab forces in the hours prior to the outbreak of hostilities and, indeed, during the war itself was a salute to the service's combined intelligence-gathering efforts—from the running of spies to the monitoring of enemy communications. Clearly, the most important of A'MAN's tools was the human element, and A'MAN's Special Tasks Section was busier than any other. After all, it had laid the groundwork with Eli Cohen and Wolfgang Lotz, and countless anonymous others.

From the reports assembled, it appears that both the MOSSAD and A'MAN were running an endless string of spies and saboteurs inside Egypt. Numerous reports have surfaced detailing the activities of A'MAN agents who not only infiltrated the upper echelons of the Egyptian military's command-and-control structure, but penetrated the political and social sphere as well, which made them privy to other vital, nonmilitary intelligence.

One reputed spy was Ali al-Atfi, the masseur to both Nasser and his successor, Anwar as-Sadat.[23] Many Egyptian security officials believe that al-Atfi relayed in-depth intelligence reports to his Israeli handlers on the impending moves—both military and political—of the Egyptian regime, and they have also accused him of slowly poisoning the Egyptian president and precipitating his death, in September 1970, of a massive heart attack. According to foreign reports, al-Atfi was recruited by A'MAN while on a vacation in Holland. He died in 1990, in Cairo's Central Prison, after serving eleven years of a fifteen-year sentence for espionage.[24]

Two other A'MAN agents who operated in the who's who of Egypt's beautiful and powerful people were Anwar Ephraim and Baruch Na'ul.[25] It is believed that Ephraim was responsible for organizing a massive and, if reports of the celebration are correct, frenzied party for the pilots and officers of the ultrastrategic Inchas Air Force Base just outside Alexandria. The party, thrown on the night of June 4, less than twelve hours before the preemptive Israeli blitz, lasted until the wee hours of the morning and included drinking, large quantities of grilled foods, and the obligatory belly dancers. As IAF pilots were being briefed for the last time, and ground crewmen were fastening runway-busting bombs to aircraft pylons, the elite of the Egyptian Air Force—the men entrusted with the security of Egypt's skies—were busy partying. Ephraim is reported to have left the sprawling installation at dawn and boarded an international flight moments before the first bombs landed on the Inchas runways, and the first MiGs, Sukhois, and Tupelovs were destroyed in their shelters.

Baruch Na'ul operated in the Alexandria area and was reported to have been a close personal friend of one of Egypt's most famous belly dancers.[26] Her body was found on the Cairo-Alexandria Highway two days before the war began. Although the Egyptian Muchabarat attempted to cover up the circumstances surrounding her death, it is believed the Na'ul killed her to keep his identity secret. The fact that A'MAN was at work in the Alexandria region, home port to the Egyptian navy, was made evident in the mounting of a major, though failed, Israeli naval commando raid on Alexandria on the first night of the war. It is believed that the audacious operation was a direct result of the years of work A'MAN and the MOSSAD had invested in photographing, monitoring, and recording events at the Alexandria base.[27]

The most important of A'MAN's *known* "human assets" in Egypt was a mysterious figure known simply as "Suleiman," or "Captain X." [28] A specialist in radio communications and a respected officer in the Egyptian army, Suleiman was recruited by A'MAN several years prior to the 1967 War when he was overheard expressing his contempt for the political nepotism and corruption within Nasser's Egypt. Luckily for the State of Israel, one man overhearing this brazen public statement was an A'MAN "headhunter" seeking talent; Suleiman was invited to the agent's house for a talk over a bottle of Arac, a sweet anise liqueur popular in the Middle East.[29] Suleiman was in. Secretly trained in coded communications in a Cairo safe house, Suleiman was the perfect "sleeper"—he was to lie low until the Egyptian army was mobilized and moved into the Sinai. Then *and only then* was he to commence communications and report all Egyptian movements to his MOD 2 handlers and technicians in Tel Aviv. His first broadcast came on May 17, 1967—the day the Egyptian army entered the demilitarized Sinai.

For the next three weeks Suleiman became A'MAN's eyes and ears in the Egyptian rear. While continuing normal duties from his post for *his* command at the feverish pace of an army poised for battle, Suleiman faithfully reported to Tel Aviv, broadcasting invaluable, detailed information on Egyptian troop strengths, movements, battle plans, and morale. Even in the chaotic first three days of the fighting, he relayed to A'MAN HQ meticulously detailed battle-field damage reports on the extent of the IAF's devastating aerial blitz and the merciless armored punch through Egyptian defenses in the Sinai desert. Tragically, he became a victim of the IDF's unstoppable juggernaut. Suleiman was one of A'MAN's most coveted agents and clearly one of its most secret; his identity was kept from cabinet ministers and even the chief of staff. It was impossible, for the obvious security considerations, to tell advancing IDF troops *not* to shoot at a particular convoy, position, or area because of the presence of a top-secret spy. The A'MAN handlers would have to pray for the best.

On June 7, Suleiman's communications and command unit found itself trapped in a chaotic logjam of burned vehicles and troops fleeing the incessant Israeli attack. As Suleiman's post made its way to the entrance of the Mitla Pass at the Parker Memorial (coincidentally the parachute landing zone of Raful Eitan's paratroopers in the opening hours of the 1956 War), the IAF appeared with a menacing roar. Before A'MAN HQ could call off the low-level strafing run by a flight of Fouga Magisters on a tank-killing sortie, Suleiman's position was pummeled by rocket and cannon fire. Hours later, when the fighting stopped on the peninsula, the A'MAN director dispatched, it is believed, a squad from SAYERET MAT'KAL to search for Suleiman.[30] His body was eventually found, and he was buried with full IDF military honors in the Sinai. Several high-ranking, though anonymous, A'MAN figures attended his funeral.

A'MAN's HUMINT success in 1967 was simply astounding. Through its agents in the field (as well as other means), A'MAN, IAF Intelligence, and the signal corps were able to determine the precise time when the first wave of Israeli Mirage IIIC, Super Mystere, Ouragon, and Vautour fighters and bombers would drop their bombs on eighteen Egyptian Air Force base runways. A'MAN's HUMINT was able to pinpoint *exactly* when the Egyptians would be most vulnerable— between 0730 and 0800. At this time, technicians manning surface-to-air radars would be most fatigued at the end of their eight-hour shift; pilots and aircrews would be wiping the crumbs from their mustaches following hearty breakfasts; fighter aircraft would be moved to outdoor service areas for maintenance; and, perhaps most importantly, senior Egyptian Air Force staff officers would be stuck in traffic jams en route to their Cairo offices. The intelligence was as accurate as it could get. The Egyptians, in effect, were caught with their pants down. Of a total of 419 Egyptian aircraft, 304 were destroyed on the ground.[31]

Information on A'MAN HUMINT activities on the Jordanian and Syrian fronts just before and during the war is sketchy at best—perhaps to protect the identities of individuals still alive or in power, or perhaps because spy-running across the Jordanian and Syrian frontiers took a backseat to other more sophisticated means of obtaining insight into the enemy's capabilities and intentions.

In the art of gathering intelligence—SIGINT, ELINT, and PHOTINT (Photographic Intelligence)—through technological means, A'MAN was far superior to its Arab foes. The man responsible for this feat was Col. Yuval Ne'eman. Born in Tel Aviv in 1925, Ne'eman was always known for his brilliance in scholarly pursuits; his friends called him "The Brain"! Although he earned a doctorate at the Imperial College in London, he also proved himself to be a courageous fighter and a charismatic leader. Being able to fight and think was a unique commodity, and Ne'eman was sent to the French Military College and made a senior A'MAN officer.

Ne'eman's impact on the development of A'MAN was profound and visionary. The technically gifted Ne'eman believed that any future war would be won— or lost—by a nation's mastery of electronics and computers.[32] Electronic watch stations and computerized observation posts that could detect even the slightest enemy move would become the equalizer in Israel's numerical inferiority to the Arabs. Yet what Ne'eman proposed cost millions—cold cash that A'MAN, let alone the State of Israel, simply did not have. Many have said that the army was reluctant to invest a cent in anything that wouldn't explode!

Ne'eman's tenacity won the day over frugal accountants, however, and A'MAN was provided with the necessary funding to build a computerized network that very few Western nations could match. Data brought in through any and all means—from a spy in an Arab capital or an article in the Arab press, to a reconnaissance patrol scanning the enemy's rear—was filtered through computer linkage systems, which helped analyze the information and distinguish fact from fiction. Israel's policymakers were given as accurate a picture on the potential for hostilities as could have been achieved by any First World intelligence service. Ne'eman invented hundreds of gadgets and novelties that helped keep Israel one step ahead of the Arabs. His electronic watch stations in Sinai, planted by IDF reconnaissance units deep inside enemy territory, were revolutionary in their technological advancement; Ne'eman's "electronic trip wire" was the basis for NATO's computerized system for tracking Soviet submarines.[33]

Ne'eman's technological impact on A'MAN intelligence-gathering capabilities was greatest in the sphere of SIGINT. Along with his trip wires planted deep beneath the sands of the Sinai, Ne'eman provided A'MAN with an ultraadvanced eavesdropping device. The "bugs" were planted in the Egyptian rear by small teams of IDF reconnaissance paratroopers and Intelligence Corps technicians who raced through the desert in laden-down jeeps. Stealthlike in their nighttime movements and nearly invisible in their French-made lizard-pattern camouflage fatigues, the lightly armed reconnaissance troopers were able to move about the Sinai desert with virtual impunity. The bug device, a miniature, highly sensitive piece of state-of-the-art electronics, was attached to an Egyptian telephone line and outfitted with an extremely potent microphone capable of picking up and recording numerous telephone conversations, while at the same time powerful enough to pick up communications from as far away as two hundred meters. (This technology would eventually be used in an electronic countermeasure employed against Arab radar batteries in the upcoming War of Attrition.[34])

One of A'MAN's major SIGINT coups during the 1967 War was the ability of technicians to monitor and intercept high-level communications between Arab field commanders and their legions in the field. A'MAN technicians and radiomen issued false orders, confused ranks already in disarray, and played with the frequencies as if they owned them. In one much publicized incident, an A'MAN radio monitor was able to "disguise" himself as a senior Egyptian army officer and guide a lost tank battalion through the sands of the Sinai—always away from the advancing Israeli lines and, after the ceasefire was declared, toward a POW depot where the T-54/55 main battle tanks were seized and the men taken into custody. In another instance, an A'MAN SIGINT officer, impersonating an Egyptian Air Force ground controller, ordered an Egyptian MiG-21 pilot to jettison his bomb load over the Mediterranean.

The SIGINT successes were also prevalent in the art of deception. Through carefully conceived broadcasts and signals, the IDF convinced the Egyptian High Command that one of their main points of thrust across the frontier would be in the south near Kusseima. This prompted Cairo to deploy numerous military forces—including an elite armored unit commanded by Gen. Sa'ad ad-Din Shazli, the Egyptian chief of staff during the 1973 War—along the southern axis.[35]

Yet the most famous case of tapping the lines occurred on the second day of the fighting. On June 6, 1967, King Hussein received a telephone call in his Amman palace from Egyptian President Nasser; the call came more than twenty-four hours after the pride of the Egyptian Air Force had been destroyed in the IAF preemptive strike, along with the air forces of Jordan, Syria, and Iraq. Although the conversation was meant to be top secret, it was being monitored and taped by two veteran intelligence officers using Second World War–era equipment.[36]

According to the most accurate account of the conversation, by noted Israeli military writer Yosef Argaman in the pages of BAMACHANE, the IDF's weekly magazine, the conversation went as follows.

Nasser: "Good morning your majesty, I understand that my brother wishes to know about the battles being waged all along the front. . . . [static] Do you know that the United States is participating with Israel in the attack? Shall we announce this?"

Hussein: "Hello, I can't make you out, the line is terrible!"
Jordanian operator: "The line between Cairo and the royal palace is very poor. I'll try to fix it."
Nasser: "Hello? Your majesty? Shall we announce that it is both America and England or just America?"
Hussein: "The United States and England."
Nasser: "Does England have aircraft carriers?"
Hussein: [Unintelligible due to static]
Nasser: "Good . . . good. So the king will make an announcement and so will I."
Hussein: "Thanks."
Nasser: "Yes, my brother, it is nothing. Be strong."
Hussein: "Your excellency Mr. President, if you have something, or some kind of an idea, anyway. . . ."
Nasser: "We are fighting with all our power and the battles are raging on all fronts—all night. If something happened in the beginning, we'll overcome it. Allah is with us. In any event I'll make the announcement [concerning the Americans] and you make the announcement. We'll also make sure that the Syrians make an announcement that American and British warplanes are using their aircraft carriers against us. We'll make the announcement, stress it to the world, and exclaim it to everyone."
Hussein: "OK, all right."
Nasser: "Does his majesty agree?"
Hussein: [Answer not recorded]
Nasser: "A thousand thanks. Be strong. We are strong today. Our aircraft are pounding the Israeli airfields from the morning's first light."
Hussein: "A thousand thanks. Be in peace." [37]

Realizing that this war was already lost, Nasser and King Hussein were contemplating the means to achieve some sort of political victory, at least in the eyes of the Arab world. The tape proved to be absolute dynamite. The commander of the eavesdropping unit said to the two technicians who monitored the conversation, "Make four copies of the tape. . . . It's worth millions!" [38]

Before the copies could be made, however, Radio Amman and Radio Cairo made the fictitious announcement to their citizens—people who had absolutely no idea of the extent of the Israeli rout. At 0900 that same day, Syria joined the party: a Ba'ath party spokesman in Damascus proclaimed that American and British warplanes were attacking the Arabs. Even the Soviet Union believed the Arab version of the unfolding events. Hours after the announcement of American and British collusion with Israel, angry mobs raced through the streets of the Egyptian capital in violent demonstrations;

in Alexandria, Egypt's second largest city, uncontrollable mobs burned down the U.S. consulate.

In light of the volatile political situation, the Israeli government decided to release the tape to the world's media—despite A'MAN director Yariv's pleading with Defense Minister Dayan to keep the conversation secret. Letting the Arabs know what A'MAN was capable of would have chilling security repercussions. Dayan, however, along with Eshkol's enthusiastic approval, ordered the tape released, and its political aftermath was astounding. According to one Israeli intelligence officer, the Arabs had been caught with their hands in the cookie jar—the leader of the Arab world was heard concocting a ridiculous tale meant to incite ignorant masses. The release of the tape drove a wedge between Egypt and Jordan, and between much of the "moderate" Arab world and the United States and the United Kingdom. The one negative effect of the released tape— the one result that Yariv had feared—was that the Arabs considerably upgraded their communications security, making A'MAN's job much harder.

"Spectacular as the conversation was," according to Brig. Gen. Ephraim Lapid, a former IDF spokesman and, during the 1967 War, the A'MAN Eavesdropping Unit's commanding officer, "it was *not* the most important conversation intercepted by A'MAN, and not even the most important bit of radio traffic intercepted during the 1967 War."[39] Nevertheless, release of the tape triggered a tremendous lift in the morale of the typical Israeli soldier. "We are capable of almost anything" became a popular catchphrase among the confident and jubilant Israeli troops. If A'MAN could tape a conversation between two Arab heads of state, only Allah knew the true limitations of Israeli intelligence.

Israel's SIGINT/ELINT/PHOTINT campaign against Egypt, Jordan, and Syria was all-inclusive and impressive. Yet it would culminate in one of the most tragic, controversial, and mysterious chapters of the intelligence war. In retrospect, perhaps Nasser's story was not so outrageous.

In May 1967, the USS *Liberty*, a former cargo vessel outfitted with top-secret intelligence-gathering equipment, set sail from Norfolk, Virginia, on what would be her final voyage; its objective was to eavesdrop on the impending war brewing in the Middle East. On June 8, less than twenty-four hours before Israel was about to grab the Golan Heights from Syria, the USS *Liberty*, alone and lightly armed, was sailing approximately fifteen miles off the coast of the Sinai, just opposite El Arish. Several crew members had requested a destroyer escort of some kind; a request had also been made to move the vessel at least a hundred miles from the fighting, but apparently this communication had been lost in the bureaucratic abyss of the Sixth Fleet HQ. At 0600, IDF/navy HQ identified the *Liberty* as a spy ship. In the navy's Haifa situation room, a red flag was placed over a plastic silhouette of the ship, identifying it as such.[40] At 1400, a flotilla of IDF/navy torpedo boats attacked the U.S. Navy spy ship; a while later, the listing vessel was strafed by low-flying IAF aircraft. Thirty-four American sailors died in that bombing.

Much has been written about the sinking of the USS *Liberty*—much fact and a great deal of fiction. Confirmed elements of the incident include the facts that the Americans were flying the Stars and Stripes; that the IDF/navy and the IAF had reconnoitered the area for nearly six hours, following the *Liberty*; and that the Israelis mistook the *Liberty* for an Egyptian naval vessel, the *el-Qusir*, which, it was reported, was shelling Israeli positions off the Sinai. According to Brig. Gen. Yeshayahu Bareket, the OC IAF Intelligence during the 1967 War, great efforts were made to identify the suspicious vessel—sailing smack in the middle of the war zone—as either friend or foe. When no positive identification could be made, the order to attack was issued.[41]

Israel later admitted guilt in the tragic episode and provided compensation to the families of the fallen sailors. Nevertheless, as far as Washington was concerned, the fact that an American ally had humiliated Soviet client states was more important than the loss of the *Liberty*.[42] The clash between allies in the waters of the Sinai also deflected attention from the covert relationship between American and Israeli intelligence forces, a relationship that was remarkable, if the reports are true.

Since the days of the MOSSAD's Reuven Shiloah and the CIA's James Jesus Angeleton, the American-Israeli intelligence relationship had developed into a dependable partnership. Militarily, the United States had begun to supply the Jewish state with arms in 1962. President Kennedy paved the way for Israel to acquire batteries of HAWK surface-to-air missiles; soon M-48 Patton tanks were also heading for Israel. *On paper* the French were still Israel's principal arms supplier and proponent in the world community; the French-Israeli alliance, especially during the Algerian Civil War, represented a Western stance against radical Pan-Arabism. Slowly, however, France's support for Israel waned as Arab oil—and the advanced French weapons that oil revenue could purchase—became more important than a traditional and beleaguered ally. The United States, under the leadership of President Lyndon B. Johnson, filled the void immediately. In 1967, the IAF was preparing its Order of Battle to accept the McDonnell-Douglas A-4 Skyhawk and was hoping to one day acquire the mighty McDonnell-Douglas F-4 Phantom. The Phantom, which would provide the IAF with speed, impressive range, durability, and, most of all, devastating firepower, also came in a highly sophisticated photoreconnaissance version—the RF-4C.

In June 1967, however, the IAF had yet to order the Phantom, and none of its variants had been incorporated into the air force's Order of Battle. But *perhaps* the IAF already had access to the mighty F-4.

According to Steven Green, in his book *Taking Sides*, a covert arrangement was forged for the USAF to assist Israel in its photoreconnaissance
efforts in the early hours of the war. It did not appear as if the IAF was lacking
in its PHOTINT abilities. The fact that targets as far away as Luxor in southern
Egypt and H-3 in western Iraq were decimated with breathtaking precision
was a testament to the skill and hard work of A'MAN and its IAF intelligence
counterparts. In the early-morning hours of June 3, however, the pilots of the
USAF 38th Tactical Reconnaissance Squadron, an element of the 26th Tactical Reconnaissance Wing, were ousted from their beds in Ramstein AFB,
in West Germany, and ordered to fly to Morón, Spain, where they would
participate in a top-secret NATO exercise. They were eventually joined by
a giant C-141 cargo plane that contained a complete WS430a photoreconnaissance system.

At the Morón airstrip, the crews were enlightened as to the true reason
behind their mission. They were told, in a top-secret briefing, that they would
be flying to a remote section of the Negev Desert near Beersheba—believed
to be Israel's sprawling Hatzerim Air Force Base—to provide tactical reconnaissance support for the IDF against Egypt and the other Arab countries.
The pilots were issued civilian clothes and identification and were flown to
Israel in a C-130 Hercules transport; their RF-4Cs were adorned with a blue
and white Star of David—the emblem of the IAF—and given tail numbers
corresponding to actual inventory numbers in the IAF.

For the next few days, the USAF "civilian fliers" scanned the skies above
the battlefield. At the end of each sortie, A'MAN photo interpreters analyzed
the thousands of feet of exposed film; during nighttime flybys, infrared film
was used to detect the heat emanating from vehicles. On June 12, the RF-4Cs
returned to Morón and then Ramstein.

This report of close-knit U.S.-Israeli military intelligence cooperation has
never been confirmed.* As mentioned in Steven Green's *Taking Sides*, it remains
a point of great secrecy and denial. Many "conspiracy theorists" have gone
so far as to speculate that the USS *Liberty*, having picked up signals from
the top-secret RF-4C transmissions, was compromising the security of the covert
operation and needed to be silenced. Perhaps the truth will never be known.

---

*In his book *Embassies in Crisis*, noted Israeli author Michael Bar-Zohar states that
the U.S. Joint Chiefs of Staff had gone so far as to prepare several contingency plans
for direct U.S. military intervention in the next Arab-Israeli war should things go badly
for Israel. Two possible scenarios included a combined large-scale paratroop drop
and naval bombardment of the Sinai; the other envisioned flying a mobile U.S. response force directly into Israel to provide a "buffer of force and fire" around large
population centers.

*   *   *

Although the 1967 War was a turning point for Israeli Military Intelligence and a victory of epic proportions, it was an extremely bloody conflict. In the six days of fighting, the IDF lost 777 dead and 2,811 wounded. Egypt lost more than 15,000 dead, 50,000 wounded, and 5,380 POWs*; Syria and Jordan together lost nearly 1,000 dead, 3,000 wounded, and 1,500 POWs.[43]

By June 10, as the smoke settled over a Middle East forever altered, Israel steeled itself for the upcoming challenges. Israel had conquered the Sinai desert, the West Bank, and the imposing Golan Heights in an astounding 144 hours. Israel's victory was A'MAN's coming of age—a zenith for a service that had used all resources at its disposal to close a vast and imposing gap. As far as most of the world was concerned, Israel's David had overwhelmed the Arab world's Goliath. Impressions would be fleeting. The true intelligence war, the dirty war against conventional soldiers entrenched in bunkers and terrorists lurking in the shadows, had only just begun.

*All of these POWs were eventually bargained off for the surviving Susannah spies, Wolfgang Lotz, and the handful of IAF pilots and IDF/navy frogmen captured during the war.

NOTES: CHAPTER TEN

1. Lon Nordeen, *Fighters Over Israel* (New York: Orion Books, 1990), 63.
2. Chaim Herzog, *The Arab-Israeli Wars* (London: Arms & Armour Press, 1982), 148.
3. One of Yariv's classmates in France's esteemed Military College was Gamal Faisal, who, several years later, as a general, was the Syrian army's chief of staff. Stewart Steven, *The Spymasters of Israel* (New York: Ballantine Books, 1980), 225.
4. Oded Granot, HEYL HA'MODE'IN: TZAHAL BE'HEILO ENTZYKLOPEDIA LE'TZAVA ULE'BITACHON (Tel Aviv: Revivim Publishers, 1981), 78.
5. Ian Black and Benny Morris, *Israel's Secret Wars: The Untold History of Israeli Intelligence* (London: Hamish Hamilton, 1991), 211.
6. *Ibid.* 212.
7. See Oded Granot, HEYL HA'MODE'IN, 78.
8. See Ian Black and Benny Morris, *Israel's Secret Wars*, 214.
9. Various ed., "19 SHANIM LE'MILCHEMET SHESHET HA'YAMIM," YISRAEL SHELANU (June 6, 1986): 8.
10. See Oded Granot, HEYL HA'MODE'IN, 79.
11. *Ibid.* 80.
12. Arieh Na'or, "MILCHAMOT HA'YEHUDIM," MONITIN (May 1991): 14.
13. Eitan Haber, HA'YOM TIFROTZ MILCHAMA (Tel Aviv: Edanim Publishers, 1987), 188.
14. Various ed., "ESRIM SHANA LE'SHESHET HA'YAMIM," MA'ARIV SHABBAT (June 5, 1987): 3.
15. Col. Trevor N. Dupuy, *Elusive Victory: The Arab-Israeli Wars, 1947– 74* (New York: Harper and Row Publishers, 1978), 229.
16. An interesting footnote to the political and military jockeying that preceded the outbreak of hostilities was the effort of Arab governments (that is, Iraq, Syria, Jordan, and Egypt) to produce propaganda films, similar to those produced by the Germans in the Second World War. The objectives of the Arab propaganda films were to (a) rally the population at home with impressive displays of Arab military power and (b) to frighten the Israeli public into panic and possible submission. Some of these films, such as a short produced by the Syrian government showing camouflage-clad troops crossing water obstacles, hurling grenades, and storming "enemy" positions with AK-47 7.62mm assault rifles blazing, were low-key. The message was clear: The mighty Arab armies would be able to defeat the IDF with little difficulty. Other films, such as one produced in Egypt, reinforced an image of Arab invincibility: Soldiers practiced bayoneting dummy soldiers adorned with a blood red Star of David and went through the motions of a judo exercise while singing a song

proclaiming that the liberation of the cities of "Haifa, Acko, and Yaffo" was at hand. Other films, however, were more devious in their meaning. As early as May 1967, newsreel films shown in Egypt and produced by the Egyptian military showed what was reported to be real attacks on Israeli positions in southern Israel. "Soldiers" of the Egyptian-sponsored Palestine Liberation Army were featured and were shown storming Israeli police forts, knifing Israeli sentries, and planting explosives along key military routes. Naturally the films were pure fiction, but they led the Egyptian public to believe that Israel was already under siege and on the verge of submission.

17. Luva Elyav, "PAGASHTI ET MUSTAFA BARZANI BE'KEN HA'NESHARIM BE'KURDISTAN," YEDIOT SHABBAT (April 12, 1991): 3; Rechavem Ze'evi, "GHANDI BE'ARETZ HA'KURDIM," MA'ARIV SHABBAT (May 16, 1991): 2; and Eilan Kfir, TZANHANIM CHI'R MUTZNACH: TZAHAL BE'HEILO ENTZYKLOPEDIA LE'TZAVA ULE'BITACHON (Tel Aviv: Revivim Publishers, 1981), 111. An indication of the close-knit relationship that had developed between these IDF visitors and their Kurdish hosts was made evident in the summer of 1968 when Lt. Col. Arik Regev was killed in a battle with Palestinian terrorists in the Jordan Valley. Days after Regev's funeral, Kurdish leader Barzani sent a telegram to the IDF chief of staff offering his deepest condolences on the loss of such a fine officer.

18. Yoni Sa'ar, "HA'SA'M'BA," BAMACHANE CHU'L (May 1984): 11.

19. See Ian Black and Benny Morris, *Israel's Secret Wars*, 219.

20. Yosef Argaman and Doram Gonet, "HA'MAFIL," BAMACHANE (June 26, 1989): 50.

21. Doram Gonet, "YOTER SURI MI'SURI," BAMACHANE (June 13, 1990): 9.

22. See Ian Black and Benny Morris, *Israel's Secret Wars*, 222.

23. Various ed., "NIFTAR HA'MASAJIST SHEL NATZER VE'SADDAT SHE'RIGEL LE'MA'AN YISRAEL," YISRAEL SHELANU (April 20, 1990): 9.

24. *Ibid.* 9.

25. Shapi Gabay, "HA'MERAGLIM BARCHU IM HA'SHACHAR," MONITIN (June 1987): 16.

26. *Ibid.* 16.

27. See Ian Black and Benny Morris, *Israel's Secret Wars*, 225.

28. Uri Dan and Y. Ben-Porat, *The Secret War: The Spy Game in the Middle East* (New York: Sabra Books, 1970), 161.

29. *Ibid.* 162.

30. In their book *The Secret War* authors Dan and Ben-Porat do not mention the unit designation "SAYERET MAT'KAL," but rather use the phrase "an Israeli parachute unit."

31. See Ian Black and Benny Morris, *Israel's Secret Wars*, 222.

32. See Stewart Steven, *The Spymasters of Israel*, 227.

33. *Ibid.* 228.

34. See Oded Granot, HEYL HA'MODE'IN, 80.

35. See Ian Black and Benny Morris, *Israel's Secret Wars*, 233.

36. Yosef Argaman, "HA'SICHA," BAMACHANE CHU'L (May 1989): 26.

37. *Ibid.* 27.

38. Yosef Argaman, ZE HAYA SODI BE'YOTER (Tel Aviv: Ministry of Defense Publications, 1990), 238.

39. See Yosef Argaman, "HA'SICHA," 60.

40. "The Attack on the *Liberty*," ABC News, 20/20, show no. 719, May 21, 1987.

41. *Ibid.*

42. Andrew and Leslie Cockburn, *Dangerous Liaison: The Inside Story of the U.S.-Israeli Covert Relationship* (New York: Harper Collins Publishers, 1991), 153.

43. Various ed., TZAVA U'BITACHON ALEPH (1948–1968): TZAHAL BE'HEILO ENTZYKLOPEDIA LE'TZAVA ULE'BITACHON (Tel Aviv: Revivim Publishers, 1981), 205.

CHAPTER 11

SPECIAL OPERATIONS: THE WAR OF ATTRITION

The 1967 Six-Day War was supposed to be the final installment in the armed conflict between Arab and Jew, but instead it opened a Pandora's box of war and bloodshed that continues to this very day. Israel's epic victory did not conquer Arab rage, or soothe it: It simply channeled the Arabs' quest for revenge into an ingenious strategy meant to eventually bring Israel to her knees. What followed became known as the "War of Attrition" and, like the 1967 War, it would have historic implications for the future of the Middle East. Unlike those epic six days of conquest, however, this war would be fought along each of Israel's many fronts; it was full-scale warfare on a very small scale.

For A'MAN, the 1967 War's fast-paced conquest of vast stretches of Arab territory reaped invaluable intelligence rewards. In the Sinai, the IDF captured thousands of Egypt's top-line Soviet-produced armored fighting vehicles, missiles, and heavy guns; the secrets behind these once-mysterious weapons systems were uncovered by A'MAN officers, IDF Ordnance Corps technicians, and anonymous figures from many NATO nations who observed firsthand these tools of war. More than five thousand Egyptian soldiers—from lowly privates to high-ranking officers, including several generals—were captured in the few brief days of combat. Each POW was filtered through a long interrogation process where name, rank, and serial number were usually accompanied by in-depth and intimate details on the Egyptian military. Valuable bits of information could be obtained with a few kind words and a pack of plain, though potent, Israeli cigarettes. The computerized network that Col. Yuval Ne'eman had helped to incorporate into A'MAN's Order of Battle was, perhaps, put to its most stringent test in the war's aftermath. Never before had so much information been funneled into such a system, and never before had so much accurate data been compiled on an enemy's military machine.[1]

Yet it was clear that not one of Israel's intelligence services—the MOSSAD, the SHIN BET, or A'MAN—was prepared for the magnitude of the victory—or for its aftermath. New battle lines were about to be drawn.

When the IDF paratroop and armor elements slammed across the Gaza Strip on the first day of the war, A'MAN and the SHIN BET agents followed close behind the fighting. Their objective was not to conquer territory but to seize the intelligence initiative.[2] They were tasked with the capture and analysis of Egyptian police files, which meticulously detailed criminal, terrorist, and espionage activities in the strip; these files included information on the fledgling Palestinian guerrillas loyal to Yasir Arafat, and on safe houses and agents of the Egyptian Muchabarat. Israeli agents also moved into the West Bank, a large and economically profitable portion of Jordan. For years, King Hussein's Muchabarat had deterred Palestinian nationalist desires that the West Bank be included in a Palestinian state; known Palestinian organizers—especially those allied to Yasir Arafat's el-Fatah or factions supported by Syria—were routinely arrested, tortured, and sometimes murdered. The Jordanian Muchabarat kept meticulous intelligence files in their West Bank headquarters; all the files fell conveniently into A'MAN and SHIN BET hands after June 10, 1967.

The Six-Day War would prove to be a turning point for the Palestinians. For the first time since 1948, the Palestinian problem once again took center stage internationally as a new refugee crisis was born. The West Bank of the Jordan River and the Gaza Strip were composed of a combined population of one million Palestinian residents, many of whom were refugees from the 1948 fighting. Controlling this enormous and hostile populace was one of the first challenges posed to the IDF. At first the problem was not addressed, since Israel did not plan to stay in the newly occupied territories for very long. It was believed that a "land for peace" deal of one sort or another would soon be achieved. But when the Palestinians awoke from their devastating defeat, it soon became evident to the Israelis—in bloody fashion—that the fledgling Palestinian guerrilla movements were preparing to embark on a full-scale terrorist campaign.

The objective of this open declaration of war was to tie down IDF forces on the West Bank and Gaza, while the rebuilding armies of Syria, Jordan, and Egypt engaged the IDF at the front lines.

For Yasir Arafat's el-Fatah and its military arm, known as the al-Asifa ("the storm"), the chances for military success seemed good. Trained in guerrilla warfare by experts from the Soviet Union, the People's Republic of China, North Korea, and North Vietnam, el-Fatah guerrillas had been taught to use population centers as impregnable veils. The enemy's unfamiliarity with their occupied lands made them perfect staging grounds for hit-and-run attacks. Arafat hoped to turn the West Bank into another Mekong Delta; Arafat's military deputy, Khalil al-Wazir (better known by his nom de guerre "Abu Jihad," or "Father Holy War"), declared himself to be a follower of such great guerrilla freedom fighters as Mao and Giap.[3]

Yet Arafat, Abu Jihad, and Abu Iyad, el-Fatah's security chief, failed to follow the first and most basic guideline of their Asian revolutionary mentors—patience! The el-Fatah leadership was so anxious for action that they sent their lieutenants throughout the West Bank and Gaza in search of volunteers for the upcoming war against Israel. Clearly their security procedures—meant to ensure that a volunteer was not an Israeli, or even a Jordanian, intelligence agent—were terribly inadequate. In fact, everything involving the freedom fighters' activities in the days following the 1967 War was hurried and accomplished with little vision. Guerrilla training lasted little more than a month, with field security and concealment classes substituted for weapons and explosives instruction. Compartmentalization and networked cells were nonexistent.[4] Their command and communications apparatus was so primitive, in fact, that most meets transpired in crowded cafes and restaurants, or even on street corners. Needless to say, picking up ringleaders and military commanders was not at all difficult for IDF troops and HA'MAN (and A'MAN) officers, especially since many of them spoke Arabic as their second language!

The status of the budding uprising was so precarious that in August 1967 Arafat himself ventured into the Israeli-occupied West Bank to establish a headquarters in the notorious casbah of Nablus, the largest West Bank city and a hotbed of Palestinian nationalism. Arafat, however, did little to further his group's cause. Instead of establishing a hardcore cadre of reliable lieutenants in the territories, he pressed the meager forces at his disposal for immediate strikes against the IDF. Within weeks, both the SHIN BET, which was slowly assuming the counterintelligence role in the territories, and A'MAN were in pursuit of the el-Fatah leader, known in the territories by his nom de guerre "Abu Ammar." On numerous occasions, IDF forces and SHIN BET squads were only minutes behind a defiant Arafat; according to numerous reports, Arafat evaded capture by masquerading as an elderly woman.[5] On one occasion, a squad from SAYERET HARUV, Central Command's paratroop reconnaissance force, stormed an el-Fatah safe house where Arafat had been only moments earlier.[6]

In the days following the 1967 victory, the Israeli intelligence community attempted to come to terms with its newfound guerrilla challenge. A'MAN had predicted the rise of a heavily armed Palestinian resistance in 1965 when the first el-Fatah attack inside Israel was perpetrated. A'MAN HQ even created its MADOR FAHA ("Hostile Terrorist Activity Department"), which removed the responsibility of tracking and infiltrating Palestinian groups from the various nation desks. This latest subdivision of the Intelligence Branch was the brainchild of Col. Shlomoh Gazit, head of A'MAN's MACHLEKET MECHKAR ("Research Department") and an eventual Military Intelligence director.[7]

In the summer months following the 1967 War, A'MAN's Arabic-speaking agents and officers were rushed to the West Bank and Gaza in order to infiltrate the forming terrorist cells. It was a task that, along with monitoring the rebuilding of Arab armies, stretched A'MAN's assets quite thinly. The force that took charge of the counterterrorist role was the SHIN BET. For years, the SHIN BET had been Israel's top-secret counterintelligence force; in the years prior to the Six-Day War it had spent the majority of its efforts tracking down Arab and Soviet bloc intelligence agents, often with astonishing success. With its new counterterrorist role, the SHIN BET mobilized all of its Arabic-speaking agents, who sifted through the seized Jordanian and Egyptian police files that identified known Palestinian leaders, criminals, deviants, and individuals who required special attention.* Arab agents inside the West Bank, who for years had been supervised by A'MAN special tasks officers, were transferred to SHIN BET jurisdiction; SHIN BET, in turn, payrolled hundreds of local informants, from smugglers to prostitutes, who were motivated by a desire for profit, or were intimidated. As a result of this counterintelligence offensive, the SHIN BET was able to execute large-scale roundups of suspects in every major West Bank city, as well as inside the refugee camps of Gaza. In some cases, local facilities were so overwhelmed by the number of people being questioned that SHIN BET agents improvised by taking over barbershops and storefronts as interrogation centers.[8]

The intelligence data obtained by the SHIN BET, analyzed by A'MAN, and then passed down to frontline IDF troops *had* to be accurate. The Jordan Valley and the West Bank were interlaced with thousands of ravines, caves, and gorges—ideal places for hiding weapons and fighters during the course of a prolonged guerrilla struggle. Even the most elite IDF troop units—reconnaissance formations able to march across dozens of square kilometers of hostile territory in a day—could not conduct a thorough sweep of this porous and inhospitable terrain. In these early days, it was impossible to combat the Palestinians with anything but solid HUMINT. SHIN BET, A'MAN, and IDF cooperation was superb.

*According to authors Ian Black and Benny Morris, in their book *Israel's Secret Wars*, SHIN BET commanders realized that the Palestinians in the newly seized territories were becoming enraged and on the verge of taking up arms. One of the reasons was the fact that tens of thousands of Israeli citizens had begun flocking to East Jerusalem, Nablus, Hebron, Bethlehem, and Ramallah on sight-seeing binges and shopping sprees. The Israelis were confident and arrogant after the IDF's victory. Local resentment, it was believed, was a breeding ground for armed struggle.

*   *   *

Even though the MOSSAD had once labeled the PLO's military effort as an insignificant threat to Israeli security, Major General Yariv was relieved that a tiresome and brutal element of his force's workload had been taken over by the SHIN BET. A'MAN needed to focus on an old and more conventional foe. Egyptian intentions to instigate a bloody "war of attrition" along the newly drawn frontiers were spelled out in the infamous "Three No's" declaration of September 1, 1967, at the Emergency Arab Summit Conference held in Khartoum, the Sudanese capital. The "Three No's" indicated that in the Arab world, there would be *NO* peace with Israel, *NO* recognition of the Jewish state, and *NO* cessation of hostilities.

On October 21, 1967, the flagship of the IDF/navy, the INS *Eilat*, was on a routine patrol of the eastern Mediterranean waters off the coast of the southern Sinai, 14.5 nautical miles from the Egyptian half of the Suez Canal off Port Said. The *Eilat* was an old ship—a Second World War–vintage British destroyer previously known as the HMS *Zealous*—yet electronically overhauled, it was the most potent naval weapon the Israelis could field at the time. At 1732, although the *Eilat*'s acquisition radar had not revealed any hostile enemy activity, a brilliant flashing object was spotted heading straight for the ship's starboard side. The *Eilat*'s captain, Cdr. Yitzhak Shoshan, ordered evasive action but it was too late. A STYX SS-N-1 Soviet-made antiship missile slammed through the *Eilat*'s thin armor and exploded inside the boiler room, resulting in an inferno. Two minutes later, as the 1,710-ton ship began to list, a second STYX struck. Two hours later a third missile hit the sinking ship. While a herculean rescue effort was underway in the rough seas, a fourth and fatal STYX struck. Of the *Eilat*'s 199-man crew, 47 were killed or missing, and 90 wounded. The missile age had dawned on naval warfare, and the fourth Arab-Israeli war was underway.

Four days later, on October 25, a heavy concentration of IDF artillery batteries launched a massive bombardment against Egyptian oil refineries in Suez. The blazing infernos lasted for weeks and crippled the Egyptian economy. Egypt retaliated with artillery barrages of its own against IDF positions along the Suez Canal. What became known as the "1,000-Days War," the War of Attrition, had *officially* begun.

Egypt may have been a defeated nation in 1967, but its army was far from destroyed. In fact, it was being rebuilt into a stronger and more capable force. According to *conservative* A'MAN estimates, Egypt would be able to resume a threatening posture to Israel by mid-1968![9] Nearly every high-ranking A'MAN officer worth his salt realized that Egypt would attempt, at one stage or another, to seek military vengeance. The Intelligence Branch's main objective centered on monitoring Egypt's acquisition of newly supplied Soviet arms, and their deployment along the embattled Suez Canal. By the winter of 1967, nearly

100,000 Egyptian troops were poised for action along the Suez Canal, their aging equipment, which had been destroyed or abandoned in the Sinai, now replaced by top-of-the-line Soviet materiel. MiG-21s replaced the MiG-17 and MiG-19; the mainstay Egyptian tank became the sturdy T-55 (and later the T-62); and hundreds of artillery batteries were being rushed straight to the front from the long and seemingly endless line of Soviet cargo ships docking in Alexandria. Initially, hundreds of Soviet advisors commanded the effort, deemed Egypt's "defensive rehabilitation" by Nasser.[10] This number would soon swell to the thousands.

One of the first priorities for Major General Yariv was coming up with a fact-based prognosis—in writing—accurately predicting Egyptian military capabilities for the coming years; the report was to be handed over to Israeli policymakers. Great resources were dedicated to increasing A'MAN's ability to gather intelligence data and analyze and delegate the necessary findings to the upper echelons of command, as well as to small-unit commanders stationed at the front. A massive search for eighteen-year-old Arabic-speaking conscripts was conducted in order to fill the Intelligence Corps ranks. Technical high school graduates and potential young people interested in electronics were also sought. To train these new personnel, a state-of-the-art intelligence school was established. In addition, Yariv undertook a dedicated effort to improve A'MAN's relationship with the military intelligence services of the NATO powers, Africa, and Asia.[11]

Intelligence Corps observation posts were soon established all along the Suez Canal. Little more than lightly defended bunkers or reinforced shacks, the early-warning positions were staffed by several combat intelligence officers and NCOs, and were located along key intersections overlooking a major town or military installation, or at a location where Israeli military planners believed a large Egyptian force might attempt an amphibious crossing into the Sinai. The man responsible for A'MAN's efforts in the Sinai was Lt. Col. Tzvi Shiler, a Romanian-born officer who, like Yariv, had served in the GOLANI Brigade and later was the intelligence officer of the conscript Paratroop Brigade and, during the Six-Day War, for Southern Command.[12]

Yet the main effort to gather data on the Egyptian forces centered on technical means. To monitor the early Egyptian effort, A'MAN responded with an increased SIGINT and PHOTINT effort. In the Sinai, A'MAN's most important stationary facility was at Umm Hushiba. Bristling with antennas and dishes, and protected by stone walls and sandbagged defenses, it was located thirty kilometers from the canal in the middle of the Sinai desert and was capable of peering deep into lower "African" Egypt. Similar positions were concealed in the desert mountains overlooking Arab Legion positions in the Jordan Valley. In the north, one of the most important of Israel's early-warning electronic positions was constructed in the imposing mountain rock atop Mt. Hermon, a snowcapped tower of stone that connected Israel, Syria, and Lebanon. From Mt. Hermon on a clear day, the Israeli soldiers manning the position could gaze through their field glasses and see the outskirts of Damascus. Clearly, the antennas sprouting atop the labyrinth of buildings and bunkers—all constructed underneath a sheet of protective brick and stone fastened with chicken wire—could "see" much farther.[13] Mt. Hermon, in fact, became known as "the eyes and ears of the State of Israel" to the select club of Israeli officials and military officers who knew the facility's true purpose.*

Even though A'MAN was satisfied with its network of intelligence-gathering bases, more devious means of monitoring enemy communications were employed as well, including planting sophisticated listening devices inside hollowed-out telephone poles.[14]

Until February 1969, the PHOTINT aspect of Israeli intelligence-gathering efforts during the War of Attrition consisted of virtually uncontested flybys of nearly every square inch of enemy territory. Arab air defenses had yet to be rebuilt, Arab fighter squadrons had yet to be replenished, and top-line Arab pilots—to replace those killed in 1967—had yet to be trained. As a result, the IAF was able to launch photoreconnaissance sorties over sensitive and soft targets alike with virtual impunity—sometimes even sheer audacity. Cairo, Alexandria, Damascus, Beirut, and Amman were frequently buzzed by low-flying Israeli aircraft; even President Nasser's presidential palace received the "treatment," as it was known in IAF Intelligence jargon. With the two valuable Sinai bases of Ophir and Refidim (Bir Gifgafa), nearly all of Egypt was within the IAF's reach. Several Mirage IIICs were modified to carry high-powered photo equipment for strategic photoreconnaissance.[15] Israeli Air Force PHOTINT provided Intelligence Corps photo interpreters with the data needed to construct highly detailed maps and target sheets.

The one unique characteristic of the intelligence campaign during the War of Attrition was the deployment of commando and special operations units. Egyptian naval commandos, special forces shock troops, and As-Saiqa ("thunder and lightning") commandos frequently raided isolated and lightly defended outposts along the Suez Canal. In most cases, these elite units were deployed in intelligence-gathering forays meant to acquire targeting information for Egyptian artillery batteries. Since the Egyptian Air Force had been decimated in 1967, and the rebuilding program could not support risky aerial reconnaissance sorties, Egyptian special forces became the fundamental tool for gathering data on the IDF deployments in the Sinai. Syrian special forces also operated along similar lines on the Golan Heights, although they sometimes depended

---

*Adjacent to the ultra-top-secret installation atop snowcapped Mt. Hermon, a modern and extremely popular ski resort and winter playground was built.

on the various Palestinian groups operating under protection from Damascus to execute the dirty deeds of cross-border intelligence-acquisition raids. Jordanian special forces employed similar techniques.

Israeli special operations were more grand in scale—more inclusive. They consisted of both the preemptive, including cross-border intelligence-gathering missions, and the retaliatory. In fact, the majority of the *known* IDF reconnaissance commando attacks against Egypt, Jordan, Syria, and Lebanon were ordered in response to either a massive artillery barrage, resulting in loss of life among Israeli soldiers, or some kind of terrorist attack that originated in one of the neighboring Arab states. The purpose of these attacks was not merely punishment: An IAF strike could have achieved that end. These deep-penetration displays of military muscle were meant to send a message to the leaders of the Arab world: If attacks against Israeli soldiers and citizens continued, every inch of their territory was vulnerable to commando attack.

Since the best of the best within Israeli society—the courageous young volunteers of the IDF's elite SAYERET—would be risked in these commando operations, the intelligence provided to them had to be very detailed and accurate. It was during this conflict that the role of the unit KA'MAN ("Intelligence officer") truly came into its own. Intelligence officers attached to the various paratroop, reconnaissance, and naval commando units were charged with integrating every detail on a potential target into a comprehensive outline that the unit's Operations officers would depend on when formulating their assault strategies. The KA'MAN became the most important figure in many of these small and select fighting formations. His responsibility was to provide all background information on the target; he must know the target almost as well as an enemy soldier stationed there. In most cases, elite unit KA'MANIM joined in the assaults.

The extent of the KA'MAN's expertise—and his Intelligence Corps training—was made evident in some of the IDF's most spectacular retaliatory raids during the War of Attrition, as was A'MAN's ability to combine endless files of SIGINT, COMINT, PHOTINT, and HUMINT data into a comprehensive and usable format. In Operation Shock, the November 1, 1968, assault on the Egyptian Nile Delta power station at Naji Hamadi and on several bridges near the town of Qina, the fourteen-man attack force from SAYERET TZANHANIM relied on aerial photographs provided by the IAF and analyzed by A'MAN, and on maps and target sheets created by the unit's intelligence officer. The operation also required that the IAF and its photoreconnaissance squadron gather meteorological data so that the helicopter pilots entrusted with ferrying the commandos to their objectives could predetermine and coordinate an optimum flight plan.[16] The raid, 350 kilometers from the front line along the Suez Canal, was the first deep-penetration heliborne raid into Egypt, and it triggered a wave of panic and fear in the Egyptian public. Following the raid, Nasser mobilized the civilian militia and brought thousands of frontline troops away from the battlefield for sentry duty inside Egypt. Beyond the physical and psychological damage the raid inflicted, there was an intelligence benefit that served A'MAN's objectives brilliantly.[17] Nasser's response to the raid provided an accurate picture of how post-1967 Egypt would respond to an attack on its soil. The raw information gathered via SIGINT and COMINT was rushed to A'MAN's Research Department.

In Operation Gift, the December 27, 1968, retaliatory raid on Beirut International Airport by a mixed force from both SAYERET MAT'KAL and SAYERET TZANHANIM, A'MAN's resources were tapped to provide the attackers with a virtual real-time assessment of civilian and military air traffic around the Lebanese capital.[18] The objective of this raid was precise—to punish the Lebanese government for supporting Popular Front for the Liberation of Palestine (PFLP) hijackings and attacks against El Al, the Israeli national carrier. Several Middle East Airlines aircraft, the Lebanese flag carrier, were to be destroyed. In order to complete this mission quickly and without loss of innocent life, the targeted aircraft had to be pinpointed so that they could be sabotaged in the minimum time span; the location of Lebanese military and gendarme units also needed to be pinpointed so that they could be isolated and covered.

Unlike Operation Shock, however, the raid on Beirut International Airport could not rely on PHOTINT, since an IAF flyby would arouse Lebanese suspicions that an attack of some type was imminent. As a result, the execution of the raid depended primarily on HUMINT, and the efforts of HATZAV to provide A'MAN with "open" information on the Lebanese airport and the Lebanese airline, and general information on the city. Travel agencies worldwide, it has been reported, were pilfered for information, and veteran travelers who had been to Beirut International Airport—such as airline flight crews —were interviewed. So accurate was the information obtained by A'MAN that the commandos were even told that the gendarmes patrolling the airport usually carried only one clip of ammunition for their 7.65mm French-made Manhurin SL automatic pistols.[19] This information was extremely important should one of the commandos engage in a firefight. "Knowledge saves lives" became a catchphrase of such operations and a secret to their success.

Another, usually forgotten, element of the success of the IDF's special operations during the War of Attrition was the work of A'MAN's BITACHON SADEH ("Field Security") department. Their agents, mainly officers and NCOs, censored word of IDF movements and actions—from careless soldiers chattering on nonsecured lines to foreign journalists filing copy—until all "friendly forces" had returned to Israeli shores.

Not all of Israel's intelligence work was so successful. In Operation Mania 6 of July 1, 1969, a joint SAYERET MAT'KAL and naval commando raid was to be made on the Egyptian man-made Green Island, a seemingly impregnable fortress that dominated the Red Sea approaches to the Suez Canal. A'MAN and the two units' intelligence officers were able to provide the commandos with a highly detailed fact sheet of the target, including the layout of its gun emplacements, a roster of the units stationed at the island (infantrymen and As-Saiqa commandos), and the physical characteristics of the imposing Egyptian position. The latter would be crucial in the nighttime hand-to-hand fighting that would take place. Nevertheless, according to numerous Israeli military analysts, A'MAN failed both SAYERET MAT'KAL and the naval commandos—without doubt the IDF's two top units. Since the island needed to be approached in a stealthlike manner to ensure the element of surprise, the naval commandos were to swim underwater to reach the target; once a beachhead had been established, the force of SAYERET MAT'KAL commandos (headed by unit chief Lt. Col. Menachem Digli) would follow in rubber dinghies.

A'MAN relied on obsolete British Second World War tidal charts to advise the naval commandos on the best day—and time—to execute the raid, as well as the ideal staging point from which to initiate the assault. The British admiralty charts proved grossly inaccurate. The naval commandos were forced to swim in strong currents, causing physical exhaustion and delaying the operation for nearly an hour. In addition, assessing Green Island as a priority-one target, requiring the talents of such a select and invaluable group of combatants, was also a mistake. The objective of the raid was to destroy a series of Egyptian 37mm and 85mm antiaircraft emplacements, but after the island was reached, the commandos found that the guns were not even in position.[20] Six commandos died in the heated battles there, in one of the most controversial and covered-up operations in Israeli military history.

Another special operation that generated much controversy and negative speculation was Operation Hell, the IDF's March 21, 1968, assault on the Jordanian town of Karameh, a major staging center and base of operations for Palestinian terrorist attacks against Israel. The fact that Karameh was home to more than two thousand heavily armed el-Fatah faithful prompted the IDF to send a combined task force of paratroopers, armored units, and reconnaissance paratroopers. The IDF task force entered the gauntlet of fortified huts, bunkers, and mountain hideouts and, in ten hours of incessant combat, destroyed the armed Palestinian presence around the town. The battles were fought at close quarters and often hand to hand.* But a Jordanian army contingent sta-

---

*One IDF officer decorated for his courage under fire during the Karameh operation was Capt. Amnon Shahak, the commander of a reconnaissance paratroop armored car force deploying French-built AML-90s. The force was called SAYERET DUCHIFAT ("Hoopoe Recon"). Shahak was the A'MAN director from 1986 to 1991 and went on to be the IDF deputy chief of staff.

tioned in the surrounding hills joined the fray, and a pitched battle developed: Jordanian Centurion MBTs engaged IDF 7th Armored Brigade Centurions; IAF aircraft were called in for close air support; and heavy artillery strikes were called in by both sides. At day's end, 150 Palestinian terrorists were killed, as were 61 Jordanian soldiers; Israeli losses were extremely heavy as well, with 28 dead and 90 wounded. Many in the Israeli defense establishment considered Operation Hell a disaster, and blamed an intelligence failure for the high loss of life. According to Major General Yariv, however, A'MAN had pinpointed the presence and location of Jordanian troop concentrations and advised the attack force commander before the operation.[21]

Nevertheless, the intelligence rewards from Operation Hell were enormous. The Israeli task force returned to Israel with 141 prisoners—Palestinian terrorists and Jordanian soldiers who were quite willing to talk. Each building in the terrorist base was thoroughly searched for any material that might be of value to the A'MAN sleuths in Tel Aviv; in many cases, entire file cabinets were tossed into the cargo sections of awaiting M-3 half-tracks. These files included a list of el-Fatah operatives throughout the world, as well as their key agents inside the West Bank and Gaza, and operational charts that revealed imminent terrorist attacks inside Israel.

One *conventional* special operation of the war stands out for its sheer audacity and great value to A'MAN's intelligence-gathering efforts. On December 14, 1969, Egyptian naval commandos crossed the Suez Canal and kidnapped an IDF officer, Capt. Dan Avidan. Vowing revenge, the IDF General Staff ordered its Operations and Intelligence branches to seek out a meaningful target along the Egyptian front. A'MAN responded to the call by locating a Soviet-built P-12 radar facility near Ras A'rab along the Red Sea coast. The radar's destruction was entrusted to the IAF. A visionary sergeant—a clerk, no less!—in IAF HQ came up with a brilliant alternative to a routine retaliatory strike: He suggested that the IAF simply steal the top-secret Soviet radar. His idea was passed along through channels, eventually reaching chief paratroop and infantry officer Brig. Gen. Rafael "Raful" Eitan and finally Chief of Staff Lt. Gen. Haim Bar-Lev. The raid was a go—it was code-named Operation Chicken 53.[22]

After training incessantly for four days (in keeping with the strict secrecy involving such operations, A'MAN's Field Security Department disconnected the phone lines for each unit involved in the raid), a combined task force of NA'HA'L and reconnaissance paratroopers set out on December 27 for Ras A'rab in three CH-53 heavy transport choppers. Aerial reconnaissance photographs of the base were extremely detailed, enabling the raiding party to coordinate its attack posture in a foolproof manner. After landing undetected at Ras A'rab, the paratroopers quickly eliminated the Egyptian defenders, many of whom

ran panic-stricken into the night. It took twenty minutes to fasten the hulking radar system to heavy cables and hook it to the CH-53; then the P-12
was lifted out of Egypt. Accompanying files, charts, manuals, and other items
of intelligence interest were also brought along for further analysis.

The IDF's abduction of the P-12 radar afforded A'MAN and the IAF a firsthand
look at the Egyptian air defense network. It was a timely piece of data, considering that Soviet military involvement in Egypt had developed into an alarming
situation for Israel: By December 1969, Soviet squadrons flew air defense
sorties over Egyptian skies; Soviet surface-to-air missile (SAM) operators manned
sophisticated SA-3 batteries throughout the nation; and more than fifteen thousand Soviet officers and NCOs helped protect Egypt from the IAF.* The NATO
powers, eager to boost their offensive capabilities against the Warsaw Pact,
analyzed the P-12, as did the world's press. The abduction of the top-of-the-
line Soviet equipment was humiliating for Egypt, whose leaders had to explain to a puzzled nation exactly how a small group of commandos managed
to pull off such a daring feat. Cairo also was forced to apologize to their patrons
in the Kremlin for the loss of their top-secret radar. To add insult to injury,
the world's press published cartoons of IAF helicopters carrying off the pyramids
and Sphinx.

The P-12 wasn't the only piece of Soviet-made high-tech military equipment that A'MAN's analysts had an opportunity to inspect. According to several reports, an Egyptian Air Force Sukhoi-7 Fitter made an emergency landing
in the Sinai during a dogfight in 1969. After being looked over by A'MAN and
the IAF, it was shipped off to the United States. (A Soviet-built Mil-8 Hip
helicopter, shot down over the Suez Canal in the 1973 War, was also shipped
back to America for CIA and DIA [Defense Intelligence Agency] analysis.)[23]

Two other Israeli intelligence operations involving A'MAN brought
foreign-produced weapons systems to the IDF's hands. The first, Operation
Noah's Ark, was a joint Israeli Foreign Ministry, MOSSAD, IDF/navy,
LA'KA'M, and A'MAN venture meant to secure a miniflotilla of French-built
fast attack craft that Israel had bought and paid for but that had been frozen
because of a French arms embargo on Israel; President de Gaulle had ordered
all arms sales to Israel halted following the IDF commando raid on Beirut
International Airport.[24] Israel, however, felt that legally the boats were hers
and was determined to continue her strategic naval plans with or without de

---

*Soviet involvement in Egyptian military affairs reached its zenith on July 30, 1970,
when a flight of IAF Phantoms engaged a flight of Soviet-piloted MiG-21Js west of
the Suez Canal and destroyed five of the Fishbeds. As an interesting aside, one of
the Phantom pilots was Aviam Sela, a man who, years later, would be accused of
running American spy Jonathan Jay Pollard for LA'KA'M.

Gaulle's permission.* Five ships had been delivered to Israel prior to the embargo, and one had slipped out of its home port of Cherbourg, on France's Normandy coast, the day the embargo was declared. Five ships remained there, however. The Cherbourg task force, consisting of A'MAN and LA'KA'M "representatives" and led by IDF/navy Adm. Mordechai Limon, head of the IDF purchasing mission in France, established a dummy Norwegian firm to acquire the five fast attack craft, while at the same time smuggling skeleton crews into France to man the ships. Food, water, and fuel had to be secretly smuggled aboard each craft, as well.

On December 24, 1969, Christmas Eve, a group of Hebrew-speaking gentlemen dressed in civilian garb boarded the impounded vessels and set sail for the open sea. The Israelis' timing was perfect, since most French families were at Christmas dinner celebrations, and security at the Chantiers de Construction Mècanique de Normandie shipyards was at its yearly low. After leaving French territorial waters, the boats sailed via Gibraltar to the open Mediterranean, where they were met by an IDF/navy armada. The "Boats of Cherbourg," as they became known, reached the IDF/navy base in Haifa on December 31.[25]

The other weapons system acquired through dubious means was also French: the Mirage IIIC. Prior to the full commencement of the War of Attrition and the 1968 French arms embargo, the IAF had purchased fifty Mirage 5J fighter bombers—aircraft that the IAF hoped would secure Israeli air superiority over the Soviet-supplied Arab air forces. When it became clear that the IAF would not be receiving these desperately needed combat aircraft, the only viable solution seemed to be for Israel to build the aircraft herself. Since Israel Aircraft Industries, headed by a remarkable American-born engineer named Al Schwimmer, did not yet have the technical facilities to design aircraft, blueprints were needed. An elaborate intelligence operation was immediately planned.

In January 1968, Alfred Frauenknecht, a Swiss aeronautical engineer, received a call from the IDF military attaché in Berne (an office under A'MAN control), requesting a meeting; initial contact had been made in 1965, during a conference in Paris for aeronautical engineers from nations who flew the Mirage.[26] Switzerland was producing the Mirage IIIC under license, and Frauenknecht was one of the heads of the aeroengines division of Sulzer, a gigantic Swiss concern that produced aircraft components for the Swiss Air Force. A Christian who had wrestled with guilt over the Swiss failure to help Jews fleeing from Nazi-occupied Europe, Frauenknecht agreed to help the attaché. Over the course

---

*Many believe that the decision to stop the once-infrangible Franco-Israeli military relationship stemmed from hurt pride. According to most accounts, French President De Gaulle *ordered* Israeli Prime Minister Levi Eshkol not to launch a preemptive strike against the Arabs in June 1967; when his demands were ignored, the French Republic felt betrayed.

of the next year, Frauenknecht microfilmed the 200,000 drawings that made up the engine's blueprints; he met several times with his handlers, who duly passed the invaluable data back to Tel Aviv.[27] Frauenknecht was eventually apprehended by Swiss authorities and imprisoned for four and a half years. His courageous assistance allowed the Israelis to produce their own version of the Mirage IIIC, known as the NESHER ("Eagle"), as well as the Israel Aircraft Industries series of Kfir fighter bombers—Israel's first truly indigenous top-of-the-line combat aircraft.

As the War of Attrition entered its final—and bloodiest—stage, it developed into a modern *and deadly* version of the trench fighting along the western front in the "war to end all wars." The IDF dug in along the Suez Canal in a series of fortified observation posts that became known as the Bar-Lev line. The positions were meant to shield IDF troops from the daily Egyptian artillery barrages. In fact, Egyptian guns were blasting the IDF front lines for days at a time, severely limiting Israeli operations. Monitoring Egyptian troop movements or deployments across the canal had become an impossible task; the intelligence officers (KA'MANIM) sat in their bunkers, able to see only the enemy's frontline positions, situated a few hundred meters away on the opposite side of the Suez Canal. To conceal their positions from prying Israeli eyes, Egyptian combat engineers constructed ten-meter-high sand walls. In order to see anything at all, the IDF had to gain higher ground, even if there was none!

The frontline intelligence officers took their high-powered field glasses and climbed atop anything that would help them peer into Egyptian territory—half-tracks, armored personnel carriers, and even bunker ventilation systems. When this proved too precarious—Egyptian mortar crews were expert at zeroing in on the reflection from field glasses, and Egyptian snipers were lethal—more innovative tools were employed. According to A'MAN specifications, the IDF Ordnance Corps modified the chassis of a Sherman tank, attaching a sixty-foot-high cherry picker to the turret area. The thin tower provided the intelligence officer, and the artillery spotter, with a platform that was nearly invisible against the desert; the tower also could be moved when Egyptian gunners located it in their sights.[28] Very few cherry pickers were available, however, and sometimes intelligence officers needed to peer deeper into enemy territory—beyond the range of issue field glasses and without launching a photoreconnaissance flight, which, in 1970, risked engaging high-altitude and extremely dangerous Soviet-produced and -manned surface-to-air missile batteries.

An innovative KA'MAN, Shabtai Bril, had been toying since the end of the Six-Day War with the idea of developing a cheap and accurate means of PHOTINT. His idea stemmed from frustration. In 1969, an agent he had been running in Egypt had brought back several photographs of Egyptian military bridges two kilometers from the canal; the photos, crucial to creating a target sheet, were too blurry to be useful.[29] Sitting in his Bar-Lev line bunker, Bril recalled an expensive toy shop he had visited in the United States, where a sales clerk had demonstrated a radio-controlled model airplane. The motorized aircraft was powered by a remote-control device equipped with four transmitting frequencies—two to power the engine, one to control the wing flaps, and a fourth serving as a reserve. With a little technical adjustment, that reserve frequency could operate a 35mm camera fitted with a zoom lens; with further adjustment, an Intelligence Corps technician could operate this device far from any potential danger.

Major Bril raised his novel idea with Col. Avraham Arnan, the head of a'MAN's Collections Department. Arnan was skeptical about toy planes replacing spies and high-flying jets; he was a man used to the exploits of brave soldiers, not gimmicks. Yet after seeing what a motorized model airplane could do, Arnan enthusiastically supported Bril's idea and rushed a memo to Major General Yariv. Someone was sent to the toy store in the United States to pick up three such models, at a cost of U.S. $850. a'MAN's Technical Department had little trouble fitting a camera to the aircraft's undercarriage. Before Arnan would authorize the aircraft's deployment over enemy territory, however, he wanted to see how the small plane would fare against determined antiaircraft fire. One of the model planes was taken to an air defense base and flown above a force of 40mm cannon batteries. "Firing like mad" for several minutes, according to one of the intelligence officers, the experienced gunners failed to score a single hit on the highly maneuverable small-silhouette device. Bril glided his model aircraft to a smooth landing without the prop-driven toy suffering a single scratch.[30]

Bril's unmanned aircraft soon materialized over the Sinai front—over the city of Isma'ilia. An Intelligence Corps officer controlled the model from a Piper Cub, holding the remote-control device in his lap and monitoring the aircraft with a pair of 120x20 field glasses. The Egyptians paid little attention to the toy buzzing their lines and failed to fire even a single shot at the small craft.[31] The photographs taken by the aircraft were of superb quality and they involved no risk to human life or top-secret equipment. Another test flight of Major Bril's low-cost, high-yielding dynamo was ordered over the eastern portion of the Jordan Valley. a'MAN HQ received detailed and focused photographs of Arab Legion firing positions facing Israel. The Jordanian antiaircraft artillery positions also failed to fire at the inconspicuous object flying over their positions. A fledgling model airplane squad was formed under special orders from Major General Yariv, but the use of unmanned prop-driven aircraft for intelligence work was still considered a sideshow—an amusing aberration from the routine dangers of intelligence-gathering work. No one in a'MAN HQ realized just how Major Bril's ideas would revolutionize modern warfare in the years to come. The age of the remote piloted vehicle (RPV) had dawned.

On July 31, 1970, Israel acquiesced to the pressures of United States Secretary of State William Rogers and agreed to a cease-fire. By then, the war had developed into a superpower test of wills, as weapons lost on the battlefield by Israel and the Arabs were being replaced immediately by Washington and Moscow. In the following weeks, with the help of USAF U-2 flights, A'MAN's primary concern was monitoring Egyptian deployments and ensuring that Egypt adhered to the agreed cessation of hostilities.[32]

Although the deafening silence of peace had overtaken the Sinai and the Suez Canal, the Palestinian terrorist offensive in Gaza, the Jordan Valley, and Lebanon was picking up momentum. Since Karameh, in fact, a revolution had overtaken the Palestinian effort. The fight for Karameh, where the Arabs gave as good as they got, was a source of tremendous pride for the Palestinians: They were no longer impudent upstarts—the Jewish soldiers no longer supermen. Soon, new "liberation" groups joined Yasir Arafat's el-Fatah in the holy struggle against Zionism. Already, el-Fatah's exclusivity had been challenged by the creation of a new Pan-Arab Palestinian liberation movement known as the Popular Front for the Liberation of Palestine (PFLP), headed by Dr. George Habash and Dr. Wadi Haddad, two Christian Palestinian doctors who used to write nationalist slogans on medicine prescriptions doled out in their Beirut clinic. The PFLP, officially created on December 11, 1967, preached a worldwide revolution; the group received assistance from Syria, its principal supporter in the Arab world, as well as from the KGB and the Eastern-bloc intelligence services. Unlike Arafat's el-Fatah, which accepted nearly every volunteer, especially the poor and illiterate, the PFLP sought out idealists and intellectuals to bring the glorious revolution to fruition. That same day, December 11, As-Saiqa ("thunder and lightning"), a group also known as "The Vanguards of the Liberation War" was formed in Damascus. A branch of the all-powerful Syrian Ba'ath party, it was a fundamental component of Syrian military operations against Israel, and was active in Lebanon as well.

The creation of new liberation groups was announced with the regularity and frequency of summer softball leagues; in the months following the Karameh battle, there were nearly twelve thousand guerrillas in Jordan, with more recruits flocking to the Hashemite kingdom from the four corners of the Palestinian diaspora. On February 22, 1969, a Jordanian-born Christian, Nayif Hawatmeh, founded the Democratic Front for the Liberation of Palestine (DFLP), a fervently Communist group whose ideology for an Arab Middle East resembled that of the socialist-minded settlers who created the kibbutz movement in Israel during the early years of the twentieth century. The DFLP also recruited ideologues, intellectuals, and men with a firm allegiance to Palestine and the international revolution.[33] On April 24, 1969, Ahmed Jibril, a former officer in the Syrian army and an aide to Habash, created his own group, the Popular Front for the Liberation of Palestine General Command (PFLP-GC), whose sole ideology was the execution of bloody and innovative attacks against Israel.[34] On February 21, 1970, the PFLP-GC carried out its first operation: A Swissair jet flying from Zurich to Tel Aviv was destroyed over the Alps by a sophisticated altimeter bomb. All thirty-eight passengers and nine crew members were killed.* Although the PFLP and the PFLP-GC groups shared differing and sometimes conflicting ideologies, their one common denominator was reliance on Jordan as a base of military operations for attacks against Israel.

During the years 1967–70, the Jordan Valley on the West Bank was turned into a bitter battlefield of terrorist infiltration and IDF pursuits. Palestinian guerrillas and agents attempted to cross the desolate mountain wilderness to the safety—and anonymity—of the West Bank's large cities, where they were to establish cells, join existing units, and perpetrate attacks inside Israel proper. To reach Israel, all that stood in the way of a Palestinian terrorist squad were the shallow waters of the Jordan River, a small contingent of Bedouin trackers, several IDF reconnaissance formations, and A'MAN's ability to intercept Palestinian radio traffic, monitor Palestinian troop movements, and infiltrate the ranks of the Palestine Liberation Organization.

Spies were especially worrisome to Arafat. Infiltration by Israeli (as well as Jordanian, Syrian, and Egyptian) intelligence agents had always been an obsessive fear of the Palestinian guerrilla formations, and, following 1967, it developed into a real problem. Arafat became so concerned that he ordered the creation of the Jihaz al-Razd ("Surveillance System"), el-Fatah's counterintelligence, counterespionage, and, in some cases, active espionage agency.[35] Several prominent el-Fatah officers would command the Razd, as it became known, including Faruq Qaddumi (a man who would become known as the Palestinian foreign minister), Abu Iyad (Arafat's deputy commander and ruthless security chief who was assassinated by an Abu Nidal gunman in Tunis in January 1991), and, of course, the infamous Red Prince—Ali Hassan Salameh. The founding fathers of the Razd were dispatched to Cairo to undergo a six-week military intelligence and security course offered by Egyptian Muchabarat officers. Between 1968 and 1970, the Razd executed dozens of known operatives and hundreds of suspected spies, some of whom were hapless souls who simply

---

*Over the course of the next two decades, the PFLP-GC would attempt dozens of such bombings. Most failed, but others, such as the December 23, 1988, bombing of Pan Am flight 103, were successful.

looked or acted suspicious.[36] The Razd became the ruthless enforcers of the Palestinian revolution.

A'MAN employed tools other than its vast HUMINT assets to keep close surveillance on the Palestinians. Israel Defense Forces patrols led by eagle-eyed Bedouin trackers were extremely successful in capturing Palestinian guerrilla squads that crossed the Jordan River; captured Palestinians were questioned by highly trained and experienced interrogators, who obtained a wealth of information for A'MAN's archives. The guerrillas' captured weapons were also analyzed, which, beyond their immediate military value, allowed A'MAN to document the trail of weapons supplied to the Palestinians; by charting the nationality and serial number of the rocket launchers, recoilless rifles, and automatic rifles, A'MAN was able to verify the extensive weapons pipeline— from their origin in Eastern Europe and Asia to the Middle East.[37] MOD 2 radiomen monitored field communications between the roaming Palestinian squads and their headquarters (as well as listening in on supposedly secure radio traffic from Jordanian patrols, which relayed information back to HQ on Palestinian units confronted in the field). KA'MANIM attached to the reconnaissance formations participated in countless pursuits in the Jordan Valley desert, meticulously documenting caves, ravines, and other hiding places that infiltrators might be able to use; and Intelligence Corps SAYARIM ("scouts") flying in Piper Cubs or Bell-205 helicopters flew over enemy terrain and reconnoitered Palestinian forward observation posts and staging areas. For more than three years, the IDF waged a bloody, costly, and hard-fought campaign in the Jordan Valley. Eventual victory belonged to both the soldiers who fought the infiltrators and the intelligence personnel who predicted the enemy's moves.

Another hotbed of Palestinian terrorist activity was the Gaza Strip. Long neglected by the Egyptians, Gaza was home to 350,000 refugees, who lived in a squalid, congested area eight kilometers wide and forty-eight kilometers long. Prior to the 1967 War, Gaza was the home base for the Palestine Liberation Army (PLA), a guerrilla contingent of the Egyptian military, and also served as a major base for the Egyptian military itself. As a result, Gaza was flooded with thousands of weapons left behind by the retreating Egyptian military and their PLA allies. Once the various Palestinian factions established cells and networks in the strip, these weapons were put to use.

By early 1970, the situation in Gaza had become intolerable. Hundreds of terrorist acts were reported: IDF soldiers were targeted for assassination and Israeli civilians were murdered. Following the 1970 murder of a Jewish family in their car, "purifying Gaza" became a national priority. The task fell on the shoulders of OC Southern Command Maj. Gen. Ariel "Arik" Sharon, a bullish figure who attacked any military problem head-on and decisively. Cooperating with the SHIN BET (who relied on an army of well-paid informants), Sharon's command divided the Gaza Strip into small squares, each one designated by a secret code name.[38] Elite units from the who's who of Israeli special forces combed through an outlined area of responsibility, map square by map square, and openly and brazenly challenged the Palestinian terrorists to fight; they were assisted by known suspects from the SHIN BET liaison and were accompanied by a HA'MAN intelligence officer seeking raw military data.* The subsequent battles were brief and one-sided. Sharon ordered the trees in the many orchards around the strip cut to the stump, which improved the soldiers' field of vision and line of fire, as well as the sealing of all caves and bunkers, which eliminated the Palestinians' main hiding places for men and arms. In fitting fashion, Major General Sharon led many patrols personally, and many of the IDF reconnaissance commandos masqueraded as locals to infiltrate marketplaces and meeting halls. Within one year, terrorist incidents dropped by more than 97 percent.[39]

The Palestinian revolution was forever changed in 1970, not by the actions of the IDF, A'MAN, or MOSSAD, but by the dynamics of a revolution expanding beyond the boundaries of the region. The PFLP's decision to internationalize military actions against Israeli interests began in July 1968 when an El Al flight from Rome to Tel Aviv was hijacked to Algeria. It would culminate more than two years later on what became known as "Skyjack Sunday," the September 6, 1970, attempted hijacking of *four* Israeli and foreign aircraft to dramatize the plight of the Palestinians on a grandiose scale. Three aircraft were seized by the PFLP: a Swissair flight from Zurich to New York and a TWA flight from Frankfurt to New York were flown to Zarqa, Jordan, and a Pan Am flight from Amsterdam to New York was hijacked and diverted to Cairo.[40] A hijack was attempted on board the fourth intended target, an El Al flight from Amsterdam to New York, but El Al sky marshals and irate passengers overpowered the two terrorists; subsequently, the aircraft was brought to London for an emergency landing. One of the passengers aboard that El Al flight, dressed in civilian clothing, was A'MAN director Major General Yariv, who was on his way to an intelligence conference with his American counterparts. In London, Yariv took charge of the chaotic situation and pleaded with British police officials to be allowed to bring the hijackers, including Miss Leila Khaled (the femme fatale of the PFLP and reported mistress of PFLP operations chief Dr. Wadi Haddad), to Israel for trial. The British refused and suffered the inevitable consequences: On September 9, a BOAC flight from Bombay to London was seized and flown to Zarqa, Jordan; once

---

*Although the information has never been declassified, the participating units are believed to have included SAYERET SHAKED, Southern Command's reconnaissance force; SAYERET HARUV, Central Command's reconnaissance force; SAYERET TZANHANIM; SAYERET GOLANI; and, according to foreign reports, SAYERET MAT'KAL.

the hostages had been removed—after baking inside the aircraft fuselage for several days—the PFLP blew up the three airliners in a dramatic statement filmed for international viewing.

For years, tension between the Jordanians and the Palestinian guerrillas, who had created their own lawless state within the monarchy, had been growing, and heading toward an inevitable showdown. "Skyjack Sunday" was an obvious challenge to Jordanian rule, one that King Hussein could not tolerate. The Jordanian army's superb Bedouin legions were thrown into the refugee camps and terrorist training centers throughout the country in pitched battles meant to once and for all destroy the fedayeen. The battles were unrivaled in their ferocity and brutality, even by Middle Eastern standards of barbarity. Thousands of Palestinians were killed and tens of thousands wounded in what became known as the Jordanian Civil War. The PLO was forced into exile in Lebanon. The display of Arab fratricide, including a Syrian invasion of northern Jordan in a show of support for the Palestinians, tore apart any hopes of Arab unity. While attempting to mediate the bloody crisis, Egyptian President Nasser suffered a fatal heart attack. The bloody civil war eventually became known as "Black September," and produced rage and violence that would haunt the Middle East for years.

In September 1972, Maj. Gen. Aharon Yariv was supposed to leave his post of A'MAN director and retire from active service to enter a political career; events on the European continent, however, would alter these plans. On September 5, a terrorist squad from the Black September organization seized most of the Israeli Olympics team in their Olympics village dormitory in Munich. Following a botched rescue attempt by West German police at Furstenfeldbruk Military Airfield near Munich, the Black September gunmen massacred eleven of the athletes before being killed or captured by German authorities. The surviving perpetrators would be released weeks later after a Lufthansa flight, from Damascus to Munich, was seized on October 29. The Olympics Massacre caused a reaction of horror and outrage around the world. Israel reeled in grief and with an obsession for revenge.

The Israeli intelligence community would never be the same.

NOTES: CHAPTER ELEVEN

1. Stewart Steven, *The Spymasters of Israel* (New York: Ballantine Books, 1980), 27.

2. Ian Black and Benny Morris, *Israel's Secret Wars:* (London: Hamish Hamilton, 1991), 239.

3. *Jerusalem Post*, April 16, 1988, 5.

4. Dr. Yuval Arnon-Ochana and Dr. Arieh Yudfat, ASHAF: DIYUKNO SHEL IRGUN (Tel Aviv: SIFRIAT MA'ARIV, 1985), 119.

5. See Ian Black and Benny Morris, *Israel's Secret Wars*, 242.

6. Ya'akov Erez and Ron Edlist, SAYEROT: TZAHAL BE'HEILO ENTZYKLOPEDIA LE'TZAVA ULE'BITACHON (Tel Aviv: Revivim Publishers, 1983), 81.

7. See Ian Black and Benny Morris, *Israel's Secret Wars*, 237.

8. David Ronen, SHNOT HA'SHABA'CH: HA'HIA'ARACHOT BE'YEHUDA VE'SHOMRON, SHANA RISHONA (Tel Aviv: Ministry of Defense Publications, 1989), 135.

9. Dan Schueftan, HATASHA: HA'STRATEGIA HA'MEDINIT SHEL MITZRAIM HA'NATZARIT BE'A'KVOT MILCHEMET 1967–70 (Tel Aviv: MA'ARACHOT, Israel Ministry of Defense Publications, 1989), 123.

10. Chaim Herzog, *The Arab-Israeli Wars* (London: Arms and Armour Press, 1982), 199.

11. Oded Granot, HEYL HA'MODE'IN: TZAHAL BE'HEILO ENTZYKLOPEDIA LE'TZAVA ULE'BITACHON (Tel Aviv: Revivim Publishers, 1981), 92.

12. *Ibid.* 165.

13. Mazal Me'ulam, "BE'YOM BAHIR EFSHAR LIROT ET DAMESEK," BAMACHANE (July 10, 1991): 9.

14. For a mention of the planting of listening devices inside Egyptian military and civilian telephone poles, see David Hutch, *Aviation Week and Space Technology* (June 30, 1975: 11). A'MAN has never admitted that it executed deep-penetration raids inside Egypt, Jordan, or Syria to plant eavesdropping devices along enemy communications lines, and, of course, A'MAN has never confirmed that it was IDF reconnaissance forces that executed this delicate operation. Nevertheless, only three reconnaissance formations known to be operating during the War of Attrition had the resources, personnel, and confidence of the General Staff to be "dropped" into the treacherous cold of enemy-held territory for such assignments; they were: SAYERET MAT'KAL, the General Staff reconnaissance unit, which was created in 1957 for just such purposes; SAYERET TZANHANIM, the conscript Paratroop Brigade's reconnaissance element; and SAYERET SHAKED, Southern Command's reconnaissance force. The identity of the true units responsible for this endeavor, however, remains classified by Israeli authorities.

15. Dani Shalom, KOL METOSEI HEYL HA'AVIR (Tel Aviv: BAVIR Aviation Publications, 1990), 26.

16. Yosef Argaman, "MIVTZA HELEM," BAMACHANE (November 2, 1988): 17.

17. Eilan Kfir, TZANHANIM CHI'R MUTZNACH: TZAHAL BE'HEILO ENTZYKLOPEDIA LE'TZAVA ULE'BITACHON (Tel Aviv, Revivim Publishers, 1981), 123.

18. Eliezer "Cheeta" Cohen and Tzvi Lavi, HA'SHAMAYIM EINAM HA'GVUL (Tel Aviv: Ma'ariv Book Guild, 1990), 357.

19. Yosef Argaman, ZE HAYA SODI BE'YOTER (Tel Aviv: Israel Ministry of Defense Publications, 1990), 281.

20. Uri Milstein, HA'HISTORIA SHEL HA'TZANHANIM—KERECH DALED (Tel Aviv: Schalgi Ltd., Publishing House, 1987), 1,485.

21. Eldar Yaniv, "YARIV: LO HAYU MECHDALIM MODE'INIM," BAMACHANE (March 23, 1987): 13.

22. Merav Arlozorov, "VE'HA'MAK'AM HUNAF," BAMACHANE (December 24, 1986): 11.

23. See Dani Shalom, KOL METOSEI HEYL HA'AVIR, 171.

24. Yossi Melman and Dan Raviv, *The Imperfect Spies* (London: Sidgwick and Jackson, 1989), 109.

25. For the best account of Operation Noah's Ark, see Abraham Rabinovich, *The Boats of Cherbourg* (New York: Seaver Books, Henry Holt and Company, 1988).

26. Abraham Rabinovich, "One Swiss Who Stopped Being Neutral," *Jerusalem Post International Edition* (week ending May 12, 1990): 12.

27. *Ibid.* 12.

28. An Intelligence Corps Sherman cherry picker is displayed at the IDF Armored Corps museum and monument at Latrun, located halfway between Tel Aviv and Jerusalem.

29. See Oded Granot, HEYL HA'MODE'IN, 100.

30. *Ibid.* 100.

31. *Ibid.* 100.

32. *Ibid.* 101.

33. Guy Bechor, LEXICON ASHA'F (Tel Aviv: Ministry of Defense Publications, 1991), 119.

34. *Ibid.* 124.

35. See Ian Black and Benny Morris, *Israel's Secret Wars*, 256.

36. Edgar O'Ballance, *The Language of Violence* (San Rafael: Presidio Press, 1979), 59.

37. Shlomoh Ben-Amnon, BE'A'AKAVOT HA'HABLANIM (Tel Aviv: Madim Books, 1970), 98.

38. Ron Ben-Yishai, "Gaza 1988: Sharon's Methods Would Not Be Efficient Now," YEDIOT AHARONOT SHEVA YAMIM (January 22, 1988): 8.

39. *Ibid.* 9.

40. Ariel Merari and Shlomi Elad, *The International Dimension of Palestinian Terrorism* (Tel Aviv: Jaffe Center for Strategic Studies, 1986), 131.

CHAPTER 12

DESTRUCTION OF THE MYTH:
THE 1973 ARAB-ISRAELI WAR

"We will chop off the hands of those who kill our children."
Israeli Prime Minister Golda Meir, October 1972

I n October 1972, during a brief and low-key ceremony in the office of
IDF Chief of Staff Lt. Gen. David "Dado" Elazar, Maj. Gen. Eliyahu
"Eli" Zeira was named the director of IDF Military Intelligence. His appointment to one of the most important positions in the Israeli defense establishment was a wise choice for a nation in the midst of a brutal and spectacular war against terrorism.

Zeira, a native-born Israeli, or sabra,* was born in Haifa in 1928 and at
the age of eighteen was accepted for service in the underground PAL'MACH,
and later in the HAGANAH. During the 1948 War of Independence, he quickly
rose through the ranks of field postings, from squad leader to company commander. He was considered a highly capable combat officer and, in 1951,
was one of the first IDF officers sent to Fort Benning, Georgia, USA, where
he underwent a comprehensive company commanders' course. Upon his return
to Israel, he was appointed director of Strategic Planning in the General Staff
Branch—an extremely prestigious title for such a young officer. Over the course
of the next twenty-five years, Eli Zeira assumed a wide array of commands,
including commander of the GIVA'ATI Infantry Brigade in 1956, commander
of the conscript Paratroop Brigade, commander of Operations in the General
Staff, deputy A'MAN commander, and, like his predecessor, Aharon Yariv, military

---

*The sabra is a cactus fruit that, like the Israeli personality bearing its name, is hard
and prickly on the outside, and soft and sweet inside.

attaché to Washington, D.C.[1] Zeira's tour of duty in the American capital provided him intimate contact with the intricacies of the Israeli-American military and intelligence alliance—a vital dose of interservice experience that would prove crucial in the years to come.

When Zeira became the A'MAN director in October 1972, he became the last link in the Israeli intelligence triumvirate destined to guide the nation through the precarious 1970s.* The MOSSAD director was Maj. Gen. (Res.) Tzvi "Tzvika" Zamir, a veteran PAL'MACH and IDF officer, an unglamorous general of whom Levi Eshkol had once commented, when asked how could he appoint such an inexperienced man to such an important post, "Don't worry, in a year or two he'll learn his job."[2] The second peg of Israel's secretive society was Maj. Gen. Aharon Yariv, who had assumed the newly formed post of special advisor on terrorist matters, a troubleshooter office of great importance created to formulate Israel's strategies to counter the stemming tide of Black September terrorism; it was answerable only to the office of the Israeli prime minister.

Yariv commanded great respect inside the Israeli defense establishment, and had the complete confidence of the Israeli political leadership. He had had eight years of experience and brilliant success as the A'MAN director during its "golden age"; many in the IDF considered his handling of the 1967 crisis the true reason for Israel's victory. Yariv was, in fact, the leader of Israel's intelligence community, and Zeira's appointment frightened him; according to several reports, Yariv was also not comfortable with the choice of Zamir as MOSSAD director. When commenting on the leadership of Defense Minister Moshe Dayan, Chief of Staff Lt. Gen. David "Dado" Elazar, and A'MAN director Zeira, Yariv declared, "Now we are heading for catastrophe, because the system is headed by three men who do not know the meaning of fear." Yariv knew that Elazar had not been Dayan's first—or even *second*—choice to be the IDF chief of staff, and that Zeira as A'MAN director was not acceptable to Elazar.[3]

Yariv's concern stemmed from the past military careers of the three IDF commanders: All PAL'MACH or elite unit veterans, these men were known for their courageous exploits under fire, not for their analytical wisdom or Solomon-like judgment. Dado and Zeira were *pure* fighters, full-fledged combatants who cared little about the political, economic, or cultural phenomena that dictated events in the Middle East. All that mattered to them was results on the battlefield; they were men who would rather lead an assault than engage in

---

*The SHIN BET, LA'KA'M, and the National Police Special Branch were also tenaciously involved in the execution of their responsibilities, but their operations were far removed from the forefront of intelligence-gathering and analysis.

abstract evaluation. They were combat leaders, and when Israel was in danger, they knew how to respond.

Indeed, in the fall and winter of 1972, Israel was under fire—in the sights of the terrorist's gun. Never before had the Jewish state felt so vulnerable; never before had terrorists proven so brazen in their actions and been able to pose such a decisive threat to Israeli security. The Black September attack in Munich united the State of Israel: Immediate destruction of Black September became the nation's number one priority. It was as if overnight the Syrian and Egyptian guns were no longer poised for battle along the Golan Heights and the Suez Canal. Egyptian soldiers, after all, did not hijack airplanes and Syrian soldiers did not gun down athletes as they sat helplessly inside the belly of a helicopter. Israel wanted to declare full-scale war against Black September.

The Munich Massacre struck Israeli premier Golda Meir very hard. She was the national matriarch, the Jewish grandmother who thought she could protect all her children. One third "iron woman," one third compassionate leader, and one third wily and hard-fighting political boss, Meir often conducted cabinet meetings, or met with generals and spy masters, in her Jerusalem kitchen while chain-smoking cigarettes and munching on homemade cakes. The deaths of the eleven Olympics athletes showed Meir as mortal, incapable of shielding all of Israel. Inevitably, she would blame the nation's intelligence services—the MOSSAD, SHIN BET, and A'MAN—for not penetrating Black September and providing warning of the impending attacks. The spies had let her down and she was adamant that heads would roll. On September 16, 1972, a government-sanctioned board of inquiry, charged with uncovering the reasons for the intelligence failure, issued their "Koeppel Report." Meir was ready to wield her ax—three MOSSAD and SHIN BET officials were sacked. With a clean slate at her disposal, Prime Minister Meir could now embark on her private holy war.

Combating Black September was no easy task, even for Israel's esteemed intelligence services. A most secretive, and adamantly denied, entity of Yasir Arafat's el-Fatah,* Black September centered around the hard-core Arafat loyalists who had survived the 1967 War, and the guerrilla campaign along the Jordanian and Lebanese frontiers, and who had proven their infrangible bond with the PLO chairman throughout the dark days of the Jordanian Civil War. What made Black September so lethal was the ability of its leadership (hard-

---

*During a televised interview of the PLO chairman by Marie Colvin for the American public television network show "Frontline"(aired on February 27, 1990), Arafat—with the help of his heavily armed bodyguards in the next room—threatened the journalist when she even mentioned Black September or terrorism.

core combatants in the ruthless Razd) to locate and recruit the most embittered and hopeless individuals willing to die for the privilege of perpetrating acts of vengeance against Israel, and also Jordan. In fact, the Hashemite kingdom was the principal target of Black September's operations. On November 28, 1971, Jordanian Prime Minister Wasfi a-Tal was assassinated as he left the lobby of a Cairo hotel; the perpetrators, Black September gunmen, were reported to have lapped up his blood in a gruesome victory display. In other acts of violence, Jordan's ambassador to Great Britain was shot in London on December 15, 1971; the Jordanian Embassy in Geneva, Switzerland, was bombed on December 16; and on February 6, 1972, five Jordanian nationals—suspected of being Israeli intelligence agents—were executed in Cologne, West Germany.[4]

Israel, however, was also a Black September obsession. On May 8, 1972, a Black September squad seized a Sabena Belgian Airlines Boeing 707 on a routine flight from Brussels, with a stopover in Vienna, to Tel Aviv. The hijacking of a foreign aircraft to Israel was as audacious a statement as any terrorist group had ever made against Israel. The hijacking, meant to secure the release of 317 jailed Palestinian terrorists, eventually failed when a force of Israeli commandos from SAYERET MAT'KAL, disguised as mechanics in white coveralls, stormed the aircraft, killing two of the skyjackers and rescuing the hostages. The operation was personally commanded by Lt. Col. Ehud Barak, the SAYERET MAT'KAL commander, a future A'MAN director, and, at the time of this book's writing, the IDF chief of staff.[5] The rescue at Lod Airport, known as Operation Isotope 1, humbled Black September but did not remove it from the forefront of terrorist operations against Israel. Four months later, the town of Munich became synonymous in the minds of Israelis with the Palestinian terrorism.

Munich, it appeared, was only the beginning of Black September's unstoppable war. On September 10, 1972, Black September terrorists hit again in an unsuccessful attempt to assassinate Tzadok Ophir, a low-level diplomat at the embassy in Brussels who was, in fact, a MOSSAD officer tasked with infiltrating Black September.

Militarily, Israel reacted to the massacre in Munich with a far-sweeping mini-invasion of Lebanon on September 16, 1972; it was known as Operation Turmoil 4. A retaliatory strike meant to destroy the growing Palestinian terrorist infrastructure in southern Lebanon, Operation Turmoil 4 also had— as a secondary objective—a crucial intelligence requirement. A foray into terrorist-dominated territory offered the Intelligence Corps a unique opportunity to obtain information from documents seized at overrun bases and first-person testimony from captured terrorists.[6] Yet before A'MAN could analyze the wealth of data obtained from Operation Turmoil 4—numerous Intelligence

Corps interrogators were dispatched to the front lines to handle the large numbers of prisoners captured*—Black September struck again. It was a relentless autumn offensive.

On September 18, Black September initiated its infamous letter-bomb campaign in which Israeli interests worldwide were subjected to hundreds of exploding parcels. This brutal tactic was highly effective. The leaders of Israel realized that Black September would *have* to be defeated. The only effective and realistic means at Israel's disposal was the elimination of the terrorist leaders, using A'MAN's assassination of Egyptian Col. Mustafa Hafaz in 1955 as a perfect example. The biblical policy of "an eye for an eye" was about to be imposed.

The Israeli hit teams tasked with the elimination of Black September's leadership (remove the head and the animal will die!) have become the subject of much publicity and romanticized speculation. The hit teams, adorned by the foreign media with such mysterious names as "Black June," "Wrath of God" (WOG), "The Avengers," and "Squad 101," never *officially* existed; Israel has never admitted its role in the selective elimination of the Black September hierarchy responsible for the Munich Olympics Massacre. Yet the track record of this enigmatic force, believed to have included mixed personnel from the MOSSAD, the SHIN BET, A'MAN, and various IDF reconnaissance formations, was efficiently lethal. On October 16, 1972, Wael Zwaiter, a translator in the Libyan Embassy in Rome and Black September's operations chief in Italy, was killed by two unidentified men; on January 9, 1973, Dr. Mahmud Hamshari, the Black September second in command in Paris, was fatally wounded by a bomb planted in the receiver of his telephone. On January 24, 1973, Abd el Hir, the Black September station chief in Nicosia, Cyprus (the most convenient espionage battleground in the Arab-Israeli conflict), was killed when a powerful bomb planted in his hotel room was detonated by a booby-trapped light switch. On April 6, 1973, Iraqi-born professor Basil al-Kubaissi, one of the more ambitious operations planners in the Black September organization, was shot dead in Paris; on April 12, Moussa Abu Zaiad, a senior Black September operations officer in Cyprus, was killed by an incendiary device

---

*One IDF operation that yielded a gold mine of intelligence rewards from captured prisoners was Operation Basket, the June 21, 1972, SAYERET MAT'KAL kidnapping of five Syrian Military Intelligence generals who were assisting Palestinian terrorist activities along Israel's northern frontier. The objective of the raid was to obtain a "human trump card" to facilitate the release of three IAF pilots held in Damascus, but A'MAN obtained valuable information on Syrian involvement in Palestinian terrorism in the process.

planted in his hotel room in Athens, Greece; and on June 28, Algerian-born Mohammed Boudia, one of the Palestinians' main contacts in Europe and the connecting factor between the PFLP, Black September, and the KGB, was blown up in his car in the Latin Quarter of Paris.[7]

Israel's warriors in the shadows suffered losses as well. On January 26, 1973, Baruch Cohen, the MOSSAD station chief in Madrid, Spain, was assassinated as he awaited a meet with a double agent in a cafe popular with university students; on March 12, Simia Glazer, a senior MOSSAD officer in Cyprus and a veteran of Menachem Begin's IRGUN, was shot by Arab assailants in the Cypriot capital.[8]

While, according to foreign reports, the MOSSAD and other "mysterious and anonymous" forces waged a brutal war on the European continent, much of A'MAN's assets were devoted to the destruction of the Palestinian terror closer to the Israeli frontiers. Militarily, the IDF was busy contemplating the destruction of Black September, and much of the PLO as well, by laying the groundwork for hard-hitting retaliatory and preemptive commando raids. Photoreconnaissance flights, flown by the newly acquired RF-4E Phantoms, were ordered over much of Lebanon, and A'MAN's SIGINT resources were mobilized to intercept any terrorist radio or telephone communications. Naturally, the agents providing A'MAN with its HUMINT edge were put to the task of penetrating the various Palestinian groups, obtaining vital information, and relaying that data back to A'MAN handlers in Tel Aviv.

Hitting the Palestinians' terrorist infrastructure in Lebanon was seen as a crucial element of Israel's overall campaign against Black September. The refugee camps of southern Lebanon were the fertile recruiting grounds for terrorist headhunters seeking talent. Training facilities throughout southern Lebanon, conveniently surrounded by a ring of United Nations' schools and hospitals, taught the devious terrorist trade to Palestinian and European anarchists, including the Irish Republican Army (bankrolled by Libyan leader Col. Muammar Qaddafi), the West German Baader-Meinhoff Gang, and the Japanese Red Army (a group that, on May 30, 1972, committed the Lod Airport Massacre on behalf of the PFLP). Spread out throughout northern Lebanon, supposedly far from the lethal reach of the IAF, were the most important Palestinian bases: command and control facilities, research and development centers, and bomb factories, which were crucial to the Palestinians' ability to wage a terrorist war in Europe. It was in these facilities that the intelligence gathered by Palestinian agents in Europe was analyzed, disseminated, and used to plan grand-scale acts of terror. It was in these facilities that explosives were planted in false bottoms of suitcases, and the tools of assassination, such as silenced Polish machine pistols, were prepared for shipment—via the diplomatic pouch of one Arab nation or another—into Europe, where they would be used for attacks against Israeli interests.[9]

In February 1973, A'MAN pinpointed two refugee camps located near the northern port city of Tripoli, Lebanon, which were of particular significance: Nahar al-Bard and al-Badawi were home to *seven* major terrorist bases. The camps not only served as staging points for attacks worldwide but as training grounds for revolutionaries from Europe, Africa, Asia, and South America.[10] One of the major considerations behind targeting the camps around Tripoli was the fact that the Nahar al-Bard camp was the principal special operations base for el-Fatah's naval forces, commanded by Ibrahim el-Muja; in October 1972, eleven terrorists from this "elite" force had departed this facility and traveled to Europe, where they began a wave of terrorism against Israeli embassies, installations, and diplomatic personnel.[11]

Since Tripoli was more than 180 kilometers from the Israeli frontier, the operation's success depended on A'MAN 's ability to provide the attack force—consisting of reconnaissance paratroopers, naval commandos, and several diverse paratroop units—with up-to-date intelligence on the layout of the seven targeted installations, the disposition of the Palestinian forces garrisoning these heavily fortified positions, and what "surprises," such as booby traps, bunkers, and camouflaged machine-gun nests, might be awaiting any frontal assault. Since the task force would be ferried to the shores of Tripoli by a miniflotilla of IDF/navy missile and patrol boats, A'MAN and MODE'IN HEYL HA'YAM ("Naval Intelligence") had to produce a comprehensive accounting of Lebanese naval activity and shore defenses and choose the most secluded and protected landing zone.[12] Israeli Air Force warplanes would be flying close air support, as well as waiting on call to transport the attackers back to Israel, so A'MAN and IAF Intelligence needed to locate Lebanese and Palestinian antiaircraft positions.[13]

The raid, code-named Operation Hood 54-55, was a bold stroke for the IDF, an energetic and innovative display of Israel's special forces capabilities. Just as had been planned in Operation Branch and promised in A'MAN HQ, the task force landed on Lebanese soil uncontested and, after a forced march through terrorist-controlled territory, attacked their objectives with split-second precision. Many of the battles were hard fought—often waged hand-to-hand with fists and rifle butts replacing weapons. Before the attackers were evacuated by helicopters, they razed most of the facilities with well-placed high-explosives. A'MAN later estimated that 37 terrorists were killed and 65 wounded. IDF losses were only eight seriously wounded.[14]

The raid on Tripoli served as a primer for Israel's many long-range, spectacular commando raids of the future. It was the first raid in the history of Israeli special operations where such a distance—180 kilometers—was crossed, and where two separate objectives were assaulted simultaneously. Operation Hood 54-55 was also the first major IDF operation against a terrorist base located in the apparently impregnable confines of the Lebanese rear. The mission served as the laboratory for more adventurous, farther-reaching raids, such as the 1976 Entebbe raid and, according to foreign reports, the April 16, 1988, assassination of Abu Jihad. First, however, there would be the Beirut raid— the culmination of the Israeli intelligence community's war against Black September.

On April 9 and 10, 1973, the IDF struck the nerve center of the Palestinian terrorist domain in Lebanon. This raid, known as Operation Spring of Youth, would be the most ambitious undertaken to date. Hundreds of Israel's best soldiers were dispatched into Beirut to assassinate three leading Black September officers, as well as destroy bases, depots, and other facilities belonging to several other Palestinian terror groups. The primary target was Objective AVIVAH—the assassinations of Abu Yusef (the el-Fatah operations chief and a key planner of the Munich Olympics Massacre), Kamal A'dwan (a senior el-Fatah operations officer responsible for running terrorist cells inside the West Bank of the Jordan River and the Gaza Strip), and Kamal Nasser (the PLO's official spokesman and a key member of Black September's operational staff) by a squad of commandos from SAYERET MAT'KAL commanded by Lt. Col. Ehud Barak. All three Palestinians lived in a luxurious block of flats on West Beirut's Rue Verdun.[15]

Objective GILAH called for the destruction of a Democratic Front for the Liberation of Palestine (DFLP) apartment complex on Rue Khartoum in West Beirut by a force of reconnaissance paratroopers commanded by Lt. Col. Amnon Shahak.* Secondary objectives included VARDAH—the destruction of the el-Fatah headquarters, which governed operations in the West Bank and Gaza, in a southern Beirut neighborhood by a force of naval commandos; TZILAH— the destruction of a major ammunition dump in northern Beirut by a force of naval commandos; and YEHUDIT—a diversionary raid against an el-Fatah ammunition dump located north of Sidon by a force of reconnaissance paratroopers.[16]

The raid was designed to be a master stroke—a one-shot deal meant to administer a fatal blow to the Black September leadership, while concurrently crippling the morale of the organization's rank and file. For Israel, the foray into the Lebanese capital *had* to work—too much was at stake for failure! The planning, coordination, and execution of the operation involved every facet of Israel's covert and conventional capabilities. A'MAN mobilized the staff at HATZAV to gather, assess, and translate all open material on the Lebanese capital; A'MAN's Eavesdropping Unit and HATZAV were ordered to apply extra effort in monitoring Palestinian radio and telephone traffic, and inter-

---

*It is interesting to note that both Ehud Barak and Amnon Shahak, commanders of "the elite of the elite" within the IDF and both highly decorated special operations officers, would become A'MAN directors and eventual chiefs of staff.

cepting any valuable bits of information. A'MAN's HUMINT sources were placed on overtime as well, and pressured to uncover any tidbit of information that might prove useful in future campaigns. A'MAN was able to discover the two addresses on Rue Verdun and Rue Khartoum, and had gathered all the necessary information on the various Palestinian targets inside Beirut before the final plan was presented to Chief of Staff Elazar.[17]

The MOSSAD was also instrumental in pulling off this most ambitious operation. Its agents infiltrated the Lebanese capital in the days prior to the raid to lay the groundwork for the task force: They rented several automobiles to ferry the commandos to and from their objectives, conducted surveillance of the targets, and mapped out escape routes by reconnoitering the bustling streets.[18] Since the commandos would reach Beirut by sea, IDF/navy Intelligence and A'MAN worked together to monitor Lebanese naval activity, the power and range of Lebanese coastal radar, and its shore defenses.

On the night of April 9, the IDF launched its daring raid into the Lebanese capital. All objectives were attended to with split-second precision. The three Black September chiefs were assassinated with little difficulty by Lieutenant Colonel Barak's commandos, all dressed in civilian clothing and carrying weapons such as the American Ingram MAC-10 .45-caliber submachine gun. The other targets were also addressed successfully, although a large battle— a pitched close-quarter fight—developed around Objective GILAH, where Lieutenant Colonel Shahak's reconnaissance paratroopers encountered stiff resistance and suffered several killed in action. After escaping through the back streets of Beirut, the Israeli commandos—and much of their supporting MOSSAD contingent—met the awaiting missile boats and returned to Israel; the seriously wounded were ferried to military hospitals by IAF transport choppers. Operation Spring of Youth, one of the most important special operations ever mounted by the IDF, was over in little more than an hour.

The intelligence rewards from Operation Spring of Youth were enormous. Each commando in Ehud Barak's force rifled through the apartments of the men they killed in search of anything of intelligence value. The fighters entered the dwellings carrying suitcases full of explosives; when they left, these suitcases were filled with documents.[19] The material was rushed to A'MAN HQ for analysis, then disseminated to military units, the SHIN BET, and foreign counterintelligence services. Although the content of the data seized was never released, it is believed to have been a virtual roster of Palestinian operatives in Israel and in deep-cover in Europe.

In the months following the raid, Black September no longer posed a serious threat to Israeli interests worldwide.[20]

Less than a month following Operation Spring of Youth, the State of Israel celebrated its twenty-fifth anniversary. It had survived a quarter century of incessant violence and had blossomed into the jewel of the Middle East.

Israel knew that its survival was dependent on the IDF, and in appreciation, a tremendous military parade was held along the walls of the old city of Jerusalem to climax the national celebration. Prime Minister Golda Meir, Defense Minister Moshe Dayan, and IDF Chief of Staff Lt. Gen. "Dado" Elazar saluted the columns of tanks, armored personnel carriers, and soldiers parading past the reviewing stand. The might of Israel was on display for the Arab world to see. The IDF had assumed a larger-than-life image of power during the 1967 War, and the raid on Beirut had reinforced this imposing image. Indeed, Operation Spring of Youth was a brilliant undertaking, an epic example of a nation's resolve to combat terrorism and an army's ability to mount incursions into the heart of enemy territory. Yet Operation Spring of Youth would have a negative impact as well: A small nation had devoted much of its limited resources to defeating a small and shadowy organization whose acts had never really threatened Israel's *physical* existence.

Even though A'MAN dedicated so much of its forces to the war against terrorism, it did continue to maintain surveillance of the opposing Arab armies. The SIGINT and ELINT positions in Umm Hushiba, Mt. Hermon, and the Jordan Valley worked around the clock monitoring military developments across the borders.[21] It appeared to most Israeli officials that the possibility of another full-scale Arab-Israeli war in the immediate future was remote at best; in A'MAN HQ it was described with the simple term SVIRUT NEMUCHA ("low probability"). After all, the Arabs were not about to risk another thrashing on the battlefield. The frontiers were quiet, and, most importantly, Black September had been defeated. A'MAN director Maj. Gen. Eli Zeira was confident that there would be no war in 1973.

Since June 11, 1967, the day the guns fell silent ending the Six-Day War, it was clear to most Israeli military planners that the Arab states of Egypt, Jordan, and Syria would somehow attempt to retrieve the vast stretches of territory they had lost. Nasser's approach was cautious, however, and attended to with the patience and guile of a Byzantine leader. The War of Attrition was the fruition of this strategy: By engaging the Israelis sporadically with massive firepower and inflicting heavy losses over an extended period of time, the Arab armies would nibble away at Israeli resolve to fight another war or keep its newly acquired territory. This would set the stage for a full-scale bid to recapture the Sinai, the Golan Heights, and the West Bank.

When Nasser died on September 28, 1970, his successor, Anwar as-Sadat, declared to the Egyptian people in a radio address that he would reinstate full-scale hostilities with Israel. Indeed, Sadat declared that 1971 would be a "year of decision." According to several reports, Sadat passed a confidential note to American President Richard Nixon in February 1971 hinting at Egypt's desire to enter into negotiations with Israel. When Jerusalem failed to respond to Sadat's overture, the course was set for war in the year of decision.

Sadat would later state, "If the war demands a million casualties we are willing to sacrifice a million dead!"[22]

The year 1971 passed without incident, however, and Israel concluded that Egypt had simply bluffed in order to retain its hold over the leadership in the Arab world. In fact, it was A'MAN's assessment that Egypt would not lead the Arab world into another "hopeless" campaign against Israel because Israel's qualitative superiority and its newly seized territorial depth gave the IDF an overwhelming edge over the Arab armies. No Arab state—not even Egypt, it was believed and hoped—would embark on war unilaterally; there would have to be a unified Arab effort, and Arab unity was a myth produced by the propagandists in Cairo. A dangerous atmosphere of overconfidence prevailed within A'MAN. The belief that there would be no war in the near future, and the listing of reasons supporting this conclusion, became known in A'MAN's vernacular as HA'KONTZEPTZIA ("The Concept"). It evolved into a cataclysmic series of errors and misconceptions that would bring the State of Israel to the brink of disaster.

Although A'MAN believed Sadat's 1971 "year of decision" to be nothing more than Arab bravado, the year did mark the beginning of Egypt's serious efforts to once again engage Israel on the battlefield. In early March, four Soviet Antonov An-22 Cock transport aircraft landed at the Cairo-West Air Base under a heavy veil of secrecy and security. At a remote section of the airfield, the An-22's cargo doors were opened and four MiG-25 Foxbat espionage aircraft (designated as the X-500) were unloaded and brought to a concrete hangar. With five camera ports for high-resolution photographic equipment, the MiG-25 was a top-secret aircraft capable of a maximum speed of Mach 3.2 at a height of seventy-three thousand feet. It was the first weapons system at the disposal of the Egyptian armed forces that totally outclassed anything in Israel's arsenal.[23]

The four X-500s "lent" to Cairo were flown by Soviet pilots and maintained by Soviet technicians *only*; Soviet-manned SAM batteries defended the base, as did, according to several reports, Soviet Spetsnaz special forces units. Egyptian President Sadat was afforded the opportunity to see this remarkable aircraft only after receiving an invitation from the Soviets. Beyond the significance of the Cairo-Moscow military relationship was the enormous intelligence value of the aircraft. Uncontested reconnaissance flights over Israel would provide the Egyptian High Command with detailed information to use in planning for the recapture of the Sinai. Egypt finally had an intelligence tool that surpassed the best at A'MAN's disposal.

Soviet-piloted Foxbat photoreconnaissance flights over virtually all of Israel began in the spring of 1971. MA'ARIV, Israel's second largest daily newspaper, went to great lengths to express national concern about the MiG-25s based in Egypt. On numerous occasions, F-4 Phantoms were scrambled to meet the high-flying Mach 3 intruder, but all attempts to intercept them were unsuccessful; once the MiGs' afterburners were ignited, even the Phantoms' AIM-7E Sparrow radar-guided air-to-air missile, with its Mach 4 speed and sixty-two-mile range, had trouble pursuing the elusive Foxbats. Foxbat flights over vast stretches of Israeli territory soon became routine. Flying parallel to the Israeli coast, the Soviet pilots were able to make precision photoreconnaissance sorties over every square mile of Israeli territory. The data was passed to Egyptian Military Intelligence, which used the information for target sheets and deployment scenarios. Yet most of the Foxbat missions were flown over the Golan Heights, where needle-sharp photographs of Israeli antitank defenses were passed on to the Syrians for their war plans, and, of course, over the Sinai desert, where top-secret Israeli defensive positions in the ultrastrategic Mitla Pass were identified. Israeli Air Force bases in the Sinai also received "the treatment," as did IDF/navy facilities at Sharm es-Sheikh, the HEYL HA'YAM's principal fleet base in the Red Sea.

Although Israeli Defense Minister Moshe Dayan was angered by the Soviet intervention on behalf of Egyptian intelligence, little was done to stop it. In fact, in a television interview Dayan reassured an anxious Israeli public by stating, "There is little to worry about with these flights, since they are only conducting reconnaissance." [24] Soviet reconnaissance of Israeli territory, and much of the eastern Mediterranean, had been going on for several years, and was therefore theoretically not worthy of unilateral Israeli military reaction.

From the sprawling Egyptian naval base at Mesra Matruh, the Soviets had been conducting photoreconnaissance flights with Tupelov Tu-16s, Ilyushin Il-38s, and Beriev Be-12s; the aircraft were adorned with Egyptian Air Force markings but flown exclusively by Soviet personnel. Although the Egyptians were told that the Soviet aerial effort was solely for targeting Israel, it was clear that most of the Soviet effort was directed at the U.S. Sixth Fleet patrolling in the eastern Mediterranean. The Soviets realized that their support for Egypt risked a superpower confrontation, and they were determined to place their forces in an advantageous strategic position. It is remarkable, however, that so much of Israel was photographed and so many sensitive locations were documented and ranged *without* a decisive IDF response. Yet, the guidelines of A'MAN's "Concept" stated that the Arabs would not initiate another war. In fact, according to "reliable" intelligence estimates updated monthly, A'MAN believed that the Arab states would be incapable of launching a major first-strike offensive against Israel until 1975 or 1976. In July 1973, Defense Minister Dayan, a man who had long believed that the potential for war *did* exist, claimed that war was not expected for the next decade. [25]

If 1971 was the year of decision, it was also the year in which A'MAN uncovered the Egyptian army's plans to launch a blitz across the Suez Canal. Large-scale Egyptian maneuvers conducted in the winter of 1971 provided A'MAN's Research and Development sections, as well as its all-important Collections Department, with the pieces to compile a step-by-step Order of Battle as to how Egypt would wage the next war. In the final half-year analysis handed to Prime Minister Golda Meir by Major General Yariv's A'MAN, the conclusion stated that Sadat and the Egyptian High Command had rejected a resumption of the War of Attrition, and plans were in motion to seize an impressive chunk of the Sinai—up to the Mitla and Giddi passes.[26] These Egyptian plans for a conquest of the Sinai were code-named Operation 41 and Operation High Minarets, but after much revision and internal Egyptian bickering, they were eventually renamed the Granite Two exercises.

The Egyptians realized after the 1967 War that the military destruction of Israel was no longer a possibility; therefore, the goal became the conquest of the Sinai.[27] The plan, code-named Operation Badr, consisted of a large-scale, two-stage amphibious crossing of the Suez Canal, with five infantry divisions spearheading the assault. Each of the five divisions was responsible for establishing separate ten-kilometer-deep beachheads, which would eventually spread out and link, creating an elongated and deep Egyptian military stand in the Sinai. Israeli counterattack capabilities were expected to be minimal, since Operation Badr was to be a *surprise* attack; the numerical backbone of the IDF Order of Battle, its reserve armor divisions, would not be in a tactical position to intervene for at least twenty-four hours. Israeli Air Force aerial superiority was to be nullified by a preemptive Egyptian Air Force strike against the Sinai air bases, and any Israeli aerial counterattack was to be decimated by a dense and apparently impregnable shield of mobile Soviet-produced SAM batteries.

While the beachhead was being established and the various Bar-Lev line fortifications were being overrun, Egyptian combat engineers were to hurriedly build pontoon bridges linking the West Bank of the canal to the newly acquired territory. The bridges would allow the second phase of Operation Badr to be implemented. The armored juggernaut of two Egyptian armies, the Second and Third—consisting of two armored divisions and two independent armored brigades, along with defending swarms of heavily armed infantrymen equipped with the modern T-62 main battle tank—would push across the IDF's second line of defenses and make a dash for the strategic Sinai passes. A concurrent Egyptian naval offensive, consisting of seaborne formations, naval commandos, and paratroop heliborne landings, would seize the strategic Sharm es-Sheikh naval facility at the southern tip of the Sinai peninsula.[28]

Attacking targets in the Israeli rear was the responsibility of Egyptian as-Saiqa commando and paratrooper units, which would be transported by helicopter deep into Israeli territory. Expert in hit-and-run warfare and sabotage, they were to attack IDF resupply convoys as well as key command and control facilities; the Egyptians had been able to discover many intended targets as a result of the Soviet MiG-25 Foxbat flybys. The special forces aspect of Egypt's master stroke was fitting. The architect of Operation Badr was Egyptian Chief of Staff Lt. Gen. Sa'ad ad-Din Shazli, a man who many have said was the Egyptian version of Israel's Ariel Sharon!

A'MAN knew of Egypt's elaborate war plans but did little with the information at its disposal. In particular, there was a lack of concern about the new weapons systems in the Arab arsenal. From 1971 to the spring of 1973, A'MAN had monitored the massive Soviet involvement in Egyptian military affairs—especially the amount and *quality* of the Soviet weapons systems incorporated into the Egyptian arsenal—but had failed to relay this data to branch and corps commands so that tactical responses could be formulated by field units. Egypt, for example, had pinned its hopes on defeating the IDF's decisive armored edge by equipping its infantry forces, which enjoyed a vast numerical superiority over the IDF, with the portable, wire-guided Sagger AT-3 antitank missile. As far back as the Second World War and the campaign in North Africa, the foot soldier had proved himself the greatest single threat to the tank. Massive infantry deployment of a deadly tank killer such as the Sagger needed a response—an IDF countermeasure that could neutralize the tank hunter teams before the loss of materiel and life was too great. Yet A'MAN dedicated little effort to formulating counterstrategy to such systems as the Sagger. As one IDF general would state, in a clear-cut example of the IDF's arrogant overconfidence, "We [the IDF command] simply did not look upon the Arabs as capable. We would say, 'Put all their paratroopers and their Saggers on a hill, and I'll wipe them out with my tanks.' "[29]

Clearly, A'MAN had little faith in the Arab fighting man and his ability to use such complex weapons systems. A'MAN had even less faith in the ability of the Arab military commanders to create a scenario to effectively engage the IDF on the battlefield.

Another weapons system that would play a prominent role in the upcoming war was the SA-6 Gainful surface-to-air missile. The mobile, three-missile radar system was supplied to Egypt and Syria by the Soviets in substantial quantities beginning in February 1972, and in vast numbers in early 1973; it was the type of system capable of determining the course of a war. Usually deployed in batteries of three, with nine radar-guided missiles overall, the SA-6's triple launchers are mounted on the chassis of a PT-76 amphibious tank, which is air portable. The acquisition of the SA-6 indicated the progressive course that the Arab armies were following in trying to achieve aerial parity with the much-vaunted IAF; according to A'MAN estimates, the Arabs would never embark on a war until Israel's aerial superiority could be matched. The Intelligence Branch, however, did not recognize the significance of the SA-6 in achieving that end.

With a wall of Soviet-built air defenses, including the SA-2 Guideline, the SA-3 Goa, the SA-6 Gainful, and an assortment of mobile, radar-guided guns, such as the extremely lethal ZSU-23-4 quad-barreled 23mm gun, the armies of Egypt and Syria finally had an equalizer to the might and guile of the IAF. The incorporation of these extremely effective weapons into the Egyptian and Syrian Orders of Battle should have raised red flags throughout A'MAN HQ, but still the "Concept" was believed with religious fervor.

Perhaps nowhere was A'MAN's glaring overconfidence more evident than in its overall view of the Arab fighting man as inferior and not worthy of serious consideration. Many A'MAN officers did not speak Arabic, and were ignorant regarding the Arabs' history, culture, religion, and literature.[30] The top echelons of A'MAN's command infrastructure, men well versed in developments in the Arab world, did not understand the true meaning of the Arab thirst for revenge. For the Arab nations the 1967 War was a humiliating defeat suffered at the hands of a small upstart army. Western sympathies—and arm sales!—to Israel helped to reinforce the old hatred of foreign intervention in Arab affairs, from the Crusades to British General Allenby entering Jerusalem. Before the reality of an Israel in the *Arab* Middle East could be accepted in Cairo and Damascus, revenge for the 1967 disaster had to be obtained. The Arab casus belli was as simple as that.

While the IDF, and specifically A'MAN, downgraded the Arab threat, the Arabs were following an opposite course of action. They had learned to respect the Israeli soldier as intelligent, resourceful, and courageous. The Egyptian soldier was told to forget the image of the Der Sturmer type of Jew fostered by Arab propagandists for twenty-five years: Israelis were not feeble, bumbling victims of the European ghettos. Also, in preparation for Operation Badr, the Egyptians sponsored an ambitious education program for their fighting men: NCOs and officers were encouraged to study technical subjects as well as the Hebrew language. Of the 800,000 Egyptian soldiers in regular service, 110,000 were graduates of universities or other institutions of higher education.[31]

The Egyptians also embarked on an aggressive program to neutralize Israeli defenses in the Sinai, while the Syrians engineered a similar effort regarding IDF obstacles in the Golan Heights. In the Sinai, the IDF had established a medieval type of defense for the Suez Canal: Top-secret oil pipelines were planted deep in the earth underneath the canal, ready to pump hundreds of thousands of gallons of highly flammable fuel into the waterway should the Egyptians attempt a crossing. The only problem with the plan was that IDF field security in the Sinai was low, and Egyptian naval commandos succeeded in neutralizing the pipes hours before the crossing in 1973.[32]

A similar impassable Israeli defense in the Sinai was a series of twenty-meter-high sand walls along the embankment, designed to make any crossing impossible. The IDF felt that this "sand defense" was impregnable; it would be impossible for any army to gain a foothold on such a steep incline while its back was to the water. The Egyptians, however, came up with an ingenious—and simple—solution: high-powered water cannons purchased from West Germany, to extinguish uncontrollable blazes, would be used to turn the sand barriers into flat puddles. Since the towns and villages along the Egyptian side of the Suez Canal were not prone to forest fires, A'MAN could not understand why Egypt had installed these water cannons so close to the front. Nothing further was done with this bit of information.

Syrian understanding of the Golan Heights defenses was equally impressive. The IDF had constructed a series of seventeen-foot-deep antitank ditches and minefields that ran across the "Purple Line" frontier with Syria. A series of fortified defensive positions, known as MUTZAVIM, were placed throughout the frontier area, overlooking the ditches and minefields, and were tasked with covering key approaches into the Golan Heights. A series of earthen ramps had also been constructed by IDF combat engineers to allow the tank units defending the volcanic heights to confront the invading armored formations from a highly advantageous hull-down firing position; these perches commanded predesignated killing grounds where the Israeli defenders could pick off large numbers of Syrian tanks. Yet when Soviet-built bridging equipment was brought up to the Golan front—an obvious move if the Israeli obstacles were to be overcome—it aroused little suspicion in Tel Aviv and prompted no reaction from A'MAN.

Although the Syrian attack plan was not as sophisticated as Egypt's, it, too, relied on the element of surprise. The war planners in both Damascus and Cairo understood that in order for Operation Badr to succeed, they would require the few days of initiative gained in a surprise attack in order to consolidate their territorial gains before the IDF reservists could be committed to the fray. One of the most important aspects of the Arab* war plans was the art of deception—political as well as military.

Throughout 1972 and 1973, Egyptian President Sadat made countless public statements proclaiming the imminent outbreak of hostilities; his calls for a

---

*Although the term *Arab* seems to denote some type of *unified* Arab world, the only two nations capable of waging direct war against Israel were Syria and Egypt. Nevertheless, Egyptian and Syrian plans required military assistance—even a token effort for publicity's sake—from nations as diverse and politically different as Algeria, Morocco, Libya, Sudan, Saudi Arabia, Jordan, and Iraq; oil and oil revenues, emanating from the Saudis and the Persian Gulf sheikhdoms, were also crucial.

jihad ("holy war") against Israel became routine and warranted little, if any, Israeli response. Initially, Sadat's saber-rattling and minimobilization of his armed forces did prompt the IDF to increase its frontline dispositions, mobilize reserve units, and prepare the national economy for war. Nothing, however, materialized. In 1972, there were twenty occasions on which the Egyptians "mobilized" for war, conducted large-scale maneuvers dangerously close to the canal area, and made civil defense preparations, such as closing Cairo airport and sounding air raid sirens.

In A'MAN's eyes, proof of Sadat's inability to attack Israel materialized in July of 1972, when Sadat ordered nearly thirty thousand Soviet military advisors *out* of Egypt.[33] The Soviets were involved in every aspect of Egyptian military life—from command and control, to the basic training of Nile Delta villagers conscripted into the infantry. The Soviets had become a miniforce of occupation, however, and were beginning to dictate Egyptian national policy and encroach on Egyptian integrity. Sadat ousted the Soviets to assert Egyptian independence, yet he quickly mended his fences with Moscow in order to guarantee the arms shipments and intelligence support without which he would be unable to wage war. Indeed, in the spring of 1973, the first shipment of SCUD-B SS-1 surface-to-surface tactical land missiles reached the port of Alexandria. The missiles, although grossly inaccurate, had a maximum range of 170 miles and, fired from portions of Egypt and Syria, could hit major Israeli population centers. Sadat assumed that the acquisition of this weapon would deter IAF deep-penetration strikes inside Egypt. The SCUDs' arrival in Egypt proved to be the determining factor in Sadat's decision to go to war.[34]

The deception's effect on A'MAN was reinforced by several provocative incidents that went unanswered by the Arabs. According to the guidelines of the "low-probability conception," A'MAN believed that the Syrians would not act unilaterally against Israel, and that the Egyptians were not ready for war. The accuracy of these assumptions was proven on February 21, 1973: A Libyan airliner on a routine flight from Tripoli to Cairo overshot Egyptian territory and wandered into Sinai airspace. The situation was considered serious, since two weeks before that radar blip crossed into Israeli-controlled airspace, Libyan strongman Col. Muammar Qaddafi had publicly vowed to crash a plane load of high explosives in the heart of Tel Aviv.

From the BOR ("pit") underneath IDF HQ, Chief of Staff Elazar ordered the aircraft intercepted. A flight of IAF fighters was scrambled; after they failed to establish radio contact with the passenger jet's pilot, Elazar ordered the aircraft blasted out of the sky. More than a hundred passengers and crew were killed. Such an incident could easily have escalated into war; indeed, the IDF expected some type of Arab military reaction. None came. Even after Operation Spring of Youth—a blatant foray into the capital city of an

Arab nation—Arab military response was limited: Libya transferred sixteen Mirage IIICs to Egypt, and Iraq sent a squadron of Hawker Hunters to the Inchas air base. A'MAN interpreted this as an inability to respond forcefully—as token moves meant for the TV news cameras. It would be a tragic miscalculation.

Sadat originally intended to go to war in May 1973. The tides for a Suez Canal crossing were perfect, an attack would coincide with Israel's twenty-fifth anniversary celebrations, and the addition of the SCUD batteries to the Syrian and Egyptian armies provided a strategic edge. At the last moment, however, at Soviet insistence, Sadat agreed to delay his attack until October.[35] Nevertheless, the IDF did believe that the Egyptian war moves that spring were genuine, and, accordingly, the proper defensive responses were implemented.

Blue-White was the code name of the contingency plan drawn up by IDF HQ to meet the possibility of a coordinated Arab surprise attack on two—or three—frontiers. The plan involved mobilizing active and reserve forces, filling equipment stores, deploying troop and vehicle transports from "dry emergency storage," and expediting military purchases. Although it was an essential reaction to the threat of war, Blue-White was not a frugal undertaking.[36] It cost approximately U.S. $35 million (approximately 60 million Israeli pounds, or lira) and constituted an enormous percentage of the yearly defense budget. This caused a fiscal uproar in Golda Meir's government—especially from a finance ministry eager to save as many shekels as possible! The Israeli treasury could not withstand many more false alarms. If the IDF was to be mobilized, it would have to be for real.

A'MAN also believed that the Egyptian and Syrian mobilizations and maneuvers of May 1973 were intended to spark interest in the Arab-Israeli conflict during the American-Soviet summit of July; such "interest" usually resulted in political pressure on Israel.[37]

The fact that A'MAN had proven itself correct in May caused its prestige to reach an unquestionable high. It was a dangerous and volatile turning point. When, in August and September, Egypt and Syria once again began their menacing troop movements, A'MAN believed that the moves were nothing more than bravado. On August 10, 1973, Israeli Defense Minister Dayan, speaking to the IDF Staff College, said, "The balance of forces is so much in our favor that it neutralizes the Arab considerations and motives for the immediate renewal of hostilities."[38]

Yet on September 13, a pitched aerial dogfight erupted in the Mediterranean skies high above Syrian territory. The IAF armada of F-4E Phantoms and Mirage IIICs was overflying Syria on a photoreconnaissance mission, gathering intelligence on various strategic targets deep inside Syrian territory. Such overflights were necessary to provide the General Staff and the Operations Branch with crucial targeting information, and were also an integral part of the IAF's intensive training program. The Syrians, too, realized the importance of the reconnaissance flights, especially since their troops were inching closer to the Purple Line, and they tried to intercept the IAF mission. In the ensuing melee, the Mirages and Phantoms shot down twelve Syrian MiG-21 Fishbeds in a matter of minutes. One IAF Mirage IIIC was hit by an Atoll air-to-air missile, and its pilot bailed out over open water and was rescued by the IAF Aeromedical Evacuation Unit.[39]

The Syrians responded to the aerial mauling by mobilizing their troops, dispatching combat formations to the Golan Heights, and promising war. These moves were viewed by A'MAN as *expected*, not as a harbinger of an imminent conflict. In A'MAN HQ, the "Concept" still prevailed.

HUMINT was a weak link in the A'MAN chain of information at this time, again because of the prevailing attitude of the Israeli leadership. From what has been reported in the Arab press or declassified by the Israelis, A'MAN's, as well as the MOSSAD's, HUMINT activities in Egypt were inadequate. According to several reports, A'MAN and the MOSSAD had pulled out many of their agents from Egypt and Syria because they felt that these nations no longer posed a threat to Israel. (Many of these top agents were needed elsewhere for the war against terrorism.[40]) Those kept behind in position and in deep cover proved ineffective. Two A'MAN agents, a senior officer in the Egyptian combat engineers and his girlfriend, had been sending highly detailed information back to Israel for several years. They were arrested in June 1973 after their code system, enciphered microdot messages on postage stamps, was uncovered; they were executed a year later.[41] Dozens of other spies— some genuine, others just unlucky victims of the Muchabarat—were either arrested, executed, or placed under such extensive surveillance that they became ineffectual.

One of A'MAN's most important agents in the period prior to the outbreak of the 1973 War was Ibrahim Shahin. A Palestinian who had been living in El Arish in the Sinai, Shahin was recruited by A'MAN Special Operations after the 1967 War; he and his wife, Inshra, were run by a highly experienced A'MAN officer known only as "Colonel Yigal."[42] Initially, the husband and wife team (eventually joined by their three teenage sons) were considered low-level agents, and provided their handlers in Tel Aviv with background information such as food prices, transport routes, and fares for travel inside Egypt. Their work was concise and capable, and they were promoted to a more advanced arena of intelligence-gathering known as "field subjects": These included providing Tel Aviv with purely military information, specifically photographs of trenches, airports, missile bases, fuel depots, and the deployments of various military units. In the course of their duty, they photographed nearly every landmark of military importance, from the Inchas air base to Sadat's presidential palace. The material they gathered was sent to Israel via a contact in

Egypt—someone they usually met in a Cairo hotel or very crowded night-club. During their espionage work, the Shahins visited Israel seven times for debriefing and instruction.[43] According to Shahin's widow,* Ibrahim had warned A'MAN of the massive Egyptian troop movements and the ominous signifi-cance of the national war footing weeks before the conflict erupted, but his reports were ignored. Some A'MAN sources, however, indicate that these re-ports did not reach Israel until after the war had actually begun.

Israel received *numerous* warnings of the impending conflict—some co-vert, some ridiculously blatant. On September 22, 1973, Egyptian President Sadat met with the PLO's deputy commander, Abu Iyad, to discuss Pales-tinian participation in the upcoming war. Sadat outlined details of the top-secret war plans to the PLO deputy chief and requested a token contingent of thirty Palestinian fighters to join the first wave of Egyptian soldiers crossing the Suez Canal; *secrecy*, Sadat stressed, was key, and he urged Abu Iyad to confide only in Arafat and Abu Jihad. Two days later a full-length descrip-tion of the Sadat-Iyad conversation appeared in the pages of the popular Beirut newspaper *an-Nahar*; "Palestine," Abu Iyad declared in an interview, "was about to be liberated and Palestinian soldiers would be at the forefront." Sadat and his generals were incensed by this foolish breach of security and com-mon sense, and they even considered delaying the proposed attack. They were sure that intelligence sources in Israel must have read the article and that ap-propriate steps were being taken. The Arabic-speaking soldiers in HATZAV did, indeed, read and translate the article, and they sent it "upstairs" for further analysis. Abu Iyad's foolish disclosures were ignored by A'MAN director Zeira and his staff, however; they were considered "terrorist bullshit." [44]

An additional warning of impending war came from another unlikely source. Two weeks before war broke out, Jordan's King Hussein made secret con-tact with Prime Minister Golda Meir and warned her of the Egyptian and Syrian plans. King Hussein had visited Cairo a few days earlier to restore diplomatic relations between Egypt and Jordan,** and, according to several reports, was briefed on the planned attack on Israel. Remarkably, when contact between Meir and Hussein was established, Major General Zeira urged his prime minister to ask the Jordanian monarch if he intended to allow Palestinian terrorists back into his country. Zeira never mentioned the Syrian war footings along the northern frontier, or the possibility of Jordanian participation should war erupt.[45] This high-level warning was also ignored.

Zeira's preoccupation with the Palestinians materialized into legitimate con-cern on September 28, 1973, when a two-man terrorist squad from As-Saiqa

---

*The ring was broken a year after the war. Shahin was arrested in August 1974 and executed three years later. His wife and their three children now live in Israel.
**Relations between Egypt and Jordan had been severed in 1972 after King Hussein proposed the formation of a joint Jordanian-Palestinian federation.

attacked a train from Czechoslovakia carrying Soviet Jews to the Schonau transit camp near Austria. The terrorists demanded that Austria close down the facility, which processed Jews en route to Israel; for the next five days the State of Israel's political and intelligence hierarchy was obsessed with this small town in Austria. Israeli Prime Minister Meir shuttled to Vienna to plead with her Austrian counterpart, Bruno Kriesky (a Jew whom Jerusalem regarded as a traitor, since he preferred the company of Arafat to any Israeli leader!), to end the ordeal and to keep the Schonau center open. While Defense Minister Dayan, MOSSAD chief Zamir, and A'MAN director Zeira pondered a response to the Palestinian attack at Schonau, Egypt was moving its invasion forces closer to the front line. It is almost certain that the As-Saiqa operation was sanctioned by Syria to create a diversion, since Palestinian groups operating under the Syrian umbrella did nothing without permission from Damascus.

On October 1, 1973, the Egyptian army began its Tahrir 41 exercises. The A'MAN fact sheet circulated to Southern Command concerning the maneuvers near the canal read: EXERCISE NAME: "Tahrir 41." EXERCISE OBJECTIVE: "The complete capture of Sinai."[46] Hundreds of thousands of frontline Egyptian troops were brought to the canal area, in addition to bridging equipment, armored formations, and SAM batteries. This was a crucial period for the Arab plan; tight security was needed. Recalling the A'MAN SIGINT victories during the 1967 War, the Egyptians conducted their communications with Syria, and among high-ranking officers, at high-level meetings— no telephones, radio, or cable systems were employed. The Egyptians and Syrians also sent many deceptive transmissions in which leaves were ordered, reservists were demobilized, and units were scheduled for routine training *far* from the front lines. Very few Syrian and Egyptian political leaders knew critical elements of the war plans—especially the time and date. Secrecy was of paramount importance.

D day was October 6, 1973, the Jewish holy day of Yom Kippur, when Egyptian and Syrian planners believed that Israeli preparedness would be at an all-time low. Commanders in the field would be issued an order changing Tahrir 41 from an exercise to full-fledged war less than twenty-four hours before H hour.

Although A'MAN maintained that the steps preceding Tahrir 41 were developments not worthy of major concern, several Israeli field officers—especially combat intelligence officers attached to frontline units—saw the writing on the wall only too clearly. On the Golan Heights, a hundred meters from Syrian tanks, the situation was growing more precarious every day. OC Northern Command Maj. Gen. Yitzhak Hofi* was outraged by Syrian troop concentrations across the Purple Line, and by the IDF failure to bolster the Golan

*Between 1974 and 1982, Major General (Res.) Hofi was the MOSSAD director.

Heights' defenses. On September 25, at an extremely tense General Staff meeting in Tel Aviv, Major General Hofi raised the possibility of a Syrian surprise attack and voiced his concern that the few infantry units and the 188th BARAK ("lightning") Armored Brigade defending the Golan Heights were grossly inadequate. In May 1973, A'MAN had obtained complete and highly detailed plans for the Syrian recapture of the Golan Heights: It involved a massive armor push through thinly defended Israeli front lines.[47] The brigade of Centurion MBTs, commanded by Col. Yitzhak Ben-Shaham, was one of the IDF's finest; it was reinforced—at Hofi's demand—by the elite 7th Armored Brigade, commanded by Col. Avigdor "Yanush" Ben-Gal (the 7th was *the* finest armored formation in the IDF's Order of Battle). This deployment—a prudent move that should have been repeated on all fronts—would prove crucial in the weeks to follow. Deputy Chief of Staff Maj. Gen. Yisrael Tal, an officer who in 1967 was instrumental in Israeli preparedness, could not believe that, in light of all the information filtering to headquarters about the Egyptian and Syrian buildup, A'MAN continued to state that a "low probability" of war *still* existed.

On October 1, 1973, an A'MAN HUMINT source sent an alarming report to Zeira that Egypt and Syria would attack that same day. The timing of the message confirmed the fears of many high-ranking officers: Tahrir 41 was a ruse meant to dissuade Israeli preparedness. At a point during the exercise, Egypt would call off its war games and embark on a bid to seize a sizable chunk of the Sinai desert. Even Cairo airport had been shut down in a rehearsed act of war's imminence.[48] Still, Zeira refused to believe that war was a possibility, reasoning that these movements were in line with the massive exercises; war would not erupt, Zeira maintained, because the Soviets—the sole arms supplier to both Egypt and Syria—*did not want* war. (The Soviets, in fact, had been told in September 1973 that war would break out on October 6. The Soviets were informed of the war plans,* and their approval and support were intrinsic elements behind Sadat's decision to initiate Operation Badr.) During this volatile period, Zeira refused to sanction additional intelligence-gathering means, such as the mobilization of A'MAN reservists and intensifying photoreconnaissance sorties over Syria and Egypt.

Not everyone in Tel Aviv was so confident with the "Concept," however. MOSSAD director Zamir believed that a conflict was not only possible, but highly probable, and his intelligence-acquisition assets were placed in high gear to determine Arab intentions. Syrian troop concentrations were most troubling and even prompted the CIA, which always worked in close liaison with the

---

*Many Western intelligence reports suggest that the KGB knew the exact dimensions of the Egyptian-Syrian plans *long* before Sadat informed Soviet Premier Brezhnev.

MOSSAD and A'MAN, to send an urgent memo to Tel Aviv warning of "something very suspicious" along the northern frontier.[49]

Remarkably, several intelligence officers were aware that the march toward war was underway along the Suez Canal and the Golan Heights, but this information was suppressed by senior A'MAN officers. First Lieutenant Binyamin Siman-Tov, a twenty-year-old KA'MAN attached to Southern Command and stationed along the front lines, was a novice at intelligence work but a capable officer; he was an exemplary graduate of BA'HAD 1, the IDF Officers' School, and had completed comprehensive Intelligence Corps instruction. His frequent trips to the no-man's-land of the Suez Canal and tenacious analysis of the data assembled by Southern Command's intelligence apparatus indicated that war was a certainty. On October 1, 1973, he fired off a report entitled "Movement in the Egyptian Army—Possibility of a Resumption of Hostilities," a detailed examination of how Tahrir 41 was a staging point for an offensive campaign. The report was labeled SODI BE'YOTER—BAHUL ("Top Secret—EXTREMELY URGENT"); this heading on the front page should have rocked the boat at Southern Command. It did not. Lieutenant Siman-Tov's superior in Southern Command, Lt. Col. David Gedaliah, ignored the report. As Southern Command's senior intelligence officer, Gedaliah should have addressed his subordinate's findings and, if he found the facts compelling, sounded an alarm loud enough to jolt the IDF out of its slumber. Undaunted, Lieutenant Siman-Tov fired off a second memorandum. This one, titled "Situation Report on the Egyptian Army: 13/9/73–2/10/73," once again earned the stamped heading of SODI BE'YOTER—BAHUL! And once again, Lieutenant Colonel Gedaliah ignored the work of the young KA'MAN ; in his daily report to the A'MAN HQ (with a copy to the General Staff), Gedaliah failed to even mention Siman-Tov's report.[50]

In A'MAN HQ, the sole voice of reason and prudence was Brig. Gen. Yoel Ben-Porat, commander of the Collections Department. On October 2, Brigadier General Ben-Porat urged Major General Zeira to begin the mobilization of key A'MAN personnel in the reserves, or overseas, but the A'MAN director balked at such a panic-inspired move. On October 4, the Soviet Union began evacuating its citizens from Egypt and Syria—a clear sign of impending war; Soviet merchant ships left the Syrian port of Latakia and the Egyptian port of Alexandria for safe mooring in international waters. Once again Ben-Porat pleaded for a limited mobilization, but once again Zeira refused, and lambasted his colleague for insolence. Outraged, but with little recourse other than to disobey his superior's command, Ben-Porat organized a secret call-up of key personnel. It was done on a "volunteer" basis; the personnel did not come to their respective bases in uniform and were not placed on the IDF payroll.[51]

On Thursday, October 4, the obvious was finally confirmed, triggering a domino effect on Israel's intelligence community. From the sprawling Umm

Hushiba facility in the Sinai, A'MAN SIGINT technicians picked up radio communications from the Egyptian army High Command instructing front-line commanders to have their soldiers refrain from the Ramadan fasting (during which Moslems do not eat or drink from dawn to dusk for twenty-eight days). Telephone intercepts from oil refineries indicated that their lights were to be extinguished at night to limit IAF accuracy during bombing runs, and major airports in Egypt were instructed to black out at a moment's notice.

For the majority of Israelis, Friday, October 5, meant one thing: getting their homes ready for the Yom Kippur holy day. It was rare that the Day of Atonement fell on the Sabbath, but last-minute preparations, mainly the purchase of food for the much-anticipated breaking of the fast on Saturday night, were attended to vigorously, especially since most IDF soldiers would be home on leave and families could be together. Pious Jews prepared for a day of prayer in synagogue; secular Jews, too, tended to revere the fast. Yom Kippur was the day when Jews, and the Jewish nation, atoned for their sins. There was no radio or television. There were no cars or buses on the nation's streets. (Israeli children, not obliged to refrain from eat or drink, looked forward to the one day in Israel where it would be safe for them to ride their bicycles in the streets unassaulted by Israel's infamous reckless drivers.) There was just prayer and the sanctity of the family. Yom Kippur eve was equally quiet. A calm engulfed Israel before the holy days, a tranquil atmosphere much different from the hectic day-to-day Israeli life. It would indeed be the calm before the storm.

At 0825 the morning of October 5, IDF Chief of Staff Lieutenant General Elazar convened an emergency meeting in his Tel Aviv office. Cigarette smoke filled the wood-paneled room and the tension was palpable. A few hours earlier, A'MAN'S MACHLEKET MECHKAR ("Research Department") had completed its analysis of a large batch of aerial photographs taken the day before on IAF flybys of Syrian and Egyptian positions. Since the dogfight of September 13, photoreconnaissance flights had been drastically scaled down in order to alleviate possible tensions and avoid engaging the massive SAM umbrellas that had been brought up to the front during the exercises. The photographs were devastating. They showed an alarming increase in the number of heavy guns at the Egyptian front, as well as the "emergency" deployment that its tank forces had assumed behind the protection of the earthen ramparts; the concentration of bridging equipment positioned at the ramparts was staggering. Many experienced photoanalysts were absolutely speechless. Nevertheless, the commander of A'MAN's Egyptian Desk, Lt. Col. Yona Bendman, had written a report in which he assessed that the probability of war was still low.[52]

When, at this General Staff meeting, Major General Zeira was asked by the IDF chief of staff if he had proof that war would not erupt, the A'MAN director answered, "No . . . but the signs are that there will not be war." Unsatisfied, Lieutenant General Elazar conferred with IAF OC Maj. Gen. Benny

Peled and his deputy, Major General Tal, after which he immediately declared KONENUT GIMEL ("Alert C") throughout the IDF. All leaves were canceled, the IAF was placed on maximum alert, mechanized elements were *flown* into the Sinai, and the Golan Heights defenses were hurriedly reinforced.[53] The reservists, however, were not mobilized. Not yet, at least.

MOSSAD director Zamir was also extremely busy on October 5. Just after midnight, Zamir was awakened with an urgent message from one of the MOSSAD's most valuable and secretive espionage agents.* The message was brief—one word, in fact. Yet when Zamir heard the word TZNON ("radish"), he knew that war was not only imminent but could break out at *any moment*. The agent indicated that additional information would be forwarded to Tel Aviv within the next twenty-four hours.[54] TZNON was the code-word warning for the immediate commencement of hostilities against Israel. It came from a reliable source and was believed with absolute confidence. Yet Zamir did not tell his prime minister, or Defense Minister Dayan; apparently the source was so confidential that the MOSSAD chief did not want the source's name or possible location filtered through Israel's political hierarchy. Zamir rushed to his counterpart in A'MAN. At last Israel knew with certainty that a conflict was but hours away. Zamir decided to race to Europe and meet with the source personally. The Israeli military needed an exact date of attack and its precise timing.

A few minutes after midnight on October 6, Zamir met his source and learned that both Egypt and Syria would be attacking later that day—at sunset! It was already Yom Kippur, and as Zamir sat in silence he realized that the timing of the attack was so perfect that it should have been obvious. Israeli preparedness would be so low on Yom Kippur—the military infrastructure so closed down—that an Arab surprise attack would be virtually guaranteed to succeed. With no radio or television to broadcast the hundreds of code names, how would the reservists be called to their units? The problem was made painfully evident to Zamir when he tried to relay the agent's information back to Tel Aviv. The cipher clerk in the Israeli Embassy was off duty until after the fast had been broken.

At 0345, MOSSAD director Zamir finally contacted Zeira—via an open, unsecured telephone line—and told the A'MAN director that there would be war in twelve hours.[55] The proof was irrefutable. The "Concept" had finally been destroyed, but now the price must be paid.

---

*The identity of the now infamous spy who sounded the alarm of impending war remains a state secret of the highest order; even the country in which he operated has been closely censored. Yet in their book *The Imperfect Spies*, authors Yossi Melman and Dan Raviv indicate that the "valued" MOSSAD source originated in Cairo, suggesting that the agent was a high-ranking member of the Egyptian leadership.

The Israeli cabinet met at 0600 on October 6, to prepare a national strategy to defeat the impending Arab attack. While the Israeli prime minister was being given the devastating news, IAF's photoreconnaissance flights were hovering above Egypt and Syria, taking the final series of aerial photographs that would prove—beyond any doubt—that war was about to erupt.[56] There could be no more mistakes. The immediate concern for the General Staff and the cabinet was mobilization of the reserves and evacuation of the thousands of settlers who lived on the Golan Heights; the thought of Israeli civilians trapped behind Syrian lines was a reality too horrible to contemplate. Another item of discussion was the possibility of unleashing the IAF on a preemptive strike to eliminate the Syrian and Egyptian missile emplacements, a "surprise" attack that would then pave the way for a second-wave attack to decimate the thousands of tanks and armored personnel carriers ready to push across the Israeli frontiers.[57] The energetic thought behind this idea did not take into consideration the Syrian and Egyptian SA-6 mobile batteries, but in any case a preemptive strike was not approved. An Israeli first strike would be seen as military provocation and therefore would be political suicide. To gain the much needed international support in this conflict, Israel would have to be the victim.

Throughout the early-morning hours of that Yom Kippur Day, men were literally pulled out of synagogues. Initially, the mobilization began on a word-of-mouth system, also spreading wild rumors and creating great anxiety. Then a remarkable emergency broadcast network began operating—for the first time ever on Yom Kippur Day. Radios were turned on and the long litany of unit code names began. Army trucks assembled reservists in town centers, and small prop-driven IAF aircraft dropped leaflets throughout Israel's major cities. Men with prayer shawls raced home and exchanged their SIDUR prayer books for kit bags and Uzi submachine guns. Eventually word got out to the entire nation. By noon, the highways leading north and south were congested with thousands of vehicles racing toward the front. Most reservists and conscripts on leave opted to forego "collection points" and hitchhike their way to the battlefield. Many reservists made it to the front in their own cars; abandoned automobiles littered the shell-marked roadways of the Golan Heights. For the first time ever on Yom Kippur Day, IAF fighters were scrambled to protect the skies of Israel.

At 1350 1st Lt. Amos Levinberg, the young Intelligence Corps commander of the SIGINT position atop MUTZAV 104, the IDF code name for Mt. Hermon, exited his heavily fortified bunker—reinforced with cast-iron doors—and gazed across the snowcapped peaks into Syrian territory. All was quiet, and Levinberg hoped for several more hours of calm.

A'MAN reports predicted a Syrian assault at sunset. A'MAN was wrong again. Seconds later, a brutal artillery barrage commenced along the frontier. Five minutes later Levinberg scanned Syrian airspace and saw four Syrian Air Force MI-8s approaching. The helicopters attempted to land on the Israeli peak. Although Mt. Hermon was one of the most strategic locations in all of Israel, it was lightly defended. One of Israel's most sensitive positions and A'MAN's most important intelligence-gathering facility was defended by thirteen soldiers from the GOLANI Brigade's Gideon Battalion and forty-one noncombatant Intelligence Corps electronics specialists—technicians *not* expert in close-combat situations. The Syrian task force, on the other hand, consisted of an elite element of the 82d Paratroop Regiment known as the Suicide Company.[58] The Syrian commandos, heavily armed and confident in their lizard-pattern camouflage fatigues, quickly seized the initiative, even though one of their helicopters was blasted out of the sky by a GOLANI soldier firing a .50-caliber machine gun. Within hours Mt. Hermon was surrounded; the last survivors fought inside the bunkers and trenches, and later ran through the darkness toward Israeli lines. More than two dozen surrendered. "The Old Man," the affectionate name for Mt. Hermon, had fallen. During the battle, the IDF lost eighteen dead and thirty-one wounded. The top-secret SIGINT devices, which monitored all audio sources of communication in much of Syria, were captured and quickly examined by Syrian and Soviet intelligence officers.[59]

The capture of Mt. Hermon was an ominous sign of how the war would progress. At 1355, the thousands of artillery pieces aimed at Israel along the Golan Heights and the Suez Canal erupted in a deafening fifty-minute symphony of destruction. In the north, Israeli positions were simply overwhelmed in most cases. The Syrian blitzkrieg was ferocious. When the Syrian guns fell silent, the IDF's 188th and 7th Armored Brigades, as well as the GOLANI Brigade and NA'HA'L Paratroop Battalion, encountered more than fifteen hundred Syrian T-62 and T-54/55s, and more than a thousand armored combat vehicles such as the BMP-1. Tens of thousands of infantrymen and special forces commandos, equipped with the lethal RPG-7 and Sagger AT-3 anti-tank guided weapon (ATGW), followed close behind. Around Nakfekh, the command center for a division headed by Brig. Gen. "Raful" Eitan, the 188th Brigade made its epic suicidal stand, and the 7th Armored Brigade made its infamous stand at the Valley of Tears.[60] Air strikes meant to stem the unstoppable tide of armor encountered a deadly gauntlet of SAMs, which inflicted a terrible toll on the once invincible IAF.

By October 8, all that stood between two Syrian armored brigades and the Sea of Galilee were eight Second World War–vintage M-51 Sherman tanks and the surviving conscripts who had evaded death on the heights by fighting continuously for more than forty-eight hours. Miraculously, the Syrians stopped short of the Jordan River crossing; Syrian 1st Armored Division commander Col. Tewfiq Jehani, fearing that the lack of IDF activity signaled an impending ambush, ordered his force's lead element, the 47th Armored

Brigade, to halt for the night. During the darkness, the first mobilized reserve units reached northern Israel, and the tide began to turn. A miracle did, indeed, occur in the holy land, but the cost was unbearable. Already, in less than forty-eight hours of fighting, hundreds of Israeli soldiers were dead.

Along the Suez Canal, the picture was equally as bleak. The Egyptian breakthrough across the canal had worked brilliantly. Naval commandos neutralized Israel's underwater fuel pipes, and the massive artillery bombardment preceding the amphibious crossing had softened IDF frontline defenses to little more than "geographic landmarks." The Egyptian Air Force had even mounted a first-strike aerial attack on the principal Sinai air bases, although damage was negligible; once outside the safety of their SAM umbrellas, the Egyptian aircraft were easy prey for IAF interceptors. On the ground, the Egyptian water pumps, the secret weapon of the war, pummeled the sand ramparts, and the bridging equipment was deployed with lethal speed. Israeli Air Force attempts to interdict the Egyptian assault were met by impassable volleys of SAMs, which resulted in the destruction of dozens of IAF aircraft. Within hours, the bridgeheads had been secured, the sixteen major Bar-Lev line positions were surrounded or overrun, and the push into the Sinai was underway. It was a major victory for Egyptian planners and the Egyptian military: For the first time since June 11, 1967, the Egyptian flag was flying over a part of the Sinai, and for the first time Israelis were being taken prisoner in large numbers. By October 8, the push toward the Mitla and Giddi passes had begun.

That night, October 8, known as LEYL METZADA ("Massada Night"), the survival of the Jewish state hung precariously in the balance. Prime Minister Meir is believed to have contemplated suicide. Defense Minister Dayan, after declaring that the Arab successes on the battlefield were paramount to the destruction of the "third temple" (a reference to the temple in Jerusalem destroyed in 586 B.C. by the Babylonians and the one torched by the Romans in A.D. 70), duly ordered up Israel's arsenal of Jericho surface-to-surface missiles, and preparation of special bomb racks on the F-4E Phantoms for the possible launch of atomic weapons.[61]

Although A'MAN failed in predicting the outbreak of war, during the eighteen-day conflict it managed to recoup its infrastructure and perform brilliantly under a combat footing. Initially, the "Concept's" faithful, the theory's greatest supporters in the A'MAN hierarchy, were so overwhelmed and shocked by the surprise Arab attack—likened by many in its magnitude to the Japanese strike on Pearl Harbor—that they were ineffective in monitoring developments on the battlefield. A'MAN officers failed to provide the division commanders with accurate information on the location of Egyptian bridges, the placement of particular Egyptian units, and the deployment of certain Arab weapons, such as the Sagger.[62] The Egyptians and Syrians deployed the potent Sagger missile in infantry teams that roamed the battlefield looking for Israeli armor.

Their effects were devastating. Two days into the war, however, A'MAN did recover. It began to appreciate the significance of handheld antitank weapons, and urgent reports were sent to both the Golan Heights and Southern Command warning frontline commanders against exposing Israeli armor in open spaces—the RPG-7 and Sagger killing ground—before a viable countermeasure could be organized. This warning would prove crucial in the upcoming tank battles, the largest fought since the Second World War.[63] They were the battles that would turn the tide of the war.

Major HUMINT victories, such as those seen during the Six-Day War, were minimal during this conflict, although most of the activities of A'MAN spies operating in the enemy rear remained highly classified. Yet the human element of A'MAN's desk officers and KA'MANIM would be crucial in transforming Israel's almost hopeless situation into a decisive military victory. A'MAN analysts attached to Northern Command were able to predict Syrian troop movements and, once the first Syrian prisoners were taken into custody and interrogated, they were able to obtain a great deal of information concerning Syrian plans. In the south, A'MAN's human element scored its greatest success overall. On October 12, while the General Staff was baffled by the course of the fighting in the Sinai, A'MAN predicted that the Egyptians would make their grand bid to grab the Sinai passes on October 14—an epic push that would attempt to alleviate the pressure on the Syrian front, which had already turned in Israel's favor. A'MAN was correct, and several armored divisions were ready. In the ensuing tank battle—a ferocious day of killing—the Egyptians lost 264 of their top-of-the-line T-62 and T-54/55 MBTs; a thousand soldiers lay dead and burned inside their decimated armored traps. Israel lost only six tanks.[64]

Indeed, October 14 was a turning point. A'MAN's SIGINT assets had been monitoring Egyptian communications closely, and had been impressed by the accurate and subdued reports being relayed to Egyptian High Command in Cairo. On October 14, however, Egyptian field officers reported grand victories and territorial gains that had never transpired. A'MAN HQ realized that this was a sign of an army that had lost control of its forces. As one A'MAN officer commented when interviewed by Israeli television in his Sinai bunker: "They're back to being themselves, and so are we!"

October 14, 1973, was also the day that the American "aerial railway" began—the massive resupply effort to replenish the IDF's depleted stocks of weapons, ammunition, and supplies. Washington *officially* announced that American air and naval assets were being mobilized to assist Israel, and stocks in Europe were rushed to Tel Aviv. Israel was no longer alone.[65] The IDF General Staff did not have to count spent shells anymore and, most importantly perhaps, American SR-71 photoreconnaissance flights over the battlefield began yielding incredibly accurate portraits of Egyptian and Syrian deployments, the details of which were duly sent to A'MAN HQ.[66]

Superpower involvement in the intelligence campaign waged by both the Arabs and Israelis was irrefutable and crucial to developments on the battlefield. The Soviets had one maneuverable photoreconnaissance satellite, the Kosmos 596, in orbit at the outbreak of the fighting; others were soon launched, allowing the Soviet military and the GRU (Soviet military intelligence) to provide the Egyptian and Syrian military commanders with timely *tactical* intelligence, such as an IDF Order of Battle and troop deployments.[67] The Americans had their own satellites over the region, including the KH-8 and KH-9 Hexagon photoreconnaissance satellites, and supplied the Israelis with highly accurate and detailed intelligence regarding the deployment of Egyptian SAM batteries throughout the front, and in particular along the strategic point where the IDF would cross the canal and invade Egypt.[68]

It is also interesting to note that the American aerial railway of C-5As and C-141s was not a one-way route; the intelligence relationship was, indeed, two way. Captured materiel, including top-of-the-line Soviet T-62s and BMP-1s, were sent back to the United States for a first-time inspection and further analysis.

Throughout the 1973 War, beyond the initial and fatal failure of A'MAN's defeated "Concept," Israeli military intelligence did succeed in analyzing and disseminating enormous volumes of data to the frontline units. Target sheets prepared by unit KA'MANIM allowed the IDF to mount deep-penetration strikes against targets in Syria and Egypt. One such raid was Operation Nightgown. At 2300 on the night of October 12, an IAF CH-53 helicopter disgorged a squad of reconnaissance paratroopers from SAYERET TZANHANIM near Kasr al-Hayr, on the main Baghdad-Damascus highway, approximately a hundred kilometers from the Syrian capital. The IDF commando force was equipped with jeeps armed with 106mm recoilless rifles, and each paratrooper carried high explosives and RPGs. Their target was a small bridge that was about to be used by elements of the Iraqi 3d Armored Division, which was being transported to the Golan fighting. As the Iraqi formations approached the lightly defended crossing, the paratroopers opened fire from three sides. A bottleneck developed and the Iraqi armor became trapped prey for the paratrooper gunners. Sappers had booby-trapped the bridge as well. As the horror of burning vehicles and trapped men turned to chaos, the paratroopers withdrew and the IAF was called in. The blazing fires proved to be perfect markers.[69]

A'MAN was also instrumental in another type of deep-penetration strike. Utilizing aerial photographs taken of the Syrian capital, the IAF mounted a bold and tenacious air strike against Syrian army General Staff headquarters on October 14: It was a raid through SAM alley into SAM city. Damage to the sprawling complex was significant but not devastating (A'MAN had learned that the Syrians were holding five IDF POWs in the building's basement).[70]

A'MAN also succeeded in monitoring developments in the other Arab states not "directly" at war with Israel. Although some reports suggest that A'MAN failed to comprehend the significance of Iraqi troop movements toward the Golan fighting, Operation Nightgown refutes this claim. The Intelligence Branch also predicted accurately that Jordan would not become a full-fledged combatant, allowing the IDF to leave only a mere company of tanks positioned along the elongated frontier opposite the Hashemite kingdom.[71] Although Jordan did send a token contingent—the elite 40th Armored Brigade—to the Golan Heights, the October conflict was not Jordan's war. In one interesting footnote to developments on Israel's eastern front, the commander of A'MAN's Jordan Desk, Col. Ze'ev "Biber" Bar-Lavi, actually saved the life of the Jordanian ruler! During the first days of the war, Colonel Bar-Lavi prevented a planned IAF attack because he knew, from various anonymous sources, that King Hussein was in the area visiting his 40th Armored Brigade. Although the IAF protested to this "Intelligence Branch intervention" in their operations, Biber obtained the necessary authorization from Chief of Staff Elazar and A'MAN director Zeira, and the air strike was canceled.[72]

Also proving itself in the war was A'MAN's PHOTINT capabilities. On the first day of the war, virtually all of the IAF photoreconnaissance aircraft were deployed over the battlefield to provide some sort of coherent picture to the IDF General Staff on enemy deployments. The aircraft ranged from the sophisticated RF-4E to a TA-4H Skyhawk trainer used by "Major Yehuda," the intelligence officer attached to the command of Brig. Gen. Dov "Dubik" Tamari, who provided the chief of staff with an accurate and detailed portrait of Egyptian movements toward the strategic passes.[73] Other PHOTINT resources deployed by A'MAN included U.S.-built, jet-powered, Teledyne Ryan 147 remotely piloted vehicles for low- and high-altitude photoreconnaissance, targeting, electronic countermeasures (ECM), and SAM suppression roles; these efforts were reinforced by U.S.-built Northrop Chukar RPVs.[74]

Unquestionably, A'MAN's greatest success during the fighting was its discovery of the Egyptian army's Achilles' heel—a soft spot on the eastern bank of the Suez Canal—along the Sinai beachhead. That point, between the Egyptian Second and Third armies around the Bitter Lakes, was where the Egyptians were most vulnerable to attack, and the IDF manipulated this weak point brilliantly. After bashing its way to the canal in some of the most fierce fighting in the history of the Arab-Israeli wars, a force of paratroopers attached to an armored division commanded by Maj. Gen. (Res.) "Arik" Sharon crossed into mainland Egypt. This Israeli bridgehead was expanded cautiously, and the counterinvasion into Egypt, along with the eventual pincer movement that trapped the Egyptian Third Army, initiated the Egyptian collapse. Among the forces protecting the Israeli foothold in Africa were A'MAN's Field Security

Unit and the Censor's Office. The Egyptians had failed to pick up on the Israeli maverick move, and it was critical that they learn about the operation from the world press.* For two days, the Censor's Office suppressed all mention of the bridgehead across the Suez Canal until it was finally discovered by the Egyptians.[75]

By the time the IDF solidified its hold inside Egypt and had reached Suez City and kilometer 101 along the road to Cairo, the only thing standing between the IDF and the capital of the Arab world was a force of ragtag Algerian soldiers equipped with nothing heavier than RPGs.[76]

On October 22, in one of the final battles of the war, a task force of GOLANI infantrymen (supported by heliborne paratroopers) recaptured the old A'MAN SIGINT and ELINT post atop Mt. Hermon. The battle against the Syrian commandos who defended the invaluable perch was close quarter, hand-to-hand, and absolutely brutal. Yet after a full day's fighting, in which a good portion of the GOLANI Brigade was either killed or wounded, the "eyes and ears" of Israel was once again flying the Star of David.[77]

The 1973 Yom Kippur War lasted eighteen long days and traumatized the Israeli nation as it had never been before. The surprise attack and the bitter combat that followed resulted in the death of 2,326 Israeli soldiers; nearly ten thousand had been injured and hundreds taken prisoner. Ultimately, however, Israel pulled off a major military miracle. At the war's end, Israeli guns were only twenty-two kilometers from Damascus, and Egypt was saved from a fatal military blow only after the Soviet Union threatened to attack Israel. Soviet paratroopers were already inside the Antonov transports, and the United States had responded by placing her forces on worldwide alert. Israel had won once again, but the Israelis would no longer feel invincible.

The Israeli showing on the battlefield was, of course, overshadowed by A'MAN's failure to predict the Arab attack and successfully monitor enemy deployments during the first dark days of the "October Earthquake." This dark period in the history of Israel's intelligence community became known as the MECHDAL, a Hebrew term defined as an "omission," "nonperformance," and "neglect." According to Israel's shocked political hierarchy, and an outraged public numbed by the surprise attack and heavy loss of life, Israel's intelli-

*During the War of Attrition, the Censor's Office had informed *all* foreign correspondents that they were forbidden to make any mention of Operation Rhodos, the January 22, 1970, commando raid on Egypt's Shedwan Island, until all IDF soldiers had returned to Israeli lines. The local CBS radio correspondent, Tony Hutch, hopped on a Cyprus Airways flight to Nicosia in order to file his story and, in the process, endangered an ongoing Israeli operation.

gence community needed to be purged. A'MAN was its likeliest and most vulnerable victim. The government of Prime Minister Meir ordered the creation of an official board of inquiry to investigate and, for obvious reasons of political survival, *identify* the guilty parties. A'MAN's reign as the nation's sole evaluator and interpreter of intelligence gathered was about to end. The commission, headed by the president of the Supreme Court, Shimon Agranat, and chaired by two former IDF chiefs of staff—Lt. Gen. (Res.) Yigal Yadin and Lt. Gen. Haim Laskov—was tasked with terminating this monopoly.

On April 2, 1974, the Agranat Commission released its initial findings. It strongly recommended the removal of A'MAN director Zeira; his deputy commander, Brig. Gen. Aryeh Shalev; Lt. Col. David Gedaliah, Southern Command's chief intelligence officer; and Lt. Col. Yona Bendman, the head of the "Egypt Desk." The commission also recommended the removal of Chief of Staff Elazar and OC Southern Command Maj. Gen. Shmuel "Gorodish" Gonen, an officer criticized for his lack of initiative during the opening hours of the war (and a fine career officer considered by many to be the personal scapegoat of Defense Minister Dayan).[78]

The Agranat Commission's findings rocked A'MAN. Its recommendations were: "To conduct fundamental changes in the structure of A'MAN and the Intelligence Corps that will guarantee [that] the sanctity of the research and analysis process will be solely in the realm of *military intelligence* (strategic intel, operational intel, and tactical intel), including reorganizing field intelligence, and that field intelligence would be properly represented at the General Staff level; proper expression and encouragement to different and opposing views—concerning enemy developments—among the various officers of the Research Department in A'MAN's analysis which is distributed to the various political and military elements; that A'MAN will dedicate proper manpower resources, including civilian elements, in the Research Department according to optimal advancement and rotation of tasks and positions; and there will be a supervising and controlling factor [quality control] in the analysis and assessment of A'MAN's work." [79]

To guarantee that the mistakes of the "Concept" would not be repeated, the powers and capabilities of the MOSSAD's Research Department and the Foreign Ministry's Research Section were greatly expanded; this allowed A'MAN to concentrate solely on military developments. In fact, A'MAN was restructured. An "Enemy Consciousness Department" was formed, known as TOD'A; its task was to collect and disseminate to combat units data on Arab military strategies and weapons. The Research Department was also changed, and divided into regional desks where more A'MAN officers would be able to concentrate on developments in their sphere of responsibility.[80] The man tasked with guiding the Research Department in the proper direction was Brig. Gen. Yehoshua Saguy, a former commander of A'MAN's BEIT HA'SEFER LE'MODE'IN

("Intelligence School"), a man who would become quite prominent in the years to come. A "Review Section," basically a watchdog office, was also created to challenge the findings of desk commanders, section leaders, and junior officers filing reports from the field. The situation of a war being predicted by a lieutenant and ignored by a colonel was never to transpire again.

The man charged with snapping A'MAN out of its post–Yom Kippur War malaise was Maj. Gen. Shlomoh Gazit. Born in Turkey in 1926, Gazit immigrated to Israel with his family in 1932. After serving in the PAL'MACH'S elite HAREL Brigade, which fought the hellish battles for Jerusalem in 1948, Gazit rose through the IDF chain of command. Although he had served in several combat postings, Gazit's calling was the covert work of intelligence; during the 1956 War he was the liaison officer to French forces and in 1963 he was named the IDF attaché to France, a most important posting considering the then close-knit military alliance between Jerusalem and Paris.[81] Gazit was an innovative officer, known for his intellect and vision, and a proponent of expanding the technical means employed by Israeli military intelligence.

In his task of rebuilding A'MAN in both structure and personality, Gazit was assisted by a new posting created—under advisement—by the Agranat Commission. The position of the KTZIN MODE'IN RASHI ("chief intelligence officer") was meant to decrease the work load of the office of the A'MAN director. The chief intelligence officer would handle the administrative and day-to-day functions of the office, allowing the A'MAN director to devote the time and efforts of himself and his staff to research and evaluation. A'MAN's first chief intelligence officer was Brig. Gen. Dov "Dubik" Tamari, a veteran paratroop and armor officer who at one time commanded the ultrasecretive SAYERET MAT'KAL General Staff Reconnaissance Unit.[82]

The lessons of the 1973 War were especially painful and tragic because every aspect of Israel's military intelligence apparatus had been operating, and the mistakes *could* have been avoided. But preconceived ideas, no matter how outrageous or outdated, are hard to change even in light of convincing evidence, and even the best espionage service can be duped or confused by an unending flow of irrelevant details and deceitful bait mixed with accurate data. War should not have come as a surprise, but it did, and its consequences were borne by the IDF's frontline soldiers and the families of those killed in battle. A'MAN, after the brilliant successes of 1967, the War of Attrition, and the campaign against Black September, had proven fallible.

Gazit and Tamari attempted to overcome the MECHDAL and return to the precarious day-to-day task of intelligence-gathering, but conflict and horror continued to plague the State of Israel. A brutal war of attrition continued along the Golan Heights in the winter of 1973–74; even though a cease-fire had been arranged, and the nation was trying to come to terms with this most unnerving of wars, Israeli soldiers were still dying on the battlefield.

Soldiers were not the only ones to die. On April 11, 1974, a terrorist squad from Ahmed Jibril's PFLP-GC attacked a block of apartment buildings in the northern border town of Qiryat Shmoneh, killing eighteen civilians, including eight children and five women. On May 15, Israel's twenty-sixth anniversary, a terrorist squad from Nayif Hawatmeh's DFLP seized a schoolhouse in the northern border town of Ma'alot and held more than a hundred students hostage. The IDF rescue attempt failed, and twenty-five students were killed and seventy wounded. On March 5, 1975, a seaborne force of terrorists from el-Fatah landed on the beach of southern Tel Aviv and seized the seafront Savoy Hotel, taking its guests hostage. Eight hostages were killed when the terrorists detonated the explosives they had planted throughout the building on top of the rescuing force from SAYERET MAT'KAL. Also dead were three IDF soldiers: two conscripts and Col. Uzi Yairi, a former commander of SAYERET MAT'KAL and one of the rising stars in A'MAN's chain of command.[83]

The MECHDAL continued to plague Israel's military intelligence.

A'MAN's fortunes would change dramatically on June 27, 1976, when four terrorists (two West Germans from the Baader-Meinhoff Gang and two Palestinians) working for the Wadi Haddad Faction of PFLP hijacked an Air France flight from Tel Aviv to Paris, following a brief stopover in Athens. The airbus was diverted first to Benghazi, Libya, and then finally to Entebbe, Uganda. A'MAN played an instrumental role in the planning and execution of the infamous rescue operation, known as Operation Thunderball, of July 3 and 4, 1976. Although the MOSSAD contributed information on the Entebbe airport, A'MAN sources obtained data on the terrorists, the Ugandan military, flight patterns, weather and climatic information, and the air defenses over the territory crossed, which the IAF would need if the journey from Israel to Uganda would be achieved without incident. Unit intelligence officers attached to SAYERET MAT'KAL, SAYERET GOLANI, and SAYERET TZANHANIM units also worked feverishly with A'MAN HQ to gather the necessary target information so that attack strategies could be formulated.

On July 4, 1976, four C-130 Hercules transports returned to Israel from Entebbe with 103 freed hostages. Israel had broken out of its post–Yom Kippur War malaise. A'MAN was also back on course, or so it appeared.

NOTES: CHAPTER TWELVE

1. Oded Granot, HEYL HA'MODE'IN: TZAHAL BE'HEILO ENTZYKLOPEDIA LE'TZAVA ULE'BITACHON (Tel Aviv: Revivim Publishers, 1981), 111.

2. Alouph Hareven, "Disturbed Hierarchy: Israeli Intelligence in 1954 and 1973," *The Jerusalem Quarterly*, No. 9 (Fall 1976): 12; Stewart Steven, *The Spymasters of Israel* (New York: Ballantine Books, 1980), 305.

3. *Ibid.* 357.

4. Samuel M. Katz, *Guards Without Frontiers: Israel's War Against Terrorism* (London: Arms & Armour Press, 1990), 25.

5. Merav Arlozorov, "HA'TRAMIT PA'ALA," BAMACHANE CHU'L (September 1987):12.

6. Yosef Argaman, ZE HAYA SODI BE'YOTER (Tel Aviv: Israel Ministry of Defense Publications, 1990), 330.

7. For the best account of Israel's hit teams roaming through Europe, see Michael Bar-Zohar and Eitan Haber, *The Quest for the Red Prince* (New York: William Morrow & Company, Inc., 1983); David B. Tinnin and Dag Christensen, *The Hit Team* (New York: Dell Publishing Co., Inc., 1976); and Uri Dan, ETZBA ELOHIM: SODOT HA'MILCHAMA BE'TERROR (Tel Aviv: Massada Ltd., 1976).

8. See Uri Dan, ETZBA ELOHIM, 93, 97.

9. See Yosef Argaman, ZE HAYA SODI BE'YOTER, 344.

10. Following Israel's "Operation Peace for Galilee" invasion of Lebanon on June 6, 1982, the extent of the Palestinians' international terrorist contacts was uncovered. Documents captured revealed that in the years between 1971 and 1982, the PLO had trained and supported terrorists from nearly every country on earth. Uri Milstein, HA'HISTORIA SHEL HA'TZANHANIM—KERECH DALED (Tel Aviv: Schalgi Ltd. Publishing House, 1987), 1,604.

11. Yosef Argaman, "HA'KAVOD HA'AVUD SHEL MIVTZA BARDAS," BAMACHANE (February 24, 1988): 16.

12. Following the raid, many IDF insiders faulted the quality of the intelligence that A'MAN handed the task force, since the landing zone chosen was not secluded but adjacent to a bustling and extremely well-lit highway. Eilan Kfir, TZANHANIM CHI'R MUTZNACH: TZAHAL BE'HEILO ENTZYKLOPEDIA LE'TZAVA ULE'BITACHON (Tel Aviv: Revivim Publishers, 1981), 140.

13. Raphael Israeli, ed., *The PLO in Lebanon: Selected Documents* (London: Weidenfeld and Nicolson, 1983), 1.

14. "Hood 54" was the attack on the Nahar al-Bard camp, and "Hood 55" was the assault on the al-Badawi camp.

15. See Uri Milstein, HA'HISTORIA SHEL HA'TZANHANIM, 1,618; and Michael Bar-Zohar and Eitan Haber, "KE'SHE'EHUD BARAK PARATZ BE'BGADEI ISHA LE'DIRAT HE'MECHABLIM," YEDIOT SHEVA YAMIM (November 30, 1990): 8.

16. Samuel M. Katz, *Follow Me! A History of Israel's Military Elite* (London: Arms and Armour Press, 1989), 113.

17. See Uri Milstein, HA'HISTORIA SHEL HA'TZANHANIM, 1,616.

18. Ronald Payne, *Mossad: Israel's Most Secret Service* (London: Transworld Publishers Ltd., 1990), 86.

19. See Uri Milstein, HA'HISTORIA SHEL HA'TZANHANIM, 1,624.

20. Israel's covert war against Black September ended on January 22, 1979, when, according to foreign reports, the MOSSAD assassinated Black September leader Ali Hassan Salameh, the infamous "Red Prince," who had masterminded the 1972 Munich Olympics Massacre. See Michael Bar-Zohar and Eitan Haber, *The Quest for the Red Prince*, 218.

21. Ian Black and Benny Morris, *Israel's Secret Wars* (London: Hamish Hamilton, 1991), 282.

22. Gad Ya'akobi, "KACH HAYA EFSHAR LIMNOA'A ET MILCHEMET YOM HA'KIPURIM," YEDIOT SHABBAT (December 29, 1989): 3.

23. Mohamed Heikal, *The Road to Ramadan* (London: William Collins Sons and Co., Ltd., 1975), 117.

24. In an interview to the Israeli television show MOKED, November 1971.

25. Ephraim Kam, "Is a Surprise Attack Inevitable?" *IDF Journal*, No. 21 (Fall 1990): 3.

26. See Ian Black and Benny Morris, *Israel's Secret Wars*, 288.

27. Brig. Gen. (Res.) Arieh Shelo, "MAKOT MITZRAIM: HA'LEKACH," BAMACHANE (May 27, 1987): 51.

28. See Ian Black and Benny Morris, *Israel's Secret Wars*, 289.

29. *Ibid.* 290.

30. Yossi Melman and Dan Raviv, *The Imperfect Spies: The History of Israeli Intelligence* (London: Sidgwick and Jackson, 1989), 215.

31. See Mohamed Heikal, *The Road to Ramadan*, 41.

32. Lt. Gen. Saad El Shazly, *The Crossing of the Suez* (San Francisco: American Mideast Research, 1980), 323.

33. See Ian Black and Benny Morris, *Israel's Secret Wars*, 298.

34. Chaim Herzog, *The Arab-Israeli Wars* (London: Arms and Armour Press, 1982), 228.

35. Brig. Gen. (Res.) Yoel Ben-Porat, "The Yom Kippur War: A Mistake in May Leads to a Surprise in October," *IDF Journal*, Vol. III, No. 3 (Summer 1986): 52.

36. *Ibid.* 52.

37. *Ibid.* 52.

38. Col. Trevor N. Dupuy, *Elusive Victory: The Arab-Israeli Wars 1947–74* (New York: Harper and Row, Publishers, 1978), 406.

39. Zeev Schiff, HEYL HA'AVIR: TZAHAL BE'HEILO ENTZYKLOPEDIA LE'TZAVA ULE'BITACHON (Tel Aviv: Revivim Publishers, 1981), 152.

40. See Ian Black and Benny Morris, *Israel's Secret Wars*, 294.

41. *Ibid.* 294.

42. Kenneth Kaplan, "Spies Report Came 'Too Late' to Prevent Yom Kippur War," *Jerusalem Post International Edition* (week ending December 9, 1989): 7.

43. Various ed., "BNEI MISHPACHTO SHEL SOCHEN YISRAELI SHE'HUTZA LE'HOREG BE'MITZRAIM, CHAYIM KA'YOM BE'YISRAEL," YISRAEL SHELANU (December 1, 1989): 2.

44. See Oded Granot, HEYL HA'MODE'IN, 105.

45. Ron Dagoni, " 'YISRAEL SHELANU': HUSSEIN HIZHIR ET GOLDA LIFNEI MILCHEMET YOM HA'KIPPURIM," MA'ARIV (October 20, 1989): 2.

46. See Oded Granot, HEYL HA'MODE'IN, 121.

47. Shlomo Nakdimon, SVIRUT NEMUCHA (Tel Aviv: Revivim Publishers, 1982), 29.

48. *Ibid.* 53.

49. Shlomo Nakdimon, "12 YAMIM LIFNEI YOM-KIPPUR KIBLA GOLDA MEIDA ISHI: MITZRAIM VE'SURIA META'AMOT MILCHAMA," YEDIOT AHARONOT, EREV YOM HA'KIPPURIM (October 8, 1989): 14.

50. Avi Shlaim, "Failures in National Intelligence Estimates: The Case of the Yom Kippur War," *World Politics* (January 1978): 354.

51. The only service untouched by the "Concept" was the IDF/navy. While A'MAN officers bickered, and failed to see the obvious, IDF/navy Intelligence predicted the inevitable commencement of hostilities and placed its forces on full alert. Indeed, the HEYL HA'YAM was the sole branch of service ready for war. During the eighteen days of fighting, the IDF/navy's SA'AR-class missile boats destroyed thirteen Syrian and Egyptian missile boats in pitched missile battles. Various ed.,"HEYL HA'YAM CHAZA ET PROTZ MILCHEMET YOM HA'KIPPURIM," HADASHOT (December 8, 1988): 5.

52. See Avi Shlaim, "Failures in National Intelligence Estimates," 355; Ian Black and Benny Morris, *Israel's Secret Wars*, 310.

53. See Shlomo Nakdimon, SVIRUT NEMUCHA, 81.

54. For the two most reliable mentions of the top-level MOSSAD agent and the code word "Radish," see Tzvi Zamir, "HA'YEDIAH SHEL HA'MOSSAD AL PROTZ HA'MILCHAMA LO HIGIYAH LE'RA'MAT'KAL BIGLALL HORA'AT-KEVA SHEL ROSH A'MAN," YEDIO SHABBAT (November 24, 1989): 4; Ian Black and Benny Morris, *Israel's Secret Wars*, 286.

55. *Ibid.* 287.

56. Eliezer "Cheetah" Cohen and Tzvi Lavi, HA'SHAMAYIM EINAM HA'GVUL: SIPURAV SHEL HEYL HA'AVIR HA'YISRAELI (Tel Aviv: Sifriat Ma'ariv, 1990), 439.

57. *Ibid.* 396.

58. See Samuel M. Katz, *Follow Me!* 117.

59. See Yossi Melman and Dan Raviv, *The Imperfect Spies*, 214.

60. For the best accounts of the armored battles fought along the Golan Heights in 1973, see Avigdor Kahalani, OZ 77 (Jerusalem: Schocken Publishers, 1981); Jerry Asher with Eric Hammel, *Duel for the Golan* (New York:

William Morrow and Company, Inc., 1987): Maj. Gen. (Res.) Moshe "Bril" Bar-Kochba, MERKAVOT HA'PLADA (Tel Aviv: Israel Ministry of Defense Publications, 1989); Chaim Herzog, *The War of Atonement* (London: Futura Publications Ltd., 1975). For the best accounts of the tank fighting in the Sinai, see Arieh Hasabiyeh, HEYL HA'SHIRION: TZAHAL BE'HEILO ENTZYKLOPEDIA LE'TZAVA ULE'BITACHON (Tel Aviv: Revivim Publishers, 1981); Elyashiv Shimshi, SA'ARA BE'OKTOBER (Tel Aviv: MA'AROCHOT-Israel Ministry of Defense Publications, 1986).

61. See Yossi Melman and Dan Raviv, *The Imperfect Spies*, 219.

62. See Ian Black and Benny Morris, *Israel's Secret Wars*, 312, 313.

63. *Ibid.* 314.

64. Various authors, KRAVOT MI'SHNEI A'AVREI HA'TA'ALAH: MILCHEMET YOM HA'KIPPURIM (Tel Aviv: KTZIN CHINUCH RASHI/A'ANAF HADRACHA VE'HASBARA, Israel Ministry of Defense Publications, 1975), 16.

65. Although the 1973 Yom Kippur War has been a source of great pride for the Arabs' ability to succeed on the battlefield, their effort was supported by *massive* Soviet-bloc assistance. Soviet advisors were prevalent in nearly every echelon of command within the Syrian military. According to several Western intelligence claims, North Vietnamese missile crews defended the skies over Damascus; Cuban armored formations participated in the fighting along the Golan Heights; North Korean pilots flew with the Egyptian Air Force; and, it is believed, East German specialists manned radio-intercept devices employed by Egyptian and Syrian military intelligence. The Soviet Union was, of course, the largest and most important Arab ally; not only were Soviet-manned SCUD batteries positioned in Egypt during the war and Soviet advisors helping in the operation of SAM batteries, but nearly every piece of Soviet-produced weaponry lost on the battlefield was *immediately* replaced by Moscow. In a message directed at Moscow's intervention, the IAF is reported to have blown away two Soviet transport planes on the ground in Aleppo, Syria. According to Edgar O'Ballance's history of the Yom Kippur War, *No Victor, No Vanquished*, the IDF deployed small groups of Arabic-speaking commandos from the "*Mektal* Israeli Intelligence Service" along the west bank of the Suez Canal to gather data on Egyptian troop deployments inside Egypt proper. While no such force as "*Mektal*" exists (nor does such a word, in fact!), it appears as if the author was referring to commandos from SAYERET MAT'KAL, the General Staff Reconnaissance Unit, whose creation in 1957 was sanctioned because it promised to be an additional source to A'MAN of unlimited potential. SAYERET MAT'KAL did, indeed, participate in the 1973 fighting—mainly in the final battle for Mt. Hermon.

66. Edgar O'Ballance, *No Victor, No Vanquished: The Yom Kippur War* (San Rafael: Presidio Press, 1978), 222.

67. Michael Russel Rip and Joseph F. Fontanella, "A Window on the Arab-Israeli 'Yom Kippur' War of October 1973: Military Photo-Reconnaissance from High Altitude and Space," *Intelligence and National Security*, Vol. 6 (January 1991): 37.

68. *Ibid.* 46.

69. Ron Ben-Yishai, "HEYL HA'AVIR HISHMID SHNEI METOSIM RUSIM," YEDIOT AHARONOT (October 5, 1987): 1.

70. Merav Halperin and Aharon Lapidot, *G-Suit: Pages from the Log Book of the Israel Air Force* (London: Sphere Books, 1990), 107.

71. See Ian Black and Benny Morris, *Israel's Secret Wars*, 315.

72. Yoni Sa'ar, "HA'SA'M'BA," BAMACHANE CHU'L (May 1984): 11.

73. Amnon Kaveh, "YEHUDA, EIN LI MODE'IN," EL-HA'MATARA, No. 17 (1990): 6.

74. See Michael Russell Rip and Joseph F. Fontanella, "A Window," 55.

75. Aharon Dolev, "TZENZUR BLI SHINA'YIM," MA'ARIV SHABBAT (August 25, 1989): 4.

76. Shapi Gabay, "KACH HITA'ANU ET HA'MODE'IN HA'YISRAELI," MA'ARIV SUCCOT (October 13, 1989): 7.

77. Avi Battleheim, GOLANI MISHPACHAT LOCHAMIM (Tel Aviv: MIFKEDET HATIVAT GOLANI-Israel Ministry of Defense Publications, 1980), 182.

78. Ariella Ringel-Hoffman, "GORODISH HIGIYAH MI'AFRIKA LE'CHUFSHA SHEL SHVUA'YIM," YEDIOT AHARONOT (April 16, 1989): 1.

79. See Oded Granot, HEYL HA'MODE'IN, 139.

80. See Ian Black and Benny Morris, *Israel's Secret Wars*, 317.

81. See Oded Granot, HEYL HA'MODE'IN, 142.

82. Emanuel Rosen, "HA'ISH SHE'HIMTZI ET HA'YECHIDA HA'MUVCHERET," MA'ARIV SOF SHAVUA, (September 19, 1990): 43.

83. Orah Arif, "ELOHIM YARAD VE'HOFIYAH A'L HA'ADAMA," YEDIOT 24 SHA'OT (April 16, 1991): 12.

CHAPTER 13

THE LEBANON QUAGMIRE

"Like a cedar that has been felled."
Headline of the Beirut daily *L'Orient Le Jour* on September 14, 1982,
covering the death of Lebanese President Bashir Gemayel[1]

It was pitch-black on the night of February 22, 1981, when the first CH-53 helicopter landed. The landing zone had been chosen well—it was isolated and protected from outside view. In a matter of seconds, a force of several dozen reconnaissance commandos from SAYERET GOLANI disembarked from the hulking crafts and began their forced march toward the night's objective: the town of el-Kfur, situated in the Nabatiya Heights of southern Lebanon.[2] The raid was an inevitable statement of retribution and deterrence.

On April 9, 1980, a three-man suicide squad from the Arab Liberation Front (ALF), an Iraqi-sponsored Palestinian terrorist group, had crossed the northern border separating Israel and Lebanon and breached the grounds at Kibbutz Misgav Am. After evading the lightly armed sentries at that border settlement, the terrorists raced toward the kibbutz nursery and quickly seized more than two dozen sleeping toddlers. A force of GOLANI Brigade infantrymen, on nearby security duty, was summoned to the embattled area immediately. Although it is an unwritten Israeli policy *never* to negotiate with terrorists, the plight of the infants, held with guns aimed at their heads, hit the Israeli leadership very hard. Such barbarity would not be tolerated, and a rescue attempt was ordered. Throughout the night, the GOLANI infantrymen played a deadly cat-and-mouse game with the heavily armed terrorists until a detachment from SAYERET MAT'KAL arrived for the final rescue assault. In the end, the death toll was one Israeli soldier, one two-year-old girl, and three terrorists.[3]

Operation New Combination, the code name for the February 22–23, 1981, raid on el-Kfur, was revenge in its simplest form. It was revenge against the ALF, revenge against Palestinian terrorism, and a stern warning to the Palestinian terrorist presence in Lebanon—a thorn in the Israeli side that, by 1981, had developed into a national obsession. Lebanon would become an obsession of equal magnitude to Israel's pledge to obliterate Black September in 1972, and, like the MECHDAL that soon followed, would develop into one of the greatest failures of Israel's intelligence community.

There was a time when Jewish newlyweds in British-mandate Palestine boarded buses or taxis and headed north to honeymoon in Beirut. The Lebanese capital was the Middle East's escape—it was a mix of the French Riviera, Switzerland, and Las Vegas, ringed by a seaside promenade. For nearly twenty years, the former French colony of Lebanon miraculously escaped the violence and destruction of the Arab-Israeli conflict. Although the small and insignificant Lebanese army played a minor role in the 1948 fighting, Lebanon was a noncombatant in the 1956 and 1967 conflagrations; the frontier separating the Jewish state from the mixed Moslem and Christian confederation was extremely quiet. Yet, perhaps, the glamor and openness that made Lebanon so attractive to tourists, European businessmen, wealthy sheikhs, and cold-war espionage agents also contributed to its tumultuous downfall. Central authority in Lebanon was extremely weak. A tense, though for a long time benign, rivalry existed between the ruling Christians and the majority Moslem populations; inter-Moslem hatred and animosities between Sunnis, Shiites, and the Druze added to this seething brotherly friction. Lebanon was a nation where smuggling was routine; the economy was booming on black market profits and drug and casino revenues; the baksheesh, a unique Middle Eastern form of bribing police or government officials, was the currency of the day. The Palestinians would change Lebanon forever.

During the 1948 Israeli War of Independence, approximately four hundred thousand Palestinians escaped north toward Lebanon.[4] They were not accepted into Lebanese society and were forced—by oppression and by the self-design of the Arab powers not willing to have the Palestinians relinquish their role as peoples without a homeland—to live in sprawling refugee camps located around the major Lebanese cities. Poverty-stricken and hopeless, the refugee concentrations swelled in and around the slums of Tyre, Sidon, Damur, Tripoli, and, of course, Beirut. The Palestinians joined the Shiite Moslems as Lebanon's underclass by design.

In 1968, however, the Palestine Liberation Organization made cosmopolitan Beirut its principal international headquarters. Offices of the various factions within the Palestinian revolution opened on the luxurious boulevards of Moslem West Beirut—a city with the charm of Paris that soon turned into an armed camp. Palestinian leaders planned their attacks against Israel in Beirut, and issued "claiming responsibility" press releases through Beirut wire services. This Palestinian presence in Lebanon troubled many in Israel; fighting a four-border war was not desired by the IDF General Staff. Yet in July 1968, the Palestinians went beyond the immediate boundaries of the region: They went international, with Beirut as their world's center.

On July 23, 1968, terrorists from Dr. George Habash's Popular Front for the Liberation of Palestine hijacked an El Al flight from Rome to Tel Aviv. They diverted the aircraft to Algiers, where the hijackers held all male passengers captive until Israel agreed to free Palestinians in her custody. On December 26, 1968, the PFLP struck once again; this time an El Al plane was attacked by machine gun–firing terrorists in Athens airport. When A'MAN learned that the terrorists had originated in the Lebanese capital, the IDF decided to retaliate with a commando strike against *Arab* civil aviation. The subsequent Operation Gift of December 28, 1968, marked the beginning of Israel's military involvement in Lebanon.

The Jordanian Civil War of September 1970 proved to be the turning point in both the Palestinian and Israeli relationships with Lebanon, as well as in Lebanon's schizophrenic internal affairs. The thousands of Palestinian guerrillas who managed to flee King Hussein's Bedouin army quickly set up bases of operation in southern Lebanon. Since Jordan was now off-limits and the Syrians forbade raids against Israel originating from its territory in order to prevent IDF reprisals, Lebanon was the Palestinians' only logical base for cross-border terrorist operations. The refugee camps near Tyre and Sidon soon became armed camps, and the northern border of Israel was transformed into a deadly battlefield. The attacks emanating from Lebanon were bloody. On May 20, 1970, fourteen schoolchildren were killed when their school bus fell into a Palestinian ambush and was rocked by a bazooka round. Israeli retaliation was also bloody. Each Palestinian incursion across the Israeli frontier, each mortar round lobbed across the fence, and each Katyusha rocket landing in an agricultural settlement was answered with an IAF air strike or IDF commando raid on Palestinian military targets in southern Lebanon. The cycle of Palestinian attacks and Israeli retaliation continued as if it were a fact of nature common to the Levantine landscape.

The need for Israel to retaliate proved to be a difficult task for the A'MAN and Intelligence Corps personnel working with the IDF Operations Branch. The Palestinian terrorist groups surrounded their facilities inside the teeming camps with rings of civilian targets. Hitting an arms dump or a command and control structure virtually guaranteed hitting civilian targets as well. Since the IDF's law of TOHAR HA'NESHEK ("purity of arms") dictated the tightly controlled use of deadly force, placing civilians in jeopardy created a supreme dilemma, not only for the pilots releasing bombs from their aircraft's pylons, but for the intelligence officers pinpointing a target on a map for eventual obliteration.[5]

On November 19, 1977, the unbelievable finally happened: An Egypt Air jetliner bearing Egyptian President Anwar as-Sadat touched down in Israel. The largest and most powerful of all Arab nations had opted for a course of coexistence over one of destruction. The Israeli government, headed by right-wing Prime Minister Menachem Begin, could not have been more receptive to the notion, and the people of Israel were ecstatic: These peace talks might provide the impetus to rid the region of its seemingly uncontrolled passion for violence.

Sadat's venture into the peacemaking arena came only four years after his venture into war. On November 9, 1977, Sadat had announced to the Egyptian people that he was "willing" to go to Jerusalem to further the cause of peace; it was the net result of top-secret negotiations conducted by Foreign Minister Moshe Dayan in Morocco and Europe.[6] The MOSSAD and A'MAN had not predicted Sadat's surprise overtures, and were undecided as to how they should view this sudden move. A'MAN concluded that there was still no positive movement in the Arabs' acceptance of Israel as a permanent fixture in the Middle East, and that Sadat was possibly using Israel's desire for peace to dupe her into a false sense of security before initiating another surprise attack. A'MAN's Research Department had uncovered troubling signs in Egypt in the days prior to Sadat's arrival in Israel: Elite Egyptian commando units were mobilized, the state of national alert was raised, and emergency stores were readied. What A'MAN did not realize was that these moves were part of the extraordinary security preparations made *for* Sadat's historic journey.[7]

As Sadat addressed the Israeli KNESSET ("Parliament"), and such notable figures as Golda Meir and Moshe Dayan, leaders whose reputations he had damaged with his October 1973 "surprise," the Palestinians plotted. They had nothing to gain by peace. Egypt would take back the Sinai, Israel would obtain a partial peace and a political foothold in the Arab world, and the Palestinians would once again be abandoned by an Arab leader. Sadat's pilgrimage of peace to Jerusalem was seen by the PLO as a sellout, a case of treachery unequaled since the Black September bloodshed. To remain in the forefront of the campaign against Israel and on the front pages of the international agenda, the PLO would have to act decisively.

A'MAN realized that the PLO would make some sort of violent statement protesting the Israeli-Egyptian peace process. A'MAN director Major General Gazit tenaciously followed Palestinian movements in Lebanon, and came up with the prediction that the most likely form of attack would come from the sea, since the long seacoast held the largest concentration of Israel's population. Nearly 2.5 million of Israel's 4 million people were spread out from Ashqelon in the south, to Tel Aviv and the suburbs in the central region, to

Haifa in the north. In the past, el-Fatah had mounted numerous seaborne attacks against Israel's coastal cities, often with devastating aftermaths. In the early-morning hours of June 24, 1974, an el-Fatah seaborne force infiltrated Israeli territorial waters and landed on the beach of Nahariya, a small Israeli city only a few dozen kilometers from the Lebanese frontier, and killed four Israelis in a block of apartment buildings before being terminated by GOLANI troopers. On March 5, 1975, an el-Fatah suicide squad landed on the beaches of southern Tel Aviv and took over the Savoy Hotel; eleven died in that operation.

Predicting that another seaborne attack was in the planning stage, A'MAN laid the groundwork for the IDF to mount Operation Sheer Joy, on February 20, 1978, in which a force of Israeli naval commandos raided the port of Tyre and sank several fishing vessels used by the el-Fatah as mother-ship platforms. Operation Sheer Joy would buy Israel less than one month of peace and security.

On the night of March 11, 1978, two rubber dinghies were dropped into the choppy waters of the Mediterranean from a small freighter anchored dangerously close to Israeli territorial waters. For more than a month, Abu Jihad, the PLO's deputy commander, had been planning his master stroke to nullify the peace process; his belief was that massive Israeli retaliation in Lebanon would torpedo Sadat's historic and precarious mission. For his grand operation, Abu Jihad had recruited thirteen hard-core terrorists from Force 17, Yasir Arafat's praetorian bodyguard unit, the most loyal and capable of all el-Fatah combatants, reserved for "special" missions or work so dirty that only a highly dedicated individual could carry it out. Abu Jihad called this special operations force the "Dir Yassin Unit of the Kamal Adwan Commando," so named for the Palestinian village where Israeli forces from Menachem Begin's IRGUN group had massacred more than two hundred civilians during the 1948 War, and for the Black September chief killed in the IDF's Operation Spring of Youth. In fact, Jihad's operation was perceived as the Palestinian version of Israel's spectacular raid on Beirut five years earlier.[8] The commander of this well-trained force was an attractive young female named Dalal Mughrabi, a native-born Israeli who spoke fluent Hebrew. She was also a cold-blooded killer.

The operation's objective was simple; so was its brutal message. The terrorists were to seize a crowded hotel on the shores of Bat Yam, a suburb south of Tel Aviv, and hold the guests hostage unless hundreds of convicted el-Fatah terrorists were released from Israeli prisons. If the terrorists' demands were not met, the hostages would be systematically executed, one every ten minutes. The Dir Yassin Unit's grand scheme proved beyond their abilities, however; severe difficulties were encountered en route to Bat Yam. One of the craft carrying the terrorists to shore capsized under the enormous weight of the ammunition and explosives it carried; two of the terrorists drowned when they failed to free themselves from the heavy web gear strapped tightly to their backs. Second, the navigation skills of the force were limited. The mother ship unloaded the two Zodiac craft approximately fifty kilometers *north* of Tel Aviv—more than a ninety-minute journey to Bat Yam. At 1600 the survivors landed on the shores of Kibbutz Ma'agan Michael, situated half-way between Tel Aviv and Haifa. Unsure of their position and unable to locate any distinguishing landmarks, the terrorists assembled their gear—each one carried a fully loaded AK-47 7.62mm assault rifle, ten banana clip magazines for the "K'latch," four Soviet-made F-1 fragmentation grenades, and blocks of the finest Czechoslovak Semtex money could buy—and headed east.[9] A few yards inland, they encountered an American nature photographer, Gail Rubin, taking pictures of the nearby wildlife. Thinking the raiders to be Is-raeli soldiers, Ms. Rubin did not flee and realized her error only when she was brusquely asked, "Where are we?" She was brutally killed seconds later.

The following chain of events developed into one of the most tragic nights in Israel's bitter history against Palestinian terrorism. The terrorists raced three kilometers eastward toward the bustling Tel Aviv–Haifa coastal highway, where they fired indiscriminately at all passing traffic until they managed to com-mandeer two buses loaded with the families of employees of Egged, the Israeli national bus company, on a day's outing. After hurriedly loading all the passen-gers onto one of the buses, Mughrabi ordered the driver to head for Tel Aviv. At the Glilot Junction, several kilometers north of Tel Aviv, a hastily assembled force of Border Guard snipers, heavily armed policemen, and IDF ground units were positioned behind barricades, ready to make a last-ditch stand. The "Country Club Junction," as the crossroads were known because of the ultraexclusive sports club located nearby, was as close to Tel Aviv as the terrorists would get. As the bus approached the gauntlet of men and weap-onry, several snipers opened fire at the vehicle's tires, causing it to veer to the center of the six-lane thoroughfare and screech to a stop. The terrorists engaged the security forces with automatic fire, and a full-blown firefight erupted, lighting the night sky with an eerie orange glow. Most of the hostages ducked under their seats for cover while others seized the moment to attack their captors. Several grenades were thrown, and the bus erupted into a blinding fireball. Thirty-seven Israelis were killed and seventy-eight were seriously wounded. Nine terrorists from the Dir Yassin Commando force were killed in the fray; two gunmen managed to escape the inferno but were rounded up several hours later wandering through the nearby sand dunes while the luxurious Tel Aviv suburbs, and much of central Israel, was under a martial law curfew. For much of Tel Aviv, it would be the longest night until the SCUDs would fall in January 1991.

The carnage, known as the "Country Club Massacre," was the worst ter-rorist attack ever perpetrated inside Israel. Both Egypt and the United States pleaded with Israeli Prime Minister Begin to show restraint in his response, but it was obvious that Israel would react to the carnage with massive retaliation of one kind or another. Prime Minister Begin, a man who had fought the world's perception of the "victim Jew" all his life, was the last man to give quarter. As the thirty-seven flag-draped caskets were lowered into the ground the following day, the Israeli public demanded retaliation, and the IDF geared itself for a major operation "up north." The Palestinians, too, understood that war was imminent; high-ranking Palestinian guerrilla leaders rushed their families out of southern Lebanon toward Beirut. The Syrians also realized that the IDF would be crossing "the frontier," and Damascus ordered its forces in Lebanon not to engage the IDF.

Realizing that immediate military action was called for, Prime Minister Begin and Defense Minister Maj. Gen. (Res.) Ezer Weizman (the former OC IAF) asked A'MAN director Gazit to provide a comprehensive list of viable targets in southern Lebanon; Prime Minister Begin *demanded* to know all options available to the IDF before authorizing any military plan.[10] After careful review of A'MAN briefs and analysis of the Palestinian Order of Battle inside southern Lebanon, the IDF Operations Branch finalized its ideas into a comprehensive offensive strategy. The plan called for an IDF invasion ten kilometers deep into Lebanese territory, up to the Litani River in the west and the Mt. Hermon frontier in the east. The objective of the invasion was the destruction of the Palestinian terrorist infrastructure in southern Lebanon.

D day was March 13, 1978, but bad weather stalled the invasion for one day. A'MAN's preinvasion reports, handed to the chief of staff twenty-four hours before the IDF's predawn artillery barrage was to begin, indicated that many of the conscript Palestinian units in the south were not running, like their commanders, but digging in for a fight; reports also indicated that terrorist bases were mined and booby-trapped.[11] The fight was expected to be a tough one.

On March 14, 1978, a seven thousand–man IDF invasion force crossed the heavily fortified frontier and began its attack into southern Lebanon; it became known in the IDF vernacular as Operation Litani. OC Northern Command, Maj. Gen. Avigdor "Yanush" Ben-Gal, one of the heroes of the 1973 War, commanded the six-pronged attack of the entire front by paratrooper, infantry, armor, combat engineering, and artillery units. The assault commenced with a massive air and artillery bombardment, followed by armored and infantry thrusts that pushed through the muddy terrain toward the Litani River. The IDF advance was slow and cumbersome, mainly to limit the number of Lebanese civilians killed in the action (or, if possible, prevent any killing). Paratrooper and infantry forces were dropped by helicopter deep behind enemy lines to ambush retreat routes; these elite units were assisted by Arabic-speaking soldiers from Unit 300, consisting of Druze, Bedouin, and Circassian volunteers and, according to foreign reports, SAYERET HA'DRUZIM, the Druze Moslem reconnaissance force.[12]

The military aspect of Operation Litani lasted only a matter of days. In the course of the fighting, IDF units killed more than three hundred terrorists, captured several hundred more, and forced more than five thousand to flee northward far from the Israeli border; twenty-one IDF soldiers were killed and one hundred twenty-one were wounded in the brief fray. The IDF remained in Lebanon, however, since Palestinian terrorists could not be permitted to return to their former bases opposite the Israeli frontier.

A primary objective of Operation Litani was the establishment of a security zone to be guarded by the Free Lebanese Army (also known as the South Lebanese Army), commanded by a renegade Christian Lebanese army officer named Sa'ad Haddad. Outraged with the Palestinians' domination of southern Lebanon, Haddad created his own mixed Shiite-Christian militia to protect the villagers of the south from PLO harassment and violence. Haddad was considered an Israeli puppet by most, and his army consisted of several hundred fighters wearing IDF surplus fatigues and deploying IDF surplus weaponry; A'MAN was responsible for their training.[13] Nevertheless, A'MAN did not have much faith in its Christian ally's ability to stop the Palestinians from returning to the south, or in its ability to control the largely Shiite population. The A'MAN director even feared that the right-wing Israeli government would make its newly controlled strip in southern Lebanon an "occupied territory" and begin the construction of settlements.[14]

In the summer of 1978, the United Nations finally intervened by creating a buffer force known as UNIFIL ("United Nations Interim Force Lebanon") to separate the Palestinians and Israelis in southern Lebanon. UNIFIL was supposed to end Israeli involvement in Lebanon, but the Jewish state had already invested a great deal of time and money in its neighbor to the north. It was an involvement that began as a golden opportunity to solidify Israel's military and political presence in the Middle East, and would develop into a catastrophe comparable to America's involvement in Vietnam.

By 1975, Lebanon was on the brink of full-scale fratricide. The Palestinians, whose armies roamed through Lebanon unmolested and unconcerned with law and order, had broken the delicate balance of power that had kept the different religions and tribal clans from open hostilities for so many tense years. Several political accords engineered by the Arab League attempted to soothe the rift between the heavily armed Palestinians and the ruling Christians, but they only delayed the inevitable.* The PLO fighters—bored, angry, heavily armed, and answerable to no one but their local commanders—instituted a reign of terror over much of Lebanon: Thousands of Lebanese

*The November 1969 "Cairo and Melkart Accords" granted the PLO virtual self-rule autonomy in the areas bordering Israel.

civilians, both Christian and Moslem, were robbed, raped, and murdered. All the local political and religious parties—Christian, Moslem, and Druze—began to form small heavily armed militias to defend their communities. The battle lines were now drawn.

By April 1975, tensions were at an all-time high in Lebanon. A series of demonstrations over food prices, fishing rights, and economic integrity resulted in the death of dozens as Christian soldiers and Moslem trade federations, supported by heavily armed Palestinians, battled in Sidon. On April 13, 1975, Palestinian fighters shot the bodyguard of Sheikh Pierre Gemayel, the Maronite Christian founder of the all-powerful Phalangist party. Heavily armed Christian gunmen soon ventured into the streets of Beirut looking for revenge.[15] In an ensuing battle, twenty-seven Palestinians—including women and children—were killed and nineteen seriously wounded. Within hours, the once bustling streets of the Lebanese capital were silent. Barricades, hastily erected, soon separated neighborhoods; citizens readied handguns and rifles for the inevitable bloodbath. The "Green Line," a boulevard separating Christian East Beirut from Moslem West Beirut, became a heavily contested no-man's-land. The Lebanese Civil War had officially begun, and the Riviera of the Middle East soon became hell on earth.

The eruption of the civil war did not surprise Israel's intelligence community. Its ferocity, however, did. The IDF Northern Command prepared itself for the new battlefield.

Israel's patriarch, David Ben-Gurion, had dreamed of the day when Israel would confront the Moslem Middle East with the support of the region's minorities: the Christians in Lebanon, the Kurds in Iraq, the pro-Western Iranians under the rule of the shah, and monarchists in Ethiopia. Until the Lebanese Civil War, however, the Christians in Lebanon had little interest in Israel and little use for the military assistance the IDF could provide. The principal Christian forces in Lebanon included the Maradas (named after legendary giants of Lebanon's prehistory), commanded by the powerful Frangieh family, whose power base was in northern Lebanon, and the port city of Tripoli in particular; the "Tigers," a pro-Western militia commanded by Danny Chamoun,* the son of former Lebanese Prime Minister Camille Chamoun; and, lastly, the Keta'ab ("of the book"), the Arabic name for the Phalangists, led by the powerful Gemayel family. Formed in 1936 by family patriarch Pierre, the Phalangists followed the fascist mold of Hitler, Mussolini, and Spain's Franco,

---

*An opposition leader in the intricate forum of Lebanese internal affairs, Danny Chamoun was assassinated on October 21, 1990, by, it is believed, Syrian agents. His death marked the end of the Israeli-Christian alliance.

and was highly organized. The three major Christian families soon found themselves in dire straits—outnumbered, outgunned, and hopelessly outfought. By September 1975, the Christian foothold in Lebanon, a mighty presence for nearly two thousand years—was tenuous.

On April 12, 1976, at about midnight, an IDF/navy missile boat placed itself on combat footing as it approached the Lebanese shore. Lights were extinguished and radio silence was maintained. The ship was not on a reconnaissance mission or even on routine patrol. It had been sent to Lebanese waters, under top-secret A'MAN directives, to pick up an important cargo—human cargo —a man who, it was thought, would help bring Ben-Gurion's "periphery doctrine" to fruition. As the Israeli missile boat's gunners aimed their .50-caliber machine guns at the coast to protect against a possible Palestinian ambush, a lone figure approached in a rubberized craft. As he was met by the ship's commander, the shivering, sea-soaked individual said simply, "I am Abu Halil, a leader of the Lebanese Phalange party. Please take me to Israel. I am on an urgent mission." [16]

Abu Halil's historic mission was not the first contact between Lebanon's Christians and the State of Israel. "Tiger" commander Danny Chamoun had contacted the MOSSAD through a European station and urgently requested Israeli military assistance in the first weeks of the civil war.[17] Even though the Chamouns were among the most pro-Western, anti-Nasserite, and anti-Palestinian of all Christian forces in Lebanon, Israeli Prime Minister Yitzhak Rabin, himself a former IDF chief of staff, frowned upon establishing a close military relationship with the Christians and becoming directly involved in the civil war.

Remarkably, Rabin and A'MAN had a history of covert contacts with the Chamouns. During the 1958 Civil War, when Rabin was OC Northern Command, Lebanese President Camille Chamoun, a man who had long called for a peace treaty with Israel, received a shipment of five hundred submachine guns from Israel. Cooperation continued in the following years, as Chamoun and the IDF helped eliminate Syrian arms smugglers bringing weapons into Lebanon.[18] Other reports indicate that both the MOSSAD and A'MAN established links with Lebanon's Christians in 1974, following the notorious Palestinian terrorist attacks on Qiryat Shmoneh and Ma'alot, both of which had emanated from Lebanese territory. Jerusalem decided to wait out the civil war, however, and determine which faction could offer the most to Israel's interests. Patience would prove to be a virtue, and Abu Halil's visit to Israel was the payoff.

Israel reacted cautiously to Abu Halil's venture. Later that spring, an IDF/navy missile boat was sent to the port of Jounieh, north of Beirut, a historic Christian enclave. On board were two important Israeli government representatives: a senior though anonymous MOSSAD official and a senior A'MAN official, Col. Binyamin "Fuad" Ben-Eliezer, a career officer who had held a wide array of postings throughout his illustrious military career, ranging from commander of SAYERET SHAKED (Southern Command's reconnaissance formation) to the IDF attaché to Singapore; prior to joining A'MAN, Fuad was commander of the Minorities "Unit 300." [19] Fuad and his anonymous MOSSAD colleague met Amin and Bashir Gemayel, Pierre's two sons and the Phalangists' two highest ranking officials. The Israelis were unimpressed. Bashir appeared seasick and childish; Amin was considered unenthusiastic and unreliable.

The Israeli intelligence contingent, again led by Fuad, returned to Lebanese waters a few weeks later. This time, however, they would evaluate the situation firsthand by visiting Lebanon on a fact-finding mission. The four Israelis, dressed in civilian clothing, and armed with only Smith and Wesson revolvers, had no idea what to expect. They were met by a luxurious yacht owned by Danny Chamoun's "Tiger" militia,[20] and landed on East Beirut's northern shore to a serenade of incoming artillery rounds and tracer fire, backlit by neon light from the city's casinos, which were still operating amid the madness. The meetings that followed were polite yet extremely serious; even Chamoun's arch rivals, Bashir and Amin Gemayel, were present in a rare and fleeting show of Christian unity. The young "Tiger" commander chaired the session, pleading with his guests for military assistance. He promised his Israeli guests, "Give us arms and we'll slaughter the Palestinians!" [21] It was an offer that took the Israeli team aback.

The visit did little to alter the Israeli intelligence perception that the Christians could not be counted on as allies.[22] The local savagery—in which corpses of dead Palestinians were butchered in the streets and young Phalangist female soldiers, noted for their beauty, carried Gucci pocketbooks filled with the chopped-off fingers of killed enemies—horrified the Israelis. The A'MAN and MOSSAD contingent was even invited to witness the siege of Tel Za'atar, a Palestinian refugee camp and military stronghold near Beirut; the siege evolved into a massacre, underscoring the Christians' conventional military shortcomings.

The opportunity to establish a non-Moslem ally in the region was too promising for Israel to abandon just because the Christians were ruthless and untrustworthy; indeed, in the Middle East such traits were often viewed as positive. Arms shipments began to trickle through to the Christians' ranks, and a "permanent" liaison was established. Israeli strategic planning along its northern front required a Christian alliance; the Phalangists and Tigers were crucial if Syrian designs on Lebanon were to be checked. The Syrians had long regarded Lebanon as a mere stretch of "Greater Syria," a parcel of land that included all of Lebanon and much of northern Israel. Damascus responded to the outbreak of civil war in Lebanon by dispatching forces of the Syrian-controlled Palestine Liberation Army (actually a unit in the Syrian army's Order of Battle) and As-Saiqa into the fray to fight alongside the Palestinians and Moslems. Syrian policy hinged on dominating Lebanon's maze of internal political rivalries.

When, in June 1976, Moslem forces, which were dominated by the Palestinians, appeared on their way to a rout of the Christians and installed their own military and political dominance over Lebanon, Damascus once again responded; this time thirty thousand Syrian soldiers invaded Lebanon in support of the Christians.

Inside the walls of the KIRYA, the Syrian move raised a red flag. Although it seemed an ironic twist of fate that the Syrians would be aiding the Christians to defeat Palestinian and Moslem forces in Lebanon, it signaled to A'MAN director Gazit that the Lebanese situation was an intricate web of deceit and madness that could not be controlled or contained by Israeli policies. It was a situation that Israel should stay out of at all costs.

The one leading Lebanese figure who personified the nation's schizophrenia was Phalangist military commander Bashir Gemayel. The handsome American-educated lawyer was as unpredictable and violently volatile as any Young Turk, while being as smooth and compromising in negotiations as a career diplomat. Known to order the execution of his political and military foes, be they Palestinian, Syrian, or Christian, Bashir was also careful to maintain a friendly liaison with his enemies. At the height of the Lebanese Civil War, one of Bashir's closest friends was Ali Hassan Salameh, the infamous "Red Prince," who as one of the commanders of Black September masterminded the Munich Olympics Massacre.[23] The two men were also highly valued CIA assets in the region.[24, 25]

Bashir's "Dr. Jekyll and Mr. Hyde" personality worried A'MAN director Gazit, but MOSSAD boss Hofi disagreed. Bashir was energetic, ambitious, and ruthless enough to assume power in Lebanon; if an alliance with Lebanon was to materialize, Israel would need *its* man in the presidential palace. Hofi felt that Bashir was the key to Israel's strategic policy in Lebanon: His army was the most powerful, his forces the most organized. But before he could dominate all of Lebanon politically and militarily, he would first have to put his own house in order: It was a thought that frightened the officers in A'MAN's Lebanon Desk. On June 13, 1978, a unit from Bashir's Phalangist militia attacked the home of Tony Frangieh, commander of the Marada militia. Frangieh, his entire family, staff, and even pets were all brutally murdered.* The Marada's power was forever weakened. A pro-Syrian force, the Marada had been a direct threat to the Maronite relationship with Israel. Frangieh's murder consolidated Bashir Gemayel's dominance over Christian Lebanon, but it also brought on the wrath of the Syrian army stationed in Lebanon. The Syrians shelled

*In February 1979, Bashir Gemayel's sixteen-month-old daughter was killed in an ambush meant for her father. The perpetrators of the attack were believed to be Frangieh loyalists.

Christian enclaves throughout Lebanon in massive bombardments; hundreds of civilians were killed and thousands wounded in the shellings.

For Israel, the new Syrian-Phalangist confrontation carved infrangible battle lines in Lebanon. Bashir's army subsequently received massive infusions of Israeli arms and assistance. A'MAN, however, did not trust the Phalangists and opposed the relationship.[26]

It was A'MAN, however, that was responsible for the early military liaison and training of select Phalangist personnel. Its officers witnessed the tribal-minded attitude of many of Bashir's men, their outright brutality, and their incompetence in the art of conventional warfare. During the Christian siege of Tel Za'atar, carried out primarily by Danny Chamoun's Tigers, so much artillery ammunition was wasted by gunners shelling destroyed targets for fun that Christian soldiers soon depleted their supplies. "They were thugs," one former A'MAN officer would later state on Israeli television, "heavily armed playboys out for the adventure and a thrill." Israel went so far as to train the Phalangists in the art of intelligence, counterintelligence, and interrogation techniques; a SHIN BET- and MOSSAD-trained secret service, headed by a Bashir loyalist named Eli Hobeika, was even created.[27]

Indeed, in the months following the Syrian invasion of Lebanon in April 1976, Christian forces began to adopt a distinctive Israeli appearance. Transported to Israel via Cyprus, thousands of Phalangists, who by the late 1970s were known to the English-speaking media simply as the Lebanese Forces (a title representing their national power and aspirations), were trained by the IDF in secret facilities in northern Israel. "Guest" soldiers received Israeli surplus uniforms bearing the name tape of the Lebanese Forces spelled out in Arabic. Lebanese Forces personnel were issued Israeli surplus helmets, web gear, and equipment; elite units within the Lebanese Forces were even given the much coveted IDF paratrooper boots. The Christian forces were also supplied with American 5.56mm M-16 assault rifles, which the IDF had found little use for, and captured AK-47 7.62mm assault rifles. The Lebanese Forces even formed conventional military units along the lines of preexisting IDF formations, such as jeep-borne antitank hunter squads and airborne-qualified commandos; a Lebanese Forces navy, equipped with ex-IDF/navy DABUR ("bee") patrol boats, guarded the Christian smuggling routes to Cyprus.[28] According to one A'MAN intelligence officer involved in their training, "If it wasn't for the fact that these soldiers spoke French and Arabic, one could mistake them for Israeli soldiers . . . in fact, they can be considered the IDF's Christian Brigade."[29]

Israel's Phalangist card was not earning great dividends in the years 1978–81, however. Palestinian terrorist attacks across the northern frontier continued. In fact, Major Haddad's militia, a sideshow compared to Israel's blossoming marriage to the Lebanese Forces, was proving itself the IDF's most capable ally as it managed to deter and intercept many terrorist infiltration attempts across the security zone. UNIFIL troopers tended to turn a blind eye to the activities of the terrorists in southern Lebanon and sometimes even supported their journeys toward the Israeli border. While Major Haddad's men were in the trenches, Bashir jockeyed for the spotlight.

Nevertheless, Bashir Gemayel was A'MAN's, and the MOSSAD's, boy in Lebanon. Israel in the 1980s was governed by a hard-line right-wing government whose inspiration for leadership stemmed from the Jews' bitter experiences in the past. Prime Minister Begin, a man haunted by the nightmare of the Holocaust and the struggle for Israeli independence against the British, likened the Christian plight in Beirut and the mountains surrounding the Lebanese capital to that of the Jews in the Warsaw ghetto in 1943[30] (an extremely ironic analogy in light of the fact that the Phalangists' founder, Sheikh Pierre Gemayel, had modeled his militia along the lines of the fascist organizations in Nazi Germany and Mussolini's Italy). The IDF chief of staff was now Lt. Gen. Rafael "Raful" Eitan, a highly decorated officer of supreme courage, who possessed an impeccable combat record; he was known simply as a "Fighter." He had commanded the 890th Paratroop Battalion at the Mitla Pass in 1956; commanded the conscript Paratroop Brigade that raced into the Sinai during the 1967 War; and, as chief paratroop and infantry officer, personally led several spectacular commando operations during the War of Attrition, including several "hairy" pursuits of terrorists in the Jordan Valley, and the December 27, 1968, Operation Gift into Beirut International Airport.* It was the 1973 War, however, that earned Raful his stripes. As commander of a mixed armor and infantry division that bore the brunt of the Syrian onslaught, his decisive leadership literally saved the front.

Major General Yehoshua Saguy was appointed A'MAN director in February 1979. Unlike Israel's previous choices for A'MAN and MOSSAD directors, Saguy was a career intelligence officer, not an ex–paratroop brigade commander or a highly decorated combat leader.[31] Although not a JOBNIK by any means—Saguy had served in a Southern Command reconnaissance force during the 1956 Sinai Campaign, as well as in an armored unit—he had served most of his twenty-eight-year career in the Intelligence Corps and A'MAN: Saguy commanded the Intelligence Corps officers' course in 1965, was Southern Command's chief intelligence officer during the 1967 War, and in 1971 was named commander of the Intelligence Corps training school. Perhaps his most important step up the A'MAN chain of command was serving as the chief

---

*Following the operation, numerous rumors circulated that Raful walked calmly into the bar at the Beirut International Airport, while commandos from SAYERET MAT'KAL were destroying thirteen aircraft from Middle East Airlines, and ordered a cup of coffee, paying for it with a ten-pound Israeli note. Although this story, which reached the pages of the international press, never happened, it followed Raful for his entire career.

intelligence officer of Maj. Gen. (Res.) Arik Sharon's armored division during the 1973 War. Sharon's division performed brilliantly during the fighting in the Sinai, and its staff of senior officers evaded the wrath of the Agranat
Commission. Following the war, Brigadier General Saguy was appointed head
of A'MAN's all-important Research Department.[32]

Saguy was a highly respected officer known for his soft-spoken manner,
and calm and deliberate reactions to developing military situations. In the post–
Yom Kippur War malaise, Saguy was also sensitive to the political aspect
of his post, even though the IDF was as apolitical a body as can exist inside
Israel. He was a company man, loyal to Prime Minister Begin and Chief of
Staff Lieutenant General Eitan. Yet A'MAN was in sharp and bitter conflict
with the prime minister and the MOSSAD over one critical matter of policy:
Lebanon.

Saguy inherited an A'MAN resolute in its opposition to the Israel-Christian
military interdependency. According to several Israeli officials, the relationship had gone too far for it to end without disaster; "like a mixed marriage
proceeding against all advice and points of logic" was how it was personified by some A'MAN officers. It was not that A'MAN objected to maintaining
a liaison, or even a "special" relationship with the Lebanese Forces; such
contact, it was agreed, could only further A'MAN's intelligence-gathering
abilities inside Lebanon and Syria. Veteran A'MAN officers with years of experience and study in the internal schisms of Lebanon continuously argued,
however, that Bashir Gemayel was dangerous. The Phalangist militia leader
maintained close ties with several Syrian elements, had a covert relationship
with the Palestinians, and even profited by smuggling Israeli arms to
Palestinian units.[33] A Phalangist-run ferry service between Jounieh and Cyprus
transported countless Palestinian terrorist personnel out of Lebanon, anonymously of course, for a hefty fee.

By 1981 A'MAN's dire predictions that Israel's march with the Christians
was a mistake still fell on deaf ears. Far from the madness of Lebanon, however,
in a land renowned for the hanging gardens of Babylon, events were brewing that would have great impact on A'MAN. Confidence in A'MAN would be
compromised in much the same way it was after the 1973 War, when the MECHDAL
left Israeli military intelligence at a low ebb. This attitude would, in turn,
influence the course of the Israeli "adventure" in Lebanon.

In the late 1970s, the two principal concerns to the State of Israel were
Lebanon and Iraq, a nation with historic implications of genocide for the Jewish
people. Although Iraq was considered a minor sideshow, there would be major
implications.

Spared the destruction of its army in the 1973 War since it sent only token units to the Golan fighting, Iraq soon emerged as having one of the strongest
military forces in the Arab world. Fueled by massive oil profits from the 1973

embargo and the Organization of Petroleum Exporting Countries (OPEC) stranglehold over the Western economies, Iraq was able to invest countless millions in her military might—purchasing weapons from any nation that accepted cash and was willing to sell arms to a one-party nation that had massacred its Kurdish minorities and brutalized its own population through terror and fear. Iraqi oil revenues were able to buy the most modern MiGs from the Soviet Union and the most capable Mirage fighter bombers from France.

That same windfall of cash, it was hoped, could also buy Iraq a nuclear weapon. Secret agreements for the building of a nuclear reactor near Baghdad were signed between Iraq and France in 1974 by French Premier Jacques Chirac and Saddam Hussein. After much fanfare, the French began to construct a seventy-megawatt reactor at the Tammuz nuclear center in the desert; it was also known as the Osirak facility. Israel realized that the reactor, allegedly to provide oil-rich Iraq with a cheap source of energy, would most likely produce nuclear weaponry. Israel's leaders were outraged by the French decision to sell the reactor to the Iraqis, but impassioned speeches by Prime Minister Begin had little effect on the French government, a nation whose anti-Israeli policies had challenged Jerusalem since the Six-Day War.

The Israeli government attempted diplomatic pressure, but the urgent messages from Jerusalem fell on deaf ears. The Israelis even pressured Washington to intercede on its behalf, but U.S. State Department efforts, too, fell short. French President Giscard d'Estaing, a notorious Arabist, continued to promise a jittery world community that the reactor under construction in Baghdad could not produce weapons-grade plutonium. He was wrong. The Iraqi leader, ignoring French warnings, deployed front companies, utilizing the treacherous cover of the Bank of Credit and Commerce International (B.C.C.I.) to purchase the technology required to build the bomb.[34]

Through the tenacious efforts of the LA'KA'M, the sole Israeli intelligence service familiar with technological and nuclear matters, Israel zealously monitored Iraqi nuclear ambitions. Although Iraq had been a nation at war with Israel since 1948—a remarkable fact considering that the two nations do not even share a common boundary—it was never considered a major threat to Israeli security until its nuclear program became active. Naturally, this warranted greater MOSSAD and A'MAN attention. Saddam Hussein, a Ba'ath party "gun" who had risen through the bullet-ridden line of the party faithful, secret service informants, and disgruntled generals to the realm of Iraqi power, had long been regarded by Israeli intelligence as a despot and megalomaniac whose ruthlessness was unrivaled—even in the Middle East. He was never considered an idiot, however; those who understood the man knew him as cool and cunning. His September 1980 invasion of Iran proved to Israel that he was a decisive risk taker determined to keep Iraq at war for the next quarter century and make it the Middle East's most powerful and feared military power. If

Iraq would invade Iran, a fellow Moslem nation, then what was in store for the Jewish state should Baghdad get the bomb? Only one course of action, it appeared, was available to Israel. Contingency plans were begun to "remove" Iraq's fledgling nuclear potential.[35]

A'MAN director Gazit was not interested in expanding the Osirak file; in fact, he vehemently opposed the implementation of a military solution to remove it.[36] The MOSSAD enjoyed substantial success in its attempts to destroy or at least stall the progression of the reactor by sabotaging key components under production in France. On April 6, 1979, anonymous individuals blew up a reactor core under construction at the French nuclear plant at Le Seyen-sur-Mer, just outside of Toulon; the attack was claimed by an unheard-of environmental group and, of course, the perpetrators were never found. Many blamed the MOSSAD for the attack.

On the night of June 13, 1980, Dr. Yahya el-Mashad was murdered in Room 904 of the sprawling Paris Meridien Hotel; he had been struck on the head with a blunt object and stabbed several times. Robbery was not the motive, since his money was still in his wallet and his papers were scattered about the hotel room. The only clue was a lipstick-stained towel near the body; perhaps it was a romantic liaison gone afoul? Dr. el-Mashad was an Egyptian-born electrical engineer who had worked for the Egyptian Atomic Energy Commission from 1961 to 1968 and had been recruited by Iraq in 1975.[37] Marie-Claude Magal, a Paris streetwalker who had been with el-Mashad and who had witnessed "elements" of the murder, was questioned by French internal security agents on July 1; she was mysteriously killed eleven days later in a hit-and-run automobile accident. Once again, the MOSSAD was blamed. In the months that followed, well-placed explosives caused significant damage to the Rome headquarters of SNIA Techint, an Italian nuclear construction company working in Iraq; several letter bombs were also sent to foreign scientists working in the Iraqi capital.[38] This new campaign was remarkably similar to the MOSSAD campaign against German scientists in Egypt in the early 1960s.

The intelligence campaign was going well, but assistance would come from a totally unexpected quarter. A'MAN director Saguy believed that it would not be necessary for Israel to launch a preemptive strike against the Osirak reactor[39] because *Iran* would make a serious effort to remove the nuclear cloud from Teheran. Saguy was right.[40] On September 27, 1980, a flight of U.S.-built F-4 Phantoms of the Islamic Revolutionary Iranian Air Force—relics of the American relationship with the shah—launched a predawn raid on Osirak; several air-to-ground missiles hit the complex, causing minimum damage. Three days later the Iranians struck again, trying to destroy the Iraqi nuclear facility with "conventional" munitions. In the IAF's eyes, the Iranian effort was amateurish but inspired. As one IAF operations officer told the author, "If the Iranians could do it, *anyone* could!"

Initially, an air strike was not the chosen course of action for the removal of the Osirak reactor. The IDF chief of staff, Lieutenant General Eitan, had been toying with the idea of dispatching a force of Israeli commandos, possibly from SAYERET MAT'KAL, into Baghdad to obliterate the facility in a spectacular ground operation; the commandos would be supporting the handiwork of intelligence personnel (and possibly Kurdish guerrillas), who would sabotage the building from the inside.[41] A'MAN estimates, however, labeled that option too risky. An air strike was seen as the only viable option.

On October 14, 1980, a top-secret planning session was conducted in Jerusalem to determine a coordinated course of action to eliminate the Iraqi nuclear threat. Several cabinet ministers, including the deputy prime minister and the minister of the interior, argued vehemently that any preemptive Israeli action would certainly stir up condemnation around the world, causing Israel to reach pariah status. If Israel had been lambasted by the Third World for defending itself in 1973, and censured in the United Nations after rescuing the hostages in Entebbe in 1976, what would the world say about a strike against an Arab capital? Other cabinet ministers were heard saying that Baghdad was not Beirut, and there could be full-scale war as a result of any unilateral action.

MOSSAD chief Hofi and A'MAN director Saguy also opposed an IAF strike, much to the surprise and anger of Prime Minister Begin and Chief of Staff Eitan. Hofi and Saguy feared that any Israeli military move might cause both Baghdad and Teheran to reach a cease-fire and devote their combined military might to the destruction of Israel; both Iran and Iraq had claimed, through their propaganda channels, that their war against each other was only a stepping-stone for the liberation of Jerusalem to restore the honor of the Arabs (for Iraq) and Islam (for Iran).[42] Both men were also concerned that a unilateral IAF strike would damage U.S.–Israeli relations, which, with the Reagan era about to commence, were developing into a full-fledged alliance. Yet there was dissension in both the MOSSAD and A'MAN ranks, especially from their deputies. Nachum Admoni, a SAYERET MAT'KAL veteran and Hofi's deputy, urged Begin to authorize the immediate destruction of the nuclear facility; "it would be a good message to send the Arabs" was his rationale. Saguy's second in command, Brig. Gen. Aviezer Ya'ari (an experienced intelligence officer who had served as chief intelligence officer in Northern Command) claimed that since any Iraqi bomb would be used against Israel, the reactor's obliteration was crucial to Israeli self-preservation.[43]

Major General Saguy, a Sephardic Jew untouched by the horrors of the Second World War, preached against the potential for a new-Holocaust scenario, stating that even if Israel destroyed the Iraqi nuclear reactor, Baghdad's seemingly endless bankroll of oil revenues would facilitate the construction of yet another Osirak; and that no matter what Israel did, Iraq would be able to produce at least one nuclear device by 1990.* Prime Minister Begin, however, fully believed that the Osirak facility represented the greatest threat to Jewish existence since Hitler. The cabinet decided on attack; it was the lesser of two evils.

The IAF OC Operations, Col. Aviam Sela, the man who would later attain infamy as the officer who recruited the American Jonathan Jay Pollard for service in the LA'KA'M, worked closely with the MOSSAD and A'MAN personnel assigned to the "Iraqi problem." [44] A'MAN and IAF Intelligence also received substantial assistance in their planning from aerial-reconnaissance photographs of the Osirak reactor taken by SR-71 Blackbird espionage flights; provided by William Casey, the new director of the Central Intelligence Agency, these photographs along with satellite intelligence were known in A'MAN jargon as "gifts." [45] Nevertheless, the IAF understood the dangers in dispatching aircraft against Iraq: During the 1967 War, the IAF lost two Vautours and a Mirage IIIC during the bombing of the H-3 airfields.

A'MAN preparations for a potential strike were all-inclusive: A wide array of HUMINT, SIGINT, and PHOTINT assets were devoted to the Iraqi reactor.** The Iraqi army Order of Battle, and data on the Iraqi air defenses and deployments around the capital city, were obtained and checked for detail and accuracy through a computerized analysis system. Open sources, usually an invaluable tool, proved ineffectual, since the Iraqis exerted tight control over the media—both the domestic press and foreign journalists. Iraq under Saddam Hussein forbade the private ownership of typewriters and the photographing of numerous locations and entities—including wildlife! Human sources were the most reliable and accessible. Italian and French personnel who had worked at the Osirak plant were questioned and, according to foreign reports, recruited for active intelligence-gathering service.[46]

Although MOSSAD director Hofi had eventually been converted to the "pro-attack" camp, A'MAN director Saguy was still an outspoken opponent of any offensive action against Baghdad. Saguy's principal concern was the failure of any attack. Many in A'MAN believed that if any of the aircraft were shot down, the magnitude of the embarrassment might be overshadowed by the brutal torture-induced death of the poor pilot. Also, if the raid failed and the reactor was not destroyed, the Israeli move might lead to the "Eastern Front"

---

*Saguy's predictions, which were virtually ignored by the Israeli political leadership, nearly came true. Following the invasion of Kuwait on August 2, 1990, Iraq's nuclear potential became an American concern and an Israeli nightmare. The full extent of Iraq's nuclear development was unveiled only after Operation Desert Storm.

**Obviously, censorship laws in Israel forbid the disclosure of the actual sources or the full extent of A'MAN'S, as well as the MOSSAD'S, intelligence-gathering efforts.

scenario, where the combined armies of Jordan, Syria, and Iraq would consolidate their forces to mount a full-scale invasion of Israel through the strategic Jordan Valley. Major General Saguy's fears were not without foundation: The three nations possessed a military might of 1.5 million men, more than seventeen hundred combat aircraft, and more than ten thousand tanks.[47]

The General Staff ordered the IAF to construct a model of the Osirak reactor with MOSSAD and A'MAN assistance, and IAF OC Maj. Gen. David Ivry was ordered to begin the selection of the crews. The fourteen pilots chosen were among the best combat aviators in the IAF, and also the most experienced; only veteran pilots would be trusted with such an important mission. According to foreign reports, the pilots were all fluent in Arabic and were trained by A'MAN to fool Saudi, Jordanian, and Iraqi ground controllers to think that they were Arab aircraft.

Although the Osirak reactor was a source of justifiable concern to Israel, it is doubtful that Israel could have even considered a military option were it not for the acquisition of two sleek and deadly combat aircraft from the United States: the McDonnell-Douglas F-15 Eagle and the General Dynamics F-16 Fighting Falcon, both received in 1979–80. The F-15, an air-superiority masterpiece capable of Mach 2.5 speeds and armed with an array of Python, Sidewinder, and Sparrow air-to-air missiles, was the most potent fighter in existence; with a range of eight hundred miles, and a midair refueling capability and additional fuel tanks, it could reach the far corners of the region. The F-16 is a pugnacious little ship with a devastating punch. Capable of Mach 2 speeds, it is one of the most maneuverable fighters; with a bomb load of twelve thousand pounds and a range of five hundred miles, it is one of the smallest and mightiest fighter bombers in the history of military aviation. These aircraft made the IAF not only the dominant air power in the region, but one of the most capable air forces in the world. The aircraft also placed Baghdad within the operational range of the HEYL HA'AVIR.

The raid on Baghdad, known in the A'MAN and Operations Branch computer as Operation Babylon, was scheduled initially for May 10, 1981. A breach in security caused its delay, however. In the middle of a top-secret meeting in the General Staff's office in early May, an anonymous general, rumored by many to have been Maj. Gen. Uri Simchoni,* the Training Branch commander, left the room to call a political leader from the Labor opposition party and inform him of the raid in an attempt to stall or cancel the operation.[48] The conversation was taped by General Staff Field Security, and the general is reported to have said: "They decided to do the thing . . . you know . . . Baghdad!"[49] A transcript of the conversation was placed on the desk of A'MAN di-

*It has never been proven that Simchoni was the guilty party.

rector Saguy, and the leak was considered so serious that the air strike was delayed while several modifications were hurriedly made to the original plan. The second date for the raid was May 31, but a summit between Prime Minister Begin and Egyptian President Sadat delayed that date, too.

Time was running out for Israel to mount its historic raid. In August or September of 1981, the Osirak reactor was to go "hot" with the insertion of uranium fuel rods into the core. Destruction of the reactor after that date would result in the release of a substantial amount of radioactive debris, causing countless deaths in Baghdad—something Israel wished to avoid at all costs. The Americans had also reviewed Israeli intelligence reports concerning the Osirak facility and, in a lengthy report complete with nineteen appendices that was handed to Prime Minister Begin by American Secretary of State Alexander Haig, presented evidence that Jerusalem's worst fears were correct: The Iraqi reactor *could* produce weapons-grade nuclear material.[50] All last-minute efforts to persuade France and Italy to cease in their nuclear programs inside Iraq had failed. Nothing outside Israeli control would stop Baghdad from acquiring the bomb.

On June 7, 1981, Operation Babylon was finally executed. At 1500, the task force of eight F-16s protected by an escort of six F-15s took off from the sprawling Etzion Air Base in the Sinai and flew a low-altitude path that evaded Arab military and radar positions by rounding the western tip of Saudi Arabia and skirting over the eastern peripheries of uninhabited desert in Jordan. The evasive maneuvers were so successful that Saudi-leased E-3A AWACS (airborne warning and control) surveillance aircraft flying over the Saudi desert failed to detect the fourteen IAF aircraft. Utilizing code names such as "ESHKOL" and "IZMAL," the task force maintained near-absolute radio silence until reaching Iraqi airspace. Just before reaching their target, the attack force split in two: The F-15s raced to twenty-five thousand feet to provide maximum air superiority protection while the Falcons headed at low altitude toward the reactor. In systematic fashion, each F-16 popped up to attack posture and then swooped in on the Osirak facility at a thirty-five-degree angle.

The first bomb hit its mark at 1734. One by one, the Falcons dropped their bomb loads inside the reactor, then veered sharply for the afterburner flight back to Israel. The Iraqi defenders never knew what hit them. In all, sixteen bombs hit the target; all of them exploded except one, believed to be a delayed-action fuse meant to make any reconstruction project all the more hazardous.* The reactor dome was shattered and the facility reduced to twisted steel, crumbling concrete, and smoking rubble.[51] Ninety minutes

---

*According to Professor Frank Barnaby, in his book *The Invisible Bomb*, on-the-spot saboteurs recruited by Israeli Intelligence—possibly French technicians—helped Is-later, the fourteen IAF aircraft arrived in Israel, while antiaircraft batteries and surface-to-air missile crews were still launching their deadly projectiles in the Iraqi capital. As they streaked over the skies of southern Israel, the pilots set off several dozen sonic booms in a fitting salute. Indeed, it was time for celebration.

Prime Minister Begin, who was awaiting the outcome of Operation Babylon in his Jerusalem home with his cabinet, was elated when Raful phoned him and announced, "Everything is in order, sir. Execution was one hundred percent, could not be better." [52] A bottle of wine was brought out and the usually divided cabinet raised their glasses to the people of Israel, to the IDF, and, of course, to the IAF.

Israel had conceived Operation Babylon as a top-secret operation; even if successful, the IDF spokesman was not to make it public. Israeli officials felt that the Iraqis would be too embarrassed by the obliteration of their ambitious venture to make press disclosures. On June 8, however, Jordan's Radio Amman announced details of the operation, claiming that it was an Israeli-Iranian conspiracy supported by the United States. The broadcast was monitored and recorded by HATZAV personnel, who were unaware that Israel had mounted its epic strike. The technicians wearing the headphones were in awe; the station watch commander rushed a tape and analysis of the broadcast, marked SODI BE'YOTER ("top secret") through channels and even attempted to contact the prime minister's military aide-de-camp. Several hours later, Israeli radio was forced to reveal the startling news to the nation. Israelis, once again, were amazed by the talents and brazenness of their air force.

In a press conference held the following day, Prime Minister Begin, IDF Chief of Staff Lieutenant General Eitan, IAF OC Maj. Gen. David Ivry, and A'MAN director Saguy addressed the world's media. Begin was proud, emotional, and absolutely defiant. He stated that Israel had nothing to apologize for, and asked the media how Israel could not keep a bomb from the hands of Saddam Hussein, a man of untold barbarity who had murdered his own friends to become the sole source of power in Iraq. Begin played to the press like a seasoned performer; his mention of the Holocaust and "Zyklon B" gas, the same gas used to end the lives of Jews in the gas chamber, brought the room crowded with hundreds of journalists to a deafening silence. [53] As Raful, a man not known for mincing words, made a brief statement and Major General Ivry provided some technical details of the operation, the A'MAN director sat

---

rael destroy the Osirak reactor by planting explosives inside the reactor's core; the device might even have been built into the structure. The charges, Barnaby states, were set off by a radio signal emanating from Israel, which was recorded by Jordanian ELINT monitors.

in glum silence. Saguy had opposed the operation, he had campaigned against it, and now A'MAN would probably lose much of its credibility. His words would be inconsequential in the future. It appeared as if a new MECHDAL was about to begin.

As it turned out, Major General Saguy's warning of international condemnation would materialize—even in the United States—although the reaction was muted. Oregon Senator Mark Hatfield, a moderate Republican, called the Osirak raid "one of the most provocative, ill-timed, and internationally illegal actions taken in *that* nation's history."[54] Of course, the United Nations General Assembly, the Arab League, the League of Non-Aligned Nations, and every international organization with access to a news agency and a telex condemned the Israeli attack as criminal!

Operation Babylon sparked major controversy in Israel. The raid was executed only three days before a national election and naturally the opposition Labor party cried foul. Shimon Peres, the party boss and prime minister "wannabe," claimed that Begin had ordered the strike in order to guarantee election for his LIKUD coalition. Although Peres was wrong, the election results produced a clear victory for Begin. One of his first moves was to appoint as the nation's defense minister Maj. Gen. (Res.) Ariel "Arik" Sharon, a man who had campaigned incessantly for the post for several years.

Sharon had already envisioned his dominance over Israel's spy masters. A'MAN's opposition to Operation Babylon had made it a weak, even ignored, element in the Sharon Defense Ministry. Longtime Sharon friend Rafi Eitan (not to be confused with the IDF chief of staff) was named as the head of LA'KA'M, and an attempt to oust MOSSAD director Hofi was immediately undertaken. Personal animosity had existed between Sharon and Hofi for a quarter of a century. In 1956, following the battle for the Mitla Pass, four battalion commanders in Sharon's 202d Paratroop Brigade had gone to the chief of staff to demand his ouster in light of his indecisive (and invisible!) command during the costly Mitla Pass battles. As a lieutenant colonel commanding operations in Central Command, Hofi led the crusade against Sharon, followed by Maj. "Motta" Gur and Raful Eitan, both future chiefs of staff. Sharon had little love for Raful either, but since he was one of the IDF's most popular chiefs, there was little the new defense minister could do about it.

With Osirak in ruin and Sharon presiding over the KIRYA, Israel could finally dedicate itself to a new political and military order in Lebanon—the intelligence community be damned.

Conflict between A'MAN and the Israeli government over the Lebanon policy had already occurred in April 1981 when the Phalangists, propped up by massive IDF assistance, began to engage Syrian forces in eastern Lebanon. The flash point was Zahle, a mountaintop city located along the ultrastrategic Beirut-Damascus Highway approximately twenty-five miles east of Beirut. With a population of two hundred thousand, Zahle was the third largest city in Lebanon and the capital of the Beka'a Valley.

Tensions had been brewing in eastern Lebanon since December 1980, when Phalangist units reclaimed the city and ambushed several Syrian positions. A full-scale conflagration erupted when the snowy ground around Mt. Lebanon thawed enough to allow a conventional military attack. On April 1, the Syrians struck. They bombarded Zahle from the air and with massive artillery shellings, then dispatched armor and commando units to decimate the inferior Christian militiamen. In Zahle, the Syrians operated with their known penchant for brutality: Crops were burned, livestock was slaughtered, and life in the once thriving town was forced to a standstill. Militarily, the Syrians proved a mighty foe—one that the Christians could not withstand alone. Syrian special forces were deployed to seize key Phalangist observation posts, including an attempt to capture "French Hill," a spartan though dominating observation post atop Mt. Senin.[55] Should Mt. Senin fall, the Christian enclave in Lebanon, from East Beirut and Jounieh to Zahle, would be permanently vulnerable to Syrian artillery.

Begin was outraged by the Phalangists' situation in Zahle. In a stormy cabinet meeting he likened their position, isolated and waiting for the slaughter, to the Jewish resistance fighters who waited in vain for Allied support during the 1943 Warsaw ghetto uprising. Israel's spy masters were quite suspicious of the whole bloody mess, however. A'MAN director Saguy viewed Zahle as a Phalangist plot to draw Israel into a Lebanon war with Syria. He believed that the Gemayels had been provided with covert assurance from an anonymous Israeli political leader that, should fighting erupt between the Phalangists and the Syrian "occupation" force, Israel would intervene militarily; MOSSAD chief Hofi was also reported to have concurred with the conspiracy theory. Saguy dispatched his chief Lebanon liaison and troubleshooter, Fuad Ben-Eliezer, to Zahle to determine whether or not the Christian plight, as presented by Begin to the cabinet, was genuine. After a quick trip to the Christian enclave, Fuad reported, with a highly detailed description, that the Christians were in relatively little danger. The cabinet ministers were never privy to this document, however.[56]

Ironically, A'MAN's controversial findings were supported by the Syrians. To Intelligence Corps personnel who analyzed Syrian moves around Zahle, two things were fundamentally clear: Syria was punishing the Phalangists by not attempting to seize Zahle, and Syria did not want a fight with the IDF.[57] To illustrate their nonaggressive stance, Syrian combat engineers dug out several emplacements for SA-6 Gainful batteries in the Beka'a Valley. The fact that the mobile SA-6 would be placed in stationary positions was a clear signal from Damascus that the weapon would not be moved to cover Israeli airspace— or even aerial portions of southern Lebanon routinely overflown by the IAF.

The A'MAN photointerpreters who examined the PHOTINT from Zahle could not miss this "we'll behave if you'll behave" message. Prime Minister Begin and Raful would have none of it, however. The IDF chief of staff, in fact, recommended that IAF fighters be dispatched to blow Syrian helicopters out of the sky.

On April 28, 1981, Raful received governmental authorization for "limited" IAF activity over Zahle. Less than four hours later, two IAF F-16 Falcons shot down two Syrian Air Force Mi-8 Hip transport helicopters. The Syrians retaliated by filling the empty SA-6 emplacements with missile batteries; mobile SA-6 batteries, commanded by Soviet advisors, were moved to the Syrian border with Lebanon; and SCUD SS-1-C surface-to-surface missile batteries were activated south of Damascus, placing much of northern Israel in their deadly range. Prime Minister Begin vowed to remove the SA-6 batteries by force and, indeed, a preemptive IAF strike was scheduled for April 30. But stormy weather and the intervention of the American ambassador, Samuel Lewis, canceled that predawn blitz, and several others that were to follow. That same day, Syrian commandos from the elite 82d Regiment captured Mt. Senin. A'MAN and the Intelligence Corps were able to monitor Syrian deployments through the use of RPV drones. Although several drones were shot down by Syrian missiles, those that survived provided accurate intelligence—both PHOTINT (real-time video transmissions) and ELINT—of SAM emplacements. The "Beka'a Valley missile crisis," as it became known, was proving to be a testing ground for the means and methods that would be used to execute the next Arab-Israeli conflict. Another march to war had commenced.

Major General Saguy's warnings were proving to be uncanny in their accuracy. Seventy-two hours after the SA-6 batteries were moved into the Beka'a Valley, Bashir Gemayel quietly withdrew his militiamen from Zahle; no massacre of the inhabitants ensued and the Christians' foothold in Lebanon was not destroyed, as predicted by Begin. With his low-key manner and calm presence, Saguy pleaded for sanity but was unheard amid the usually tumultuous Israeli power structure. Aside from the fact that Israel's Lebanon policy was steering the nation toward certain war, Saguy's A'MAN was against Israel's one-way traffic of money and material to the Phalangists, arguing that "the merchandise was not worth the price"; there were more economical means available for Israel's frugal Ministry of Defense to further national security. According to intelligence reports, the Phalangists maintained eight thousand men under arms and had an annual operating budget of $50 million; these funds, furthered by Israeli assistance, emanated from profits earned by the Gemayels' traditional "economic activities"—prostitution, narcotics, smuggling, and protection money from merchants living in Gemayel-controlled areas.[58]

A'MAN viewed the Phalangists as unscrupulous and untrustworthy, and preferred a relationship with Major Haddad's small militia; after all, A'MAN was concerned with military developments and threats, not grand political schemes. The political makeup of the region was a MOSSAD concern and Bashir Gemayel was *their* man. Saguy charged his most trustworthy aides—Arabists, Lebanon Desk veterans, and other assorted experts—with evaluating the political future of Lebanon. Their findings, handed to Major General Saguy in a lengthy top-secret report, concluded that there was no chance of Lebanon ever becoming a Christian-dominated state ruled by the Phalangists.[59] A Gemayel in the president's chair would provoke the Druze (the historic nemesis to the Maronites), the Sunnis, the Palestinians, the Communists, the Nasserites, and, most importantly, the Shiite Moslems—a neglected majority that had been awakened by Ayatollah Khomeini's Islamic revolution in Iran.

A'MAN predictions fell on deaf ears. Although Begin did not remove the Syrian SA-6 batteries by force, he did decide to play the brinksmanship game with Damascus. On May 28, 1981, he approved the renewal of aerial attacks against Palestinian terrorist facilities in southern Lebanon; the aerial blitz lasted until early June. Three days following the destruction of the Osirak facility, with the sense of Israeli military might at an all-time high, the IAF renewed its campaign against terrorist positions in southern Lebanon. On July 14, a Syrian Air Force MiG-23 Flogger tasked with intercepting an IAF raid was blown out of the sky. On July 15, however, the Palestinians returned the fire and upped the ante with an artillery barrage of Nahariya, on the Mediterranean coast. A'MAN suggested that the IAF retaliate by hitting a long list of military targets it had pinpointed throughout southern Lebanon, but Raful wanted to hit the terrorists where they lived—the headquarters of Arafat's el-Fatah and Nayif Hawatmeh's DFLP, both situated in the heavily populated area of West Beirut.[60]

Although IAF OC Major General Ivry was not a proponent of hitting the Lebanese capital, he faithfully followed his orders and on July 17 Beirut was bombed. According to estimates by the Red Crescent, the Palestinian/Lebanese version of the Red Cross, more than a hundred people were killed and six hundred seriously wounded. Palestinian units in southern Lebanon followed suit by launching a massive Katyusha rocket attack on Galilee. The barrages were incessant and lasted for ten days. Several Israeli settlements along the northern frontier were evacuated, and the physical and psychological damage to such embattled towns as Qiryat Shmoneh and Ma'alot was ravaging. The situation was so volatile that the United States government sent a special envoy to the region, Ambassador Philip Habib, to discuss a cease-fire and a disengagement agreement.

Although the summer of 1981 passed quietly, the new Israeli defense minister was contemplating the "once and for all" destruction of the Palestinian military presence on the Israeli frontier. Removing the terrorists, in Sharon's words, included Beirut and a new political order in Lebanon![61]

On October 6, 1981, Egyptian President Anwar as-Sadat was assassinated while reviewing a military parade celebrating Egypt's surprise assault on Israel eight years earlier. Sadat, following his Nobel Peace Prize–winning pilgrimage, had become one of the most endeared of all world leaders; his humble roots, charisma, and uncanny ability in handling the media were truly unique. Most importantly, he was an extremely popular figure in the American capital and knew how to convince congressional leaders, the State Department, and even the president to exert pressure on Jerusalem. Perhaps the only man capable of stopping a war in Lebanon was now dead.

That October the newly appointed OC Northern Command, Maj. Gen. Amir Drori, was ordered by Defense Minister Sharon and Chief of Staff Eitan to begin consideration of war plans for Lebanon. Drori, a diligent commander who, as OC GOLANI Brigade during the 1973 War, had witnessed war's wrath firsthand, was more concerned about defending Galilee than organizing an invasion. But he ordered his staff to pull out several contingencies prepared by the Operations Branch for a war in Lebanon: Little Pines, which included a conquest of southern Lebanon up to the Sidon area; Medium Pines, which included confrontation with the Syrians in the Beka'a Valley and a push up to Beirut; and Big Pines, which included confrontation with Syrian forces throughout Lebanon and a campaign against the terrorists inside Beirut. Plans for a full-scale war with Syria, including battles that would spill over to the Golan Heights, were also examined.[62]

The Syrians, too, were preparing for war. On March 11, 1982, a force of Syrian Military Intelligence officers established an ELINT and VISINT ("visual intelligence") gathering post inside Beaufort Castle, the Crusader fortress towering 717 meters above sea level in southern Lebanon, which enjoyed a commanding view of virtually all of Galilee. For years it had been a Palestinian observation post from where much of the Katyusha fire directed at Israel had been coordinated.[63] A Syrian presence in Beaufort Castle had ominous meaning, however. War was no longer a possibility but an inevitability.

The PLO was preparing for the ultimate showdown as well. It, too, had intelligence assets monitoring political developments inside Israel, and, from its impervious perch atop Beaufort Castle, kept close tabs on major IDF military moves around Israel's northern boundaries. In fact, some of the PLO's best intelligence on Israeli desires and intentions came from none other than Bashir Gemayel, who leaked data on his contacts with the Israelis to his friends in the PLO. Arafat could do little with the information at his disposal, however, since preventing a war was beyond the means of the self-proclaimed president of Palestine. With little recourse other than to bolster his defenses in Lebanon, Arafat assumed full military control of the PLO. He ordered his forces, as well as those under the command of various other factions, to deploy as *conventional* fighting formations. Even though the Palestinians had little training in the art of fighting a conventional battle, and even less experience, Arafat was convinced that the "pure guerrilla" hit-and-run tactics employed so successfully by the North Vietnamese would not work against the mighty IDF; his recollections of the bitter Jordan Valley campaign reinforced these beliefs.

The PLO chairman realized that the IDF, under the command of Sharon and Eitan, was determined to launch a war in Lebanon and make a grand bid to take Beirut. In a dramatic move, Arafat created an army of last stand in the south to stall any IDF advance until international political pressure and the United Nations could drive a wedge between any Israeli juggernaut and his home lair. From Beirut to the Israeli frontier, Arafat put three "brigades" together: the Yarmouk, the Kastel, and the Karameh. Several support units, including a "tank regiment" consisting of obsolete T-34s purchased from Romania and Hungary, were hastily created, as were artillery companies equipped with Katyusha rocket tubes purchased in North Korea, which were each assigned civilian targets in northern Israel.[64] Arafat was so confident in the PLO's transformation from terrorist force to conventional army that he mobilized his naval nucleus, based in the Syrian navy home port of Latakia, and an air wing, Force 14, commanded by the mysterious Colonels "Tarik" and "Awida," which trained in Algeria and South Yemen on MiG-23 fighters for "conventional" combat and turboprop transports crammed with explosives for suicide kamikaze sorties.[65] Palestinian guerrillas did receive a great deal of foreign instruction in the People's Republic of China, Vietnam, North Korea, East Germany, Czechoslovakia, Cuba, Poland, and, of course, the Soviet Union.

In all, there were more than fourteen thousand well-trained, heavily armed Palestinian fighters stationed throughout the southern half of Lebanon, with an additional nine thousand Palestinian fighters interspersed throughout northern Lebanon, primarily based around Tripoli.[66] The PLO's Order of Battle consisted of a hodgepodge combination of different factions, rival commanders, and miscellaneous loyalties, including el-Fatah, whose forces in Lebanon included ten thousand fighters divided into four "infantry" brigades, one armored "force," and one "artillery" force; As-Saiqa, consisting of three thousand fighters divided into three infantry battalions and one "militia" home-guard force; the PFLP, consisting of twelve hundred revolutionary guerrillas divided into four infantry battalions; the PFLP-GC, consisting of nine hundred "commandos" not organized into conventional units; the DFLP's fifteen hundred fighters divided into four infantry battalions; the Abu Abbas Faction of the PLF forces, including nine hundred fighters; the Popular Struggle Front forces, consisting of four hundred fighters; and the Arab Liberation Front forces, commanded by military intelligence officers from the Iraqi army, including one thousand fighters conventionally trained in Lebanon.[67]

Augmenting the Palestinian military presence in Lebanon, and particularly troubling to the IDF, was the considerable Syrian deployment. Beyond the nineteen SA-6 batteries stationed throughout the Beka'a Valley, Damascus maintained a forty thousand–man garrison inside Lebanon; they primarily defended the western border, since it was feared that any IDF invasion of Syria might attempt to seize Damascus through Lebanon. In the Beka'a Valley, the Syrians based one tank division, the 1st Armored; the 91st Tank Brigade; the 76th Tank Brigade; the 58th Mechanized Brigade; the 62d Independent Brigade; and ten commando battalions—primarily antitank shock troops armed with RPG-7s and Saggers. In and around Beirut, the Syrians deployed the 85th Infantry Brigade inside the Lebanese capital, as well as one tank brigade, one mechanized brigade, and, it is reported, twenty commando battalions.[68]

A'MAN's misgivings about Israel's unstoppable Lebanon adventure did not prevent the agency from carrying out its intelligence-gathering duties and formulating an accurate and highly detailed description of Palestinian and Syrian strengths throughout Lebanon. The IDF liaison with Major Haddad's militia inside southern Lebanon had produced a frontline Israeli observation post just meters from the enemy lines. A'MAN deployment of RPVs provided an inexpensive and safe means for obtaining PHOTINT and, through the use of video equipment, real-time VISINT. The two principal RPVs deployed by A'MAN squadrons in the months prior to the Lebanon war were the Israel Aircraft Industries Scout, which carries a photolens TV camera mounted in a large transparent bubble under the fuselage, and the Tadiran Mastiff Mks. I and II, which carries two TV cameras and various electronic warfare, ELINT, and electronic countermeasure packages, laser-designation systems, and forward-looking infrared (FLIR). Both "mini-RPVs" are similar, with small signatures and several payloads, including, it has been reported, explosive warheads.[69] Palestinian and Syrian positions, their staging areas and command centers, were pinpointed by A'MAN's Lebanon Desk and Research Department, and the information was disseminated to the Operations Branch for tactical planning.

There would be very few *military* surprises awaiting the IDF in Lebanon, but A'MAN director Yehoshua Saguy still believed that Israel would be unable to achieve its objectives—the destruction of the Palestinians in Lebanon and a new Christian political order—through invasion.[70]

From January 1982 until June, the Israelis planned and prepared for the inevitable conflict. In the middle of January, the Israeli defense establishment paid its largest and most important visit to Lebanon to confer with Lebanese Forces commander Bashir Gemayel and Phalangist patriarch Sheikh Pierre Gemayel in the family lair at Bekfaya, northeast of Beirut. The covert party included Defense Minister Sharon, MOSSAD's chief man in Lebanon, Nahik Nevot, A'MAN director Saguy, and various other "spooks" and "soldiers" crucial to the formulation of Israel's Lebanon strategy.[71] The Israelis were quite clear about their intentions to rout the PLO, but stressed that they would not enter Beirut because it would incur the political wrath of the United States; it was also emphasized during the meeting that Israel did not intend to seize an Arab capital city. Israel expected the *Christians* to "take care" of matters in Beirut, since, according to Maj. Gen. Yehoshua Saguy, any advance that deep inside Lebanon would only result in an inescapable quagmire. As the A'MAN director had predicted all along, both Pierre and Bashir Gemayel were noncommittal about sending Christian forces into the fray. They even warned Sharon that, should Israel win its war and should the Phalangists assume control over the presidential palace, Jerusalem should not expect the signing of a peace treaty between Lebanon and Israel. The handwriting was on the wall—and it read impending disaster. MOSSAD chief Yitzhak Hofi became a "convert" to A'MAN's pessimistic camp, but Begin and Sharon would have none of it. The planning continued.

The meeting in Bekfaya, conducted under a tremendous veil of secrecy and tight security, should have cemented the covert alliance between the Phalangists and Israel. Weeks later, however, the wily Bashir Gemayel would play both sides against the middle. In February, Gemayel met with "Abu Zaim," the nom de guerre for the PLO's director of Military Intelligence, and informed him that Israel was planning to conquer Lebanon and destroy the Palestinians "once and for all." In their lengthy discussions, Bashir suggested to "Abu Zaim" that only the PLO and the Phalangists, working together, could forestall a holocaust in Lebanon.[72] Bashir was clearly carving out his own political niche inside the intricate framework of Lebanon: Israel was just a patron of convenience, not the ally that Jerusalem had hoped it to be.

At the same time that Bashir was meeting with the Palestinians, A'MAN director Saguy was conferring with the American secretary of state, Alexander Haig, to "feel out" America's view of any possible Israeli action in Lebanon. Haig, an experienced military officer and a former commander of NATO, was a staunch supporter of the Jewish state. He told Saguy that the Reagan administration would support a massive Israeli military move only if the Palestinians committed a flagrant violation of the cease-fire accords that special ambassador Philip Habib had carved out in July 1981. Haig's statement greatly pleased the A'MAN director. Realizing that the Palestinians were not about to instigate a violation of the cease-fire and risk annihilation, Saguy hoped that war could, perhaps, be avoided. Sharon and Begin, however, would have differing views on what would constitute a flagrant cease-fire violation.

On April 3, 1982, an Israeli diplomat in Paris, Ya'akov Bar-Simantov—who was, in fact, the MOSSAD station chief—was shot dead by a mysterious group calling itself the "Lebanese Armed Revolutionary Faction."[73] Although the assassination of a MOSSAD official was not a legal or acceptable reason for war, only the fact that the group claiming responsibility was not part of the PLO (or any Palestinian movement for that matter) prevented the defense minister from initiating conflict at that time. In fact, the murder of Bar-Simantov worried the Palestinians more than it did the Israelis. In a top-secret document uncovered by A'MAN after the Israeli invasion, PLO's deputy commander Abu Jihad wrote to his comrades in the Palestinian Communist party, the Democratic Front for the Liberation of Palestine, the Abu Abbas Faction of the Palestine Liberation Front, and As-Saiqa, pleading for restraint in attacks against Israel and especially Israeli diplomats; the edict was published on April 5, 1982.[74]

Other potential provocations also failed to bring about full-scale war. On April 21, an Israeli soldier serving with the Haddad liaison inside the security zone enclave was killed when his jeep struck an antivehicle mine: The IAF responded with an air strike on major PLO targets in southern Lebanon. The PLO did not fire back into Israel, although Arafat did place his forces throughout Lebanon on full combat alert. The PLO had even learned from French Intelligence,* in a report leaked through the Lebanese government, that the IDF might not promote a ground campaign, but instead initiate a major aerial blitzkrieg meant to obliterate all stationary and mobile Palestinian positions throughout Lebanon. Arafat took the French report quite seriously and ordered legions of antiaircraft gunners, many manning Soviet 23mm cannons mounted on flatbed trucks and station wagons, to protect the camps of southern Lebanon. Young men, dressed in camouflage lizard-pattern fatigues, were seen roaming the camps of southern Lebanon wearing field glasses around their necks and carrying SA-7 Strella handheld surface-to-air missiles.

Indeed, Israel's next move would come from the air. On May 9, a day before Defense Minister Sharon had called on the Israeli cabinet to authorize—at least!—the Little Pines operation, the IAF once again went into action over the skies of southern Lebanon. This time, the avalanche of bombs prompted the PLO to respond with a limited artillery bombardment of their own into northern Galilee; no cities were hit—or even targeted—in what appears to have been a message missed by Jerusalem.

The Israeli cabinet met on May 10 to discuss the implementation of one

*There has been much speculation about the relationship between the PLO and the various French intelligence services, especially the Direction Generale de la Securite Exterieure ("DGSE"), the French government's foreign intelligence–gathering apparatus, and the Service de Documentation Exterieure et de Contre-Espionnage ("SDECE"), the French counterintelligence service. A covert bond, it is believed, was created in the early 1980s to prevent Palestinian attacks from transpiring on French soil. The French were to refrain from arresting known Palestinian officials involved in anti-Israeli and anti-Western acts of terrorism in exchange for receiving an unwritten "gentleman's agreement" that the Palestinians would avert bloodbaths on the streets of Paris.

of the Pines strategies, but A'MAN's deputy commander, Brig. Gen. Aviezer Ya'ari, warned that any military action would mean confrontation with Syria—something the IDF wanted to avoid at all costs. At an unusually stormy meeting of the IDF General Staff on May 13, Defense Minister Sharon provided his generals with his version of how a Lebanon war should be executed: It called for a push all along the coastal plain to Beirut and then a linkup with the Phalangists.[75] Saguy, speaking in a deliberate, eloquent, and hard-hitting fashion, presented A'MAN's case against Big Pines, arguing that it was not in Israel's strategic interest to engage the Syrians. The Phalangists, he warned, would not fire a shot in anger against the Palestinians, and, most importantly, the PLO would not be destroyed by any Israeli action. As Saguy spoke, the General Staff, the men tasked with executing the conflict, sat in silence, absorbing the information and opinions. Saguy warned that a Lebanon adventure would also cause national opinion to splinter into a thousand separate directions. His words were prophetic.

On June 3, 1982, three gunmen from the Fatah–The Revolutionary Council* (FRC) shot the Israeli ambassador to the Court of St. James in the head as he left a reception in London's fashionable Dorchester Hotel. The FRC is one of the cover names employed by Abu Nidal, the nom de guerre of Sabri al-Banna, one of the most notorious of all Palestinian terrorists. The FRC had dedicated itself to the destruction of Yasir Arafat's PLO, which Abu Nidal viewed as selling out to the moderates. Abu Nidal had been sentenced to death—in absentia—by a PLO tribunal for treason. The Fatah Revolutionary Council had but one purpose in authorizing an attack against the Israeli ambassador to Great Britain, Shlomoh Argov: to provoke an Israeli assault on Arafat's fortress in Lebanon and thereby weaken his two most bitter enemies. Abu Nidal realized that gunshots on a London street corner would start a war in Lebanon that, perhaps, would engulf the entire Middle East.

The fact that the perpetrators of the Argov shooting belonged to Abu Nidal, an anti-Arafat anti-PLO force, did not matter to Jerusalem. SHIN BET officials expert in tracking the comings and goings of all the major terrorist groups clearly informed the prime minister that the guilty party was *not* regular PLO, but Chief of Staff Eitan was ordered to dispatch the IAF anyway. Although he had been sanctioned to hit terrorist targets that A'MAN had identified in southern Lebanon, Raful suggested an alternative—hitting PLO headquarters in Beirut. Begin agreed. At 1500 on June 4, a flight of IAF aircraft pummeled the PLO's main command and control center in fashionable West Beirut. Less

*Other names for the group include the Abu Nidal organization, Black June Organization, Arab Revolutionary Brigades, Revolutionary Organization of Socialist Muslims, and Black September Organization.

than an hour later, thousands of artillery shells and Katyusha rockets rained down on western Galilee. The residents of much of northern Israel were forced to seek safety in their bomb shelters; several civilians were killed in the Palestinian barrages. The IAF was, once again, called in for retaliatory strikes.

With the chiefs of Israel's two most important intelligence services silenced by the tides of war, the Israeli cabinet met in Prime Minister Begin's Jerusalem home on the night of June 5 to plan the strategy for the invasion of Lebanon. Not a word was mentioned about Beirut, and "contact" with the Syrians was to be avoided at all costs. The operation would be a brief and decisive action, Begin promised—much like Operation Litani but with more permanent effects. The stamp of approval was given.

Late at night on June 5, as conscript IDF units were hurriedly moved into attack position along the northern frontier and reservists were being mobilized for the fray, Lieutenant General Eitan met with Bashir Gemayel to inform him of the impending assault. Eitan asked Gemayel to order his forces to open fire along the "Green Line," which separated the Moslem and Christian halves of Beirut; Eitan also "requested" Phalangist permission for the IDF to deploy from Jounieh and cut Lebanon—and any Palestinian escape route—in half.[76] Both requests were brusquely denied. A'MAN was right. Israel would be fighting this battle alone. At 1100 on the morning of June 6, the first IDF armored units crossed the barbed-wire fence separating Israel from Lebanon and headed north. Operation Peace for Galilee, the name coined for the war, was officially underway. Israel's sixth major conflict in her thirty-four years of existence would also be her most controversial and most bitterly fought.

Operation Peace for Galilee was a full-frontier assault waged along a four-tier axis: UGDAT MORDECHAI, a mixed armored and infantry division, commanded by Brig. Gen. Yitzhak Mordechai, was responsible for the advance up the coastal plain toward Tyre, the refugee camps, Sidon, Damur, and, eventually, Beirut; UGDAT KAHALANI, a mixed armored and infantry division, commanded by Brig. Gen. Avigdor Kahalani, would thrust across the frontier in the central axis toward Nabatiya and the mountain passes that commanded the Lebanese coastal roads; UGDAT EINAN, an armored division, commanded by Brig. Gen. Menachem Einan, would follow Brigadier General Kahalani's advance, then veer off the ultrastrategic Beirut-Damascus Highway; and UGDAT BEN-GAL, a division-sized force of armor and infantry units, commanded by Maj. Gen. Avigdor "Yanush" Ben-Gal, would assault the main Syrian concentrations in the Beka'a Valley. A fifth division, UGDAT YARON, commanded by the chief paratroop and infantry officer, Brig. Gen. Amos Yaron (a SAYERET MAT'KAL veteran[77]), was to be landed amphibiously at the tributary waters of the Awali River north of Sidon, to drive an armored wedge between Beirut and retreating Palestinian guerrillas from the south.

The initial IDF assaults did not materialize as planned. As a result of Sharon's outlandish self-imposed veil of secrecy regarding the full extent of the conflict, most commanders did not know their true objectives. Many were not even issued formal orders. Therefore, deep-penetration heliborne landings were conducted when the timing was *politically* feasible, not militarily necessary; and the amphibious force landed on the *second* day of the fighting, not prior to the invasion, as it should have. Nevertheless, the IDF's armored juggernaut proved to be an impervious force. Long columns of indigenously produced MERKAVA ("Chariot") main battle tanks, supported by even longer columns of M113 APCs, pushed across Palestinian positions. The combined aerial and armor assault proved to be too much for most Palestinian defenses, and the push to Tyre and the surrounding refugee camps was accomplished within hours. Many in the Israeli cabinet confidently predicted that Israeli forces could wrap things up within twenty-four hours!

Yet all was not going well. The war was not turning out to be the lightning-fast, antiseptic conflict that many in the Israeli cabinet had envisioned. On the night of June 6, a task force from SAYERET GOLANI was to capture Beaufort Castle—one of the icons of the Palestinian terrorist dominance over southern Lebanon for so many years. The Flying Leopards, the unit's endearing nickname, were to scale the 717-meter-high fortress during daylight at 1100, but a traffic jam of armored personnel carriers delayed their escorts, who did not reach their objective until late afternoon. The subsequent battle was a fierce display of tenacity and courage. It was waged in the darkness of caves and passageways carved by the Crusaders and illuminated only by the muzzle blasts of automatic weapons and the detonation of fragmentation grenades. The firefights continued into the night; Beaufort Castle was not reported secured until 0630 on June 7. Seven SAYERET GOLANI fighters, among the best soldiers in the IDF, died for the mountaintop perch.[78] The cost for this objective was unbearable to such a small unit, and would prove a harbinger of worse to come.

In the west, Palestinian units around the Tyre refugee camps were not fighting in their hastily assembled conventional formations as Arafat had ordered, but had shed their uniforms and were engaging the advancing IDF armor columns as guerrillas. Once again, the RPG-7 and AT-3 Sagger were proving to be decisive tank killers, and Israeli casualties began to mount. By June 7, the four Israeli divisions were making good progress; Amos Yaron's tanks and paratroopers had landed near Sidon and were pushing around the coastal city for the linkup with the vanguard of UGDAT MORDECHAI. In the east, units from UGDAT EINAN had already engaged Syrian armor elements and seized the strategic town of Jezzine and were moving along the Beirut-Damascus Highway. The Syrians viewed these developments as crucial. An IDF move *through* Lebanon in order to attack Syria from the loosely defended western frontier had always been a nightmare scenario in Damascus. With a full IDF division closing in on the main artery to the Syrian capital, combat with Israel was seen as an act of national preservation. On the night of June 8, Syrian antitank commandos were ordered to engage the IDF in the treacherous terrain of eastern Lebanon. Just as A'MAN had predicted, war with Syria was unavoidable.

In the early-morning hours of June 9, IDF commanders received the green light to turn Operation Peace for Galilee into an epic crusade. Forces operating along the coast were told to push on toward Beirut; Major General Ben-Gal was ordered to enter the Beka'a Valley; and, most significantly, IAF OC Maj. Gen. David Ivry was ordered to once and for all move against the Syrian SAMs.

Just after midday on June 9, the skies over the Beka'a Valley became very active. Israeli Air Force communications and electronic intelligence aircraft—such as the Grumman E-2C Hawkeye, an Israel Aircraft Industries–modified Boeing 707, and Grumman OV-1 Mohawks—hovered within range of the Syrian SAM batteries in order to identify and record the location of the missile-site radars; by the first day of the war, the Syrians had moved five new SA-6 batteries into Lebanon from permanent fixtures atop the Golan Heights.[79] Once the electronic battlefield had been illuminated, a fleet of RPVs was dispatched to act as aerial decoys—Israel's propeller-driven version of the Trojan horse deception—causing Syrian missile operators (and their Soviet advisors) to track the unidentified targets emanating hostile signatures, and ready the missiles for launch. With the Syrians showing their hand, IAF antiradiation sorties, flown by F-4 Phantoms, were able to drive home their AGM-45 Shrike missiles to the center of the surface-to-air radar dish with little difficulty. Once the radars were destroyed, an aerial armada of Phantoms, F-16s, Skyhawks, and Kfirs were thrown into the fray to hit the defenseless Syrian ground targets. Devastation was complete. In less than two hours, the IAF destroyed nineteen SAM batteries, and on the following day, eleven more.

The Syrians responded to the IAF blitzkrieg in a grand, albeit haphazard, fashion. In a desperate bid to catch the attacking IAF fighter bombers in the middle of an aerial bombardment, the Syrian Air Force scrambled its might for one epic engagement. From air bases located throughout Syria, legions of MiG-21 and MiG-23 fighters (and even MiG-25s) raced toward the Beka'a Valley. Yet before the MiGs' Atoll air-to-air missiles could acquire the Israeli attack planes, the IAF F-15 and F-16 killer groups appeared. Controlled and coordinated by high-flying E-2C Hawkeyes, the superior Eagles and deadly Fighting Falcons went to work. In chaotic air-to-air dogfights, the size of which had not been seen since the Second World War, the IAF shot down twenty-two Syrian aircraft without suffering a single loss. The following day, the IAF blew another twenty-six Syrian MiGs and Sukhois out of the sky. The military campaign for Lebanon, it appeared, had already been won.

In the following three days, the IDF continued its advance through the Lebanese heartland toward the capital. Yaron's paratroopers fought the brutal battles around Sidon before linking up with UGDAT MORDECHAI on June 9, at the Palestinian killing fields around Damur, and then joined Kahalani's armor and GOLANI units for the push to Beirut.[80] As A'MAN had predicted, the Palestinians did not throw down their arms and retreat in a replay of Operation Litani: They gave as good as they got and fought with impressive determination. Many Palestinian units, like those defending the Ein el-Hilweh refugee camp, fought to the death in combat that was block to block, house to house, and, in many cases, room to room. As the IDF advanced farther north toward Beirut, resistance increased—by both Palestinian and Syrian units who suddenly found themselves backed to a wall. In the village of Kfar Sil, located at the southern outskirts of Beirut and home to many of the PLO's top commanders, a mixed task force of paratroopers and GOLANI infantrymen encountered the deadly obstacle of Force 17 and As-Saiqa fighters who were deployed with Syrian commandos in a classic antitank ambush. The combat in Kfar Sil was pure terror. Men and machine fought each other at point-blank range; the town's main street, a mere kilometer in length, took the Israelis nineteen hours to seize. The battle was characterized by IDF Chief of Staff Eitan as the toughest of the entire war.[81] By June 11, the IDF had reached the outskirts of the Lebanese capital.*

In the Beka'a Valley and the Shouf Mountains, fierce battles were also raging between Israeli and Syrian units. In several now historic armor battles, IDF MERKAVAS engaged Syrian T-72s in close-quarter tank killing grounds. In the battles of Sultan Yaqoub and Ein Zehalta, tank fought tank and helicopter fought tank. It was the first time in military history where antitank helicopter gunships, such as the American AH-1S Cobra flying with the IAF and the Soviet Mi-24 Hind operating with the Syrian Air Force, were used with such lethal effectiveness.

By June 11, 1982, the day the first United Nations cease-fire was implemented, the war had already turned into a stalemate. In the following weeks, the IDF inched its way closer to the Lebanese capital to force Arafat and his fourteen thousand strong out of the city. The IDF laid siege to the embattled city in an all-inclusive manner: Ground units sealed all roads and mountain passes; the IAF maintained a tenacious airborne vigil; and the IDF/navy's fleet of missile boats and patrol craft closed the Lebanese shoreline.

Even though the IDF chief of staff had "linked up" with Bashir Gemayel at Ba'abda, along the cut Beirut-Damascus Highway in a highly publicized embrace, Christian participation in the fighting *never* materialized. A'MAN had

*On June 10, 1982, Maj. Gen. Yekutiel "Kuti" Adam, the deputy chief of staff, was killed in Lebanon as he gazed upon battlefield developments from a forward observation post. One of the most respected officers ever to serve the IDF, Major General Adam was slated as Yitzhak Hofi's replacement as the next MOSSAD director.

been correct. Israel was walking the political tightrope all alone and with little room to maneuver.

From the outset, it was clear that Lebanon would leave a lasting impression on the Israeli military psyche. A'MAN realized that Operation Peace for Galilee was a different kind of war for the IDF. Lebanon was not the Golan Heights and not the desert wasteland of the Sinai. It was a populated battlefield—a maze of minefields and killing grounds interlaced with populated villages, rife with black market goods and narcotics—in a nation not ruled by law for nearly a decade. Lebanon was the first war in which the Israeli soldier was both warrior and heavily armed tourist.

The one aspect of the Lebanon war that proved unique as well as threatening to IDF operational security was the legions of foreign journalists equipped with video recorders and access to satellite feeds outside of Israeli control. When Israel invaded Lebanon, it became the world's first "semi-real-time" war: Journalists shot their stories and then filed them hours later to satellite stations for nightly viewing on major networks. Journalists working out of Israel were subjected to A'MAN's censorship guidelines, but those in Lebanese territory or behind Syrian lines were free to file their scoops without security examination. Although the Beirut satellite feed was destroyed during the civil war, one still operated in Damascus and reporters not wishing to have their work cut by the IDF Censor's Office simply drove to the Syrian capital. Much news footage around the world was shown with clips removed by the IDF Censor's Office—to the chagrin of network executives who did not appreciate the need for military security.

Although the IDF did not forbid fraternization between Israeli troopers and Lebanese civilians and journalists, it was not recommended. Nevertheless, Lebanon was Israel's first war in which temptation proved a major threat to operational security. A'MAN Field Security units were hard at work throughout Israeli lines trying to ensure that classified information never reached the enemy, or an evening news broadcast. Throughout the roads, towns, and cities of Lebanon, plastered over street signs, billboards, and portraits of Yasir Arafat, were BITACHON SADEH ("Field Security") posters stating, "All The Honor To The Soldier Who Knows To Keep A Secret." [82]

A'MAN and HA'MAN operated brilliantly during the conflict—especially in the HUMINT and VISINT arenas. During the first several weeks of Operation Peace for Galilee, the IDF captured nearly four thousand terrorists and suspected terrorists; policemen from the National Police Border Guard's 20th and 21st companies, a force of a few hundred men, also captured nearly four thousand terrorists and suspects in "snare and seize" operations. All captured individuals needed to be interrogated, and the information quickly disseminated through the intricate network of A'MAN offices, territorial and unit desks, and frontline commanders. Also caught in the massive dragnet was an international roster of terrorists from all over the globe who had trained in the "Palestinian terrorist universities" in southern Lebanon: They included Japanese Red Army assassins, Spanish Basque ETA (Evzkadi Ta Askatasuna) bombers, and members of the Irish Provisional Republican Army who "studied" in Lebanon, courtesy of Libyan oil revenues.

Israel has been tight-lipped about the foreign terrorists it captured in Lebanon, but according to foreign reports that circulated in the international media during the war, "the counter-intelligence services of most Western European nations were hard at work as a result of the data uncovered by the IDF." According to different reports that have never been confirmed by intelligence sources, several Cuban, East German, and Asian instructors were also captured by the Israelis. In a rare midwar interview, A'MAN director Saguy admitted that the IDF did capture an impressive number of foreign terrorists, including South Americans, Africans, and Turks; he also mentioned that the IDF monitored Italian, German, and "Sandinista" personnel evacuating Beirut.[83] A'MAN also uncovered foreign volunteers in the PLO ranks, including terrorists from Somalia, India, Pakistan, and Bangladesh, as well as documentation proving that foreign exchange programs existed between the PLO and the Indian and Pakistani military.

Perhaps more important than the personnel seized and then transferred to the sprawling Ansar detention facility near Tyre were the voluminous files "liberated" from the various camps and bases. The IDF onslaught was so swift that Palestinian officers did not have time to burn or remove files; some files contained the only copies of certain documents, and so could not be destroyed! These documents allowed A'MAN (as well as the MOSSAD, the SHIN BET, and the Israeli National Police) to uncover so much data on the terrorist infrastructure, as well as its networks located inside Israel and throughout the world, that its effectiveness as a fighting entity was severely weakened. The captured documents also uncovered the vast Soviet-bloc involvement in the Palestinian terrorist groups, including the conventional military training of Palestinian officers in armor courses in Hungary, air defense courses in Vietnam, company commanders' courses in Bulgaria and the People's Republic of China, combat engineers' courses in East Germany, a staff college course in Yugoslavia, and sabotage and sapper training in Cuba.[84]

In Lebanon, the IDF also captured enough guns, tanks, and weapons systems to equip a major-sized army. Hundreds of tanks, from T-62s to T-54s, which once belonged to Syrian armor units, were transported back to Israel, where they were examined, displayed, and dispatched to HEYL HA'CHIMUSH ("Ordnance Corps") depots for repair and deployment in IDF units. According to Western intelligence reports never confirmed by the Israelis, the IDF captured several T-72 MBTs (before Operation Desert Storm, the most modern Soviet tank not yet touched by Western analysts) and secretly shipped them to the United States for examination. The IDF, however, suffered intelligence losses as well. During the deadly tank battle for Sultan Yaqoub in the Beka'a Valley, an IDF M-60 tank equipped with boxes of top-secret Blazer reactive armor (as well as top-secret Arrow antitank shells) was captured by the Syrians. The tank and its defenses were shipped back to Moscow and, within a matter of years, the Soviet Union began manufacturing the reactive armor kits for their T-80 MBTs.[85]

Hundreds of Palestinian and Syrian heavy guns were also captured, as were tens of thousands of weapons and tons of explosives and Soviet-bloc ammunition. Seizing so much war materiel allowed A'MAN to formulate a "cradle-to-grave" arms chart, systematically describing how the various Palestinian terrorist factions acquired arms. Some weapons captured were American M-16 5.56mm assault rifles and M-60 7.62mm light machine guns originally supplied to the Lebanese, Jordanian, and Saudi Arabian armies but diverted to the Palestinians in Lebanon; other American weapons had serial numbers placing them as missing in Vietnam![86] (Many of the Soviet weapons seized in the sprawling refugee camps would later be dispatched to Central America in the triangular U.S.-Israeli-Iranian "Iran-Contra" arrangement.)

The most important A'MAN contribution during Operation Peace for Galilee was its deployment of the RPV for intelligence-gathering missions. Although its role in the destruction of the Beka'a Valley SAMs had secured the MA'Z'LA'T (Hebrew acronym for "RPV") as an impressive electronic countermeasure tool, the real-time intelligence-gathering value of the high-flying drones as they buzzed enemy positions over Lebanon was truly revolutionary. Controlled by an Intelligence Corps NCO or officer wielding a joystick and paying close attention to a video monitor, a drone was dispatched from a forward position close to the front lines and flown over a stretch of enemy territory; a video image from the ship's cameras and electronic sensors was transmitted throughout the entire flight and simultaneously relayed to a mobile forward command post (either a truck or an M113 APC); the visual data was then conveyed to Intelligence Corps officers in a territorial desk, or sometimes back to Tel Aviv, where the data was analyzed and disseminated to front-line unit commanders.[87] The entire process could be instantaneous (real-time), or it could take several hours. In many cases, RPVs flew over heavily fortified positions, such as Palestinian sniper dens and Syrian artillery pits, and helped the IAF or IDF artillery batteries zero in for the eventual kill.* Since

---

*The art of deploying the RPV as a real-time intelligence-gathering/targeting tool was not lost to the United States military. During the subsequent U.S. Marine operations in Lebanon between 1983 and 1984, and the January 1991 Operation Desert Storm, Israeli-produced RPVs, such as the Israel Aircraft Industries Pioneer, were deployed with great success by the U.S. Navy and Marine Corps to pinpoint enemy targets without endangering reconnaissance flight crews or long-range reconnaissance patrol (LRRP) teams.

the RPV produced very little noise, had a small radar signature, and was extremely maneuverable, it was unlikely to be noticed electronically by enemy surface-to-air radar operators, or visually by tank commanders standing in their turrets. The RPV became the most cost-effective and successful intelligence-gathering tool ever employed in military history.

One perfect example of the RPV's invaluable role as an intelligence platform was seen on June 10, 1982. According to the October 1982 edition of the esteemed London-based *Military Technology Magazine*, a Scout RPV flying over the Beka'a Valley located a Syrian tank column attempting to reinforce the beleaguered 1st Armored Division: The IAF was called in and, in a matter of minutes, seventy T-62s were destroyed.[88] Sometimes, situations changed too quickly for the information to be put to deadly use. On numerous occasions, it has been reported, the motorcade of PLO chairman Arafat was monitored by an Intelligence Corps officer looking at the video images being transmitted by a high-flying Scout RPV. Yet before the data could be funneled through command channels to IAF aircraft poised for action over Lebanon, the PLO leader had found safe shelter.

The IDF siege of Beirut, which was considered the least violent means to push the PLO out of the city, eventually succeeded in forcing Arafat's hand. On June 27, 1982, Arafat agreed to evacuate the PLO from Beirut, although the actual withdrawal, conducted under the supervision and protection of U.S. Marines, Italian infantrymen, and French paratroopers, did not commence until August 22, 1982. The Syrians, too, agreed to pull their forces out of the Lebanese capital. Over the course of twelve days, 14,938 Palestinian and Syrian fighters departed Beirut in a dramatic withdrawal. The majority of the Palestinians departed by sea. In tearful good-byes followed by maddening volleys of automatic fire aimed toward the heavens (a Palestinian symbol of victory), 8,144 members of the various factions within the PLO boarded hired Greek freighters and headed to yet another exile—their third diaspora since the 1967 War. The commanders and special operations forces went to Tunis, the capital of Tunisia, where the PLO would establish yet another headquarters to direct the struggle against the Zionist enemy. Other fighters went to Algeria, Libya, Iraq, South Yemen, and any other country willing to have them. Arafat, too, departed by sea. As the defiant PLO chairman prepared to board the ship that would take him to his new Tunis lair, an IDF sniper positioned in one of the deserted and bombed-out buildings managed to place Arafat in the cross hairs of his 7.62mm high-powered marksman rifle. But all Israeli soldiers—even special operations snipers—were under strict orders not to "take out" terrorist chiefs, in order to preserve the precarious cease-fire arrangement brokered by the United States.[89] Not only would Arafat live to fight another day, but he would return to Lebanon months later in an ill-fated bid to consolidate his forces in and around Tripoli.

Another observer to the withdrawal of Palestinians from Beirut was Maj. Sa'ad Haddad, who had been invited by the IDF top brass to witness the PLO's departure from his land. Only the Phalangists refrained from open celebration. Their victory appeared hollow, their political and military agenda yet to be written.

Along the winding Beirut-Damascus Highway, more than 6,200 Syrian soldiers and guerrillas from the Palestine Liberation Army boarded buses, trucks, and tanks for the slow and precarious journey to the Syrian capital. In a remarkable, and tense, scene, Syrian BTR-60s and T-62s passed a long line of Israeli soldiers watching the historic event from the curb. The spectators standing less than two yards from the mile-long convoys included Brig. Gen. Amos Yaron and Brig. Gen. Menachem Einan. Both men were veteran combat officers and realized that the Syrian departure was a temporary respite. Now, perhaps, it was Israel's turn to depart as well.

The departure of the Palestinian and Syrian forces marked a turning point for Lebanon, and certainly the Middle East. On August 23, 1982, Bashir Gemayel was elected Lebanon's president. For the Gemayels, men who had worked their entire lives to see a Maronite-dominated Lebanon, the nation was now their own. For Begin and Sharon, the dream of an Israeli-Maronite alliance had finally materialized. It would, however, be short-lived. Days after his election, Bashir Gemayel informed Begin and Sharon that he would need a year's grace period before his government could even consider signing a peace accord with Israel. More importantly, Gemayel scoffed at Israel's request that Maj. Sa'ad Haddad be named military commander of southern Lebanon; instead, the Lebanese president-elect vowed that the renegade officer would be brought up on charges of treason and sentenced to death![90]

The ascension of Bashir Gemayel to the "Lebanese throne" shocked many seasoned intelligence officers in A'MAN, and especially the field KA'MANIM in Northern Command who were responsible for the day-to-day liaison with the Phalangist units "operating" in the field. The Phalangists had not fired a single shot, yet had managed to win the grand Lebanese sweepstakes. For the first time, open dissension was heard in the IDF camp, as senior officers vehemently disagreed with Israel's backing of just "one horse" in the mad reality of Lebanese politics. Although the Sharon-Begin-Eitan triumvirate was still in full support of Bashir, A'MAN officers began to contemplate the possibility of renewing military contacts with Danny Chamoun. Beyond any political situation, the IDF's principal concern was still the protection of northern Israel from terrorist attack; after all, this had been the prime objective of going to war in Lebanon. In the south, Israeli-backed Major Haddad began to consolidate his ragtag army and move northward—which was, in fact, a blunt message sent directly to the Gemayel clan in Bekfaya. Bashir was not the only man inside Lebanon's Christendom with whom Israel could work. Bashir could be expendable. Indeed, contacts were also established with Walid Jumblatt's Druze forces and Nabih Berri's Shiite Moslem Amal movement.

Yet Israel was not about to relinquish its seven-year investment in the Phalangists so quickly. On September 12, 1982, Defense Minister "Arik" Sharon and the MOSSAD's Nahik Nevot met with Bashir Gemayel in a typical Middle Eastern *sulkha*—the Arabic term for a meal and meeting where old animosities and angers are quickly forgotten—to advance the Israeli-Christian relationship to full-fledged military cooperation.[91] The topic of the meeting in Bekfaya was the question of the Palestinian terrorists, Lebanese Nasserites, and Syrian agents still at large in West Beirut. Sharon demanded that the Lebanese Forces clean up the western half of the city through force. Gemayel is reported to have supported this notion of settling old scores with great enthusiasm and spoke of turning the Moslem and Palestinian areas into a wasteland! Gemayel would not live to carry out this grand plan.

On September 14, at 1610, a powerful bomb destroyed the Phalangist party headquarters just as the Lebanese president-elect was concluding a fire-branding address to the party's leadership about the "Palestinian problem." The three-hundred-kilogram bomb had been planted by Habib Shartouni, an agent for the Syrian Socialist Nationalist Party ("SSNP"); the blast killed Bashir Gemayel and twenty-seven other party faithfuls. The Syrians had long viewed the brash and independent Gemayel as a threat to their goals: They were determined to dictate the course of Lebanese internal affairs, no matter what means were employed. Syria was a powerful factor in Lebanon's history that Israel had fatally underestimated. Defeated in the conventional fight for Lebanon, the Syrians had managed to destroy Israel's long-sought political objectives in the millisecond it took a bomb to explode.

Realizing that the assassination of the Phalangist leader would result in violence, IDF troopers stationed throughout Lebanon geared up for the inevitable carnage. Both Begin and Sharon, numbed at seeing their hard work destroyed by one deliberate act of destruction, knew that the Phalangists would seek revenge for the assassination of their leader and would probably target the Palestinians—even though they were not responsible for Bashir's death. With the PLO no longer a military presence in the city, the Palestinians were the logical scapegoat. A'MAN assessments concurred, predicting that Phalangist anger would result in a major massacre. A'MAN recommended that the IDF enter West Beirut *immediately* to protect the city's Moslem inhabitants and prevent the expected bloodbath. Saguy, in fact, viewed these circumstances as Israel's golden opportunity to distance herself from the Phalangists and cut the nation's losses before a major catastrophe came about.[92]

Before sunrise on September 15, squads of IDF paratroopers supported by armored units crossed the once infrangible Green Line and took up defensive positions throughout West Beirut. There was minor resistance to the Israeli move, mainly from the Nasserite Mourabitoun militia, but on the whole the operation went unopposed. An eerie calm engulfed the schizophrenic city. Almost everyone in the know realized that some sort of retribution was inevitable. One day later, the silence would end with volleys of automatic gunfire and unanswered cries for mercy.

From their observation post on a rooftop adjacent to the Shatilla refugee camp, Brigadier General Yaron and several A'MAN officers curiously watched as squads of heavily armed Lebanese Forces militiamen, dressed in full combat gear, entered the dusty shantytown. The Phalangists had been "allowed" to enter the West Beirut camps by Defense Minister "Arik" Sharon, but he had failed to inform A'MAN officers of the arrangement.[93] Ostensibly, the Christian soldiers were there to root out PLO stragglers who had failed to evacuate the Lebanese capital, but A'MAN officers followed the Christian troop movements closely; these were the troops who failed to participate in any phase of the conventional fighting during the summer months. Brigadier General Yaron warned Phalangist internal security chief Eli Hobeika that no innocent civilians were to be harmed, but Yaron's stern pleas for restraint were ignored. Hobeika simply shrugged off Yaron's warning and ordered his men to enter both the sprawling Sabra and Shatilla camps.

The killings in the camps commenced at 0700 on September 16. Several hours later, IDF Intelligence Corps radio monitors working out of the Aley HQ heard the Phalangists openly discussing a *dabha* ("massacre") transpiring inside Sabra and Shatilla; that fact was leaked to the esteemed military correspondent of the Israeli daily newspaper HA'ARETZ (a newspaper frequently called "the *New York Times* of Israel"), but little interest was displayed in the story. Indeed, it would take several days for the magnitude of the butchery to reach the world and the Israeli military and defense establishment. The two Israeli generals stationed near the two adjacent camps, in the southwestern portion of Beirut, had tried to force the Phalangists out of the camps, but their hands were tied by political sensitivities and standing orders not to enter either facility. In more than forty-eight hours of systematic slaughter, the Phalangists killed between four hundred and a thousand men, women, and children; an exact body count will never be known, but A'MAN estimates base the final toll at seven hundred to eight hundred dead.[94]

When the smoke cleared, the media was allowed to enter the camp and witness and film the bullet-ridden corpses filling the dust-filled alleyways. International reaction was that of pure horror. Initially, the Palestinians identified the perpetrators as "commandos from Major Haddad's militia," but Haddad's legions had not advanced that far; more importantly, they never would have perpetrated such carnage to retaliate the death of their arch rival Bashir Gemayel. It was obvious that the Phalangists had committed the atrocities, but the IDF was receiving the blame abroad and, remarkably, at home. The IDF chief of staff, Eitan, was not about to let the acts of brutal men stain the honor and pride of an army that maintained the highest moral standards of any fighting force in the world. During the invasion of Lebanon he had issued strict orders that Israeli soldiers restrain from harming innocent Lebanese civilians; in fact, many IDF troopers were killed by Palestinian fire as a result of overcautiousness when they held their fire in order to shield civilians.

An angry Raful flew to Beirut to scold his Phalangist counterpart, Gen. Fadi Frem, and demand that the Lebanese Forces admit their role in the massacre. Frem refused. So, too, did Sheikh Pierre Gemayel, who argued that any admission of guilt would harm the chances of his son Amin being elected as Lebanon's new president; Eli Hobeika violently vowed that he would not allow his men to be scapegoated. A'MAN had been exonerated: Their predictions had come true. Although the Military Intelligence director had tried unsuccessfully to prevent just such a disaster, the dead civilians did little to appease the soldier spies at A'MAN and HA'MAN headquarters.

Several days later in Tel Aviv's Kings of Israel Square, nearly four hundred thousand men, women, and children (roughly 10 percent of the entire Israeli population) participated in the nation's largest demonstration. Israelis were angry at their sanctimonious nation's relationship with a "bunch of thugs," according to one placard proudly displayed in the rally, and their military's involvement in such an abominable crime against humanity. In well-choreographed chants, the crowd began to scream "BEGIN, RAFUL VE'SHARON TZU MIYAD ME'LEVANON" ("Begin, Raful, and Sharon get out of Lebanon NOW!"). The chorus of rage engulfed the vibrant city. The cries for an end to the madness were also heard clearly in A'MAN HQ, in the KIRYA just a few blocks away.

The Sabra and Shatilla massacre had irreversible effects on the future of Lebanon and the realization of Israel's military aims as set forth in Operation Peace for Galilee. The Multi-National Force of Italian, French, and American soldiers, which had disembarked on Beirut's shores less than two weeks earlier in order to supervise the withdrawal of the Syrians and the Palestinians, now returned to protect the Palestinians (and the Lebanese, too—from each other), as well as to prop up the fledgling Lebanese government. Indeed, Amin Gemayel fulfilled his father's wishes and was elected, through deceit and the bayonet, as Lebanon's next president. The Syrians, provided with the golden opportunity to regroup their forces, were able to find new, more deadly surrogates in the Lebanese chaos and continue the conflict: the Druze, Shiites, and remaining Palestinian forces loyal to Damascus were soon on war's footing. Civil war once again erupted in Lebanon as tens of thousands of Israeli soldiers sat tight, praying for Jerusalem to bring them home. By December 1982, Operation Peace for Galilee had cost the casualty-conscious Israel Defense Forces 368 dead and 2,383 wounded.[95] More casualties would soon follow, nearly 500 more, as the conflict against the Shiites was set to begin. Already, journalists in Israel were calling Lebanon "Israel's Vietnam."

Lebanon proved to be the political death of Menachem Begin: The national outrage, and perhaps a sense of responsibility, humbled the once wily and undaunted political warlord. Acquiescing to public and opposition demands, Begin appointed a judicial board of inquiry to examine Israel's connection to the Sabra and Shatilla killings. Known as the "Kahan Commission," the board was chaired by Supreme Court president Yitzhak Kahan, Supreme Court justice Aharon Barak, and Maj. Gen. (Res.) Yona Efrat. It was tasked with uncovering all facts and factors relating to the massacre, as well as any possible Israeli role in the killing; the commission would also focus on and help uncover the relationship between the Phalangists and the Israeli intelligence community.[96] The Kahan Commission investigated the covert and convoluted details of Israel's Lebanon adventure for four months, hearing the testimony of fifty-eight witnesses—thousands of pages of transcripts. Naturally, the findings centered on Ariel Sharon, whom the commission labeled "remiss in his duties," and suggested—in terms uniquely delicate for Israeli politics—that the defense minister resign. He did not, and Begin was forced to remove him from office through edict. Chief of Staff Eitan and Major Generals Drori and Yaron all received mild rebukes.

A'MAN director Saguy would become the national scapegoat for the Lebanon disaster. He was found "grossly negligent" in his duties for not preventing the massacre and was forced to resign his post and retire from the IDF; he subsequently entered politics and, at the time of this book's writing, is a member of parliament. The one man who had campaigned for three years against Israel's involvement with the Christians was now held singularly responsible for the national failure. He would be the third A'MAN director forced to resign under controversial political circumstances. Israel's most important intelligence-gathering service was also at its most vulnerable.

Saguy was succeeded by Maj. Gen. Ehud Barak, the Young Turk officer who, as commander of SAYERET MAT'KAL, had revolutionized the abilities of the IDF special forces and special operations to mount intelligence-gathering forays deep behind enemy lines.[97] Barak, the IDF's most decorated and enigmatic soldier, was tasked with putting A'MAN's house back in order. His combat experience and highly respected career in the operational and planning departments of the Intelligence Corps and A'MAN were seen as the ideal resume. It would be a difficult task at a most difficult time, but perhaps Barak was the ideal choice as A'MAN director. He was a man of decisive action who in his career had commanded some of the most spectacular operations in Israeli military history, including Operation Isotope 1, SAYERET MAT'KAL's May 9, 1972, rescue of a hundred hostages aboard a Sabena Belgian Airliner at Israel's Lod Airport; Operation Basket, the June 21, 1972, kidnapping of five Syrian intelligence officers; and Operation Spring of Youth, the IDF's epic commando foray into Beirut. As a senior A'MAN officer in 1976, Barak was instrumental in the preparation and planning of Israel's Entebbe rescue.[98]

Indeed, A'MAN needed a charismatic and swashbuckling officer. The mid-1980s would prove a decisive period in Israeli military history.

On May 17, 1983, Lebanon—under the control of Amin Gemayel—and Israel signed accords to formally end the state of war that had existed between the two nations since 1948. The agreement sparked anger from Damascus and resulted in the Druze openly engaging the Christian-dominated and, now, American-trained and -supplied Lebanese army. A Syrian-sponsored rebellion against forces loyal to Yasir Arafat, led by renegade Palestinian Col. "Abu Mussa," besieged the PLO's final foothold in Lebanon in Tripoli, eventually forcing Arafat out of Lebanon for the second time in two years. Also, the Syrian-Iranian alliance that had been formed during the Iran-Iraq War was now earning rewards with the Shiite Amal and Hizbollah movements declaring a *jihad* ("holy war") against the State of Israel.

Naturally, A'MAN was troubled by the Syrians' ability to continue the war in Lebanon without actually participating in the fight. The IDF was concerned that the Syrians would manipulate the Lebanese internal strife, convincing them to make a military move against Israel either through southern Lebanon, or with a bid to retake the Golan Heights. To prevent any Syrian military surprises, Intelligence Corps observers, fully trained combat soldiers, monitored Syrian lines tenaciously. The "observers"—trained to operate observation equipment, guidance systems, and communications equipment; proficient in topography, field skills, and camouflage; and knowledgeable about the intricacies of the enemy's army—infiltrated Syrian lines to set up permanent listening and observation posts.[99] The most important monitoring position was atop Jebel Barouk, the former Syrian intelligence ELINT and VISINT observation post in the central Beka'a Valley. With the use of electro-optic equipment and TV cameras, Intelligence Corps personnel were able to clearly observe distant Syrian positions.[100] The highly detailed reports were sent back to A'MAN HQ, corroborated with data gathered by HUMINT, PHOTINT, and VISINT means, and then disseminated downward. In the course of the eventual Israeli withdrawal from Lebanon, which transpired from May 1983 to May 1985, the Intelligence Corps created a new term in the tradecraft glossary: VIDINT, for video intelligence. HA'MAN crews equipped with video cameras roamed nearly every inch of Lebanese territory under IDF control, videotaping the topographical signatures for future use—"just in case Israel would need to return for some unfinished business."[101]

Militarily, the IDF and A'MAN were in good shape to keep the north of Israel safe and monitor hostile developments in Lebanon. Yet the Syrians would not engage the Israeli military in open warfare. Instead they employed a long litany of proxy agents. And Israel's new enemies were not willing to play by conventional military rules: They had their own bloody and fanatic agenda. On November 4, 1983, a Shiite suicide truck bomber driving a green Chevrolet pickup crammed with half a ton of high explosives rammed the gate at the IDF/Border Guard/SHIN BET HQ near Tyre. Twenty-eight Israeli security officers were killed. The modus operandi was identical to that of the April 18, 1983, bombing of the U.S. Embassy in West Beirut, and the October 23, 1983, truck bombings of the French and U.S. Marine barracks. Israel's second Lebanon war had begun. It continues to this day.

Many historians and scholars have labeled the events in Lebanon the greatest failure in the history of Israeli intelligence. However, the mistakes made by both the MOSSAD and A'MAN were not ones of negligence or corruption, but of idealistic intentions and national security necessities. The feudal hell that is Lebanon has undone many great powers and, if history is any indicator, may harm others in the future.

NOTES: CHAPTER THIRTEEN

1. Various ed., "Sectarian with a New Vision," *Time* (September 27, 1982): 28.

2. Merav Arlozorov, "SOGRIM MA'AGAL," BAMACHANE (February 23, 1988): 13.

3. Emanuel Rosen, "HA'KLAF HA'CHAZAK SHEL SHOSHELET DAYAN," MA'ARIV SOF SHAVUA (February 5, 1988): 7.

4. United States Department of State, Bureau of Public Affairs, *Background Notes: Lebanon*, United States Government Printing Office (September 1984): 4.

5. Reuven Gal, *A Portrait of the Israeli Soldier* (New York: Greenwood Press, 1986), 240.

6. Yechiam Fadan, ed., "BITACHON YISRAEL: 40 SHANA LU'ACH IRU'IM," SKIRAT HODSHIT, Vol. 35, No. 3–4 (April 25, 1988): 76.

7. Oded Granot, HEYL HA'MODE'IN: TZAHAL BE'HEILO ENTZYKLOPEDIA LE'TZAVA ULE'BITACHON (Tel Aviv: Revivim Publishers, 1981), 145.

8. Samuel M. Katz, *Guards Without Frontiers: Israel's War Against Terrorism* (London: Arms and Armour Press, 1990), 159.

9. Ian Black and Benny Morris, *Israel's Secret Wars* (London: Hamish and Hamilton, 1991), 361.

10. *Ibid.* 362.

11. Eilan Kfir and Ya'akov Erez, TZAVA U'BITACHON (1968–81): TZAHAL BE'HEILO ENTZYKLOPEDIA LE'TZAVA ULE'BITACHON (Tel Aviv: Revivim Publishers, 1984), 159.

12. SAYERET HA'DRUZIM is one of the most remarkable of all IDF units. It was formed in 1968, at the suggestion of a Druze officer, Maj. Muhamed Mulla, who saw the need for the creation of an airborne-qualified reconnaissance force of Druze soldiers who could infiltrate the Druze Mountains in Lebanon and Syria for sabotage and intelligence-gathering operations should war erupt with Syria. SAYERET HA'DRUZIM has since flourished into one of the IDF's premier reconnaissance forces; they have participated in the War of Attrition, the 1973 War, the 1982 Lebanon War, the Intifadah, and countless "security" operations in between. Salim Kadur, "SAYERET HA'DRUZIM: HA'YACHSANIM SHEL HA'YACH'SAR," BAMACHANE (April 11, 1986): 42.

13. Yossi Melman and Dan Raviv, *The Imperfect Spies* (London: Sidgwick and Jackson, 1989), 284.

14. See Ian Black and Benny Morris, *Israel's Secret Wars*, 363.

15. Barbara Newman with Barbara Rogan, *The Covenant: Love and Death in Beirut* (New York: Crown Publishers, Inc., 1989), 22.

16. Ze'ev Schiff and Ehud Ya'ari, *Israel's Lebanon War* (New York: Simon and Schuster, 1984), 11.

17. In their book *Israel's Secret Wars*, authors Ian Black and Benny Morris claim that the Chamouns' contact with the MOSSAD came in Europe—probably in Paris. In their book *The Imperfect Spies*, authors Yossi Melman and Dan Raviv claim that the initial Christian contact with the MOSSAD came through the service's "Beirut Station," which was commanded by the elusive David Kimche. An English-born agent and senior MOSSAD official, Kimche was affectionately (or negatively!) known as "the man with the suitcase" because of his penchant for disappearing on top-secret missions without informing anyone. The *true* semantics of the beginning of the Christian-MOSSAD relationship, however, remain a secret to this day.

18. Jonathan C. Randal, *Going All the Way: Christian Warlords, Israeli Adventurers, and the War in Lebanon* (New York: Vintage Books, 1984), 200.

19. Tzvi Lavi, MI'UTIM: TZAHAL BE'HEILO ENTZYKLOPEDIA LE'TZAVA ULE'BITACHON (Tel Aviv: Revivim Publishers, 1983), 153.

20. See Ze'ev Schiff and Ehud Ya'ari, *Israel's Lebanon War*, 15.

21. *Ibid.* 16.

22. It is interesting to note that in the late 1980s, once the Christians' "Israel card" had been played, Lebanese Forces commanders turned to Saddam Hussein and Iraq, the arch rival of Syria for military dominance of the Arab world, for military aid. The Christians received tremendous supplies of ammunition and arms, including FROG-7 Soviet-produced surface-to-surface missiles, which were even fired at Damascus! Philippe Perinet, *"Armes! Petrole! Passeports! L'incroyable Imbroglio Du Proche-Orient,"* *Raids*, No. 41 (October 1989): 9. The subsequent carnage was absolute and ended only after Lebanese Forces commander Gen. Michelle Auon was forced to flee Lebanon. Syria finalized its subjugation of its neighbor to the east in January 1991, as a gift for its participation in the anti-Iraq coalition in Operation Desert Storm.

23. Michael Bar-Zohar and Eitan Haber, *The Quest for the Red Prince* (New York: William Morrow and Co., Inc., 1983), 208.

24. Bob Woodward, *Veil: The Secret Wars of the CIA 1981–87* (New York: Pocket Books, 1987), 270.

25. Other CIA assets in the Middle East included Jordan's King Hussein and Morocco's King Hassan II. In fact, it was King Hussein who urged the Lebanese Christians to seek Israeli military assistance in their struggle against the Palestinians and Syrians. See Yossi Melman and Dan Raviv, *The Imperfect Spies*, 286.

26. See Ian Black and Benny Morris, *Israel's Secret Wars*, 367.

27. See Yossi Melman and Dan Raviv, *The Imperfect Spies*, 287.

28. Ned Kelly, "Salty Crusaders: Sailing with the Christian Militia," *Soldier of Fortune* Magazine (December 1986): 55.

29. See Jonathan Randal, *Going All the Way*, 211.

30. *Ibid.* 214.

31. The chief intelligence officer at the time was Brig. Gen. Chaim Binyamini, an ex-reconnaissance paratrooper who personally led several spectacular commando operations during the 1967 War and the War of Attrition. See Oded Granot, HEYL HA'MODE'IN, 164.

32. *Ibid.* 146.

33. See Yossi Melman and Dan Raviv, *The Imperfect Spies*, 288.

34. Jonathan Beaty and S. C. Gwynne, "Not Just a Bank," *Time* (September 2, 1991): 57.

35. See Ian Black and Benny Morris, *Israel's Secret Wars*, 333.

36. *Ibid.* 333.

37. Steve Weissman and Herbert Krosney, *The Islamic Bomb: The Nuclear Threat to Israel and the Middle East* (New York: Times Books, 1981), 239.

38. Angus Deming, Milan J. Kubic, and Timothy Nater, "What Israel Knew," *Newsweek* (June 22, 1981).

39. See Steve Weissman and Herbert Krosney, *The Islamic Bomb*, 5.

40. In the weeks prior to the first Iranian raid on the Osirak facility, A'MAN director Saguy, in an interview with the Israeli press, even encouraged the Iranians to respond militarily by stating, "If I were an Iranian, *I*, too, would be worried about the Iraqi reactor." Shlomo Nakdimon, *First Strike* (New York: Summit Books, 1987), 155.

41. See Yossi Melman and Dan Raviv, *The Imperfect Spies*, 269.

42. Press release from the Iraqi Information Office, London, Great Britain, September 1980.

43. Shlomo Nakdimon, "TEISHA SHANIM LE'HAFTZATZAT HA'KUR HA'IRAQI: HADLAFOT," YEDIOT AHARONOT MOSAF SHAVU'OT (May 5, 1990): 1.

44. *Ibid.* 1.

45. Ronald Payne, *Mossad: Israel's Most Secret Service* (London: Bantam Press, 1990), 141.

46. See Ian Black and Benny Morris, *Israel's Secret Wars*, 333.

47. According to The International Center for Strategic Studies, as mentioned in BAMACHANE (February 27, 1991): 18.

48. See Shlomo Nakdimon, "TEISHA SHANIM," 1.

49. *Ibid.* 1.

50. *Ibid.* 1.

51. Lon Nordeen, *Fighters Over Israel* (New York: Orion Books, 1990), 167.

52. See Shlomo Nakdimon, *First Strike*, 224.

53. Much to the horror of the IDF Military Censor's Office, during his question-and-answer session with the press, Begin committed a military security blunder by disclosing a strictly held intelligence source when he stated, "Iraqi officials had pressured French technicians to get the reactor hot by July." *Ibid.* 239.

54. Steven Stasser, "A Risky Nuclear Game," *Newsweek* (June 22, 1981).

55. See Ze'ev Schiff and Ehud Ya'ari, *Israel's Lebanon War*, 32.

56. Shimon Shiffer, KADUR SHELEG SODOT MILCHEMET LEVANON (Tel Aviv, Edanim Publishers, 1984), 41.

57. See Ze'ev Schiff and Ehud Ya'ari, *Israel's Lebanon War*, 33.

58. Yehuda Tzur, "BEIN HA'MOSSAD LE'A'MAN," AL HA'MISHMAR (March 25, 1983): 3.

59. Oded Granot, "KVAR BE'CHODESH YULI, BE'A'AKAVOT TAKRIOT BE'SHUF, HIZHIR AGAF HA'MODE'IN MIPNEI SHITUF PE'ULAH IM HA'FALANGOT," MA'ARIV (February 11, 1983): 17.

60. See Ze'ev Schiff and Ehud Ya'ari, *Israel's Lebanon War*, 37.

61. *Ibid.* 42.

62. Ze'ev Klein, ed., HA'MILCHAMA BE'TERROR: U'MEDINIUT HA'BITACHON SHEL YISRAEL BE'SHANIM 1979–1988 (Tel Aviv: Revivim Publishers, 1988), 73.

63. See Yechi'am Fadan, ed., BITACHON YISRAEL, 83.

64. Richard A. Gabriel, *Operation Peace for Galilee* (New York: Hill and Wang, 1984), 48.

65. Guy Bachur, LEXICON ASHAF (Tel Aviv: Israel Ministry of Defense Publications, 1991), 174.

66. See Richard Gabriel, *Operation Peace for Galliee*, 49.

67. Gen. Dr. Mustafa Tlas, ed., *The Israeli Invasion into Lebanon* (Tel Aviv: Israel Ministry of Defense Publications, 1991), 458. This is a Hebrew translation of the original manuscript published in Syria by the Syrian defense minister and former chief of staff.)

68. See Richard Gabriel, *Operation Peace for Galilee*, 55.

69. Bill Gunston, *An Illustrated Guide to the Israeli Air Force* (London: Salamander Books Ltd., 1982), 156–157.

70. Eitan Haber, "HARBEI LIFNEI ARGOV," YEDIOT AHARONOT SHEVA YAMIM, (May 31, 1985): 14.

71. See Ian Black and Benny Morris, *Israel's Secret Wars*, 373.

72. See Ze'ev Schiff and Ehud Ya'ari, *Israel's Lebanon War*, 88.

73. Neil C. Livingstone and David Halevy, *Inside the PLO* (New York: William Morrow, 1990), 80.

74. See Ze'ev Klein, ed., HA'MILCHAMA BE'TERROR, 63.

75. See Ian Black and Benny Morris, *Israel's Secret Wars*, 374.

76. See Ze'ev Schiff and Ehud Ya'ari, *Israel's Lebanon War*, 106–107.

77. According to the film "Uzi," produced by the Israel Broadcast Agency, and televised on Israeli national TV on April 16, 1991.

78. Yigal Serena, "KUDKUD NOKEM KOREH," YEDIOT AHARONOT SHABBAT (June 6, 1987): 8.

79. Helena Cobban, *The Superpowers and the Syrian-Israeli Conflict* (New York: Praeger, 1991), 40.

80. See Ze'ev Schiff and Ehud Ya'ari, *Israel's Lebanon War*, 123.

81. *Ibid.* 190.

82. Emanuel Rosen, "TZAHAL MIMESH ET IKRON HA'HAFTA'AH—HA'OYEV HUFTAH MI'HA'MILCHAMA, ME'HIKFA, UME'YADAE'HA," BAMACHANE (July 28, 1982): 7.

83. Mordechai Barqay, "RA'AYON IM ROSH A'MAN," DAVAR (September 17, 1982): 19.

84. Raphael Israeli, ed., *The PLO in Lebanon: Selected Documents* (London: Weidenfeld and Nicolson, 1983), 81–147.

85. See Ze'ev Schiff and Ehud Ya'ari, *Israel's Lebanon War*, 179.

86. During the first three months of Operation Peace for Galilee, many of these weapons were displayed in Tel Aviv's Exhibition Park, and Intelligence Corps NCOs described the history of these guns and weapons systems to general audiences.

87. Hanoch Shinman, "EINAYIM SHELI," BAMACHANE (December 22, 1982): 12.

88. See Ze'ev Klein, ed., HA'MILCHAMA BE'TERROR, 70.

89. See Ian Black and Benny Morris, *Israel's Secret Wars*, 382.

90. *Ibid.* 383.

91. See Ze'ev Schiff and Ehud Ya'ari, *Israel's Lebanon Wars*, 254.

92. *Ibid.* 255.

93. Gideon Doron and Reuven Pedatzur, "Israeli Intelligence: Utility and Cost-effectiveness in Policy Formation," *International Journal of Intelligence and Counter-intelligence*, Vol. 3, No. 3, 347.

94. Although the tragic Sabra and Shatilla camp massacres have come to personify Lebanese brutality, Israeli and, later, Italian and French units from the Multi-National Force (MNF) uncovered an enormous ammunition dump concealed underneath the camps' catacombs and sewer system. Bruno Vespa, *Italia/Libano: Per La Pace* (Rome: Edizioni Fotogramma, 1983), 21.

95. See Richard A. Gabriel, *Operation Peace for Galilee*, 236.

96. See Ian Black and Benny Morris, *Israel's Secret Wars*, 388.

97. Emanuel Rosen, "HA'ISH SHE'HIMTZI ET HA'YECHIDA HA'MUVCHERET," MA'ARIV SOF SHAVU'A (September 19, 1990): 42.

98. Naomi Levitzki, "ALUF TEFLON," HADASHOT SHABBAT (July 21, 1989): 4–5.

99. Ron Schwartzman, "Observers Behind Syrian Lines," BAMACHANE (June 8, 1983): 17–18.

100. *Ibid.* 17.

101. Baruch Ron and Yair Silbersheleg, "LE'HAKDIM TMUNA LE'MAKA," BAMACHANE CHU'L (August 1984): 16.

CHAPTER 14

TERRORISTS AND UPRISINGS: A'MAN IN THE NEW WORLD ORDER

The Israeli intelligence community's "Lebanon MECHDAL" opened a Pandora's box of scandal and controversy that has yet to relinquish its grip. Whereas Operation Peace for Galilee rocked the foundations of A'MAN and the MOSSAD, subjecting the agencies to a period of self-doubt and public criticism, Israel's third intelligence force, the SHIN BET, was also exposed to public scrutiny and embarrassment in a harbinger of worse to come.

On April 12, 1984, four Palestinian terrorists seized the Number 300 intercity bus traveling between Tel Aviv and the southern Israeli city of Ashqelon and ordered it toward the Gaza Strip and the Egyptian frontier. The IDF and Border Guard police units stopped the bus on a small stretch of roadway at the Dir el-Balach Junction just outside the gates to the Gaza Strip, and a tense hostage standoff ensued. At 0443 on April 13, a force from, according to foreign reports, SAYERET MAT'KAL, commanded by chief paratroop and infantry officer Brig. Gen. Yitzhak Mordechai, stormed the bus and reportedly killed all four Palestinians aboard. A female soldier hostage, Cpl. Irit Portugez, was also killed in the assault. It was later revealed that two of the terrorists had indeed been killed by the well-placed ordnance of the commandos, but two others were captured alive. After a violent interrogation by Brigadier General Mordechai, the two survivors were taken into custody by SHIN BET agents, brought to a nearby citrus grove, and murdered. This incident would have remained concealed were it not for the Israeli daily newspaper HADASHOT ("News"), which made the decision to publish a front-page photograph of two SHIN BET security men with a visibly shaken Majdi Abu Shma'aha, one of the hijackers, in custody *without* submitting the story to A'MAN's Military Censor's Office prior to publication.[1]

The subsequent "Bus Number 300 Affair" rocked the very foundations of the SHIN BET; the agency's veil of secrecy was so absolute that many Israelis had not even known of the organization's existence. Journalist, and then government, scrutiny of SHIN BET activities uncovered further violations of the law, including the detention and torture of Lt. Iza'at Nafsu, a Circassian officer in the IDF who was accused of contact with the enemy while serving in southern Lebanon as part of the liaison with Major Haddad's forces. Espionage, agent-running, and the other dirty tricks involved in the IDF's and A'MAN's semipermanent observation facilities in southern Lebanon opposite Palestinian lines were commonplace, and Nafsu was accused, mainly because he was Circassian,* of being an el-Fatah agent. The popular IDF officer was brutally tortured by SHIN BET agents, who are also reported to have falsified much of the evidence used in the conviction. Nafsu was sentenced to eighteen years imprisonment in 1980, but was released in 1987 after the true story of his ordeal was uncovered.

The SHIN BET, too, had been badly bloodied in the Lebanon quagmire. They were dispatched into the Levantine wilderness to assist IDF and Border Guard forces in the identification and apprehension of known terrorist leaders, from PLO stragglers to Israel's new and lethal foe, the Amal and Hizbollah Shiite militiamen. On November 4, 1983, several SHIN BET officers were killed in the Hizbollah suicide truck-bombing attack on the IDF administrative headquarters near Tyre. For the SHIN BET, Lebanon was an anonymous and thankless campaign where interservice cooperation and tireless efforts proved insufficient, since they failed to prevent heavy casualties and an inevitable Israeli defeat.

The 1982 Israeli invasion of Lebanon was supposed to have eliminated the threat of Palestinian terrorism from the northern Israeli frontier, but Lebanon, Israel would learn, possessed an uncanny ability to rebound from invasion and counterattack in brutal fashion. The Phoenicians, Egyptians, Persians, Babylonians, Greeks, Romans, Arabs, Crusaders, Turks, French, Syrians, and, now, Israelis had all learned this costly lesson. The deadly capabilities of Israel's new northern frontier were underscored on March 10, 1985, when a suicide car bomber detonated his vehicle next to a convoy of IDF Ordnance Corps personnel. The attack resulted in thirteen IDF dead and twenty seriously wounded.[2] Galilee, once again, was besieged.

---

*The Circassians, along with the Druze Moslems (who are conscripted) and Bedouins of Galilee and the Negev, are the non-Jewish minorities who serve in the IDF and the National Police Border Guards.

Inside its self-established security zone in southern Lebanon, the IDF battled a savage war of attrition against the Shiite villages harboring the Hizbollah faithful—those same villages that in 1982 had welcomed the IDF invasion as liberation from PLO imprisonment. For IDF Military Intelligence, the "Shiite Campaign" was like nothing ever endured before. The superior technical means that A'MAN and the Intelligence Corps had deployed to defeat the Palestinians and Syrians in Operation Peace for Galilee were useless against the shadowy Shiite gunmen and car bombers, whose compartmentalized ultrasecretive cells and cryptic communications would have made the most sophisticated espionage service envious; it was a terrorist organization that could not be compromised by gadgets. Hizbollah had to be defeated through HUMINT means; their cells, mosque meetings, and communications network, including liaison with Iranian officials, needed to be infiltrated. Unfortunately for A'MAN, Hizbollah was not an entity that could easily be infiltrated. According to one Israeli intelligence expert, "Terrorist affiliations and Shiite terrorist bonds are based on religious or family bonds. One becomes a full-fledged member by birth, and even the most sophisticated intelligence service cannot falsify that reality for its own objectives."[3]

A'MAN did try, however, to obtain intelligence on the Shiite guerrillas through informers and spies, but this practice had limited success, since the local villagers feared Hizbollah much more than the IDF, A'MAN, or even the SHIN BET, and were *very* wary of betraying their own. It was a catch-22 situation: As one IDF officer serving in the security zone stated, "How do you deter people who *want* to martyr themselves?" A rare insight into A'MAN's HUMINT practices in southern Lebanon was gained when one recruited agent related his tale to a Syrian Ba'ath party newspaper. The agent, whose name was never disclosed, stated that he had been recruited by a "Major Ghazi," an Israeli Druze, who was an officer in IDF Military Intelligence. To "observe" the comings and goings of suspected guerrillas in his home town of Nabatiya, the agent was paid fifteen hundred Lebanese pounds; the more information received, the greater the financial reward. The agent did, indeed, disclose the whereabouts of several Hizbollah arms caches of B-7 antitank weapons, assault rifles, and grenades.[4] The agent, fearing for his own safety, then escaped to Damascus and turned himself in to Syrian authorities.

Hizbollah's methods of attack were also impossible to predict. The ability to strike on the spur of the moment in all weather and at all hours proved impossible for IDF intelligence assets to monitor and prevent. According to Brigadier General Y., commander of the IDF General Staff's Operations Unit, "Hizbollah enjoys striking at close range, at night (unlike the Palestinian terrorist groups), and with the minimum of conventional military preparation."[5]

The problem of engaging a virtually invisible enemy was an enormous operational strain for the beleaguered IDF units stationed in the security zone, and a costly one as well. The car bombings and hit-and-run attacks perpetrated by the ready-to-be-martyred militiamen continued in an indiscriminate and bloody fashion. On March 17, 1985, a Hizbollah terrorist squad ambushed an IDF patrol in the Shiite stronghold of Jibchit, located in southwestern Lebanon; the town was the largest Shiite center close to the security zone and was also home to Sheikh Abdul Karim Obeid, a senior Hizbollah commander. On April 9, 1985, a female Shiite suicide bomber blew herself up, together with two IDF troopers manning a roadblock, near Jezzine. Such attacks accelerated the IDF withdrawal to the safety of their self-declared security zone.

The Intelligence Corps and A'MAN relied on observation posts and heavily fortified towers located in villages and towns to monitor the late-night movements of the guerrillas. Infrared and night scopes used by the Intelligence Corps observers denied the Shiite terrorists their most popular form of camouflage—darkness. It was in this bitter campaign that the unit intelligence officers came into their own. KA'MANIM joined active patrols to observe enemy methods of deployments in the field. The KA'MAN's most valuable means of gathering intelligence, however, was through retaliatory raids against known Hizbollah villages following an attack on IDF personnel. The search and seizure operations that characterized the IDF's iron fist policy in dealing with Shiite terrorism afforded the unit intelligence officer the opportunity to interrogate suspects and examine seized documentation. A'MAN was, however, able to follow the terrorists' armaments acquisition program through open sources. For example, HATZAV personnel, reading through the pages of the Italian newspaper *Corera de-la Sera*, were able to uncover the fact that the Iranian government, acting on behalf of Hizbollah, had purchased several hang gliders from the French firm *Da Bufel* and had them sent to Lebanon.[6] As will be seen later in this chapter, the hang glider would prove itself a most lethal platform for terrorist attack. The data compiled by A'MAN was disseminated to field units—especially IAF Air Defense units stationed in northern Israel, which were not used to engaging airborne targets.

Following the IDF's retreat to the security zone, defense of the zone fell mainly to the remnants of Haddad's pro-Israeli militia. Major Sa'ad Haddad had died of cancer on January 13, 1984, and command of the newly revamped "South Lebanon Army" (SLA), with its arms and Israeli training, was transferred to Gen. Antoine Lahad. Haddad's death created a vacuum along the embattled "Purple Line"—not militarily but psychologically, causing an undermining of Israeli confidence.[7] A'MAN involvement in the SLA increased. It was the only true barrier between the Israeli frontier and the legions of Palestinian and Shiite guerrillas who consolidated positions in the south abandoned by the IDF.

Terrorism, in fact, remained at the forefront of the Israeli intelligence community's agenda. While the Palestinians in Lebanon, Tunisia, and elsewhere in the Middle East regrouped and planned, the Shiites initiated a war against Israel and the West. It would be a conflict that would test the talents and imagination of A'MAN's soldier spies far beyond the boundaries of the State of Israel and in close cooperation with Israel's most important military ally.

On June 14, 1985, TWA Flight 847, a routine shuttle connection between Athens and Rome, was hijacked moments after its landing gear folded up for the sixty-minute journey. The aircraft was seized by two Arab men, Lebanese Shiites armed with 9mm automatic pistols—which had been easily smuggled on board through the lax security apparatus at the airport most favored by Middle Eastern terrorists—and forced to head for Beirut. The Lebanese initially balked at the aircraft's "request" to land at Beirut International Airport, but the pilot, John Testrake, running out of fuel and with a fragmentation grenade held to his head, landed there anyway. The aircraft was refueled and two masked Hizbollah gunmen, armed with AK-47s, boarded the aircraft. Over the next several hours, the hijacked aircraft proceeded to zigzag across two continents, eventually landing in Algiers. After freeing several hostages, mainly women and children, as a humanitarian gesture, the terrorists proceeded to bind and beat a twenty-three-year-old U.S. Navy diver, Robert Stethem, and then shoot him in the head and dump his body onto the darkened tarmac.[8] The aircraft later returned to Beirut, where the hostages were conveniently distributed throughout the Shiite slums of western Beirut.

The hijacking was clearly an American matter: The aircraft was a United States carrier, the murder victim was a United States serviceman, and the only hostages detained were Americans. But Israel was the deciding factor in the situation. During the hijackers' first stopover in Beirut, they aired their demands to the international press: Israel was to release seven hundred Shiite holy warriors whom they had captured in southern Lebanon, and the United States was to denounce its support of the Jewish state. If the demands were not met, the hostages would be systematically murdered. Israel found itself in the middle once again.

Initially, the United States planned a military solution to the crisis. A reaction center was quickly set up in the office of the Joint Special Operations Agency, an entity established in 1984 to advise the Joint Chiefs of Staff on possible military solutions in terrorist and hostage-holding scenarios. Israel realized that the Americans would probably not sit still for this latest outrage and volunteered the use of its territory as a staging ground for the American Delta Force and SEAL Team 6 commandos. A'MAN and MOSSAD assets, mainly SIGINT and background data, were of tremendous assistance to the Pentagon planners, but a military response was never implemented. Political maneuvering and American pressure on Israel to release the seven hundred Shiites ended the ordeal days later.

Nevertheless, the TWA hijacking crisis brought the United States and Israel in a zenith of antiterrorist and shared-intelligence cooperation. The special relationship was known only by a handful of individuals in Washington (defense secretary Caspar Weinberger, assistant secretary of defense for international security policy Richard Armitage, Joint Chiefs of Staff Gen. John Vessey, and CIA director Bill Casey and his deputy Bill Gates); the Israeli end of the operation was handled by defense minister Lt. Gen. (Res.) Yitzhak Rabin, former MOSSAD officer and Foreign Ministry official David Kimche, IDF Chief of Staff Lt. Gen. Moshe Levy, and, of course, A'MAN director Maj. Gen. Ehud Barak.[9] Barak, the ex–SAYERET MAT'KAL commander and the IDF's most decorated soldier, took over the reins at A'MAN in 1983. He was a man of action, especially involving counterterrorist operations. The American responsible for the Israeli liaison was a charismatic marine officer serving on the National Security Council (NSC), Lt. Col. Oliver North. Through Lieutenant Colonel North in the NSC and Maj. Gen. Uri Simchoni, the IDF attaché in Washington,[10] the special NSC/A'MAN relationship was nurtured. A series of spectacular events in the autumn of 1985 would test this newfound intelligence alliance in glorified fashion.

The year 1985 would be one of decisive action in Israel's war against terrorism, as the Palestinians, too, engaged in the international hunt for the headlines.

On the night of September 10, 1985, an IDF/navy patrol boat, utilizing extremely accurate intelligence, seized a Lebanese ferry ship, the SS *Opportunity*, running what the IDF angrily called the "Terrorist Express," traveling between the Phalangist-controlled port of Jounieh and Larnaca, Cyprus.[11] The crew of the IDF/navy vessel, heavily armed and wearing flak vests, boarded the *Opportunity* and found one extremely important passenger: Faisal Abu Sharah, a senior officer in Force 17; at the time of his capture, he was military chieftain of the sprawling terrorist-recruiting centers at the Sabra and Shatilla refugee camps in Beirut. The crewmen quickly blindfolded Abu Sharah and brought him to an IDF detention center in Israel, where for twenty days he underwent a series of questioning sessions by A'MAN personnel; he was later transferred to a SHIN BET facility somewhere in Israel. Defense Minister Yitzhak Rabin signed an administrative detention order to hold Abu Sharah for at least six months. He was eventually tried and convicted of membership in a hostile organization, and sentenced to eight years' imprisonment.

Abu Sharah was a twenty-one-year veteran of el-Fatah and had been a Force 17 officer since 1972. He had been sent to the Eastern bloc for advanced training and was even part of Yasir Arafat's personal entourage for more than a year. The capture of so senior a commander sounded an alarm throughout the Palestinian diaspora; such men were not routinely rousted from their slumber on board Phalangist-hired ferries and brought back to Israel. In PLO offices from Amman to Tunis, Algiers to South Yemen, agents of Abu Iyad's Intelligence and Security Apparatus, the PLO's principal post-Razd intelligence and counterintelligence arm of el-Fatah, conducted a search for Israeli intelligence agents who had infiltrated the Palestinians' ranks.

Although no traitors were found (several unfortunate individuals were questioned and "attended to"), Force 17 commanders were convinced that their colleague had been captured as a result of the work of the MOSSAD or A'MAN and ordered their agents to seek out and assassinate Zionist agents. Palestinian agents conducted surveillance in all Mediterranean ports used by their officers, with special attention dedicated to Jounieh and Larnaca.

On September 25, 1985, three Israeli civilians, two middle-aged men and a woman, enjoying a brief vacation in Larnaca harbor, Cyprus, were taken hostage on board their yacht by three Force 17 gunmen who believed them to be MOSSAD agents. After a brief standoff with Cypriot police units who were not at all interested in engaging the terrorists, the two Palestinians and Ryan Michael Edison, a British Neo-Nazi National Front faithful who had volunteered for el-Fatah in 1982 and served with Force 17 in North Yemen and Tunisia, opted to murder the three Israelis and then politely surrender to authorities. The PLO immediately denied any involvement in the botched operation, but the three Force 17 gunmen confessed to everything, including their orders to kill MOSSAD agents.

The murders occurred on Yom Kippur Day, and the audacity of the attack outraged the usually low-key Israeli prime minister, Shimon Peres. On September 26, Peres summoned seven of his senior cabinet ministers to discuss retaliation. Some figures, such as Ezer Weizman, opposed any Israeli action, since, it was argued, a retaliatory strike might dampen the mood for peace negotiations that were emanating from several Arab capitals at the time, and damage Israel's weak relationship with Hosni Mubarak's Egypt. "Arik" Sharon, the coalition government's leading hawk, urged the prime minister to authorize a strike against PLO offices in Amman and Jordan, and the office of Abu Jihad, the PLO deputy and military commander, in particular; Force 17 maintained a quasiheadquarters in the Jordanian capital and had threatened, through third parties, to intensify its terrorist war against Israel if Abu Sharah was not released.[12] Peres opted for the compromise solution proposed by Rabin: The IAF would mount an air raid on the PLO headquarters at Hammam ash-Shatt, situated on the Mediterranean coast twelve miles south of Tunis.

From an intelligence point of view, Tunis was an ideal choice for a target. With a weak military, Tunisia was much less a gamble than hitting a PLO office in Jordan and risking an engagement with the Royal Jordanian Air Force or their America-supplied HAWK SAM batteries. For A'MAN, Tunisia was also an "easier" hostile state on which to gather intelligence. Of all the Arab and

North African states, Tunisia was the most open nation, a semiautocracy, more prone to advancing tourism than maintaining a police state or engaging in military folly. In the "open sources" archives of HATZAV, there was reported to be plentiful information on Tunis, and the PLO compound, in particular. The Israeli intelligence community, both the MOSSAD and A'MAN it has been reported, maintained an impressive HUMINT infrastructure inside the Tunisian capital—an operation that greatly intensified following the PLO's 1982 move to Tunis. HUMINT sources were able to provide A'MAN with highly detailed information concerning the layout of the PLO complex. Remarkably, both the MOSSAD and A'MAN had recruited a number of Tunisian government and security officials, utilizing the tradecraft ruse known as "false flag"; the agents were told that they would be spying for a "European" government.[13] While these false-flag victims were motivated primarily by greed, some Tunisian assets were, indeed, recruited with the knowledge that they would be working for Israeli intelligence.[14] *

Major General Ehud Barak's A'MAN was not solely concerned with detailing the target for the attacking Israeli pilots. A'MAN had to provide an exhaustive operational intelligence report to the IAF on possible hostile forces or actions that might be encountered en route to or returning from the target. SIGINT efforts were intensified to provide an accurate electronic portrait of the Tunisian Air Force and their air defenses (just in case), and data on the Libyan Air Force and their air defenses (in case the flight of attacking aircraft was intercepted by Colonel Qaddafi's fighters over the Mediterranean) needed to be examined and detailed as well.

In the last days of September an IDF/navy missile boat carrying a helicopter and a force of commandos from the IAF's elite Aeromedical Evacuation Unit (AEU) headed for on-call status off the coast of Malta. If any aircraft were shot down over enemy territory, the AEU would quickly rescue the pilots.[15]

At dawn on October 1, 1985, eight F-15 Eagles took off from an anonymous air base in northern Israel, followed, forty minutes later, by a flight of F-16 Falcons. Halfway to Tunis, just beyond the waters off Crete, the F-16s were refueled by a Boeing 707 tanker, and then the menacing formation split into a low-level pattern for the stealthy, radar-evading journey to Tunis. According to foreign reports, a Boeing 707 ECM platform flew over the Tunisian capital, jamming radars and rendering air defenses useless, while a Grumman

<hr>

*An article in *Defense and Foreign Affairs Weekly*, Vol. XII, No. 29 (August 4–10, 1986) suggested that Israel's intelligence-gathering abilities in North Africa were augmented by the MOSSAD's close-knit relationship with the Moroccan foreign espionage service, the Directorate-General for Studies and Documentation (DGED). The report also claimed that the MOSSAD and A'MAN were responsible for the training of Moroccan intelligence and security units.

E-2C Hawkeye, the IAF's AWACS, circled the city directing the attack. At 1000, the F-16s swooped in from the heavens and began a precision run against three installations: Arafat's headquarters, situated in three one-story buildings; the Force 17 command office (where its commander, Abu Tayeb, sat); and the offices of the el-Fatah operations chief, Abu Muatassem, whose unit was responsible for actions in southern Lebanon and for the planning of terrorist attacks against Israel in the Mediterranean.[16] The attacking aircraft flew so low that eyewitnesses on the ground could identify the IAF Star of David on the wings and fuselages.

The F-16s unloaded a deadly array of bombs directly on target. The devastation was complete. Arafat's command center was reduced to a pile of twisted steel and disintegrated concrete. In the attack, sixty-five people, including ten Tunisian security guards, were killed; A'MAN had taken painstaking precautions to prevent the unnecessary deaths of civilians, as did the attacking IAF aircraft. Although the PLO claimed that the air strike killed *only* innocent civilians, the flag-draped funerals that soon followed indicated that some important senior officers had found their details in the rubble, including four men instrumental in the Palestinians' naval effort against Israel.

Mysteriously, or "coincidentally," Arafat had left his complex only moments before the first bombs hit their mark. Visibly shaken as he observed the damage, Arafat vowed revenge. It would not be long in coming. On the night of October 6, 1985, two Israeli merchant seamen in Barcelona, Spain, were kidnapped and murdered by Force 17 assassins.[17] The chain of events was escalating into uncontrollable violence, involving a most dangerous and cold-blooded faction of Arafat's PLO.

On the night of October 6, 1985, the Italian cruise liner *Achille Lauro* was in the middle of its eleven-day cruise. The ship's 750 passengers were enjoying gourmet Italian cuisine and the calming Mediterranean waters, and were preparing to land at Port Said the following morning, where they would make a short land trip to Cairo, then travel to Israel and rejoin the ship in Ashdod, a major Israeli port south of Tel Aviv. The next morning 666 passengers departed, leaving 97 passengers and 315 crew members on board for the short hop to Israel. Also on board the luxury liner were four young men who kept to themselves, remaining in their cabins for most of the journey. Although they spoke Arabic to one another, they claimed to be Norwegian students. The four were, in fact, gunmen from the Abu Abbas Faction of the Palestine Liberation Front.

Their mission, which according to intelligence sources was planned as far back as 1984—to be ordered only after a major Israeli incident such as the bombing of the PLO's Tunis HQ—was a complex, highly imaginative gamble that would result either in a bloodbath or a victory for Palestine. Supplied with explosives and weaponry, the four were dispatched to Genoa on October 4. According to the plan, when the *Achille Lauro*'s passengers disembarked at Ashdod, the four heavily armed gunmen would take them hostage and demand that Israel release 150 Palestinian terrorists held in Israeli jails.

Abu Abbas, the pudgy terrorist chieftain who had once worked for Ahmed Jibril's PFLP-GC, realized that this operation was a tremendous gamble. Topping the list of the terrorists to be released was Sami Kuntar, a man involved in one of the most brutal terrorist incidents ever recorded in Israeli history. On the night of April 22, 1979, four seaborne PLF terrorists landed on the Nahariya shore and proceeded to attack a block of apartment buildings. Indiscriminately searching for victims, they came upon the Haran family and, after hearing the sirens of encroaching police vehicles, took Danny Haran and his four-year-old daughter to the shoreline for a final stand against the Israeli security forces. Smadar Haran had managed to hide when her husband and daughter were abducted, but tragically suffocated her infant daughter while trying to stifle the baby's screams. As a force of GOLANI infantrymen inched their way toward the beachfront, Kuntar took a boulder and smashed it into the head of the four-year-old Haran girl; he then aimed the barrel of an AK-47 at the head of Danny and put the bereaved parent out of his misery. Seconds later, a firefight erupted and two terrorists were killed and two seized.[18] The horrific details of the murders in Nahariya prompted even the most liberal of Israelis to demand the death penalty, and made Abu Abbas a wanted man.[19]

Unfortunately for Abu Abbas, his four-man squad never made it to Ashdod. At dinnertime on the night of October 7, the four terrorists were cleaning their weapons and preparing explosive charges when a steward inadvertently entered their stateroom. A comical moment of shocked silence ensued, but the terrorists realized that their cover had been blown. In an impromptu attempt to save themselves, they gathered their gear and proceeded to take control of the ship. According to A'MAN radio intercepts and information revealed by Italian Defense Minister Giovanni Spadolini, the terrorists, utilizing the ship's sea-to-shore radiotelephone, contacted a PLF controller in Genoa, who, in turn, called Arafat's HQ in Tunis for final instructions.[20]

Initially, the *Achille Lauro* seajacking appeared to be solely an Israeli matter. A'MAN radiomen had monitored the announcement that the ship had been seized by *Palestinian* gunmen, that the vessel was extremely close to Israeli territorial waters, and, it appeared, that the terrorists would demand the release of their jailed comrades in Israel in exchange for the safe return of the ship and the hostages. But, in an odd twist of fate that in many ways paralleled the hijacking of TWA Flight 847, the seizure of the *Achille Lauro* developed into an *American* matter. The ship was in no position to continue on to Ashdod, and, with the majority of the hostages being American tourists, it was clear that demands and responses would be coming from Washington—especially after the gunmen collected all the passports and isolated the Americans, separating those with Jewish names for "special treatment." Hours later, after the *Achille Lauro* was refused permission to dock in the

Syrian port of Tartus, the enraged terrorists singled out a wheelchair-bound sixty-nine-year-old American named Leon Klinghoffer as the first hostage to be killed. The youngest of the terrorists, al-Hassan, shot Klinghoffer point-blank in the forehead and chest; the gunman's clothing was splattered with the victim's blood. After joking in Arabic with his comrades, he ordered a group of terrified waiters to throw the body and wheelchair overboard. The body washed up several days later on a Syrian beach.

The Italians, who had initially balked at claiming responsibility for the incident, now prepared to dispatch commandos from the "Groupe Interventional Speciale" of the national Carabinieri to mount a seaborne rescue operation; at the same time, IDF/navy vessels were dispatched to follow and monitor the hijacked liner. Yet it was the Americans who made it clear that they would take the active role in any rescue bid. From Charleston Air Force Base, elements of the U.S. Navy's SEAL Team 6 were flown to the British Royal Air Force Base in Akrotiri, Cyprus, as were members of the U.S. Army's ultrasecretive Delta Force, flown out from their home base in Fort Bragg, North Carolina.[21] The Americans would, indeed, act militarily, but before the campaign was executed over the Mediterranean skies, it would first be waged in the top-secret decision centers in Tel Aviv and Washington.

From the outset of the bungled drama, it was obvious to A'MAN that the perpetrators of the seajacking were members of the Abu Abbas Faction of the PLF. A'MAN's Eavesdropping Unit was monitoring all Palestinian radio networks, and one of their monitors had picked up a cryptic message from an anonymous figure named "Abu Khaled," sent to the hijackers via Radio Monte Carlo, the PLO's principal radio station transmitting from Cyprus to the "Occupied Territories" and Lebanon. A quick search through the Intelligence Branch files and the name "Abu Khaled" appeared next to a photograph of Abu Abbas. The data was transmitted to Washington and the U.S. Navy's Sixth Fleet.

The Americans were unable to locate the *Achille Lauro*, but the Israelis were—a DABUR patrol craft had tailed the slow-moving *Achille Lauro* and was relaying its position back to Tel Aviv. To the IDF/navy and A'MAN, it was apparent that the *Achille Lauro* hijackers were confused about what they should do and so were sailing what seemed to be the safest course back to Egypt. The Americans by now were in hot pursuit of the *Achille Lauro*, with SEAL Team 6 commandos poised on a naval platform to launch a heliborne raid on the ship. The frogmen would be dropped from a chopper into the Mediterranean, swim to the ship underwater, then board the ship and quickly eliminate the terrorists. The only scenario that would prevent an American rescue operation was a turnabout in the terrorists' position: In the eyes of the Arab world, the United States could not attack the terrorists if they signaled that they would surrender.

On October 8, 1985, A'MAN monitors discovered that "Abu Khaled" had departed his Tunis lair and headed to the Egyptian harbor at Port Said, ostensibly, as he told members of the Arab press, to oversee the situation as a third-party observer on *humanitarian* grounds. In fact, he had been dispatched by Arafat to see the situation through to an acceptable end.[22] Even before the cowardly killing of Leon Klinghoffer was made public, the botched hijacking was a crushing embarrassment for Arafat's PLO, and it had to end as soon as possible if the organization was to maintain the "moderate" image it was touting in the capitals of Western Europe.

In Port Said, Abbas was afforded "diplomatic" status and all the provisions of a dignitary. His first request was use of the shore-to-ship telephone so that he could contact his men. Abu Abbas assumed the security of PLF communications to be absolute. Little could he know that his conversation was being taped by A'MAN. Major General Barak released the tape eight days later during a live Israeli television broadcast. As Barak discussed the terrorists' true objectives, he hit the "play" button on a cassette tape player; the conversation went as follows:

> Port Said: "This is 'Abu Khaled' speaking to the ship. How do you hear me? Over."
> Ship (code-named "Jihad"): "Send."
> Port Said: "You had better calm down. 'Abu Khaled' requests that you *protect* the passengers and keep them safe."
> Ship: "We'll call you back."
> (A brief pause interrupts the communication.)
> Port Said: "Who is this on the line . . . is this Majid [the code name of one of the terrorists]?"
> Ship: "Yes . . . yes . . . yes!"
> Port Said: "How are you, Majid?"
> Majid: "Praise Allah."
> Port Said: "Listen very carefully. You must treat the passengers *very* well. You must also apologize to them, the ship's captain, and the ship's crew and explain to them that *our* objective was not to seize the ship. Explain to them what our initial objective *was*. Do you hear me?"
> Majid: "Yes, yes, we spoke with them and explained that we did not intend to seize the ship. Can you please send me a sign that 'Abu Khaled' is, indeed, transmitting these messages? Over."[23]

Throughout the ordeal, the communications and liaison channel that had been established between the Israeli intelligence community and the NSC remained a viable routing of top-secret information and classified cables. In fact, from the first time that Lt. Col. Oliver North contacted IDF attaché Major General Simchoni in Washington, a secure line had been kept open between

A'MAN HQ in Tel Aviv, the Israeli Embassy in Washington, and the White House.[24] That communications link would prove invaluable the following day.

Lieutenant Colonel North had learned through the American intelligence apparatus of a series of secret deals between Egyptian President Hosni Mubarak, Italian Premier Craxi, and PLO chairman Arafat, calling for the safe return of the ship and hostages to Egypt, and for the terrorists' *safe* passage back to Tunis. It appeared that terrorism had once again won the day; even the SEAL Team 6 commandos were being ordered home. Frantic diplomatic efforts were made to convince the Egyptians to release the *Achille Lauro* seajackers to either American or Italian custody. Egyptian President Mubarak cabled the White House to inform the national security advisor, Bud McFarlane, that diplomatic pressure was in vain, since the terrorists, having departed the hijacked vessel by means of a tugboat, were already *out* of Egypt en route to Tunis. McFarlane did not believe Mubarak and ordered North to "clarify the situation."

The first confirmation of deceit was relayed to the White House by the American ambassador in Egypt, Nicholas Veliotes, who, fearing a Palestinian fait accompli, boarded the *Achille Lauro* off Port Said. Once on board, the horrified U.S. ambassador learned of Klinghoffer's murder; using the same ship-to-shore telephone that the terrorists had used to communicate with Abu Abbas, Veliotes issued the following, now infamous, demand to his colleagues in Cairo: "I want you to contact the Egyptian foreign minister, tell him what we've learned, tell him the circumstances, tell him that in view of this and the fact that we, and presumably they, didn't have those facts, we insist that they prosecute those *sons of bitches*! The second thing: I want you to pick up the phone and call Washington and tell them what we've done. If they want to follow up, that's fine." [25] Indeed, the hunt was now on.

North contacted his most reliable intelligence source, A'MAN, and asked the Israelis if they had a "handle" on the four terrorists. Simchoni, speaking from the embassy, said he needed to call Tel Aviv but would get back to the White House a half hour later. A'MAN radio intercepts, gathered through a sprawling COMINT facility in the Negev Desert,[26] were remarkable in their ability. Not only could A'MAN eavesdrop on seemingly secured communications conducted between Mubarak and his close governmental and security officials, but could also monitor a telephone conversation between the commander of the Egyptian Muchabarat and a "volunteer" Egypt Air pilot who was to fly the four terrorists, Abu Abbas, and O'zzudin Badrak Kan, the PLF's chief of military operations,[27] to Tunis. Not only was the flight plan discussed, but important details, including the fact that heavily armed Egyptian As-Saiqa commandos would also be on board, were disclosed. Even though U.S. Secretary of Defense Weinberger, a man not known for his pro-Israeli sympathies, had ordered the U.S. intelligence apparatus *not* to be in contact with A'MAN

HQ, the SIGINT intercept from the Negev was rushed, via Tel Aviv and Major General Simchoni, to Lieutenant Colonel North's desk.[28]

The subsequent action taken by the United States was a dramatic and bold statement of not only America's sincere resolve to combat terrorism but of the energetic and innovative means employed by Lieutenant Colonel North to execute the American decision. Through a special link established between Major General Barak and North (who was in the White House situation room), A'MAN was able to supply the Americans with the Egypt Air Boeing 737's tail number, and radio and radar call signs, only moments after it took off from Cairo airport. The data that A'MAN commander Barak supplied to Lieutenant Colonel North was immediately transmitted to the aircraft carrier USS *Saratoga*, which, in turn, launched Grumman E-2C Hawkeyes to conduct aerial surveillance of the congested air lanes and F-14 Tomcat fighters to intercept the Egypt Air jet. A'MAN, too, was utilizing its HUMINT and SIGINT abilities in and around Egypt to track the Boeing 737's coordinates.[29]

A'MAN was by no means a passive observer to the American effort. When the U.S. Navy needed time for its scrambled aircraft to locate and intercept the Egyptian aircraft, Israel's specially modified intelligence-gathering Boeing 707 was launched and flown over the Mediterranean. Arabic-speaking experts sitting at computerized consoles monitored *all* military and civilian communications within its still-classified range, as well as transmitting some deceitful messages of its own. An A'MAN officer, utilizing the frequency of the Tunis air traffic controller and speaking in a perfect Tunisian dialect, informed the pilot of the Egypt Air jet that he was denied permission to land.[30] As the perplexed Egyptian pilot flew in circles around the island of Crete, pondering what to do, a flight of sleek swept-wing Tomcats flew beside the plane and forced it to land at the NATO air base in Sigonella, Sicily. Awaiting the aircraft on the ground were units from SEAL Team 6 and Delta Force, who had been ordered back into the Mediterranean once Lieutenant Colonel North's plan was put into motion.

It appeared, if only for a brief and long overdue instance, that the American and Israeli intelligence communities had scored an astounding victory over terrorism. Palestinian terrorism was dealt a humiliating blow equal in magnitude to the failed hijacking to Entebbe in 1976. For the United States, the intelligence alliance with Israel had produced invaluable dividends—especially considering that many of the American intelligence assets in the region, both human and on file, were lost when Hizbollah destroyed the U.S. Embassy in Beirut in April 1983, and when "Islamic Jihad" kidnapped William Buckley, the CIA station chief in Lebanon, and tortured him to death. Yet as thumbs-up signs were displayed in Washington, and A'MAN officers slapped one another on the back for a job well done, a major snag emerged to jeopardize the short-lived American-Israeli coup.

Just as the American commandos, weapons poised for action, approached the stopped airliner, an imposing force of Italian Carabinieri was on its way to the tarmac to save Abu Abbas. While events were unfolding over the Mediterranean, the Italians and Egyptians, with PLO insistence, had concluded a top-secret, face-saving arrangement. The Italians could keep the four seajackers, but Abu Abbas and his military operations chief were to be provided with a diplomatic escape—allowing Yasir Arafat to deny any connection to the botched operation. The Americans wanted Abbas; so, too, did the Israelis, who had long sought his capture or "permanent disappearance."

The black-clad American commandos boarded the aircraft and, after a tense confrontation with the Egyptian commandos and Abu Abbas, were prepared to remove the human bounty and shuffle them on board an awaiting C-141B transport back to Washington for judicial action. But troops from the Carabinieri (Italy's elite paramilitary police force) intervened, forming a defensive ring around the American commandos. A very tense standoff ensued. The shouting match between the American commanding officer, General Stiner, and his Carabinieri counterpart was so loud that it could be heard over the 737's engines.[31] In the end, however, General Stiner was forced to call his men off. Italian Premier Craxi was determined to show his constituents that Italy was not an American puppet; the Americans understood that the apprehension of one of the world's most notorious terrorist warlords was not worth the eruption of combat between two NATO allies. As four nervous Palestinians were taken into Italian custody, a smiling Abu Abbas and O'zzudin Kan were escorted to a secluded airstrip at Sigonella, where they boarded a flight to Rome, then to Yugoslavia and on to Baghdad; Abu Abbas was carrying *Iraqi* diplomatic credentials. Triumph had been tarnished by political cowardice.

The seizure of the *Achille Lauro* seajackers was an important military victory for the Reagan administration and was an astounding demonstration of A'MAN's abilities to watch over its backyard, but it provoked controversy nonetheless. First, Major General Barak's disclosure of the tape between Abu Abbas and the seajackers—the proverbial "smoking gun evidence"—on Israeli national television was considered a tremendous breach of security by many hard-line intelligence traditionalists.[32] They argued that the disclosure provided the enemy with a glimpse into A'MAN's capabilities that would damage future intelligence-gathering operations. Many also criticized disclosing the covert intelligence relationship with the United States. Yet the decision to order Major General Barak to release the tape came from Defense Minister Rabin, who, as IDF chief of staff during the 1967 War, was also behind the decision to release the explosive President Nasser–King Hussein tapes.

Although the *Achille Lauro* incident had ended in severe humiliation for Yasir Arafat's PLO, revenge would come from an organization not known for its PLO sympathies. On November 23, 1985, Egypt Air Flight 648, the very Boeing 737 that had been forced to land at Sigonella, was hijacked during a flight from Athens to Cairo by terrorists belonging to the Abu Nidal Faction; the aircraft was ordered to Malta, where the terrorists killed eight hostages, including four Egyptian security agents and an Israeli female passenger whose body was dumped on the tarmac. The following day, Egyptian commandos from Force 777, that nation's elite counterterrorist hostage rescue force, stormed the aircraft in a misguided and poorly executed rescue bid resulting in fifty-eight dead and twenty-three wounded.

Abu Nidal's next expression of revenge against the American-Israeli collusion to humiliate the Palestinian cause was particularly bloody. At 0903 on the morning of December 27, 1985, four Middle Eastern men who had been milling suspiciously about Rome's Leonardo da Vinci International Airport pulled Kefiyeh scarves over their faces and produced a deadly arsenal of assault rifles and grenades from their travel bags. Their target, the El Al check-in counter where passengers were preparing to relinquish their suitcases for a security check. The Palestinians fired indiscriminately into the crowd; according to one witness, the people were dropping like tin cans at a shooting alley. El Al's SHIN BET–trained security guards immediately returned fire and managed to kill three of the terrorists and critically wound the fourth. In the five minutes of gunfire, fifteen innocent travelers were killed and seventy-four wounded.

Seconds after the first grenade exploded at the departure terminal in Rome, three Arab men wearing jeans and combat jackets entered the second-floor departure area of Vienna's Schwechat International Airport and attacked the El Al ticket counter crowded with passengers. In a 120-second firefight, Austrian paramilitary policemen and El Al security guards killed two of the terrorists and wounded the third. Two civilians were killed and forty-seven were seriously wounded in the attack. Had the El Al security personnel not intervened, the terrorists intended to seize hostages and two aircraft and then crash-land them into Tel Aviv.[33]

The three Abu Nidal operations underscored the fact that the success of antiterrorist cooperation, perfected by Lieutenant Colonel North and A'MAN, lasted only as long as the recess between attacks and atrocities. Indeed, the attacks would continue. On April 2, 1986, a bomb ripped through TWA Flight 840 as it prepared to land in Athens, Greece, and caused four passengers, *all Americans*, to be sucked out of the gaping hole. The grisly bombing was believed to be the work of the "Arab Organization of 15 May," a small terrorist faction commanded by Hussein al-Umari (better known by his nom de guerre Abu Ibrahim); a pro-Iraqi, pro-Libyan group, it is known for its bombing attacks against airliners. On April 6, 1986, a powerful bomb ripped through the La Belle Disco in West Berlin, a night spot extremely popular with American military personnel; the bomb was planted by a Libyan-backed Palestinian agent.

Two people, including an American soldier, were killed; 150 others were seriously wounded.

American intelligence had been monitoring Libya's supportive role in Palestinian terrorist operations worldwide since the *Achille Lauro* fiasco and was now determined to exact some military payback. On April 9, 1986, President Reagan authorized a retaliatory military strike on Libya, and Lieutenant Colonel North once again contacted his friends in A'MAN for help.[34] According to reports, A'MAN performed virtually all of the United States' intelligence-gathering operations in the counterterrorist arena. A'MAN's Boeing 707 spy planes were dispatched to the Libyan coast for close monitoring operations. Two Boeing 707s, in fact, operating in tiring twelve-hour shifts, remained over Libyan waters from April 10 until the American attack five days later. The Arabic-speaking NCOs on board the flying electronic platform were able to eavesdrop on virtually all of Libya's military communications.[35] The data that A'MAN obtained was disseminated through the already well-tested channels from Tel Aviv to the National Security Agency, based at Fort Meade, and then on to the NSC office inside the White House. The data collected was checked and rechecked in Washington, then rushed to the Pentagon, where it would prove invaluable to the American raid on Qaddafi's compound and various other targets inside Libya.

The *Achille Lauro* affair and the subsequent Operation El Dorado Canyon highlighted the *known* aspect of the secret intelligence cooperation between the United States and Israel, but the affairs also highlighted a major A'MAN weakness, which needed to be addressed before the situation became desperate. Since the 1982 Lebanon war, A'MAN and the Intelligence Corps had noticed a sharp decrease in the number of Arabic-speaking personnel it was able to recruit into its ranks. The importance of Arabic-trained personnel for intelligence work was made evident by the officers who tapped into Egyptian, Palestinian, and Libyan signal communications, as well as those serving on board the Boeing 707 SIGINT, COMINT, and ECM craft. By 1985–86, the shortage of Arabic-speaking conscripts had reached crisis proportions. According to Rahamim Rajua'n, one of Israel's veteran Arabic teachers, "The phenomenon exists because of the hatred of Arabs among the younger generation of Israel and has resulted in a hatred of the Arabic language. The number of Arabic speakers has been declining for years; even families who had come from Arab countries are now ashamed of their native tongue."[36] The IDF Military Intelligence has attempted to remedy the situation by introducing, with Rahamim Rajua'n's supervision, a computer-assisted instructional program in Arabic. To augment this system, the female reservists usually assigned to searching Arab women crossing the Adam or Allenby Bridge from Jordan into Israel were deployed for their Arabic skills.[37] A'MAN's manpower (or womanpower!) problems at home did not reflect the ability of its personnel serving abroad. Nevertheless, repeating the victory of the *Achille Lauro* incident would not be easy.

On February 4, 1986, IAF warplanes intercepted a Libyan Airlines executive jet in the skies near Cyprus and forced it to land at an anonymous air base in northern Israel. The flight, between Tripoli, Libya, and Damascus, was brought down, ostensibly, in retaliation for the Rome and Vienna airport massacres. Through highly guarded HUMINT sources on the ground in Libya, A'MAN believed that the small jet was carrying several top-ranking Palestinian terrorists, including the PFLP-GC's Ahmed Jibril, Abu Nidal, and the PFLP's Dr. George Habash, who had attended a terrorist convention in Libya.[38] As the aircraft taxied on the darkened airfield, a force of 150 heavily armed commandos boarded the aircraft hoping to seize several of the world's most wanted terrorist chieftains. To their horror, neither Jibril, Abu Nidal, nor Dr. George Habash was on board, just several high-ranking officials from the Syrian Ba'ath party. After several hours in Israel, the passengers received a humble apology and were cleared for takeoff. Analysts in Israel labeled the fiasco a new MECHDAL; according to CBS News, the mistaken seizure was a crushing embarrassment to the MOSSAD. Nevertheless, Dr. George Habash exonerated the Israeli intelligence community when he released a statement admitting to having *almost* boarded the aircraft with one of Abu Nidal's aides. His travel plans had changed at the last minute.[39]

The incident underscored Israel's resolve to combat terrorism, and the tenacious efforts of the new A'MAN director to bring an innovative edge to Israel's war against the terrorists, but it also underscored the precarious line between brilliant success and disastrous, and embarrassing, failure. Syria vowed revenge and, ominously, nearly achieved it, as well as igniting a full-scale Middle Eastern bloodbath.

On April 17, 1986, an El Al security agent who was screening and searching passengers about to board Flight 016, the daily New York–London–Tel Aviv flight, came across a pretty twenty-year-old pregnant Irish woman named Anne-Marie Murphy. As she stood in a small screen-covered booth, the security agent went through his long list of rehearsed questions, such as, "Are these bags yours?" "Did you pack them yourself?" "Have the packed items of luggage left your possession at any time?" "Has anyone given you a parcel, a letter, or a gift to give someone in Israel?" Alone and pregnant, and not Jewish, Anne-Marie Murphy was already considered suspicious by the SHIN BET–trained agent.

The questioning paid off. Murphy revealed that the father of her child was a thirty-year-old Jordanian-born Palestinian who didn't use El Al himself because, since he was an Arab, the painstaking security procedures bothered him. Upon closer examination of her purse, given to the unknowing Ms. Murphy by her lover, the agent discovered a false bottom and 1.5 kilograms of high-grade Czechoslovakian-produced Semtex attached to a highly sophisticated altimeter detonating device. Hindawi, an agent for Syrian Air Force Intelligence, had set the groundwork for the mass murder of the flight's 375 passengers.[40] Hindawi was arrested outside the Syrian Embassy in London; the affair led to a disruption of diplomatic relations between the United Kingdom and Syria.*

In February 1986, Maj. Gen. Amnon Shahak was appointed IDF director of Military Intelligence. Lieutenant General Dan Shomron, the hero of Entebbe, was named the IDF's thirteenth chief of staff; Maj. Gen. Ehud Barak was named his deputy and eventual successor. In the wake of "Barak's A'MAN," Shahak was an obvious choice. Like Barak, he had been a reconnaissance paratrooper with exemplary combat records in both conventional and counterterrorist operations (many of which remain classified to this day); like Barak, Shahak was also one of the IDF's most decorated soldiers.

Amnon Shahak, the twelfth director of Israeli Military Intelligence, was born in 1944, in the port city of Haifa. A student in the Haifa Military Academy, at the age of fourteen young Amnon was already learning the art of marksmanship and parachuting while children his age were playing ragtag soccer matches in neighborhood streets.[41] A veteran paratroop, NA'HA'L, and reconnaissance officer, Amnon Shahak was twice awarded the IDF's second-highest medal for valor, the I'TUR HA'OZ ("Courage Medal")—the first for his courageous command of a force of reconnaissance paratroopers operating out of French AML-90 armored cars under heavy artillery fire during the IDF's March 21, 1968, commando raid on the Palestinian stronghold in Karameh, Jordan; the second for his decisive leadership under fire as commander of Objective GILAH—the attack on the headquarters of Nayif Hawatmeh's DFLP on April 9–10, 1973, during Operation Spring of Youth.[42]

A'MAN's principal concern during Shahak's tenure as commander centered on Syria, and technical means of gathering intelligence on Israel's dangerous northern neighbor. The most pressing concern for Israel's soldier spies was Syria's ability to surprise the IDF in a bid to snatch a portion of the Golan Heights. The Syrians had undergone a massive arms-acquisition program to reach strategic parity with Israel; matching Israel man for man and tank for tank on the battlefield became an obsession for Syrian President Hafez el-Assad and his defense minister, Gen. Mustafa Tlas, as the Syrian military absorbed hundreds of modern T-72 tanks, MiG-29s, and various Soviet and French attack helicopters. Most troubling to A'MAN was the Soviets' decision to sell Syria the deadly and highly accurate S.S. 23 surface-to-surface missile, which could reach *any* target inside Israel. The missiles, aimed at Tel Aviv and Jerusalem, were even more threatening considering that the Syr-

---

*Some Western intelligence agents believe that extremists in Syrian Air Force Intelligence, commanded by Brig. Gen. Mohammed Khouli, sanctioned the bombing to initiate a full-scale war with Israel.

ians were under an intensive program, together with West German firms, to produce chemical and biological warfare materials—and the plants were located in northern Syria far from the range of IAF F-16s.[43]

Major General Shahak inherited the reins of A'MAN during a most crucial and controversial period of history for Israel's intelligence community. A *major* embarrassment and scandal occurred on November 21, 1985, when Jonathan Jay Pollard, a U.S. Navy analyst, was arrested by FBI agents outside the Israeli Embassy in Washington, D.C. LA'KA'M's spy in America had been caught, and the political fallout of one ally spying on another was hard to sweep under the rug. Although Pollard's arrest was a severe blow to Rafi Eitan's LA'KA'M, the MOSSAD, too, would suffer several embarrassing incidents, the most important of which was its semi-involvement in the growing "Iran-Contra" scandal that was developing on Washington's Capitol Hill. A'MAN would not be immune to failure. Although IDF Military Intelligence had invested enormous man-hours and resources to monitor Syria's possible path to war, it failed to prevent a lone terrorist attack that would have enormous political and military repercussions.

For many years, the only small aircraft flying in the skies over Lebanon were IAF RPVs on intelligence-gathering or ECM sorties. On November 25, 1987, however, there were no Israeli RPVs in the Levantine skies when Israeli soldiers serving along the Lebanese border heard the muted noise of a small engine overhead. There had been two instances in Israel's sordid war with Palestinian terrorists in which ingenious means were employed to overcome the security fence of northern Israel: In March 1981, terrorists from the Abu Abbas Faction of the PLF had utilized two one-man hang gliders, but the devices were forced down; and, in April 1981, PLF terrorists tried once again to reach Israel in a hot-air balloon, which was blown out of the sky by IDF gunners. Every soldier serving along the embattled border knew of these two failed PLF attempts; naturally, engine sounds in the middle of the night were highly suspicious. Immediately, alarms were sounded through IDF Northern Command and much of the frontier area was placed on full battle stations alert.

At 2235, Khaled Akov, a terrorist in Ahmed Jibril's PFLP-GC, silently rode the Lebanese winds across the Israeli border in a red and white ultralight hang glider, landing in a thorny field near the town of Kiryat Shmoneh. High on amphetamines and heavily armed with silenced pistols, grenades, and an AKMS 7.62mm assault rifle, the tenacious Akev opted to bypass the northern Israeli town and proceed instead to Camp Gibor, a military base and home to a NA'HA'L infantry unit.[44] Akov could not have chosen a more opportune target, since the Camp Gibor had grievous security shortcomings. The sentry on duty left his post when he heard gunshots off in the distance, and the base's personnel, instead of manning defensive positions as such an alert warranted, were in their tents reading, relaxing, and playing backgammon. In a matter of minutes, the lone Palestinian gunman killed six Israeli soldiers and wounded seven others before Sgt. Gideon Bashari killed him with a burst of 5.56mm fire from his GLILON assault rifle. A'MAN had warned Northern Command about the potential for such an attack, but the best intelligence in the world is worthless if it is ignored.[45] That fateful evening, known in the Israeli vernacular as "The Night of the Hang Glider," would trigger the "Years of the Uprising," a violent statement of Palestinian resentment and anger that would take years—and Iraqi aggression—to neutralize.

The common history was that Palestinian terrorists never attacked Israeli soldiers; instead they took civilian hostages to manipulate publicity on the international media stage. The killing of six Israeli soldiers, however, tore a permanent hole in the IDF's superman-like veil. The actions of one courageous—though drugged—gunman was a desperately needed boost to Palestinian morale, and soon the Israeli soldier patrolling the streets of Nablus, Hebron, or Gaza was no longer seen as a feared icon but as a legitimate and vulnerable target. A few days later, following the accidental traffic death of a Palestinian worker, the angry and hopeless youth of the territories began to hurl rocks and Molotov cocktails at hapless IDF troopers incapable of handling massive civil unrest. Palestinian youths cruelly taunted the Israeli soldiers with cheers hailing the death of the six NA'HA'L troopers near Kiryat Shmoneh. Soon gunfire could be heard, and the sight of Israeli soldiers using their weapons against Palestinian demonstrators filled TV screens worldwide. A modern version of David and Goliath was unfolding "real-time" through satellite feeds. Israel was in for its worst public relations disaster in the nation's history.

Trouble had, indeed, been brewing inside the territories for quite some time. Although the SHIN BET had kept close tabs on the increasing numbers of terrorist acts perpetrated by clandestine Islamic fundamentalist groups, the Intifadah ("Uprising"), as it became known, was more a unified chaos than a meticulously followed formula for revolution. The Shabab—the Palestinian youth movement members who fought in the Uprising—had presented the IDF, considered by many to be the world's most experienced army, with one of its most critical operational challenges. And the IDF would fail. In essence, the Intifadah was an internal security matter, but the SHIN BET was overwhelmed by the unprecedented mass resistance. There was little A'MAN could do, either. Its main concern was to ensure that the PLO, who also had been caught completely by surprise by the Intifadah's eruption, did not capitalize on its momentum. A'MAN would have its hands full in the months to come.

It is interesting to note that A'MAN, in several of its semiannual status reports submitted to Israel's political hierarchy, had warned since 1985 of the possibility that an outbreak of some kind would erupt in the occupied territories. Colonel Reuven Levi, a well-respected A'MAN officer who during Israel's

Lebanon adventure was responsible for liaison with his Lebanese Forces counterparts, wrote of the potential for massive civil unrest and the need for the IDF and the political planners to prepare themselves for such an eventuality. Like his unheeded warnings about the involvement in Lebanon, Levi's calls for preventive actions were ignored. When, in 1988, he advised OC Central Command, Maj. Gen. Amram Mitzna, that there was no *military* solution to the Palestinian uprising, he was held in disfavor because his assessment went against the intelligence community's perception of the situation.[46]

Indeed A'MAN's role in combating the Intifadah became extremely controversial—especially regarding the relationship of the inhabitants of the territories and the Palestine Liberation Organization. As far back as 1986, A'MAN had prepared several extremely sensitive and top-secret reports that openly contradicted the government view of the PLO as a murderous group of thugs dedicated to the destruction of the Jewish state.[47] "In fact," according to one Israeli intelligence officer, "the official view of A'MAN became that they wanted peace in return for a state." Prime Minister Yitzhak Shamir, himself a veteran MOSSAD officer, attempted to stifle the report, since it would, in effect, be a de facto legitimization of the PLO.[48] It would not be the first time (or the last time) that intelligence reports had been ignored or politically compromised.[49]

Yasir Arafat and the PLO went to extraordinary efforts to prove to the world they were controlling events inside the territories. To display leadership, however, Arafat had to show muscle through military attacks mounted across the Israeli frontiers. Such an operation was Abu Jihad's department.

Abu Jihad ("Father Holy War") was the nom de guerre for Khalil al-Wazir, an Arafat loyalist since the earliest days of el-Fatah, when he founded the Kuwat al-Asifa ("storm troops") in Algiers in 1963. A rising star in the *military* ranks of the organization, Abu Jihad traveled to the People's Republic of China, North Vietnam, and North Korea in pursuit of assistance and training.[50] In the next twenty years, Abu Jihad was behind countless terrorist operations— some insignificant, others extremely bloody and spectacular. His specialty was the seaborne assault. He conceived the March 1975 Savoy Hotel operation and, of course, the March 1978 Country Club Massacre. Abu Jihad seemed obsessed with duplicating the IDF's Operation Spring of Youth, a one-shot assault that achieved remarkable results and inspired awe around the world. Abu Jihad's fascination with Israel's grand statement in Beirut was fitting, since his role as the PLO deputy commander was secured following the assassination of Abu Yusef. In early 1984, Abu Jihad conceived a plan that would make Spring of Youth look like a Boy Scout outing.

For his master stroke, Abu Jihad sought a select group of volunteers (the families of whom were usually awarded handsome dowries of foreign currency or plane tickets to more prosperous areas of the Middle East) who would be willing and able to kill. This force had to embody the hatred of the Palestinian people and their willingness to martyr themselves for the cause. Abu Jihad needed to look no farther than the teeming squalor of the Ein el-Hilweh refugee camp in Lebanon—one of the world's most lethal breeding grounds for terrorists—for his force; in all, twenty-eight men were recruited and would be known as "The Holy Martyrs of Ein el-Hilweh." [51]

From Lebanon, the men were transported to the Algerian port of Annaba, a major Force 17 facility—one believed to be far away from the prying eyes and ears of Israeli intelligence—to undergo intensive military training, which included infantry assault, weapons proficiency, cold killing, communications, sabotage and explosives, high-speed driving, navigation, seamanship, and even Hebrew. Beyond the exhaustive training, the twenty-eight terrorists were also given extensive intelligence material on Tel Aviv. Months into their training, a Force 17 intelligence officer showed the forces photographs and videotape of Israel's largest city, with landmarks, neighborhoods, and beachfronts highlighted; the film intelligence was supplied by PLO agents in Israel and by Western European tourists duped or paid to work on behalf of the Palestinian revolution.[52] A great deal of fanfare and preparation went into premission planning, but this operation would be like no others. This time, the Palestinians would strike at the nerve center of the Israeli defense establishment: the KIRYA.

The terrorists were to be ferried from Algeria to Israel by means of a mother ship, then land on the beaches of Bat Yam, a few miles due south of Tel Aviv, in rubber dinghies. They were to seize a bus, race through the streets of Tel Aviv, and crash through the gates of the IDF General Staff headquarters and Israeli Defense Ministry inside the walled confines of the KIRYA; following a battle with the facility's defenders, the terrorists were to seize the compound. After booby-trapping the buildings, they would take Israeli Defense Minister Lt. Gen. (Res.) Yitzhak Rabin and much of the IDF General Staff hostage; they would be systematically executed if Israel did not release 150 convicted el-Fatah terrorists in Israeli prisons. D day was April 21, 1985—the thirty-seventh anniversary of Israeli independence.

On the night of April 13, Abu Jihad boarded the thousand-ton, sixty-meter-long Panamanian-registered ship SS Attaviros and addressed his force one last time with a low-key motivational speech. He inspected the ranks and then saluted the Palestinian flag, which was quickly hoisted above the ship's deck. Abu Jihad watched the ship set sail and was driven back to headquarters to await the onset of el-Fatah's attack.

According to foreign reports, A'MAN had obtained advance warning of a possible Palestinian attack, believed to be a seaborne infiltration attempt, which would coincide with independence day celebrations. Coastal defenses had been reinforced. At 2315 on April 20, the slow-moving Attaviros was located in the southern Mediterranean by the INS Moledet ("Homeland"), a SA'AR fourth-class missile boat of the IDF/navy.[53] Armed with a deadly array of Gabriel and Harpoon surface-to-surface missiles, cannons, and air defense weapons, the *Moledet* far outclassed the *Attaviros*; this disparity became obvious when the mother ship attempted to engage the missile boat. A brief and deadly battle erupted. With a few well-placed rounds of 76mm fire by the *Moledet*'s main armament gun, the *Attaviros* began to sink. In all, twenty Palestinians were killed in the exchange and eight were pulled from the sea. They were interrogated by A'MAN personnel and, in an attempt to receive light sentences, "sang like canaries." They disclosed *all* details of the mission as well as the fact that the entire affair was the grand design of Abu Jihad. For years, there had been an unwritten "accepted-by-all-sides gentlemen's agreement" that the top leadership of either side was not to be targeted for termination. Since Rabin, in essence, was one of the objectives in the foiled operation, his Palestinian counterpart, Abu Jihad, was now considered fair game.

Israel, however, was patient; Abu Jihad's death sentence may have been written but it was not yet signed. The Intifadah changed everything. In the winter of 1987–1988, when the Palestinian uprising was in a stalled and confused state, Abu Jihad decided that the PLO needed to assume a dominant role in the struggle by sending elite squads of terrorists across Israel's frontiers. On December 26, the pro-Arafat Abu Abbas Faction of the Palestine Liberation Front attempted to infiltrate a three-man squad into the Jordan Valley through Jordanian territory. The attack failed miserably and resulted in King Hussein clamping down on all Palestinian activities inside his kingdom. Abu Jihad then turned to the quiet Egyptian frontier, although several attempts there ended in embarrassing failure.

At 0630 on March 7, 1988, three heavily armed Force 17 commandos slinked across the desert frontier separating Egypt and Israel. They proceeded to commandeer a car and raced through the Negev Desert toward the city of Beersheba. Their crossing had been identified by IDF units, and a general security alert was sounded throughout southern Israel. Realizing that a hostage-rescue operation might be required, the YA'MA'M, the Border Guard Police's antiterrorist unit, was placed on full alert. In the ensuing chain of events, the terrorists seized an intercity bus carrying workers from their homes in Beersheba to the nuclear reactor in Dimona and took the passengers hostage. The IDF troops immobilized the bus, and a standoff ensued. At 1015, the terrorists executed one of their hostages and promised that more would be killed if their demands were not met. A rescue assault was then ordered. The ordeal was over in a matter of seconds as the YA'MA'M commandos succeeded in killing all three of the terrorists; two female hostages, however, were killed in the assault. Upon further examination, A'MAN learned that the terrorists had been under the personal command of Abu Jihad. Israeli tolerance ended at that moment. A death sentence had been signed in Jerusalem.[54]

Abu Jihad was by no means an easy target. For an assassination operation to succeed, it would require *extremely* accurate intelligence, and an innovative plan that would be deniable. The MOSSAD was utilizing its Tunisian and North African assets to provide the planned strike force with as much support as possible, including, according to foreign reports, a plant within the PLO who relayed information on the day-to-day movements of Abu Jihad. A'MAN intensified its intelligence-gathering campaign against the North African state. Naval frogmen from HA'KOMMANDO HA'YAMI routinely mapped Tunisian beaches and other landing areas, and monitored Tunisian naval facilities and coastal defenses. Commandos from SAYERET MAT'KAL also operated virtually unhindered in Tunisia, mapping out targets (such as PLO installations) and Tunisian military posts that might one day be used in a combined Arab effort against Israel.[55] The ability of the IDF's special operations forces to covertly gather firsthand intelligence and assist A'MAN in its responsibilities proved to be a major factor in the Intelligence Branch's success. These same units would play a major role in the operation whose groundwork they helped prepare.

The IDF knew of Abu Jihad's obsession with Operation Spring of Youth and, in an ironic twist of fate, was determined to repeat its success in Tunis. The operational plan called for a force of naval commandos to deploy from four missile boats—including the INS *Aliyah* and INS *Geula*, which could both carry helicopters—and secure a beachhead for the SAYERET MAT'KAL commandos, who would be driven to the targeted home of Abu Jihad by a group of MOSSAD agents who were responsible for renting vehicles and securing escape routes. The assassination was to take only a matter of minutes, since the MAT'KAL commandos were not expecting much resistance from Abu Jihad's security contingent. One IAF ECM Boeing 707, utilizing the civilian identification number 4X-007 and carrying A'MAN director Major General Shahak, MOSSAD director Nachum Admoni, and IDF Deputy Chief of Staff Maj. Gen. Ehud Barak, would provide an electronic blanket over the Tunisian capital, rendering much of the Tunisian security and military communications useless during the raid. A second Boeing 707, utilizing the civilian identification number 4X-497 and carrying IAF OC Maj. Gen. Avihu Ben-Nun, would coordinate all ground, sea, and aerial activities. To make sure that all was in order for "his" operation, the SAYERET MAT'KAL commander flew to Tunis, with a *genuine* passport, to examine the area for himself. A MOSSAD welcoming committee met him at the airport and took him first to the exclusive Sidi Bouseid suburb of Tunis, where Abu Jihad's home was, and then to the proposed landing site—a deserted strip of beach at Ras Carthage, located approximately forty kilometers north of the city.[56]

In early April 1988, as the Israeli cabinet was beginning to debate the assassination operation, the participants conducted a dress rehearsal of the raid in the city of Haifa, with the town atop Mt. Carmel imitating the hilly confines of the Tunisian capital quite convincingly. Utilizing intelligence obtained by the MOSSAD, the IDF Ordnance Corps even constructed a scale model of

Abu Jihad's home. The dry run was executed with split-second precision. The commandos, wearing Nomex coveralls and carrying silenced weapons with laser range finders and sights, were able to eliminate Abu Jihad with little difficulty. The operation was on. Under a veil of enormous security, the commandos boarded their missile boat ferries and headed out to sea.

On April 13, 1988, the A'MAN director was interviewed in the pages of BAMACHANE, the IDF's weekly magazine. He said, "I do believe that commando assault operations are highly successful. They do have a strong deterrent impact on terrorists, and therefore, I regard them as a highly important tool. I don't think that the IDF has stopped thinking about them, or that we will stop conducting them." That same day, April 13, 1988, the Israeli cabinet approved the operation in Tunis.[57] D day was April 16.

In the late-night hours of April 15, two naval commandos reached the Ras Carthage beach after a brisk underwater swim. They produced weapons from special plastic cases and checked the perimeter for any sign of life. After ensuring that the coast was clear, they signaled to the missile boats for the remainder of the naval commando and SAYERET MAT'KAL force to race to shore. They were met on the beach by MOSSAD agents driving three rented vehicles. With the two Boeing 707s hovering in a civilian flight path between southern Sicily and northern Tunisia, the North African skies—and all communications below—belonged to the IAF. MOSSAD agents had tapped into telephone lines and blocked all outgoing calls from the Sidi Bouseid suburb.[58]

A few hours later, the assault force, divided into four teams, was parked outside Abu Jihad's home, awaiting his return from a PLO staff meeting. The commandos sat nervously inside their vehicles for nearly forty-five minutes; at 0130, Abu Jihad's motorcade finally arrived. They would have to wait another sixty minutes, however, until he went to bed and it would be safe to strike. At 0230, as the lights inside Jihad's home were extinguished, the commandos exited their vehicles. While one force eliminated Abu Jihad's driver and bodyguard, the strike force burst into the luxurious home and within seconds reached the bedroom where Abu Jihad and his wife, Umm Jihad ("Mother Holy War"), were sleeping. Before the noise of footsteps could awaken the PLO military commander, he was cut down by seventy-five bullets. According to Abu Jihad's widow, one of the commandos was a woman and the entire operation was videotaped.[59] The operation lasted a matter of seconds, and before the alarm could be sounded, the commandos and their MOSSAD comrades were making their hasty withdrawal back to Israel. The raid was a brilliant success, although one for which Israel has yet to claim responsibility.

The assassination of Abu Jihad was a daring display of a nation's resolve to pay back the perpetrators of terrorism. The foray into Tunis had *enormous* intelligence rewards as well. While one force of SAYERET MAT'KAL commandos eliminated the guards, and the other two executed Abu Jihad, another force searched the premises for anything that might be of intelligence value. Although the inventory remains classified, it has been reported that a comprehensive list of all the PLO's agents in Western Europe was seized.[60]

If Abu Jihad could be targeted because of his desire to inflame the fires of the Intifadah, then Israel could strike at the man who started it all in the first place.

In the early hours of December 9, 1988, the first anniversary of the eruption of the Intifadah, an IDF task force of naval commandos and reconnaissance infantrymen from SAYERET GOLANI landed on the Lebanese coast, three kilometers from Damur. After a forced march, the GOLANI commandos stormed the headquarters and principal training facility of Ahmed Jibril's PFLP-GC in Na'ameh; their objective, according to foreign reports, was to kill the dangerous terrorist chieftain.* A'MAN's HUMINT, SIGINT, COMINT, and VISINT resources were pushed to their maximum capabilities prior to the raid to provide the strike force with an *extremely* detailed layout of the PFLP-GC position; photos and videotape taken during Israel's occupation of the area were also examined. Preoperational intelligence needed to be detailed: The PFLP-GC Na'ameh base was an impregnable fortress complete with heavily fortified caves and a series of tunnels, plowed deep underground, which had been designed by Vietnamese advisors. Jibril had prepared a gauntlet of death and, indeed, the battle for the base would be extremely brutal and hard fought. To destroy the tunnels, which had posed such a problem for the IDF operational planners, the GOLANI commandos deployed "kamikaze dogs"; carrying explosives and gas canisters that could be detonated by remote control, the dogs were trained to follow a laser beam toward the target.[61]

Much of the battle was fought underground and in pitch-darkness; the GOLANI fighters wore special image-enhancing goggles, and their weapons were fitted with laser sights.** In several hours of fighting, much of the base was destroyed or damaged, but only seven terrorists were killed. The lone IDF casualty was the task force commander, twenty-nine-year-old Lt. Col. Amir Meital, who was killed by a burst of automatic fire. The mission concluded with a dramatic rescue of two trapped GOLANI commandos.

Two weeks later, Pan Am Flight 103, on a routine flight from Frankfurt and London to New York and Detroit, exploded high above the sleepy Scot-

---

*According to reports that would surface later, another possible objective of the raid was to *kidnap* Jibril and use him to bargain for two missing IDF servicemen believed held by the PFLP-GC.
**Although the IDF does not confirm the use of such equipment by its special forces units, several laser sights and weapons were captured by PFLP-GC personnel and displayed by Ahmed Jibril in a press conference.

tish hamlet of Lockerbie, killing all 270 passengers and crew. The PFLP-GC, operating under Iranian and Syrian auspices, was widely believed to be the group responsible for the bombing, although recent evidence has now indicated that Libyan intelligence was involved; in November 1991, the U.S. Justice Department even indicted two Libyan intelligence officers as the perpetrators of the crime. A massive investigation was conducted by the intelligence services of the United States, Great Britain, Germany, and Israel. Physical evidence—remarkably, a computer chip used in a bomb's detonator mechanism, obtained from the wreckage of a UTA French Airlines DC-10 airliner—linked the two incidents. Both aircraft were destroyed in exactly the same manner.

On July 31, 1989, a force of commandos from SAYERET MAT'KAL (according to foreign reports) was landed by helicopter just outside the southern Lebanese town of Jibchit, and proceeded to kidnap the regional Hizbollah commander, Sheikh Abdul Karim Obeid, in order to obtain a bargaining chip against the pro-Iranian Hizbollah terrorists who were holding six IDF as hostages.[62] The kidnapping operation, like the strike at Jibril's headquarters, was yet another example of the IDF's ability to mount daring commando operations based on accurate, precise intelligence. Spectacular operations and dedicated intelligence work was not an Israeli exclusivity, however. The Palestinians were conceiving spectacular raids of their own.

To the experienced individual, the signs of impending trouble were clear. For much of the month of May 1990, sunbathers along Israel's lengthy Mediterranean coastline witnessed aerial patrols by Sea Scan jets, low-flying Bell-212 helicopters, AH-S1 Cobra attack choppers, and Dornier light observation piston-engine aircraft. Joining the watch were speedy DABUR patrol craft, armed with 20mm cannons, which anchored close to shore; lightly armed police coastal patrol craft joined the windsurfers, fishermen, and bronzed sun worshippers in the shallow waters in the shadows of five-star luxury hotels. The danger of a Palestinian terrorist attack along Israel's vulnerable coastline was ever-present, and the increased patrols were an added, though routine, precaution meant to provide increased protection during the volatile month of May, historically a tinderbox period for violence in the Middle East. May was the month in which the State of Israel declared her independence some forty-three years before.

In May 1990 a lone madman—rejected by the IDF for mental instability, no less—gunned down a group of Arab workers who were awaiting offers for employment along a busy interchange in a southern Tel Aviv suburb, killing seven of them. Inevitably, the murders' byproduct was an escalation of the already deadly Intifadah in the West Bank and Gaza Strip. May 1990 was also the month of the Arab summit in Baghdad, the Iraqi capital. Amid the usual calls for Israel's destruction from the leaders of the Arab states were more subdued calls for action from the men in the background. The commanders of the various Palestinian liberation groups gathered with Libyan leader Muammar Qaddafi and Iraqi strongman Saddam Hussein to chart the course of a deadly campaign against the "Zionist Entity." Indeed, May was to be a monumental month.

In May 1990, however, all facets of A'MAN were finely tuned—highly accurate and ready for all contingencies. Through a host of HUMINT, ELINT, and SIGINT means, the IDF was able to learn of a planned Palestinian terrorist attack involving a seaborne infiltration attempt near a major population center. The information was rushed to Israeli Defense Minister Yitzhak Rabin.[63] Coastal defenses were reinforced, and patrol craft in the choppy Mediterranean waters were placed on their highest state of alert.

The vigilant efforts paid off in the early-morning hours of May 30. It was the Jewish holiday of SHAVUOTH ("Feast of the Tabernacles"), and since it was a hot and sunny day, most Israelis, in their truly secular tradition, were celebrating the religious holiday by preparing for a long day of sun and fun on the beach. Conservative estimates placed nearly a quarter of a million sunbathers along the Tel Aviv shoreline.

At 0643, a rusty Libyan freighter, which had set sail from the port of Benghazi a few days earlier, dropped anchor approximately 120 miles off the Tel Aviv coast. In the dawn's calm waters, this mother ship unloaded six speedy motor craft, each manned by a highly trained squad of Palestinian terrorists from the Abu Abbas Faction of the Palestine Liberation Front, commanded by the notorious Abu Abbas. Each craft was heavily armed with mounted 107mm Katyusha rocket launchers, 23mm cannons, RPG-7 antitank grenades, PK 7.62mm machine guns, and SAM-7 Strella surface-to-air missiles. The small boats, painted with a rubbery compound to make them more difficult to detect by radar, headed for the Israeli coastline, but four of the vessels suffered mechanical difficulties and were forced to return to the mother ship. The mission was not aborted, however, and the two remaining vessels split course; one headed north toward Herziliya and Netanya. Ten minutes later, an IDF/navy DABUR patrol craft spotted the fast-moving boat twenty nautical miles off the coast near Kibbutz Ga'ash, just north of Tel Aviv. The DABUR fired several warning shots to stop the craft, and the terrorists were ordered to disrobe, enter the water, and not resist capture. Once aboard the Israeli vessel, the terrorists admitted to their inquisitive captors that they were not the only Palestinians in the Mediterranean waters that day.

Immediately, the wheels of the elaborate and well-rehearsed Israeli security apparatus were set in motion. Police units prepared roadblocks, and many beaches were evacuated—especially around Tel Aviv; antiterrorist and special forces units were placed on their highest state of alert. Helicopter gunships and reconnaissance aircraft were also summoned. Three hours later, the second ship was spotted off the coast of Nitzanim, approximately five miles from the southern port city of Ashdod, heading at top speed for shore. Although the slower DABUR could not catch the speedy craft, the IDF/navy patrol craft did manage to force the terrorists away from a crowded beach club, and toward deserted sand dunes nearby. Cobra helicopter gunships kept the Palestinians at bay with accurate bursts of cannon and missile fire until the "cavalry" arrived. The Israeli response force, which included the National Police Border Guard antiterrorist unit, the YA'MA'M, as well as other elite units, who for security reasons remain anonymous, began to hunt down the intruders amid the sandy dunes and thick foliage. Also taking part in the operation were soldiers from the GIVA'ATI Infantry Brigade, who were helilifted to the beach from anti-Intifadah duties in the Gaza Strip. The battle was brief and completely one-sided; four terrorists were killed and twelve captured in a matter of minutes. Through highly accurate intelligence work and a brilliantly executed military operation, the Israel Defense Forces had prevented a horrendous massacre.

Captured terrorists usually talk, and those caught near Ga'ash and the sand dunes at Nitzanim offered their Military Intelligence interrogators a wealth of information concerning the training methods of the PLF, their seaborne capabilities, the complicity of the Libyans, and, most importantly, the *true* objective of their well-planned operation: Tel Aviv. In their Libyan training camp, the terrorists had been shown video clips of the city's beachfront hotels, public parks, and squares by the PLF's naval commander, Abu al-Kassam, who also supplied them with highly detailed maps of these targets. They had been ordered to shell the fully-booked luxury hotels and the adjacent homes from the sea, then machine-gun every soul they saw on the beach once they landed. In a quickly organized press conference, A'MAN director Major General Shahak offered indisputable evidence that the objective of the mission was the indiscriminate murder of countless civilians. Shahak reiterated Libyan complicity, informing the gathered fourth estate that the commander of Libya's naval commandos, the mysterious Colonel Zuhair, had supplied the terrorists with training facilities, the fiberglass motorboats, and operational assistance. According to Mohammad Ahmad al-Hamadi Yusef, one of the terrorists captured on that fateful day, "We were told not to leave anyone alive. Kill them all . . . children, women, elderly people." [64]

Through the interrogation of the surviving terrorists, A'MAN was able to piece together a remarkable chronology of their preparation in Libya. On April 27 the terrorists had carried out a large-scale exercise of their planned assault together with the Libyan navy, including an amphibious landing under fire; on April 28 the force was taken to a mountainous zone and trained in urban fighting; on May 26, they were taken to the Libyan navy's naval commando base near Benghazi, where they were informed for the first time that their date with destiny would, indeed, be in a few days. After Abu Abbas addressed the group with a fire-branding speech as to the importance of their mission, they boarded the mother ship secretly, under cover of darkness, using Zodiac craft.[65]

Oddly enough, Military Intelligence's handling of this affair would become controversial, since reports indicated that A'MAN had tracked the Libyan mother ship ever since it departed Benghazi on May 27. Once out of the government, however, Rabin would say that A'MAN had known of the planned attack for well over five months.[66]

The attempted assault on Tel Aviv's crowded beach was a signal that the stagnation of the peace process would result in deadly acts that threatened the stability of the region. As Colonel Y., head of the Intelligence Corps' Terror Department, commented: "The fact that there are 20,000 individuals drawing salaries from 15 various Palestinian organizations and are available for terrorist attack must send off alarm signals which cannot be ignored."[67]

Terrorists, however, would not be the only threat to Tel Aviv. A situation was brewing hundreds of miles to Israel's east that would place the nation, and its intelligence community, in one of the most awkward and unenviable positions in that nation's history.

The foiled attack on the Tel Aviv shoreline coincided with the Arab League summit being held in grand opulence in the Iraqi capital. Since the Abu Abbas Faction of the PLF is a pro-Iraqi and Iraqi-sponsored and -protected organization, it is believed that the attack was sanctioned by Saddam Hussein to deflect attention from his true intention at the time of the diplomatic conference: the destruction of Kuwait. Trouble had been brewing for some time between the oil-rich sheikhdom and the Iraqi Republic, which historically had considered Kuwait its "19th Province"; OPEC price-fixing, economic maneuvering, and a massive war debt (after eight years of pointless conflict with Iran) had left Iraq virtually bankrupt. Such tensions were usually glossed over by the Kuwaitis, and nothing much was expected of these differences either. On August 2, 1990, however, Saddam Hussein's massive million-man army launched an invasion of Kuwait and seized the nation in a matter of hours. The attack caught virtually everyone by surprise—*especially* the Israeli intelligence community.

Between 1988 and 1990, Israel's intelligence community—principally the MOSSAD—had been rocked by a series of scandals and embarrassments that prevented it from faithfully monitoring developments in Baghdad. In June 1988, the first "intelligence disaster" occurred in London, when British police arrested Ismail Hassan Sawan, a Force 17 terrorist, when a weapons cache was found in his London apartment. Under interrogation, Sawan admitted that he was, in fact, a MOSSAD agent. He felt that the British, whose intelligence services enjoyed a close working relationship with Israel, would understand his Israeli allegiance and release him immediately. Nothing could have been farther from the truth. The disclosure of Israeli intelligence personnel operating freely on British soil sent shock waves through Great Britain; under the recommendation of MI5, the British internal secret service, Britain expelled five Israeli "diplomats," all believed to be MOSSAD agents. The most important to leave was Arieh Regev, the MOSSAD's liaison with British Intelligence.[68]

The second embarrassment to tarnish the MOSSAD's image was a January 1989 court battle in which the Israeli Supreme Court overturned an IDF Military Censor's Office decision to censor thirty-eight passages from an article in the Tel Aviv newspaper HA'IR, in which the MOSSAD was severely criticized for failed operations in Germany and Greece, and the outgoing MOSSAD director, Nachum Admoni, was even identified by name.

The final MOSSAD attempt at damage control came at the time when much of the world was in the throes of sending armed forces to Saudi Arabia to combat Saddam Hussein. In September 1990, the Israeli government went to extraordinary efforts to stop the publication of a book, *By Way of Deception: The Making and Unmaking of a Mossad Officer*, written by a Canadian-born Israeli, and failed MOSSAD collections officer, Victor Ostrovsky. The book, a small dosage of historical and common fact laced with seemingly fictitious assertions meant to cause controversy that would result in large book sales, was filled with a wide variety of supersensitive secrets, including the actual names of dozens of agents still serving in the field, secret code names for various A'MAN units, locations of premises, and controversial claims that Israeli intelligence *allowed* a Shiite suicide truck bomber to hit the U.S. Marine barracks in Beirut by not handing down valuable intelligence to the Americans.[69] Although serving in the MOSSAD for a mere seventeen months (from October 1984 to March 1986),* Ostrovsky seemed to have gathered an enormous bank of data on the MOSSAD's inner workings and dark personal secrets. Although the book was clearly the work of a bitter man out for revenge against a system whose standards for competence had compromised his career, the MOSSAD and the Israeli government's highly publicized attempts to stop the book's release in the United States led to undue publicity and, inevitably, its spot on international best-seller lists. Much to the MOSSAD's chagrin, the book was translated into several languages—although not into Hebrew—and film rights were even sold.

Yet the blame for the "Iraqi MECHDAL" cannot lie solely with the MOSSAD and its in-house problems.[70] A'MAN, too, was supposed to deal with such a

---

*According to Ostrovsky, it was his role in the failed monitoring of the Libyan jet forced to land in Israel in February 1986, that led to his disgraced dismissal from the MOSSAD.

regional crisis. The Intelligence Branch had even gone "space age" to ensure that, in the age of long-range missiles in the hands of Iraq, Syria, and Saudi Arabia, Israel would not be caught in a tragic surprise attack. On September 19, 1988, the State of Israel entered the international space race when a SHAVIT ("Comet") rocket launched a 343-pound OFEK-1 (the name means "Horizon" in Hebrew) satellite. The OFEK-1 was the prototype for an Israeli photo-reconnaissance satellite to be used for purely military intelligence purposes. Israel announced that future space vehicles would indeed have military applications.[71] On April 3, 1990, Israel kept its promise when the OFEK-2 was launched; the satellite proceeded to circle the earth in an elliptical trajectory between two hundred and fifteen hundred kilometers above the earth's surface.

Remarkably, the launching of the OFEK-2 came one day after Saddam Hussein warned that his secret weapons would destroy "half of Israel with chemical agents if this nation [Israel] becomes involved in an attack against Iraq."[72] Those threats were more than veiled promises: They followed an intensive Iraqi arms buildup in long-range surface-to-surface ballistic missiles; science fiction–type long-range cannons*; and binary, chemical, and, in a glimpse of Armageddon, attempts to produce nuclear weapons.

As far back as 1989, Iraq had prepared itself for a possible military confrontation with Israel. In an ominous move meant to counter the IDF's supreme advantage in technological and human intelligence resources, Iraqi Air Force Dassault-Breguet Mirage F.1CR jets, piloted by Jordanian airmen, began photoreconnaissance flights over the elongated Israeli-Jordanian frontier in July 1989. Although many in the Israeli defense community believed that the reconnaissance aircraft, part of a joint Iraqi/Jordanian squadron, were being flown to give the economically handicapped Royal Jordanian Air Force extra flight hours, the sorties were conducted over ultrastrategic elements of the Israeli border, including, it has been reported, the Dimona nuclear reactor in the Negev Desert. According to Major General Shahak, A'MAN was able to determine from the altitude and flight pattern of the Jordanian/Iraqi aircraft that they were gathering PHOTINT and ELINT data.[73] When the Iraqi mischief along Israel's frontier was uncovered, *Jordanian* aircraft were used to obtain the data. This was the beginning of a Jordanian alliance with Iraq that would last even through the dark days of the Gulf War. In addition, Iraqi intelligence officers frequently conducted intelligence-gathering reconnaissance from the Jordanian border and, with the dispatching of Palestinian terrorist

---

*According to foreign reports, the MOSSAD was responsible for the assassination of Dr. Gerald Bull, the brilliant Canadian-born ballistics expert who was the architect of Iraq's supergun, with 350mm artillery aimed at Israel.

squads, were believed to be involved in testing Israel's security apparatus and border defenses.

Yet what truly alarmed A'MAN was the subsequent discovery of modified SCUD missile launchers, aimed at Israel, positioned in the western Iraqi H-2 and H-3 airfields.[74] A'MAN director Shahak was troubled by this new development, and realized that the Intelligence Branch could not adequately cover Iraq with its meager operating budget. Clearly, added SIGINT and HUMINT operations were required. Shahak urged Defense Minister Rabin to authorize additional funds, but the former chief of staff refused emphatically. Israel would pay the price in the months to follow.

After the invasion of Kuwait, Iraqi military prowess rippled to the rest of the Arab world, especially the Palestinians. Their uprising in a state of self-defeat and exhaustion, the Palestinians found new inspiration in Saddam Hussein's cocky nature and self-professed military might. The Intifadah, as a result, escalated into a full-scale bloody conflagration. Israelis became victims in the cities and in their homes, bullets and bombs replacing stones and Molotov cocktails. Many *military* orders to the uprising's leaders now originated in Baghdad from Palestinian terrorist warlords who quickly allied themselves with Saddam Hussein. The Palestinians inside Israel also became intelligence operatives for the Iraqi military, providing targeting data for striking at Israel.[75] Iraq used the plight of the Palestinians as the basis of its terms for withdrawal from Kuwait. Israel, relying on urgent shipments of American Patriot antiballistic missiles, distributed gas masks to its civilians and prayed for peace.

As a result of this new and undecided "equation" in the Middle East, the message of the OFEK-2's launching was striking: The Israeli-made rocket could ferry a spy satellite over Iraq, but it could not guarantee peace or keep Israel's frontiers safe. That responsibility fell to the Israel Defense Forces, who, in turn, relied on Israeli Military Intelligence. At no time in the State of Israel's history, perhaps, was the need to gather, analyze, and disseminate accurate military intelligence so important.

As the American-led coalition rushed to draw its epic line in the sand of the Saudi desert, Israel was forced to gear up for a conflict that threatened to bring a shower of chemically tipped missiles onto ground zero of its largest cities. From the onset of the crisis in the gulf, it was obvious to the Israeli defense establishment that, should the shooting start, Israel would be the first target of Saddam's arsenal in an effort to convert an inter-Arab struggle into the final Arab-Israeli war. As a result, A'MAN rededicated itself to monitoring developments in Iraq (including, according to foreign reports, HUMINT assets in the Kurdish mountains), as well as reassessing the conventional Iraqi military and examining and categorizing every bit of information regarding Saddam Hussein's army, including its Order of Battle, weapons systems, ability to mobilize and move its million-man force, and its battle doctrine and strategy.[76] All the information gathered by the Collections Department and other highly classified means was rushed to the "Desk" for analysis.

A'MAN's principal concern was the Iraqi Air Force. The intelligence officers were trying to determine whether or not Saddam Hussein's extended-range SCUD missiles had chemical capabilities, but it was known with certainty that his Mirage F-1 and Sukhoi Su-24 Fencers could deliver lethal NBC (nuclear-biological-chemical) payloads. Although the IDF General Staff had supreme confidence in the IAF for air defense, if just *one* Iraqi aircraft managed to break through Israel's aerial gauntlet it could kill hundreds in a gas, chemical, or biological bombing run. Realizing that the IAF might not only have to engage Iraqi—and, possibly, Jordanian—combat aircraft in defense of Israel's territorial integrity, but also over Iraq during a retaliatory strike, A'MAN needed to supply the IAF with accurate data on the technical abilities of the Iraqi Air Force, as well as its strategic attributes and the ever-important "nontangibles."

In this regard, Israeli Military Intelligence was able to come through with flying colors. On October 11, 1989, Maj. Bassem Adel, a Syrian Air Force MiG-23 Flogger-G pilot, had defected to Israel along with his aircraft. The MiG-23 was the most prevalent combat aircraft in the Syrian Order of Battle, and in the Iraqi Air Force as well. The defection was an important intelligence coup. Israeli Air Force technicians were able to take apart the aircraft and put it back together following a meticulous examination. The Flogger was flown by an Israeli test pilot in January 1990, and its aerodynamic abilities, combat envelope, and pronounced limitations were all recorded for the first time by a Western nation. That data was processed through the various IAF fighter squadrons, as well as IAF Air Defense units. The end of the cold war and the unification of the two Germanies provided A'MAN and the IAF with another preview of a frontline Soviet-built warplane, when Israeli intelligence experts were invited to examine an ex–East German Air Force MiG-29 Fulcrum, the most modern air-superiority fighter in both the Syrian and Iraqi air forces.[77]*

The other aspect of the intelligence war in which A'MAN displayed considerable success was monitoring the movement of Iraqi missiles to their launchers—critical knowledge for countering a surprise attack; in fact, A'MAN director Shahak made this ability *public* to allay the growing fears inside Israel. In an interview, Shahak stated, "A'MAN has learned that since the invasion of Kuwait, the Iraqis had moved 'missiles' from its central storage facility

---

*Military cooperation between the German and Israeli intelligence services regarding Soviet-built equipment was fully uncovered in autumn 1991 when a covert shipment of ex–East German equipment was discovered on an Israeli ship in Hamburg.

at Taji, to several locations including concrete-bunker positions in the western portion of the country which are pointing directly at Israel."[78]

The developments in Iraq, unclear as they were, prompted grave concern inside the walls of the KIRYA. Israel wanted to keep this latest Arab dispute from being termed an *Arab-Israeli* conflict, thus denying Saddam Hussein his bargaining position—offering to withdraw from Kuwait if Israel would unilaterally withdraw from the occupied territories. Therefore, a preemptive strike by Israel was politically out of the question. Yet Israel knew that the deadline for the Iraqi withdrawal was nearing and that United States President George Bush would not back down in his promise to use military means to force Iraqi capitulation. There would *probably* be war and, as Israeli Defense Minister Moshe Arens would state on national TV: "If somebody in Iraq decides to push a button and launch a ballistic missile, that missile will probably land somewhere in Israel." With realistic A'MAN estimates of the range of Iraqi missiles and the knowledge that the Iraqi military could produce thirteen thousand tons of chemical agents annually, the likelihood of the region's first chemical war seemed strong. The order was given to begin the distribution of gas masks to the Israeli public.

A'MAN'S, as well as the MOSSAD'S, inability to obtain a reliable flow of accurate intelligence on Iraq was considered by many intelligence veterans in Israel to be a MECHDAL equal to what happened in 1973 and 1982. The most verbal proponent of this opinion was former A'MAN director, and member of the KNESSET's Intelligence Section of the Foreign and Security Affairs Department, Maj. Gen. (Res.) Yehoshua Saguy, who unequivocally declared, "The Iraqis had caught us with our pants down."[79]

Yet spying on Iraq, a nation that did not border Israel, was of monumental difficulty for Israel's espionage services. Saddam Hussein's Ba'ath party had created the most notorious police state in the region, paling even Syria, where people routinely disappeared and where allegiance to the regime was in many ways measured by a person's desire to inform on friends and family. Iraq was *not* a nation where intelligence agents could be easily recruited, since everyone in the country was under constant suspicion anyway, and people were trained not to trust anyone. According to one western joke circulating in Baghdad, "There are 32 million people in Iraq: 16 million citizens and 16 million pictures of Saddam." As one intelligence officer commented, it is virtually impossible to ask someone to spy on the Iraqis when, under Section 225 of the Iraqi emergency laws, mild criticism of the regime warrants the death penalty. Nevertheless, some contradicting claims were made that A'MAN and MOSSAD had extraordinary success in infiltrating the highest echelons of the Iraqi military.[80]

As the countdown for war continued, Israel prepared itself for the inevitable conflict. January 15, 1991, was Iraq's final day to unilaterally withdraw its forces from Kuwait before United Nations resolutions would sanction the use of military force. On January 2, 1991, the IAF OC Maj. Gen. Avihu Ben-Nun conducted a dramatic news briefing from the inside of a protective aircraft shelter at an anonymous air force base in central Israel. Fearing a surprise Iraqi missile attack, the IAF had mobilized its forces and placed attack squadrons on twenty-four-hour-a-day alert to be scrambled the moment American satellites picked up the launch of an Iraqi missile toward Israel. Israeli Air Force pilots sat inside their cockpits in full flight gear in eight-hour shifts to ensure maximum readiness; since a SCUD's flight time from western Iraq to Tel Aviv was little more than four minutes, every second counted. Although the fact that Israeli pilots were sitting in their cockpits poised for a strike against Iraq might have been considered—under normal circumstances—a military secret, the censor's office allowed the release of the information to allay public panic.

Since the British Mandate's "emergency regulations," declared at the onset of the Second World War and kept in practice following the 1948 War of Independence, military censorship has been a way of life in Israel. In the following years, a strange marriage of convenience existed between the censor's office and journalists. Both Israelis and foreign correspondents working out of Israeli desks had to sign legal contracts ensuring that their stories on military and security matters would be submitted to the censor's office either in Jerusalem or Tel Aviv for approval. Under the governmental accords, the defense minister and IDF chief of staff are responsible for appointing a high-ranking officer, with the rank of brigadier general, as chief censor.[81] A full-fledged part of A'MAN, the censor's office has incredible powers that, although they are seldom implemented to their full legal limit, include the right to shut down newspapers or publications in violation of censorship guidelines, and the right to listen in on telephone calls (mainly by journalists) and read telex type. They can deny a journalist, film crew, or historian the right to publish or display the identification of military units (designations, insignia, and code names), full names of intelligence and high-ranking IDF officers, and any mention of Israel's *alleged* nuclear weapons program. In the winter of 1991, the censor's office would face a new challenge.[82]

When 1991 began, much of Israel had prepared for potential chemical war by sealing one room—semihermetically—inside their homes with plastic sheets and tape. On January 17, however, it appeared for a brief moment that the sealed rooms would not be needed. The American and coalition preemptive raid against Iraq was believed to have crippled Saddam Hussein's ability to wage war. On Israeli television, the nightly newscaster, relieved that Israel had been spared, closed his broadcast with "God Bless America." The jubilation would be short-lived. At 0143 on January 18, the scream of air-raid sirens could be heard in every corner of Israel. Within four minutes, Iraqi

SCUD missiles slammed through several Tel Aviv neighborhoods, as well as parts of Haifa in the north. The IDF spokesman, Brig. Gen. Nachman Shai, ordered the code word NACHASH TZEFA ("poisonous snake"), which indicated a genuine attack, to be broadcast over all TV and radio stations.

The promised Israeli retaliation never materialized. The first night of SCUD attacks, televised live throughout the world courtesy of CNN, had miraculously caused little damage and no fatalities; most importantly, the warheads did not carry chemical or biological agents. It was as if Israel had a divine veil of protection.

Not only did the actual missile attack catch A'MAN, in its former director's words, "with its pants down," but the phenomenon of hundreds of journalists covering a war, real-time, placed an unprecedented strain on military security. So unprepared was the IDF Military Censor's Office during the initial Iraqi blitz that television correspondents filed "live on the air" coverage of the attacks, in which they foolishly told their audiences where the missiles had impacted. Several American news networks even showed satellite imagery maps with the *exact* location of SCUD hits, much to the delight of Iraqi intelligence agents abroad who naturally relayed the data back to the missile crews operating out of H-2 and H-3.[83] As the conflict grew and SCUDs continued to fall on Israel, the censor's office quickly mobilized all available personnel and ensured that the thousand foreign journalists covering the war from Israel were sufficiently supervised.

From January to March, according to the IDF's chief censor, Brig. Gen. Yitzhak Shani, the censor's office cut 593 of the 95,000 telephone calls placed by journalists to their desks abroad. In some cases, reprimands were given. CNN and NBC were denied access to the international satellite facility in the Ayalon Valley for failure to submit stories for the censor's inspection before airing them on American TV. Theodore Stanger, *Newsweek*'s Jerusalem bureau chief, had his press credentials suspended after reporting the location of a joint U.S. Army–IAF Patriot missile battery.[84]

Foreign journalists were not the only ones to jeopardize military security. During the conflict, A'MAN's Field Security Eavesdropping Unit (known by its Hebrew acronym I'T), which monitors IDF telephone and radio communications, was forced to impose stockade sentences on several soldiers in various branches of service who violated security by discussing military developments over the telephone. In one instance, the commander of a corps had his office telephone cut off for sixty days because he, too, had blatantly violated security regulations.[85] To enforce its traditional message of "All The Honor To The Soldier Who Knows How To Keep A Secret," Field Security officers also resorted to their old trick of posing as civilian drivers and, after picking up a soldier hitchhiker, talking to him about military matters. If the soldier divulged anything more than could be ascertained by his beret color or unit patch, he was given at the least a warning; in more serious infractions, the soldier received a fine or even time in the stockade.

Operation Desert Storm presented the Israeli defense establishment with a dilemma: When do political considerations outweigh a nation's inherent right of self-defense? After all, *restraint* is not part of Israel's security doctrine. The IDF had several contingency plans on the books to strike the Iraqi missile sites, including the heliborne landing of special forces in western Iraq, to operate much like Captain Sterling's Long-Range Desert Group of the Second World War, using jeeps for sweeping search and destroy operations. Other plans included an Entebbe-like commando raid on Baghdad involving SAYERET MAT'KAL, deep-planted MOSSAD agents, and A'MAN personnel; the objective of such a raid was believed to be the assassination of Saddam Hussein.[86] The most likely of Israeli military responses would have been an air raid against the launch sites in western Iraq, but the Americans refused to provide the IAF with the all-important identification friend or foe (IFF) codes needed to prevent an accidental dogfight between IAF and coalition aircraft. To keep Israel out of the war and preserve its Arab anti-Iraq coalition, the United States sent Delta Force commandos on hit-and-run raids to destroy the SCUD launchers; the British sent in their SAS units on the same assignments.

Active Israeli participation in the war never materialized. Even though thirty-eight SCUDs hit Israel, including one whose warhead was filled with stones, Israel chose restraint, hoping to score political points for the future. After nearly a month of being crammed in their sealed rooms for the nightly SCUD raid, Israelis were finally allowed to resume normal lives. A'MAN, too, emerged from its isolation relatively unscathed; its failure to predict the oncoming conflict could have been debilitating for the agency. In March 1991, Defense Minister Moshe Arens announced to the Israeli KNESSET that in the near future Israel would launch another spy satellite. The defense minister explained that during the war in the Persian Gulf, even though Israel possessed intelligence not available to the Americans, the IDF was still at the mercy of the Pentagon for the acquisition of data from intelligence satellites.[87] In the future, Israel would be self-reliant in this intelligence area. But the IAF was taking no chances. It was learned that, following the war, the IAF mounted reconnaissance flights over western Iraq to ensure that Baghdad no longer posed a threat to the Jewish state.

A'MAN will require that intelligence edge if past mistakes are not to be repeated. According to Brig. Gen. Oren Shachar, the chief intelligence officer, "Iran has emerged as a new strategic threat to Israel—operating with great intensity against the IDF in Lebanon, via its Hizbollah surrogates, and maintains a deadly surface-to-surface capability."[88] Syria, too, despite its appearance of warming up to the West, has entered the regional peace talks backed by an impressive and deadly arsenal, poised for action against Israel. In May 1991, the Syrians ordered their first batch of heavily modified SCUD-B missiles from North Korea. The SCUDs, produced by the most advanced weapons' producer in the Third World, have a range of six hundred kilometers and could accurately hit any target in Israel.[89]

Even though the technical means at Israel's disposal are far more advanced than the forefathers of Israeli Military Intelligence could have ever foreseen, the challenges facing A'MAN have become more dire and immediate than ever before.

NOTES: CHAPTER FOURTEEN

1. Various ed., "ZE HA'MECHABEL SHE'HUKA LE'MAVET BE'YADEI KOCHOT HA'BITACHON," HADASHOT (May 29, 1984): 1.
2. Ze'ev Klein, ed., HA'MILCHAMA BE'TERROR: U'MEDINIUT HA'BITACHON SHEL YISRAEL BE'SHANIM 1979–1988 (Tel Aviv: Revivim Publishers, 1988), 145.
3. Various ed., "Relying on RUMINT," Newsweek (February 27, 1989): 27.
4. Minar Press, "Agent Confesses and Reveals the Practices of Zionist Intelligence," Tishrin (Damascus daily in Arabic; December 27, 1984): 8.
5. Baruch Ron, "EICH HEIM OVDIM," BAMACHANE CHU'L (February 1987): 7.
6. Sharon Sadeh, "GAM HIZBOLLAH ROCHSHIM GILSHONIM," BAMACHANE (October 25, 1989): 6.
7. Much controversy has followed Major Haddad to the grave. In several reports, he is held responsible for the massacre of more than fifty "regular" Lebanese soldiers on October 7, 1976 (one of the reasons, perhaps, why Bashir Gemayel wanted him tried for treason), and the abduction of Palestinian women. Most shockingly, it was later revealed that Major Haddad, A'MAN's principal ally in Lebanon, was in close contact with agents of Syrian Air Force Intelligence, the Syrian government's principal foreign espionage service, and the PLO's Intelligence and Security Apparatus (ISA), the forerunner of the Jihaz al-Razd. Ehud Ya'ari, "SA'AD HADDAD; SDAKIM," MATARA, No. 6 (1990): 4.
8. Steven Emerson, Secret Warriors: Inside the Covert Military Operations of the Reagan Era (New York: G. P. Putnam and Sons, 1988), 202.
9. Neil Livingstone and David Halevy, "Striking Back: Oliver North's Secret War on Terror," Soldier of Fortune (December 1989): 60.
10. Major General Uri Simchoni was one of the IDF's commando geniuses and, like his commander, was expert in the art of antiterrorist and intelligence A'MAN warfare. An ex-paratrooper, Simchoni was the GOLANI Brigade's intelligence officer during the 1967 War and, in 1970, was appointed the commander of SAYERET EGOZ ("Walnut Recon"), Northern Command's paratroop reconnaissance force, where he commanded countless counterterrorist forays into the notorious "Fatahland" strip of southern Lebanon. Ya'akov Erez and Ron Edlist, SAYEROT: TZAHAL BE'HEILO ENTZYKLOPEDIA LE'TZAVA ULE'BITACHON (Tel Aviv: Revivim Publishers, 1983): 66.
11. Yigal Serena, "CHATIFATO U'MISHPATO SHEL HA'KATZIN ABU SHARAH," YEDIOT: SHEVA YAMIM (January 20, 1989): 26.
12. Milan J. Kubic, "Targeting the PLO," Newsweek (October 14, 1985): 53.
13. Ron Dagoni, "SARIM BE'TUNISIA HUFA'ALU BE'SHERUT HA'MOSSAD," MA'ARIV (November 8, 1988): 1.

14. Ian Black and Benny Morris, *Israel's Secret Wars: The Untold History of Israeli Intelligence* (London: Hamish Hamilton, 1991), 454.

15. William E. Smith, "Israel's 1,500-Mile Raid," *Time* (October 14, 1985): 42.

16. Haim Raviv, "MUSHEVET ASHA'F BE'TUNIS," BAMACHANE (October 10, 1986): 5.

17. Various ed., *International Terror: July 1968–July 1986* (Tel Aviv: IDF Spokesman's Office, 1986), 45.

18. The other surviving terrorist of the attack was released in May 1985, in Ahmed Jibril's controversial prisoner exchange, where 1,150 convicted Palestinian terrorists were swapped for three IDF POWs. Fern Allen, "A Widow and Bereaved Mother Commemorates Murdered Family," *Jewish Week* (January 9, 1987): 3.

19. Yehuda Ariel, "TRAGEDIA VE'GVURA BE'RECHOV JABOTINSKY 61 BE'NAHARIYA," HA'ARETZ (April 23, 1979): 3.

20. Neil C. Livingstone and David Halevy, *Inside the PLO* (New York: William Morrow & Co., Inc., 1990), 253.

21. David C. Martin and John Walcott, *Best Laid Plans: The Inside Story of America's War Against Terrorism* (New York: Harper and Row, Publishers, 1988), 238.

22. See Neil C. Livingstone and David Halevy, *Inside the PLO*, 254.

23. Yosef Walter, "TZAHAL HIKLIT SICHOT HA'CHOTFIM IM MEFAKDAM," HA'ARETZ (October 17, 1985): 3.

24. See Neil C. Livingstone and David Halevy, "Striking Back," 76.

25. William E. Smith, John Borrell, and Dean Fischer, "The Voyage of the *Achille Lauro*," *Time* (October 21, 1985): 33.

26. See Neil C. Livingstone and David Halevy, "Striking Back," 77.

27. Daniel P. Bolger, *Americans at War 1975–1986: An Era of Violent Peace* (Novato, California: Presidio Press, 1988), 376.

28. See Neil C. Livingstone and David Halevy, "Striking Back," 77.

29. See Steven Emerson, *Secret Warriors*, 214.

30. See Neil C. Livingstone and David Halevy, "Striking Back," 80.

31. See Daniel P. Bolger, *Americans at War*, 376.

32. Ze'ev Schiff, "HA'MODE'IN—A'D KAMA LA'CHSOF," HA'ARETZ (October 23, 1985): 7.

33. See David C. Martin and John Walcott, *Best Laid Plans*, 267.

34. Neil C. Livingstone and David Halevy, "Bombs Over Benghazi," *Soldier of Fortune Magazine* (January 1990): 24.

35. *Ibid.* 26.

36. Eli Tabor, "Hatred for Arabs is Causing the Young to Hate Their Language as Well" (in Hebrew), YEDIOT AHARONOT (June 6, 1985): 13.

37. Tali Zelinger, "Female Reservists to Study Arabic for Intelligence Purposes" (in Hebrew), DAVAR (June 7, 1988): 2.

38. Shapi Gabai, Yosef Walter, Oded Granot, Rafael Mann, Yanon Shenkar,

Ron Dagoni, and Yehoshua Bitzur, "HABASH: A'AMADETI LA'TUS IM OZRAV SHEL ABU-NIDAL BE'MATOS SHE'YURAT," MA'ARIV (February 5, 1986): 1–9.

39. *Ibid.* 9.

40. Yosef Harif, "SURIA NITFASA AL CHAM," MA'ARIV (April 25, 1986): 4.

41. Yair Amikam, "A'MAN: ROSH CHADASH," YEDIOT AHARONOT (February 2, 1986): 13.

42. For a mention of his medal in Karameh, see Eilan Kfir, TZANHANIM CH'IR MUTZNACH: TZAHAL BE'HEILO ENTZYKLOPEDIA LE'TZAVA ULE'BITACHON (Tel Aviv: Revivim Publishers, 1981), 217; for a mention of Shahak's medal in Operation Spring of Youth, see Menachem Michelson, NA'HA'L NOA'R HALUTZEI LOCHEM: TZAHAL BE'HEILO ENTZYKLOPEDIA LE'TZAVA ULE'BITACHON (Tel Aviv, Revivim Publishers, 1981), 171.

43. Yohanan Lahav, "Sunday Times: YISRAEL SHOKELET HAFTZATZAT MIFA'ALEI HA'GAZ BE'SURIA," YEDIOT AHARONOT (January 10, 1988): 1.

44. Various ed., "MECHDAL LEYL HA'GALSHANIM," YISRAEL SHELANU (December 4, 1987): 2.

45. See Ian Black and Benny Morris, *Israel's Secret Wars*, 462.

46. Emanuel Rosen, "LO HE'IMINU LO SHE'TIFROTZ INTIFADAH A'ACHSHAV HU MUITRAD," MA'ARIV SOF SHAVU'A (December 7, 1990): 10.

47. Robert I. Friedman, "Smearing the PLO," *The Village Voice* (February 14, 1989): 8.

48. *Ibid.* 10.

49. On March 15, 1989, months after the assassination of Abu Jihad in Tunis, A'MAN director Shahak advised the Israeli cabinet that it was the estimation of Israeli Military Intelligence that it would be *impossible* to enter into meaningful negotiations with the Palestinians if the PLO were not included in the talks. "Otherwise," Shahak added, "the Intifadah could continue for years." Joel Brinkley, *The New York Times* (March 26, 1989): A-3.

50. Various ed., "Father of the Holy War," *Jerusalem Post* (April 17, 1988): 15.

51. Haim Raviah and Eilan Kfir, "HA'MATARA: TEVACH BE'MAT'KAL," HADASHOT (April 23, 1988): 3.

52. *Ibid.* 3.

53. Sigal Buchris, "KA'ASHE LE'TA'AER MA HAYA KOREH EILU," BEIN GALIM, No. 180 (April 1990): 47.

54. Three years after the assassination of Abu Jihad, the Israeli government still refused to admit officially that it was responsible for the killing. A'MAN's Military Censor's Office, however, did permit publication of press reports about the operation, provided that the account stated that the information was listed as "according to foreign reports." See Ian Black and Benny Morris, *Israel's Secret Wars*, 471.

55. Neil C. Livingstone and David Halevy, "Israeli Commandos Terminate PLO Terror Chief," *Soldier of Fortune Magazine* (December 1989): 77.

56. *Ibid.* 78.

57. See Ian Black and Benny Morris, *Israel's Secret Wars*, 470.

58. Alex Fishman, "HARUG MISPAR 142," HADASHOT (April 22, 1988): 10.

59. Marie Colvin, "Abu Jihad Knew Hit Team Was in Town," *London Sunday Times* (April 24, 1988): a-15.

60. Various ed., "YISRAEL TAFSA BE'TUNIS RESHIMAT SOCHNAEI ASHAF BE'ARETZ U'BE'SHTACHIM," YEDIOT AHARONOT (May 8, 1988): 1.

61. Dafna Vardi, "NICHSHAL HA'NISAYON SHEL TZAHAL LE'FOTZETZ MATEH JIBRIL BE'EMTZA'UT KLAVEI NEFETZ," AL HA'MISHMAR (December 11, 1988): 1.

62. Various ed., "SAYERET MAT'KAL BITZA'A CHATIFAT HA'SHEIKH OBEID," YEDIOT AHARONOT (July 30, 1989): 1.

63. Joshua Brilliant, "Palestinian Terrorists Told to Kill Everyone They Saw in Beach Area," *Jerusalem Post International Edition* (week ending June 16, 1990): 2.

64. Interview on Israeli TV news, MABAT, June 4, 1990.

65. Shani Payis, "EIZE CHAG YACHOL HAYA LIHIOT LANU," BEIN GALIM, No. 182 (January 1991): 8.

66. Ron Ben-Yishai, "BE'TNA'IM MESUYAMIM MECHABLIM YECHOLIM LACHDOR LE'SHETACH YISRAEL," YEDIOT AHARONOT SHABBAT (June 1, 1990): 1.

67. Joshua Brilliant, "Terrorism Will Increase," *Jerusalem Post International Edition* (week ending June 30, 1990): 2.

68. See Ian Black and Benny Morris, *Israel's Secret Wars*, 447.

69. Victor Ostrovsky and Claire Hoy, *By Way of Deception: The Making and Unmaking of a Mossad Officer* (New York: St. Martin's Press, 1990), 321.

70. According to reports that have surfaced since the war's end, the only viable work the MOSSAD compiled on Iraq was totally incorrect; a top-secret report claimed that Iraq would not be able to build a nuclear bomb for at least five years. Naomi Levitski, "MERAGLIM LO MUSHLAMIM," HADASHOT MOSAF SHABBAT (August 30, 1991): 6.

71. William J. Broad, "Non-superpowers Are Developing Their Own Spy Satellite Systems: Programs May Rewrite the Diplomatic Equation," *The New York Times* (September 3, 1989): A16.

72. Joel Brinkley, "Israel Puts a Satellite in Orbit a Day After Threat by Iraqis," *The New York Times* (April 4, 1990): A3.

73. Joshua Brilliant, "Gas Mask Distribution Begins," *Jerusalem Post International Edition* (week ending October 13, 1990): 4.

74. Peter Allen Frost, "The JDW Interview," *Jane's Defence Weekly*, Vol. 14, No. 14 (October 6, 1990): 676.

75. Arielah Ringel Hoffman, "HA'IM HAYA KAN MECHDAL MODE'INI," YEDIOT AHARONOT 24 SHA'OT (February 21, 1991): 1.

76. Eitan Haber, "MA YADA HA'MODE'IN VE'MA LO," YEDIOT AHARONOT (February 15, 1991): 11.

77. Shaul Ben-Haim, "MUMCHIM YISRAELIM BADKU MATOSEI MIG 29 BE'GERMANIA," MA'ARIV (November 16, 1990): 1.

78. See Joshua Brilliant, "Gas Mask," 4.

79. Various ed., "ROSH A'MAN LE'SHA'AVAR, YEHOSHUA SAGUY: HA'IRAQIM TAFSU OTANU IM HA'MICHNASAYIM LE'MATA," YISRAEL SHELANU (August 16, 1991): 12.

80. Various ed., "HUSNI MUBARAK MAZHIR ET SADDAM HUSSEIN: HA'MODE'IN HA'YISRAELI CHADAR LE'TZAVACHA," YISRAEL SHELANU (October 10, 1990): 6.

81. Various ed., "TZENZURA: MA ZE, BE'E'TZEM," BAMACHANE (May 4, 1988): 7.

82. In a highly controversial decision, the censor's office decided to prohibit the publication of a novel called *The Blue and White File*, written by Chagai Tayumkin, an investment advisor whose military service, completed in 1975, was in the Field Security Section of the IDF's sprawling Computer Center. The decision to censor the work of fiction, removing 160 pages from a 220-page manuscript, was a troubling precedent to many, especially since it appeared that the main problem with the story line—about a Romanian intelligence agent planted in the ranks of the SHIN BET—was that it dealt with that agency's inept personnel. Michal Goldberg, "HA'TZENZURA ASRA LE'FARSEM SEFER RIGUL DIMYONI A'L HA'SHA'BA'CH," YEDIOT AHARONOT (June 5, 1991): 7.

83. Yoav Caspi, "EIN SHIDURIM HAYIM," BAMACHANE (January 30, 1991): 17.

84. Dan Izenberg, "Censor Cut 593 Media Calls," *Jerusalem Post International Edition* (week ending March 16, 1991): 6.

85. Yoav Caspi, "PE GADOL," BAMACHANE (June 26, 1991): 55.

86. Joshua Hammer, Douglas Waller, Jeffrey Bartholet, and Theodore Stanger, "Will Israel Hit Back," *Newsweek* (February 11, 1991): 33.

87. Various ed., "ARENS: YISRAEL TISHAGER LAVYAN RIGUL," DAVAR (March 7, 1991): 1; various ed., "ARENS: BE'KAROV TIHIYE LANU YECHOLET MODE'YINT BE'ZMAN AMITI," YEDIOT AHARONOT (April 16, 1991): 4.

88. Yoav Caspi, "IRAN: HA'NE'ELAM HA'BA," BAMACHANE (March 20, 1991).

89. Ron Ben-Yishai, "TZFON-KOREA ASU'YA LI'MKOR LE'SURIA TILIM LE'TVACH 600 KM," YEDIOT AHARONOT (May 10, 1990): 5.

Postscript

The importance of A'MAN to the future of Israeli survival was dramatically reiterated in the summer of 1990 when the Intelligence Corps was transformed from a mere corps, such as the Artillery Corps, Armor Corps, and Combat Engineers, to the IDF's fourth branch of service, joining the IDF, IAF, and IDF/navy. HA'MAN personnel were even awarded their own beret, a dark green one, to illustrate their new status. The decision to transform Israeli Military Intelligence into an equal power player in the IDF came out of necessity, to meet the increased threat that the proliferation of ballistic missiles and chemical agents, and the growing surge of religious fanaticism, brings to the Middle East. For A'MAN and HA'MAN to contribute decisively to the defense of the Jewish state will require greater manpower and a larger share of Israel's defense budget.[1]

Indeed, decisive action would be the catchphrase for Israel's soldier spies as a new age dawned on the IDF. On April 1, 1991, Lt. Gen. Ehud Barak was appointed the IDF's fourteenth chief of staff. The most decorated soldier in Israel's history, Barak is also the first member of the top-secret club— a veteran of the SAYERET MAT'KAL and Intelligence Corps operations departments—to assume command of the IDF. From Beirut to Tunis, Barak's signature has adorned many of Israel's most spectacular operations; most of the actions behind his decorations are still considered state secrets of the highest order.[2] He is a man who has addressed military problems with lightning speed and stealth, innovative brilliance, and deadly firepower. To see Israel through the next four years of its precarious existence in a hostile region, his General Staff, too, needed to be cut from the same "Mission Impossible" cloth—especially his A'MAN director.

While forming his General Staff during the Gulf War, Barak, as one of his prerequisites to being a successful chief of staff, named Maj. Gen. Uri Saguy as his Intelligence Branch director. One of the brilliant and analytic minds in the IDF, Saguy has a combat record that is long and illustrious. A veteran GOLANI officer, he commanded SAYERET GOLANI during the tumultuous years of counterterrorist operations along Israel's northern frontier in Fatahland in 1971, as well as serving as a battalion commander during the 1973 War; on July 4, 1976, Saguy commanded the GOLANI contingent to Operation Thunderball in Entebbe.[3] His operational common sense and cool head made him a desired commodity during Israel's times of crisis. During the 1973 War he was ordered away from his unit at the front so that he could advise the Operations Brigade in the General Staff on long-term planning; during the 1982 Lebanon War, he was the commander of the General Staff Operations Brigade. Realizing that Saguy had long dreamed of becoming OC Northern Command, Barak told the forty-eight-year-old general, "I know that your big dream has always been to have Northern Command. I know that they promised it to you and I think you deserve it. I am also telling you that if you really want it, it's yours. Nevertheless, I need you to be my A'MAN Director."[4]

Major General Uri Saguy took command of an A'MAN racing toward the twenty-first century, trying to achieve technical mastery over its adversaries in the region. Israel Aircraft Industries continues to provide Israeli Military Intelligence with high-flying espionage platforms, from the new Phalcon ECM ELINT Boeing 707 to the Searcher, an RPV equipped with state-of-the-art electronic and optical gear, and capable of remaining airborne for more than twenty-four hours. Spy satellites, of course, are expected in the coming years. Yet it is the human element of A'MAN's work that will keep the nation at peace, and defend it in case of war. From the eighteen-year-old conscript sitting at his desk in HATZAV, to the seasoned spy runner standing alone on a dark winter night awaiting the meet with his agent, it is the men and women of A'MAN, HA'MAN, the KA'MANIM, and photointerpreters who will provide Israel with the ability to monitor the enemies of the Jewish state and deal with them accordingly.

Chief of Staff Barak and A'MAN director Saguy, both combat veterans, realize that it is the soldiers and spies, not the satellites or communications gear, who achieve the victories, and risk paying the ultimate price. In the course of Israel's turbulent history, over seventeen thousand soldiers have fallen in battle—an incredible price for such a small country to bare. Among this vast number of dead is Eli Cohen, a man whose courage helped bring A'MAN out of its primitive genesis into its age of brilliance. On May 19, 1991, in a small and brief ceremony, Lieutenant General Barak honored Eli Cohen, presenting him with the posthumous rank of lieutenant colonel. Eli Cohen inspired a generation of soldiers and spies.[5] His legacy continues to this day in Israeli Military Intelligence.

In a recent interview to celebrate "Intelligence Corps Day," A'MAN director Saguy was asked, "What will be the next surprise—like the 1973 War, the Intifadah and the Iraqi invasion of Kuwait—to hit A'MAN?" A brief pause, a brief smile, and Saguy simply retorted, "If I knew I would prevent it!"

One new responsibility for A'MAN will be to forewarn Israeli policy makers of threatening developments in the wake of the dismantling of the Soviet Union. According to Maj. Gen. Amnon Shahak, former A'MAN director and current deputy chief of staff, "There is great concern that *unemployed* Soviet nuclear scientists will become atomic free agents, selling their services to such Arab states as Iraq and Syria, looking to produce a nuclear bomb . . . and the Israeli military should put a lot of thinking and planning in order to cope with it."[6] Another A'MAN fear is that a Soviet nuclear worker from the Moslem republic of Kazakstan will provide nuclear weapons secrets to the Islamic Republic of Iran or, worse, to a fundamentalist Moslem terrorist group such as Hizbollah.

Intelligence work is a crapshoot. Nevertheless, in the coming years of potential peace or protracted conflict, A'MAN remains Israel's most important and vulnerable espionage and intelligence-gathering service.

NOTES: POSTSCRIPT

1. Various ed., "HEYL HA'MODE'IN YAHAFOCH LE'ZARUA'A REVI'IT BE'TZAHAL," YISRAEL SHELANU (June 23, 1989): 11.

2. Ron Ben-Yishai, "RA'MAT'KAL CHADASH LE'TZAHAL," YEDIOT AHARONOT (April 1, 1991): 2.

3. Ron Levi, "SIVUV HA'MINU'IM HA'GADOL BE'TZAVA MATCHIL HA'YOM, "DAVAR" (March 3, 1991): 12.

4. Emanuel Rosen, "HA'MAZAL SHEL URI SAGUY," MA'ARIV SHABBAT (August 9, 1991): 9.

5. Various ed., "SGAN ALUF L'ELI COHEN ZA'L," MA'ARIV (May 20, 1991): 6.

6. Uri Dan, "Israelis Say Arabs May Recruit Soviet Nuclear Experts," *New York Post*, December 27, 1991, p.4.

APPENDIX:

IDF MILITARY INTELLIGENCE DIRECTORS

1948–49	Lieutenant Colonel Isser Beeri
1949–50	Colonel Chaim Herzog
1950–55	Colonel Binyamin Gibli
1955–59	Major General Yehoshofat Harkabi
1959–62	Major General Chaim Herzog
1962–63	Major General Meir Amit*
1964–72	Major General Aharon Yariv
1972–74	Major General Eli Zeira
1974–79	Major General Shlomoh Gazit
1979–83	Major General Yehoshua Saguy
1983–85	Major General Ehud Barak**
1985–91	Major General Amnon Shahak
1991–	Major General Uri Saguy

*MOSSAD Director from 1963–1986.
**IDF Chief of Staff from 1991.

Adam, Monya. KESHER AMITZ. Israel Ministry of Defense Publications, Tel Aviv, 1986.

Adan, Avraham ("Bren"). *On the Banks of Suez*. Arms and Armour Press, London, 1980.

Allon, Yigal. *Shield of David*. Weidenfeld and Nicolson, London and Jerusalem, 1970.

———*The Making of Israel's Army*. Vallentine, Mitchell and Co. Ltd., New York, 1970.

Amir, Aharon. *Lebanon, Country, People, War*. Hadar Editors, Tel Aviv, 1979.

Arad, Yitzhak. *1000 Days: June 12, 1967–August 8, 1970*. Israel Ministry of Defense Publications, Tel Aviv, 1971.

Argaman, Yosef. ZE HAYA SODI BE'YOTER. Israel Ministry of Defense Publications, Tel Aviv, 1990.

Asher Jerry, and Hammel, Eric. *Duel for the Golan*. William Morrow and Company Inc., New York, 1987.

Avigur, Shaul, Slotzki, Yehuda, and Rivlin, Gershon (Colonel). KITZUR TOLDOT HA'HAGANAH. Israel Ministry of Defense Publications, Tel Aviv, 1984.

Avneri, Arieh. HA'MAHALUMA. Revivim Publishers, Israel, 1983.

Bachur, Guy. LEXICON ASHA'F. Israel Ministry of Defense Publications, Tel Aviv, 1991.

Banks, Lynne Reid. *Torn Country*, Franklin Watts, New York, 1980.

Bar On, Mordechai. *Six Days: Israel Defense Forces*. Israel Ministry of Defense Publications, Tel Aviv, 1968.

Bar-Zohar, Michael. *The Avengers*. Hawthorn Books, Inc., New York, 1967.

———*Spies in the Promised Land: Isser Harel and the Israeli Secret Service*. Houghton Mifflin Company, Boston, 1972.

Bar-Zohar, Michael, and Haber, Eitan. *The Quest for the Red Prince*. William Morrow and Company Inc., New York, 1983.

Battleheim, Avi. GOLANI: MISHPACHAT LOCHAMIM. MIFKEDET HATIVAT GOLANI Israel Ministry of Defense Publications, Tel Aviv, 1980.

Becker, Jillian. *The PLO: The Rise and Fall of the Palestine Liberation Organization*. Weidenfeld and Nicolson, London, 1984.

Ben Amnon, Shlomoh. *Following the Arab Terrorist*. Madim Books, Tel Aviv, 1978.

Ben David, Ofer. HAMA'ARACHA BELEVANON. Tel Aviv, 1985.

Ben-Hanan, Eli. *Our Man in Damascus: Elie Cohen*. Steimatzky Ltd., Jerusalem, 1980.

Benziman, Uzi. *Sharon: An Israeli Ceasar*, Adama Books, New York, 1985.

Bercuson, David J.. *The Secret Army*, Stein and Day Publishers, New York, 1984.

Bethell, Nicholas. *The Palestine Triangle*, André Deutsch Ltd., London, 1979.

Binur, Yoram. *My Enemy, Myself.* Doubleday, New York, 1989.

Black, Ian, and Morris, Benny. *Israel's Secret Wars: The Untold History of Israeli Intelligence.* Hamish and Hamilton, London, 1991.

Blitzer, Wolf. *Territory of Lies.* Harper and Row, New York, 1989.

Bolger, Daniel P. *Americans at War: 1975–1986, An Era Of Violent Peace.* Presidio Press, Novato, California, 1988.

CIA: Translator and Editor—Melman, Yossi. *Israeli Foreign Intelligence and Security Service Survey.* Zmora Bitan, Tel Aviv, 1982.

Cobban, Helena. *The Palestine Liberation Organization: People, Power and Politics.* Cambridge University Press, London, 1984.

Cockburn, Andrew and Leslie. *Dangerous Liaison: The Inside Story of the U.S.-Israeli Covert Relationship.* Harper Collins, New York, 1991.

Cohen, Eliezer "Cheetah," and Lavi, Tzvi. HA'SHAMAYIM EINAM HA'GVUL. Ma'ariv Library, Tel Aviv, 1990.

Cohen, Yerucham. LE'OR HA'YOM UBE'MACHSHECHA. Amikam Publishers, Tel Aviv, 1969.

Cordesman, Anthony H., and Wagner, Abraham R. *The Lessons of Modern War, Volume 1: The Arab Israeli Conflicts, 1973-1989.* Westview Press/Mansell Publishing Ltd., San Francisco/London, 1990.

Dan, Ben. *The Spy from Israel.* Vallentine, Mitchell and Co., London, 1969.

Dan, Uri. ETZBA ELOHIM: SODOT HA'MILCHAMA BE'TERROR. Massada Ltd., Tel Aviv, 1976.

Dan, Uri and Ben-Porat, Y. *The Secret War: The Spy Game in the Middle East.* Sabra Books, New York, 1970.

Dayan, Moshe. *Diary of the Sinai Campaign 1956*, Weidenfeld and Nicolson, London, 1966.

———*Story of My Life*, Weidenfeld and Nicolson, London, 1976.

Deacon, Richard. *The Israeli Secret Service.* Sphere Books, Ltd., London, 1979.

Dekel, Ephraim. A'ALILOT SHAI. IDF/Ma'arachot Publications, Tel Aviv, 1953.

Dietl, Wilhelm. *Holy War.* Macmillan Publishing Co., New York, 1984.

Dobson, Christopher, and Payne, Ronald. *The Carlos Complex: A Study In Terror.* Hodder and Stoughton Ltd., London, 1977.

———*Counterattack*, Facts on File Inc., New York, 1982.

Dror, Yosef. HA'KOMMANDO HA'YAMI. Ha'Kibbutz Ha'Me'uchad Publishing, Tel Aviv, 1981.

Dror, Tzika. HA'MISTA'ARAVIM SHEL HA'PAL'MACH. HA'KIBBUTZ HA'MEUHAD. Publishing House Ltd., Tel Aviv, 1986.

Dupuy, Trevor N. *Elusive Victory: The Arab-Israeli Wars 1947–74.* Harper and Row Publishers, New York, 1978.

Eisenberg, Dennis, Dan, Uri, and Landau, Eli. *The Mossad: Israel's Secret Intelligence Service Inside Stories.* Signet, New York, 1979.

Eitan, Rafael. RAFUL: SIPURO SHEL CHAYAL. Ma'ariv, Tel Aviv, 1985.

Emerson, Steven. *Secret Warriors: Inside the Covert Operations of the Reagan Era.* G. P. Putnam and Sons, New York, 1988.

Ennes, James M. Jr. *Assault on the* Liberty. Ivy Books, New York, 1979.

Erez, Ya'akov, Edlist, Ron, and Lavi, Tzvi. SAYEROT MI'UTIM TZAHAL BE'HEILO ENTZYKLOPEDIA LE'TZAVA U'LE'BITACHON. Revivim Publishers, Tel Aviv, 1983.

Eshed, Hagai. MI NATAN ET HA'HORA'AH. Edanim/Yediot Aharonot Publishers, Tel Aviv, 1979.

———— MOSSAD SHEL ISH ECHAD—REVUEN SHILOACH AVI HA'MODE'IN HA'YISRAELI. Edanim/Yediot Aharonot Publishers, Tel Aviv, 1988.

Gabriel, Richard A. *Operation Peace for Galilee.* Hill and Wang, U.S.A, 1984.

Gal, Reuven. *A Portrait of the Israeli Soldier.* Greenwood Press, New York, 1986.

Galber, Yoav. LAMA PIRKU HA'PAL'MACH. Schocken Publishing House Ltd, Tel Aviv, 1986.

Golan, Aviezer. MILCHEMET HA'A'ATZMA'UT. Israel Ministry of Defense Publications, Tel Aviv, 1985.

———— *Operation Susannah.* Harper and Row, New York, 1978.

Goodman, Hirsh, and Mann, Shlomoh. HEYL HA'YAM TZAHAL BE'HEILO ENTZYKLOPEDIA LE'TZAVA U'LE'BITACHON. Revivim Publishers, Tel Aviv, 1982.

Granot, Oded. HEYL HA'MODE'IN TZAHAL BE'HEILO ENTZYKLOPEDIA LE'TZAVA U'LE'BITACHON. Revivim Publishers, Tel Aviv, 1981.

Gur, Mordechai. *The Battle for Jerusalem*, Popular War, New York, 1974.

Haber, Eitan. HA'YOM TIFROTZ MILCHAMA. Edanim/Yediot Aharonot Publishers, Tel Aviv, 1987.

Harel, Isser. BITACHON VE'DEMOKRATIA. Edanim/Yediot Aharonot Publishers, Tel Aviv, 1989.

———— RIGUL SOVIETI. Edanim/Yediot Aharonot Publishers, Tel Aviv, 1987.

Harel, Yehuda. *Growing Achievement.* Citation Madim Books, Tel Aviv, 1970.

Hasabiyeh, Arieh. HEYL HA'SHIRION: TZAHAL BE'HEILO ENTZYKLOPEDIA LE'TZAVA U'LE'BITACHON. Revivim Publishers, Tel Aviv, 1981.

Herzog, Chaim. *The Arab-Israeli Wars.* Arms and Armour Press, London, 1982.

———— *The War of Atonement.* Weidenfeld and Nicolson, London, 1975.

Hirst, David. *The Gun and the Olive Branch.* Faber and Faber Ltd., London, 1977.

Insight Team of the *Sunday Times*. *The Yom Kippur War*. Doubleday and Company, New York, 1974.

Israeli, Rafael. *The PLO in Lebanon: Selected Documents*. Weidenfeld and Nicolson, London, 1983.

Kfir, Eilan. TZANHANIM CH'IR MUTZNACH TZAHAL BE'HEILO ENTZYKLOPEDIA LE'TZAVA U'LE'BITACHON. Revivim Publishers, Tel Aviv, 1981.

Klein, Zeev (Ed.). HA'MILCHAMA BE'TERROR U'MEDINIUT HA'BITACHON SHEL YISRAEL BE'SHANIM 1979-1988. Revivim Publishers, Tel Aviv, 1988.

Laffin, John. *The War of Desperation 1982–1985*. Osprey, London, 1985.

Lanir, Zvi. *Fundamental Surprise: The National Intelligence Crisis*. United Kibbutz Publications, Tel Aviv, 1983.

Laquer, Walter. *A World of Secrets: The Uses and Limits of Intelligence*. Basic Books Inc., New York, 1985.

Laskov, Haim. *Military Leadership*. Israel Ministry of Defense Publications, Tel Aviv, 1985.

Levy, Moshe. *The 48th Soul*. Ma'arachot/Israel Ministry of Defense Publications, Tel Aviv, 1981.

Livingstone, Neil, C., and Halevy, David. *Inside The PLO*. William Morrow and Co., Inc., New York, 1990.

Lossin, Yigal. *Pillar of Fire*. Shikmona Publishing Company Ltd., Jerusalem, 1983.

Lotz, Wolfgang. *The Champagne Spy*. St. Martin's Press, New York, 1972.

Lovich, Netanel. *The War for Independence*. Masada, Tel Aviv, 1966.

Markovitzki, Ya'akov. HA'YECHITDOT HA'YABASHTIOT HA'MEYUCHADOT SHEL HA'PAL'MACH. Israel Ministry of Defense Publications, Tel Aviv, 1989.

Marshall, S.L.A. *Sinai Victory*. The Battery Press, Nashville, 1985.

Martin, David C., and Walcott, John. *Best Laid Plans: The Inside Story of America's War against Terrorism*. Harper and Row, New York, 1988.

Melman, Yossi. *The Master Terrorist: The True Story behind Abu Nidal*. Adama Books, New York, 1986.

Melman, Yossi, and Raviv, Dan. *The Imperfect Spies: The History of Israeli Intelligence*. Sidgwick and Jackson, London, 1989.

——SHUTAFUT O'YENET. Edanim/Yediot Aharonot Publications, Tel Aviv, 1987.

Merari, Ariel, and Elad Shlomi. *The International Dimension of Palestinian Terrorism: JCSS Study No. 6*. The *Jerusalem Post* and Westview Press, Jerusalem, 1986.

Michelson, Menachem. HA'NA'AA'L: NO'AR HALUTZEI LOCHEM TZAHAL BE'HEILO ENTZYKLOPEDIA LE'TZAVA U'LE'BITACHON. Revivim Publishers, Tel Aviv, 1981.

Milstein, Uri. *A History of the Paratroopers: Volumes 1–4*. Schalgi Publishing House Ltd., Tel Aviv, 1985-89.

Nakdimon, Shlomo. *First Strike*. Summit Books, New York, 1987.

——SVIRUT NEMUCHA. Revivim Publishers House, Tel Aviv, 1982.

Na'or, Mordechai. HA'HAGANAH. Israel Defense Forces, Tel Aviv, 1973.

Neff, Donald. *Warriors at Suez.* Linden Press, New York, 1981.

Netanyahu, Benjamin. *Terrorism: How the West Can Win,* Farrar, Straus, and Giroux, New York, 1986.

Newman, Barbara, with Rogan, Barbara. *The Covenant: Love and Death in Beirut.* Crown Publishers, Inc., New York, 1989.

Nordeen, Lon. *Fighters over Israel.* Orion Books, New York, 1990.

O'Ballance, Edgar. *No Victor. No Vanquished: The Yom Kippur War,* Presidio Press, Novato, California, 1978.

———*The Language of Violence,* Presidio Press, Novato, California, 1979.

Ohana, Arnon-Yuval, and Yodfat, Arieh. ASHA'F—DIYUKONO SHEL IRGUN. Ma'ariv Library, Tel Aviv, 1985.

Ostrovsky, Victor, and Hoy, Claire. *By Way of Deception: The Making and Unmaking of a Mossad Officer.* St. Martin's Press, New York, 1990.

Pa'il, Meir, Dr. (Colonel), Battleheim, Avi, and Eilon, Avraham. HATIVOT HA'CHI'R–GOLANI–GIVA'ATI: TZAHAL BE'HEILO ENTZYKLOPEDIA LE'TZAVA U'LE'BITACHON. Revivim Publishers, Tel Aviv, 1982.

Parry, Albert. *Terrorism: From Robespierre to Arafat,* Vanguard Press, New York, 1976.

Payne, Ronald. *MOSSAD: Israel's Most Secret Service.* Bantam Press, London, 1990.

Posner, Steve. *Israel Undercover: Secret Warfare and Hidden Diplomacy in the Middle East.* Syracuse University Press, New York, 1987.

Rabinovich, Abraham. *The Battle for Jerusalem.* The Jewish Publication Society, New York, 1972.

———*The Boats Of Cherbourg.* Seaver Books, Henry Holt and Company, New York, 1988.

Randal, Jonathan C. *Going All the Way: Christian Warlords, Israeli Adventurers, and the War in Lebanon.* Vintage Books, New York, 1984.

Rika, Eliyahu (Major). PARPAR HA'SHACHAR. Yorikel Publishing, Tel Aviv, 1987.

Rivlin, Gershon. *The Tenth Anniversary of the Israel Defense Forces.* Israel Ministry of Defense Publications, Tel Aviv, 1958.

Ronen, David. SHNOT HA'SHA'BA'CH.: HA'HA'A ARACHOT BE'YEHUDA VE'SHOMRON, SHANA RISHONAI Israel Ministry of Defense Publications, Tel Aviv, 1989.

Ruey, Natan. HEYL HA'KESHER VE'HA'ELEKTRONIKA TZAHAL BE'HEILO ENTZYKLOPEDIA LE'TZAVA U'LE'BITACHON. Revivim Publishers, Tel Aviv, 1982.

Schiff, Zeev. *A History of the Israeli Army 1870-1974.* Straight Arrow Books, San Francisco, 1974.

———HEYL HA'AVIR: TZAHAL BE'HEILO ENTZYKLOPEDIA LE'TZAVA U'LE'BITACHON. Revivim Publishers, Tel Aviv, 1981.

Schiff, Zeev, and Ya'ari, Ehud. *Intifadah: The Palestinian Uprising—Israel's Third Front.* Simon and Schuster, New York, 1989.

———*Israel's Lebanon War.* Simon and Schuster, New York, 1984.

———*October Earthquake: Yom Kippur 1973.* University Publishing Projects Ltd., Tel Aviv, 1974.

Segev, Shmuel. BODED BE'DAMESEK: CHAYAV VE'MOTAV SHEL ELI COHEN. Keter Publishing House, Jerusalem, 1986.

Shalom, Dani. KOL METOSEI HEYL HA'AVIR. Bavir Aviation Publications, Tel Aviv, 1990.

Shazly, Sa'ad es-Dinn. *The Crossing of the Suez.* America-Mideast Research, San Francisco, 1980.

Shiffer, Simon. KADUR SHELEG. SODOT MILCHEMET LEVANON. Edanim. Yediot Aharonot Publishers, Tel Aviv, 1984.

Shimshi, Elyashiv. *Storm in October.* MA'ARACHOT/Israel Ministry of Defense Publications, 1986.

Sitton, Rafi and Shoshan, Yitzhak. ANSHEI HA'SOD VE'HA'STAR. Edanim/Yediot Aharonot Publishers, Tel Aviv, 1990.

Steigman, Yitzhak (Major). ME'A'ATZMA'UT LE'KADESH: HEYL HA'AVIR BE'SHANIM 1949-1956. Israel Ministry of Defense Publications, Tel Aviv, 1990.

Sterling, Claire. *The Terror Network: The Secret War of International Terrorism.* Berkley Books, New York, 1982.

Steven, Stewart. *The Spymasters of Israel.* Ballantine Books, New York, 1980.

Stevenson, William. *90 Minutes at Entebbe,* Bantam Books, New York, 1976.

Tadmor, Joshua. *The Silent Warriors.* The Macmillan Company, Toronto, 1969.

Tlas, General Dr. Mustafa (ed.). *The Israeli Invasion to Lebanon.* Israel Ministry of Defense Publications, Tel Aviv, 1991.

(Various Editors). TZAVA U'BITACHON ALEPH (1948–1968): TZAHAL BE'HEILO ENTZYKLOPEDIA LE'TZAVA U'LE'BITACHON Revivim Publishers, Tel Aviv, 1981.

———TZAVA U'BITACHON (1968–81) TZAHAL BE'HEILO ENTZYKLOPEDIA LE'TZAVA U'LE'BITACHON. Revivim Publishers, Tel Aviv, 1984.

Weizmann, Ezer. *On Eagles' Wings.* MacMillan Publishing Company Ltd., New York, 1976.

JOURNALS

BAMACHANE - IDF Weekly Magazine
BEIN GALIM - IDF/Navy Bi-monthly Magazine
BITON HEYL HA'AVIR - Israel Air Force Magazine
IDF Journal - Bi-monthly English Language Military Magazine
MA'ARACHOT - IDF Senior Command Publication
SKIRAT HODSHIT - IDF Officer Corps Magazine
Mention must also be given to the fine military correspondents working for the Israeli daily newspapers YEDIOT AHARONOT, MA'ARIV, HADASHOT, HA'ARETZ, DAVAR, and *The Jerusalem Post* from which much material was obtained.

About the Author

Samuel M. Katz served in the Israeli Defense Forces at the height of
Israel's involvement in Lebanon. He has had a lifetime interest in Israeli
military matters and has written over a dozen books and articles on
the subject. His books include *Israel Tank Battles, Follow Me! A
History of Israel's Military Elite, Guards without Frontier,* and three
illustrated books in the Motorbooks POWER Series: *Israel's Army,
Israel's Air Force, and Israel's Special Forces.* He has written articles
for *Air Force Magazine, Military Illustrated, Air and Space, Smithson-
ian,* and *Bamachane* (the IDF Weekly). He also serves as technical advisor and writer for the Discovery Channel series "World of Valor"
and "Those Who Dare." Katz lives with his family in New York City.